2020 EDITION

ECONOMICS

COURSE COMPANION

Jocelyn Blink
Ian Dorton

OXFORD
UNIVERSITY PRESS

OXFORD
UNIVERSITY PRESS

Great Clarendon Street, Oxford, OX2 6DP, United Kingdom

Oxford University Press is a department of the University of Oxford. It furthers the University's objective of excellence in research, scholarship, and education by publishing worldwide. Oxford is a registered trade mark of Oxford University Press in the UK and in certain other countries

First published in 2020

British Library Cataloguing in Publication Data
Data available

978-1-38-200496-1 (print)
10 9 8 7 6 5 4 3

978-1-38-202022-0 (enhanced digital)
10 9 8 7 6 5 4 3 2

Paper used in the production of this book is a natural, recyclable product made from wood grown in sustainable forests. The manufacturing process conforms to the environmental regulations of the country of origin.

Printed in the UK by Bell and Bain Ltd, Glasgow

Acknowledgements

The publisher and authors are grateful to those who have given permission to reproduce the following extracts and adaptations of copyright material:

Agazzi, Isolda: adapted from article 'TRADE: Whither African Cotton Producers After Brazil's Success?', 23 March 2010, Inter Press Service, www.ipsnews.net, reprinted by permission.

American Cancer Society Cancer Action Network (ACS CAN) and American Lung Association: excerpts from press releases 'American Cancer Society Cancer Action Network Urges Oregon Legislature to Pass $2 Tobacco Tax Increase in 2019', 29 January 2019, ACS CAN, www.fightcancer.org, and 'American Lung Association 'State of Tobacco Control' Report Finds Oregon Can Do More to Prevent, Reduce Tobacco Use', 30 January 2019, American Lung Association, www.lung.org, reprinted by permission.

BBC News: adapted excerpts from article 'Scotland ends cheap booze as minimum price starts', 1 May 2018, BBC News, www.bbc.co.uk/news, reprinted by permission.

Carrington, Damian: excerpt from article 'Why the Guardian is changing the language it uses about the environment', 17 May 2019, *The Guardian*, www.theguardian.com, copyright Guardian News & Media Limited 2019, reprinted by permission.

Commerce Commission New Zealand: excerpt from 'Avoiding anti-competitive behaviour', © Crown Copyright, https://comcom.govt.nz/business/avoiding-anti-competitive-behaviour, reprinted under the terms of the Creative Commons Attribution 4.0 International (CC BY 4.0).

European Commission: excerpt from press release 'Antitrust: Commission confirms sending a Statement of Objections to Microsoft on the tying of Internet Explorer to Windows', Brussels, 17 January 2009, and press release 'Antitrust: Commission fines Google €1.49 billion for abusive practices in online advertising', Brussels, 20 March 2019, reprinted by permission.

FP Canada: adapted excerpts from article 'One-in-five Canadians with debt will need to liquidate assets to pay it down in 2019', 13 March 2019, FP Canada (formerly Financial Planning Standards Council), www.fpcanada.ca, reprinted by permission.

Friedman, Milton: excerpt from *The Counter-Revolution* in Monetary Theory, first published by The Institute of Economic Affairs, London, 1970, reprinted by permission.

Jing, Li: excerpt from article 'China softens 'iron fist' pollution fight', 15 March 2019, Diálogo Chino, www.dialogochino.net, reprinted by permission.

Krugman, Paul: quotation © The Nobel Foundation, reprinted by permission.

Lewis, Leo and Robertson, David: adapted excerpts from article 'Copper breaches $8,000 barrier but hot metal prices may soon cool', 7 April, 2010, *The Times*, www.thetimes.co.uk, reprinted by permission of The Times / News Licensing.

Monbiot, George: excerpt from article 'Finally, a breakthrough alternative to growth economics – the doughnut', 12 April 2017, *The Guardian*, www.theguardian.com, copyright Guardian News & Media Limited 2019, reprinted by permission.

Naidoo, Prinesha: excerpt from article 'South African Business Confidence Falls to Almost Two-Year Low', 13 March 2019, copyright © 2019, Bloomberg.com, reprinted by permission of Bloomberg L.P., all rights reserved.

New Economics Foundation: 'How is the Happy Planet Index calculated?', http://happyplanetindex.org/about, reprinted by permission.

O'Halloran, Barry: adapted excerpts from article 'Consumer confidence slumps amid Brexit uncertainty', 4 March 2019, *The Irish Times*, www.irishtimes.com, reprinted by permission.

Organisation for Economic Co-operation and Development (OECD): excerpt from article 'Few countries are pricing carbon high enough to meet climate targets', 18 September 2018, www.oecd.org.

Ostrom, Elinor: quotation © The Nobel Foundation, reprinted by permission.

Prieur, Danielle: article 'Tree prices are rising and it's because of changing supply and demand', 28 November 2018, WMFE, www.wmfe.org, reprinted by permission.

Raworth, Kate: excerpts from 'Why it's time to vandalize the economic textbooks' from www.kateraworth.com, reprinted by permission.

Raworth, Kate: excerpts from *Doughnut Economics: Seven Ways to Think Like a 21st-Century Economist*, copyright 2017 by Kate Raworth, reprinted by arrangement with Chelsea Green Publishing, White River Junction, VT, www.chelseagreen.com, and published by Random House Business, reprinted by permission of The Random House Group Limited, © 2017.

Reuters: excerpt from article 'U.N. urges new resource accounting, cites BP spill', 13 July 2010, from Reuters.com, © 2010 reuters.com, all rights reserved, used under licence, reprinted by permission of PARS Intl. Corp.

Stern, Professor Nicholas: excerpt from Royal Economic Society (RES) public lecture in Manchester, 2007, reprinted by permission.

SWNS: article about helium shortage written by Berny Torre, 22 January 2019, reprinted by permission.

United Nations: excerpts and icons from 'Goal 14: Conserve and sustainably use the oceans, seas and marine resources' and 'Goal 13: Take urgent action to combat climate change and its impacts', United Nations Sustainable Development Goals (www.un.org/sustainabledevelopment), © 2019 United Nations, reprinted by permission of the United Nations. The content of this publication has not been approved by the United Nations and does not reflect the views of the United Nations or its officials or Member States.

United Nations Framework Convention on Climate Change (UNFCCC): excerpts from 'Summary of the Paris Agreement' from *Climate: Get the Big Picture*, https://unfccc.int/resource/bigpicture.

WWF: adapted excerpts from 'Overfishing', https://www.worldwildlife.org, reprinted by permission.

Course Book definition

The IB Diploma Programme Course Books are designed to support students throughout their two-year Diploma Programme. They will help students gain an understanding of what is expected from their subject studies while presenting content in a way that illustrates the purpose and aims of the IB. They reflect the philosophy and approach of the IB and encourage a deep understanding of each subject by making connections to wider issues and providing opportunities for critical thinking.

The books mirror the IB philosophy of viewing the curriculum in terms of a whole-course approach and include support for the IB leaner profile and the IB Diploma Programme core requirements.

IB mission statement

The International Baccalaureate aims to develop inquiring, knowledgable and caring young people who help to create a better and more peaceful world through intercultural understanding and respect.

To this end the IB works with schools, governments and international organisations to develop challenging programmes of international education and rigorous assessment.

These programmes encourage students across the world to become active, compassionate, and lifelong learners who understand that other people, with their differences, can also be right.

The IB learner profile

The aim of all IB programmes is to develop internationally minded people who, recognising their common humanity and shared guardianship of the planet, help to create a better and more peaceful world. IB learners strive to be:

Inquirers They develop their natural curiosity. They acquire the skills necessary to conduct inquiry and research and show independence in learning. They actively enjoy learning and this love of learning will be sustained throughout their lives.

Knowledgeable They explore concepts, ideas, and issues that have local and global significance. In so doing, they acquire in-depth knowledge and develop understanding across a broad and balanced range of disciplines.

Thinkers They exercise initiative in applying thinking skills critically and creatively to recognise and approach complex problems, and make reasoned, ethical decisions.

Communicators They understand and express ideas and information confidently and creatively in more than one language and in a variety of modes of communication. They work effectively and willingly in collaboration with others.

Principled They act with integrity and honesty, with a strong sense of fairness, justice, and respect for the dignity of the individual, groups, and communities. They take responsibility for their own actions and the consequences that accompany them.

Open-minded They understand and appreciate their own cultures and personal histories, and are open to the perspectives, values, and traditions of other individuals and communities. They are accustomed to seeking and evaluating a range of points of view, and are willing to grow from the experience.

Caring They show empathy, compassion, and respect towards the needs and feelings of others. They have a personal commitment to service, and act to make a positive difference to the lives of others and to the environment.

Risk-takers They approach unfamiliar situations and uncertainty with courage and forethought, and have the independence of spirit to explore new roles, ideas, and strategies. They are brave and articulate in defending their beliefs.

Balanced They understand the importance of intellectual, physical, and emotional balance to achieve personal well-being for themselves and others.

Reflective They give thoughtful consideration to their own learning and experience. They are able to assess and understand their strengths and limitations in order to support their learning and professional development.

Contents

Access your support website for additional support material here:
www.oxfordsecondary.com/9781382004961

This book is designed to be a companion to you as you embark upon your study of the International Baccalaureate Diploma Programme in economics. Through its overarching emphasis on key economic concepts, we hope that it will help you become, in the words of the IB learner profile, "internationally-minded people who, recognizing their common humanity and shared guardianship of the planet, help to create a better and more peaceful world".

Economics has a vital role to play in promoting international cooperation and mutual understanding because of its focus on global issues. To achieve this understanding, you need to learn to consider economic theories, ideas and events from the points of view of different stakeholders in the world economy.

The first attribute of an IB learner is to be an inquirer. The scope for inquiry in economics is tremendous. In this book, we aim to provide you with the essential theory included in the syllabus. To be able to understand and apply economic theory, you need to "tell a story". This means that you present the theory in the context of real-world examples. In this book we give you many examples, some of which are theoretical/hypothetical and some of which are real-world examples. However, it is your responsibility to build up your own awareness of real-world issues through your own inquiries.

This course book has been designed to facilitate your learning of economics in a number of ways:

- The study of the subject at both standard and higher level is encompassed and there is a focus toward the Approaches to Learning (ATL) skills.
- Given the importance of the nine key concepts addressed in the economics syllabus, we introduce these in some depth in the first chapter. From this point on, you will see "concept icons" throughout the companion to remind you to make the link between economic theory and these key concepts.
- We provide many stimuli for you to carry out your inquiries through the "Economics in Action" boxes. These investigations are important for two main reasons. Developing your awareness of real-world examples will make you a more informed global citizen, able to debate

contemporary economic issues in a knowledgeable and critical way. Equally, your knowledge of real-world issues and your ability to evaluate real-world issues critically using economic theory are stepping stones to successful assessment in IB Economics.

- Opportunities are provided to learn and practise the skills of evaluation and synthesis – key skills needed to become an informed student of economics. As you expand your knowledge of economics and gain the ability to evaluate these ideas you will develop a balanced view of alternative viewpoints and become critical thinkers.
- The importance of Theory of Knowledge (TOK) is emphasized, a core element of the IB Diploma Programme model. This will help you to understand that TOK exists in and applies to economics as it does in all academic areas.
- You will learn that economics is based on the collection of empirical evidence and the development of models which may differ, depending on the assumptions upon which they are based. You will also become aware of the inherent biases in economics and that there are conflicting schools of thought within the discipline.
- Opportunities are created to discuss ethical issues, such as the responsibilities for climate change, inequities in the distribution of income and wealth and the responsibility of policy makers to address poverty.
- There are biographies of several famous economists, which bring to light the fact that economic theory is devised by real people, people not unlike you.
- A number of data response exercises are included that are modelled on the final IB examination. Each exercise comprises a brief case study of economics in the real world and so will help you to develop your knowledge of real-world issues.
- Sample examination questions are included throughout the companion, both in exercises and at the end of each chapter. There is also assessment advice for external assessment throughout the book.
- There is a valuable final chapter containing advice on internal assessment, examination technique and extended essay writing.

The order of topics in this companion is not exactly as it appears in the IB syllabus. In a few places, the topics have been rearranged so that they are presented where they are most useful.

Economics is, by nature, a dynamic subject. As a result, theories evolve and change, and new theories are introduced to explain new evidence. It is not expected that you will rely entirely on this one course book as your only resource. To benefit fully from an economics course at any level, you should draw on a wide variety of resources and approaches.

Jocelyn Blink and Ian Dorton

1 WHAT IS ECONOMICS?

By the end of this chapter, you should be able to:

→ Define, and give examples of, social sciences

→ Define economics

→ Understand the social nature and scope of economics

→ Identify the nine central (key) concepts of IB economics

HL Define, give examples of, and distinguish between needs and wants; goods and services; and economic goods and free goods

HL Define opportunity cost and understand its link to scarcity and choice

HL Explain the basic economic questions; "What to produce?", "How to produce?" and "How much to produce?"

HL Distinguish between microeconomics and macroeconomics

HL Describe, and give examples of, the factors of production

HL Explain that economists are model builders and that they employ the assumption of *"ceteris paribus"*

HL Distinguish between positive economics and normative economics

HL Explain, illustrate, and analyse production possibilities curves in terms of opportunity cost, scarcity, choice, unemployment of resources, efficiency, actual economic growth and growth in production possibilities

HL Distinguish between different economic systems: free market economy, planned economy and mixed economy

HL Compare and contrast the advantages and disadvantages of planned and free market economies

What is economics?

Economics is known as a *social science*. This means that it is the study of people in society and how they interact with each other. Other social sciences include sociology, political science, psychology, anthropology and history. As the discipline of economics has evolved, certain branches of the discipline have incorporated the findings of many of these other social sciences in order to explain economic behaviour better.

The Earth is, to all intent and purposes, finite. This means that we only have a finite amount of resources. Since we need to use these resources to produce the goods and services that we need or want, the quantity of goods and services available to us is also finite. Goods are physical objects that are capable of being touched (tangible), such as mobile phones, vegetables and cars. Services are intangible things that cannot be touched, such as mobile-phone repairs, car insurance and haircuts.

Although the resources used to produce goods and services are finite, human needs and wants are infinite. Needs are things that we must have to survive, such as food, shelter and clothing. Wants are things that we would like to have but which are not necessary for our immediate physical survival, such as televisions and mobile phones.

Scarcity exists because of the conflict between the finite resources available to the world's population and its infinite material needs and wants. This is where economics comes in. Economics is *the social science that examines the way that people behave and interact with each other to overcome the problems that arise as a result of the basic economic problem of* ***scarcity***.

It should be obvious that because of scarcity, **choices** have to be made. Therefore, we can say that economics is *the study of the choices that people make in overcoming the problems that arise because resources are limited, while needs and wants are unlimited*. Needless to say, the choices made by groups of people can have significant impact on other groups of people, and also on the environment. This must be taken into account when examining economic issues.

Exercise 1.1
ATL Thinking and Communication

1. Make a list of your own needs.
2. Make a list of the needs that your grandparents may have had when they were your age.
3. Explain the reason for any differences between your lists for parts 1 and 2.
4. Make a list of the needs of a person the same age as you, living in another continent.
5. Explain the reason for any differences between your lists for parts 1 and 4.

What are the costs of the choices that economic agents make?

All economic agents, whether they are consumers, producers or the government, must make choices about how to allocate the scarce resources available to them. For example, in very simple terms, consumers have to decide which goods and services to buy. Producers have to decide which products to produce and how to produce them. Governments have thousands of decisions to make in trying to allocate the resources available to them.

Whenever a **choice** is made by an economic agent concerning the use of its resources, something is given up, or sacrificed. This leads us to a key economic concept, known as **opportunity cost**. Opportunity cost is defined as the next best alternative foregone when an economic decision is made. This may sound quite complicated but simply means that opportunity cost is what you give up in order to have something else. For example, if you decided to buy a new sweater for $30 rather than use the $30 to have a meal out, then you have sacrificed the meal out. Therefore, the opportunity cost of the sweater is the meal out that you have gone without. It is not the $30, as opportunity cost is never expressed in monetary terms. When we discuss opportunity cost, we can also use the word "trade-off". When you choose one option, you are trading it off for the option you do not select.

Consider the example of a government with limited revenues that is faced with the decision of whether to spend EUR 900 million on kindergarten for all children aged 3–6 years old or spend that same amount of money on upgrading its military aircraft fleet. If it spends the money on the aircraft, the opportunity cost of that decision is the kindergarten education that is not available to the children. If it spends the money on the kindergartens, the opportunity cost is clearly the improvements to the military aircraft. Obviously, this is a very difficult decision for a government, who will be confronted by political lobbies (special interest groups) from the different sides who are trying to get the government to spend on what they feel is best for the country. This is an example of the **interdependence** that exists between different groups within an economy; the decisions of one economic agent inevitably impact on other agents.

Consider another example of an industrial firm producing toys. At its annual general meeting, the directors must choose between spending $150,000 on a new technology that will reduce its CO_2 emissions or spending that money on new machinery that will result in greater **efficiency** for the firm by allowing more of its toys to be produced with the same inputs. If the company spends on the technology that favours the environment, the opportunity cost would be new machinery (and the possible additional profits from producing more toys). If it spends on the new machinery, the opportunity cost would be the technology to reduce emissions (and the gains to the environment).

These are good examples of the dilemmas that all economic agents face when making choices – because resources are limited, we can't meet our infinite wants and needs. When we decide in favour of one **choice**, we necessarily sacrifice something else. Trade-offs always have to be made. Again, economics studies how these choices are made.

Does everything have a cost in economics?

If secondary education is "free" in your country, this simply means that you do not have to pay money to get it. However, education can never be considered free because the resources that go into providing education could be used for something else, and so there is an **opportunity cost**. Let's say that someone offers you a "free lunch", because you do not have to pay for it. However, the resources that went into that lunch could have been used for something else, and so there is an opportunity cost of those resources. This is why economics is famous for the expression: "There is no such thing as a free lunch".

In economics, the only things that can be considered to be "free" are those things that are so abundant that there is no scarcity. If there is no **scarcity** of a good, and everyone can have as much of the good as they want, then we call it a *free good*. An example of a free good might be air, since air is everywhere around us and there is no competition for the air. We can have as much as we want. However, if we change the good to "breathable" air, then we might find that it is becoming an *economic good*. An economic good is one that is scarce and whose use involves an opportunity cost. Breathable air might not be free in many cities where pollution levels make it difficult to breathe, and so breathable air may be scarce. This leads to an important question, which is whether the current patterns of consumption and production of today's populations are threatening air quality for future generations. This is the issue of **sustainability**. To what extent are we actually threatening future generations while meeting the wants and needs of current generations?

What is the basic economic problem?

We have already seen that resources are relatively scarce and wants are infinite, which leads to **choices** to be made. These **choices** are often expressed in terms of three questions and represent the basic economic problem:

- *What should be produced and in what quantities?*

  Using these scarce resources, how many computers should be produced, how many bicycles, how much wheat and how much milk? This has to be decided for all economic goods.

- *How should things be produced?*

  There are many different ways of producing things and there are different combinations of resources that may be used in production. Should sports shoes be produced by an automated production line or by manual workers? Should crops be grown with a high usage of fertilizer or grown organically?

- *For whom should things be produced?*

  Should they go to those who can afford them or be shared out in some "fair" manner? How will the total income (the national income) of the economy be distributed? Will teachers get higher incomes than nurses?

Whatever the system used to allocate resources, these questions need to be answered. There are two theoretical allocation (rationing) systems – the free market system and the planned economy. In reality, all economies are mixed economies, which are a combination of the free market and planning. The extent to which governments should **intervene** in any economy is a constant source of debate and will be addressed throughout this course book.

> **Note**
> The free market system and the planned economy are discussed in more depth on pp. 20–22.

What is the difference between microeconomics and macroeconomics?

Economics can be split up into two main areas: microeconomics and macroeconomics.

Microeconomics	Macroeconomics
Microeconomics deals with smaller, discrete economic agents, such as consumers and producers, and the choices they make in response to **change** in a dynamic world. Microeconomics looks at the way consumers and producers come together in individual markets. At the consumer level, microeconomics examines the way in which people make choices about which goods and services to buy in order to improve their **well being**, given their budget constraints. When looking at producer behaviour, microeconomics examines how firms make decisions, such as what goods and services to produce and how to improve **efficiency**, given their limited resources. Microeconomics also considers individual industries to see how producers interact and compete with each other and how government **intervention** may affect producers.	Macroeconomics looks at the factors affecting the economy as a whole, such as economic growth and the way that **well being** is impacted by economic growth. The economic problems of unemployment (joblessness), inflation (rising prices across the economy) and deflation (falling prices across the economy) are examined in macroeconomics. It looks at the role of official policies, such as taxes and interest rates, in influencing economic activity. It also looks at the way that income is distributed throughout an economy.

Governments throughout the world, to varying degrees, intervene in markets and in economies with their government policies. In terms of microeconomics, there are numerous reasons why governments intervene in markets. For example, it may be to make sure that products meet certain standards in order to protect the **economic well being** of consumers, it may be to discourage consumers from consuming certain products, it may be to promote **sustainability** in the way that producers produce their products, or it may be to prevent large firms from abusing their ability to influence markets.

In terms of macroeconomics, governments may intervene to try to encourage businesses to produce more in order to increase Gross National Income (or Gross National Product); they may intervene to try to make the conditions in the labour market more **equitable** (fair) for workers; they may try to reduce the level of unemployment to improve the **economic well being** of workers or raise taxes on high income people to achieve greater **equity** (fairness).

Throughout the course, the debate about the extent to which governments should intervene in markets or in the economy is a key area for discussion and evaluation.

Exercise 1.2

ATL Thinking and Communication

Look back at the first few pages of this chapter to find references to the nine central concepts. These are in bold. Without doing any research (and without reading on!), try to explain what you think each of these concepts means, in terms of economics.

What are the nine central concepts of this IB Economics course?

Throughout this course, we will refer to nine central concepts that overarch economic issues. These will be presented in bold letters throughout the course book.

Icon	Key concept	Description
	Scarcity	Scarcity is a central concept in economics. Scarcity refers to the limited availability of economic resources relative to society's unlimited demand for goods and services. Thus, economics may be defined as the science that studies human behaviour as a relationship between ends and scarce resources which have alternative uses.
	Choice	Since resources are scarce, economics is a study of choices. It is clear that not all needs and wants can be satisfied. This necessitates choice and the idea of opportunity cost. Economic decision makers continually have to make choices between competing alternatives. Economics studies the consequences of these choices, both present and future.
	Efficiency	Efficiency is a quantifiable concept, determined by the ratio of useful output to total input. Allocative efficiency refers to making the best possible use of scarce resources to produce the combinations of goods and services that are optimum for society, thus minimizing resource waste.
	Equity	In contrast to equality, which describes situations in which economic outcomes are similar for different people or different social groups, equity refers to the concept or idea of fairness. Fairness is a normative concept as it means different things to different people. In economics, inequity is often interpreted to refer to inequality which may apply to the distribution of income, wealth or economic opportunity. Irrespective of economic system, inequity (or inequality) remains a significant issue both within and between societies.
	Economic well being	Economic well being is a multi-dimensional concept relating to the level of prosperity and the quality of living standards enjoyed by members of an economy. It includes: • present and future financial security • the ability to meet basic needs • the ability to make economic choices permitting achievement of personal satisfaction • the ability to maintain adequate income levels over the long term. There are broad disparities in economic well being both within and across nations.
	Sustainability	Sustainability in economics refers to the ability of the present generation to meet its needs without compromising the ability of future generations to meet its own needs. It refers to limiting the degree to which the economic activities of the current generation create harmful environmental outcomes. These might involve resource depletion or degradation that will negatively affect future generations. Sustainability is proving increasingly important in all economic analysis as planetary boundaries are pushed to the limit.
	Change	An understanding of the concept of change is essential in economics. The economic world is in a continual state of flux, and economists must be aware of this and adapt their thinking accordingly. The concept of change is important both in economic theory and in the empirical world that economics studies. In economic theory, economics focuses not on the level of the variables it investigates, but on their change from one situation to another. Empirically, the world that is studied by economists is always subject to continuous and profound change at institutional, structural, technological, economic and social levels.
	Interdependence	Consumers, firms, households, workers and governments (all economic actors) interact with each other within and, increasingly, across nations in order to achieve economic goals. The greater the level of interaction, the greater the degree of interdependence. In a highly interdependent economic world, decisions by certain economic actors will generate many, and often unintended, economic consequences for other actors. A consideration of possible economic consequences of interdependence is essential when conducting economic analysis.
	Intervention	Intervention in economics usually refers to government involvement in the workings of markets. While markets are considered the most efficient mechanism to organize economic activity, it is often recognized that they may fail to achieve certain societal goals, such as equity, economic well being or sustainability. Failure to achieve such goals may be considered to be sufficient reason for government intervention. In the real world, there is often disagreement among economists and policymakers on the need for, and extent of, government intervention.

▲ **Table 1.1** The nine central concepts in IB Economics, *IB Economics Guide* (2020), International Baccalaureate Organisation

Exercise 1.3

ATL Thinking and Communication

For each of the following headlines, work in groups to complete the table. One has been done for you as a sample (shown in red). Please note that there is no right answer; just think about possible options!

Headline	Reflection	Which central concept(s) might be relevant? Why?	Do you think this is a microeconomics or a macroeconomics issue? Why?
The car industry is pressuring the government to remove regulation on CO_2 emissions, which the firms say is reducing profits.	Why do you think firms might want fewer regulations? The firms probably want to make higher profits. OR Firms in other countries do not have the same regulations, so they have an advantage. AND The firms do not care if their emissions may be impacting on climate change because it does not really affect them.	**Intervention** is definitely relevant since the government recognises that the car market poses a threat to sustainability **Efficency** might be relevant, as firms think that if the regulations are removed then they will have lower costs and be more efficient. **Sustainability** is definitely relevant. Regulations are often designed to reduce emissions to prevent climate change which will certainly threaten future generations. **Interdependence** may be relevant as the producers in one country are dependent on the activities of producers in another country because they have to compete with them.	This is microeconomics, because it is dealing with one group of firms, the car industry.
President Lessing lowers income taxes to stimulate consumer spending.	Why do you think lower taxes would encourage consumers to spend more?		Micro or macro?
The Nasarawan government has blocked a merger between the two largest mobile service providers to protect consumers.	Why do you think consumers need to be "protected" from a merger?		Micro or macro?
Unemployment climbs to its highest rate in two years.	Can you suggest two problems that might occur as a result of higher unemployment?		Micro or macro?
In 2017, a leading soft drinks producer reported that it spent approximately $4 billion (US$) on advertising globally.	Why would a company spend this much money on advertising? Try to think of possible advantages and disadvantages of this.		Micro or macro?
Prime Minister Cornish has announced that she will put a 10% tariff (tax) on imported shoes.	Can you suggest two reasons for putting a tax on imported shoes?		Depending on the reasons for the tariff, this could be a micro issue or a macro issue.

What are the factors of production that are used to produce goods and services?

We have already established that **scarcity** is the fundamental problem addressed in economics and that humans must make **choices** about how they are going to allocate their limited resources to meet their unlimited wants and needs. But what are those "resources"? In economics, the resources used to produce goods and services are classified into four categories known as the four factors of production.

Land

Land includes all the resources provided by nature that are used to produce goods. It includes the soil on which agricultural products are grown, anything that is grown on the land and used in the production of other goods, and anything that is found under the land, including oil, minerals and elements. It therefore includes all natural resources. This factor of production may be referred to as "natural capital".

> **Note**
>
> An orange that you pick off the tree in the garden to eat is not a factor of production because it is not being used to produce another good. However, the oranges that are sold to firms from an orange grove in Spain would be considered a factor of production because these oranges will be used to produce orange juice, for example.

Labour

Labour includes all the human resources used in producing goods and services. It is the physical and mental contribution of the existing workforce to production. Labour may also be referred to as "human capital".

Capital

Capital, which may also be referred to as "physical capital" is the factor of production that includes all the buildings, offices, factories, machines, tools, infrastructure and technologies, and buildings that are used to produce goods and services. Anything that has been made by humans, and is used to produce a good or a service, is referred to as capital. When firms spend money on capital, this is known as investment.

Entrepreneurship (management)

Management is the organizing and risk-taking factor of production. Entrepreneurs organize the other factors of production – land, labour and capital – to produce goods and services. They may use their personal money and the money of other investors to develop new ways of doing things and new products, buy the factors of production, produce the goods and services and, hopefully, make a profit. As a profit is never guaranteed and money may be lost, this is the risk-taking part of the role of the entrepreneur.

What is the methodology of economics?

How do economists build models?

Given the complexity of economic relationships, economists aim to simplify such relationships by focusing on a few specific factors at a time and developing a model. A model is a simplification of reality, often expressed in the form of a mathematical analysis and equations or a diagram. We use economic models as the basis for our analysis.

It must be pointed out that every model that has been created by economists has been specifically chosen to highlight certain factors. By definition, this means that other factors are left out, or ignored. It must also be acknowledged that in order to simplify complex reality, economists make assumptions.

This can help us to understand why there can be significant disagreement between economists. In developing their theories, economists make **choices** about which relationships they seek to examine and they make assumptions to explain what is likely to happen. These **choices** and assumptions differ, and so we have contrasting models.

In order to make predictions about how economic agents are likely to behave, economists often use the *ceteris paribus* assumption. This is a Latin term which means "all other things being equal". When economists want to test the effect of one variable on another, they need to isolate the effect of the one variable by assuming that there is no change in any of the other variables.

Let's consider an example. How would you expect people to behave if the price of a product such as ice cream falls? Typically, when the price of a product falls, people wish to buy more of the product because they can afford more. You will see that this is known as the "law of demand". An economist would say. "A decrease in the price of ice cream leads to an increase in quantity demanded, *ceteris paribus*". It is necessary to say *ceteris paribus*, because there are many things that affect the amount of ice cream – not just the price. Demand for ice cream could be affected by the weather, or current trends in diets. Ice-cream sellers might lower their prices, but if there is very bad weather or a public health campaign against high-calorie foods, then people might not buy more ice cream. By saying *ceteris paribus*, we assume that nothing else has changed. The *ceteris paribus* assumption allows economists to use their models to predict how people will behave.

What is the distinction between positive economics and normative economics?

There are two standard ways in which economists approach the world. Positive economics is concerned with describing and analysing economic relationships and making factual and objective claims. Positive

Note

In any economics course, there is extensive use of economic models. However, in many cases, the assumptions behind the models are not understood, or not questioned. In this course, we want to make sure that you are aware of competing models, and that you can understand how the assumptions made by different economists can lead to different economic theories. You should also grow to realise that when economic models are used to help people make choices, or businesses develop business plans, or governments set policies, there is often an ideological (political) bias due to the framing of the model.

economics uses the scientific method by using logic to make hypotheses and then collecting empirical evidence in order to refute the hypothesis or develop predictive models and theories. Positive statements are concerned with the facts and what actually is happening, or what will happen. They may be used to explain causal relationships. Examples of positive statements include:

- The unemployment rate in Spain is higher than the unemployment rate in Austria.
- An increase in income tax will cause a fall in consumer spending.
- The burning of coal, natural gas, and oil for electricity and heat is the largest single source of global greenhouse gas emissions.

Normative economics is concerned with how things should be, and necessarily involves subjective value judgments. A normative statement may usually be recognised because it includes opinion-based words like "should", "ought", "too little" or "too much". Examples of normative statements include:

- "The Spanish government has put too little emphasis on lowering unemployment."
- "Governments should increase the use of renewable energies by putting higher taxes on fossil-fuel based energy."

It is worthwhile to point out that positive statements can be true or false, and can be fact-checked. For example, a newspaper might have a headline stating that the unemployment rate had fallen to 4%, but the data might be incorrect. On the other hand, normative statements cannot be true or false, as they are based on subjective judgments.

Even when they are correct, positive economic statements may be misleading, and can contain some normative assumptions. For example, assume that the headline about the unemployment rate is actually a fact. At first glance, this would suggest a positive outcome, as the reduction of unemployment is usually seen to be a good thing. However, if the unemployment rate decreased because more people were hired into low pay, part-time jobs with no job security, this might result in longer term problems and not be a good thing, on balance.

It is important to recognize that when governments develop their policies, they are using the positive economic statements and theories about what are likely to be the outcomes, but they are heavily influenced by their own values and ideological objectives. And when we judge economic policies, we are also influenced by our own personal viewpoints.

As noted earlier, the debate about the extent to which government should **intervene** in markets or in the economy is a key area for discussion and evaluation. This is of course an area of normative economics.

TOK

To what extent does the distinction between positive and normative statements exist in other academic disciplines?

How can we illustrate the concepts of scarcity, choice, opportunity cost and efficiency?

You will now be introduced to the first "model" that economists use, known as the production possibilities curve (PPC). This simple model may be used to illustrate the concepts of **scarcity**, **choice**, **opportunity cost** and **efficiency**. The definition of a production possibilities curve is that it is a curve showing the maximum combinations of two types of output that can be produced in an economy in a given time period, if all the resources in the economy are being used efficiently and the state of technology is fixed.

The PPC for an imaginary economy is illustrated in Figure 1.1.

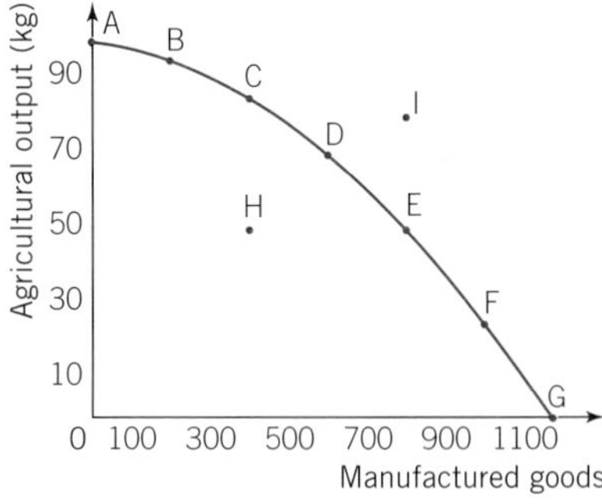

▲ **Figure 1.1** Production possibilities curve

With the current amount of scarce resources (land, labour, capital and entrepreneurship) that are available in this imaginary economy, it can produce a limited amount of manufactured goods and agricultural products. The PPC itself shows the maximum quantity of both products that can be produced; this is known as the *potential output*. You should be able to see that the economy could produce 100 kg of agricultural products (point A), but to do so, the economy would be using all of its resources and so no manufactured goods could be produced. Similarly, the economy could produce 1175 units of manufactured goods, but then no agricultural output would be able to be produced (point G). More realistically, the economy would allocate its resources to produce somewhere along the curve, for example at point E, producing 50 kg of agricultural products and 800 units of manufactured goods.

How can the PPC model be used?

Note that the PPC model contains several assumptions:

- It is assumed that the economy produces only two goods.
- It is assumed that the resources and state of technology are fixed.
- It is assumed that all the resources in the economy are fully employed.

Despite its simplicity, the PPC model is extremely useful in illustrating several key economic concepts.

Scarcity: This imaginary economy does not have enough resources to produce as many agricultural products and manufactured goods as it would like. The PPC illustrates this constraint. The economy cannot produce 800 kg of agricultural products and 80 kg of units of manufactured goods because it does not have enough resources. We say that all the points beyond the PPC are unattainable given the current resources and state of technology.

Choice: The PPC clearly shows that a choice has to be made between the two types of output that are competing for the economy's resources. If, for example, some of the workers in the economy (labour) are producing agricultural products, then they cannot be used to produce manufactured goods. So choices have to be made as to which combination of output is to be produced using which resources.

Opportunity cost: Let's say that the economy is operating at point D, with 70 kg of agricultural products and 600 units of manufactured goods. It would be possible to increase the production of manufactured goods to 800 units by shifting some of the resources away from agricultural output, but only if the economy sacrificed the production of agricultural products. To move from point D to point E, the opportunity cost of the extra 200 manufactured goods would be 20 kg of agricultural products.

Efficiency: If the economy is using all of its resources to the fullest extent possible and operating on the PPC, we say that there is *productive efficiency*. The economy could of course operate at point H, making 50 kg of agricultural products and 400 units of manufactured goods, but this would imply a lack of productive efficiency, as not all resources would be working to the fullest extent possible. It could be that there are unemployed workers or factories not operating in the economy, so not all labour and capital are being used to the fullest extent possible. It could also mean that the economy is not making the best use of the available resources. For example, the land on which the factories are built might be used more effectively to produce agricultural output.

So, point H illustrates unemployment of resources, or inefficient use of resources. By using the factors of production more efficiently, the economy could move closer to the PPC, increasing its output of agricultural output and manufactured goods. Any points underneath the PPC are possible, but would indicate a lack of **efficiency**, and some waste of resources. A movement from any point inside the PPC towards the PPC means that more output is being produced. This is known as *actual economic growth*.

The PPC only indicates what a hypothetical economy could produce; it says nothing about where the economy should produce, or which point would be in the best interests of society. Furthermore, even though operating on the PPC indicates productive **efficiency**, and technically there is no waste, this is not necessarily a desirable outcome. Productive **efficiency** means that the economy is using all of its factors of production to the fullest extent possible. This could well involve a rate of resource use and extraction that damages the environment and poses a threat to **sustainability**. This may reduce production possibilities in the future, and certainly impose costs on the future **economic well being** of society.

Why is the PPC concave?

In moving from point A to point B, the economy produces an additional 200 units of agricultural output at an **opportunity cost** of 5 kg of agricultural products. In moving from point B to point C, there is again an increase of 200 units of agricultural output, but the **opportunity cost** of these additional 200 units has risen to 10 kg of agricultural products. In moving from point C to point D, the economy again produces an additional 200 kg of agricultural output, but this time, the economy has to give up 15 kg of agricultural products. Using the diagram, we can see that as we move the resources from producing agricultural products to producing manufactured goods, the **opportunity cost** increases. This accounts for the concave shape of the PPC.

The reason why the **opportunity cost** increases is due to the fact that not all the factors of production used to produce agricultural output are equally suitable for producing manufactured goods. To produce the first 200 manufactured goods, some of the workers and other resources such as the land itself could be reasonably easily re-allocated to producing manufactured goods. For example, if factories to produce manufactured goods were built on the less fertile agricultural land, then not much agricultural output would have to be sacrificed. However, to go on increasing the production of manufactured goods, the resources taken away from producing agricultural output would be less and less suitable for producing manufactured goods, and so the **opportunity cost** of re-allocating them would be higher.

If the **opportunity cost** were constant, with each additional unit of manufactured goods costing the exact same amount of agricultural output, the PPC would be a straight line (as shown in Figure 1.2).

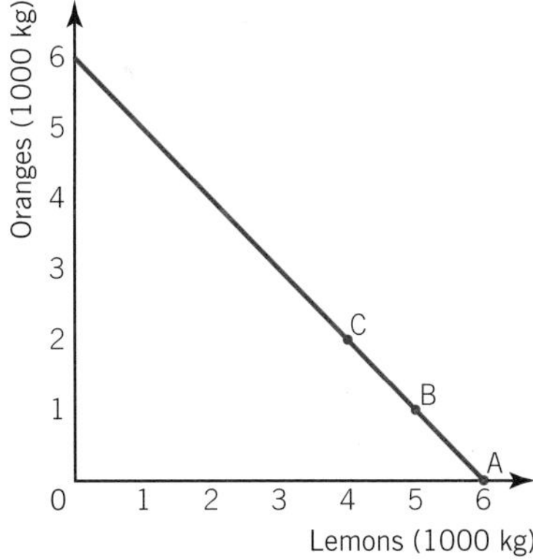

▲ **Figure 1.2** Constant opportunity cost

In the hypothetical economy shown in Figure 1.2, the **choice** of output is between oranges and lemons. In this case, we may assume that the factors of production used to produce oranges (agricultural land, climate, farming skills, machinery) are identical to those producing lemons. Therefore, to increase the production of lemons, the factors of production producing oranges could be readily substituted without facing increasing **opportunity costs**. In moving from point A to point B, producing 1000 kg of oranges incurs an **opportunity cost** of 1000 kg of lemons. In moving from point B to point C, the same quantity of lemons is sacrificed, and so on.

A straight line PPC indicates constant **opportunity costs**, whereas the concave PPC indicates increasing **opportunity costs**.

Are the unattainable points beyond the PPC always unattainable?

Remember that the PPC is drawn on the assumption that the factors of production and the state of technology are fixed. However, these can certainly change. If there is an improvement in the quality or an increase in the quantity of the factors of production, or technological

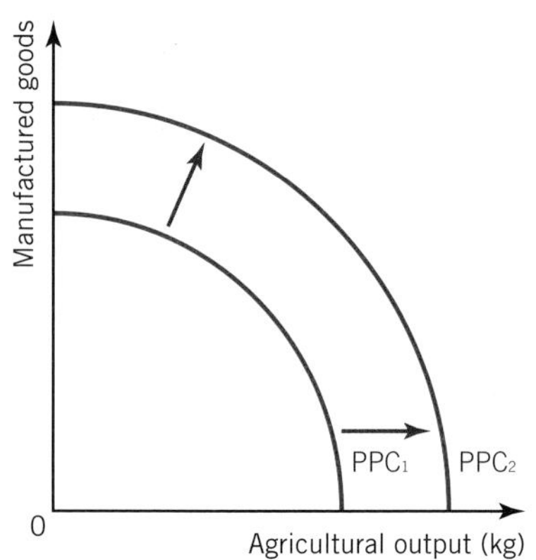

▲ **Figure 1.3** An increase in production possibilities

Exercise 1.4

ATL Thinking and Communication

Come up with as many different ways as you can to explain how the quality or the quantity of an economy's factors of production could be increased or improved.

Now imagine that you represent the government of your country. Explain what policies you could adopt to increase the production possibilities for your country. What possible limitations would you face in putting your policies into action?

advancements, then the PPC would shift outwards from PPC_1 to PPC_2, as shown in Figure 1.3.

This is referred to as a growth in production possibilities. This could come about from hundreds of reasons. For example:

- changes in the education system could improve the quality of labour
- policies to increase immigration could improve the quantity and also the quality of labour
- a better-educated population could develop improved technologies
- new forms of energy could be found, or developed, increasing the quantity of natural resources.

Unfortunately, an economy's PPC could also shift inwards if there is a reduction in the quantity or worsening of the quality of the factors of production. Wars, epidemics and natural disasters could all have a negative impact on all the factors of production, thus reducing an economy's production possibilities.

Assessment advice

The choice of agricultural products and manufactured goods is only one of infinite pairs of goods that you could choose to illustrate the PPC theory. The key thing is that the two items you choose would both be using the economy's factors of production. In effect, they are "competing" to use the same factors of production, and this explains why there is a trade-off. If the resources are used to produce one good, then they cannot be used to produce the other – a trade-off must be made. Other examples you might see in textbooks or on the Internet include:

- capital goods versus consumer goods
- military goods versus civilian goods (often referred to using the metaphor "guns versus butter")
- Good X versus Good Y. (It is recommended that you do not use this one. Whenever you draw and explain a diagram in economics, you want to be able to "tell a story" and weave in an example. This is difficult to do if you are using generic products like Good X and Good Y!)

Exercise 1.5

ATL Thinking and Communication

1. Consider a hypothetical economy which produces only two types of output – consumer goods (goods used by consumers) and capital goods (goods used by producers). Because resources are scarce, they cannot produce as much of each of these as they would like. The following table illustrates the possible combinations of consumer goods and capital goods that can be produced.

Combination	Consumer goods (units)	Capital goods (units)
A	0	200
B	50	180
C	100	150
D	150	100
E	200	0

a) Draw a diagram to illustrate the economy's production possibilities curve.

b) Use values from the table or the diagram to explain the concept of opportunity cost.

c) On your diagram, add a point "F" that is inside the curve. Describe how the economy is using its resources at point F.

d) On your diagram, add a point "G" that is beyond the curve. Explain why this point is currently not attainable.

e) Explain what would have to happen for the economy to reach point G.

2. Using a (new) PPC diagram, explain what would happen if an economy experienced a devastating natural disaster. Be sure to explain your reasoning.

What is the circular flow of income model?

Another model to illustrate how an economy might work is the circular flow of income model. This will be developed further when macroeconomics is the focus, but at this point it is worthwhile to have an overview of the model, as it can illustrate the interdependence that exists between key economic decision makers. As with the PPC model, there are certain assumptions behind this model. A simple two-sector model of the economy is shown in Figure 1.4.

The two sectors are households and firms. In this simplified model, households have two roles: it is assumed that they are the owners of all the factors of production and they are the people who buy the nation's output of goods and services.

The firms are the productive units; they hire the factors of production from households and use these factors to produce the nation's output of goods and services, which are sold to the households (arrow 3), and receive the expenditure by the households on these goods and services (arrow 4).

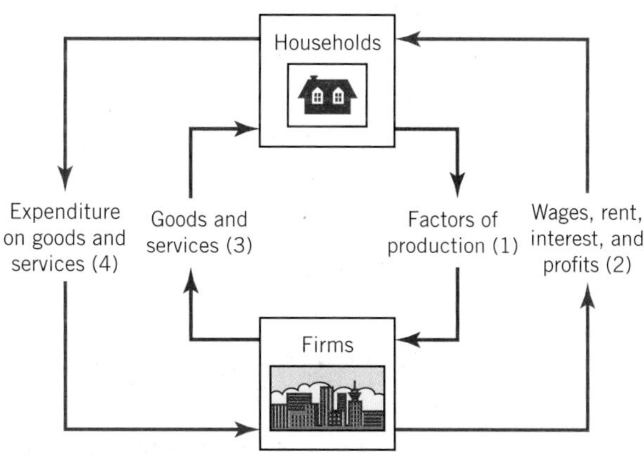

▲ **Figure 1.4** Two-sector circular flow of income model

Households supply their factors of production to the firms (arrow 1) and, in turn, they receive income for their factors (arrow 2). (See box at the top of the next page for a summary of the factors of production provided and the income received.)

The red arrows show how the income flows through the economy between these two sectors, and illustrates the **interdependence** between the households and firms.

The factors of production provided by households and payments provided by firms are shown below:

Factors of production – provided by households.	Payments to the factor – provided by firms
Labour	Wages
Land	Rent
Capital	Interest
Entrepreneurship	Profits

This very simple model contains only two sectors. It suggests that **all** income earned by the households is spent on domestically produced goods and services. Clearly, households and firms are not the only two sectors acting in an economy and consumers do not spend all their incomes on domestically produced goods. We expand on the model by introducing three additional sectors: the government, the financial sector and the foreign sector.

Consumers do not spend all their income on domestically-produced goods and producers do not pass on all their income to the domestic households. Income leaves the sector via the three additional sectors. The income that leaves is known as a *leakage*. There are three leakages:

1. **Taxes:** some of the income from both households and firms goes to the government sector in the form of taxes.
2. **Saving:** both households and firms save some of their income in financial institutions. Examples of these include banks, stock markets and pension funds. These make up the financial sector.
3. **Imports:** both households and firms spend some of their money on foreign goods and services. The foreign producers that receive this income constitute the foreign sector.

The three sectors are also responsible for introducing income into the circular flow. The income that comes in is known as an injection. There are three injections.

- **Government spending.** The two sector model includes only the spending by households and firms. Governments at all levels (local district councils to national governments) spend on all kinds of things including education, health care, the maintenance of law and order, infrastructure and salaries for government workers. As you will see in later chapters, governments are able to spend more than they earn in order to deliberately influence the level of leakages and injections in an economy and thereby affect the level of national income.

  It is important to point out that there is a category of government spending known as transfer payments that are not included as an injection into the circular flow. Transfer payments are payments to individuals that are not the result of an increase in output. They are payments for which no good or service is exchanged. Examples of transfer payments are pensions, unemployment benefits and child allowance payments. Governments tax the income of some households and transfer this income to others through the payments. As it is a transfer of income rather than income in exchange for output, this spending does not represent an injection.

- **Investment.** The financial sector lends money to firms, which they use to start up or expand their businesses by buying capital. This spending by firms on capital is referred to as investment.
- **Exports.** Foreign households and firms buy the country's exports, injecting money into the economy.

Figure 1.5 shows the circular flow of income model with the five sectors – households, firms, the foreign sector, financial institutions and the government sector – taking into account the leakages and injections.

Each sector is associated with one leakage and one injection. However, there is no reason to assume that each sector's leakage will be equal to its corresponding injection. Governments are able to spend more money than they earn in taxes by borrowing money (this is known as *running a budget deficit)*. Countries can certainly spend more on imports than they earn from their exports and experience trade imbalances. Banks lend more money than they have as savings held in their institutions.

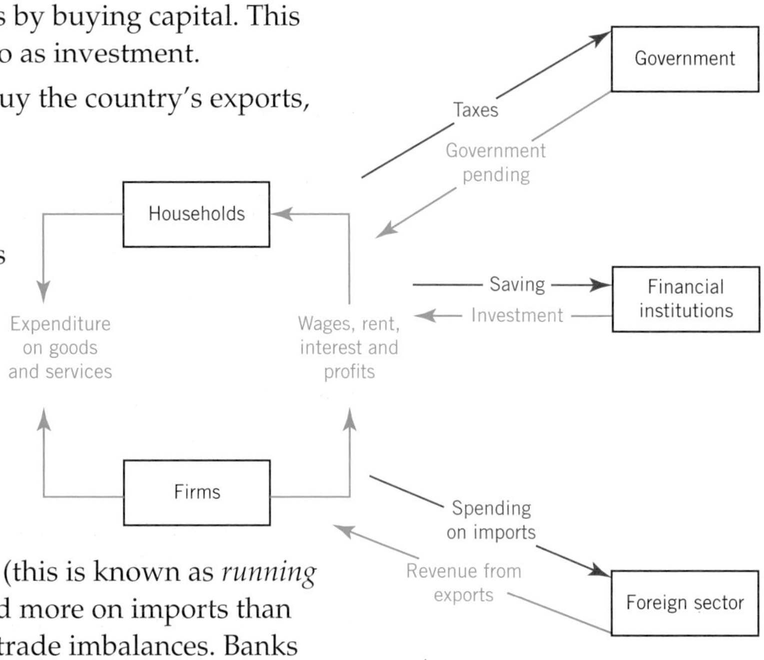

▲ **Figure 1.5** Circular flow of income

What can the four-sector circular flow of income model tell us?

This four-sector model is clearly a simplification of a complex economy, but is used to illustrate some important conclusions.

The amount of income flowing in the circular flow can be referred to as the national income, or Gross National Income (GNI). When national income is rising, we say that the economy is growing. If national income is falling, the economy may be in a recession.

The economy is said to be in equilibrium when leakages are equal to injections. This means that if leakages and injections remain equal, the economy will not grow or shrink. If leakages rise, without a corresponding increase in injections, then national income will fall to a new equilibrium, as there will be less income circulating. If injections rise with no corresponding rise in leakages, then the economy will grow by moving to a higher level of national income. If it is assumed that economic growth is a key objective for an economy (an assumption we will question later), the circular flow of income model is widely used to explain how growth can occur. This will be developed further in later chapters.

The model is also useful in showing the **interdependence** that exists between the five sectors.

Let's look at some of the ways in which households and the other sectors are interdependent:

- Households are dependent on the firms to pay for their labour and to provide them with goods and services. If firms cannot start up and grow to create jobs, then households will not earn money. This will affect their spending on goods and services which will in turn harm the firms. Reduced incomes will reduce the amount that households pay to the government in taxes, and it will harm foreign producers because they will not be able to afford as many imports.
- Households are dependent on the financial sector as a place to borrow money to pay for products that their current income does not allow them to buy and as a place to store their savings safely. If the financial institutions make it too difficult to borrow money, then they may not be able to buy houses or cars or use their credit cards to finance their spending. If the money that they can earn from saving their money (the interest) is low, then their savings will not grow, and this will damage their ability to spend on goods and services in the future. Because the decisions taken by the financial sector affect households directly, then firms, the government, and the foreign sector will also be affected.
- Households are dependent on foreign producers to provide them with imports that they cannot get at home, or that are better and/or less expensive than the products they can buy at home. They are also dependent on foreign countries as places to travel. The incomes of the foreign producers are dependent on the ability of the country's households and firms to buy their products.
- Households are dependent on the government for a myriad of things. For example, governments provide law and order, regulations to make people's lives better and safer, education and valuable infrastructure. And clearly governments are dependent on the households to provide tax revenues to finance their expenditure.

The circular nature of the flow of income means that decisions taken anywhere on the cycle will have an impact on all other areas of the cycle.

Exercise 1.6
ATL Thinking and Communication

Draw your own version of the circular flow model, including the five sectors, the leakages and the injections. Using your diagram, explain or illustrate how a decision by the government to lower household income taxes might affect the five sectors of the circular flow.

What are rationing systems?

Economics is often referred to as a study of rationing systems. Since the resources in an economy are relatively scarce, there must be some way of rationing those resources and the goods and services that are produced by them.

In theory, there are two main rationing systems and we shall look at them now:

What is a planned economy?

In a planned economy, sometimes called a centrally planned economy or a command economy, decisions as to what to produce, how to produce, and for whom to produce, are made by a central body, the government.

All resources are collectively owned. Government bodies arrange all production, set wages, and set prices through central planning. Decisions are made by the government on behalf of the people and, in theory, in their best interests.

The quantity of decisions to be made, data to be analysed and factors of production to be allocated are immense. This makes central planning very difficult. If one then adds the need to forecast future events accurately in order to plan ahead, the task becomes almost impossible to achieve with any decent level of efficiency.

In the 1980s, almost one third of the world's population lived in planned economies, mainly in the USSR and China. These days, there are very few countries that rely solely on planning. In Eastern Europe, the countries of the old USSR now have clear market segments. The same is true in China.

Did you know?

As a result of planning problems and an emphasis on industrial production, there were chronic shortages of consumer goods in the USSR and queues were a part of daily life. It is estimated that the average Russian woman would spend two hours every day lining up to buy essential goods.

What is a free market economy?

In a free market economy, sometimes called a private enterprise economy or capitalism, prices are used to ration goods and services. All production is in private hands and demand and supply are left free to set wages and prices in the economy. The economy should work relatively efficiently and there should be few cases of surpluses and shortages.

Individuals make independent decisions about what products they would like to purchase at given prices and producers then make decisions about whether they are prepared to provide those products. The producers' decisions are based upon the likelihood of profits being made. If there are changes in the pattern of demand, then there will be changes in the pattern of supply in order to meet the new demand pattern. For example, let us assume that producers have been making both roller skates and skateboards and find that they are equally profitable in the quantities currently supplied. Now assume that tastes change and skateboards are seen to be more fashionable. There will be an increased demand for skateboards and a fall in the demand for roller skates. Shops will experience a shortage of skateboards to sell and a surplus of roller skates that are not being sold. In order to rectify this, they will raise the price of skateboards, reducing the quantity demanded, and lower the price of roller skates in order to clear the surplus. Producers, whose costs have not changed, will realise that there is now more profit to be made in producing skateboards than there is in producing roller skates and will increase their production of skateboards and reduce their production of roller skates. Resources will be moved from producing roller skates to producing skateboards. Thus, we can see that a change in the demand of consumers sends "signals" that bring about a chain of events that re-allocates factors of production and makes sure that the wishes of the consumers are met. The free market system is a self-righting system.

When consumers and producers work to their own best interests, the market produces the "best" outcome for both. As the father of modern economics Adam Smith said, "Every individual… generally, indeed, neither intends to promote the public interest, nor knows how much he is promoting it… he intends only his own gain, and he is in this… led by an invisible hand to promote an end which was no part of his intention." This is often used as a justification for arguing that there should be minimal government interference in the economy.

In a market economy, it is said that resources will be allocated efficiently. However, sometimes it takes a long time for resources to be reallocated from the production of one good or service to another. This is likely to create negative consequences for the stakeholders involved.

How realistic are planned and free market economies?

In reality, all economies are mixed economies. What is different is the degree of the mix from country to country. Some countries, such as China, have high levels of planning and government involvement in the economy. Even in the seemingly free economies, such as the USA, the UK or even Hong Kong, government intervention is very much a part of the economic system. Some degree of government intervention is deemed essential, since there are some dangers that will exist if the free market is left to operate without interference. Some of the disadvantages of pure free markets and planning are shown in Table 1.2.

Disadvantages of pure free markets	Disadvantages of planning
Demerit goods (things that are bad for people, such as drugs or child prostitution) will be over-provided, driven by high prices and thus a high profit motive.	Total production, investment, trade, and consumption, even in a small economy, are too complicated to plan efficiently and there will be misallocation of resources, shortages, and surpluses.
Merit goods (things that are good for people, such as education and health care) will be underprovided, since they will only be produced for those who can afford them and not for all people.	Because there is no price system in operation, resources will not be used efficiently. Arbitrary decisions will not be able to make the best use of resources.
Resources may be used up too quickly and the environment may be damaged by pollution, as firms seek to make high profits and to minimize costs.	Incentives tend to be distorted. Workers with guaranteed employment and managers who gain no share of profits are difficult to motivate. Output and quality may suffer.
Some members of society will not be able to look after themselves, such as orphans, the sick and the long-term unemployed, and will not survive.	The dominance of the government may lead to a loss of personal liberty and freedom of choice.
Large firms may grow and dominate industries, leading to high prices, a loss of **efficiency** and excessive power.	Governments may not share the same aims as the majority of the population and yet, by power, may implement plans that are not popular, or are even corrupt.

▲ **Table 1.2** Disadvantages of pure free markets and planning

Thinking outside the box

Remember that every economic model is based on certain assumptions. In her 2017 book, *Doughnut Economics: Seven Ways to Think like a 21st-Century Economist*, Kate Raworth of the University of Oxford's Environmental Change Institute, provides compelling challenges to the assumptions presented in the standard circular flow of income model. At the root of her argument is the idea that the circular flow of income model focuses only on economic growth as the key economic goal. Her analysis shows how the preoccupation with economic growth is the cause of the growing social and economic inequalities and massive environmental challenges facing the global community.

She points out four clear flaws related to the assumptions of the circular flow model: (https://www.kateraworth.com/2012/07/23/why-its-time-to-vandalize-the-economic-textbooks/)

1. It assumes that the economy is independent of the environment, with a closed flow of income cycling between the five sectors. There is no reference to the energy and natural materials that are necessary for economic activity, and there is no understanding of the environmental threats such as climate change involved in using the energy and other natural resources. Later, you will see that economists do try to account for the costs to the environment in treating the consequences as something known as "externalities". However, Raworth points out that this type of analysis treats the negative consequences as external side effects of economic activity and argues that this thinking is a key reason for the threats to sustainability we are facing. As Raworth says, "How can it make sense to treat the fundamental resource on which all life depends as a factor external to the system?"
2. The circular flow of income model includes only incomes that are paid for (monetized) in formal markets – such as incomes paid to teachers, factory workers, shop workers or bankers. It ignores the fact that the monetized economy would not function without the unpaid work of the "care economy". This includes all the services provided by parents and carers (largely women) in having and raising children, managing households, looking after sick people so that they can return to work and looking after elderly people. In many low-income countries, where people can't afford necessities and governments are unable to provide things which people in richer countries take for granted, such as water supplies, heating materials and food, millions of women and girls spend hours walking miles each day carrying huge loads of water, food or firewood on their heads, often with a child on their back. All this work done in the unpaid ("non-monetized") sectors everywhere in the world is ignored in the circular flow model. And as Raworth says, "If we ignore it, we ignore many of life's most valued goods and services, and misunderstand the working lives of many of the world's women."
3. Related to the previous point, there are further kinds of non-monetized resources and work that are very significant to the working of the economy. The circular flow of income assumes that all work done is compensated for by income received and all natural resources are exchanged in markets. However, a great deal of work is done for objectives not related to earning an income. This includes all the voluntary work that contributes to the functioning of a society. It includes all the work done to contribute to the world's sharing of knowledge and information, including the common pool of information on the Internet (for example, Wikipedia). Rowarth refers to the results of this non-monetized work as "the commons", and defines it as "the shareable resources of nature or society" that we can all use without relying on a government or a firm to provide them. The "commons" also includes the natural resources, such as the sea, that are not formally owned, but which are used for economic activity.
4. In the circular flow of income, firms pay wages, rent, profit and dividends to households. In the "real world" the majority of people receive comparatively low wages in comparison to the very large rents and dividends which go to the relatively fewer wealthy people who can afford to own land and capital. This has given rise to troubling power imbalances and growing social and economic inequalities both nationally and internationally that cannot be ignored.

George Monbiot summarizes the criticisms of the circular flow: "It depicts a closed flow of income cycling between households, businesses, banks, government and trade, operating in a social and ecological vacuum. Energy, materials, the natural world, human society, power, the wealth we hold in common … all are missing from the model. The unpaid work of carers – principally women – is ignored, though no economy could function without them." (*The Guardian*, 12 April 2017)

One of the principal uses of the circular flow model is to analyse how the economy can experience economic growth, and it is usually assumed that the primary objective of any economy should be to achieve economic growth. For decades, it has been assumed that economic growth can solve all problems. However, given the massive negative consequences of this approach in terms of climate change and other environmental crises, along with the tremendous social and economic hardships faced by people across the globe, there has been increasing pressure for a new approach to economic theory.

Raworth believes that students of economics require a more realistic "picture" of the economy. She presents her model, called the "Embedded Economy" (Figure 1.6) to show that the economy nests within society and within the living world. This model recognises the diverse ways in which the economy can meet people's needs and wants. It shows that people are much more than simply workers supplying our labour in return for incomes to buy goods and service. Instead, we are members of societies functioning within the Earth's ecosystem. The embedded economy shows that households, the state (government), markets and the commons are all interdependent in supplying and consuming the things we need to meet our material and non-material needs and wants. At a time when we are facing tremendous environmental challenges, the embedded economy model is valuable in demonstrating that the economy cannot be examined without considering the extent to which economic activity both uses up the world's natural resources and causes possibly irreparable damage to global ecosystems.

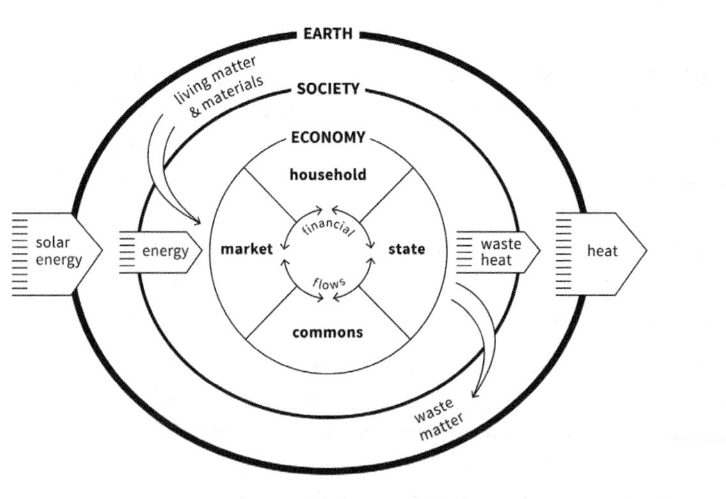

▲ Figure 1.6 The embedded economy, Raworth (2017)

Exercise 1.7

ATL Thinking and Communication

Read the article below and answer the questions that follow:

Should we be concerned about the world's supply of helium and indium?

A leading British academic last night (MON) warned the world's Helium supply is on course to run out in just 10 years.

Professor David Cole-Hamilton urged people not to let off birthday party balloons into the atmosphere as the inert gas was needed for MRI scans and deep sea diving.

There is no chemical way of manufacturing helium; the supplies on Earth come from the very slow radioactive alpha decay that occurs in rocks.

Prof Cole-Hamilton, Emeritus Professor of Chemistry at the University of St Andrews in Scotland, added supplies of Indium, which is used to create smartphone and TV screens were due to run out in 20 years.

He said: "By having Helium balloons at your birthday party you may prevent people from having an MRI scan.

"We are recycling it from the MRI scans and most of it from the deep sea diving but we are not recycling from the balloons.

"In both of those applications it's recycled, however Helium is very very light, if it gets into the atmosphere it can escape.

"If we recycle I think we would be fine but if we gradually put balloons up in the atmosphere then the timescale will be shorter.

"The timescale is shorter than Indium – it is ten years."

The Professor explained the world had about six years of Helium supply from a mine in Tanzania with the rest coming from the US.

Smartphones could become unaffordable without better recycling of the chemicals in them, he added.

Prof Cole-Hamilton said Indium, which is currently obtained from zinc ore mining, was the first of some 30 elements used to make smartphones that will run out at current rates of recycling.

He said: "That ore will run out in about 20 years in the rate we are using it.

"We will be able to [build mobile phones] but it will become much more expensive.

"We would have to pay more for it and probably people at the lower end of the economic activity spectrum would find each much more difficult but may they would keep their phones for longer.

"But I think that won't happen because scientists are waking up to the fact that this is a problem."

Describing what he believes needs to happen to avoid elements running out, he said: "We have to first of all reduce the number of mobile phones. We exchange one million mobile phones in the UK every month.

"Secondly, we should be able to replace the battery, then we have to recycle all the elements that are in it and we have to look for replacements which are more abundant."

Asked who was responsible, he said: "The consumer and of course, the manufacturers because they want to sell more phones, they want you to change your mobile more often.

"We have to have a proper process for recycling materials."

Source: SWNS

1. Write down definitions of the following words, and use the information from the text to illustrate the meaning of the terms:
   a) Scarcity b) Opportunity cost c) Sustainability

Assessment advice: Essay questions (Paper 1 HL and SL)

The first examination paper you will write in your final IB Diploma Programme economics exam will be the essay paper, Paper 1. You will find more information about this paper in Chapter 32, but we introduce you to the topic here. Paper 1 consists of three essay questions in total and you will be required to answer one of them. The questions may be drawn from any of the four areas of the syllabus, Introduction to Economics, Microeconomics, Macroeconomics and The Global Economy. Each question has a part (a), worth 10 marks, and a part (b), worth 15 marks. You will have 75 minutes to write the essay that you choose.

In part (a) you will be expected to define key terms, fully explain relevant theory, and illustrate the theory with an appropriate diagram(s). You should explain how the diagram relates to the theory. Do not just stick the diagram at the end of the answer: explain it! Although you do not have to give examples, you may find that it is easier to explain the theory through the real-world examples that you know and it may also make your understanding more clear to the examiner. Please note that the questions do not specifically ask you to draw a diagram. However, if there are relevant diagrams, you would be expected to draw them and use them as part of your response. Some examples of possible part (a) questions are as follows:

EXAMINATION QUESTIONS

Paper 1, part (a) questions

1. Explain how an economy might experience a growth in production possibilities. [10 marks]
2. Explain the idea of opportunity cost. [10 marks]
3. Distinguish between constant opportunity cost and increasing marginal opportunity cost. [10 marks]

Note

Each of these questions requires a diagram!

2 THE EVOLUTION OF ECONOMIC THINKING

By the end of this chapter, you should be able to:

→ Describe the basic ideas of Adam Smith
→ Explain the meaning of *laissez-faire* economics
→ Describe the evolution of microeconomic and macroeconomic thinking through the nineteenth century
→ Describe the thinking behind Keynesian economics
→ Describe the thinking behind monetarist/new classical economics
→ Describe the growing role of behavioural economics
→ Understand the concept of a circular economy.

There are full-length university courses on different aspects of the history of economic thought, and it is impossible to give the topic full justice within just a few pages. In this chapter, we introduce you to several names and theories associated with the evolution of modern economic thought. Some are treated in slightly more depth than others, and most are returned to later in the book. What is important at this stage is that you have some understanding of the evolution of the economic theory that we study today.

At the end of the chapter, you will see that the rapid changes in the world, and the tremendous threats that we are facing in terms of socioeconomic inequalities and threats to sustainability, may not be able to be explained through traditional, "orthodox" economic theories. This has raised demands for a more "heterodox" approach to economics: one which incorporates a range of economic theories and questions the assumptions of many of the earlier models that have driven much of the decision-making of businesses and policy makers.

As Ha-Joon Chang shows in his excellent book, *Economics: The User's Guide* (highly recommended!), there many different ways of "conceptualising and explaining the economy". This gives rise to very different economic theories and models, none of which is "right". As he notes, "all theories, including natural sciences like physics, necessarily involve abstraction and this cannot capture every aspect of the real world". But what is most important is his comment that "this means that no theory is good at explaining everything. Each theory possesses particular strengths and weaknesses, depending on what it highlights and ignores, how it conceptualises things, and how it analyses relationships between them."[1] The fact that no one theory is "right" is what should encourage students of economics to adopt a heterodox approach where they consider issues from a variety of perspectives, using a range of theories.

The cover of *Economics: The User's Guide*, by Ha-Joon Chang

Let's look at some of these different theories and their origins.

Where did "modern" economics begin?

Classical economics – the eighteenth century

Until the beginning of the industrial revolution and the birth of capitalism, the prevailing view of economics was that there was a certain amount of gold and silver in the world, and that the amount of gold and silver a nation state had was the only measure of its worth. Under this theory of what is now known as *mercantilism*, rulers aimed to accumulate wealth by obtaining more gold and silver through trade. The goal was to maximize exports to earn more gold and silver, and use barriers to imports such as customs and tariffs to prevent gold and silver from leaving the economy. The government was heavily involved in controlling aspects of the economy. Having colonies abroad was one important way in which countries were able to produce and export goods to accumulate more gold and silver.

In 1776, the first "revolution" occurred in economic thought and the *classical school* of economics was born. The "father" of classical economics is Adam Smith, a moral philosopher from Scotland, who published what is often referred to as the first book on modern economics, *An Inquiry Into the Nature and Causes of the Wealth of Nations,* in 1776. Smith's book, more commonly known as *The Wealth of Nations,* completely changed the way that economic activity was understood and became the backbone of economic theory for the classical school until later in the nineteenth century. Although there have been changes in economic thought since then, his observations form the basis of many of the theories that we still study today and his book is still considered to be extremely influential in terms of its contributions to economic thought.

[1] *Economics: The User's Guide* by Ha-Joon Chang, Pelican Books, 2014

In comparison to the mercantilist theories that preceded him, Smith observed that the wealth, or prosperity, of a nation is not based on its accumulation of gold and silver. He proposed that a country's wealth is based on the value of the goods and services that it produces. In modern terminology, we would say that a country's wealth is based on its Gross National Product. Smith argued that the priority of governments should be to maximize the country's output, and he wrote about how production and productivity (output per worker) could be increased.

One of his major contributions to economic theory was through his identification of the benefits of specialization and the division of labour. His famous illustration of these benefits was through a story about a factory with ten workers making pins. In his story, he identifies approximately eighteen separate steps involved in manufacturing a pin. If each worker works alone and completes all eighteen steps, Smith suggested that they could each make ten to twenty pins for a total of 100 to 200 pins. However, when they divide up the tasks, with each one specializing in one or two of the steps, they can make 48,000 pins, or an average of 4,800 pins per person[2]. The labour productivity of the workers, when they divide up the job and specialize in one or two tasks, is about fifty times higher than the work done if they operate individually. While he observed that this was just a simple example, his more technical observations about the benefits of the division of labour were significant in explaining how production and productivity across an economy could grow. As output increases, there are further and further divisions of labour and increases in productivity, leading to higher profits and the accumulation of capital to develop even better production technologies and more output. Overall, this would result in greater wealth and prosperity for the nation as a whole. Contrary to earlier thought, the wealth was not increased merely through trade and the acquisition of more gold and silver; wealth is increased by producing more output.

"It is not from the benevolence of the butcher, the brewer, or the baker, that we can expect our dinner, but from their regard to their own interest"

—Adam Smith, *An Inquiry Into the Nature and Causes of the Wealth of Nations* (1776).

Another theory introduced by Smith, and developed by other classical economists, is the "labour theory of value". According to this theory, the value, or price of a good is the sum of the value of all the labour that was used in producing the good. So, for example, the price of a bushel of corn was determined by all the labour costs of the inputs involved in producing that bushel. Contrary to theories that were developed later, the value of a product was determined primarily from factors relating to the supply of the product.

One of Smith's most notable contributions to the discipline of economics is the metaphor of the "*invisible hand*". He observed that when private producers are left alone to decide what to produce and how to produce it, they are guided by an "invisible hand". They are not told what to produce by a government or any other authority. They choose what to produce based on what consumers want. In pursuing their own "self-interest" (ie higher profits for themselves), Smith observed that producers

[2] Book 1, *The Wealth of Nations*, Adam Smith

also benefit consumers because the competition between the producers gives them the incentive to come up with better and cheaper products. So when producers seek to maximize their profits, they also maximize the satisfaction of consumers. This satisfaction or pleasure that consumers get from consuming products is known in economics as *utility*. And when producers supply the goods that give consumers the most utility, they create jobs and wealth for the nation as a whole. What was particularly innovative was the notion that markets are self-regulating, and will lead to an optimum outcome without government intervention. An economy based on free markets and competition is one which leads to full employment of resources and greater prosperity for the economy.

In *The Wealth of Nations*, Smith also showed how a country's prosperity grows through trade with other countries. He advocated that countries specialize in the production of goods which they produce more efficiently than other countries, export their surpluses to other countries and import goods which other countries produce more efficiently. This was contrary to previous views under mercantilism where governments restricted imports from other countries in order to protect their own producers. Smith's writings promoted the notion of free trade, or trade without government protectionist policies.

The conclusion that society as a whole prospers from the forces of competition and the invisible hand is the basis for the *laissez-faire* theory for which the classical economists are famous. *Laissez-faire* translates literally from French as "let do", but the term is used in English to refer to the capitalist economic system where production, consumption and trade take place in free markets with as little government intervention and as few regulations as possible.

This does not mean to say that Adam Smith advocated no government intervention whatsoever. In Smith's view, government responsibilities lay in the areas of defence, universal education, the provision of essential infrastructure such as roads and bridges, the establishment of legal rights and the punishment of crime. He wrote extensively about these obligations of governments in facilitating the pursuit of prosperity for nations.

How did Classical Economics develop in the nineteenth century?

Classical economics was developed in the nineteenth century through the work of many famous economists, including David Ricardo, Thomas Malthus, John Stuart Mill and Jean-Baptiste Say.

The classical economist David Ricardo is well known for the work he did on international trade. Similar to Smith, he agreed that countries should specialize in the production of different goods and trade freely

Exercise 2.1

ATL Thinking and Communication

1. In 1958, the political philosopher Leonard Read wrote an essay called "I, Pencil" to celebrate what he viewed as the tremendous benefits to be gained as a result of the "invisible hand". Writing in the first person, from the perspective of a simple lead pencil, Read aimed to show that no one person in the world has the knowledge and ability to single-handedly make an entire lead pencil from scratch. It is a cleverly crafted story illustrating the vast complexity of the supply chain and the author's wonder at the huge variety of resources, workers, machinery, technologies and skills that come together around the world to create a pencil. The essay is written as a tribute to the creativity that is unleashed through free markets. Read the story and try to identify the benefits of the "invisible hand" observed by the author.
2. A more modern interpretation of the essay "I, Pencil" was made in the form of a video celebrating the genius behind a smartphone (unsurprisingly called "I, Smartphone"!). Watch the video and comment on the similarities between the stories of the pencil and the smartphone. https://www.youtube.com/watch?v=V1Ze_wpS_o0&feature=youtu.be

to increase global output. However, where Smith focused on what came to be known as the "absolute advantage" of one country compared with another country, Ricardo developed the law of "comparative advantage". This theory is the basis of most international trade theory today, and is one we develop later in the book.

Much of classical economics is based on the work of Jean-Baptiste Say, who is famous for "Say's law of markets". A Frenchman who was known to be very much in favour of free markets and free trade, Say was strongly influenced by the writings of Adam Smith.

"It is worthwhile to remark that a product is no sooner created than it, from that instant, affords a market for other products to the full extent of its own value."

–Jean-Baptiste Say, *A Treatise on Political Economy* (1803).

According to Say's law, it is the production of goods that is actually the source of all demand in an economy. This main theory has been paraphrased by others as meaning "supply creates its own demand". This can be linked to the circular flow model in the previous chapter. The model shows that the economic activity of production creates incomes equivalent to the value of the output. These incomes are then used to consume other goods and services. By supplying goods, producers are effectively creating the purchasing power for consumers to demand other goods. Total demand in the economy comes about as a result of production.

Importantly, Say's theory is used to argue that there cannot be any overproduction of goods within the economy and that economic growth is achieved by focusing on increasing production as a means of generating further demand for products. The conclusion of Say's law, with its focus on the supply side of the economy, is consistent with classical economics in rejecting government interventions that restrict the operating of free markets.

What was the neoclassical school of economics?

The neoclassical school of economics emerged in 1870, with the work of William Jevons, Léon Walras and Carl Menger. These three economists were operating independently in three different countries, yet they shared some common conclusions and approaches.

A significant difference between the neoclassical and the classical theories relates to the determination of the value or price of a product. As noted earlier, Smith and other classical economists supported the labour theory of value which concluded that the value of a product is determined by the costs of labour and other inputs in the production process, so their focus was primarily on the production side. In contrast, the neo classical economists rejected the labour theory of value. They argued that the value of a good is determined by the value that consumers place on the good, based on the amount of utility that it brings them. They therefore placed significant importance on the demand for the product. Neoclassical economists believed that utility could be measured and given a monetary value. This is one small sign of the increasing importance of mathematical analysis in the neoclassical school.

The work of Jevons, Menger and Walras introduced what is known as *the marginal revolution*, because of their idea of "marginal decision-making". Put very simply, this means that consumers decide whether to consume the "next" unit of a good depending on how much utility that extra unit brings them; producers decide whether to produce the "next" unit of a good depending on the extra cost of producing that good. An example of a neoclassical "marginal" theory was the development of the theory of diminishing marginal utility that is explained in the box below.

Law of diminishing marginal utility

Imagine that you have just completed a sports event on a very hot day. When you finish, someone offers you a bottle of water. It is likely that this bottle of water will give you a huge amount of pleasure, or joy, or satisfaction. The bottle of water is extremely useful to you. Economists use the term "utility" to explain this satisfaction, or usefulness that a product gives you.

After you have finished the bottle of water you are offered a second bottle of water. You are still hot and a little thirsty, so you drink the second bottle. However, the benefit that this second bottle brings you is less than the first bottle. Economists use the term "marginal utility" to refer to the extra utility that you gain from consuming an extra unit of a product, the extra satisfaction. If you are offered a third bottle in a few moments, you may still feel thirsty, but the pleasure that this third bottle brings you is considerably less than the satisfaction that you gained from the first bottle, when you were so hot and thirsty. This very simple story illustrates the concept of diminishing marginal utility, which was an extremely important theory developed by neoclassical economists.

This marginal revolution marked a significant change between the theories of classical economics and the much more mathematical, scientific work of neoclassical economics. Although the classical school considered both supply and demand, they considered them separately, and placed more importance on the supply side because of their belief in the labour theory of value. Rejecting the labour theory of value, neoclassical economists placed more emphasis on the demand side, and developed complex mathematical functions to explain the interaction between production (supply) and consumption (demand) decisions to understand how prices were determined and hence how resources are allocated in individual markets.

For us, perhaps the most notable contributions to the neoclassical school came from the work of Alfred Marshall, whom some regard as the actual founder of the neo classical school. In his *Principles of Economics* (1890), Marshall was the first to present the visual supply and demand graphical model, which we still use today, to illustrate how prices are determined in a market. Marshall's original diagram is shown in

Note

The terms demand and supply are central to economic analysis. Demand is defined as the quantity of a good or service that consumers are willing and able to purchase at different prices in a given time period, so the "demand side" refers to the behaviour of consumers. Supply is defined as the quantity of a good or service that producers are willing and able to supply at different prices in a given time period, so the "supply side" refers to the behaviour of producers. We look at these in much more detail in Chapters 3 and 5.

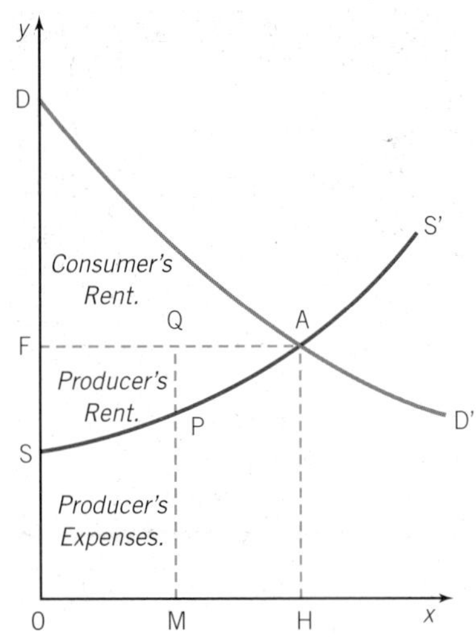

▲ **Figure 2.1** The "first" supply and demand diagram

Figure 2.1. Instead of the pages and pages of writing that characterized earlier works of economics, Marshall's work was filled with diagrams to illustrate the theories and models. This was further evidence of the change in the way that economists approached the world, using mathematics and a much more scientific approach to explain economic behaviour.

In building their models to explain producer and consumer behaviour, it was necessary for neo classical economists to make assumptions. These assumptions, which continue to underpin contemporary economic theories, are based on the idea that both consumers and producers are assumed to be *optimizers* in seeking the best outcome for themselves; consumers are assumed to want to maximize utility and producers are assumed to want to maximize their profits.

In maximizing utility, consumers are assumed to behave in a rational way. This means that they are self-interested (in some interpretations, this is referred to as selfish behaviour). When faced with choices, it is assumed that consumers have full information about their options and they are assumed to be able to make judgments instantly about the marginal utility of consuming an extra unit of a product. Producers are also assumed to be rational when making choices about how to maximize their profits, and it is assumed that producers are able to calculate accurately the marginal cost of producing an extra unit of a good. In modern terminology, the assumptions built into the neoclassical model are referred to as "rational choice theory".

The neo classical model is consistent with Adam Smith's notion of the "invisible hand". When producers are rationally trying to maximize their profits (acting in their own self-interest), they will compete with each other, thereby producing the best possible products at the lowest prices in order to give consumers the opportunity to choose their products rationally. According to the model, this process will produce the best possible outcome from society's point of view.

Up until the time of the "marginal revolution" and the models presented by the neo classical economists, the discipline of economics was formally referred to as "political economy" and the approach to the subject was largely philosophical. With its heavy reliance on mathematical models, equations and diagrams, neo classical economics effectively allowed the discipline of economics to be viewed as a science. From this point on, the discipline became known by its modern term "Economics". This was part of a move to remove the subjective, normative questions from the study and give it more objectivity and rigour as a science in comparison with the philosophical approach taken by the classical economists.

Karl Marx (1818–83)

Best known not as an economist or philosopher but as a revolutionary communist, Karl Marx's works inspired the foundation of many communist regimes in the twentieth century. He had a massive influence upon the shape of the world in that century. Although he was originally trained as a philosopher, Marx eventually turned more towards economics and politics. He attempted to prove his theories using mathematics. He felt that this was important, since he said that his book, *Das Kapital*, was a "scientific description" of the course that history would take.

Marx saw "capitalism", the free market system, as being only one of a series of methods of production. Marx predicted that there would be an inevitable breakdown of capitalism, for economic reasons, and that communism would be the natural end result. He issued the rallying cry, "the proletarians have nothing to lose but their chains ... working men of all countries, unite!"

Marx predicted that, eventually, society's ability to produce would grow faster than its ability to consume, causing growing unemployment. Thus the free market could not be depended upon to serve the best interests of workers and there would be a need for the government to take over the means of production, in a system known as communism.

The ideas of Marx continue to have a prominent role in economic and political debate today, with his views being associated with perspectives on the "left" of the ideological spectrum.

So what happened in the twentieth century?

In the first few decades of the twentieth century, the neo classical faith in the ability of the free market to bring about the best outcomes prevailed. Since individual markets were seen to move towards equilibrium when left alone to the forces of demand and supply, it was believed that the economy as a whole would move towards a general equilibrium with full employment of resources, without government intervention. While there would be up and down cycles in terms of economic growth, if there was any over-supply in the economy ("gluts"), the prices would drop, encouraging consumers to buy and eliminating the surpluses. The "orthodox" or generally accepted view remained that governments need not intervene – *laissez faire*.

The theory could also be applied to labour markets and used to explain why unemployment would not be a long-run problem. If there was unemployment of labour (ie an oversupply of labour), it would be a short-run phenomenon. Like any other market, if there was too much labour, then the price of labour (wages) would fall and producers would want to hire more workers at the lower price, thus eliminating the unemployment. There would be no need for the government to intervene to try to correct the problem of unemployment; market forces would do it automatically.

What is Keynesian macroeconomics?

In the 1920s and 1930s, the British economist John Maynard Keynes (pronounced Canes) was responsible for the next "revolution" in economic thinking and "Keynesian economics" emerged as a new school of thought. With his focus on the workings of the economy as a whole, Keynes is often considered to be the "father of macroeconomics".

John Maynard Keynes (1883–1946)

Keynes was born in Cambridge, England into a highly intellectual family, and was educated in the elite academic institutions of Eton and Cambridge. Although highly intelligent, Keynes did not focus exclusively on academics, but found ample time for literary pursuits and political activities. He was well-known for his involvement with the progressive literary Bloomsbury Group in London, which included many other intellectuals such as Bertrand Russell and Virginia Woolf. He joined the British civil service in 1906. In order to enter the civil service, he had to write entrance examinations and, ironically, he was not as successful in his economics exam as one might expect – but, as he explained later, "I evidently knew more about economics than my examiners."

Following a short period with the civil service, Keynes went back to Cambridge and then went to work at the British Treasury (the government department responsible for government spending and taxation). He was a key representative of the British Treasury at the Paris Peace Conference in Versailles in 1919, but he was very much against the conclusions of the Conference in which Germany was expected to make massive payments (reparations) to the Allied countries for World War I. As a result, he resigned from the Treasury and wrote *The Economic Consequences of the Peace*. His argument was that it would be impossible for Germany to pay the amounts that the Allied countries demanded it pay. He predicted that the consequences would be very damaging and he turned out to be quite right.

The view for which Keynes is most well-known, and most relevant to our introductory economics course, was published in 1936 in *The General Theory of Employment, Interest and Money*. As you should know now, the governing orthodoxy at the time was that of *laissez-faire*, which argued that government intervention in the economy should be carefully limited and focused on the supply side of the economy. This means that governments did have a role, but the role was in helping create the conditions necessary for maximum production. Put very simply, this would involve education to create skilled workers, infrastructure to make production and exchange possible, and the establishment of laws and the maintenance of order in order to guarantee stability. Keynes changed the focus and put forward the radical idea that it was demand, rather than supply, that determined the overall level of national income and more importantly, that governments had a key role to play in managing the level of *total demand* (known as "aggregate demand") in the economy. Keynes' *General Theory* grappled with the problem of mass unemployment during the Great Depression. He observed that the persistent levels of high unemployment of the 1920s were not going to disappear if left to market forces, as the *laissez-faire* economists would have people believe.

Contrary to what earlier economists theorized, Keynes argued that the problem during the Great Depression was one of insufficient demand in the economy. The demand from consumers and businesses was not enough to buy up the total output of goods and services being produced in the economy, resulting in a "general glut". With excess supplies, firms would lay off workers, who would then have even less purchasing power to buy up goods and services, resulting in further falls in demand for goods and services and even less demand for workers. The solution, as Keynes saw it, was for the government to intervene to increase total

demand in the economy by spending more money itself and lowering taxes to allow households and businesses to spend more. Increasing aggregate demand was advocated as a means of bringing the economy out of the depression.

This ran counter to the neo classical economists in two ways. Firstly, it went against the notion of **automatically** stabilizing markets; rather than leaving the economy alone, Keynes argued that it was an obligation for governments to intervene. Keynes acknowledged that while market forces might eventually result in full employment of all resources in the long run, this could take an unacceptably long time, with consequences too damaging (in terms of high and prolonged unemployment) for governments to accept. The policies that Keynes recommended were fiscal policies, related to government spending and taxation, and monetary policies, related to interest rates and the money supply.

Secondly, until the time of Keynes, it was felt that all economic agents (households, firms and the government) should operate within their means, and not spend more money than they had. In contrast, Keynes proposed that in order for governments to stimulate the economy by increasing overall demand, they should go into debt and "run budget deficits". That is, they should spend more money than they earn from taxation revenue by borrowing money to make up the shortfall. The assumption was that in times when the economy was growing well, the government would take in more money in taxes and spend less so that the debts could be paid.

Keynesian economics is also referred to as "demand-side" theory, or "demand management". Observing that economies typically pass through *business cycles* fluctuating between rapid rates of growth (with low unemployment and rising inflation) and slow growth, or recessions (with high unemployment), Keynes advocated "counter-cyclical" government policies. During an economic downturn, or recession, with high unemployment, governments should increase aggregate demand by using expansionary fiscal policy (increasing government spending and decreasing taxes) and expansionary monetary policy, operated by the country's central bank (increasing the money supply and decreasing interest rates). During a rapidly growing, or booming economy, where an economy risks rapidly rising prices (inflation) governments should decrease aggregate demand by using contractionary fiscal policy (decreasing government spending and increasing taxes) and contractionary monetary policy (increasing interest rates and decreasing the supply of money).

Keynesian economics gained widespread acceptance and became the dominant economic school of thought until the 1970s, when economic realities could not so easily be explained by Keynesian theories. For example, Keynesian economics implied that economies could **either** face the problem of high unemployment during a downturn in the business cycle or the problem of high inflation during an upturn in the business cycle, and that if governments managed the level of aggregate demand, they could reduce the swings in economic activity to minimize both of these problems. Up until the late 1960s and early 1970s, those policies seemed to work and countries employing these policies enjoyed strong economic growth with low unemployment and low inflation. However, around this time, many economies began to face the problem of high unemployment **and** high inflation (known as *stagflation*), which Keynesian theory was unable to explain adequately. In fact, it was argued that governments using Keynesian policies were making the economic problems even worse. This cleared the way for a new way of looking at macroeconomics.

"Inflation is always and everywhere a monetary phenomenon."

–Milton Friedman, *The Counter-Revolution in Monetary Theory*, 1970.

What is Monetarism (New Classical Economics)?

Monetarism emerged as the main challenge to Keynesianism in the late 1960s. This school of thought was made famous by the economist Milton Friedman, who received a Nobel Prize in Economics in 1976. Monetarists believe that the main determinant of economic growth is the total amount of money in the economy and so their focus was mainly on monetary policy.

Monetarists were most concerned with the issue of inflation in an economy, and observed that inflation was caused by too much growth of the money supply. In their view, a country's central bank should **not** use monetary policy to try to deliberately increase aggregate demand in the economy by increasing the supply of money, as this would simply lead to higher and higher inflation. They believe that central banks **should** increase the money supply, but by a strictly controlled steady amount consistent with the rate of growth of national income. When money supply increases by more than the amount of output, then the economy faces a situation of "too much money chasing too few goods". As a result, prices rise rapidly.

In the view of the monetarists, the best way to achieve economic growth is for the government to steer clear of demand management and for the central bank to control the growth of the money supply. Expansionary policies would only result in inflation.

A slight twist on the name, the new classical school builds on the work of the neo classical school and similarly argues that the economy will move automatically to a level of national income where all resources are fully employed. The new classical school revives the notion of rationalism through its theory of "rational expectations". Applied to macroeconomics this assumption leads new classical economists to have similar conclusions about inflation as the monetarists. When governments employ expansionary policies, households and businesses will anticipate that inflation will occur and, acting in a rational manner, will behave in a manner that will actually cause wages and prices to rise. For example, if governments use expansionary policies, workers will rationally *expect* inflation to occur and so will demand higher wages.

If workers demand higher wages, producers will charge higher prices to cover their higher costs.

Economist Robert Lucas Jr. received a Nobel Prize in Economics in 1995 for having "developed and applied the hypothesis of rational expectations, and thereby having transformed macroeconomic analysis and deepened our understanding of economic policy"[3].

Economists in the new classical school of thought are similar to the monetarists in their conclusion that governments should never try to manage the level of demand in the economy. They go back to the classical and neo classical economists in arguing that the only way that government can promote economic growth is by using policies that focus on the supply side of the economy by creating incentives such as tax cuts for businesses to become more efficient and for workers to work harder.

So what has happened so far in the twenty-first century?

What is behavioural economics? (Economics meets psychology!)

As you know by now, the neo classical approach makes the assumption that consumers behave rationally. That is, whenever a consumer makes a choice to consume a good or service, it is assumed that they have carried out an internal calculation of the benefit or utility that the product gives them in relation to the amount it costs to buy the product, in an intelligent, logical and selfish way.

However, in the real world, humans do not necessarily behave in this rational way and are not able to make these instant cost–benefit analyses. When faced with the millions of choices that we make on a day-to-day basis, we do not necessarily make intelligent and logical decisions, and we certainly do not have perfect information about relative prices of goods and the utility that each product will give us. Furthermore, we do not act in a purely self-interested way; we do actually care about how our choices affect others.

Challenges to the assumptions of consumer rationality have given rise to a branch of economics known as "*behavioural economics*". This is a branch of economics which incorporates the insights of psychology and recognizes that the choices which consumers make are governed by many factors that are not consistent with the assumptions behind the neoclassical models.

Richard Thaler is regarded as a pioneer in the field of behavioural economics and won a Nobel Prize for his work in 2017. He argues that

[3] https://www.nobelprize.org/prizes/economic-sciences/1995/press-release/

assumption of rational choice means that neoclassical models are based on people that do not actually exist!

Given that humans are not necessarily rational, they do not necessarily always make the best choices about what to consume, and what not to consume. Behavioural economics aims to understand the decision-making process of **actual** human beings (rather than so-called "rational" human beings). It then uses this understanding to help consumers make better choices and to help governments design policies that will encourage consumers to make better choices.

In the terminology adopted by Richard Thaler and his colleague Cass Sunstein in their book, *Nudge: Improving decisions about health, wealth and happiness*, consumers can be "nudged" to make choices **voluntarily** that are better for them and indeed, better for society. For example, when governments legislate that processed foods must have the nutritional values printed on their labels, they are then "nudging" consumers to make healthier eating choices.

The work on nudge theory by behavioural economists has had a big impact on governments and organisations all around the world, which are now nudging people in countless ways to help people make "better" decisions. These have contributed to improvements in people's standards of living, their health, their communities and the environment.

Nudge theory is not without its critics. Any form of government intervention may be accused of taking away individual rights. There is also the concern that governments do not actually know what is best for people and so cannot be trusted to choose how to nudge people. This is a good example of the debate between those who believe that governments have an important role to play in the functioning of markets and those who believe that market forces operate efficiently on their own. However, behavioural economists argue that the belief that markets operate efficiently on their own is based heavily on the assumption that consumers act rationally and this assumption can be easily challenged. Their vast experimental work shows how the insights from psychology can be used to select carefully designed and tested interventions to nudge consumers in the right direction, without taking away their rights to choose.

What is the circular economy? (Reframing economics in the twenty-first century)

There is increasing awareness that tremendous challenges to sustainability are the result of the fact that economic activity tends to take place within what is described as a "linear" economy. This has led to calls for a different approach to economic activity. One idea that has gained widespread support is that there is a need to move from a linear economy to a "circular" economy. This is best explained through the use of diagrams.

▲ **Figure 2.2** The take, make, waste approach

The linear economy, described as a "take-make-waste" approach, is shown in Figure 2.2. We take natural resources from the environment and use them to produce new products. Once used, these products are disposed into the environment where they end up in landfill sites or are incinerated, creating even more pollution. This type of economy is responsible for the overexploitation and degradation of natural resources. Moreover, it is resulting in unmanageable accumulations of waste with accompanying health and environmental risks. This presents tremendous challenges to sustainability.

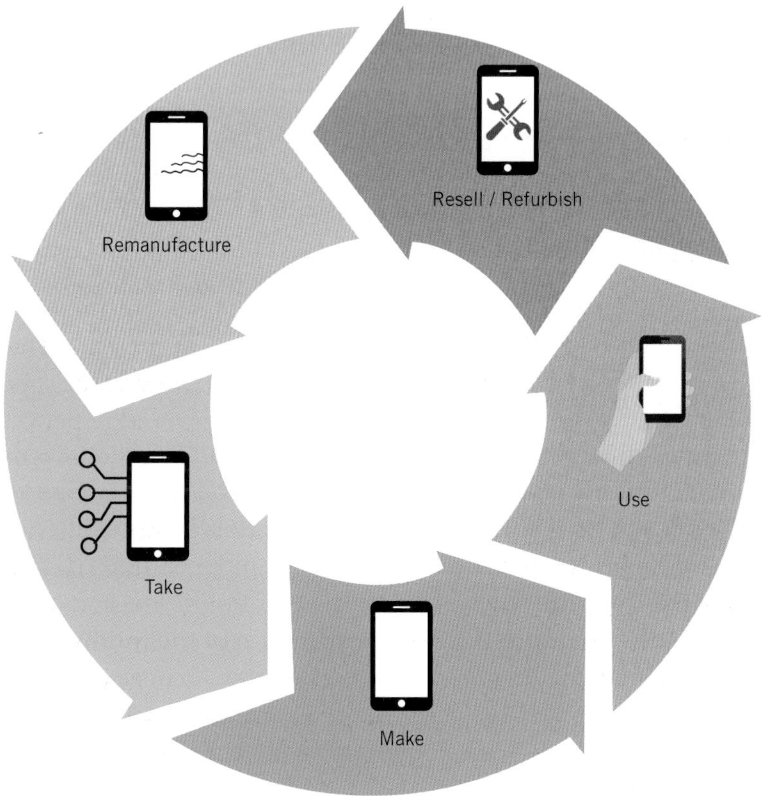

▲ **Figure 2.3** The circular economy

In contrast, the circular economy shown in Figure 2.3 is described as a "regenerative" and "restorative" approach. Products are specifically designed to be long-lasting and the materials for new products come from reusing and recycling old products. There is much more emphasis on the design, maintenance, repair, refurbishment and remanufacture of products.

Did you know?

This is the Olusosun landfill site in Lagos, Nigeria. It is the largest landfill site in Africa. Approximately 10,000 tons of garbage ends up in this site every day. Much of this is electronic waste, such as computers, printers, phones and TVs, which arrives from all over the world on container ships. Because developments in technology are so rapid, there is a constant demand for new products, and people are throwing out old devices in shorter and shorter amounts of time, resulting in the global challenge of waste management.

Note

See chapter 28 for more on the Sustainable Development Goals.

The principles of the circular economy are consistent with many of the Sustainable Development Goals (SDGs). Throughout the world, governments are increasingly encouraging, or even requiring, the adoption of circular economy principles. For example, in 2019, the European Union released a comprehensive report on the implementation of its Circular Economy Action Plan.

From the perspective of businesses, there are great potential gains from adopting circular economy models, in terms of cost savings and compliance with national environmental regulations. Many companies have also adopted principles of circular economy.

Economics in action — ATL Thinking, Communication and Research

1. How has a country of your choice implemented circular economy principles? To what extent has it been successful in moving away from the linear economy?
2. How has a company of your choice implemented circular economy principles? To what extent has this benefited the company?

Key concept
INTERDEPENDENCE

Kate Raworth's "embedded economy" model illustrated in Chapter 1 is another depiction of a circular economy, and the key feature is the interdependence that exists between the economy, society and the environment. Economic activity which does not appreciate this interdependence will increase the challenges confronting the globe today.

Key concept
EQUITY

Raworth argues that economics must take a radically different approach that can deal with the challenges of the twenty-first century. She shows that policies based on traditional economic models have resulted in a narrow preoccupation with economic growth and a careless disregard for the negative consequences of "extreme inequalities of income and wealth coupled with unprecedented destruction of the living world". According to Raworth, the goal must be changed. It cannot simply be to achieve economic growth, or increases in economic output. "*For the 21st century, a far bigger goal is needed: meeting the human rights of every person within the means of the planet. Instead of pursuing ever-increasing GDP, it is time to discover how to thrive in balance*"[4]. For Rowarth, this can only happen when one views the economy as operating within society and within the Earth's ecosystem.

Economics students demand an education that reflects post-crash world

https://www.theguardian.com/sustainable-business/economic-students-demand-education

Raworth has developed a ground-breaking diagram to show the challenges that we face and illustrate the world that she thinks we need. With its two concentric circles, Raworth's model looks like a doughnut (Figure 2.4), and she has used this metaphor of a doughnut to describe her vision.

[4] **Source:** *Doughnut Economics: Seven Ways to Think Like a 21st-Century Economist,* by Kate Raworth, Random House, 2017

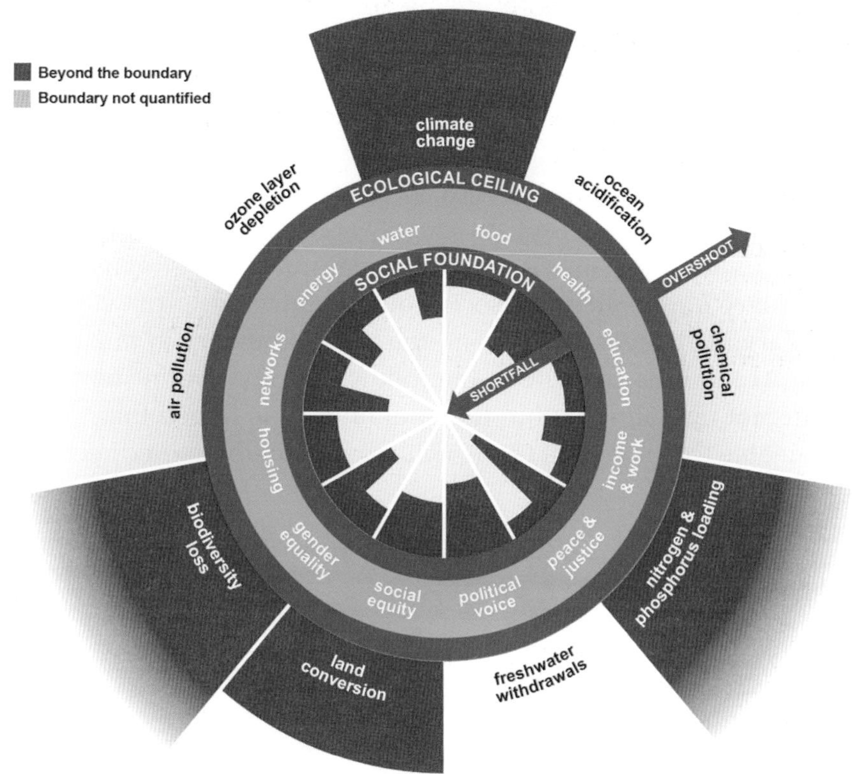

▲ **Figure 2.4** The doughnut economy, Raworth (2017)

The inner ring is the "social foundation". These are the "basics in life" that we should rightfully demand for everyone: "sufficient food; clean water and decent sanitation; access to energy and clean cooking facilities; access to education and to healthcare; decent housing; a minimum income and decent work; and access to networks of information and to networks of social support." In addition, the model shows that people should be entitled to gender equality, social equity, political voice, peace and justice. Anyone living within this boundary, in the hole in the doughnut, would be in a state of deprivation. These are not radical or unrealistic goals; the UN Sustainable Development Goals (SDGs), includes all of these, with a view to achieving the goals by 2030.

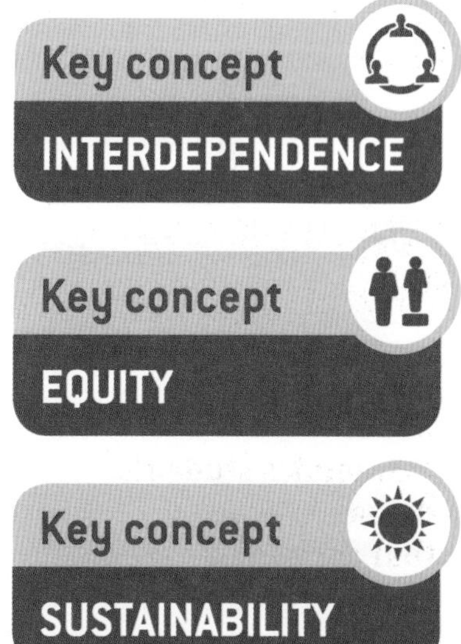

The outer ring of the diagram illustrates the Earth's environmental limits, or boundaries. If we move beyond this outer ring, we are putting the Earth's ecosystems, and our ability to live within this ecosystem, under great threat. Therefore, the "safe place" is within the two rings, in the doughnut. It is Raworth's view that economic goals, models and theories must be adapted to ensure that we operate within this safe place, working towards a world where people's human needs and rights are met within the environmental limits of the earth.

Economics in action

ATL Thinking, Communication, Research

How are we doing today in terms of operating in the ecologically safe and just space for humanity?

As Raworth points out, with advancements in the ability to gather data, we are able to measure reasonably accurately how we are doing against each of the metrics in the doughnut, and although many things have improved in the social foundation, we are still within the boundary in all areas and beyond the outer boundary in threatening ways. At the time of writing, the following information shows that we are **not** operating within the doughnut. It is hoped that the UN Sustainable Development Goals will move us in the right direction.

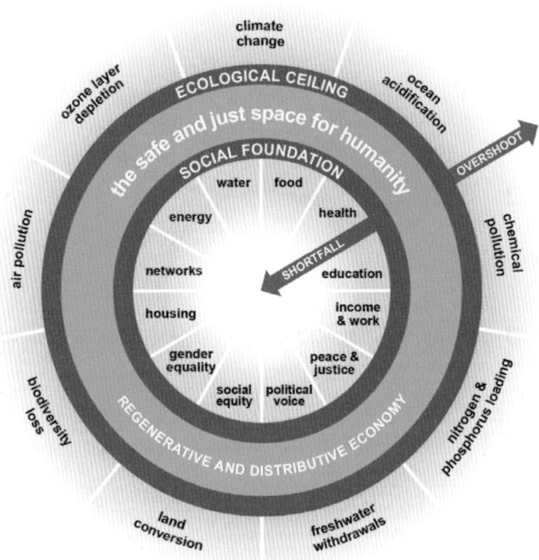

"Many millions of people still live well below each of the social foundation dimensions.

- Worldwide, one person in nine does not have enough to eat.
- One in four lives on less than $3 a day.
- One in eight young people cannot find work. One person in three still has no access to a toilet.
- One in eleven has no source of safe drinking water.
- One child in six aged 12–15 is not in school, the vast majority of them girls.
- Almost 40% of people live in countries in which income is distributed highly unequally.
- More than half of the world's population live in countries in which people severely lack political voice.

It is extraordinary that such deprivations continue to limit the potential of so many people's lives in the 21st century. Humanity

Theory of knowledge

To what extent have individuals shifted the paradigms of economics?

Many economists argue that economics as a social science is in its infancy, and that with time, as empirical testing methods and the quality of data improve, it will become more reliable in making accurate predictions. Do you agree with this statement?

has, at the same time, been putting Earth's life-giving systems under unprecedented stress. We have transgressed at least four planetary boundaries:

- climate change,
- land conversion,
- nitrogen and phosphorus loading,
- biodiversity loss."

Source: *Doughnut Economics: Seven Ways to Think Like a 21st-Century Economist*, by Kate Raworth, Random House, 2017

Inquiry:

The information above was given in Rowarth's book published in 2018. How are we doing now?

To answer the question, you could take a look at the progress towards the Sustainable Development Goals We come back to the SDGs in several chapters, and look at them in more detail in Chapter 28. However, given their importance, it would be valuable for you to have a look at them on your own now.

So what is the conclusion on economic thinking?

Whilst there have always been debates among different branches of economics and different schools of thought, many students of economics have grown increasingly frustrated with the focus and assumptions of mainstream economics (the theories that tend to be taught in high schools and universities). It has been argued that we are facing growing real-world crises, such as climate change and tremendous socioeconomic inequities, because businesses and governments have been using narrow economic theories as the basis on which to make their decisions.

The movement of students calling for change has grown and spread to many countries across the globe. There are demands to see the discipline of economics taught with much more questioning of the assumptions, and including many more varied schools of thought.

In our brief look at the origins of economic thought, we have looked at several which have gained the status of "mainstream" economics. However, there are many more approaches and schools of thought including Developmentalist Economics, Feminist Economics, Austrian Economics, Institutional Economics, Complexity Economics, Islamic Economics, Cooperative Economics and many more. Sadly, we do not have the time to go into all of them, but it is essential that you are aware that this multitude of approaches exists, and that economics is not all **just** new classical economics. With the growing awareness of the importance of circular economics, we may be looking at the next paradigm. Hopefully, students of IB Economics will accept the challenge of moving this forward!

Inquiry

Possible CAS activity

The demands by students all around the world that the teaching of economics adapts to the real world rather than clings to the assumptions and theories of new classical economics developed into the Rethinking Economics network (www.rethinkeconomics.org).

Task: Research the "Rethinking Economics" network to try to learn more about their recent work. They may even have a group near you. Joining up could be a worthy CAS project.

Exercise 2.2

ATL Thinking and Communication

Using information from this chapter, create an annotated timeline of the evolution of economic thinking from 1750 up to the present time.

Assessment advice

It is possible that a part (a) essay question in Paper 1, either HL or SL, could ask for a description of any of the areas of economic thought that have been looked at in this chapter. Some of the areas, such as Keynesian, New Classical, and Behavioural economics will appear later in this course book.

3 DEMAND

REAL-WORLD ISSUE: How do consumers and producers make choices in trying to meet their economic objectives?

By the end of this chapter, you should be able to:

- → Define a market
- → Define demand
- → Explain the Law of Demand
- → Identify and explain the non-price determinants of demand
- → Distinguish between a shift of a demand curve and a movement along a demand curve
- → Understand the relationship between an individual consumer's demand and market demand
- HL Understand the income and substitution effects
- HL Understand the concept of rational consumer choice
- HL Define and explain behavioural economics
- HL Explain some limitations of the assumptions of rational consumer choice
- HL Define and explain bounded rationality, bounded self-control, bounded selfishness and imperfect information
- HL Define and explain cognitive biases
- HL Define, explain and give examples of choice architecture
- HL Define, explain and give examples of nudge theory

In the next chapters, we look at the way in which consumers and producers interact with each other. We examine the "market mechanism" as the way in which resources are directed to meet the needs and wants of people in an economy. The standard models that we use in analysing markets are based on the neoclassical school of thought. However, we will also look at how the assumption behind these models can be questioned.

What is a market?

A market is where buyers and sellers come together to carry out an economic transaction. Markets may be physical places where goods and services are exchanged for money, but there are other ways that economic transactions may be made. In modern times, products are increasingly sold in on-line markets, through the use of credit cards or money transfers.

There are many different forms of markets, such as:

- product markets, where goods and services are bought and sold
- factor markets, where factors of production are bought and sold, such as the labour market
- stock markets, where shares in companies are bought and sold
- international financial markets, where international currencies are traded, such as the foreign exchange market.

At the core of standard market theory are the concepts of demand and supply.

What is demand?

Demand is the quantity of a good or service that consumers are willing and able to purchase at different prices in a given time period. For example, a group of people may buy 150 cans of a soft drink at $1.20 each, each afternoon. We would say that their demand for soft drinks at a price of $1.20 would be 150 units per afternoon.

The important phrase here is "willingness and ability". It is not enough for consumers to be willing to purchase a good or service. They must also have the financial means to buy the product; that is, the ability to buy. This is known as "effective demand" and it is this that economists consider when discussing demand. It is not effective demand if you would like to purchase a motorcycle, but you do not have the financial means to do so.

How does the Law of Demand work?

The Law of Demand simply states that "as the price of a product falls, the quantity demanded of the product will usually increase, *ceteris paribus*". It is sometimes expressed even more simply as "the demand curve normally slopes downwards".

The Law of Demand may be illustrated using either a demand schedule or a demand curve. The example in Table 3.1 illustrates the effective demand for soft drinks at a sports event.

Exercise 3.1

ATL Thinking and Communication

1. Make a list of twenty goods or services that you would like to buy.
2. Separate the list into two columns – effective demand and ineffective demand.
3. Briefly explain why the goods and services are in the columns that they are.

Note

As you read earlier, *ceteris paribus* is an assumption that means "all other things being equal". This assumes that when there are a number of different factors that determine something, only one is changing and all of the others are held constant. Thus, in this case, price is changing but any other determinants of demand are assumed to be unchanging.

Price of soft drinks ($ per can)	Quantity demanded of soft drinks (cans per day)
2.00	100
1.20	150
0.80	225
0.40	400

▲ **Table 3.1** A demand schedule for soft drinks

The quantity of soft drinks demanded increases as the price falls. The table showing these changes is known as a demand schedule. The same information can be shown in graphical form, using a demand curve. This is a curve that shows the relationship between the price of a product, which is placed on the vertical axis, and the quantity demanded of the same product over time, which is placed on the horizontal axis. This is shown in Figure 3.1.

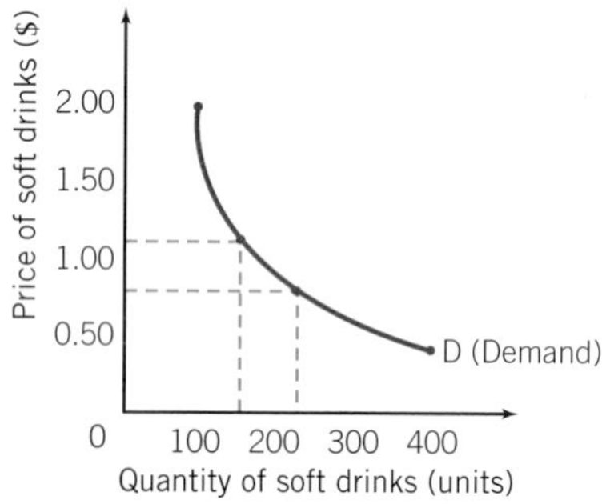

Price of soft drinks ($)
2.00
1.50
1.00
0.50
0
100 200 300 400
Quantity of soft drinks (units)
D (Demand)

▲ **Figure 3.1** A demand curve for soft drinks

As we can see from the diagram, demand curves are normally convex to the origin. However, for ease of analysis, economists usually draw them as straight lines, although they still call them curves! We will do the same.

As we saw in the example, in the Law of Demand, a change in the price of the product itself will lead to a change in the quantity demanded of the product, ie a movement along the existing demand curve. The phrase "*change in the quantity demanded*" is important, since it differentiates a change in price from the effect of a change in any of the other determinants of demand. In Figure 3.1, a change in the price of soft drinks from $1.20 to $0.80 leads to *an increase in the quantity demanded* of soft drinks from 150 cans to 225 cans.

Note

For more on the law of diminishing marginal utility, see p. 31.

Note

Higher Level students are given more explanation for the Law of Demand on p. 53.

There is some common sense in understanding why a decrease in the price of a product leads to an increase in quantity demanded. After all, this is what drives promotions or sales in shops; more consumers are likely to buy a product when the price drops. Furthermore, since additional units of a product are likely to bring consumers less utility, the price would have to be lower to give consumers the incentive to buy more.

What are the non-price determinants of demand?

When economists talk about a *change in demand*, they are actually referring to a shift of the demand curve to the right or left. This is different to the phrase *change in the quantity demanded*, which we came across earlier.

There are a number of factors that determine demand and lead to an actual shift of the demand curve to either the right or the left. Whenever we look at a change in one of the determinants, we always make the *ceteris paribus* assumption. If we do not, then the analysis becomes too complicated and it is almost impossible to identify the effect of a change in any one of the determinants. The determinants of demand are outlined below.

1. Income

There are two types of products to consider when we are attempting to understand how a change in income affects the demand for a product. These are normal and inferior goods.

Normal goods

For most goods, as income rises, the demand for the product will also rise. When people have higher incomes, they can afford to buy more goods, so the demand will increase. Such goods are known as normal goods. As income rises, the demand curve for a normal good will shift to the right. The size of the shift in demand will depend upon the good itself. An increase in income may cause a small shift to the right in the demand curve for salt, but a larger increase in the demand for cinema tickets.

The demand curve for air travel is shown in Figure 3.2. In this case, an increase in income shifts the demand curve for air travel to the right (D to D_1), so more air travel is demanded at every price.

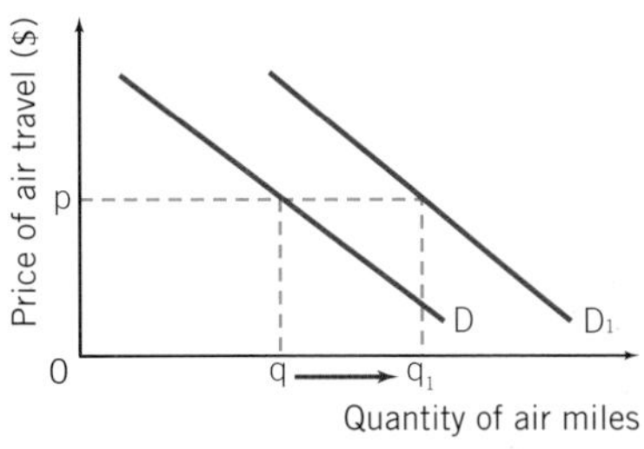

▲ **Figure 3.2** The demand for air travel

Inferior goods

If a product is considered to be "inferior", then demand for the product will fall as income rises and the consumer starts to buy higher priced substitutes in place of the inferior good.

Examples of inferior goods may be cheap wine or "own brand" supermarket detergents. As income rises, the demand curve for the inferior good will shift to the left. When income gets to a certain level, the consumer will be buying only the higher priced goods and the demand for the inferior good will become zero. Thus the demand curve will disappear.

2. The price of related goods

There are three possible relationships between products. They may be substitutes for each other, complements to each other, or unrelated.

Substitutes

If products are substitutes for each other, then a change in the price of one of the products will lead to a change in the demand for the other product. For example, if there is a fall in the price of chicken in an economy, then there will be an increase in the quantity demanded of chicken and a fall in the demand for beef, which is a substitute.

This would lead to a movement along the demand curve for chicken and a shift to the left of the demand curve for beef. This is shown in Figure 3.3.

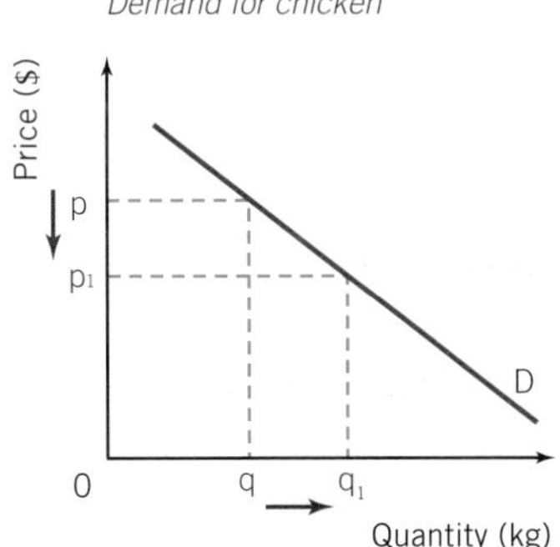

▲ **Figure 3.3** The demand for chicken and beef

A fall in the price of chicken from p to p_1 leads to an increase in the quantity demanded of chicken from q to q_1. This change in the price of a substitute means that some consumers will switch from buying beef to buying chicken and there will be a fall in the demand for beef, at all prices. Therefore, the demand curve for beef will shift to the left from D

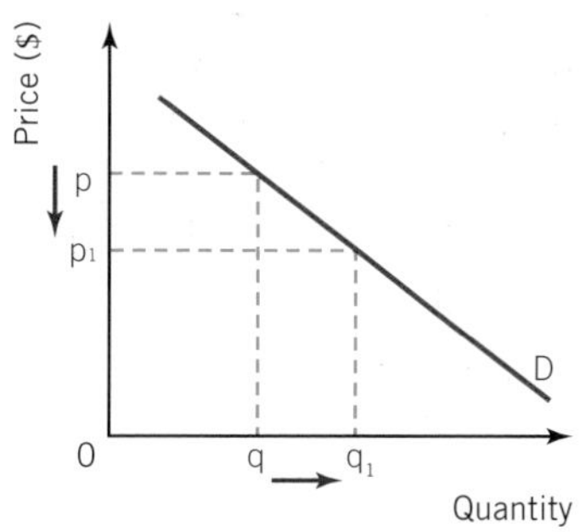

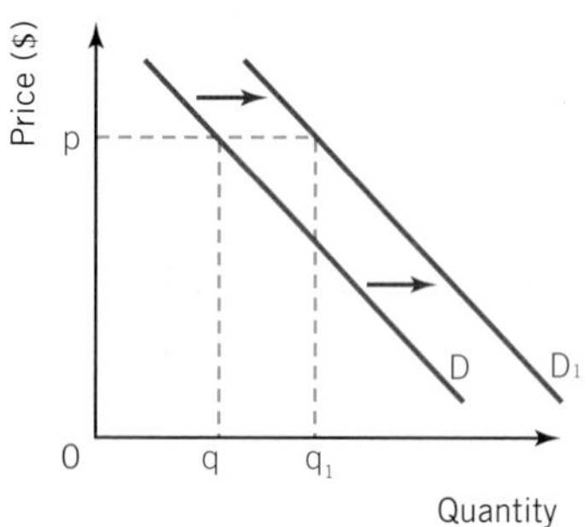

▲ **Figure 3.4** The demand for Games consoles and Games

to D_1. Even though the price of beef has not changed from p, there is a fall in demand from q to q_1.

In the same way, an increase in the price of a substitute product will lead to a fall in the quantity demanded of that product and an increase in demand (shift of the demand curve to the right) for the substitutes whose prices have not changed.

Complements

Complements are products that are often purchased together, such as printers and ink cartridges. If products are complements to each other, then a change in the price of one of the products will lead to a change in the demand for the other product. For example, if there is a fall in the price of games consoles in an economy, then there will be an increase in the quantity demanded of games consoles and an increase in the demand for the games themselves, which are complements.

This would lead to a movement along the demand curve for games consoles and a shift to the right of the demand curve for games. This is shown in Figure 3.4.

As we can see, a fall in the price of games consoles from p to p_1 leads to an increase in the quantity demanded of consoles from q to q_1. This change in the price of a complement means that consumers will now buy more games to go with the additional consoles that they are buying and there will be an increase in the demand for games, at all prices, and the demand curve for games will shift to the right from D to D_1. Even though the price of games has not changed, there is an increase in demand from q to q_1.

In a similar fashion, an increase in the price of a complementary product will lead to a fall in the quantity demanded of that product and a fall in demand (shift of the demand curve to the left) for the complements whose prices have not changed.

Unrelated goods

If products are unrelated, then a change in the price of one product will have no effect upon the demand for the other product. For example, an increase in the price of toilet paper will have no effect upon the demand for pencils. We say that the two products are unrelated.

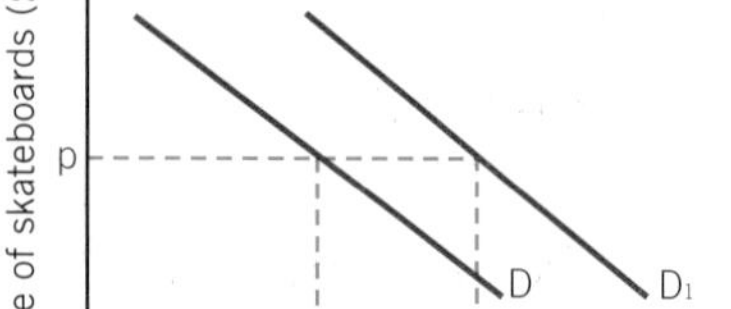

▲ **Figure 3.5** The demand for skateboards

3. Tastes and preferences

Consumer tastes and preferences have a powerful influence on consumer demand. If tastes change in favour of a particular product, then more will be demanded at every price. When tastes change so that a given product becomes less popular, then demand will fall and the demand curve shifts to the left. Clearly, there are many forces acting on tastes and preference, including marketing and advertising, peer pressure and media influence.

The demand curve for skateboards is shown in Figure 3.5. If there is an advertising campaign to encourage the purchase of skateboards, or if the world skateboarding championships are televised and this leads to more people wishing to skateboard, then there will be a shift of the demand curve for skateboards to the right. This means that more skateboards will be demanded at every price.

Demand for Men's Grooming Products Market to Witness Rapid Surge During the Period 2017–2027

https://consumerreportsreview.com/demand-for-mens-grooming-products-market-to-witness-rapid-surge-during-the-period-2017–2027/

Ketchup tries to keep up with changing tastes

https://www.marketplace.org/2019/07/03/ketchup-flat-sales-condiment-alternatives/

Did you know?

In 2017, the British Broadcasting Corporation (BBC) aired Blue Planet 2, a documentary narrated by David Attenborough. The programme highlighted the devastating impact of plastic pollution on the world's oceans and environment. The show was watched by 62% of the UK population and received widespread global attention.

The increased public awareness of the issues has impacted many markets, reducing the demand for single-use plastics and creating a large increase in demand for refillable water bottles.

4. Future price expectations

If consumers think that the price of a product will increase in the future, then they may well demand more of that product in the present, taking advantage of the current lower prices. This will lead to a shift of the demand curve for the product to the right.

For example, when announcements are made about increased taxes being placed on cigarettes from a certain date in the future, there is usually bulk buying of cigarettes before that date. The demand curve for cigarettes shifts to the right.

In the same way, if consumers expect the price of a product to fall in the future, then they may well demand less of that product in the present, postponing their demand until a future date. This will lead to a shift of the demand curve for the product to the left.

For example, with "Black Friday" taking place in late November in many countries, people's demand for all kinds of electrical products falls in the weeks before "Black Friday", as they postpone their present consumption, waiting for the lower prices that will be available. The demand curves for those products shift to the left.

Economics in action

ATL Thinking, Communication and Research

1. Investigate "Black Friday".
2. Explain why you think "Black Friday" may have come into existence.

Economics in action

ATL Thinking, Communication and Research

1. Research changes in the demographic structure of your country, relating to the percentage of people under the age of 16 and over the age of 60, over the last 50 years.
2. Explain how you think that the changes may have affected the demand for any three products of your choice.

5. Number of consumers

If there is an increase in the number of consumers of a product, then there will be a shift of the demand curve to the right. This often relates to the size of the population and demographic changes in a country. Obviously, if the population of a country is growing, then the demand for most products will increase and their demand curves will start to shift to the right.

In the same way, if the age structure of the population of a country starts to alter, then this will affect the demand for certain products. For example, in many European countries, the percentage of older people in the economies is starting to increase. This will be reflected in the demand patterns for certain products, such as holidays targeted at senior citizens, walking frames or mobility scooters, where the demand curves should shift to the right.

What is the distinction between a movement along a demand curve and a shift of the demand curve?

As we have now seen, sometimes there are movements along an existing demand curve and sometimes the demand curve actually shifts to the left or the right. Distinguishing one from the other is very simple.

A change in the price of the good itself leads to a movement along the existing demand curve, since the price of the good is on one of the axes. This is shown in Figure 3.6, where a fall in the price of soccer boots from p to p_1 leads to an increase in the quantity demanded from q to q_1.

A change in any of the non-price determinants of demand will always lead to a shift of the demand curve to either the left or the right. For example, as shown in Figure 3.7, a government policy requiring cyclists to wear safety helmets would lead to a shift to the right of the demand curve for safety helmets from D to D_1. Thus, more would be demanded at each price, and at the existing price of p, demand would increase from q to q_1.

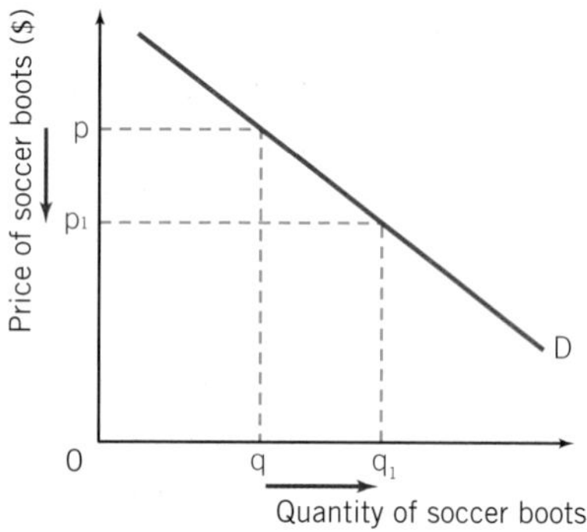

▲ Figure 3.6 The demand for soccer boots

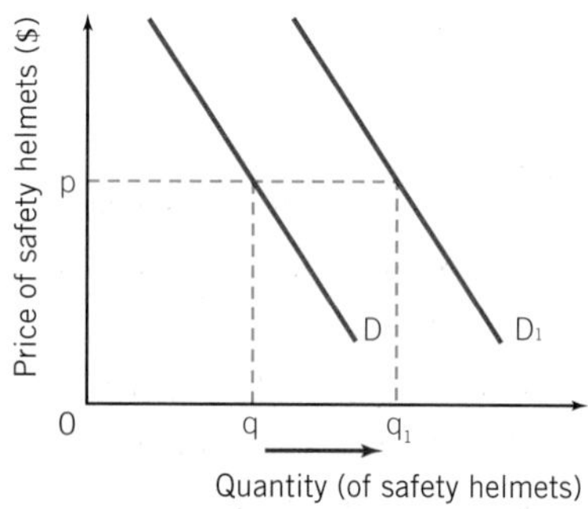

▲ Figure 3.7 The demand for safety helmets

Theory of knowledge

In the physical sciences, scientists discover laws. Let's look at an example. Imagine that your economics teacher is standing at the front of the class explaining the price mechanism when all of a sudden she floats off into the air, seemingly defying the law of gravity. Could this happen? No, because the law of gravity is 100% valid. If exceptions were to emerge then the law would not be valid and would have to be scrapped.

In economics we also have laws, such as the "Law of Demand", but there may be exceptions. For example, an economist named Thorsten Veblen identified a different situation where he claimed that the quantity demanded rose as price rose. These have come to be known as Veblen goods. In his book, *The Theory of the Leisure Class*, he reported that some products become more popular as their prices

rise. Part of the reason for this he attributed to **conspicuous consumption**; the fact that people gain satisfaction from being seen to consume expensive products by other people. He said, "failure to consume in due quantity and quality becomes a mark of inferiority and demerit". As the price of a Veblen good rises, such as a Louis Vuitton handbag, people with high incomes begin to buy more of the product because it has a "snob value"; it is a "good of ostentation".

As we can see in Figure 3.8, at low prices, a typical Veblen good will have a normal demand curve, with the quantity demanded falling as the price rises. However, as the price continues to rise the product eventually achieves "snob value" status and further price rises start to lead to increases in the quantity demanded by those who want to be seen to consume the good. Can you think of any goods which might be considered to be Veblen goods?

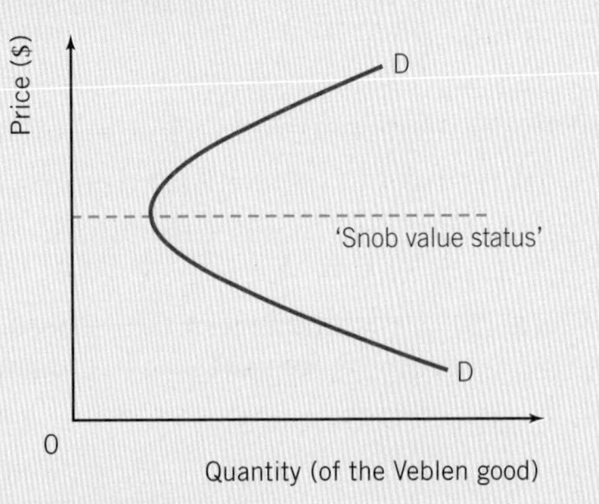

▲**Figure 3.8** The demand for a Veblen good

Exercise 3.2

ATL Thinking and Communication

Using fully labelled diagrams, illustrate what may be the outcome in each of the questions given below. (Remember to use a ruler and include accurate labels.)

1. What would happen to the demand for bicycles if there were a large increase in the tax on electric scooters?
2. What would happen to the demand for foreign holidays if there were an increase in incomes?
3. What would happen to the demand for video games if there were a significant fall in the price of games consoles?
4. What would happen to the demand for cars if there were a significant increase in the level of income tax?
5. What would happen to the demand for ice creams if the price of ice creams were to go up?
6. What would happen to the demand for a certain brand of bottled water if there were an article about the lack of purity of the source of the water in a national newspaper?
7. What would happen to the demand for carrots if there were an increase in the size of the population?

Now write an explanation of **any one** of the above and then share it with another class member, or present it to the whole class.

Thorstein Veblen (1857–1929)

Thorstein Veblen was born in the USA, the son of Norwegian immigrants. He studied at Carleton College, Yale, Cornell and John Hopkins universities. He was a true "social" scientist, arguing that "human nature" was too simplistic an explanation as a basis for economic actions and that economics must be shaped by culture.

His two most famous publications were *The Theory of the Leisure Class* (1899) and *The Theory of Business Enterprise* (1904). His main interest lay in such questions as: "What is the nature of economic man?", "Why does a community have a leisure class?" and "What is the economic meaning of leisure itself?" Unlike Karl Marx, Veblen did not believe that the lower classes would eventually want to overthrow the upper class; instead, he believed that the lower classes would work hard in order to move up the class structure. Veblen thought that the presence of the upper class set an example and gave the working class an aim.

What is the relationship between an individual consumer's demand and market demand?

Up to this point, we have mostly looked at the demand curves for individual consumers. However, it is possible to construct the demand curve for a whole market by a process known as *horizontal summing*. This process is best understood by looking at an example. Table 3.2 shows the demand of three different consumers for a product. We will assume that the three consumers are the only ones in the market in question. By adding up the individual demands at each price, it is possible to calculate the total market demand.

Price ($)	Consumer A demand	Consumer B demand	Consumer C demand	Market demand
1	600	400	600	1600
3	400	300	450	1150
5	200	200	300	700

▲ **Table 3.2** Individual demand schedules and the market demand schedule

Figure 3.9 shows the individual demand curves of the three consumers that are identified in table 3.2. All of the demand curves follow the Law of Demand. At a price of $5, consumer A will purchase 200 units, consumer B, 200 units and consumer C, 300 units. Since they are the only consumers in the market, the total market demand, at a price of $5, will be 700 units. At a price of $3, total market demand will be 400 + 300 + 450 = 1150 units. In the same way, at a price of $1, total market demand will be 600 + 400 + 600 = 1600 units.

All of the other points on the market demand curve may be gained by summing the points on the individual demand curves. This is the process of *horizontal summing*, because it is the values on the horizontal axes for the individual demand curves that are added together to get the market demand curve. The figures on the vertical axis are common to all of the demand curves and so do not change.

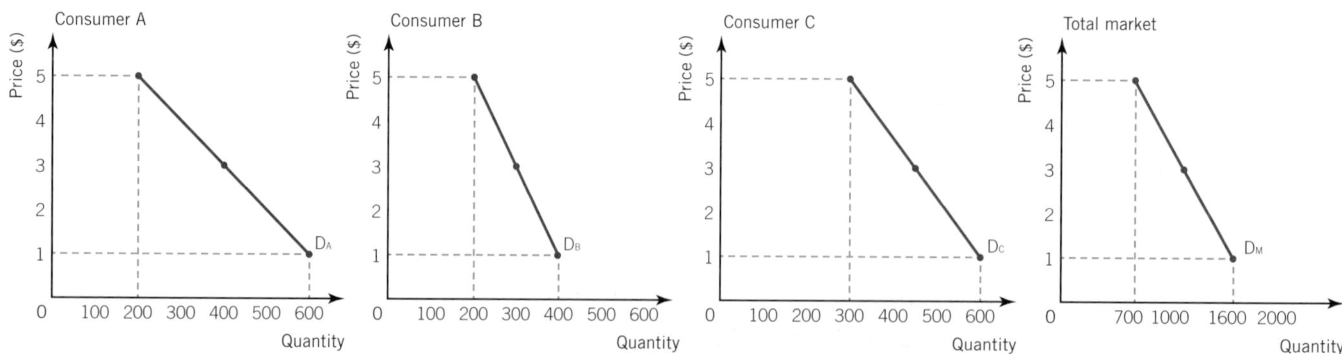

▲ **Figure 3.9** Individual demand curves and the market demand curve – horizontal summing

How do economists explain the Law of Demand

One explanation of the Law of Demand suggests that, when the price of a product falls, there is an increase in the quantity demanded of the product for two reasons:

1. *Income effect*: When the price of a product falls, then people will have an increase in their "real income", which reflects the amount that their incomes will buy. With this increase in real income, the people will be likely to buy more of the product, thus partly explaining the reason for an increase in quantity demanded when there is a fall in the price of a product.

   If someone buys 14 caffe latte coffees each week and they pay $2.95 for each cup, then their total spending is $41.30 per week. If the price of the coffee is reduced to $2.45, then they will save $0.50 per cup, a total of $7.00 per week. In effect, the person now has $7.00 more income to spend each week. Her "real income" has increased by $7.00. The income effect means that she may now buy more coffees, thus increasing the quantity demanded.

2. *Substitution effect*: It is argued that people receive a certain amount of satisfaction (or benefit) when they consume a product. This satisfaction is known as *utility*. In Chapter 2, you read about the law of diminishing utility. Here is an extension of that reasoning in relation to the law of demand.

   When the price of a product falls, people will still gain the same amount of satisfaction (utility) from the product as before, but they will be paying less for it. So, their ratio of satisfaction to price will have improved. This means that the product will now be relatively more attractive to people compared with other products, whose prices have stayed unchanged. So it is likely that consumers will purchase more of the product, substituting it for products that have a poorer ratio of satisfaction to price.

   If a person receives 10 utils (a measurement of satisfaction) from a cup of caffe latte and the cost is $1.95, then the ratio of satisfaction to price is 1 util to $0.195. If the price of the coffee falls to $1.45, then the ratio changes to 1 util to $0.145. The consumer is paying less to get the same amount of satisfaction and so the coffee will be more attractive. It will be a "better deal".

The final outcome of a fall in price on the quantity demanded of a product will, in the end, be a combination of the income effect and the substitution effect.

Exercise 3.3
ATL Thinking and Communication

Which phone should I buy?

Homo economicus will:

- *know exactly what she wants from her phone*
- *research the capabilities of all the different phones*
- *understand all the information that is provided*
- *be able to compare all the models*
- *know the prices of each and every phone on the market*
- *know how long each phone will last*
- *know what she will need from her phone in two years*
- *be able to know which phone makes her happiest.*

In pairs, discuss how realistic the statements above are. What difficulties might *homo economicus* face?

What are the key assumptions behind the theory of demand?

As was explained in the first chapter, economic models are developed to explain economic behaviour. In creating these models certain assumptions have to be made in order to test and validate the hypotheses that are needed to generate economic theories.

In *neoclassical theory*, key assumptions are made about the way in which consumers, as economic "agents", make their choices. In this standard economic model, it is assumed that consumers behave *rationally*. This means that faced with an economic decision, consumers are able to consider all the possible options and work out which option will give them the most satisfaction, or utility. In other words, consumers will always seek to *maximize their utility*. In making their decisions, it is assumed that consumers act only in their own self-interest; they do not take into account the interests of others. Furthermore, it is assumed that when making decisions or choices, consumers have access to all the relevant information about each of their choices. This is known as the assumption of *perfect information*. In the standard model, this rational consumer is known as *homo economicus*. When faced with choices, it is assumed that *homo economicus* will make intelligent, logical and well-considered decisions that give them the most utility.

What is behavioural economics?

Richard Thaler is regarded as a pioneer in the field of behavioural economics and won a Nobel Prize for his work in 2017. He refuted the notion that consumers are "rational maximizers" who are essentially mathematical machines able to carefully calculate every decision to enable them to maximize their utility. He observes that a problem with the field of economics is that it studies the behaviour of people that simply do not exist, presenting the view that there is no such person as *homo economicus*. We are all *homo sapiens*! In everyday English, he uses the terms "Econs" for *homo economicus* and "Humans" for "real people". According to Thaler, Econs and Humans exhibit the following characteristics:

Econs (non-existent, according to Thaler)	Humans (all of us!)
• Are rational • Have perfect information • Are extremely intelligent, and able to perform complex calculations quickly • Seek to maximize their own utility • Make decisions based on their own self-interest • Have consistent preferences over time • Have no self-control problems • Are unbiased	• Have bounded rationality • Have incomplete information • Are not as intelligent as Econs • Have limited ability to carry out complex calculations • Are social beings, and make decisions in a social context • Change their tastes over time • May have self-control issues

How realistic are the key assumptions of the rational consumer model?

One key assumption of the standard economic model that is challenged by what actually happens in the real world is that of *perfect information*. This is the assumption that all economic agents have access to all the same information at the same time. This would imply that consumers have perfect information about the price and quality of all products in the market. There are several problems associated with this. One is that in the real world, there are "information asymmetries" where different economic agents (consumers, producers and the government) have different levels of information available to them where economic transactions are concerned. Another relates to the fact that even if all the information were available, humans face limits in terms of how they can actually process the information that is available to them. In today's world, with the Internet providing access to seemingly infinite information, we often face the situation of information overload. Therefore, in the real world, consumers make decisions based on *imperfect information*.

Consumers face huge challenges in making economic choices and are unable to make decisions in the rational manner assumed by the standard economic model. The term *bounded rationality* is used to explain the notion that the rationality of consumers is limited by the information that they have, and the fact that they do not have the time nor the cognitive abilities to weigh up all the options.

In the standard economic model, humans act in their own self-interest. In other words, consumers are assumed to act selfishly, only taking their own objective of utility maximization into account when making choices. In fact, humans do care about others. We volunteer work, we give to charities, we buy Fairtrade products because we are concerned about the wellbeing of farmers. All of these show that the assumption of self-interest may be challenged. The term *bounded selfishness* is used to explain that humans do not always act in their own self-interest as assumed by the neoclassical model.

Finally, it is assumed that when acting rationally, consumers are able to demonstrate perfect willpower. In reality, consumers are unlikely to be able to do this. We use the term *bounded self-control* to illustrate this natural tendency to give in to temptation sometimes.

Exercise 3.4 ATL Thinking and Communication

Economic Man vs Humanity: a Puppet Rap Battle

Watch this creative rap video from Kate Raworth, the author of *Doughnut Economics*, to understand limitations of the assumption of rational human behaviour:

https://youtu.be/Sx13E8-zUtA

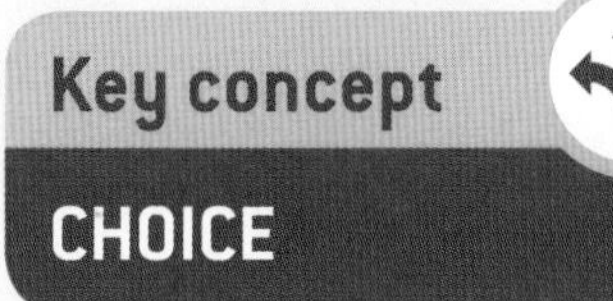

Higher Level

Exercise 3.5

ATL Thinking and Communication

Would you like a Caffe Latte, Americano, Cappuccino, Espresso, Flat White, Long Black, Mocha, Macchiato, Mochaccino, Frappuccino, Small, Medium, Large, Takeaway?

Is it possible to have too much choice? What problems do people have to face when they are presented with a vast range of choices? Does it make the decision easier or more difficult?

How can the "Dual System Model" explain how humans actually act?

In order to explain why Humans make decisions that are different from Econs, behavioural economics draws on the experimental work of psychologists Daniel Kahneman and Amos Tversky who developed the "dual system model". According to this model, individuals actually have two different systems of thinking, known as System 1, the fast thinking system, and System 2, the slow thinking system.

In his book, *Nudge*, Richard Thaler calls System 1 the "Automatic System" and System 2 is the "Reflective System". The Automatic System involves fast decisions that are essentially subconscious. The Reflective System involves slow decisions that are much more controlled. The characteristics of each of the types of thinking system are illustrated below:

You would use automatic thinking to:

- Answer the question, "What is three plus four?"
- Get home from school on the route that you have taken every day for the last year
- Speak in your mother tongue
- Do your grocery shopping.

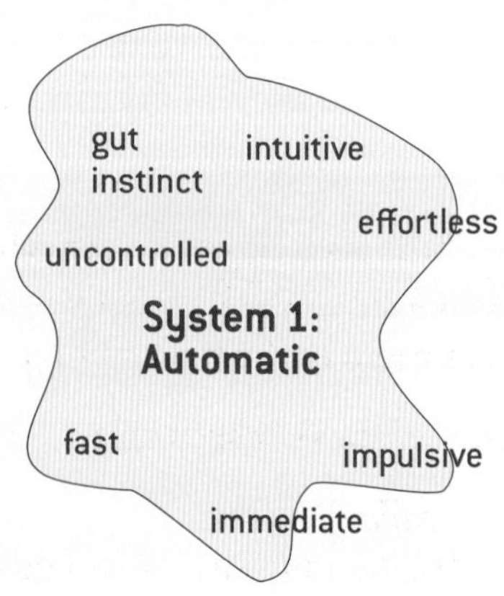

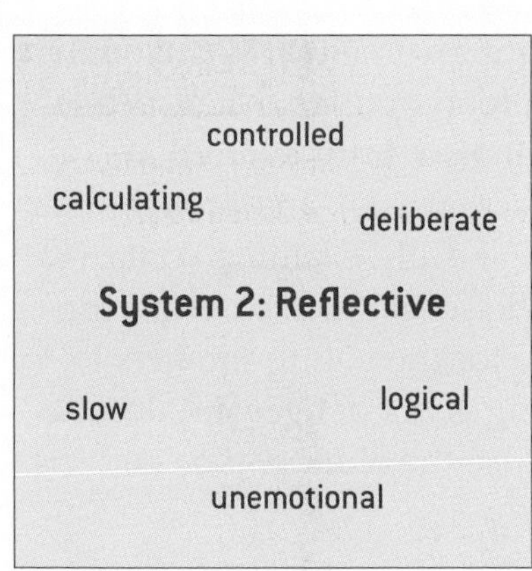

You would use reflective thinking to:

- Answer the question, "What is 1989 times 31?"
- Choose your IB subjects
- Have a conversation in a second language in which you are not fluent.

▲ Figure 3.10 The Automatic System and the Reflective System

Neoclassical economists would claim that rational consumers make all their decisions using reflective thinking. However, this is obviously not the case. When people have important and complex decisions to make, they usually use elements of the Reflective System and take their time to make a decision. However, sometimes they let the Automatic System take over and this can result in poor decision-making.

This is particularly a problem when we make a short-term decision too quickly, without considering the long-term effects. For example, if you have decided to go on a diet to become more healthy and you are offered something like a doughnut that you eat because you just can't resist it, then you are using your automatic thinking. Obviously, you should reflect on the decision and come to the rational decision that the short-term benefit from the doughnut is not worth the longer term loss of remaining overweight.

Exercise 3.6
ATL Thinking and Communication

Try to think of a choice that you have made and then regretted afterwards. Using the terms System 1 thinking and System 2 thinking, explain how you might have chosen differently.

On a day to day basis, we make thousands of decisions, and have to cope with a tremendous amount of information. In order to make them quickly, we employ certain mental "rules of thumb". The rules of thumb that we use to make quick decisions are also known as "*heuristics*". A heuristic may be defined as a mental shortcut that allows people to make decisions and solve problems quickly and efficiently. However, there are "*cognitive biases*" implicit in the short cuts we employ that may be problematic and result in poor decisions. If we let our impulsive automatic thinking take over when making an important decision, we might make choices that we will regret later. Impulse buying is an example of this.

What are the cognitive biases that affect decision-making?

Psychologists have identified many biases that affect consumer choices. Behavioural economics uses the understanding of these biases to help consumers make better choices.

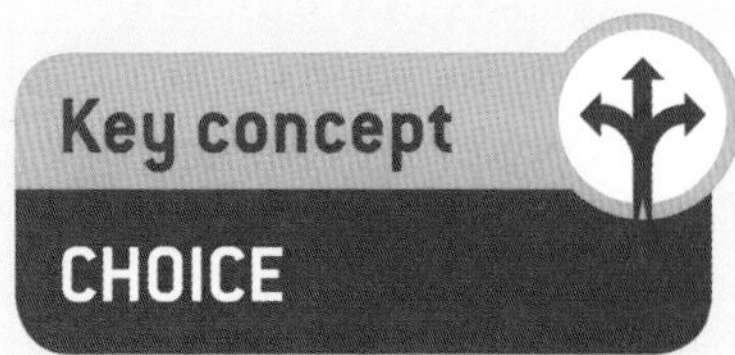

Some of these biases are:

- *Availability bias*
  The availability of recent information and examples tends to over-influence people's decision making. If there is a case of salmonella

in one part of a country, consumers might assume that it will occur nearby and they might choose different food options as a response, even if there is absolutely no risk in their area. It turns out that consumers are actually quite poor at assessing risk and probabilities, relying on recent examples rather than carefully-examined data. A common example is young smokers, who see a much older person who is also a smoker. It is quite possible for the young smokers to delude themselves into thinking smoking is not dangerous, despite all the information to the contrary, because the older person is perfectly healthy.

- *Anchoring bias*
  Anchoring occurs when we are given the value of something, and then use this value as a reference point to influence future choices or decisions. Once an anchor value has been set in our minds, we tend to rely too much on it, and this can lead to poor decisions. Supermarkets use awareness of this bias in their pricing. Consumers anchor certain prices in their minds, and when there is a sale and the price drops, the consumers feel that they are getting a very good deal and may purchase more than they really need. Salespeople use this when prices are negotiable by offering a very high starting price and then accepting a lower price that is still higher than what the product should cost.

- *Framing bias*
  The way that information is presented to us influences our choices. In many cases, especially where data is presented, a given piece of information may be presented in either a positive way or a negative way. When information about a product is framed in a very positive manner, it will lead consumers to think more positively about the product. Evidence of this can be seen in all kinds of marketing and advertising. If you see that a particular yoghurt is labelled as "90% fat free", it will be a lot more appealing than a label which says, "contains 10% fat". Although the product would be identical, the framing of the information induces a cognitive bias.

- *Social Conformity/Herd behavior*
  As consumers, we naturally want to fit in. The way that others behave can exert a powerful influence on our own choices. It can be very gratifying and rewarding to be like others. There is evidence of this herd behaviour (wanting to be part of a "herd") everywhere. An obvious example would be changing clothing fashions. Producers are able to convince people to buy more clothes in order to fit into the new styles, even when their own clothes are perfectly good! This is also known as the "*Bandwagon Effect*" and is used to describe the behaviour of people when they join a perceived majority of people in doing something, even if it is against their best-interest.

Economics in action

ATL Thinking, Communication and Research

Several cognitive biases have been listed here.

- Find your own examples of how these cognitive biases influence people.
- These are not the only cognitive biases that influence the decisions that consumers make. Research others, and explain their influence.

- *Status Quo/Inertia bias*
  It is often the case that consumers, faced with a bewildering set of choices, would prefer to maintain the status quo by doing nothing. An example would be what a consumer might do when their mobile phone contract expires. It could be a very good time for the consumer to investigate other options, and maybe consider entering into a contract with another mobile service provider. However, faced with the challenge of researching into all the available options, it is quite likely that the consumer will prefer just to stick with the same provider, even if something else might actually provide more utility.

- *Loss aversion bias*
  Experiments show that humans feel that losses are far more significant than gains. It has been estimated that the pain that people feel from losing something is psychologically about twice as powerful as the pleasure that they get from gaining something. This leads to the situation where people might make poor choices because they fear that they will lose something, even if their reasoning is not well-informed. This is linked to the status quo bias, as consumers may be reluctant to change the status quo due to the fear of loss. Businesses can take advantage of this bias by making consumers feel that they will lose something if they don't purchase a good. If you see a sign saying, "Buy now before stocks run out!", you should be aware that the producer is trying to make you feel that you will lose out if you don't take advantage of their offer.

- *Hyperbolic discounting*
  This is a very fancy name for something that everyone can relate to. It refers to the tendency of humans to prefer smaller short-term rewards over larger later rewards. If your Economics IA is due the day after tomorrow and you haven't even started it, you should probably get started right away – at least decide on the article you are going to analyse. However, you decide that you would prefer to go out this evening and enjoy yourself, as you convince yourself that you will do a much better job in the morning. This is an example of hyperbolic discounting – you prefer the short-term reward of a night out, rather than the longer-term reward of getting the work finished. This cognitive bias is even more powerful when the reward is much further in the future.

How can behavioural economics be used to help consumers make better choices?

Given the many cognitive biases which cause consumers to make poor choices sometimes using their System 1 (automatic) thinking system, behavioural economics aims to help consumers make better choices. One way of doing this is to alter the *choice architecture* that consumers face.

Exercise 3.7

ATL Thinking and Communication

This picture was taken in a local supermarket. How has the company taken advantage of cognitive biases to try to get consumers to buy the product?

Research Black Friday and Singles' Day. How do retailers take advantage of any of the cognitive biases on these days?

What is choice architecture?

Choice architecture is the theory that the decisions that we make are heavily influenced by the ways in which the choices are presented to us. We make many decisions every day but we might not realize the extent to which those choices are influenced by the way that someone, referred to as a "choice architect", presents the choices to us.

A very simple example from supermarkets can be used to explain the term. When you shop in a supermarket, you will find all kinds of products right at the cash desk that encourage you to "impulse buy". They are not there by accident; the "choice architect" has placed them there because it is assumed that while you are waiting there, you will be tempted to buy those products. This is especially the case if they are chocolate bars or candies and you are waiting with a small child who will have a temper tantrum if you don't buy them!

An example of an area where choice architecture can be observed is when a *default choice* is changed. There are two ways of explaining the default choice. One is that it is the pre-set option that is effectively selected if the decision-maker does nothing. In other words, it is what you get if you do nothing. For example, Google is the default search engine on many browsers – it does not have to be selected, it opens automatically. The second is that it is the choice that is always followed unless a deliberate decision is made to change it. In other words, you carry on making the same choice because it is a habit. For example, if you always get a caffè latte when you go to the coffee shop, then it becomes your default option.

Although the default options do not always result in a good outcome, they are very popular for many reasons. The status quo bias described earlier can be very powerful. Consumers may not have the time or the resources to research alternatives, they may lack the cognitive skills to understand the alternatives, they may lack the courage to make changes, they are comfortable with what they normally choose and they generally like the easier options!

Consider the case of organ donation. There is always a shortage of organs for organ transplants. One way to increase the supply of organs available for transplants is to increase the number of people that consent to donate their organs in the event of their death. There are different systems for doing this. One system is the opt-in/opt-out approach. If a country operates an opt-in system, it is the responsibility of people to actively sign up to the organ donation register. This allows hospitals to use their organs for transplants after death. In an opt-out system, organs will automatically be donated unless people make a specific request before death that their organs should not be taken. If a country operates an opt-in system, then opting-in is the default option. If people do nothing, then their organs cannot be used, as they will not have given their consent. Changing the default option from opt-in to opt-out is seen as one way of using choice architecture to increase the number of people who consent to having their organs donated.

Another way in which choice architects can influence consumers is through *mandated choice*. These are situations where people are required by law to make a choice in advance. In the example of an organ donation, people are required by law to indicate if they are willing to become an organ donor in the event of their death. The way that the government can do this is by requiring people to tick a box to say whether or not they are willing to be donors when they renew their driver's licences. Although many people would like to be organ donors, when left to themselves to register as donors, many do not make the effort to indicate this choice. When the choice architects force people to make the choice, the number of organ donations increases substantially.

Economics in action

ATL Thinking, Communication and Research

A global problem is a lack of organs for organ transplants. Using the theory of choice architecture, explain the ways that different governments approach this problem and identify which method you think is the best. Justify your choice.

How can people be encouraged to make better choices?

Nudge theory was developed by behavioural economist Richard Thaler. The theory suggests that the choice architecture offered to people can be carefully designed to gently encourage (nudge) the people to voluntarily choose the option which is better for them. Behavioural economics in general, and nudge theory in particular, became much more well-known and accessible to the general population following the publication of Richard Thaler and Cass Sunstein's book *Nudge: Improving decisions about health, wealth and happiness*.

The cover of *Nudge*, by Richard Thaler

The key to nudge theory is that consumers maintain their *consumer sovereignty* (their right to choose) but are encouraged to make better decisions. A commonly cited example of this relates to the positioning of food in a school cafeteria. If healthy foods are placed in a very convenient, easy-to-reach, easy-to-see place, evidence shows that students will consume more of them. They are not forced by anyone to choose the healthy foods, but the placement "nudges" the students subconsciously to choose them. The key thing is that the students are not forced to choose the healthy option, but they do it themselves. The argument is that students are more likely to pick up healthy habits if they are making the choices themselves.

When designing positive choice architecture, the "architects" must essentially override certain cognitive biases. If consumers use their System 1 thinking system and subconsciously fall back on rules-of-thumb which cause them to make poor decisions, then they may need to be nudged towards better decisions.

More Evidence That Menu Design Can Nudge Us Toward Better Choices

https://www.forbes.com/sites/maisieganzler/2019/07/25/more-evidence-that-a-menu-design-can-nudge-us-toward-better-choices/#2d7a916b52a1

A good example where nudges have been used to help people make better decisions is in the area of pension savings. In many more economically developed countries, governments provide pension schemes that are designed to allow people to have a decent standard of living when they retire. However, these pensions schemes are under considerable threat due to the fact that people are living longer, and governments are unable to finance the pensions. Therefore, there is a need for people to set up private savings schemes to ensure that they have enough money when they retire. A rational "Econ" would be able to calculate how much they are going to earn over their working life, work out how much they will need when they retire, and have the will-power to set aside just enough money each month to ensure that they have enough money when they retire. But we know that humans do not work like this. Despite all good intentions to save, there are several reasons why people do not save for their future.

Firstly, because of the hyperbolic discounting bias, people do not like to save for the future, because it means that they are giving up rewards in the present. The further away retirement is (that is, the younger people are), the less likely they are to save money. The temptation will always be to say that they will start saving later. Secondly, if people have to cut their spending in order to save, they are likely to consider this as a loss and because of the loss aversion bias they are not likely to be prepared to accept this loss of consumption in the present.

Richard Thaler and fellow behavioural economist Shlomo Benartzi developed the "Save More Tomorrow (SMT)" scheme in the United States as a way of nudging people to save money for retirement. Under this scheme, which companies can offer their employees, people are encouraged to start saving early in their working lives. This scheme addresses the problem of the hyperbolic discounting bias which discourages people from saving early. In the beginning, the pension contributions are quite small. But whenever the workers get a pay rise, there is an automatic increase in the pension contribution. Without doing anything deliberate, those workers will be saving more. However, because they are not experiencing a loss in income (the extra saving comes from the salary increase) the loss aversion bias is addressed. Each time there is a pay increase, there is an "automatic escalation" of the pension contribution. Another key element of the scheme is that workers can opt in to the scheme, and opt out at any time. This maintains their consumer sovereignty, which is considered to be a requirement when a policy is considered a "nudge". Research shows that this scheme, along with other nudges designed by behavioural economists, has had tremendous success in raising pension contributions. The change in choice architecture, which nudges people towards an easy choice of opting into a scheme, will help people to guarantee a more comfortable future.

The work on nudge theory by behavioural economists has had a big impact on governments and organizations all around the world who are now nudging people in countless ways to help people make "better" decisions. These have contributed to improvements in people's standards of living, their health, their communities and the environment.

Nudge theory is not without its critics. Any form of government intervention may be accused of taking away individual rights. There is also the concern that governments do not actually know what is best for people and so cannot be trusted to choose how to nudge people. This is a good example of the debate between those who believe that

Theory of knowledge

Nudge theory has been described as *libertarian paternalism*. How can both words, "libertarian" and "paternalism" be perceived negatively? Despite the fact that both of the words have some negative connotations, proponents of nudge theory are happy to call it "libertarian paternalism". How do they justify this?

Economics in action

ATL Thinking, Communication and Research

There are countless examples of the ways in which nudge theory has been adopted, by both governments and organizations all around the world. Compile a list of examples from three different countries, and explain how your chosen "nudges" meet the requirements of getting consumers to voluntarily change their behaviour in a positive way. Try to find nudges from different areas, eg nudges to help make people happier, nudges to help improve communities, nudges to promote sustainability.

governments have an important role to play in the functioning of markets and those who believe that market forces operate efficiently on their own. However, behavioural economists argue that the belief that markets operate efficiently on their own is based heavily on the assumption that consumers act rationally and this assumption can be easily challenged. Their vast experimental work shows how the insights from psychology can be used to select carefully designed and tested interventions to nudge consumers in the right direction, without taking away their rights to choose.

Economics in action

ATL Thinking, Communication and Research

Nowadays, many people are "voting with their dollars" (or renminbi or pesos or rupees or euros) where they indicate their beliefs to producers by buying (or not buying) their brands. This has also been referred to as ethical consumption or "belief-driven buying".

In the 2018 "Edelman Earned Brand Report" based on surveys of consumers from Brazil, China, France, Germany, India, Japan, the UK and the US, it was demonstrated that an average of 64% of consumers choose, switch, avoid or boycott a brand based on its stand on societal issues.

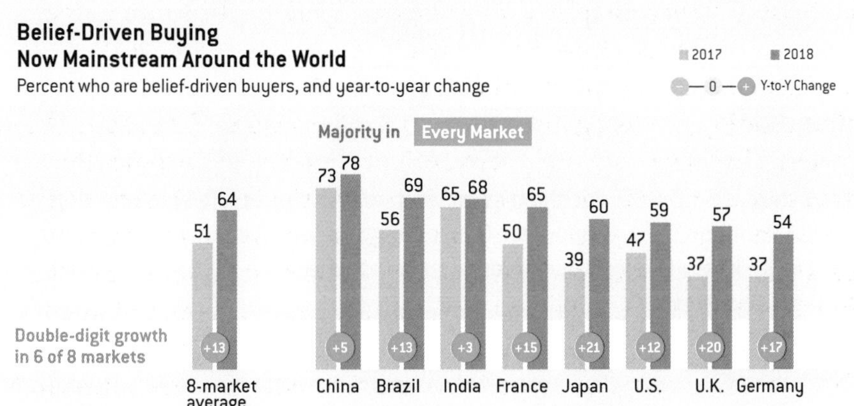

As the graph suggests, the percentage of consumers who care enough about issues to change their buying habits has grown in all eight of the surveyed economies. This suggests that demand can be a force for positive change on the issues related to social justice that consumers care about.

For example, consumer concern about the impact of single-use plastics was instrumental in incentivizing coffee chains to promote the use of reusable cups and stop offering plastic straws to their customers. Producers, seeking to maintain demand, are paying much more attention to their use of plastics at all levels of production, and this may be instrumental in reducing plastic waste. In this way, consumer demand can contribute to positive changes in terms of sustainability.

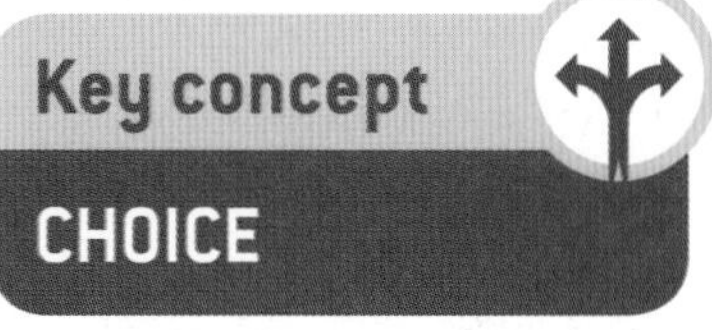

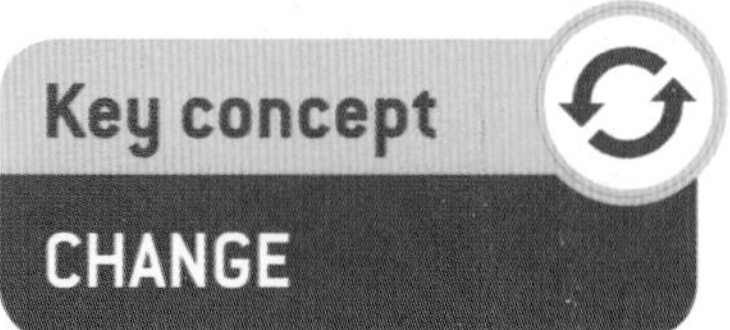

Of course, the cynical among us will say that the producers have no genuine interest in the environment or other social issue and they are only doing it to increase their profits. But if positive change is the result, does it matter what their main goal is? (There is no right answer to this question!)

---

1. Have you ever purchased a product because the company showed concern for an issue that you care about? Ask around to see if others have done the same.
2. Have you ever thought about not buying a product because the company showed a lack of concern about something that you think is important? Ask around to see if others have done the same.
3. Find an example of a company that has responded to consumer concerns about a social issue by changing what it produces or the way it produces.
   - Which social issue is the company responding to (eg sustainability, gender equity, racial equity)?
   - How is it responding?
   - How can you determine if the company behaviour is contributing to a positive change?

Theory of knowledge

Utilitarianism is a philosophy stemming from the English philosophers and economists, Jeremy Bentham (1748–1832) and John Stuart Mill (1806–1873). It has applications in economics. Utilitarianism tries to answer the question, "What should a person do?" The utilitarian answer is that the person should act to try to produce the best consequences from his or her actions.

In terms of consequences, a utilitarian person attempts to evaluate all of the good things and bad things produced by an act, whether they happen after the act has been performed or during its performance. Utilitarians believe that an action is right if the happiness produced by it is greater than the unhappiness. They believe that if all individuals were to follow this ethos, then the outcome would be the greatest good for the greatest number of people.

Happiness is sometimes referred to as utility and attempts to measure positive and negative happiness are often calculated in utils, which are measures of happiness, and negative utils, which are measures of unhappiness.

The consumption of products can be measured in utils and it is assumed that the marginal utility, the extra utility gained from consuming an extra unit of a product, will decrease as consumption increases. People will get less happiness from eating a second ice cream than they did from consuming the first one.

It is this theory that has been used in economics, in a simplistic sense, to explain why the demand curve slopes downwards. Consumers will only purchase more of a product if it is cheaper, since they receive less extra utility as they increase their consumption, and so will not pay as much for it.

1. Research the basic concept of utilitarianism.
2. You have $20 and are considering going out for the evening or giving the money to the World Wildlife Fund. Consider who would benefit from the two options and try to give util values to the options in order to decide the right course of action. (Itemize all those who would benefit and lose from each option.)
3. Drink five glasses of mineral water and attempt to give a marginal utility value to each glass. How does your marginal utility change as you consume each extra glass of water? How would this affect the amount that you are prepared to pay for a glass?
4. Does utilitarianism assume rational consumer behaviour?

Assessment advice: Paper 1 – Essay questions

You have already been introduced to Paper 1, which is divided into two parts. In Chapter 1, there were examples of part (a) questions. In part (b) you are expected to go a little further.

Part (b) invites the use of the skills of evaluation and synthesis. These are higher order skills that you should practise a great deal. Evaluation is a process that involves careful consideration of a topic or issue with a view to forming a balanced conclusion. Questions that begin with "evaluate", "discuss", "to what extent", "compare", "contrast", "compare and contrast", "examine" and "justify" are all questions requiring this higher order skill.

In part (b), you will also be expected to identify and develop relevant real-world example(s) to support your argument or conclusion. These should be the examples that you have come across through the inquiries that you have carried out throughout your economics course.

Remember that in part (a) and part (b) answers, it is necessary that you use diagrams to support your explanations. There will be very few questions where a diagram is not appropriate and needed.

EXAMINATION QUESTIONS

Paper 1, part (a) questions

1. Distinguish between a shift of the demand curve for a product and a movement along the product's demand curve. [10 marks]
2. With reference to two different determinants of demand, explain why the demand for environmentally friendly products might increase. [10 marks]

Paper 1, full question – HL Only

a) Describe two cognitive biases that influence consumers when making consumption choices. [10 marks]

b) Using real-world examples, evaluate the effectiveness of nudge theory in helping consumers to make better choices. [15 marks]

Higher Level

Assessment advice: Paper 2 – Data response

This is the first of many data response part questions that you will be doing in this course. On your second examination paper (Paper 2), you will be asked to choose one of two, multi-part, data response questions. The data response questions will all follow exactly the same pattern, which you will come to recognize. Each question will have seven part questions, labelled (a) to (g). The first part, (a), requires simple knowledge and understanding, usually asking for definitions from the text.

The second part, (b), may require a simple calculation or diagram from the text or data. The next four parts, (c) to (f), require an explanation of something from the text or data, usually involving a diagram and explanation. Part (g) requires a longer response to the data including synthesis and evaluation. The questions in the exercise below are typical of questions (a) and (c).

So, in Paper 2, key skills involve writing clear and succinct definitions, drawing neat and well-labelled diagrams, and using the information from the text to support your analysis. Soon, you will add the skills of synthesis and evaluation to this list. For further information about answering data response questions, see Chapter 32.

Data response exercise

Read the following article and answer the questions below:

Tree prices are rising and it's because of changing demand and supply by Danielle Prieur (WMFE)

If you're shopping for a pre-cut Christmas tree this year, expect to pay a little more than usual.

The National Christmas Tree Association's Director Tim O'Connor says there's a number of factors driving up Christmas tree prices in Florida. The first is an increased **demand** for the trees among Millennial customers. The second is a shortage in the noble conifer:

"It takes 8–10 years to grow a tree. And when you think back 8–10 years ago, growers were not profitable, the economy wasn't great, and they planted less trees back then. And so today, the trees that weren't planted, are just not there."

Jodi Utsman owns Santa's Christmas Tree Forest in Eustis, Florida. She says they won't run out of pre-cut trees because they ordered them from farmers in Michigan and North Carolina last June. But she says they've had to change their prices to reflect rising costs.

"Growers have increased prices on us on the ones we purchase from growers and the shipping costs have also risen. So the combination has driven the prices up a bit this year."

The National Christmas Tree Association estimates about 2.7 million trees were sold across the country last year alone.

Source: WMFE.org 28 November 2018

1. Define demand. [2 marks]
2. With the help of a diagram, explain what has happened to the demand for Christmas trees. [4 marks]

4 A CLOSER LOOK AT DEMAND: ELASTICITY OF DEMAND

REAL-WORLD ISSUE:

How do consumers and producers make choices in trying to meet their economic objectives?

By the end of this chapter, you should be able to:

- → Explain the concept of elasticity
- → Define elasticity of demand
- → Define and calculate price elasticity of demand (PED)
- → Explain and illustrate the theoretical range of values for price elasticity of demand
- → Explain and illustrate the relationship between price elasticity of demand and total revenue when demand is price elastic and when it is price inelastic
- HL Explain and illustrate different values of price elasticity of demand along a straight-line, downward-sloping demand curve
- → Explain the determinants of price elasticity of demand
- → Understand the importance of price elasticity of demand for firms and government decision-making
- HL Explain the likely differences in price elasticity of demand for primary commodities and manufactured goods
- → Define and calculate income elasticity of demand (YED)
- → Explain the possible range of values for income elasticity of demand
- HL Understand the importance of income elasticity of demand for firms and in explaining sectoral changes in the structure of the economy.

What is elasticity of demand?

Economists use the concept of *elasticity* to measure how much something changes when there is a change in one of the determinants. Elasticity is a measure of responsiveness.

Key concept
CHANGE

Elasticity of demand is a measure of how much the demand for a product changes when there is a change in one of the factors that determine demand. We will look at two elasticities of demand:

- price elasticity of demand [PED]
- income elasticity of demand [YED].

What is price elasticity of demand and how do we measure it?

Price elasticity of demand is a measure of how much the quantity demanded of a product changes when there is a change in the price of the product. It is usually calculated by using the following equation:

$$\text{PED} = \frac{\text{Percentage change in quantity demanded of the product}}{\text{Percentage change in price of the product}}$$

For example, a publishing firm discovers that when they lower the price of one of their monthly magazines from $5 to $4.50, the number of magazines that are bought by customers each month rises from 200,000 to 230,000. With this information, we can calculate the price elasticity of demand for the magazine in question:

1. The price has fallen by 50¢ from an original price of $5, which is a change of −10%. This is calculated by the equation

$$\frac{-50}{500} \times 100 = -10\%.$$

2. The quantity demanded has increased by 30,000 from an original demand of 200,000, which is a change of +15%. This is calculated by the equation

$$\frac{+30{,}000}{200{,}000} \times 100 = +15\%.$$

3. If we put the two values above into the equation for PED, we get PED = +15%/−10%, which gives a value of −1.5.
4. The negative value indicates that there is an inverse relationship between price and the quantity demanded. However, in order to simplify matters, economists usually ignore the negative value that comes from the equation and simply give the answer as a positive figure. Thus, in this case, the PED for the monthly magazine would be 1.5.

Exercise 4.1

ATL Thinking and Communication

Which do you think would have the bigger impact on consumers' willingness and ability to buy the following products? Why? (Explain your reasoning.)

1. A 10% increase in the price of bottled water from $2.00 per bottle to $2.20 per bottle.
2. A 10% increase in the price of an economy-sized car from $10,000 to $11,000.

What is the range of values of price elasticity of demand in theory?

The possible range of values for price elasticity of demand can, in theory, go from zero to infinity. Practically speaking, the actual PED values for a product will lie in between these two extreme theoretical values.

If PED is equal to zero, then a change in the price of a product will have no effect on the quantity demanded at all. The percentage change in quantity demanded would therefore be zero and so would the value on the top of the PED equation. Since zero divided by anything is zero, no matter what the percentage change in price, the PED value will be zero. A demand curve with a PED value of zero is shown in Figure 4.1 and, in this case, demand is said to be perfectly inelastic – it is completely unresponsive to price changes. Whether price is P_1, P_2, or any other price, the quantity demanded will be Q.

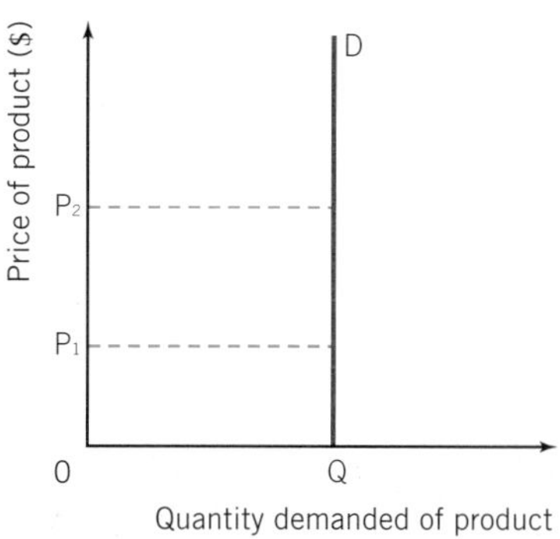

▲ **Figure 4.1** A perfectly inelastic demand curve

A PED value of infinity is best explained by using a diagram and the situation is shown in Figure 4.2. In this case, demand is said to be perfectly elastic. At the price P_1, the demand curve goes on forever and so the quantity demanded is infinite. However, if price is raised above P_1, even by the smallest amount, demand will fall to zero, an infinite change. Because of this, the value in the numerator of the equation would be infinity. Since infinity divided by anything is infinity, no matter what the percentage change in price, the PED value will be infinity.

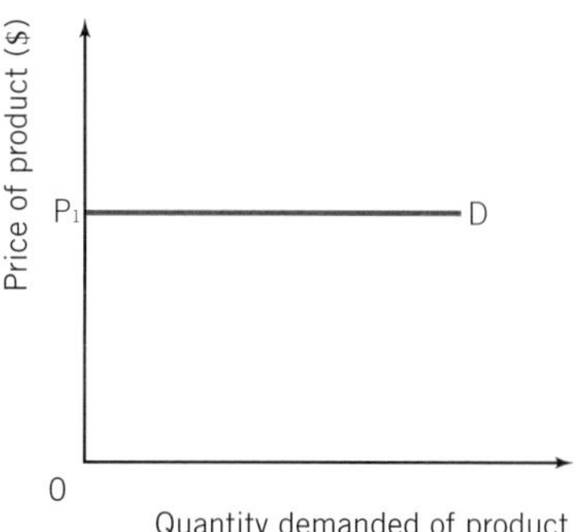

▲ **Figure 4.2** A perfectly elastic demand curve

As stated before, it must be remembered that the extreme values of PED are simply theoretical and there are no single products that would possess a PED value of zero or infinity. Normal products have values of PED between the two and we will now look at those values. The range of values of PED is normally split into three categories.

1. *Inelastic demand*: The value of PED is less than one and greater than zero. If a product has inelastic demand, then a change in the price of the product leads to a proportionally smaller change in the quantity demanded of it. This means that if the price is raised, the quantity demanded will not fall by much in proportion, and so the total revenue gained by the firm (the number of units sold x the price of the product) will increase.

   For example, when the price of a carton of strawberry yoghurt is raised from \$1 to \$1.20, the firm finds that quantity demanded per week falls from 12,000 cartons to 10,800 cartons. Thus, a 20% increase in price is causing a 10% fall in the quantity demanded. We can work out the PED by using the equation:

$$PED = \frac{\%\ \Delta \text{ in Quantity Demanded}}{\%\ \Delta \text{ in Price}} = \frac{10\%}{20\%} = 0.5 \text{ (Where } \Delta \text{ is "change")}$$

   As we can see, the PED is 0.5, less than one, so the demand for the yoghurt is inelastic. Before the price increase, the total revenue gained by the firm was 12,000 × \$1 = \$12,000. After the increase, the total revenue becomes 10,800 × \$1.20 = \$12,960. The firm has increased revenue by raising the price. This is shown in Figure 4.3.

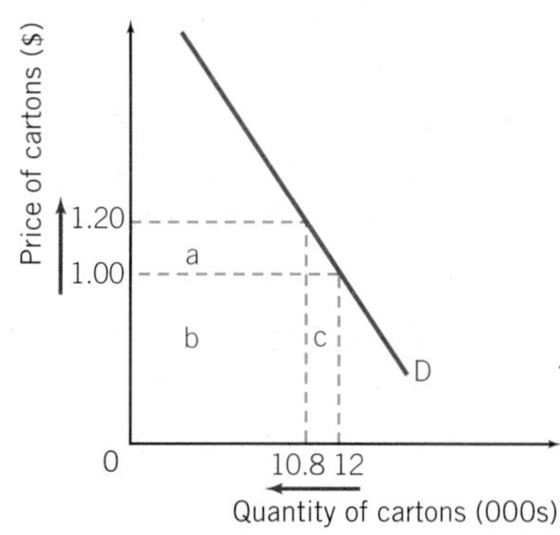

▲ **Figure 4.3** The demand for strawberry yoghurt

The "revenue boxes" in the diagram clearly show why a price increase causes an increase in total revenue, when the demand for a product is inelastic. In this case, before the price rise, the firm was getting revenue equal to "revenue box b" + "revenue box c". After the price increase, the firm loses "revenue box c", because quantity demanded falls to 10,800 cartons, but gains "revenue box a", because the remaining cartons are now sold at $1.20 each. Since "revenue box a" (10,800 × 0.20 = $2,160) is clearly larger than "revenue box c" (1,200 × $1 = $1,200), the firm's total revenue rises by $960.

Thus, if a firm has relatively inelastic demand for its product and wishes to increase total revenue, it should raise the price of the product.

2. *Elastic demand*: The value of PED is greater than one and less than infinity. If a product has elastic demand, then a change in the price of the product leads to a greater than proportionate change in the quantity demanded of it. This means that if price is raised, the quantity demanded will fall by more in proportion, and so the total revenue gained by the firm (the number of units sold × the price of the product) will fall.

For example, when the price of a hot dog is raised from $2 to $2.10, a hot-dog seller finds that quantity demanded per week falls from 200 hot dogs to 180 hot dogs. Thus, a 5% increase in price is causing a 10% fall in the quantity demanded. We can work out the PED by using the equation:

$$\text{PED} = \frac{\%\,\Delta \text{ in Quantity Demanded}}{\%\,\Delta \text{ in Price}} = \frac{10\%}{5\%} = 2$$

As we can see, the PED is 2, greater than 1, so the demand for the hot dog is elastic. Before the price rise, the total revenue gained by the hot-dog seller was 200 × $2 = $400. After the increase, the total revenue becomes 180 × $2.10 = $378. The seller has caused a fall in revenue by raising the price. This is shown in Figure 4.4.

The "revenue boxes" in the diagram clearly show why a price increase causes a decrease in total revenue, when the demand for a product is elastic. In this case, before the price rise, the hot dog seller was earning revenue equal to "revenue box b" + "revenue box c". After the price increase, the hot-dog seller loses "revenue box c", because quantity demanded falls to 180 hot dogs, but gains "revenue box a", because the remaining hot dogs are now sold at $2.10 each. Since "revenue box a" (180 × $0.10 = $18) is clearly smaller than "revenue box c" (20 × $2 = $40), the hot-dog seller's total revenue falls by $22.

Thus, if a firm has elastic demand for its product and wishes to increase total revenue, it should not raise the price of the product.

3. *Unit elastic demand:* The value of PED is equal to one. If a product has unit elastic demand, then a change in the price of the product leads to a proportionate, opposite, change in the quantity demanded of it. This means that if price is raised by a certain percentage, then the quantity demanded will fall by the same percentage, and so PED is

Exercise 4.2

ATL Thinking and Communication

A firm producing decorative candles lowers the price of one of its scented candles from $4 to $3.60 and finds that the weekly quantity demanded of the candles goes up from 600 per week to 630.

1. Calculate the percentage changes in price and quantity demanded.
2. Calculate the price elasticity of demand for the scented candles.
3. Calculate the change in total revenue that the firm will experience following the fall in price.
4. Draw a "revenue box" diagram to illustrate the effect on quantity demanded and total revenue following the price change for the scented candle.
5. Was the firm sensible to lower the price of the scented candles? Explain your answer.

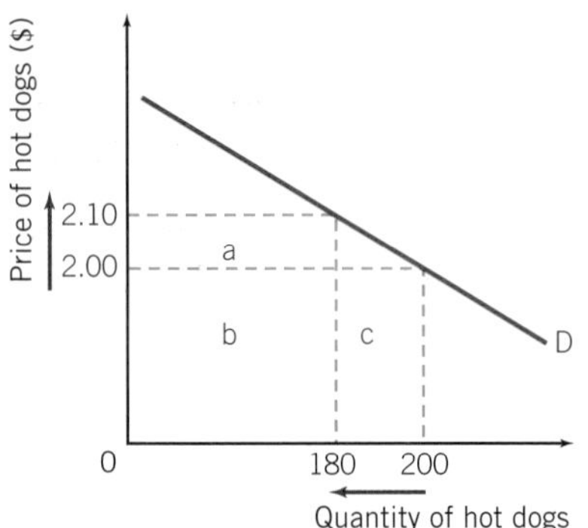

▲ Figure 4.4 The demand for hot dogs

equal to 1 and the total revenue gained by the firm (the number of units sold × the price of the product) will not change. A curve that has unit elasticity at every point is shown in Figure 4.5. It is known as a rectangular hyperbola.

The rectangular hyperbola is drawn in such a way that price multiplied by quantity at any point is constant. This means that the total of the "revenue boxes" always has the same area and if the revenue does not change when price changes, then PED must be unity. Thus, in Figure 4.5, the two rectangles a + b have the same area as the two rectangles b + c, and so since revenue does not change when price changes, PED must be unity.

Exercise 4.3

ATL Thinking and Communication

A pizzeria lowers the price of its most popular takeaway pizza, the Margherita, from $5 to $4.50 and finds that the weekly quantity demanded of the pizzas goes up from 60 per week to 72.

1. Calculate the percentage changes in price and quantity demanded.
2. Calculate the price elasticity of demand for the pizzas.
3. Calculate the change in total revenue that the pizzeria will experience following the fall in price.
4. Draw a "revenue box" diagram to illustrate the effect on quantity demanded and total revenue following the price change for the Margherita.
5. Was the firm sensible to lower the price of the Margherita? Explain your answer.

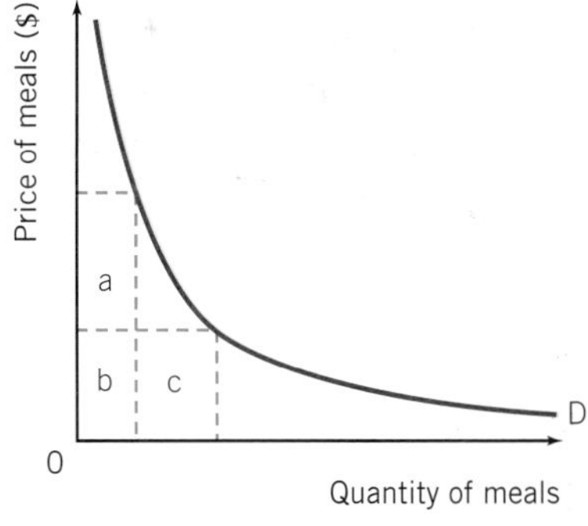

▲ **Figure 4.5** A rectangular hyperbola where PED = 1 at every point

What do PED values mean?

Price elasticity of demand	Value (ignoring the negative sign)	Meaning	Change in price	Effect on total revenue (TR)
Inelastic	0 < PED < 1	% Δ in price < % change in Qd	Price ↑	TR↑
Inelastic	0 < PED < 1	% Δ in price < % change in Qd	Price ↓	TR↓
Elastic	1 < PED < ∞	% Δ in price > % change in Qd	Price ↑	TR↓
Elastic	1 < PED < ∞	% Δ in price > % change in Qd	Price ↓	TR↑
Unity	PED = 1	% Δ in price = % change in Qd	Price ↑	No change in TR
Unity	PED = 1	% Δ in price = % change in Qd	Price ↓	No change in TR

▲ **Table 4.1** The meaning of PED values

Exercise 4.4

ATL Thinking and Communication

Economists often use the language of mathematics and symbols to express theoretical relationships. For each of the rows in Table 4.1, turn the mathematical expression into a sentence.

For example:

1. When demand for a product is inelastic, the value of PED lies between 0 and 1. This means that if the price of a product increases, there will be a proportionately smaller fall in quantity demanded. This would result in an increase in producer's revenue.

A mathematical note about elasticity: Why are there different values of price elasticity of demand along a straight-line, downward-sloping demand curve?

It is a common mistake for students to assume that elasticity is a measure of the slope of the demand curve and that the value is always the same at any point on the curve. This is not the case. For a straight-line, downward-sloping demand curve, the value of PED falls as price falls. This is shown in Figure 4.6.

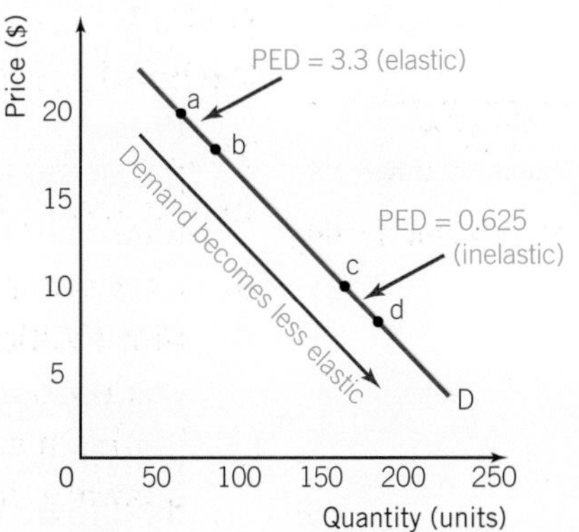

▲ **Figure 4.6** PED values for a normal demand curve

Higher Level

When price falls from \$20 to \$18, quantity demanded increases from 60 to 80 units. Thus the PED value is:

$$PED = \frac{\%\Delta QD}{\%\Delta P} = \frac{33.3\%}{10\%} = 3.3$$

The value of PED is 3.3, elastic, when we move from point a to point b.

When price falls from \$10 to \$8, quantity demanded increases from 160 to 180 units. Thus, the PED value is:

$$PED = \frac{\%\Delta QD}{\%\Delta P} = \frac{12.5\%}{20\%} = 0.625$$

The value of PED is 0.625, inelastic, when we move from point c to point d.

Thus, we can see that the value of PED falls as we move down a demand curve. It is logical that this should happen. Low-priced products have a more inelastic demand than high-priced products, because consumers are less concerned when the price of an inexpensive product rises than they are when the price of an expensive product rises.

What are the determinants of price elasticity of demand?

Different products will have different values for PED. For example, the demand for a restaurant meal may have a PED value of 3, ie the demand is elastic, whereas the demand for petrol may have a PED value of 0.4, which is inelastic. What actually determines the value of PED for a product? There are a number of determinants:

1. The number and closeness of substitutes

The number and closeness of substitutes that are available is certainly the most important determinant of PED. It is fair to say that the more substitutes there are for a product, the more elastic the demand will be for it. Also, the closer the substitutes available, the more elastic the demand will be.

For example, there are many different brands of butter available on the market and so an increase in the price of one brand will lead to a large number of customers changing their demands to another brand. Thus, the demand for products with lots of substitutes, such as brands of household products, types of meat and types of fruit, will tend to have elastic demand.

Products with few substitutes, such as oil, will tend to have relatively inelastic demand, with the quantity demanded falling relatively little as the price goes up.

2. The necessity of the product and how widely the product is defined

Food is a necessary product. Indeed, if we do not have food, then we will die, so it is very necessary. Thus we would expect the demand for food to be very inelastic, which it is. However, if we define food more

narrowly and consider meat, we would expect the demand to be less inelastic, since there are many alternatives, such as vegetables. Once again, if we then define meat more narrowly and consider chicken, beef, lamb and pork, we could once again reasonably assume that the demand for each would be relatively elastic, since the consumer can easily change from one type of meat to another, if the price of one rises. As the product is defined even more narrowly, into chicken products and then identical, but branded, chicken products, demand becomes even more elastic. This is shown in Figure 4.7.

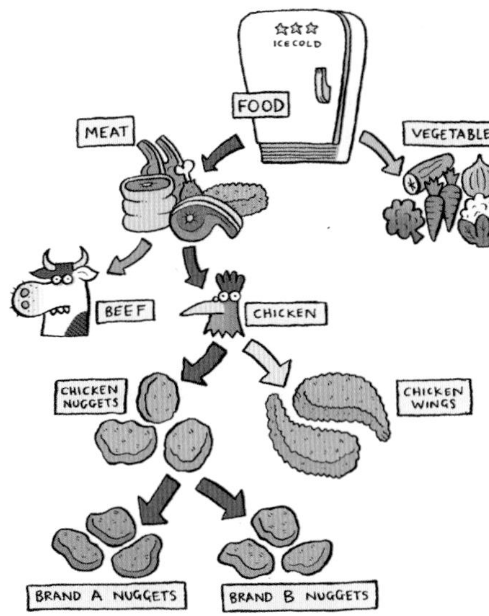

▲ **Figure 4.7** Level of definition

It is worth remembering that for many goods, necessity will change from consumer to consumer, since different people have different tastes and necessity is often a subjective view.

For example, in Malaysia, chicken is very popular among the population and so the demand for it is less elastic than it would be in Italy, where it is not valued as highly. Necessity may go to extremes when individuals consider products to be very "necessary", such as habit-forming or addictive goods – **for example,** cigarettes, alcohol or chocolate. Such products tend to have inelastic demand.

3. The proportion of income spent on the good

If a good costs very little and constitutes a very small part of a person's budget, then a change in price may cause very little change in quantity demanded, ie the demand will be quite inelastic.

For example, if a person earning a relatively good salary buys a coffee on the way to work each day and it costs $1.50, then a 10% increase in price to $1.65 will be unlikely to curtail her expenditure on coffee. It is worth considering that behavioural economists might explain this in terms of the *status quo bias*.

4. The time period considered

As the price of a product changes, it often takes time for consumers to change their buying and consumption habits. PED thus tends to be more inelastic in the short term and then becomes more elastic, the longer the time period it is measured over.

For example, when heating oil prices rose sharply in Austria, the demand for oil that winter changed by a proportionately smaller amount than the change in price. Demand was relatively very inelastic, since people did not really have many alternative products that they could switch to. They still needed heating oil for their central heating. However, over the next few years, the demand for heating oil began to fall as people started to change their heating systems to ones that used gas, coal or wood. The PED, when measured over a longer time period, was certainly more elastic.

Exercise 4.5

ATL Thinking and Communication

For each of the following pairs of goods, identify the one that you would expect to have the higher price elasticity of demand and explain your choice by referring to at least one of the determinants of elasticity. There may not necessarily always be a "correct" answer. It may depend upon your viewpoint and reasoning.

1. Heineken beer vs beer
2. A prescription tablet to reduce blood pressure vs a tablet to reduce headache pain
3. Milk vs orange juice
4. A motor car vs a daily newspaper

Exercise 4.6
ATL Thinking and Communication

Estimates based on studies of the US population suggest that a 10% increase in the price of cigarettes would reduce overall consumption by adults by 3% to 5%. The same 10% increase would reduce the consumption by youths by 13%.

1. Calculate the price elasticity of demand for cigarettes among US adults and among US youths.
2. Suggest possible reasons for the different magnitude of elasticity between the two groups.
3. Explain two possible reasons why a government would place a tax on cigarettes.

Why is a knowledge of price elasticity of demand important for decision making by governments and firms?

An understanding of price elasticity of demand can be very useful for firms and also for the government.

For firms, as we have seen, the main use is for predicting the effects of their pricing decisions on quantity demanded and also on total revenue.

For governments, they need to be aware of the possible consequences on a number of economic variables when they impose indirect taxes, such as sales taxes, on products. If a government puts a tax on a product, then its price will usually rise. This means that the quantity demanded of the product in question is likely to fall and this will have consequences for the amount of tax revenue that the government will receive. (This is dealt with in more detail in Chapter 8.) There will also be consequences for employment in the industry concerned. If the demand for the product is very elastic, then a price increase as a result of the imposition of a tax on the product will lead to a relatively large fall in the demand for the product. This means that the demand for workers in the industry is likely to fall significantly, increasing unemployment in the economy.

Since governments are not usually keen to increase unemployment, they may place higher taxes on products where demand is relatively inelastic, so that the demand for the product will not fall by a significant amount, and will thus not lead to high unemployment. However, the choices that governments face about which products to tax and how much tax to place on a good depends on much more than simply the elasticity.

Higher Level

What is the difference between the price elasticity of demand for primary commodities and manufactured products?

"Primary commodities" is another term for raw materials, such as cotton or coffee. Such products tend to have inelastic demand as they are necessities to the "consumers" who buy them and they have few or no substitutes. It must be noted that consumers of primary commodities are not everyday households. The consumers of primary commodities are manufacturing industries which process the raw material into finished products. They require the primary commodities in order to produce their processed products. For example, if there is an increase in the price of green coffee (raw coffee beans), then the coffee processing companies who buy the green coffee to make instant coffee for consumers have little choice but to continue buying the coffee, and thus the quantity demanded will fall by a proportionately smaller amount. For those coffee processing companies, there are no substitutes for the raw coffee beans. Similarly, if there were to be a decrease in the price of green coffee

the processing companies would not want proportionately more coffee as their production targets would already have been set and they have no use for further inputs, regardless of the price.

On the other hand, demand for manufactured goods tends to be more elastic, as there are usually many more substitutes available to consumers, since the product can be differentiated by different producers. This ties in with the determinant of PED mentioned earlier – "the number and closeness of substitutes". For example, if the price of one branded vacuum cleaner increases significantly, consumers have the option of many other brands and will be likely to switch their purchasing to one of those. For most consumer goods, there are many ways that producers can differentiate their products, giving consumers lots of choice.

Processing coffee beans

What is income elasticity of demand (YED) and how do we measure it?

Income elasticity of demand is a measure of how much the demand for a product changes when there is a change in the consumer's income. It is usually calculated by using the equation below:

$$\text{YED} = \frac{\text{Percentage change in quantity demanded of the product}}{\text{Percentage change in income of the consumer}}$$

Take an example. A person has an increase in annual income from \$60,000 per year to \$66,000. She then increases her annual spending on holidays from \$2,500 to \$3,000. With this information, we can calculate her income elasticity of demand for holidays.

1. Her income has risen by \$6,000 from an original income of \$60,000, which is a change of +10%. This is calculated by the equation $\frac{+6{,}000}{60{,}000} \times 100 = +10\%$.
2. The quantity demanded of holidays has increased by \$500 from an original demand of \$2,500, which is a change of +20%. This is calculated by the equation $\frac{+500}{2{,}500} \times 100 = +20\%$.
3. If we put the two values above into the equation for PED, we get +20%/+10%, which gives a value of 2.

What is the range of values for income elasticity of demand?

In YED, the sign obtained from the equation (ie whether it is positive or negative) is important. The sign of YED tells us whether the product we are looking at is a normal good or an inferior good.

Remember that the demand for a normal good rises as income rises and the demand for an inferior good falls as income rises.

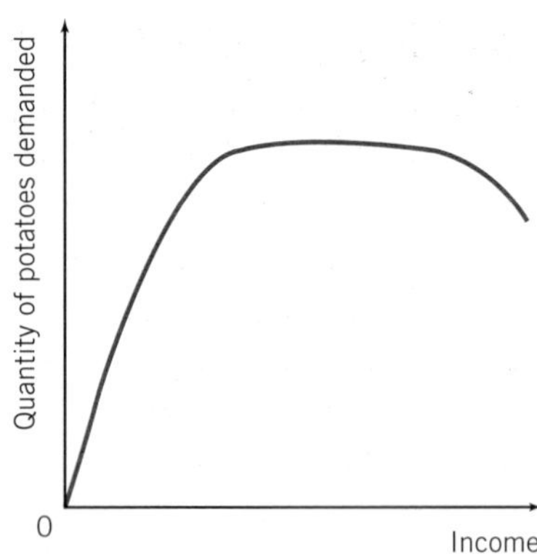

▲ Figure 4.8 An Engel Curve showing the relationship between income and the demand for potatoes

Exercise 4.7
ATL Thinking and Communication

A consumer had an increase in income, following a salary rise, from $80,000 per year to $100,000 per year. In the following year, her expenditure on holidays increased from $8,000 to $10,000, her expenditure on gym membership remained the same, and her expenditure on locally produced clothes fell from $2,000 to $1,500.

1. Calculate her income elasticity of demand for holidays.
2. Explain what the value of her income elasticity of demand for holidays means.
3. Calculate her income elasticity of demand for gym membership.
4. Explain what the value of her income elasticity of demand for gym membership means.
5. Calculate her income elasticity of demand for locally produced clothes.
6. Explain what the value of her income elasticity of demand for locally produced clothes means.

For normal goods, the value of YED is positive (ie the demand increases as income increases). If the percentage increase in quantity demanded is less than the percentage increase in income, then a YED value between zero and one is obtained and the demand is said to be income-inelastic.

If the percentage increase in quantity demanded is greater than the percentage increase in income, then a YED value greater than one is obtained and the demand is said to be income-elastic.

Necessity goods are products that have low income elasticity. The demand for them will change very little if income rises. For example, the demand for bread does not increase significantly as income rises, because people feel that they already have enough bread and so will not increase consumption significantly. Demand will be income-inelastic.

Superior goods are products that have high income elasticity. The demand for them changes significantly if income rises. As people have more income and have satisfied their needs, they begin to purchase products that are wants, ie non-essential, in greater number. For example, the demand for holidays in foreign countries is likely to be income-elastic.

For inferior goods, the value of YED is negative, because the demand decreases as income increases. People start to switch their expenditure from the inferior goods that they had been buying to superior goods, which they can now afford. For example, the demand for inexpensive jeans falls as income rises because people switch to buying branded jeans.

An Engel Curve shows the relationship between income and the demand for a product over time. It is named after Ernst Engel, a nineteenth-century German economist. Such a curve is shown in Figure 4.8. We can see that as the income in a country rises over time, the demand for potatoes may increase, then become constant, and then begin to fall as people begin to buy superior products instead, such as pasta.

What do YED values mean?

Type of good	YED value	Meaning
Inferior	YED < 0	A given increase in income will lead to a proportionately smaller fall in demand
Necessity	0 < YED < 1	A given increase in income will lead to a proportionately smaller increase in demand
Luxury	YED > 1	A given increase in income will lead to a proportionately larger increase in demand

▲ Table 4.2 The meaning of YED values

Why is a knowledge of income elasticity of demand important?

1. *For decision making by firms*

   A knowledge of YED can be useful for firms when they are planning which markets to enter and which products to sell. Products that have a high YED will see large increases in demand as income levels in a country rise and so their markets will grow quickly. The research department of a company will aim to be aware of the YED of their products and the changing incomes of their target consumers in order to make the most of the possible opportunities. For example, consider the market for smartphones; as incomes in a particular country are growing, there is likely to be a proportionately larger increase in the demand for smartphones. The producers of smartphones will look to expand their sales in rapidly growing economies to take advantage of rising incomes.

   As you are probably aware, producers often manufacture several versions of their product in order to appeal to consumers of different incomes. They also want to be able to take advantage of their knowledge of changing incomes to increase production of certain products and decrease production of others. If a country is expected to go into a recession, where national income (GNP) is actually falling, then producers will want to increase their production of inferior goods, whose demand increases as incomes fall.

2. *For explaining sectoral changes in the structure of the economy*

   Production in economies is usually separated into three sectors:

   - Primary sector – this consists of agricultural and fishing industries and extraction industries such as forestry and mining. Their products are known as primary products.
   - Secondary (manufacturing) sector – these are industries that take primary products (raw materials) from the primary sector and use them to manufacture producer goods, such as machinery or consumer goods such as electronic goods or clothing. The secondary sector also includes the construction industry.
   - Tertiary (service) sector – these are industries that produce services or intangible products, such as financial services, education, information technology and mass media to name just a few.

   Sectoral change refers to the shift in the relative share of national output and employment that is attributed to each of the production sectors as an economy develops over time.

   As countries grow and living standards improve, there is a change in the proportion of the economy that is produced in each sector. This does not mean that any sector is getting smaller, just that the relative proportion of output coming from this sector is likely to change. This may be explained using YED. As an economy grows, and incomes increase, the demand for primary products, such as agricultural

Exercise 4.8

ATL Thinking and Communication

Orange, a computer manufacturer, produces a very basic laptop computer at a low price of $300 but also produces a more sophisticated model at a price of $2,500 (and many other models in between!). At the end of 2017, Orange had sold 10,000 of the low-priced laptop and 800 of the higher-priced model.

In 2018, the country experienced economic growth of 5%. This economic growth of 5% is equated with an increase in national income of 5%. At the end of 2018, Orange had sold 9,000 of the cheaper model, and 900 of the more expensive laptop.

1. Calculate the YED for each model.
2. What does the value of YED for each model signify?
3. What is Orange likely to do if economists predict a recession in the following year?

products, does not greatly increase, because they have income-inelastic demand. When incomes grow, people do not tend to buy many more agricultural products. So, the extra income tends to be spent on manufactured products, such as mobile phones and other electronics, that have income-elastic demand. It follows that output in the primary sector will be growing, but output in the secondary sector will be growing more quickly. So output may be growing in all sectors in the economy, but the proportions of the total product from each sector will change.

As a country develops further, the same YED explanation may be used to account for the growth of the service sector. As we know, services tend to have high YED and so, as income grows, there will be faster growth in this sector, reflecting the high YEDs. There will be high growth in industries such as entertainment, education and healthcare.

Therefore, the tertiary sectors of an economy tend to grow at a faster rate when a country grows, and the living standards of its populations increase, since the demand for tertiary products grows more rapidly.

It is worth noting that in our increasingly globalized world, where it is easier and easier to import goods and services from other countries, it is not necessarily the income of each individual country that determines how its own sectors may grow. It is more the case that global incomes are growing, leading to increased demand for manufactured goods and even greater increases in the demand for services from all different countries.

Exercise 4.9

ATL Thinking and Communication

The following data illustrate how the structure of the Bangladesh economy has changed since 1970. The three pieces of the pie indicate the amount of GDP generated from each of the three sectors.

Source: *https://data.worldbank.org/*

Using numbers from the charts in your explanation, comment on the changes that have occurred. How might income elasticity of demand have contributed to the change in the structure of the economy?

Assessment advice: Using the language of economics

Whenever you are discussing any type of elasticity in an examination question, you must try to be very precise with language. Elasticity measures the responsiveness of change, and it is the percentage change or proportionate change that is significant. Never say that a small change in price (or income) causes a large change in the quantity. Be specific – say that a given price change causes a proportionately smaller (or proportionately larger) change in quantity. Or say that a given percentage change in price leads to a smaller (or larger) percentage change in quantity. Or you could give values. For example, say that a 10% increase in price leads to a change in quantity that is greater (or less) than 10%. The adjectives "small" and "big" are just too imprecise.

EXAMINATION QUESTIONS

Paper 1, part (a) questions – HL & SL

1. Explain the determinants of price elasticity of demand. [10 marks]
2. A businessperson wants to increase her revenues. Explain why knowledge of price elasticity of demand would be useful. [10 marks]
3. Explain the concept of income elasticity of demand. [10 marks]
4. Using income elasticity of demand, explain the difference between normal, necessity and inferior goods. [10 marks]

Paper 1, full question – HL & SL

1. **a)** Explain the concept of elasticity of demand. [10 marks]

   b) Using real-world examples, discuss why it may be important for a firm to have knowledge of price elasticity of demand. [15 marks]

5 SUPPLY

REAL-WORLD ISSUE:
How do consumers and producers make choices in trying to meet their economic objectives?

By the end of this chapter, you should be able to:

- → Define supply
- → Explain the Law of Supply
- → Illustrate a supply curve
- → Explain the non-price determinants of supply
- → Distinguish between a shift of a supply curve and a movement along a supply curve
- → Understand the relationship between an individual producer's supply and market supply
- HL Explain the assumptions underlying the Law of Supply – diminishing marginal returns and increasing marginal costs.

Supply is defined as the quantity of a good or service that producers are willing and able to supply at different prices in a given time period For example, firms may be willing and able to produce 4,000 frozen pizzas per week, at a price of $3 each. We would say that their supply of frozen pizzas at a price of $3 would be 4,000 units each week.

The important phrase here is "willingness and ability", as it was in demand. It is not enough for producers to be willing to produce a good or service; they must also be able to produce it, ie they must have the financial means to supply the product, the ability to supply. This is known as *effective supply* and it is this that is shown on a supply curve.

How does the Law of Supply work?

The Law of Supply simply states that "as the price of a product rises, the quantity supplied of the product will usually increase, *ceteris paribus*". It is sometimes expressed even more simply as "the supply curve normally slopes upwards".

The Law of Supply may be illustrated using either a supply schedule or a supply curve. The example in Table 5.1 illustrates the effective supply for frozen pizzas in a small town.

Price of frozen pizzas ($)	Quantity supplied of frozen pizzas (per week)
3.50	4,400
3.00	4,000
2.50	3,500
2.00	2,750
1.50	1,750

▲ **Table 5.1** A supply schedule for frozen pizzas

As shown, the supply of frozen pizzas increases as the price increases. A table showing such changes is known as a supply schedule. The same information can be shown in graphical form, using a supply curve. The supply schedule and supply curve show the sum of all individual producers' supply, and is known as the market supply. This is a curve that shows the relationship between the price of a product, which is placed on the vertical axis, and the quantity supplied of the same product over time, which is placed on the horizontal axis. This is shown in Figure 5.1.

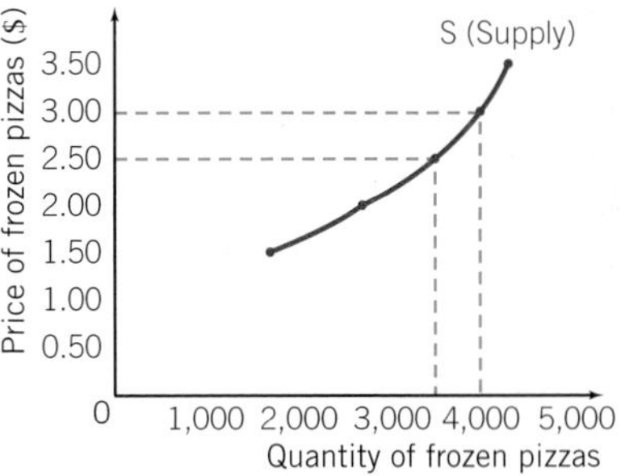

▲ **Figure 5.1** A supply curve for frozen pizzas

Supply curves tend to be curved and get steeper as price rises. However, for ease of analysis, economists often draw them as straight lines, and so shall we from now on.

As we have seen, in the Law of Supply a change in the price of the product itself will lead to a change in the quantity supplied of the product, ie a movement along the existing supply curve. The phrase "change in the quantity supplied" is important, since it differentiates a change in price from the effect of a change in any of the other determinants of supply. In Figure 5.1, a change in the price of frozen pizzas, from $2.50 to $3.00, leads to an increase in the quantity of frozen pizzas supplied, from 3,500 pizzas per week to 4,000 pizzas per week.

In the neoclassical model, it is assumed that producers are rational "maximizers". That is, their only goal is to maximize profits. So since rising prices can translate into higher profits for producers, they will wish to increase supply to take advantage of the higher potential profits. For Higher Level students, the link between price, quantity and the Law of Supply is explained in more depth at the end of this chapter.

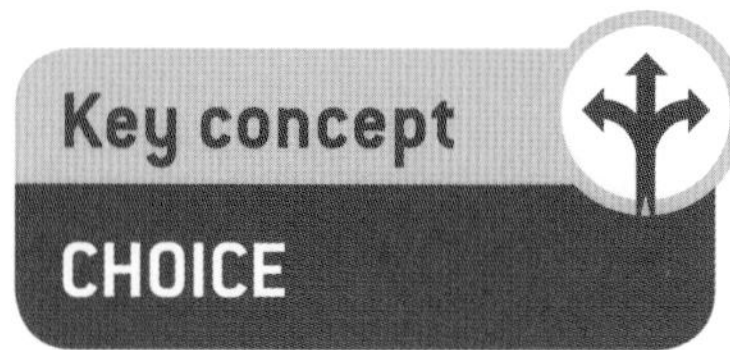

Exercise 5.1

ATL Thinking and Communication

It is important to be aware that the supply curve that we draw is based on the assumption that rational producers choose to maximize profits. In many situations, this will not be the case. Can you think of other goals that owners of firms might have? Try to find examples of firms whose main goal may not in fact be profit maximization. HL students will look at this in some more depth later.

What are the non-price determinants of supply?

There are a number of factors that determine supply and lead to an actual shift of the supply curve to either the right or the left. Whenever we look at a change in one of the determinants, we always make the *ceteris paribus* assumption. If we do not, then the analysis becomes too complicated and it is almost impossible to identify the effect of a change in any one of the determinants. The determinants of supply are outlined below.

1. The cost of factors of production

If there is an increase in the cost of a factor of production, such as a wage increase in a firm producing textiles, which is labour-intensive, then this will increase the firm's costs. This means that they can supply less, shifting the supply curve to the left. This is shown in Figure 5.2.

▲ **Figure 5.2** The supply of textiles

A rise in the level of wages in the textile firm means that the firm must now supply fewer textiles at all prices and the supply curve will shift to the left from S to S_1. A fall in the cost of factors of production will enable firms to increase their supply, shifting the supply curve to the right.

2. The price of related goods – competitive and joint supply

Competitive supply – Often, producers have a choice as to what they are going to produce, because the factors of production that they control are capable of producing more than one product. For example, a producer of roller skates may also be able to produce skateboards with a minimal change in production facilities. In this case, if the price of skateboards rises, because there is more demand for them, then it may well be that the producer will be attracted by the higher prices and aim to supply more skateboards and fewer roller skates.

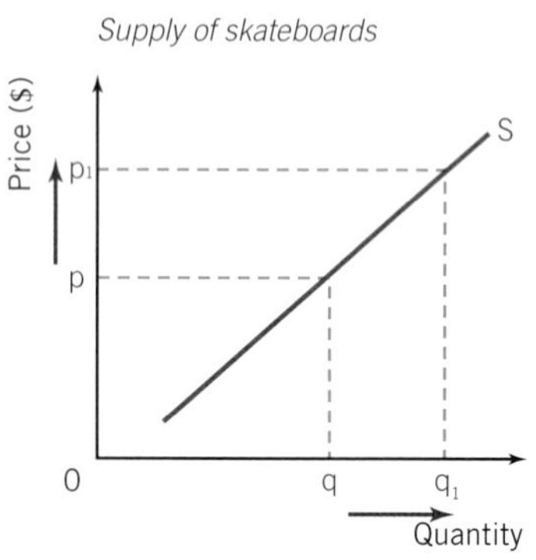

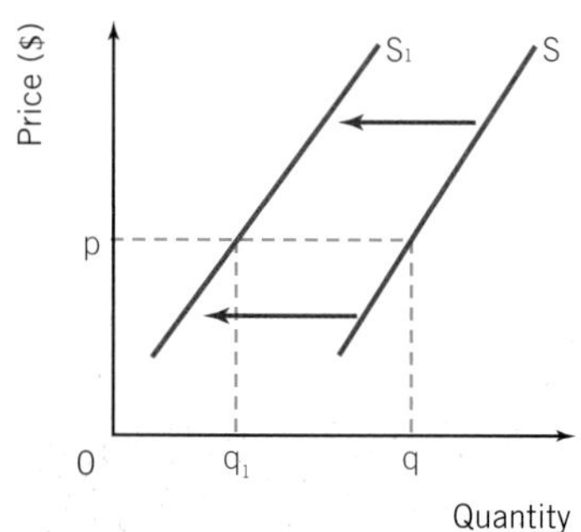

▲ **Figure 5.3** The supply of skateboards and roller skates

This would lead to a movement along the supply curve of skateboards and a shift to the left of the supply curve of roller skates. This is shown in both the graphs in Figure 5.3.

As you can see, a rise in the price of **skateboards** from p to p_1 leads to an increase in the quantity of skateboards supplied from q to q_1. This change in the price of skateboards means that some producers will now supply fewer roller skates, since they are manufacturing skateboards. There will be a fall in the supply of **roller skates**, at all prices, and the supply curve will shift to the left from S to S_1. Even though the price of roller skates has not changed, there is a fall in the supply from q to q_1.

In this case, skateboards and roller skates are "competing" for the factors of production that the firm has in their control. Thus, it is often said that products are in *competitive supply*.

Joint supply – Sometimes, when one good is produced, another good is produced at the same time. If this happens, then the goods are said to be in joint supply. You might hear the term "by-product" where products that are in joint supply are concerned. For example, when sugar is refined, molasses (a kind of black treacle) is created. Molasses is said to be a by-product of sugar and the two products are in joint supply.

When crude oil is treated to produce petrol, other goods are inevitably produced as well, such as diesel. If the demand for one good in joint supply increases, then the supply of the other good(s) will also increase. So if there is an increase in the demand for petrol, there will be an increase in the quantity supplied of petrol, but also, the supply of diesel will increase as it is in joint supply with petrol. This is shown in Figure 5.4.

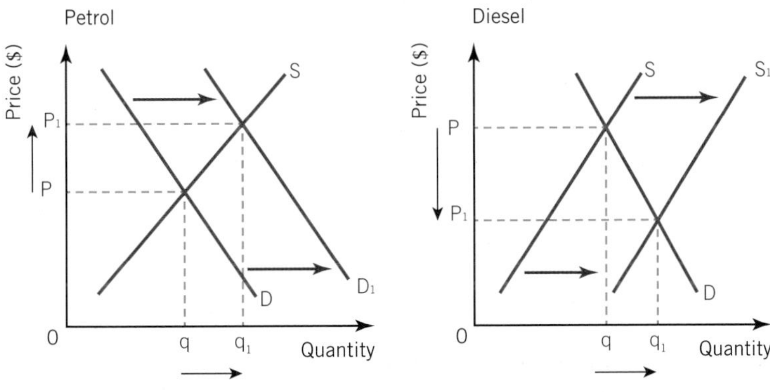

▲ **Figure 5.4** Joint supply

An increase in the demand for petrol shifts the demand curve for petrol from D to D_1. The quantity supplied of petrol will increase from q to q_1, in response to the increase in price from p to p_1. Because diesel is in joint supply, there will be an automatic increase in the supply of diesel and the supply curve will shift to the right from S to S_1, lowering the price of diesel to p_1 and increasing the quantity demanded and supplied to q_1.

3. Government intervention – indirect taxes and subsidies

In many countries, governments intervene in markets in ways that alter the supply. The two most common ways are through indirect taxes and subsidies.

Indirect taxes – Indirect taxes (expenditure taxes) are taxes on goods and services that are added to the price of a product. The producers are the ones that have to pay the taxes to the government, so the taxes effectively increase the costs of production to the firms. Therefore, they have the effect of shifting the supply curve upwards by the amount of the indirect tax. Less of the product will be supplied at every price.

Subsidies – Subsidies are payments made by the government to firms that will, in effect, reduce their costs of production. This then has the effect of shifting the supply curve downwards by the amount of the subsidy. More of the product will be supplied at every price.

We will look at indirect taxes and subsidies in much more detail in Chapter 8.

4. Expectations about future prices

Producers make decisions about what to supply based on their expectations of future prices. However, the effect that expectations might have on production decisions might vary. Producers who expect the demand for their product to rise in the future may assume that the higher demand will lead to a higher price. If it is possible to store the product they might then withhold the product from the market in order to be ready to be able to supply more in the future, to gain from the higher price.

Alternatively, supply might be increased to be able to meet the demand at higher prices. Similarly, if market research suggests that demand for a product will fall in the future, then producers will be likely to reduce their supply of the product. Producers' expectations and confidence in the future may exert a strong effect on their production decisions.

5. Changes in technology

Improvements in the state of technology in a firm or an industry should lead to an increase in supply and thus a shift of the supply curve to the right. In the unlikely event of a backward step in the state of technology, the supply curve would shift to the left. Although this is unlikely, natural disasters, such as hurricanes or earthquakes, may have the effect of moving technology backwards in an area or country.

Beer supply threatened by future weather extremes

https://phys.org/news/2018-10-beer-threatened-future-weather-extremes.html

6. Weather or natural disasters

In markets vulnerable to weather conditions, such as agricultural markets, the weather can have an impact on supply. Extremely favourable weather could lead to "bumper crops" with increased supply while poor weather, such as drought, can lead to significant cuts in supply. Scientists are predicting significant challenges in the production of agricultural output as a result of climate change.

What is the distinction between a movement along a supply curve and a shift of the supply curve?

As you may have noticed above, sometimes there are movements along the existing supply curve and sometimes the supply curve actually shifts to the left or the right. Distinguishing between the two is very simple.

A change in the price of the good itself leads to a movement along the existing supply curve, since the price of the good is on one of the axes. This is shown in Figure 5.5, where a fall in the price of soccer boots from p to p_1 leads to a fall in the quantity supplied from q to q_1.

A change in any of the other determinants of supply will always lead to a shift of the supply curve to either the left or the right. For example, as shown in Figure 5.6, an increase in the cost of the rent of the land occupied by a large car firm will have the effect of shifting the supply curve to the left from S to S_1. Thus, less will be supplied at each price and at the existing price of p, supply will fall from q to q_1.

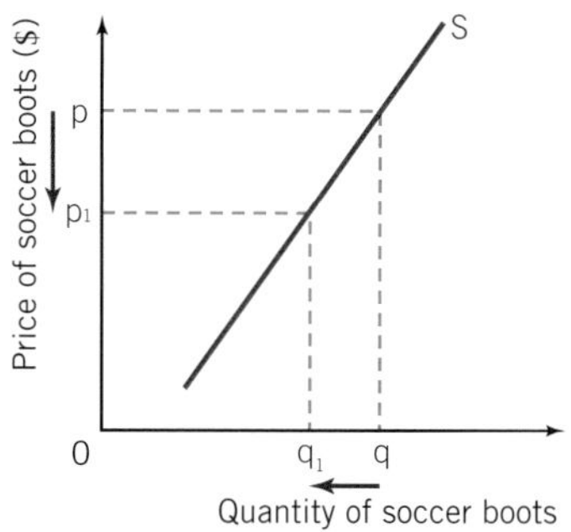

▲ **Figure 5.5** The supply of soccer boots

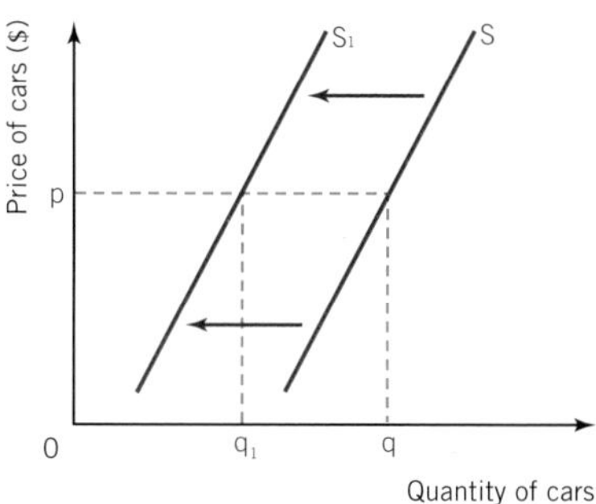

▲ **Figure 5.6** The supply of cars

Exercise 5.2

ATL Thinking and Communication

Using fully labelled diagrams, illustrate what may be the outcome in each of the questions given below, (Remember to use a ruler and include accurate labels.)

1. What would happen to the supply of bicycles if there were a large increase in the tax on bicycles?
2. What would happen to the supply of foreign holidays if there were a fall in the price of foreign holidays?
3. What would happen to the supply of vinyl records if there were a significant increase in the price of the components used to make vinyl records?
4. What would happen to the supply of cars if the government were to subsidize car production in order to encourage employment in the car industry?
5. What would happen to the supply of white bread if a firm were to discover that there has been a large increase in the demand for brown bread, which they could also produce?
6. What would happen to the supply of a certain brand of bottled water if there were an improvement in the technology used to produce it?
7. What would happen to the supply of carrots if the farmer decided to preserve the environment by farming in a more traditional manner, instead of making more profits?

Now write an explanation of **any one** of the above and then share it with another class member, or present it to the whole class.

What is the relationship between an individual producer's supply and market supply?

We have mostly looked at the supply curves for individual producers. However, it is possible to construct the supply curve for a whole market by the process of *horizontal summing* that we came across in the theory of demand. This process is best understood by looking at an example. Table 5.2 shows the supply of three different producers of a product. We will assume that the three producers are the only ones in the market in question. By adding up the individual supplies at each price, it is possible to calculate the total market supply.

Price ($)	Producer A supply ('000s)	Producer B supply ('000s)	Producer C supply ('000s)	Market supply ('000s)
1	200	200	300	700
3	400	300	450	1,150
5	600	400	600	1,600

▲ **Table 5.2** Individual supply schedules and the market supply schedule

Figure 5.7 shows the individual supply curves of the three producers that are identified in table 5.2. All of the supply curves follow the Law of Supply. At a price of $1, Producer A will produce 200,000 units, producer B 200,000 units and producer C 300,000 units. Since they are the only producers in the market, the total market supply, at a price of $1, will be 700,000 units. At a price of $3, total market supply will be 400,000 + 300,000 + 450,000 = 1,150,000 units. In the same way, at a price of $5, total market supply will be 600,000 + 400,000 + 600,000 = 1,600,000 units.

All of the other points on the market supply curve may be gained by summing the points on the individual supply curves. As with demand, this is the process of *horizontal summing*, because it is the values on the horizontal axis for the individual supply curves that are added together to get the market supply curve. The figures on the vertical axis are common to all of the supply curves and so do not change.

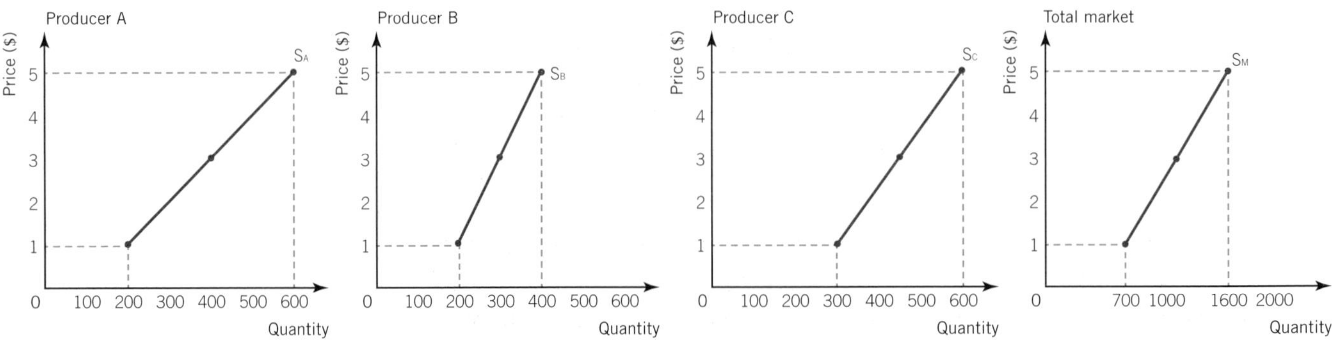

▲ **Figure 5.7** Individual supply curves and the market supply curve – horizontal summing

How do economists explain the Law of Supply?

There are a number of steps needed to explain the Law of Supply.

1. *The short run*

   Economists consider two different time periods when looking at production – the short run and the long run. They are distinguished by their definitions. The short run is defined as the period of time in which at least one factor of production is fixed. All production takes place in the short run. The long run is the period of time in which all factors of production are variable, but the state of technology is fixed. All planning takes place in the long run.

   Because we are explaining the Law of Supply, and thus production, we shall focus on the short run, where all production takes place. When a firm is producing, some of its factors of production will be fixed in the short run, ie the firm will not be able to increase the quantity of certain factors quickly, even if the price goes up and the producer wishes to produce more. Often the fixed factor is some element of capital or land, but this is not always the case. It could be a type of highly skilled labour, such as a specialist machine worker. Therefore, if a firm wishes to increase output in the short run, it may only do so by applying more units of its variable factors to the fixed factors that it possesses, while it plans ahead to change the number of fixed factors that it has.

   The length of the short run for a firm will be determined by the time it takes to increase the quantity of the fixed factor. This will vary from industry to industry. For example, a small firm involved in gardening may find that its fixed factor is the number of lawn mowers that it has available and that it takes a week to order and get delivery of a new lawn mower. Thus, its short run is one week. On the other hand, a national electricity provider is constrained by its fixed factor, the number of electricity generating plants that it has. Building a new electricity generating plant may take up to two years (more if a nuclear plant is built) and so its short run is a lot longer.

2. *The law of diminishing returns*

   In the short run, if a firm increases output by adding more and more units of a variable factor to its fixed factors, it is logical to assume that the output from each unit added will eventually fall. To understand this fully, we need to consider the concepts of total, average and marginal product.

   Total product (TP) is the total output that a firm produces, using its fixed and variable factors in a given time period. As we have already said, output in the short run can only be increased by applying more units of the variable factors to the fixed factors.

Average product (AP) is the output that is produced, on average, by each unit of the variable factor. AP = TP/V, where TP is the total output produced and V is the number of units of the variable factor employed.

Marginal product (MP) is the extra output that is produced by using an extra unit of the variable factor. MP = ΔTP/ΔV, where ΔTP is the change in total output and ΔV is the change in the number of units of the variable factor employed.

For example, a firm has four machines (fixed factors) and increases its output by using more operators to work the machines. Production figures for each week are given in Table 5.3.

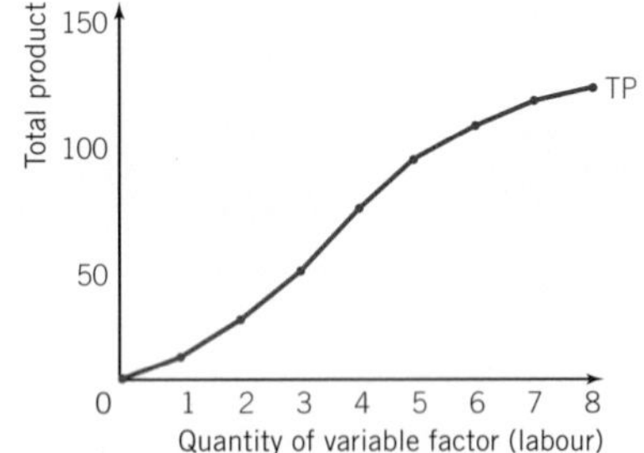

▲ Figure 5.8 The total product curve

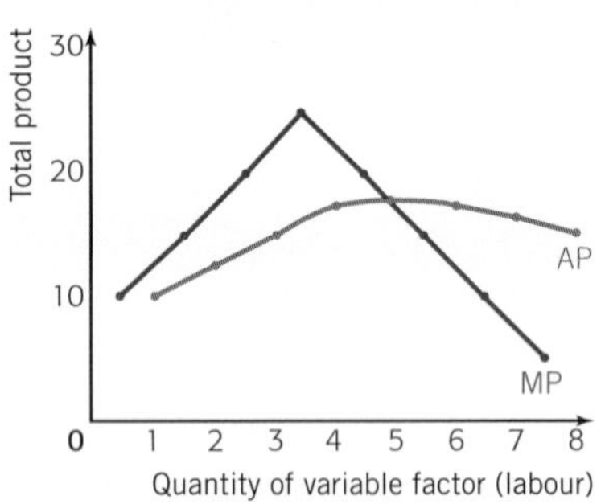

▲ Figure 5.9 Average and marginal product curves

Quantity of labour (V)	Total product (TP)	Average product (AP)	Marginal product (MP)
0	0		
			10
1	10	10	
			15
2	25	12.5	
			20
3	45	15	
			25
4	70	17.5	
			20
5	90	18	
			15
6	105	17.5	
			10
7	115	16.43	
			5
8	120	15	

▲ Table 5.3 Total, average and marginal product per week

We can plot the TP, AP and MP figures to produce curves as in Figures 5.8 and 5.9.

From the table, we can deduce the following definitions.

The hypothesis of eventually diminishing marginal returns – as extra units of a variable factor are added to a given quantity of a fixed factor, the output from each additional unit of the variable factor will eventually diminish.

The hypothesis of eventually diminishing average returns – as extra units of a variable factor are added to a given quantity of a fixed factor, the output per unit of the variable factor will eventually diminish.

The two hypotheses look at the same relationship from different angles. The whole concept is really a matter of common sense. Consider an example.

A young entrepreneur named Ben sets up a new business, which is a small hamburger stand on a busy street corner. The stand consists of a very small shop, containing a refrigerator, a grill and some countertops for preparing the burgers. There are also the implements for making burgers. These are all the fixed factors. When he starts out, Ben works alone and prepares everything himself. He makes the burgers, cuts the onion, lettuce and tomatoes, heats the buns, and sells the hamburgers to the customers. He can make 20 burgers per hour.

Ben finds demand to be high and he cannot make enough burgers, so he hires his friend, Caroline, to help. They divide up the jobs and manage to produce 50 burgers each hour. The hamburgers become even more popular and Ben and Caroline agree that they need another worker, so Nick joins them. They divide up the work again, with each specializing in a task, and produce 90 burgers each hour. Demand continues to rise, so they bring in Niki. With the four working together, they produce 124 burgers per hour.

When Ben worked alone, his output was 20 burgers per hour. When Caroline joined him, the total output was 50 burgers per hour. This means that Caroline's marginal product was 30 burgers. When Nick joined, the total number of burgers per hour rose to 90, so Nick's marginal product was 40 burgers. When Niki joined (we are adding units of a variable factor), the total output of burgers rose to 124 per hour, making the marginal product 34 burgers. Note that the marginal product fell when Niki was added to the workforce. Was this because Niki was inefficient? No. So why was this? Well, it was efficient to add extra people up to three workers, but because the space in the shop, the counter tops, and the grill, are all fixed, it became less efficient when there were more people. They started to get in each other's way and so could not increase the output of burgers by as great an amount as when the previous worker was added.

Whether we measure it from the amount added by the extra variable factor (marginal product) or the amount added per unit of the variable factor (average product), logic tells us that inefficiency must eventually begin to occur.

3. *Increasing marginal costs*

   Firms have many different ways of measuring costs when producing whatever good or service they provide. Higher level students will look at more ways to measure costs later in Chapter 11, but for now we are interested in *marginal costs.*

   Marginal cost (MC) is the increase in total cost of producing an extra unit of output. $MC = \frac{\Delta TC}{\Delta q}$, where ΔTC is the change in total cost and Δq is the change in the level of output.

   If we add some costs to the example from Table 5.3, then we can identify what happens to marginal cost as output increases.

To increase output, we need to add more units of a variable factor to fixed factors

↓

Eventually, output from each extra unit of the variable factor falls, as inefficiency sets in (law of diminishing returns)

↓

Logically, the cost of producing more output, MC, will go up

↓

So, firms will only produce more if prices rise to cover the increased MC

Thus, the supply curve will slope upwards

▲ **Figure 5.10** The Law of Supply

Total product (TP) or Output (q)	Total cost (TC) ($)	Marginal cost (MC) ($)
0	400	
		200/10 = 20
10	600	
		200/15 = 13.33
25	800	
		200/20 = 10
45	1,000	
		200/25 = 8
70	1,200	
		200/20 = 10
90	1,400	
		200/15 = 13.33
105	1,600	
		200/10 = 20
115	1,800	
		200/5 = 40
120	2,000	

▲ **Table 5.4** Marginal costs

Assessment advice: Paper 2 HL & SL – Data response

Four parts of the data response paper, (c) to (f), require an explanation of something from the text or data, usually involving a diagram and explanation.

These answers require accurately labelled diagrams, preferably with information from the text, They do not require a lot of depth in the explanation. They require you to explain briefly a change indicated on your diagram, using concise economic terminology and a reference to your diagram. See the example on the next page.

Increasing marginal costs is clearly related to diminishing marginal returns. If the output produced by each additional worker (MP) begins to fall, yet each worker costs the same, then the cost of producing each extra unit (MC) begins to increase. We can see that, because of the law of diminishing returns, as output increases, marginal costs will begin to increase also. It therefore follows that firms will only be prepared to supply more and increase output, if the prices that they will receive for their products are also going up as output increases. That way, the firms will be able to cover their marginal costs with the price.

We can show the whole process of the Law of Supply by using a flow chart as shown in Figure 5.10.

EXAMINATION QUESTIONS

Paper 1, part (a) questions

1. Distinguish between a shift of the supply curve for a product and a movement along the product's supply curve. [10 marks]
2. With reference to two different determinants of supply, explain why the supply of coffee beans might decrease. [10 marks]

Exercise 5.3

Here is a worked example. It should be noted that this example is much simpler than one you would be asked to do in the exam, as in this case, we are just looking at a change in one "side" of the market – the supply side.

Washington to eliminate the tax on diapers

The mayor of Washington D.C, has just announced that the state will be removing the sales tax on babies' diapers, in an attempt to help families to save money. It has been calculated that on average, families can spend more than $500 per child on diapers. This is particularly harmful to low income families. As the mayor said, *"Elimminating the diaper tax is one more way we can make it affordable to raise children right here in D.C.*

Adapted from: https://deist.com/story/19/03/20d-c-is-eliminating-the-sales-tax-on-diapers/

Using a supply diagram, explain the effect of the removal of the sales tax on diapers.

Answer:

Sales taxes are a determinant of supply. If the D.C. government removes the sales tax on diapers, it will increase the supply of diapers, shifting the supply curve to the right (S_1 to S_2), ceteris paribus.

Everything highlighted are things that examiners will look for, and are good practice (but there is not one mark for each highlight):

- Good to include specific economic terminology, eg "determinant of supply"
- Necessary to say exactly what is happening in the diagram
- Valuable to include the reference to the diagram. ($S_1 \rightarrow S_2$)
- Pleasing to see the reference to *ceteris paribus*, as it shows you are aware that you are isolating the effect of one change in the supply
- Necessary to have accurate labels on the axes, and valuable if you show that you know it is the price per unit, and indicating the actual market (price per diaper, US$)
- Necessary to have accurate labels on the curves, with an indication that there has been a change (S_1 to S_2)
- An arrow to show the change that is occurring in the market.

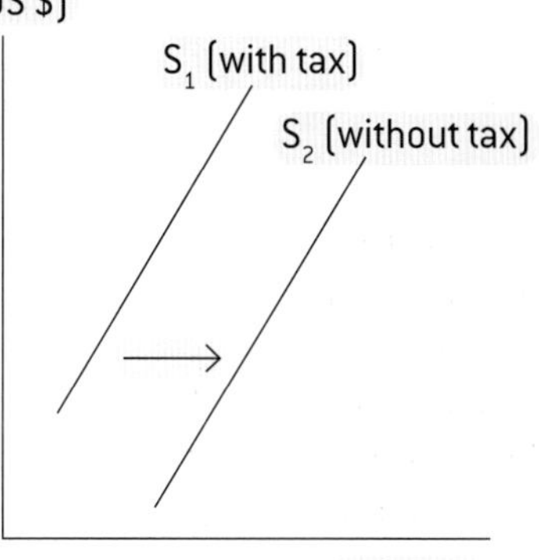

Bonus question: Do you think that the demand for diapers is likely to be elastic or inelastic? Explain your reasoning.

Now you try it!

Exercise 5.4

Paper 2 – 4 mark question

Italy sees 57% drop in olive harvest as result of climate change, scientist says

Extreme weather blamed for plunge in country's olive harvest – the worst in 25 years. Olive trees across the Mediterranean have been hit by freak events that mirror climate change predictions – erratic rainfalls, early spring frosts, strong winds and summer droughts.

Using a supply diagram, explain the change in the market for olives in Italy as indicated by the article.

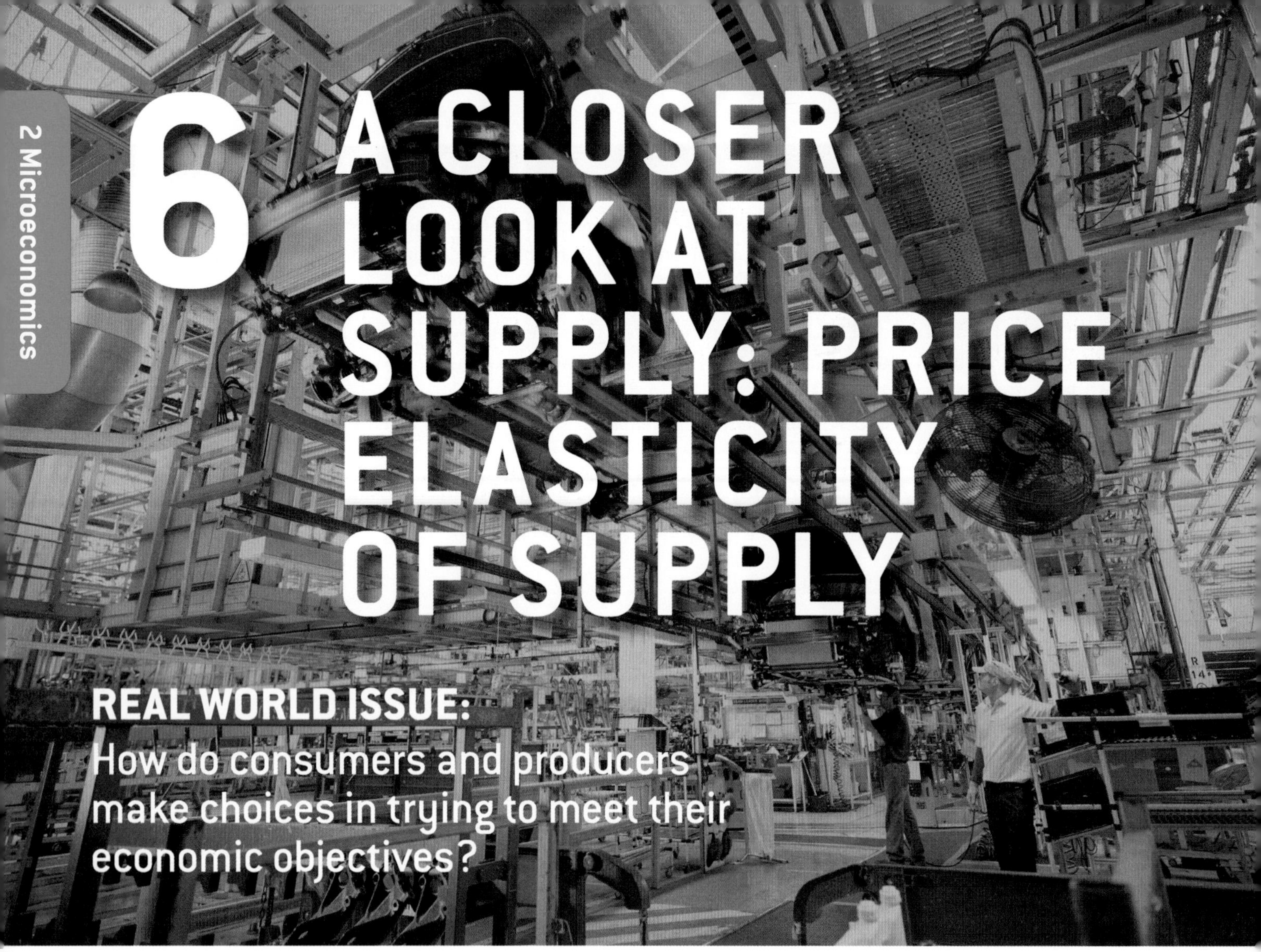

6 A CLOSER LOOK AT SUPPLY: PRICE ELASTICITY OF SUPPLY

REAL WORLD ISSUE:
How do consumers and producers make choices in trying to meet their economic objectives?

By the end of this chapter, you should be able to:

- → Define and calculate price elasticity of supply (PES)
- → Illustrate different values of price elasticity of supply using supply curves
- → Explain the determinants of price elasticity of supply
- HL Explain the likely differences in price elasticity of supply for primary commodities and manufactured goods

If the price of a product increases, producers will want to increase the quantity they supply in order to increase their profits. However, the ability of the producers to increase the quantity supplied in response to higher prices depends on the *price elasticity of supply* for their product.

What is price elasticity of supply (PES)?

Price elasticity of supply is a measure of how much the supply of a product changes when there is a change in the price of the product. It is usually calculated by using the equation below:

$$\text{PES} = \frac{\text{Percentage change in quantity supplied of the product}}{\text{Percentage change in price of the product}}$$

For example, a publishing firm realises that they can now sell their monthly magazine for $5.50 instead of $5.00. In light of this, they increase their supply from 200,000 to 230,000 magazines per month. With this information, we can calculate the price elasticity of supply of the magazine in question.

1. The price has risen by 50¢ from an original price of $5, which is a change of +10%. This is calculated by the equation:

$$\frac{+50}{500} \times 100 = +10\%$$

2. The quantity supplied has increased by 30,000 from an original supply of 200,000, which is a change of +15%. This is calculated by the equation:

$$\frac{+30{,}000}{200{,}000} \times 100 = +15\%$$

3. If we put the two values above into the equation for PES, we get 15%/10%, which gives a value of 1.5.

What is the range of values of price elasticity of supply?

The possible range of values for price elasticity of supply usually goes from zero to infinity. Unlike PED, we will come across examples of both extreme values as we continue our study of economics.

If PES is equal to zero, then a change in the price of a product will have no effect on the quantity supplied at all. Thus the percentage change in quantity supplied would be zero and so would the value on the top of the PES equation. Since zero divided by anything is zero, no matter what the percentage change in price, the PES value will be zero. A supply curve with a value of zero is shown in Figure 6.1 and, in this case, supply is said to be perfectly inelastic – it is completely unresponsive to price changes. Whether price is P_1, P_2 or any other price, the quantity supplied will be Q.

In the very short run, sometimes known as the immediate time period, it is impossible for firms to increase their supply straight away, no matter what happens to price, and so the supply curve would look like the one in Figure 6.1, until new factors of production could be employed. Thus, a perfectly inelastic supply curve is a possibility.

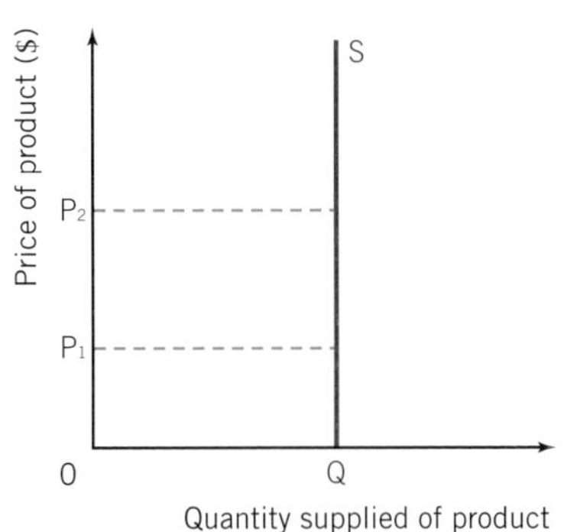

▲ Figure 6.1 A perfectly inelastic supply curve

An example of perfectly inelastic supply would be the number of tickets available for a sporting or entertainment venue with a maximum capacity. For example, Manchester United plays its home soccer games at Old Trafford stadium, which (currently) has 74,944 seats. Therefore, the supply is perfectly inelastic at a quantity of 74,944 seats. No change in price could affect the quantity supplied.

A PES value of infinity is best explained by using a diagram and the situation is shown in Figure 6.2. In this case, supply is said to be

▲ Figure 6.2 A perfectly elastic supply curve

perfectly elastic. At the price P_1, the supply curve goes on forever and so the quantity supplied is infinite. However, if price falls below P_1, even by the smallest amount, supply will fall to zero, an infinite change. Because of this, the value on the top of the PES equation would be infinity. Since infinity divided by anything is infinity, no matter what the percentage change in price, the PES value will be infinity.

In international trade, it is often assumed that the supply of commodities, such as wheat, available to a country for import is infinite. The consumers in the country can have all that they want as long as they are prepared to pay the current world market price. Thus, the market in the country will have a "world supply" curve that is perfectly elastic at the current world market price.

Note

We will deal with this in more detail in Chapter 24.

Normal products have PES values between zero and infinity and we will now look at those values. The range of values of PES is normally split into three categories:

1. *Inelastic supply*: The value of PES is less than one and greater than zero. If a product has inelastic supply, then a change in the price of the product leads to a less than proportionate change in the quantity supplied of it, and so the value of PES is greater than zero and less than one.
2. *Elastic supply*: The value of PES is greater than one and less than infinity. If a product has elastic supply, then a change in the price of the product leads to a greater than proportionate change in the quantity supplied of it, and so the value of PES is greater than one and less than infinity.
3. *Unit elastic supply*: The value of PES is equal to one. If a product has unit elastic supply, then a change in the price of the product leads to a proportionate change in the quantity supplied of it and so the value of PES is equal to one.

Examples of supply curves with different values of PES are shown in Figure 6.3.

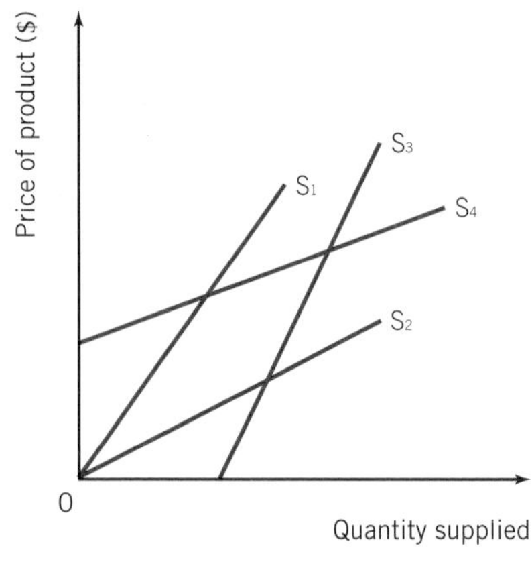

▲ Figure 6.3 Supply curves with different values of PES

In Figure 6.3, curves S_1 and S_2 have a PES value equal to one along their entire length. This is because the percentage change in price is always equal to the percentage change in quantity supplied. For mathematical reasons, it is correct to say that any straight-line supply curve, passing through the origin, has an elasticity of supply of one.

Curve S_3 has a PES value of less than one along its entire length. This is because the percentage change in price is always greater than the percentage change in quantity supplied. For mathematical reasons, it is correct to say that any straight-line supply curve starting from the x-axis has a PES value less than one.

Curve S_4 has a PES value of greater than one along its entire length. This is because the percentage change in quantity supplied is always greater

than the percentage change in price. For mathematical reasons, it is correct to say that any straight-line supply curve starting from the *y*-axis has a PES value greater than one.

What are the determinants of price elasticity of supply?

Different products will have different values for PES. For example, the supply of cans of a soft drink may have a PES value of 2, ie the supply is elastic, whereas the supply of electricity may have a PES value of 0.5, which is inelastic. What actually determines the value of PES for a product? There are a number of determinants:

1. *How much costs rise as output is increased*: If total costs rise significantly as a producer attempts to increase supply, then it is likely that the producer will not raise the supply and so the elasticity of supply for the product will be relatively inelastic. It would take large price rises to make increasing the supply worthwhile.

   If, however, total costs do not rise significantly, then the producer will raise the quantity supplied and take advantage of the low increase in costs to benefit from the higher prices, thus making more profits. Total costs will not rise significantly if the costs of factor inputs do not increase quickly as the firm uses more of them.

   There are a number of factors that assist in preventing a significant rise in costs, such as:

   a. **The existence of unused capacity**
   If a firm has a lot of unused capacity, ie if it has significant productive resources that are not being fully used, then it will be able to increase output easily and without great cost increases. In this case the elasticity of supply for the product will be relatively high.

   If a firm is producing at capacity, then it is difficult to increase supply without a significant increase in productive resources, which will be expensive. It is therefore unlikely that the firm will increase supply. PES will be relatively inelastic.

   b. **The mobility of factors of production**
   If factors of production are easily moved from one productive use to another then PES will be relatively elastic. For example, assume that it is easy to shift production from manufacturing one-litre plastic bottles to manufacturing two-litre plastic bottles. If the price of two-litre bottles goes up, then the extra cost of switching to the larger bottles will not be great and it will be easy for the producer to increase the quantity of two-litre bottles.

2. *The time period considered*: The amount of time over which PES is measured will affect its value. In general terms, the longer the time period considered the more elastic the supply will be.

   In the immediate time period, firms are not really able to increase their supply very much, if at all, if price increases, since they cannot

Exercise 6.1
ATL Thinking and Communication

A firm producing stuffed toys experiences an increase in the demand for its main product, a cuddly dog, because of an increase in its popularity. The price of the toy rises from $15 to $18. In response, the firm increases its output of the toy from 5,000 per week to 5,500 per week.

1. Calculate the price elasticity of supply for the toy dog.

Key concept

EFFICIENCY

EXAMINATION QUESTIONS

Paper 1, part (a) questions

1. Explain the determinants of price elasticity of supply. [10 marks]
2. Explain the likely value of price elasticity of supply for primary commodities. [10 marks]

Paper 1, part (b) question – HL

Contrast the price elasticities of demand and supply for primary commodities with those of manufactured goods.

Higher Level

Key concept

SUSTAINABILITY

immediately increase the number of factors of production that they employ. The value of PES will be very inelastic.

In the short run, firms may be able to increase the quantity of some of the factors that they employ, such as raw materials and labour, but they may not be able to increase all of their factors, such as the number of machines that they use or the size of their factory. The value of PES will be more elastic than the immediate time period.

In the long run, firms may be able to increase the quantity of all of the factors that they employ and so the value of PES will be much more elastic. We will look at time periods and production in much more detail in Chapter 8.

3. *The ability to store stock*: If a firm is able to store high levels of stock (inventories) of their product, then they will be able to react to price increases with swift supply increases and so the PES for the product will be relatively elastic.

Is there a difference in the price elasticity of supply for primary commodities and manufactured products?

We have already discovered in Chapter 4 that primary commodities is another word for raw materials, and that they tend to have inelastic demand as they are necessities to the consumers who buy them and they have few or no substitutes. But what about the price elasticity of supply of primary commodities?

Commodities tend to have inelastic supply as a change in price cannot lead to a proportionately large increase in quantity supplied. For example, if there were to be an increase in the demand for cocoa, and therefore an increase in the price of cocoa, producers would be unable to respond with a proportionate increase in the quantity as it takes time to grow the cocoa. It would take time to re-allocate resources to the production of cocoa or it might not be possible or desirable to re-allocate resources to the production of more cocoa. Similarly, if there were to be a fall in the price of cocoa then the quantity supplied would not adjust accordingly as the cocoa crop might already have been harvested.

On the other hand, the supply of manufactured goods tends to be more elastic as it is easier to increase or decrease quantity supplied in response to a change in price. This relates to the earlier determinants of PES. With manufactured goods, it is likely that there may be unused capacity in the industry, factors of production are more mobile, and it is relatively easy to store high levels of stock. If any, or all, of these determinants is fulfilled, then supply will tend to be relatively elastic.

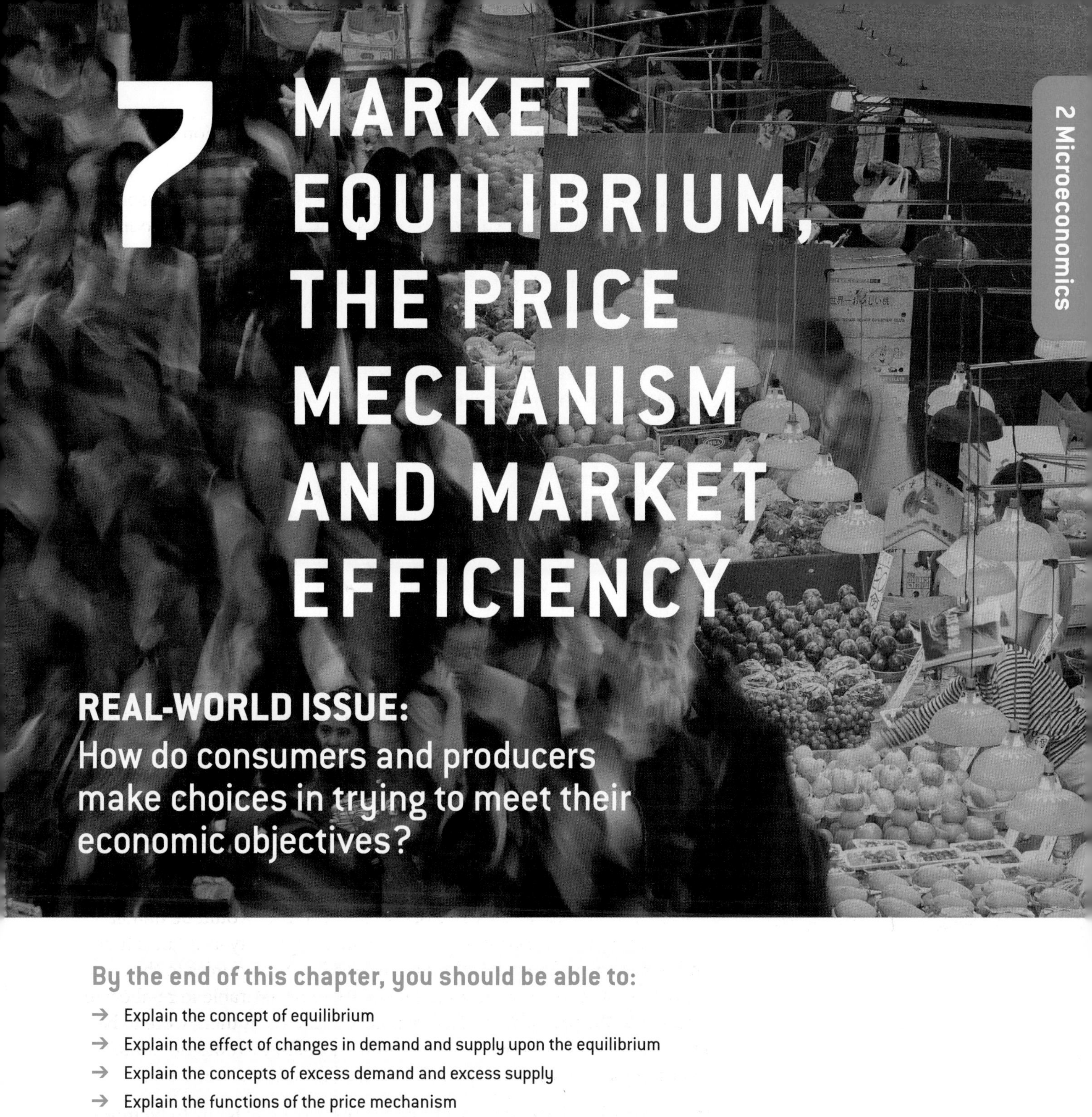

7 MARKET EQUILIBRIUM, THE PRICE MECHANISM AND MARKET EFFICIENCY

REAL-WORLD ISSUE:
How do consumers and producers make choices in trying to meet their economic objectives?

By the end of this chapter, you should be able to:

- → Explain the concept of equilibrium
- → Explain the effect of changes in demand and supply upon the equilibrium
- → Explain the concepts of excess demand and excess supply
- → Explain the functions of the price mechanism
- → Explain the concepts of consumer and producer surplus
- → Explain the concept of social/community surplus
- → Explain the concept of allocative efficiency.

Clearly, when consumers and producers make choices, they cannot make them in isolation. The interdependence of consumers and producers is illustrated when we bring demand and supply together in one model.

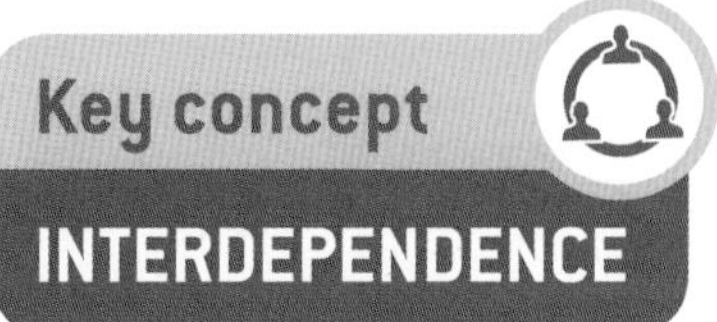

What is equilibrium to an economist?

The concept of equilibrium is very important in economics. Equilibrium may be defined as "a state of rest, self-perpetuating in the absence of any outside disturbance". For example, a book is in equilibrium if it is lying on a desk. Unless someone comes along and moves it (an "outside disturbance"), then it will continue to lie there ("a state of rest"). If someone does move it, then it is in disequilibrium until it is put down somewhere else, at which time it is in a new equilibrium situation.

Economists spend a lot of time considering situations where equilibria change and the reasons why the changes take place. They then use the information to begin to predict changes in equilibrium situations that may be caused by a certain action. They can begin to formulate economic policy.

Let us look at demand, supply and the equilibrium for coffee.

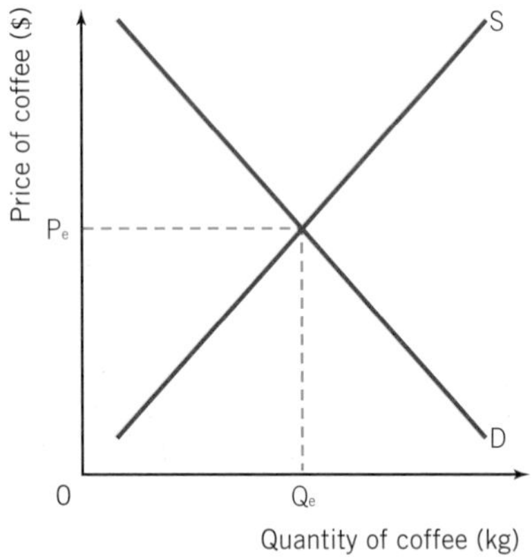

▲ **Figure 7.1** The market for coffee

In Figure 7.1, both the demand and supply curves for coffee are in the same diagram and we see that, at the price P_e, the quantity Q_e is both demanded and supplied. We would say that the market is in equilibrium at the price P_e, since the amount of coffee that people wish to buy at that price, Q_e, is equal to the amount of coffee that suppliers wish to sell at that price. The price P_e is sometimes known as the *market-clearing price*, since everything produced in the market will be sold. The market is in equilibrium, since it will stay like this, in each time period, until there is an "outside disturbance".

The equilibrium in this situation is "self-righting", ie if you try to move away from it, without an outside disturbance, it will return to the original position. This is best explained through diagrams.

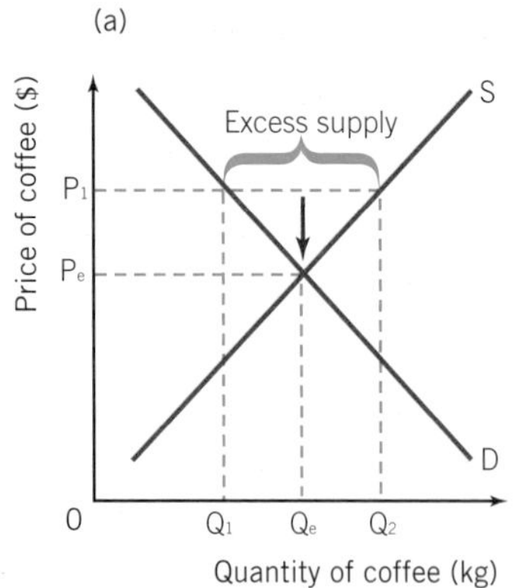

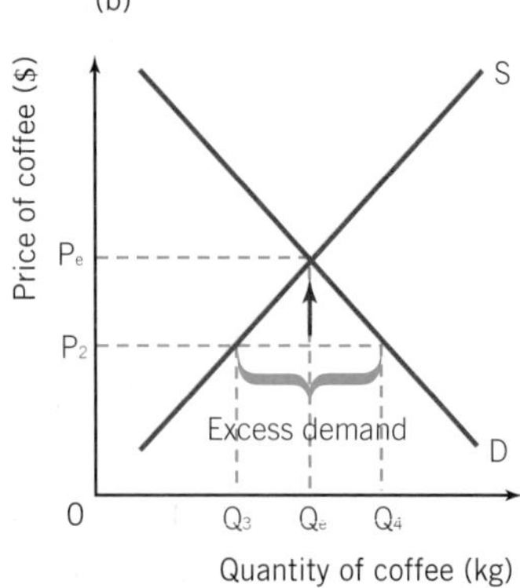

▲ **Figure 7.2** The market for coffee

Diamond prices are falling: producers grappling with too much supply

https://www.ig.com/uk/investments/news/investing/2019/07/16/diamond-prices-are-falling--producers-grappling-with-too-much-su

In Figure 7.2, we can see what will happen if the producers try to raise or lower the equilibrium price. In diagram (a), the producers have tried to raise the price to P_1. However, at this price, the quantity demanded will fall to Q_1 and the quantity that producers supply rises to Q_2. We now have *excess supply* of Q_2–Q_1. An excess supply exists where more of a good is being supplied at a given price than is being demanded. In this case, more is being supplied than demanded at the price P_1. In order to eliminate this surplus, producers will need to lower their prices. As they do so, the quantity demanded will increase and the quantity supplied will fall. This process will continue until the quantity demanded once again equals the quantity supplied. This will be back at the equilibrium price and so the situation is self-righting, if price is raised for no external reason.

In diagram (b), the producers have tried to lower the price to P_2. However, at this price, the quantity demanded will rise to Q_4 and the quantity that producers supply falls to Q_3. We now have *excess demand* of Q_4–Q_3. An excess demand exists where more of a good is being demanded at a given price than is being supplied. In this case, more is being demanded than supplied at the price P_2. In order to eliminate this shortage, producers will need to raise their prices. As they do so, the quantity demanded will fall and the quantity supplied will increase. This process will continue until the quantity demanded once again equals the quantity supplied. This will be back at the equilibrium price and so, once again, the situation is self-righting.

Can Metals Supply Keep Up With Electric Vehicle Demand?

https://www.forbes.com/sites/woodmackenzie/2019/07/24/can-metals-supply-keep-up-with-electric-vehicle-demand/#7af704c76c9b

How does the equilibrium change when there are changes in demand and supply?

Key concept

CHANGE

As we know, the equilibrium may be moved by any "outside disturbance". In the case of demand and supply, this would be a change in any one of the determinants of demand or supply, other than the price of the product itself, which would lead to a shift of either of the curves.

Take the example of an increase in income for consumers of foreign holidays, which is a normal good. When income increases, then there will be an increase in the demand for holidays and the demand curve for holidays will shift to the right, *ceteris paribus*, as shown in Figure 7.3.

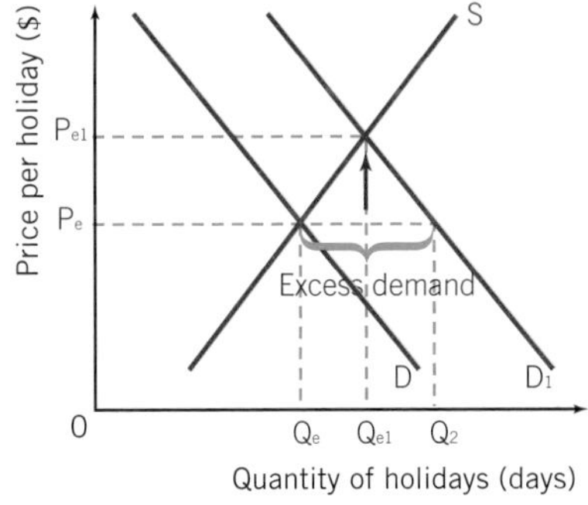

▲ Figure 7.3 The market for foreign holidays

When the demand curve shifts from D to D_1, price initially remains at P_e and so we find that Q_e continues to be supplied, but demand now increases to Q_2. This means that at the original equilibrium price, there is now a situation of *excess demand*. In order to eliminate this excess demand, it is necessary for price to rise until the quantity demanded once again equals the quantity supplied. Thus, price will rise until it reaches P_{e1}, the new equilibrium price, where Q_{e1}, the new equilibrium quantity, is both demanded and supplied.

Whenever there is a shift of the demand or supply curve, the market will, if left to act alone, adjust to a new equilibrium, market-clearing price.

Assessment advice: What is good about this answer?

- Good to include specific economic terminology, "tastes and preferences" as a "determinant of demand"
- Necessary to say exactly what is happening in the diagram
- Valuable to include the references to the diagram
- Pleasing to see the reference to *ceteris paribus*, as it shows you are aware that you are isolating the effect of one change in the determinants of demand
- Necessary to have accurate labels on the axes, and valuable if you show that you know it is the price per unit, and indicating the actual market (price of microwave popcorn, EUR per package)
- Necessary to have accurate labels on the curves, with an indication that there has been a change (D_1 to D_2)
- An arrow to show the change that is occurring in the market.

Exercise 7.1

ATL Thinking and Communication

Using fully labelled diagrams, illustrate what will happen to the equilibrium price and quantity in each of the markets below, and then explain what has happened. A worked example for the first question is given below. You should try to use this as a template to do the remaining two questions.

1. The media has published an article saying that eating microwave popcorn results in a higher risk of dementia (popcorn market).
2. a) An early drought has severely harmed the olive harvests in Italy (olive market).
   b) Without drawing a diagram, how would this then affect the olive oil market? Why?
3. There has been an improvement in production technology in the textile industry (textile market).

Model answer:

If there is a media report pointing out that microwave popcorn might contribute to dementia, it means that there is likely to be a change in tastes and preferences, which is a determinant of demand. Demand is likely to fall from D_1 to D_2 ceteris paribus, as shown in the diagram.

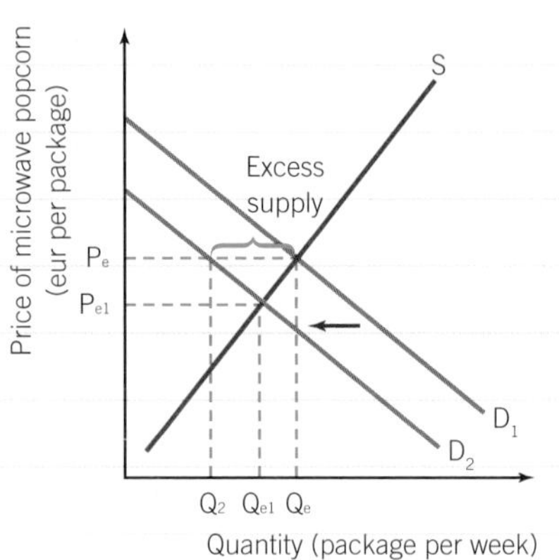

Even though the demand curve has shifted, supply remains the same. Therefore, at the original equilibrium price (P_e), Q_e is still supplied, but the quantity demanded has decreased to Q_2 and so there will now be excess supply. In order to eliminate this excess supply, the price will fall until the quantity demanded once more equals the quantity supplied at a new price of P_{e1} and a new quantity of Q_{e1}.

Thinking outside the box

As we have seen, economic models are based on a set of assumptions. In the case of this equilibrium analysis, there are key assumptions used to develop the theory of demand and the theory of supply. If the assumptions may be challenged, then the conclusions of the analysis may also be questioned.

For example, behind the theory of demand are the assumptions that consumers act rationally, seeking to maximize their own utility, making all decisions with perfect information. (Remember that in Chapter 3, we looked at the limitations of these assumptions.) Behind the theory of supply is the assumption that producers act rationally, seeking to maximize their profits. If these assumptions are not valid, then conclusions based on the theory may have limited validity. This is something we will come back to later.

What is the price mechanism and what are its functions?

We have seen how the forces of supply and demand, otherwise known as the "price mechanism", move markets to equilibrium. It is now important to see how this price mechanism helps to allocate scarce resources.

Price has three significant functions in a market:

1. *To signal information to consumers and producers – the signalling function*
   The price of a good is an important piece of knowledge for consumers and producers. Prices are set by the actions of consumers and producers in a market, and so they reflect the changing circumstances in markets, acting as a signal to those in the market to act in some way.
2. *To ration scarce resources – the rationing function*
   We know that resources are scarce in the world (see Chapter 1) and need to be allocated through some mechanism. Prices help to allocate and ration scarce resources. If the demand for a good is significantly greater than the supply, prices will be relatively high and the low supply will be rationed to those consumers who are prepared to pay the high price.
3. *To give incentives to consumers and producers – the incentive function*
   Prices act as an incentive for both consumers and producers. Lower prices give consumers an incentive to buy more of a good, because they will receive more utility (satisfaction) from the good for their money spent. Higher price will act as a disincentive, since the utility in relation to the money spent falls.

   For producers, if there is an increase in the price of a good, due to an increase in demand for the good, then this gives a sign to producers that consumers wish to buy this good. Since we can assume that producers are rational and wish to maximize their profits, then a higher price will give producers an incentive to produce more of the good. Therefore, producers will allocate more resources towards those goods where the demand is highest, since this is where they will be able to make more profit.

Resources are allocated, and re-allocated, in response to changes in price. The key thing is that there is no central planning agency that specifically tells producers to produce more of the good; it is the increase in price that serves as a signal to producers, creating the incentive for the producers to produce more of the good. Referring to the ideas of Adam Smith, whom we mentioned on p. 27, it is as if there is an *invisible hand* in the economy moving the factors of production around to produce the goods and services wanted by the buyers in the economy.

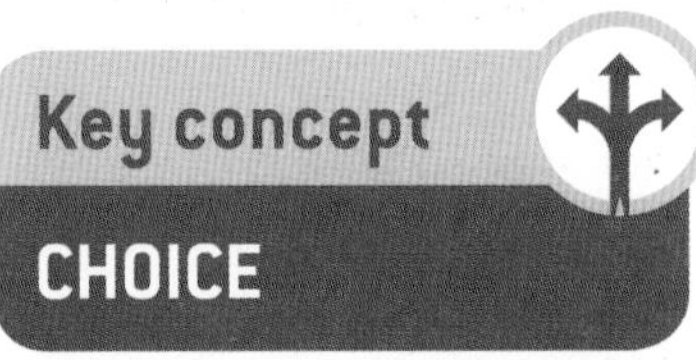

Exercise 7.2

ATL Thinking and Communication

Refer back to the example of skateboards and roller skates described in non-price determinants of supply in Chapter 5 on page 82. The example traced changes in the markets for two related goods. Now be creative and think of your own example using two related, but different, goods.

1. Draw and fully label supply and demand diagrams for your two products. Now think of a reason for a change in consumer preferences for your goods, such as one of your products becoming more or less fashionable. Using your diagrams, explain the effect that the change in consumer taste has on the prices of both products.
2. Using your diagrams and the concepts of the signalling and incentive functions of price, explain how resources are allocated according to the price mechanism.

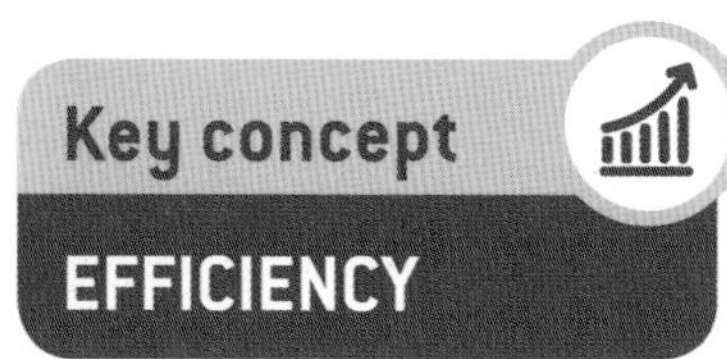

What is market efficiency?

What are consumer and producer surplus?

Consider Figure 7.4 illustrating the market for thingies, an imaginary product.

As we can see, the equilibrium price of thingies is $10 and the equilibrium quantity demanded and supplied is ten thingies per week. This is determined by the forces of demand and supply. At the equilibrium point, there are some consumers who would have been prepared to pay a higher price for their thingies.

▲ Figure 7.4 The market for thingies

This is clearly shown by the demand curve. For example, at a price of $15, there would still be five thingies demanded; and at a price of $17, there would be demand for three thingies. However, the consumers do not have to pay $15 or $17; they just have to pay the equilibrium price. This means that all of the consumers who purchase the first nine thingies have made a gain. They have paid a price below the one they were prepared to pay.

This illustrates the concept of *consumer surplus*. This is defined as the extra satisfaction (or utility) gained by consumers from paying a price that is lower than that which they are prepared to pay.

In this case, one consumer was willing to pay as much as $19 for a thingy, but as he only has to pay $10, he is gaining. The total consumer surplus is usually shown by the area under the demand curve and above the equilibrium price. In Figure 7.5, the consumer surplus is shown by the shaded triangle abc.

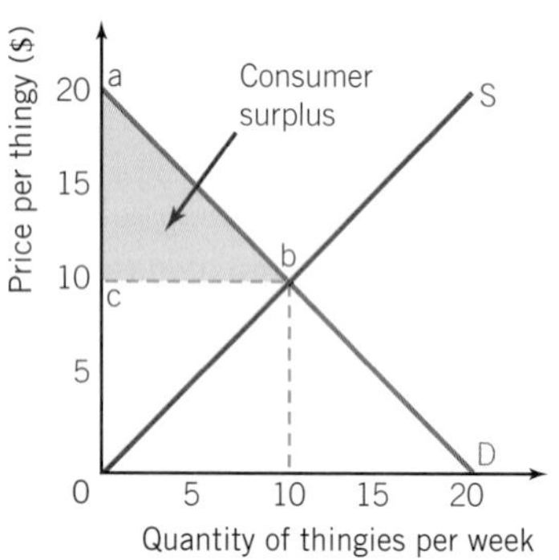

▲ Figure 7.5 Consumer surplus in the market for thingies

It should also be clear that, at the equilibrium point, some production of thingies would take place at a price lower than $10.

This is clearly shown by the supply curve. For example, at a price of $5, there would still be five thingies supplied and at a price of $3, there would be a supply of three thingies. However, the producer does not have to sell for $5 or $3; she can sell her thingies at the equilibrium price. This means that she will have made a gain on each of the first nine thingies in terms of what she would have accepted for them. She has received a price higher than the one she was prepared to accept.

This illustrates the concept of *producer surplus*. This is defined as the excess of actual earnings that a producer makes from a given quantity of output, over and above the amount the producer would be prepared to accept for that output.

In this case, the producer is willing to supply a thingy for as little as $1, but as she receives $10 for each thingy, she is gaining. The total producer surplus is usually shown by the area under the equilibrium price and above the supply curve. In Figure 7.6, the producer surplus is shown by the shaded triangle bcd.

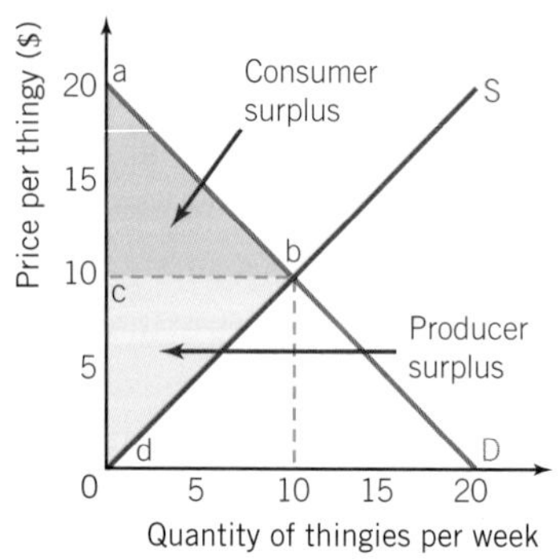

▲ Figure 7.6 Producer surplus in the market for thingies

What is community (social) surplus and how does it relate to allocative efficiency?

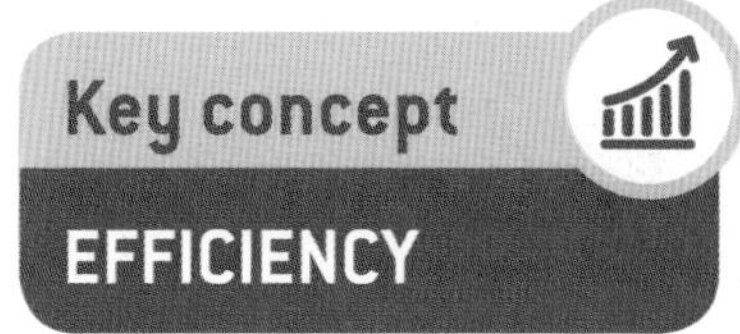

When a market is in equilibrium, with no external influences and no external effects, it is said to be socially efficient or in a state of *allocative efficiency*. This means that the resources are allocated in the most efficient way from society's point of view. The concept of allocative efficiency is quite different from the everyday meaning of "efficiency" that you might be familiar with. In everyday language someone is viewed as operating efficiently if s/he produces the maximum output with a given level of input. In economic terms this kind of efficiency is known as productive efficiency. We will address productive efficiency later with Higher Level students.

Consider Figure 7.7 which shows the consumer surplus and producer surplus when a market is in equilibrium. The sum of consumer and producer surplus is known as community (social) surplus; this is the total benefit to society. At the equilibrium, where demand is equal to supply, community surplus is maximized. This is the point of allocative efficiency. Given this supply and demand situation there is no other combination of price and quantity on the diagram that could give a greater community surplus. This is therefore the optimal allocation of resources from the point of view of society as a whole. Perhaps consumers would prefer lower prices and producers would prefer higher prices, but with these demand and supply curves this is the allocatively efficient price and quantity since community surplus is maximized.

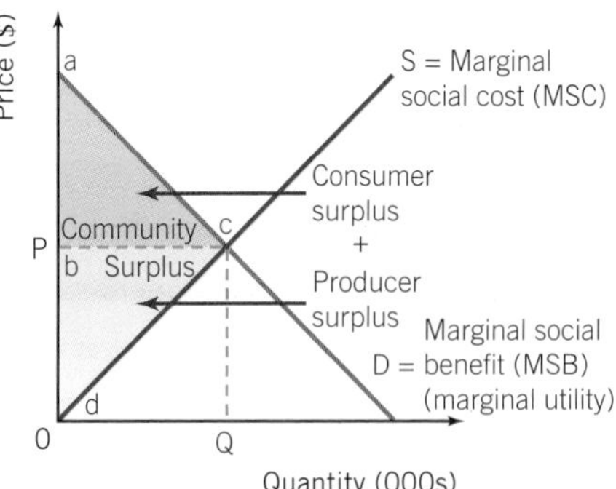

▲ **Figure 7.7** Community surplus

We introduce some more sophisticated language here which we will come back to in later chapters. As we learnt earlier, the supply curve for a market is largely determined by the industry's costs of production. When we assume that the costs of the industry are equal to the costs to society, then the supply curve represents the social cost curve. In efficiency analysis we call this the marginal social cost curve (MSC). The demand curve is determined by the utility, or benefits, that the consumption of a good or service brings to the consumers. Again, if we assume that the benefits in the market are equivalent to the benefits to society, then the demand curve represents the social benefits. In efficiency analysis we refer to the demand curve as the marginal social benefit curve (MSB).

To conclude this introduction to efficiency analysis, a free market leads to allocative efficiency. Community surplus is maximized, so it is the optimum allocation of resources from society's point of view. This occurs where demand is equal to supply, or, where marginal social benefit is equal to marginal social cost.

Higher Level

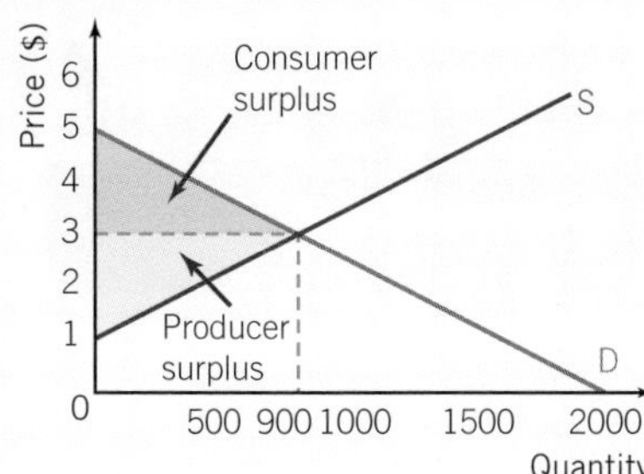

▲ **Figure 7.8** Calculating consumer and producer surplus

How do I calculate consumer surplus and producer surplus?

In Paper 3, you may be asked to calculate the area of consumer surplus and/or producer surplus from a demand and supply diagram. This is best shown through an example.

In Figure 7.8, we are given the demand and supply curves for a product. If we are asked to calculate the consumer and producer surplus in the market, then there are three easy steps to do so.

1. Identify the equilibrium price and quantity demanded and supplied. This is where the demand and supply curves intersect and so in this case, a quantity of 900 units is demanded and supplied at a price of \$3.
2. Calculate the consumer surplus.
   Consumer surplus is shown by the area above the equilibrium price and below the demand curve, so it will be the area of the triangle indicated in Figure 7.8.

   The area of a right-angled triangle is equal to ½ base x height. In this case, the base of the triangle is 900 units and the height is \$2. Thus, the area will be:

   $$\left(\frac{1}{2} \times 900\right) \times \$2 = \$900$$

   This is the amount of consumer surplus – the total amount consumers were willing to pay and have not had to do so.
3. Calculate the producer surplus.
   Producer surplus is shown by the area below the equilibrium price and above the supply curve, so it will be the area of the triangle indicated in Figure 7.8.

   In this case, the right-angled triangle is upside-down, but the process is the same. The base of the triangle is 900 units and the height is \$2, the same as for consumer surplus. Thus, the area will be:

   $$\left(\frac{1}{2} \times 900\right) \times \$2 = \$900$$

   This is the amount of producer surplus; the extra earnings that producers receive over and above the minimum amount they would be prepared to accept.

   In this case, consumer and producer surplus are the same amount. However, this is not always the case and the amounts will depend upon the relative price elasticities of demand and supply for the product.

Exercise 7.3

ATL Thinking and Communication

The diagram below shows the market for a product.

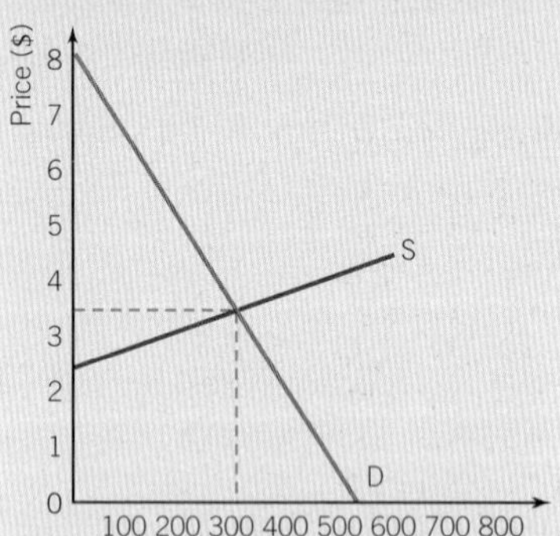

1. Identify:
   a. the equilibrium price
   b. the equilibrium quantity demanded and supplied.
2. Calculate the amount of consumer surplus in the market.
3. Explain what the amount signifies.
4. Calculate the amount of producer surplus in the market.
5. Explain what the amount signifies.
6. Explain why the consumer surplus is much larger than the producer surplus.

Assessment advice: Paper 2 HL & SL – data response

Whenever you can, in all diagrams, you should use values from the text on your axes and label the axes accordingly, eg in question 2 below, the axes would be "price of copper/tonne ($)" and "quantity of copper (thousands of tonne)". In question 4 below, evaluation may be best achieved by considering the short-run and long-run effects and also by looking at how the various stakeholders are affected. For more advice on evaluation, see Chapter 32. Where appropriate, diagrams should also be used in question 4. In order to achieve the top marking level (above 12 marks), it is necessary to make direct reference to the text.

Data response exercise

This data response exercise is similar to, but smaller than, what you will encounter in your IB examination in Paper 2. Remember that you answer one question that has question parts ranging from (a) to (g). Question 1 is similar to question part (a). Questions 2 and 3 are similar to questions parts (c) to (f), and question 4 is similar to question part (g).

Read the following article and answer the questions.

Copper breaks through $8,000 per tonne barrier but hot metal prices may soon cool

The price of copper passed $8,000 a tonne for the first time in 20 months yesterday, but hopes that it was proof of a sustained global recovery promptly suffered a setback when copper traders said that it may be about to fall steeply again.

Copper prices on the London Metal Exchange hit $8,009.75 a tonne in early trading yesterday, the highest level since August 2008, before slipping back to $7,970 a tonne at the end of the day. The price rise was driven in part by renewed confidence in the American economy after strong employment data published recently.

But it is **demand** from China that has been the main driving force behind the recovery in copper prices from last year's low prices of under $3,000 a tonne. Traders in South-East Asia said yesterday that even if the Chinese economy continued to storm ahead at its present pace, copper demand was likely to fall because so many big construction projects, which use large amounts of copper wiring, were now finished.

Moreover, preparations for the Shanghai Expo have been keeping copper prices up since last summer. When the pavilions open their doors in three weeks' time, building will have stopped and with it the significant demand for copper will also fall. Indeed, after the expo closes at the end of October, the market could be swamped with recycled metal.

A fall in demand is also expected from Chinese utility companies, which are responsible for more than half the country's copper needs. Huge quantities of electricity cable were laid as the government made orders for massive investments in infrastructure. Many of those projects were brought forward as part of last year's $586 billion stimulus programme, but this is government spending that is already beginning to be reduced. Overall investment in the Chinese power grid is expected to fall by a quarter this year and cable producers are already talking about buying 10 percent less copper.

However, those who argue that copper prices will not fall dramatically observe that high rates of **economic growth** mean that Chinese consumer spending is the strongest in the world. Property prices continue to rise and new buildings require miles of copper wiring. And, at the end of every new power socket is a demand for new washing machines, fridges and other products that need copper, which should help to keep the price up.

Source: Adapted from *The Times Online*, April 7, 2010, Leo Lewis and David Robertson

1. (i) Define the term *demand*, indicated in bold in the text. [2 marks]
   (ii) Define the term *economic growth*, indicated in bold in the text. [2 marks]
2. Using a supply and demand diagram, explain one possible reason for the increase in copper prices. (Be sure to use the information from the text.) [4 marks]
3. Using a demand and supply diagram, explain why the price of consumer goods such as new washing machines might be expected to rise. [4 marks]
4. Using information from the text/data and your knowledge of economics, evaluate what is likely to happen in the copper market in the coming months. [15 marks]

A special note about commodity prices

As you learned earlier, commodities (raw materials) tend to have low price elasticity of demand and low price elasticity of supply. Make sure you can explain why this is the case. This combination of relatively inelastic demand and inelastic supply for commodities means that any changes in the demand or supply of a commodity will result in large swings in prices. This is referred to as "price volatility". Consider the changes in the price of copper in the article above. In April 2010, the price was around $8,000 per tonne, which was the highest price since August 2008. The previous year the price had reached a low of $3,000 per tonne. Thus, within two years, there were fluctuations in price (up or down) of more than 150%. Part of the reason for the large fluctuations lies in the low elasticities of supply and demand.

As you can see in Figure 7.9, a change in demand will result in changing prices for copper. In the case of copper and the article in Chapter 3 the increase in demand, largely due to demand from China, resulted in a shift in demand from D_1 to D_2. The resulting change in price of $5,000 per tonne in one year is very large. But, as the article implies, what goes up also comes down!

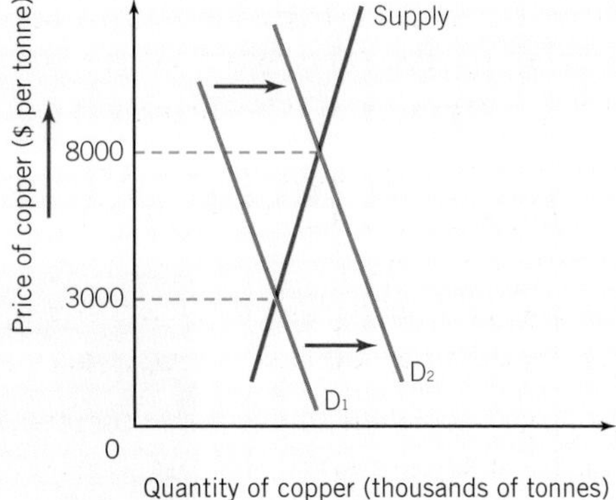

▲ **Figure 7.9** The market for copper

The graph below provides some more up-to-date data about copper prices, which illustrates the price volatility.

Source: https://www.macrotrends.net/1476/copper-prices-historical-chart-data

For copper producers and copper-producing countries, the upswings in price might be very good in terms of generating large revenue gains but the same producers are very vulnerable to the inevitable downswings in prices. The volatility of commodity prices and the vulnerability of commodity producers is a topic that we shall return to later in the companion.

Economics in action

ATL Thinking, Communication and Research

Choose an industrial commodity, other than oil, that is used in the production of a product which consumers buy. Select a commodity where there is some evidence of volatile prices.

1. Who are the main producers?
2. What is it used for?
3. Provide information to illustrate the volatile prices.
4. What factors explain the volatile prices?
5. Which stakeholders are impacted by the volatile prices? In what way are they impacted?

Assessment advice: Internal assessment (IA)

Having covered basic demand and supply, you are now able to start preparing for the task of writing your IA commentaries. It would not be advisable to attempt a proper commentary at this stage, as you don't really have enough conceptual knowledge to write a sufficiently sophisticated piece. Nonetheless, you can do a basic commentary using demand and supply analysis to explain the movement of the price of a particular good or service. In this chapter, for example, there have been references to a number of markets such as LCD televisions and copper.

To find an article, go to a search engine that specifically finds news items and type in the words "price" plus the name of a good you might want to research. Commodities such as oil and rubber are possibilities, as are any currently popular items. Entering "supply" and "demand" is also a possibility. Make sure that you get an actual news item that comes from a media source. Do appreciate that it usually takes quite a bit of time to find an appropriate article, and you may have to read through several before you choose one that really works.

An appropriate article will explain why the market is changing, and you have to turn this into economic analysis. That is, you have to identify any determinants of demand and supply that might be changing and explain why they are changing. You should support your answer with neatly labelled and accurate diagrams. Also remember to note the *ceteris paribus* assumption where appropriate.

When you complete your actual IA commentaries for the IB, you will be required to make a link between the information in your article and one of the key concepts of the course. When you are considering whether an article is a good one to use, try to see if you can link it to one of the key concepts.

It is difficult to evaluate a great deal at this stage, but you could attempt to do so by:

- explaining how different stakeholders might be affected by possible price changes
- explaining the most important reasons for any changes in the market
- looking at how the market might change in the long run.

Note

You will find more information about internal assessment in Chapter 32.

8 METHODS OF GOVERNMENT INTERVENTION IN MARKETS

REAL-WORLD ISSUE:

When are markets unable to satisfy important economic objectives and does government intervention help?

By the end of this chapter, you should be able to:

→ List possible reasons for government intervention in markets
→ Define and give examples of an indirect tax
→ Explain the difference between a specific tax and a percentage tax
→ Explain, and illustrate, how the imposition of an indirect tax may affect consumers, producers and the government
→ Explain the importance of elasticity in understanding the effect of a specific tax on the demand for, and supply of, a product
→ Explain the significance of the elasticity of demand and supply in assessing the incidence of an indirect tax
→ Discuss the consequences of an indirect tax on the stakeholders in a market
HL Calculate the effects on stakeholders of imposing an indirect tax
→ Define and give examples of a subsidy
→ Explain, and illustrate, how the granting of a subsidy may affect consumers, producers and the government
→ Discuss the consequences of a subsidy on the stakeholders in a market
HL Illustrate and calculate the effects on stakeholders of subsidies
→ Explain, distinguish between, illustrate and give examples of maximum and minimum price controls
HL Calculate the effects on stakeholders of minimum and maximum prices
→ Discuss the consequences of price controls on the stakeholders in a market.

Governments may intervene in individual, microeconomic markets for a number of reasons. They may wish to support households, support firms, influence consumption and/or production, protect consumers from the problems associated with monopoly power, promote well-being and equity or simply earn government revenue to use for other purposes. We need to consider some of the ways that governments may intervene in markets and try to assess how effective the methods may be in achieving the desired aims. In this chapter, we consider four different types of government intervention in markets: indirect taxes, subsidies and minimum and maximum prices.

What is the effect of indirect taxes on the demand for, and supply of, a product?

An *indirect tax* is one imposed upon expenditure. There are different names for indirect taxes, including "goods and services tax" (GST), "value added tax" (VAT), sales tax, consumption tax and excise tax.

One of the reasons that governments impose indirect taxes is to provide the government with revenues needed to carry out their many responsibilities. Other taxes which generate income include: direct tax (household income tax and corporate tax, property tax and social insurance tax). Table 8.1 indicates how important indirect taxes are in generating revenue for governments. In the case of Chile, it accounts for over half of government revenue.

Country	Indirect taxes as a % of total revenue
Chile	54.1
Mexico	38.6
United Kingdom	32.9
Japan	21.0
U.S.A	17.0

▲ **Table 8.1** Indirect tax rates in selected countries 2018

Source: OECD, https://taxfoundation.org/sources-of-government-revenue-oecd-2018/

Another important reason for setting taxes is to discourage the consumption of certain goods. While a government may place a "standard" indirect tax on all goods and services, they may place an extra tax on goods that may be considered undesirable.

An indirect tax is placed upon the selling price of a product, so it raises the firm's costs and shifts the supply curve for the product vertically upwards by the amount of the tax. Because of this shift, less of the product will be supplied at every price.

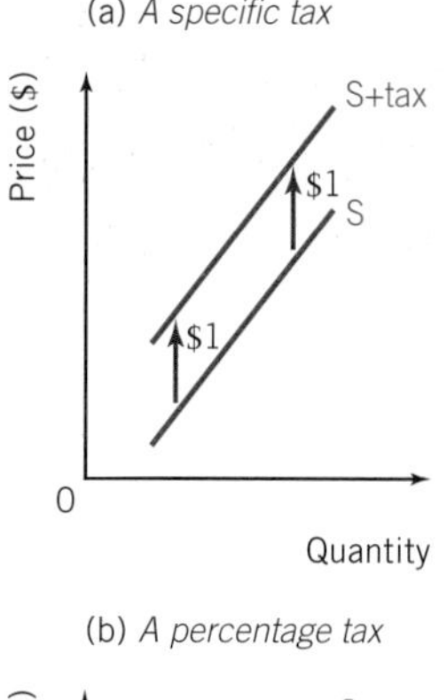

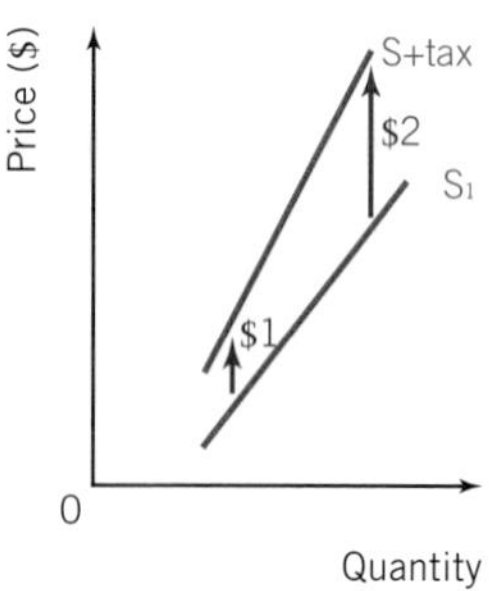

▲ **Figure 8.1** The effect on a supply curve of different types of indirect taxes

There are two types of indirect taxes to consider:

1. *A specific tax*: This is a specific, or fixed, amount of tax that is imposed upon a product; for example, a tax of $1 per unit. It thus has the effect of shifting the supply curve vertically upwards by the amount of the tax, in this case, by $1. This is shown in Figure 8.1(a). S is the original supply curve and S + tax is the curve after the tax is imposed.
2. *A percentage tax* (also known as an *ad valorem tax*): This is where the tax is a percentage of the selling price and so the supply curve will shift as shown in Figure 8.1(b). It is clear from this that the gap between S_1 and S + tax will get bigger as the price of the product rises. If the percentage tax is 20%, then at a price of $5, the tax on the product will be $1. If the price of the product is $10, then the tax becomes $2. The gap between the supply curves widens because it is a percentage tax.

When an indirect tax is imposed on a product, we need to consider what the effect will be on consumers, producers, the government and the market as a whole. In order to do that, we add the demand curve to the graph and consider the following questions:

- What will happen to the price that the consumers pay?
- What will happen to the amount received by the producer?
- How much tax will the government receive?
- What will happen to the size of the market, and so employment?

If we take a normal demand and supply curve and then assume that the government imposes a specific tax on a product, we get the diagrams shown in Figure 8.2 (a), (b) and (c).

The market is in equilibrium, with Q_e being supplied and demanded at a price of P_e. After the tax of XY per unit is imposed, the supply curve shifts vertically upwards from S_1 to S_1 + tax. The producers would like to raise the price to P_2 and so pass on all of the cost of the tax to the consumers. However, as we can see in Figure 8.2(a), at that price, there is an excess supply and so price has to fall until a new equilibrium is reached, which is at a price of P_1, where Q_1 is both demanded and supplied.

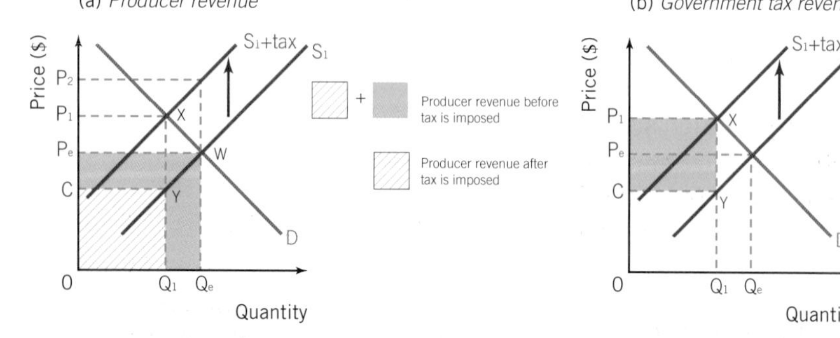

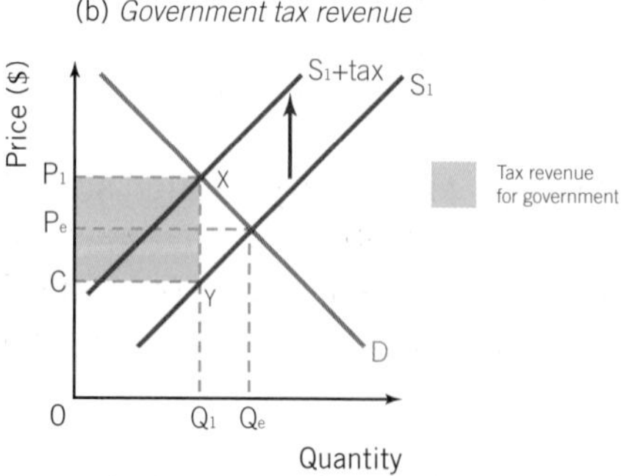

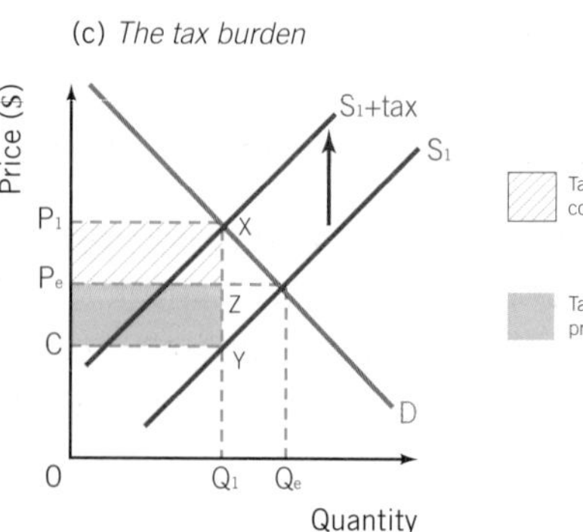

▲ **Figure 8.2** The imposition of a specific tax on a product

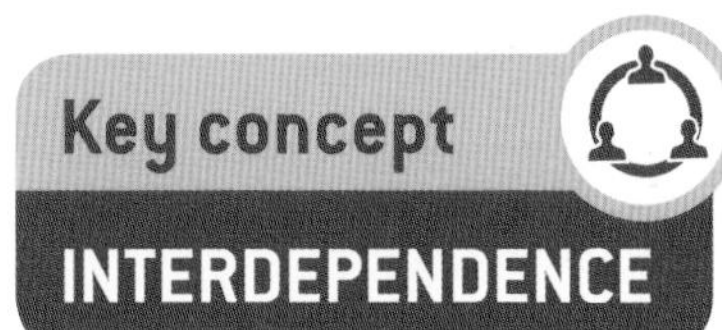

We can now address the questions that we asked previously. From Figure 8.2(a), we can see that the price of the product for the consumers rises from P_e to P_1, which is their share of the tax, and is about half of the whole tax of XY. Producers now receive C per unit, after paying the tax of XY to the government. Thus, they contribute the rest of the tax, P_eC per unit. The revenue for producers falls from $0P_eWQ_e$ to $0CYQ_1$. This is shown in the blue striped section in the diagram.

From Figure 8.2(b), we can see that the government will receive tax revenue equal to CP_1XY and that the market falls in size from one producing Q_e units to one producing Q_1 units. This may well have implications for the level of employment in the market, as firms might employ fewer people.

Figure 8.2(c) shows us that, in this case, the burden of the indirect tax is shared fairly evenly between the consumers and the producers.

Economics in action — ATL Thinking, Communication and Research

Conduct an investigation to find a real-world example by researching cigarette taxes in a country or region of your choice.

As part of your investigation, you should try to answer the following questions:

- How much is the tax on a packet of cigarettes?
- Has the tax changed over recent years? If so, why?
- Is there an increase or decrease in the tax?
- Who benefits and who suffers from the tax?

Finally, link your analysis to one or more of the nine key concepts.

Who pays what share of the indirect tax?

The share of the tax burden will not always be equal between producers and consumers. It will vary with the relative values of price elasticity of demand and supply for the product, as will government revenue, and the effect on the size of the market.

Let us look at two different situations. In the first case, consider a market where the price elasticity of demand is relatively elastic and the price elasticity of supply is relatively inelastic, ie where the value of PED is greater than the value of PES. This is shown in Figure 8.3.

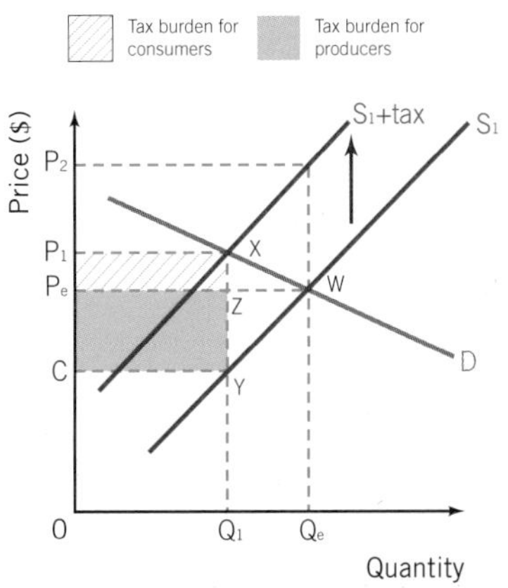

▲ **Figure 8.3** The imposition of a specific tax on a product where PED is greater than PES

The market is in equilibrium, with Q_e being supplied and demanded at a price of P_e. After the tax of XY per unit is imposed, the supply curve shifts vertically upwards from S_1 to S_1 + tax. The producers would like to raise the price to P_2 and so pass on all of the cost of the tax to the consumers.

However, at that price, there is an excess supply and so price has to fall until a new equilibrium is reached, which is at a price of P_1, where Q_1

is both demanded and supplied. However, in this case, the producers cannot pass on a lot of the burden of the tax, because demand is very elastic and too many of the consumers would stop buying the product. Thus, the producers have to bear most of the burden of the tax themselves. The price of the product for the consumers rises just a little from P_e to P_1. Producers now receive C per unit, after paying the tax of XY to the government. Thus, they contribute the majority of the tax, P_eC per unit. The income of producers falls a great deal, from $0P_eWQ_e$ to $0CYQ_1$. The consumers' share of the tax is P_eP_1XZ. The government will receive high tax revenue equal to CP_1XY and the market falls in size from one producing Q_e units to one producing Q_1 units. This will once again have implications for the level of employment in the market.

In this case, the burden of the indirect tax is much heavier on the producers than on the consumers. This is because of the difference in the values of the elasticities.

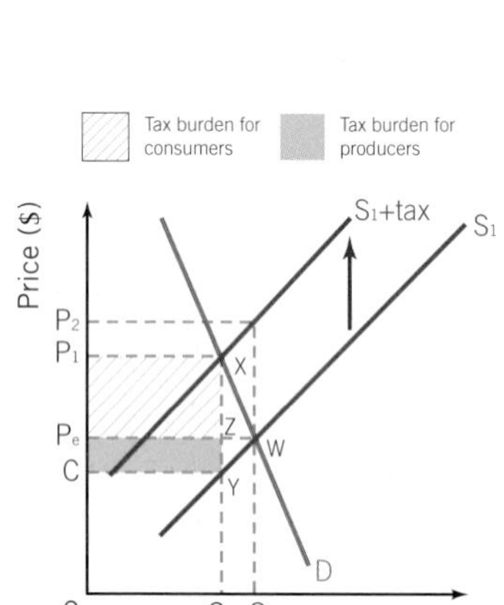

▲ **Figure 8.4** The imposition of a specific tax on a product where PED is less than PES

In the second case, consider a market where the price elasticity of demand is relatively inelastic and the price elasticity of supply is relatively elastic, ie where the value of PED is less than the value of PES. This is shown in Figure 8.4.

The market is in equilibrium with Q_e being supplied and demanded at a price of P_e. After the tax of XY per unit is imposed, the supply curve shifts vertically upwards from S_1 to S_1+ tax. The producers would like to raise the price to P_2 and so pass on all of the cost of the tax to the consumers. However, at that price, there is an excess supply and so price has to fall until a new equilibrium is reached, which is at a price of P_1, where Q_1 is both demanded and supplied.

In this case, the producers can pass on a lot of the burden of the tax, because demand is fairly inelastic and so consumers are not very responsive to the increase in the price. Thus, the consumers have most of the burden of the tax passed on to them. The price of the product for the consumers rises substantially from P_e to P_1. Thus, they contribute the majority of the tax, P_1P_e per unit. Producers now receive C per unit, after paying the tax of XY to the government. The income of producers falls a small amount, from $0P_eWQ_e$ to $0CYQ_1$. The government will receive high tax revenue equal to CP_1XY and the market falls in size from one producing Q_e units to one producing Q_1 units. This will once again have implications for the level of employment in the market.

In this case, the burden of the indirect tax is much heavier on the consumers than on the producers. We can use the examples above to derive a set of rules relating to the incidence of indirect taxes on producers and consumers:

1. Where the value of PED is equal to the value of PES for a product, then the burden of any tax imposed will be shared equally between the consumers and producers of the product.

2. Where the value of PED is greater than the value of PES for a product, then the burden of any tax imposed will be greater on the producers of the product than on the consumers.
3. Where the value of PED is less than the value of PES for a product, then the burden of any tax imposed will be greater on the consumers of the product than the producers.

This is one of the reasons why governments tend to place indirect taxes on products that have relatively inelastic demand, such as alcohol and cigarettes. By doing this, demand changes by a proportionately smaller amount than the change in price and so the government will gain high revenue and yet not cause a large fall in employment. You should be able to think of some other good reasons why governments put taxes on such goods. These will be addressed further when we study macroeconomics.

Exercise 8.1

ATL Thinking and Communication

1. A product has relatively inelastic demand and also relatively inelastic supply. Draw a diagram to show this and then show the effect of the imposition of a **percentage tax** on the product. Label the diagram carefully and state the areas corresponding to:
   a. the original revenue of the producer
   b. the revenue of the producer after the tax is imposed
   c. the tax revenue received by the government
   d. the amount of the tax paid by the consumers
   e. the amount of the tax paid by the producers.

   Would it be sensible for a government to tax a product with such elasticities? Explain your answer.

2. A product has relatively elastic demand and also relatively elastic supply. Draw a diagram to show this and then show the effect of the imposition of a **specific tax** on the product. Label the diagram carefully and state the areas corresponding to:
   a. the original revenue of the producer
   b. the revenue of the producer after the tax is imposed
   c. the tax revenue received by the government
   d. the amount of the tax paid by the consumers
   e. the amount of the tax paid by the producers.

   Would it be sensible for a government to tax a product with such elasticities? Explain your answer.

How do you calculate the effects on stakeholders of imposing an indirect tax?

Higher Level

In HL paper 3 you may be asked to calculate possible effects from an indirect tax diagram, in terms of price, quantity, consumer expenditure, producer revenue, government revenue, consumer surplus or producer surplus.

Here is an example of the kinds of questions that you may face and suggested responses.

EXAMINATION QUESTIONS

Below is the market for aerated drinks in a country. A specific indirect tax has been imposed by the government.

Answer the following questions:

1. Label the demand and supply curves.
2. Indicate the original equilibrium price and quantity on the graph.
3. Indicate the new equilibrium price and quantity on the graph, following the imposition of the indirect tax.

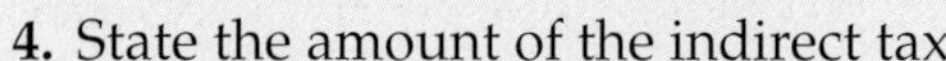

4. State the amount of the indirect tax.
5. Calculate the government revenue from the tax.
6. Calculate the amount of tax paid by:
   a) consumers
   b) producers.
7. Calculate the change in consumer expenditure after the tax.
8. Calculate the change in producer revenue after the tax.
9. Illustrate the area showing the loss of consumer surplus.
10. Illustrate the area showing the loss of producer surplus.

Suggested answers

The required diagram is shown here:

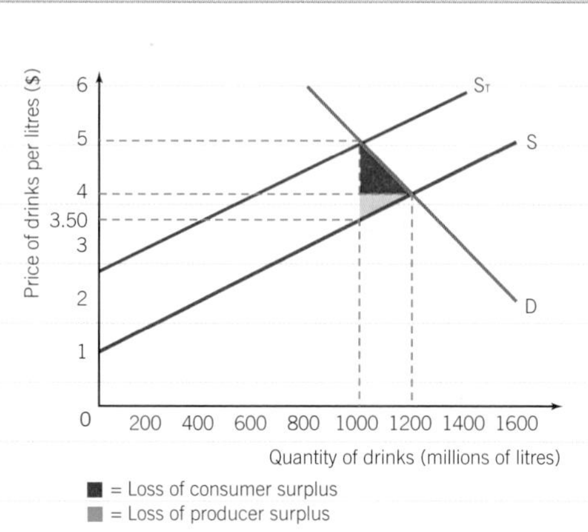

For question 1, the curves are labelled D, S and S_T.

For questions 2 and 3, the original equilibrium price and quantity are shown as $4 and 1,200 million litres of drinks. The new equilibrium price and quantity are shown as $5 and 1,000 million litres of drinks.

For question 4, the amount of the tax is shown by the vertical difference between the supply curves and so it is $5 - $3.50 = $1.50. (The tax amount per unit does not change, since it is a specific tax.)

For question 5, the government revenue will be the number of drinks purchased after the tax multiplied by the amount of the tax. So, it will be 1,000 million x $1.50 = $1,500 million.

For question 6(a), consumers will pay the increase in price x the number of drinks purchased after the tax. The price rises from $4 to $5, so the amount of tax paid will be $1 x 1,000 million = $1,000 million.

For question 6(b), producers will bear the amount of the tax that they cannot pass on to the consumers. This will be $1.50, the amount of the tax per unit, less $1, the amount of the tax per unit paid by the consumers. So, the producers will pay $0.50 per unit in tax. Since they now supply 1,000 million litres of drinks, they will pay $0.50 x 1,000 million = $500 million.

For question 7, consumer expenditure before the tax was 1,200 million x $4 = $4,800 million. Consumer expenditure after the tax was 1,000 million x $5 = $5,000 million. Therefore, consumer expenditure on aerated drinks increased by $200 million.

For question 8, producer revenue before the tax was 1,200 million x $4 = $4,800 million. Producer revenue after the tax was 1,000 million x $3.50 = $3,500 million. Therefore, producer revenue from aerated drinks decreased by $1,300 million.

For questions 9 and 10, the loss of consumer surplus is shown by the red shaded area and the loss of consumer surplus is shown by the blue shaded area.

Note

In an IB examination, you are not allowed colour pencils, and so you would need to use stripes or to label the vertices, eg triangle abc.

What is the effect of a producer subsidy on the demand for, and supply of, a product?

A *subsidy* is an amount of money paid by the government to a firm, per unit of output. There are a number of reasons why a government may give a subsidy for a product and the main ones are:

1. To lower the price of essential goods, such as rice, to consumers. In this way, the government hopes that the consumption of the product will be increased, encouraged by the lower price.

2. To guarantee the supply of products that the government thinks are necessary for the economy. This may be because the goods are essential for the economy, such as a basic food supply or a power source like coal. It may also be that the industry creates a lot of employment that would be lost, thus causing economic and social problems.

Note

This is dealt with in more detail in Chapter 24.

3. To enable producers to compete with overseas trade, thus protecting the home industry.

If a subsidy is granted to a firm on a certain product, then the supply curve for the product will shift vertically downwards by the amount of the subsidy, because it reduces the costs of production for the firm, and more will be supplied at every price. As with indirect taxes, the amount of the subsidy that is passed on to the consumers in the form of lower prices, and the amount that is retained by the producers, will depend upon the relative elasticities of demand and supply.

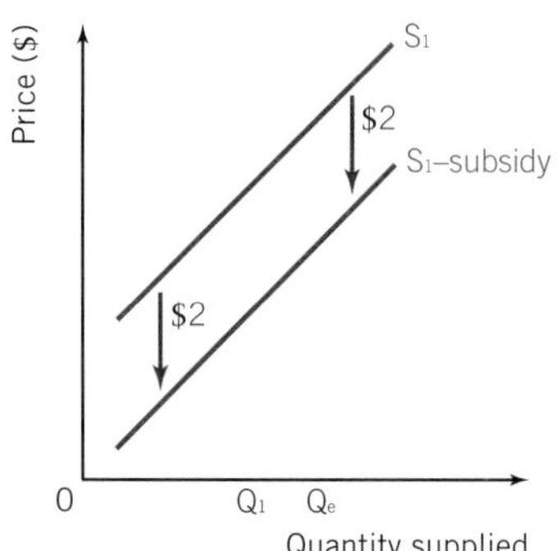

▲ **Figure 8.5** The effect on a supply curve of a specific subsidy

Although percentage subsidies are sometimes granted, they are rare and so we will concentrate on specific subsidies. A *specific subsidy* is a specific amount of money that is given for each unit of the product; for example, a subsidy of $2 per unit. It thus has the effect of shifting the supply curve vertically downwards by the amount of the subsidy, in this case by $2, at every price. This is shown in Figure 8.5. S_1 is the original supply curve and S_1 – subsidy is the curve after the subsidy is granted.

If we take a normal demand and supply curve and then assume that the government grants a specific subsidy on a product, we get the diagrams shown in Figure 8.6(a), (b) and (c).

(a) *Increase in producer revenue*

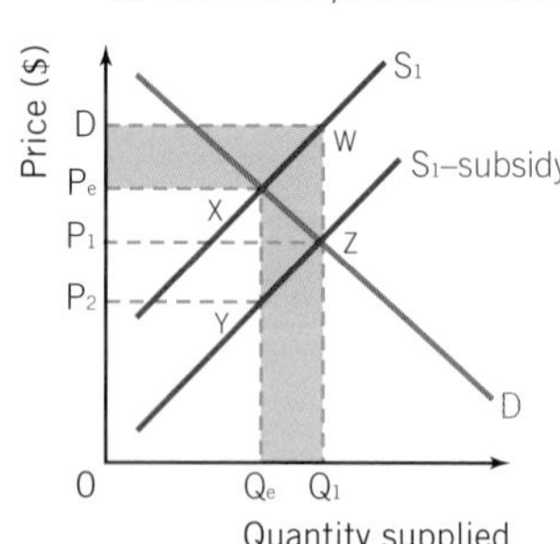

(b) *Change in consumer expenditure*

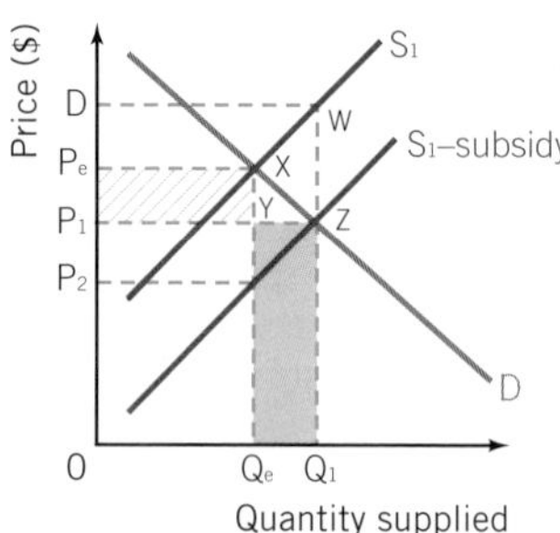

(c) *Amount of government subsidy*

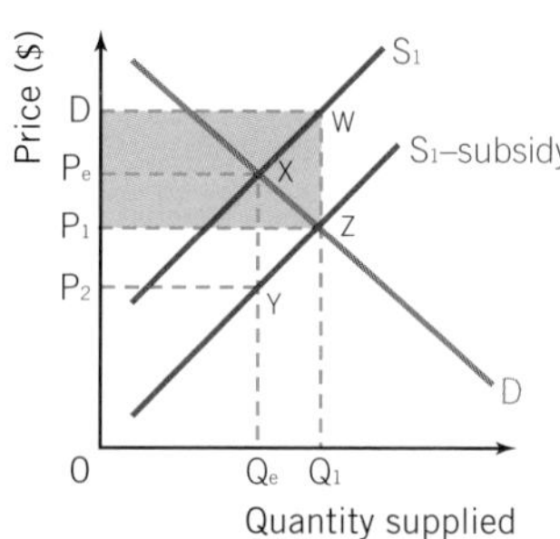

▲ **Figure 8.6** The granting of a specific subsidy on a product

The market is in equilibrium with Q_e being supplied and demanded at a price of P_e. After the subsidy of WZ per unit is granted, the supply curve shifts vertically downwards from S_1 to S_1 – subsidy. As we can see in Figure 8.6(a), the producers lower their prices and increase output until a new equilibrium is reached, which is at a price of P_1, where Q_1 is both demanded and supplied.

From Figure 8.6(a), we can see that the price to consumers falls from P_e to P_1, not the whole amount of the subsidy, which would need a fall to P_2. The income of the producers rises from the original amount of $0P_eXQ_e$ to $0DWQ_1$. The consumers pay $0P_1ZQ_1$ for their purchases and P_1DWZ is paid to the producers by the government as the subsidy on the Q_1 units.

From Figure 8.6(b), we can see that the consumers get to buy the original Q_e units at a lower price, P_1, thus saving the expenditure P_1P_eXY. However, they do purchase more units, Q_eQ_1, because the price is lower,

spending Q_eYZQ_1 extra. Total consumer expenditure may increase or fall, depending upon the relative savings and extra expenditure.

Figure 8.6(c) shows us that the total cost of the subsidy to the government is P_1DWZ. This money has to be found from somewhere and so there is an *opportunity cost* here. Once again, the government must either take money away from other areas of expenditure, such as building infrastructure or providing public amenities, or it must raise taxes.

Exercise 8.2

ATL Thinking and Communication

Working through this question successfully will enable you to illustrate and calculate the effects on stakeholders of the granting of a subsidy.

Below is the market for a prescription drug in a country. A specific subsidy has been granted by the government to make the drug more easily accessible for those who need it.

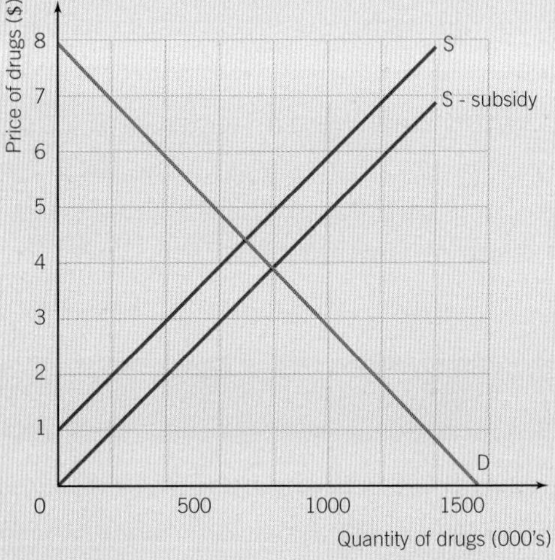

1. Determine the equilibrium price and quantity in the market, before the granting of the subsidy.
2. Determine the new equilibrium price and quantity in the market, following the granting of the subsidy.
3. Calculate the increase in producer revenue after the subsidy is given.
4. Calculate the change in consumer expenditure after the subsidy is given.
5. Calculate the total expenditure of the government on the subsidy.
6. Explain why both consumers and producers will benefit from the granting of the subsidy.
7. Identify possible losers from the granting of the subsidy and explain why they may lose.

Higher Level

There are a number of things that need to be evaluated when a government is considering the granting of a subsidy:

- The opportunity cost of government spending on the subsidy in terms of other alternative government spending projects. The government is making a choice when they go for the subsidy. There are obviously many other projects upon which government money may be spent, which will then not happen.

Key concept
EFFICIENCY

- Whether the subsidy will mean that firms do not have an incentive to gain efficiency, if they do not have to compete with foreign producers in a "free market".
- Although a subsidy allows consumers to buy products at a lower price, they may also be the taxpayers who are funding the subsidy. Who is paying the taxes?
- What damage will it do to the sales of foreign producers who are not receiving subsidies from their governments? There is a great deal of international debate concerning the billions of dollars of subsidies that high-income countries give to their farmers. These subsidies lead to overproduction, which has implications for sustainability. It is also argued that this is highly damaging to small-scale farmers in developing countries, who do not receive subsidies themselves and then have to compete with the low prices charged by the farmers who do receive subsidies. It raises the concept of equity.

  High-income country farmers are accused of dumping their products in developing countries. That is, they are accused of selling such products at prices beneath their costs of production. This is a major issue of contention at the World Trade Organization (WTO).

Economics in action

ATL Thinking, Communication and Research

As part of their commitments to the Sustainable Development Goals, governments around the world are adopting policies to encourage the development of green/renewable energies. One way to encourage green energy is through the provision of subsidies.

Conduct an investigation to find a real-world example by researching environmental subsidies in a country or region of your choice.

As part of your investigation, you should try to answer the following questions:

- How much is the subsidy?
- Has the subsidy changed over recent years? If so, why?
- Who benefits and who suffers from the subsidy?

Finally, link your analysis to one or more of the nine key concepts.

Exercise 8.3 ATL Thinking, Communication and Research

Read the following text and answer the questions which follow:

Cotton producers hope to benefit from Brazil's subsidy battle with US

African cotton-producing countries are happy with Brazil's success in its case with the World Trade Organisation against the United States' continued use of subsidies in cotton production.

"True, we don't benefit directly from the WTO ruling," said Prosper Vokouma, representative of Burkina Faso to the United Nations in Geneva and coordinator of the C4. The C4 is the grouping of four cotton-exporting African countries of which Benin, Burkina Faso, Mali and Chad are the members. "But it has helped put the issue of the 'white gold' on the WTO agenda."

"The WTO ruling gives legitimacy to the C4's demands," Vokouma says. "It is a strong criticism of the massive and distorting subsidies. The WTO dispute settlement body has confirmed that US subsidies damage other countries' producers because of their impact on world market prices."

"We know that the US has a bad conscience regarding this issue. Some 2,500 large farmers share more than $3 billion between them every year, whereas 20 to 30 million African cotton producers live in misery because the product of their hard work is not even enough to feed them," says Vokouma.

Studies by international organisations show that the total abolition of US subsidies would increase the world cotton price by 14%.

According to the charity Oxfam, this would translate into additional revenue that could feed one million more children per year, or pay the school fees of two million children in West Africa.

Source: Adapted from: http://www.ipsnews.net/2010/03/trade-whither-african-cotton-producers-after-brazilrsquos-success/

1. Using an appropriate diagram, explain why "US subsidies damage other countries' producers because of their impact on world market prices" and how "the abolition of US subsidies" could "increase the world cotton price by 14%".
2. Comment on the advantages and the disadvantages of the abolition of US cotton subsidies.
3. The article was written in March 2010. Research the current situation with regard to US cotton subsidies. Have the C4 countries in Africa experienced a positive change in their circumstances?

Why, and how, do governments impose price controls?

Key concept
INTERVENTION

Although it may seem to be an optimum situation, the free market does not always lead to the best outcomes for all producers and consumers, or for society in general. Hence governments often choose to intervene directly in the market in order to achieve a different outcome. There are two key situations where this occurs:

- maximum prices
- minimum prices.

We now look at each of these situations in turn.

What are price ceilings (maximum prices) and what are their effects on markets?

This is a situation where the government sets a maximum price, below the equilibrium price, which then prevents producers from raising the price above it. These are sometimes known as ceiling prices, since the price is not able to go above "the ceiling" that has been put in place by the government.

Maximum prices are usually set to help consumers and they are normally imposed in markets where the product in question is a necessity and/or a *merit good* (a good that would be underprovided if the market were allowed to operate freely). For example, governments may set maximum prices in agricultural and food markets during times of food shortages to ensure affordable food, or they may set maximum prices on rented accommodation in an attempt to ensure affordable accommodation for those on low incomes.

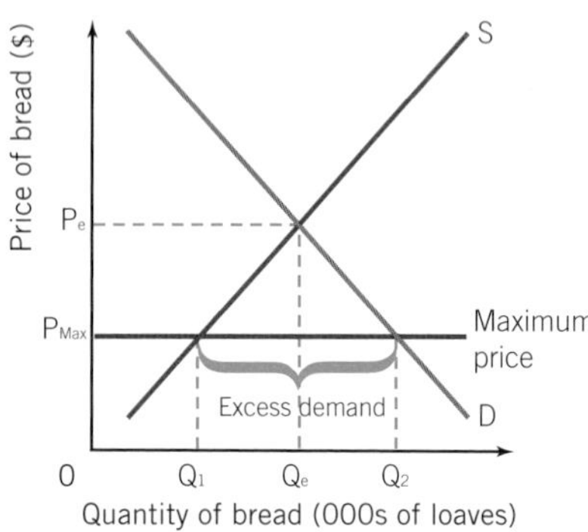

▲ Figure 8.7 The market for bread

Figure 8.7 shows the situation that may exist if the government were to implement a maximum price in the market for bread.

Without government interference, the equilibrium quantity demanded and supplied would be Q_e, at a price of P_e. The government imposes a maximum price of P_{Max} in order to help the consumers of bread. However, a problem now arises. At the price P_{Max}, Q_2 will be demanded because the price has fallen, but only Q_1 will be supplied. Thus, we have a situation of excess demand. If the government does not intervene further, they will find that consumption of bread actually falls from Q_e to Q_1, even though it is at a lower price.

The excess demand creates problems. The shortages may lead to the emergence of a black market (an illegal market), in which the product is sold at a higher price, somewhere between the maximum price and the equilibrium price. There may also be queues developing in the shops and producers may start to decide who is going to be allowed to buy. Since these problems are not really "fair" for the consumers, the government may now need to make attempts to eliminate, or at least reduce, the shortage.

There are a number of ways in which the government may try to do this. Essentially, it has two options. First, it could attempt to shift the demand curve to the left, until equilibrium is reached at the maximum price, but this would limit the consumption of the product, which goes against the point of imposing the maximum price.

Second, the government can attempt to shift the supply curve to the right, until equilibrium is reached at the maximum price, with more being supplied and demanded. There are a number of ways of doing this.

1. The government could offer subsidies to the firms in the industry to encourage them to produce more.
2. The government could start to produce the product themselves, thus increasing the supply. This is known as *direct provision*.

3. If the government had previously stored some of the product, then they could release some of the stocks (stored goods) onto the market. However, if the product were perishable, like bread, this would not be possible.

As we can see in Figure 8.8, if the government is able to shift the supply curve to the right, by subsidising, direct provision or using stored bread, then equilibrium will be reached at P_{Max}, with Q_2 loaves of bread being demanded and supplied. However, it is fair to say that this may well mean that the government incurs a cost, especially in the case of a subsidy, and that this will have an opportunity cost. If the government spends money supporting the bread industry, it may have to reduce expenditure in some other area, such as education or health care.

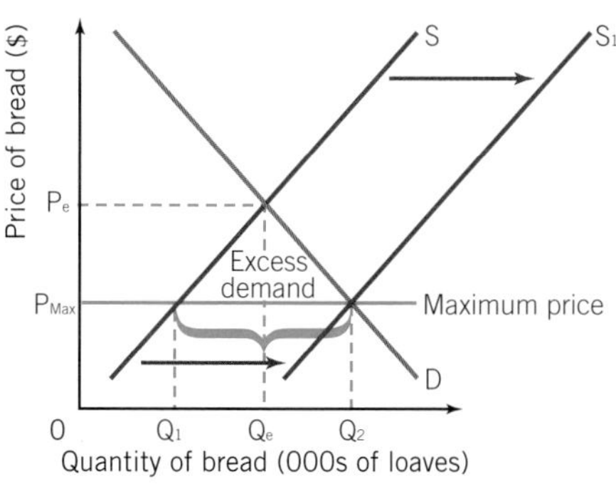

▲ **Figure 8.8** Government action to solve the problem of excess demand

Exercise 8.4

ATL Thinking and Communication

A government wishes to keep the cost of cheap rented accommodation low in a city, by imposing legal maximum rents on properties of a certain size. In doing this, they aim to:

- provide low-cost rental accommodation for people on low incomes
- provide more rental accommodation for people on low incomes.

1. Draw a diagram to show the effect of the maximum rent legislation on the market for rented accommodation.
2. Explain the situation facing those people who rent out their properties.
3. Explain the situation facing those people who wish to rent properties.
4. Suggest measures that the government might take to ensure that they achieve both of their stated aims above.

Key concept

EQUITY

Economics in action

ATL Thinking, Communication and Research

The example of bread as a maximum price, used above, is hypothetical and is there to help us understand the theory. The example of rent controls is theoretical, but there are many cities around the world that implement some sort of rent control.

Conduct an investigation to find a real-world example of a maximum price. You may choose to investigate rent controls as your example. As part of your investigation, you should try to:

- identify the reasons for the government intervention
- illustrate the market on a diagram
- discuss the advantages and disadvantages for relevant stakeholders
- link your analysis to one or more of the nine key concepts.

Higher Level

How do you calculate the effects on stakeholders of imposing a price ceiling?

In HL paper 3 you may be asked to calculate possible effects from the price ceiling diagram including the possible shortage, and changes relating to expenditure.

Here is an example of the kinds of questions that you may face and suggested responses.

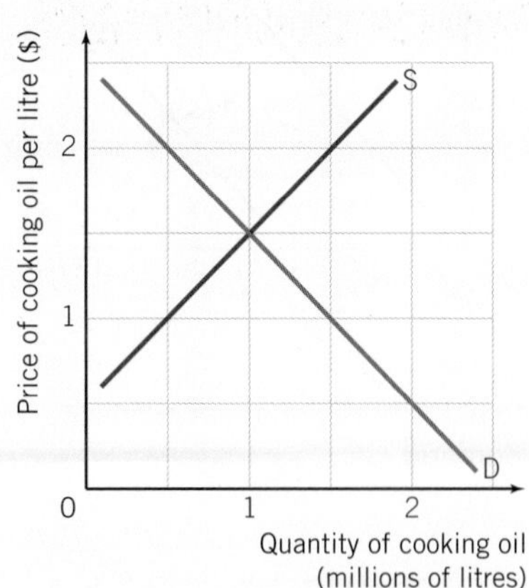

Below is the market for cooking oil in a country.

The government of the country decides to impose a legal price ceiling of $1 per litre.

1. Indicate the equilibrium price and quantity on the graph.
2. Show the price ceiling on the diagram.
3. Explain how much cooking oil will be demanded and supplied following the imposition of the price ceiling.
4. Calculate the change in consumer expenditure on cooking oil following the imposition of the price ceiling.
5. Explain **two** measures that the government may take to achieve their aim of giving less expensive cooking oil to more people.

The required diagram is shown here:

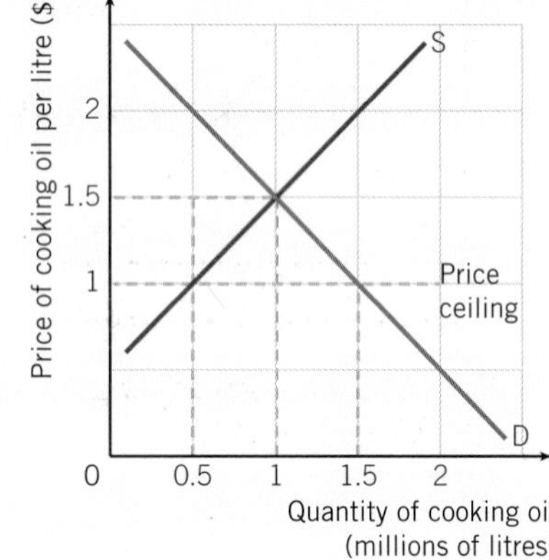

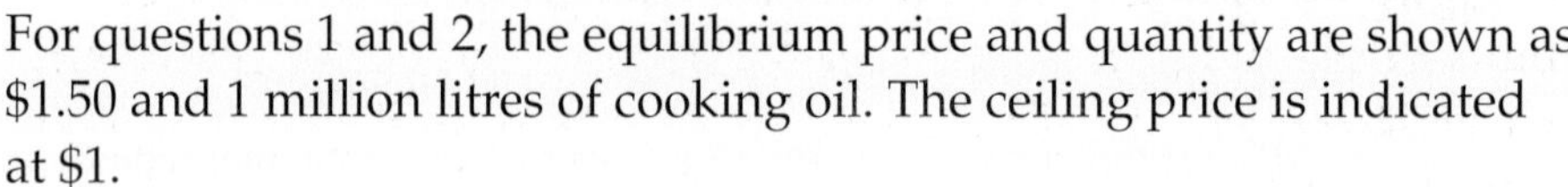

For questions 1 and 2, the equilibrium price and quantity are shown as $1.50 and 1 million litres of cooking oil. The ceiling price is indicated at $1.

For question 3, you could explain that at the maximum price of $1, 1.5 million litres of cooking oil will be demanded but only 0.5 million litres will be supplied. This means that there will be an excess demand for cooking oil of 1 million litres.

For question 4, consumer expenditure before the maximum price was 1 million × $1.50 = $1.5 million. Consumer expenditure after the maximum price was 0.5 million × $1.00 = $0.5 million. Therefore, consumer expenditure on cooking oil has fallen by $1 million.

For question 5, you could explain that if the government wants to achieve its aim then they need to eliminate the excess demand. This might be done by:

a. direct provision of cooking oil by the government, ie the setting up of government-owned cooking oil manufacturers
b. granting subsidies to cooking oil producers in order to encourage greater supply.

What are price floors (minimum prices) and what are their effects on markets?

This is a situation where the government sets a minimum price, above the equilibrium price, which then prevents producers from reducing the price below it. These are sometimes known as floor prices, since the price is not able to go below "the floor" that has been put in place by the government.

Minimum prices are mostly set for one of two reasons.

- To attempt to raise incomes for producers of goods and services that the government thinks are important, such as agricultural products. They may be helped because their prices are subject to large fluctuations, or because there is a lot of foreign competition. When equilibrium prices are low, the economic well being of producers may be harmed.
- To protect workers by setting a minimum wage, to ensure that workers earn enough to lead a reasonable existence. Very low equilibrium wages may be seen as unfair to those workers who receive them, raising issues of equity.

Figure 8.9 shows the situation that might exist if the government were to implement a minimum price in the market for wheat.

Without government interference, the equilibrium quantity demanded and supplied would be Q_e, at a price of P_e. The government imposes a minimum price of P_{Min} in order to increase the revenue of the producers of wheat. However, a problem now arises. At the price P_{Min}, only Q_1 will be demanded because the price has risen, but Q_2 will now be supplied. Thus, we have a situation of excess supply. If the government does not intervene further, they will find that consumption of wheat actually falls from Q_e to Q_1, albeit at a higher price.

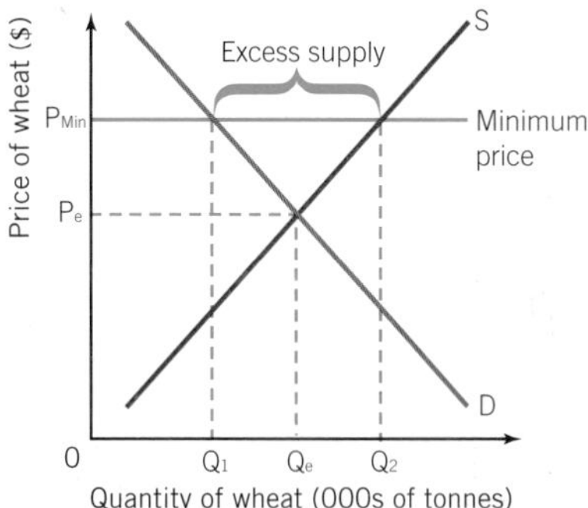

▲ **Figure 8.9** A minimum price in the market for wheat

The excess supply creates problems. Producers will find that they have surpluses and will be tempted to try to get around the price controls and sell their excess supply for a lower price, somewhere between P_{Min} and P_e.

In order to maintain the minimum price, it is likely that the government will have to intervene. This is shown in Figure 8.10.

The government would normally eliminate the excess supply by buying up the surplus products, at the minimum price, thus shifting the demand curve to the right and creating a new equilibrium at P_{Min}, with Q_2 being demanded and supplied. The new demand curve would be D + government buying.

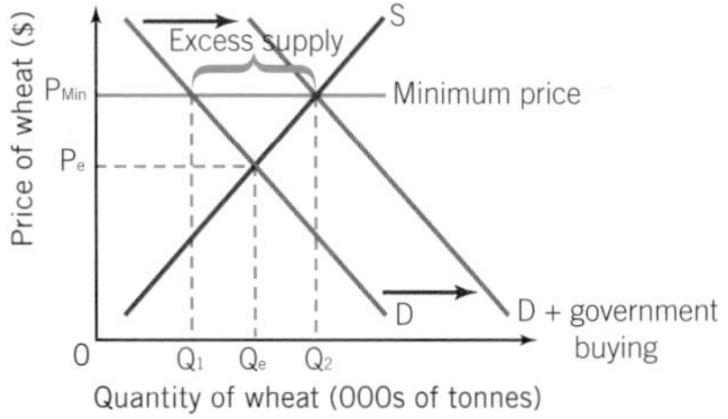

▲ **Figure 8.10** Government action to solve the problem of excess supply

The government could then store the surplus, destroy it or attempt to sell it abroad. However, storage tends to be rather expensive and destroying products is considered to be wasteful. Selling abroad is always an option, but it often causes angry reactions from the foreign governments involved, who claim that products are being dumped on their markets and will harm their domestic industries.

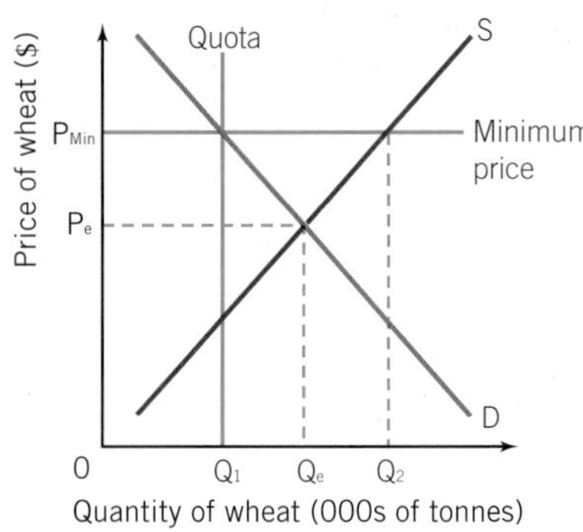

▲ **Figure 8.11** A quota to maintain a minimum price

There is bound to be an opportunity cost whenever governments spend money in any given area. In this case, the cost of buying up and storing surpluses must be paid and so the government may well have to cut back on expenditure in some other area, such as funding for teacher training, or raise taxes.

There are two other ways that the minimum price can be maintained. First, producers could be limited by quotas, restricting supply so that it does not exceed Q_1. This is shown in Figure 8.11. This would keep price at P_{Min}, but would mean that only a limited number of producers would receive it.

Second, the government could attempt to increase demand for the product by advertising or, if appropriate, by restricting supplies of the product that are being imported, through protectionist policies, thus increasing demand for domestic products.

If governments do protect firms by guaranteeing minimum prices, problems are likely to occur. Firms may think that they do not have to be as cost-conscious as they should be and this may lead to inefficiency and a waste of resources. It may also lead to firms producing more of the protected product than they should and less of other products that they could produce more efficiently.

Are minimum prices only implemented to help producers or workers?

No! Typically, we assume that minimum prices are imposed to help certain producers who would struggle to survive by selling at the equilibrium price or to help workers who might not be able to afford a decent standard of living if they were paid the equilibrium wage. However, there are examples where governments have set minimum prices to prevent people from consuming a product in order to help them to make better choices. Two examples where minimum prices are used to reduce consumption are the cases of alcohol and cigarettes.

Consider the example of minimum prices on alcohol. It may be the case that certain types of alcohol are very affordable (ie very inexpensive), resulting in overconsumption and problems affecting those people who drink too much alcohol. Overconsumption of alcohol can also obviously result in larger problems for society. (This is known as a "market failure" and will be addressed in much more detail in the next chapter.)

To prevent suppliers such as supermarkets from selling alcohol at low prices, governments might set a minimum price above the market equilibrium price, thereby forcing suppliers to sell at a higher price.

Such a policy might be very important from society's point of view, but consumers who enjoy the product, and producers who profit from the sale of the product, will certainly be against such government intervention.

Exercise 8.5

Read the following text and answer the questions which follow:

Scotland ends cheap booze as minimum price starts

Adapted from BBC, May 1, 2018, https://www.bbc.com/news/uk-scotland-43948081

The price of cheap, high-strength alcohol has gone up in Scotland as long-awaited legislation on minimum pricing comes into force. The law, which sets a floor price for drinks depending on how many units of alcohol they contain, was passed five years ago but could not be brought into effect because of ongoing legal battles with the Scotch Whisky Association. The government has called the new law a significant step in tackling Scotland's "unhealthy relationship" with alcohol and said that the move would cut consumption and save lives.

The government said the idea was to target booze that attracted problem drinkers. It has been concerned that a two-litre bottle of strong cider (7.5 abv), which contained more than the weekly recommended limit for alcohol (14 units), could be bought for as little as £2.50. It will now cost at least £7.50. Own-brand vodka, gin and whisky will also rise in price by as much as £3 a bottle, as will some cheap wines and multi-pack beers. The new law is not a tax and any extra revenue from higher prices will go to the supermarkets.

Scotland's Health Secretary has said: "This policy targets hazardous and harmful drinkers. It is geared towards making sure that by increasing the price, we will reduce consumption."

The medical profession has welcomed the move. Figures show that more than 80% of assault victims in hospital emergency departments had been drinking, as had the people who had assaulted them.

One spokesperson from the medical profession has said: "Young people will start drinking at an early age and inevitably they don't have a lot of money to do that. So they are probably drinking the cheap alcohol. The new law will make that much more expensive. We are not aiming to get the whole population to stop drinking but it will have an impact on the people who are currently experiencing the most harm. The hope is that the higher price will be a real disincentive to them."

1. Using an appropriate diagram, explain the effect of the minimum price on "strong cider". Be sure to use actual numbers from the text on your diagram.
2. Which stakeholders are likely to benefit from the minimum price policy? Why?
3. Which stakeholders are likely to suffer from the minimum price policy? Why?

Economics in action

ATL Thinking, Communication and Research

The example of wheat as a minimum price, used above, is hypothetical and is there to help us understand the theory.

Conduct an investigation to find a real-world example of a minimum price. As part of your investigation, you should try to:

- identify the reasons for the government intervention
- illustrate the market on a diagram
- discuss the advantages and disadvantages for relevant stakeholders
- link your analysis to one or more of the nine key concepts.

Exercise 8.6

ATL Thinking, Communication and Research

A government wishes to increase earnings for those workers who are on low wages, by introducing minimum wage legislation in order to raise wage levels above the equilibrium wage. In doing this, they aim to:

- ensure higher wages for low-paid workers
- increase the number of workers employed.

1. Draw a diagram to show the effect of the minimum wage legislation on the market for low-paid workers.
2. Explain the consequences of the minimum wage for the workers.
3. Explain the situation facing the employers.
4. Suggest measures that the government might take to ensure that they achieve both of their stated aims above.

Exercise 8.7

ATL Thinking and Communication

Below is the market for carrots in a country.

The government of the country decides to impose a legal price floor of $3.00 per bushel of carrots.

1. Indicate the original equilibrium price and quantity on the graph.
2. Show the price floor on the diagram.
3. Explain how many carrots will be demanded and supplied following the imposition of the price floor.
4. Calculate the change in producer revenue from carrots following the imposition of the price floor.
5. Explain two measures that the government may take to achieve their aim of giving more revenue to the carrot farmers.

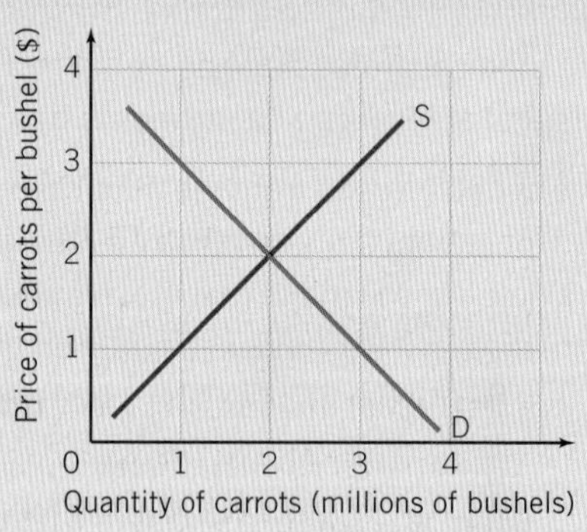

EXAMINATION QUESTIONS

Paper 1, full questions

1. a) Explain the possible effect on consumers and producers when a specific tax is imposed on cigarettes. [10 marks]

   b) Using real-world examples, evaluate the possible outcomes of imposing such a tax. [15 marks]

2. a) Explain why a government might grant a subsidy to producers of wheat. [10 marks]

   b) Using real-world examples, discuss the consequences of such a subsidy. [15 marks]

3. a) Explain the role of prices in allocating resources in an economy. [10 marks]

   b) Using real-world examples, discuss the consequences of the setting of a maximum price in a market. [15 marks]

So why do governments intervene in markets?

In this chapter, we have looked at four types of government **intervention** in markets. In the next chapter, we will extend our analysis of government intervention to look at further situations where markets fail to achieve socially efficient levels of output.

While there is much controversy surrounding the issue of government intervention, with free market economists often opposed to the types and extent of government intervention, it is valuable to look at some of the reasons for government intervention in the context of some key concepts.

1. To help consumers make better **choices**
   - Indirect taxes reduce the quantity of a product sold in a market, and so will make certain goods less attractive. This can help to achieve a government's goal of reducing the consumption of goods which may be harmful to consumers.
   - Minimum prices to increase the price of goods that are harmful to consumers will discourage them from buying as much of the product.
   - Subsidies on healthy products will make them more affordable and give consumers the incentive to increase their consumption.
2. To promote **sustainability**
   - Indirect taxes may be imposed on production processes or products that threaten sustainability. Taxes such as carbon taxes which raise the costs of production may encourage firms to produce using more sustainable practices.
   - Subsidies may be given to producers whose production methods or final goods are favourable to the environment.
3. To promote **equity** and **economic well being**
   - Minimum wages are one way of trying to ensure that workers earn a **fair** payment for their labour.
   - Minimum prices are one way of trying to ensure that producers earn a fair payment for their products.
   - Maximum prices on necessity goods and rental accommodation may make such things affordable for low income households.

Data response exercise

This data response exercise is similar to what you will encounter in your IB examination in Paper 2. Remember that you answer one question that has question parts ranging from (a) to (g). Question 1 is similar to question part (a). Question 2 is similar to question part (b). Question 3 is similar to questions parts (c) to (f), and question 4 is similar to question part (g).

Read the text below and answer the questions that follow:

Assessment advice

If the market is given to you in part (a), as in the market for cigarettes in question 1(a), you should state any assumptions that you might make in answering the question. In this case, since the incidence of an indirect tax varies according to the price elasticity of demand, you would need to state your assumption about the nature of the price elasticity of demand for cigarettes.

Please note that in essay question 3 the two parts of the question come from different chapters. You must be aware that question setters try to cover different areas of the syllabus within questions and therefore you must be able to make links between the different topics. Since one of the core concepts in economics is the allocation of scarce resources, this is a topic that you should try to include in all different topics/chapters.

Key concept

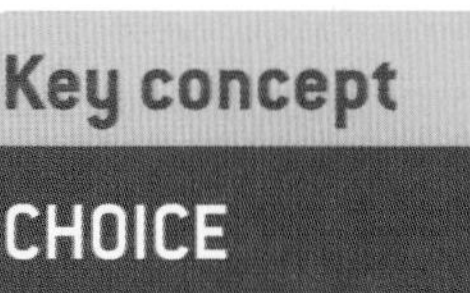

CHOICE

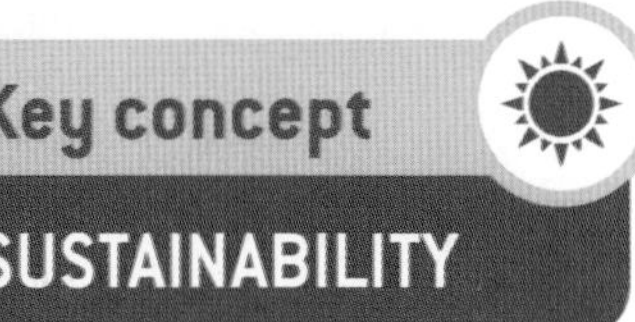

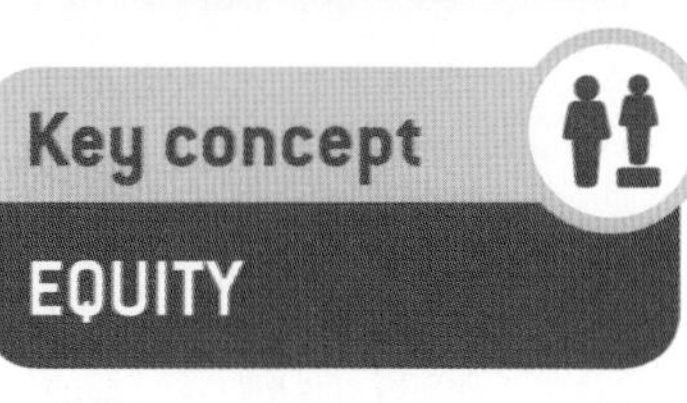

Group urges Oregon to hike cigarette taxes $2 a pack

The American Cancer Society Cancer Action Network (ACS CAN) urged Oregon lawmakers to prioritize and pass a $2 tobacco tax increase on all tobacco products, including electronic cigarettes, in the 2019 session.

Governor Kate Brown's 2019 budget includes this **indirect tax** increase to fund the state's Medicaid program, the organization said in a news release, which continues below.

"Oregon has not raised its tobacco tax significantly since 2002. Our cigarette tax is $1.33 per pack, which ranks us 32nd in the nation and is not high enough to have a significant public health benefit and reduce tobacco use," said an Oregon government relations director for ACS CAN. "For a state that prides itself on being so healthy, we should not be toward the bottom of the pack."

Data from ACS CAN shows Oregon has room to improve on several key tobacco control efforts to fight cancer, including its tobacco tax. Increasing the price of tobacco products with regular and significant tax increases is proven to help people quit and prevent kids from starting.

New projections from ACS CAN show the tremendous public health benefits of increasing the **specific tax** on cigarettes by $2:

- 31,300 adults who currently smoke would quit;
- 19,200 kids under age 18 would not become new daily smokers;
- Youth smoking rates would decrease nearly 21 percent;
- 13,700 lives would be saved from a premature smoking-related death.

Tobacco use is the No. 1 cause of preventable death and disease and each year, 5,500 Oregonians die from smoking. Roughly 28 percent of all cancer deaths in Oregon are caused by smoking, the group said.

Tobacco use remains Oregon's and the nation's leading cause of preventable death and disease, taking an estimated 480,000 lives every year in the U.S., according to a report released Tuesday night by the American Lung Association.

This year's "State of Tobacco Control" report finds that Oregon earned failing grades on its efforts to reduce and prevent tobacco use. The organization called on the Oregon Legislature to increase tobacco taxes and use the tax revenue to adequately fund anti-smoking projects, such as increased negative advertising.

The need for Oregon to protect youth from tobacco is more urgent than ever, the group said, with youth e-cigarette use reaching epidemic levels due to a 78 percent increase in high school e-cigarette use from 2017 to 2018, according to the Centers for Disease Control and Prevention.

That equals one million additional kids beginning to use e-cigarettes, placing their developing bodies at risk from the chemicals in e-cigarettes, as well as a lifetime of deadly addiction.

"Tobacco use is a serious addiction and we need to invest in the proven measures to prevent and reduce tobacco use," said the Senior Director of Advocacy for the American Lung Association in Oregon. "The 'State of Tobacco Control' report provides evidence-based policies that are proven to reduce tobacco use and save lives."

Increasing tobacco taxes is one of the most effective ways to reduce tobacco use, not only among low-income individuals but also for youth. Multiple studies have shown that every 10 percent increase in the price of cigarettes reduces consumption by about 4 percent among adults and about 7 percent among youth.

"To protect youth from a lifetime of nicotine addiction, the Lung Association in Oregon encourages Oregon legislators to increase tobacco taxes by $2 per pack. This step is critical as current tobacco use among youth is skyrocketing," said Nyssen.

Source: Adapted from "Group urges Oregon to hike cigarette taxes $2 a pack", *KTVZ.COM news sources,* Posted: Jan 29, 2019

https://www.ktvz.com/news/group-urges-oregon-to-hike-cigarette-taxes-2-a-pack/995101133

1. Define the following terms indicated in bold in the text:
   a. Indirect tax [2 marks]
   b. Specific tax [2 marks]
2. a. Using information from the text (paragraph 12), calculate the price elasticity of demand for adult smokers and the price elasticity of demand for youth smokers. [2 marks]
   b. Draw a demand and supply diagram to show how increased negative advertising (paragraph 8) might affect the market for cigarettes. [3 marks]
3. Using a demand and supply diagram, explain how the increased $2 tax on cigarettes will affect the market for cigarettes in Oregon. [4 marks]
4. Using real-world examples, discuss the likely effects on the market for cigarettes of the changes in legislation suggested in the article. [15 marks]

9 MARKET FAILURE

REAL-WORLD ISSUE:
When are markets unable to satisfy important economic objectives and does government intervention help?

By the end of this chapter, you should be able to:

- → Define market failure
- → Explain and give examples of merit goods, demerit goods and public goods
- → Define, distinguish between, illustrate and give examples of positive and negative externalities of production and consumption
- → Explain and give examples of the meaning of common pool resources
- → Explain and evaluate policies available to governments in response to externalities and common pool resources
- → Discuss the importance of international cooperation in addressing sustainability
- HL Explain, using examples, asymmetric information as a market failure.

Why do governments put regulations on the amount of permissible CO_2 emissions? Why do governments build public sporting facilities? Why do governments ban certain drugs? You most certainly have opinions in response to each of these questions. In this chapter, you will learn how to approach such issues using economic theory.

In the "real world" markets are not perfect. That is, they are not allocatively efficient (see Chapter 7). There are a number of things that prevent markets from being perfect and, therefore, from allocating resources in an optimal manner. If this is the case, then community surplus is not maximized and we say that this is a market failure. When markets fail, governments are often expected to intervene in order to attempt to eliminate the market failure and move towards the optimal allocation of resources.

We need to look at the reasons why markets might fail and the possible options that governments have to try to correct that failure.

Why is the existence of externalities a market failure?

An externality occurs when the production or consumption of a good or service has an effect upon a third party. If the effect is harmful, then we talk about a *negative externality*. This means that there is an external cost that must be added to the private costs of the producer or consumer to reflect the full cost to society. If the effect is beneficial, then we talk about a *positive externality*. This means that there has been an external benefit to add to the private benefits of the producer or consumer.

We have already come across marginal social cost (MSC) in Chapter 7. MSC is equal to marginal private cost (MPC) plus or minus any external cost or benefit of production. If there are no externalities of production, then MSC = MPC. The MPC is essentially the "private" supply curve that is based on the firm's costs of production.

We have also come across marginal social benefit (MSB). MSB is equal to marginal private benefit (MPB) plus or minus any external cost or benefit of consumption. If there are no externalities of consumption then MSB = MPB. The MPB is essentially the "private" demand curve that is based on the utility or benefits to consumers.

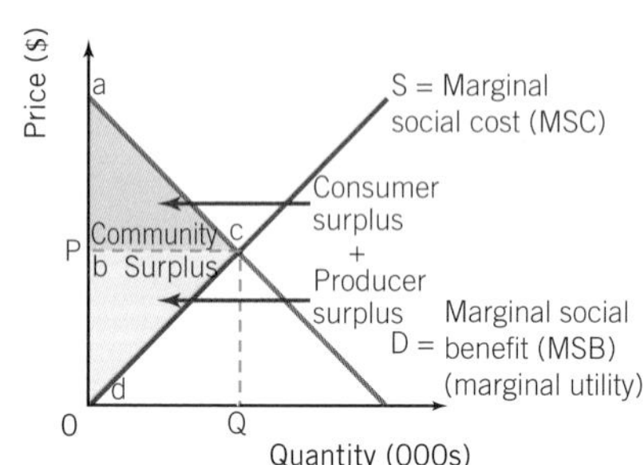

▲ **Figure 9.1** Social efficiency

Thus, if no externalities exist in a market, then MSC = MSB and we have social efficiency and so maximum community surplus, as in Figure 9.1. If externalities do exist, then MSC does not equal MSB and so we have a market failure and an inefficient allocation of society's resources.

Externalities may be split into four types.

What are positive externalities of consumption?

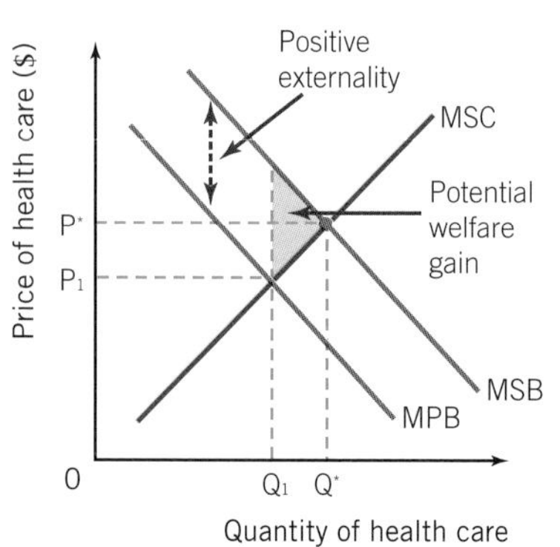

▲ **Figure 9.2** A positive externality of consumption

There are certain goods or services which, when consumed (used) are beneficial to those who consume them, but will also provide external benefits to third parties. For example, when people "consume" health care, they aim to make their own health better but they also create a positive externality for society. If people are healthier, then they will not pass on illnesses to other people. A healthier workforce means a higher level of human capital, which means that the economy will be more productive. This may be to the benefit of the whole population. Thus, the marginal social benefit of consuming health care is greater than the marginal private benefit enjoyed by the consumers themselves. This is shown in Figure 9.2.

Key concept
EQUITY

Key concept
ECONOMIC WELLBEING

In a free market for health care, people will consume where the marginal social cost (in effect, the supply curve) meets the marginal private benefit curve (in effect, the demand curve) at the quantity Q_1 and price of P_1. However, the socially efficient, or socially optimum, level of consumption would be Q*, where MSB = MSC. There is a potential welfare gain, shown by the shaded triangle, because for the units from Q_1 to Q*, MSB is greater than MSC. We say that the market fails because too little of the product is produced; there is an *underallocation* of resources to this market. If the consumption of health care increases from Q_1 towards Q*, then welfare in society will increase. (This potential welfare gain is also known as a *welfare loss* as society is losing the welfare that would be achieved if the market was operating at the socially efficient level.)

Another important example of a positive externality of consumption is education, which has a significant effect on the well being of society when its consumption is increased. Health care and education are both examples of *merit goods*.

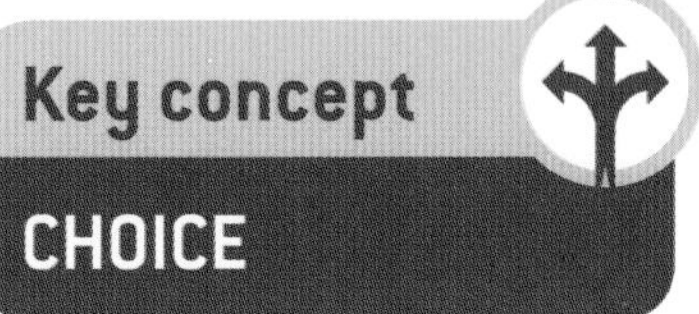

Merit goods

Merit goods are goods that are beneficial to consumers, but people might not consume them enough, either because they underestimate the potential benefits or because they choose to ignore the potential benefits. That is, consumers have imperfect information about the potential benefits. Therefore, the demand for the good is lower than it "should" be from society's perspective.

Governments aim to bring about an increase in the quantity of merit goods consumed. This will benefit the consumers themselves, but more importantly, higher consumption will bring higher benefits to society as a whole.

Some examples of merit goods and their possible private and social benefits are given below:

Product	Possible private benefits	Possible benefits to society as a whole
A university education in engineering	The joys of pursuing a career in a chosen field. Better job prospects.	More people educated in engineering at university may contribute to important technological innovations.
Measles vaccines	Less risk of contracting measles. Better health.	If a certain percentage of the population is immunized against measles, then it reduces the risk of a measles outbreak.
Sports facilities	Enjoyment of physical activity. Better health.	A "fitter" population is a more productive population.

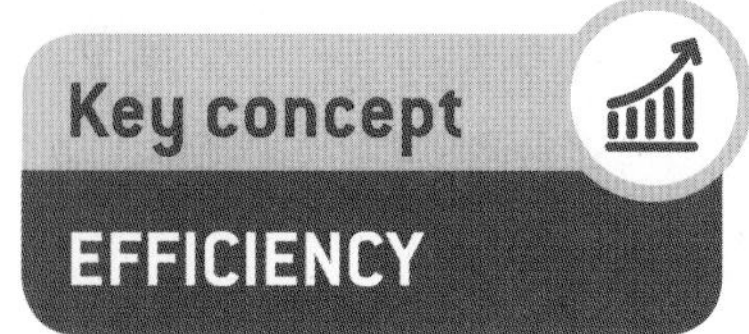

It is worth drawing a link to the Production Possibilities Curve (PPC) model in Chapter 1. Any improvement in the quality and quantity of an economy's factors of production will shift out the PPC, increasing the economy's production possibilities. By this reasoning, we can see that any improvements in the health and education of an economy's population will improve the quality of labour, thereby shifting the PPC with potential benefits for the well being of the whole economy.

In this presentation of the essential theory, the examples of health care and education are very broad indeed. Each category could be broken into a large number of smaller markets. For example, under the general topic of health care, one could talk about positive externalities of consuming measles vaccines or flu injections or anti-malaria tablets, or prostate cancer screening or dementia screening. Any sub-market within the healthcare industry may be seen to create benefits, not only for the consumers themselves but for society as a whole because it benefits from healthier citizens. Under education, one could examine the positive externalities of kindergarten education, high school education, tertiary education, education for girls, adult education and so on. Any sub-market within the education industry can be seen to create benefits not only for those people getting the education, but also for society as a whole that benefits from better educated citizens. Any one of these sub-markets would make an interesting area for investigation.

Key concept
INTERVENTION

How can the government achieve the potential welfare gain related to positive externalities of consumption and an under consumption of merit goods?

If a government wishes to increase the consumption of merit goods that create positive externalities of consumption, then there is a number of options. We examine the possible policies in the context of the overall healthcare market. You should then be able find other relevant examples to which you can apply the theory.

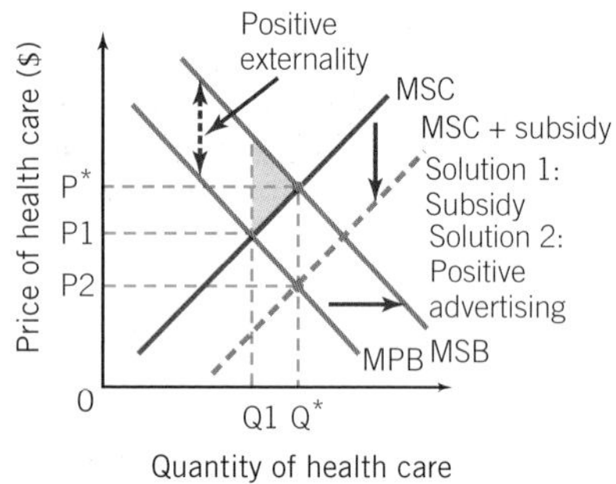

▲ Figure 9.3 Measures to promote positive externalities of consumption

- *Subsidies (or direct provision by the government)* – The government could subsidize the supply of health care. This is shown in Figure 9.3. A subsidy would shift the MSC curve downwards and, in this way, the socially efficient level of consumption at Q_1 could be reached, with a price of P_2. Indeed, it may be that the government deems the importance of health care to be so great that it will subsidize it to the point where it is free to the consumer, or the state will supply it at no direct cost to the consumer.

One key problem with such a solution is cost and the opportunity cost involved. As you know, governments have limited resources and must make choices about how to allocate their budgets. Any increase in any aspect of spending on health care is likely to require a cut in spending elsewhere.

Political considerations should also be taken into account. We must not make the assumption that spending on health care is always and everywhere a government priority. Different political parties might take different stands on their government's responsibility to provide it. Another political consideration is the time involved in making and changing government policy. This is even more the case if there is a change in government following an election.

- *Improving information about the benefits of the products through public awareness campaigns* – Since consumers might have imperfect information about the potential benefits of consuming a particular merit good, the government could use public awareness campaigns to make people more aware of the benefits. This would shift the MPB curve to the right, towards the MSB curve, and would thus increase welfare.

  The problem here is that there may be a high cost to providing the advertising and, although the effect may be beneficial in the long run, it takes a long time to have an effect and so the short-run benefits may be minimal.

- *Legislation* – The government could pass laws insisting that citizens have vaccinations against certain diseases, or have regular health checks, but this will only be successful if the government provides the service free of charge. Also, people often resent laws of this sort being imposed by the government. They may see it as an infringement of their civil liberties.

  The extent to which the government will intervene depends on the external benefits, and of course there are always challenges in being able to accurately measure these. In the case of merit goods, such as health care and education, the positive externalities are significant. Indeed, economic growth is heavily dependent on the productivity of labour, which is of course dependent on the education and health of the people. Therefore, it is generally a government priority to have an effective system for providing education and health care. The extent to which this is done through direct provision by the government or through the private sector will vary from country to country. This highlights one of the central themes of economics which is the extent to which governments should intervene in the allocation of resources.

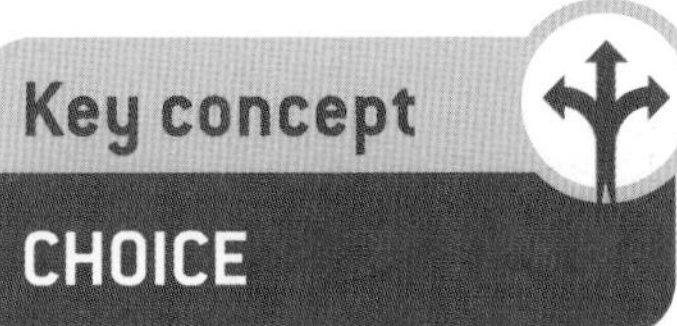

Economics in action

ATL Thinking, Communication and Research

At the time of writing, there has been considerable international attention given to the topic of measles vaccines and whether or not they should be compulsory. Using the economic theory that you have learned, evaluate the view that governments **should** make it compulsory for all children to be immunized against measles. (To do this, you will need to be aware of the arguments **against** compulsory immunizations.)

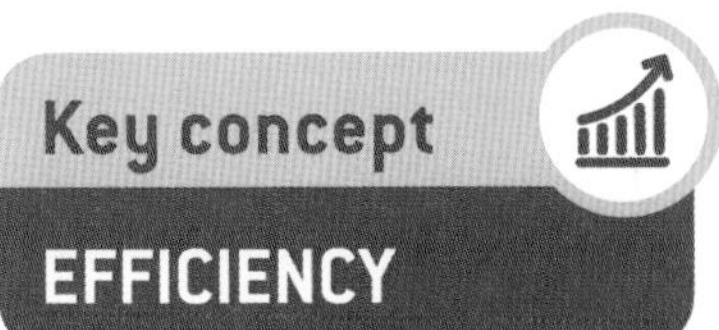

What are positive externalities of production/external benefits?

These occur when the production of a good or service creates external benefits that are favourable for third parties. Let us suppose that a large printing firm provides high-quality training for its employees. This is a cost to the firm. When employees leave the printing firm and go to other firms, there is a benefit to the other firms who do not have to spend money on training their new workers. This is a positive externality of production to the new firms. Society has gained from the training given by the printing firm, even though the firm itself has not. Thus the marginal private cost of the firm is greater than the marginal social cost. This is shown in Figure 9.4.

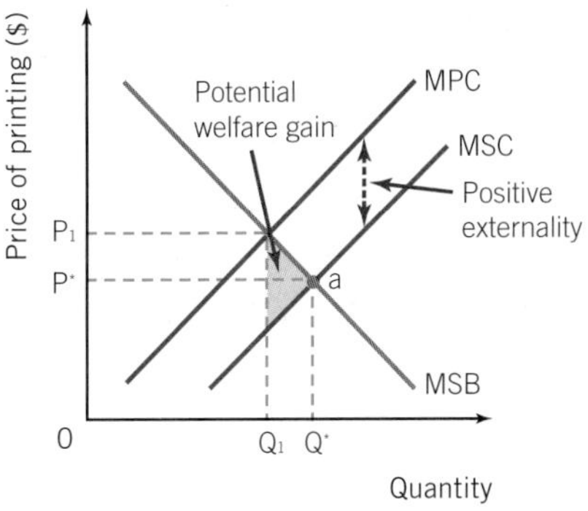

▲ Figure 9.4 A positive externality of production

As we can see, the printing firm produces where its marginal private costs (in effect, the supply curve) meet the marginal social benefits (in effect, the demand curve) at a level of output, Q_1. This is below the socially efficient level, Q*. Between Q_1 and Q* there is a *potential welfare gain* shown by the shaded triangle. If output could be increased to Q* then welfare would be gained, because for all the units from Q_1 to Q*, MSB is greater than MSC. (This is also known as a *welfare loss,* as society is losing the welfare that would be achieved if the market was operating at the socially efficient level.) Again, this is a market failure because in a pure free market, there would be an under allocation of resources to this market. Firms will not want to engage in as much training as would be desirable, from society's point of view.

How can the government achieve the potential welfare gain related to positive externalities of production?

The government has a number of policy options:

- *Subsidies* – The government could subsidize firms that offer training. If this were to happen, then the MPC curve would be shifted downwards by the subsidy and, if a full subsidy were given, then MPC would be the same as MSC and the socially efficient point "a" would be reached.

  There are two main problems with this solution. First, it is very difficult for the government to estimate the level of subsidy deserved by every individual firm. Second, the cost of the subsidies would imply an opportunity cost. The government would be forced to make a **choice** about its spending, and cut back on spending in other areas.

- *Direct provision* – The government could provide vocational training through the state, by setting up training centres for workers in certain industries.

  Although this is a possibility, the costs would be high, the trainers may lack the expertise found in the firms, and it may dissuade firms from offering training of their own.

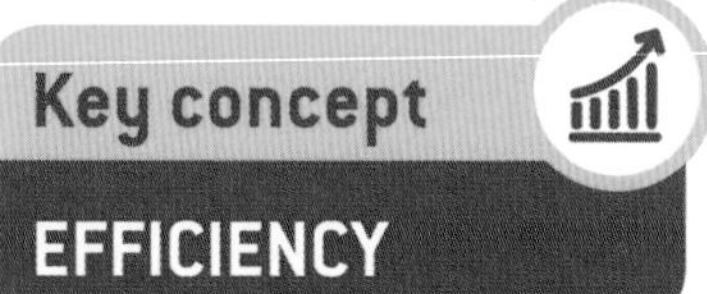

Regardless of the costs, or who pays these costs, economies benefit enormously from the training and retraining of labour. Any improvements in the quality of labour, a factor of production, can shift out an economy's PPC. Later, we will also see that as technological change is rapidly changing the nature of employment, replacing many workers with machinery, it is extremely important that workers are provided with retraining opportunities. Without systems in place to provide these opportunities, there is a grave risk that people who lose their jobs due to changing technologies will remain unemployed and see reductions in their economic well being.

What are negative externalities of consumption?

Key concept

EQUITY

There are many things that, when they are consumed by individuals, adversely affect third parties. Examples of this would be cigarettes and "second-hand smoking", petrol or diesel for driving cars and air pollution, and alcohol and anti-social behaviour. The negative externalities of consumption produced here mean that the marginal social benefits in each case are less than the marginal private benefits. The private utility is diminished by the negative utility suffered by the third parties. This is shown in Figure 9.5 with cigarettes as an example.

People who smoke choose to do so because they enjoy some private benefits of smoking. However, this will reduce the benefits (create losses) for other people through passive smoking, or second-hand smoking. Other than simple discomfort at the smell of cigarettes, the costs to others are significant and include lung cancer, bronchial illnesses and asthma, to name a few. Because there is a free market, consumers will maximize their private utility (benefit) and consume at the level where MSC = MPB. They will ignore the negative externality that they are creating. This means that they will over-consume cigarettes by smoking Q_1 cigarettes at a price of P_1. The socially efficient output is at Q^* and so there is over-consumption of Q_1 to Q^*. Since MSC is greater than MSB for these units, there is a welfare loss to society and a market failure. Too many resources are allocated to this market and the good is over-produced.

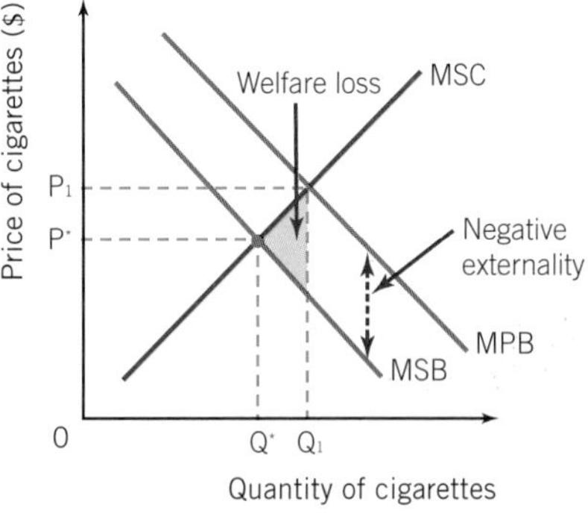

▲ Figure 9.5 A negative externality of consumption

There are many products whose consumption creates significant environmental problems that impact others today, and through the impact on the environment are also creating threats to sustainability. For example, the waste that is created and the greenhouse gases that are emitted from consuming goods and services are negative externalities of consumption. This may be seen as a situation of inter-generational inequity, as our actions today are damaging the ability of future generations to meet their needs.

Demerit goods

Demerit goods are goods that are harmful to consumers, but people who consume them are either unaware of the possible harm, or they ignore the possible risks. That is, consumers have imperfect information about the potential costs to themselves, and to others. Therefore, the demand for the good is higher than it "should" be from society's perspective. Demerit goods also create negative externalities when they are consumed.

It is worth noting that not all goods that create negative externalities of consumption are demerit goods. For example, the petrol that is consumed when a car is driven causes external costs for third parties as a result of the emissions, but it does not cause a particularly harmful effect to the driver. Therefore, petrol is not considered to be a demerit good.

Governments aim to bring about a reduction in the quantity of demerit goods consumed. This will benefit the consumers themselves, but more importantly lower consumption will reduce the welfare loss to society as a whole.

Examples of demerit goods:

Product	Examples of the possible harm to the consumer	Examples of the possible harm to third parties
Cigarettes	Respiratory illnesses, cancer, death, damage to unborn children.	Unpleasant smell (small cost). All the same problems as the harm to consumers as a result of passive smoking.
Alcohol	Health consequences, such as hangovers, liver disease, high blood pressure.	Problems to society as a result of excessive (binge) drinking, such as aggressive behaviour, domestic violence, costs of medical care.
Unhealthy food (eg sugary drinks, food with high sugar or fat content)	Possible health consequences, such as high blood pressure, problems associated with being overweight.	Health care costs are borne by society.

How can the government reduce or eliminate the welfare loss related to negative externalities of consumption and an overconsumption of demerit goods?

The government will act to reduce or eliminate the negative externality and, once again, there is a number of policy options. Let's examine the possible policies in the context of the cigarette market. Then you will be asked to carry out your own case study.

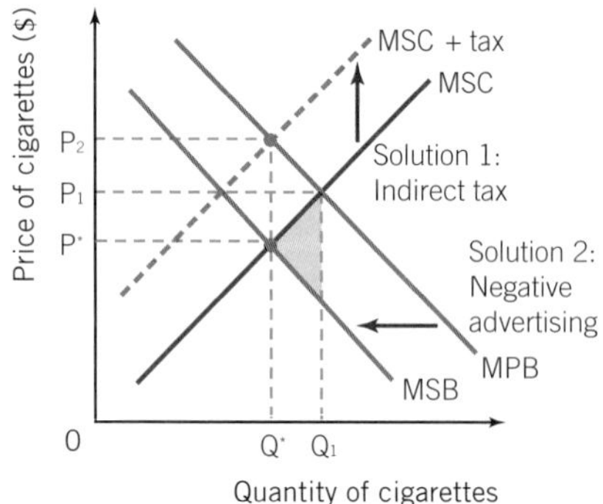

▲ Figure 9.6 Measures to reduce negative externalities of consumption

- *Market based approach: Indirect taxes:* The government could impose a Pigouvian tax on cigarettes, in order to reduce consumption. A Pigouvian tax is an indirect tax that is imposed on any market that creates negative externalities, in order to eliminate the externality. This is shown in Figure 9.6. If the government imposes an indirect tax, then that will shift the MSC curve upwards to MSC + tax. This will reduce consumption to the socially efficient level of output Q*, but the price to the consumers will be P_2. The government will gain significant revenue and this may be used to correct some of the negative externalities caused by smoking.

  However, the inelastic demand for cigarettes (and other demerit goods) tends to mean that taxes do not manage to reduce quantity demanded very much and so, while government revenue is raised, quantity demanded does not fall to the socially efficient level.

  Also, if taxes are raised too much then experience suggests that people start to look for other sources of supply, where the product is cheaper. If neighbouring jurisdictions have lower taxes, then it may be easy for consumers to travel to purchase the product elsewhere. If this happens, not only is consumption not reduced, but the government does not gain the tax revenues.

A significant criticism of indirect taxes is that they are *regressive*. That is, their impact is greater on lower income people than higher income people. Higher income and lower income people pay the same amount of tax, but this takes up a larger proportion of income from lower income people. Thus, they are criticised for being inequitable.

- *Legislation/regulation*: Another approach is to create legislation (laws) and regulations to alter the behaviour of consumers. This is known as a "command and control" approach. In the example of cigarette smoking, there are several examples of laws which reduce the demand for cigarettes, such as age restrictions, bans on smoking in public places, laws about advertising tobacco products and laws about cigarette packaging.

  Increased regulations or legislations may be met with opposition from those who argue that they take away the rights of consumers to choose for themselves.

  When regulations are effective in changing the behaviour of consumers, this will have a negative effect on the producers of the product. In many cases, this causes the producers of the product to lobby the government to prevent them from bringing in new legislation. For example, when governments have tried to implement new legislation to reduce the demand for cigarettes, large cigarette companies have used their lobbying power and legal teams to prevent them from doing so.

  Regulations may also be difficult to enforce; it will be necessary for the government to allocate resources to ensure that stakeholders comply with regulations, and have mechanisms in place to punish those who do not comply.

Note

It is worth looking up the term "nanny state" to see how people object to governments telling them how to behave!

Exercise 9.1

ATL Thinking and Communication

Paper 2 – 4 mark question

New York City bans alcohol advertisements on city property

New York City has banned the use of alcohol advertisements on public properties such as bus shelters, newsstands, recycling bins and Wi-Fi kiosks. Public officials have said that the loss of $2.7 million in alcohol advertisement revenues is justified by the costs of overconsumption.

Using an MSC/MSB diagram, explain what New York City officials hope to accomplish by the ban on advertising.

- Education/raising awareness: Given that in the real world, consumers do not necessarily have perfect information of the damage that demerit goods might cause them, it is possible that governments could increase the information available to consumers by using the education system (a longer-term solution) or funding public awareness campaigns in order to reduce demand, thus shifting the MPB curve to the left, as shown in Figure 9.6. Ideally, revenues gained from the taxes placed on cigarettes could be used to finance the necessary spending to raise awareness.

  In addition to the costs involved, there is some doubt as to the effectiveness of education and public awareness campaigns in terms of reducing cigarette consumption. Many teenagers, for example, seem prepared to accept the dangers of smoking and are little affected by measures to put them off. Behavioural economics examines this seemingly irrational behaviour by consumers and has several explanations. It is possible that consumers are aware of the potential risks, but manage to convince themselves that they will not be affected. Or, they reason that the consequence will be felt too far in the future to worry about it.

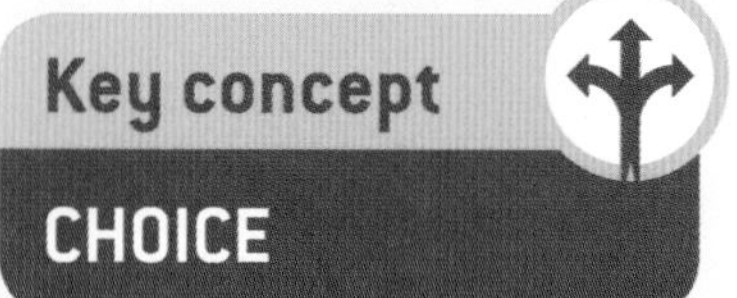

Higher Level

- Consumer nudges: Behavioural economics has shown that consumers do not always have perfect information and do not always make rational choices. They may be poor at judging the utility of a product when the benefits are enjoyed in the present, while the consequences might not occur for some time. Consumers are also subject to peer pressure and enjoy conforming to things that appear to be enjoyed by others in society. Consumers also have limited will power. In short, consumers do not always have perfect information and do not always make rational choices. Governments and other organizations have much work to do in encouraging people to make better choices, so that their own well being is improved, as well as the well being of society as a whole.

  The work of behavioural economics has been prominent in getting governments to use "consumer nudges" to encourage consumers to reduce their consumption *voluntarily*.

  In the case of cigarettes, research showed that cigarette companies were using innovative design of cigarette packages as a form of advertising to get around advertising bans. As a result, laws have been put into place requiring cigarette packs to be a plain dull colour, with graphic images (rather than simple warnings) showing the dangers of smoking. This is designed to nudge consumers to choose not to smoke. The idea behind nudge theory is that consumers still have their freedom of choice, but they are nudged to choose differently. Not surprisingly, the cigarette industry has mounted massive campaigns against governments choosing this approach, arguing that it is taking away **their** freedom to pursue profits.

Economics in action ATL Thinking, Communication and Research

There are many examples of products which create negative externalities of consumption. These may be related to goods whose consumption creates health problems, or those which create environmental problems. There is actually substantial overlap between the two.

Choose a product whose consumption creates negative externalities and address the following questions to build up a case study.

a. Illustrate how the consumption of your product creates a market failure. Be sure to specify the external costs, and who "pays" these external costs.
b. Investigate different policies that governments have used to reduce this market failure. Try to identify three different policies, noting where these have been implemented.
c. Evaluate the success of these policies, considering the following questions:
    - What barriers did the governments face in trying to implement policies?
    - To what extent have they been successful in reducing consumption?

Economics in action ATL Thinking, Communication and Research

Increasing rates of obesity across the world are a pressing global issue. How can it be seen as an economic problem in the context of market failure? What types of policies are governments implementing to fight obesity?

What are negative externalities of production?

These occur when the production of a good or service creates external costs that are damaging to third parties. These relate mainly, but not exclusively, to environmental problems, where economic activity has resulted in clear threats to sustainability.

This may be argued to occur because, in the absence of government intervention, profit-maximizing producers only take into account their private costs of production and are unconcerned about the costs that may impact upon other people now and in the future.

Let's look at a very simple example to understand the theory. Consider a paint factory that emits fumes which are harmful to people in the area, then there is a cost to the community that is greater than the costs of production paid by the firm. The firm has its private costs but then, on top of that, is creating external costs. Thus, the marginal social cost of the production is greater than the marginal private cost. The marginal social cost is equal to the marginal private cost plus the external costs. This is shown in Figure 9.7.

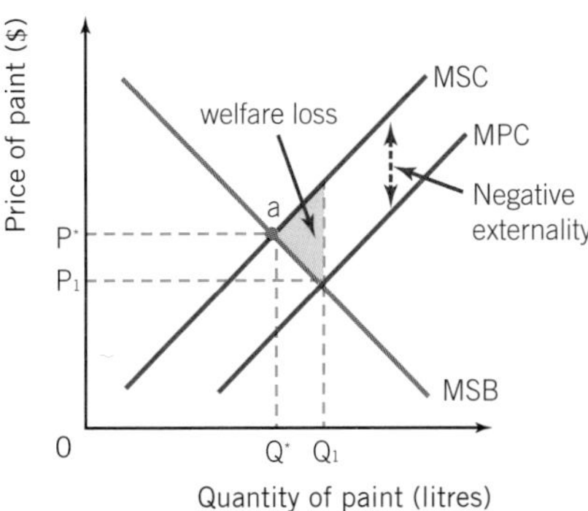

▲ Figure 9.7 A negative externality of production

As we can see, the marginal private costs of the firm are below the marginal social cost, because there is an extra cost to society caused by the pollution that is created, such as respiratory problems for people in the neighbourhood of the polluting firm. The firm will only be concerned with its private costs and will produce at Q_1. It is not producing at the socially efficient output, Q*, where the marginal social cost is equal to the marginal social benefit and so it is a market failure. There is a misallocation of society's resources; too much paint is being produced at too low a price. There is a *welfare loss* to society of the extra units from Q_1 to Q*, because the MSC is greater than the MSB for those units. This is shown by the shaded triangle.

Before we look at how governments may tackle problems associated with negative externalities, we must look at a related issue.

What are common pool resources?

Key concept SUSTAINABILITY

Key concept CHOICE

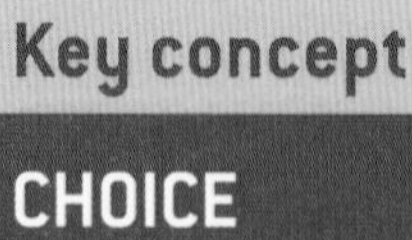

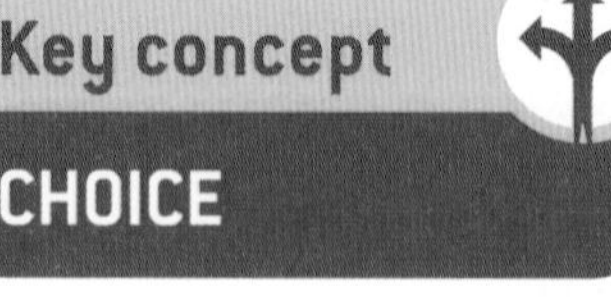

We can link the theory of negative externalities to what are known as *common pool resources*. Common pool resources are typically natural resources, such as fishing grounds, forests and pastures where it is very difficult, or very expensive, to exclude people from using them. Thus, they are considered to be *non-excludable*. In addition, if one person uses the good, it reduces the value of that resource to others. In this sense, common pool resources are said to be *rivalrous*. Because they are non-excludable and rivalrous, the main consequence is that in the absence of effective management, common pool resources are inevitably degraded.

In 1968, biologist Garrett Hardin wrote a paper entitled *The Tragedy of the Commons*, examining the consequences of the non-excludability of common resources. In this work, Hardin challenged the notion that rational decisions by producers and consumers acting in their own self-interest would result in the best possible outcomes for society as a whole.

The tragedy of the commons is best explained with the example given by Hardin. In the example, there are a number of cattle herders, who can all take their cattle to graze on a large area of fertile pasture land that is open to everyone (open access). Acting rationally and wanting to maximize their own self-interest, each cattle herder will want to graze increasing amounts of cattle on the land, since every extra cattle will earn them more money. However, when all the other cattle herders think in the same way, and the number of grazing cattle grows, the overgrazing will result in soil degradation. The previously fertile land will become infertile and be of no use to any of the herders. No individual farmer would take into account the eventual cost of the total destruction of the resource. The cumulative effect of all rational producers acting in their own self-interest results in a fall in social welfare and therefore is a "tragedy of the commons".

> "Each man is locked into a system that compels him to increase his herd without limit – in a world that is limited. Ruin is the destination toward which all men rush, each pursuing his own best interest in a society that believes in the freedom of the commons. Freedom in a commons brings ruin to all."
>
> *Garrett Hardin, The Tragedy of the Commons, 1968*

Some producers might see that this was happening and could voluntarily reduce their production to prevent the degradation of the resource. Yet this would give rise to the "free rider problem". Those that do not change their behaviour would benefit from those who do. In the absence of intervention, a profit-seeking producer would not do this if others were going to continue to reap the benefits.

There are ample examples of the tragedy of the commons. Commercial fishers, taking into account only their own costs of production, have the incentive to catch as many fish as they can, ignoring the external costs. These might include, for example, the collapse of fishing stocks and the ultimate loss of livelihood to fishers in the future, along with many other ecological problems. Profit-seeking forestry companies want access to as much timber as possible, at the lowest private costs, ignoring the external (social and ecological) costs associated with deforestation.

Key concept
EQUITY

This explanation illustrates that the use of common pool resources may be examined in the context of the theory of negative externalities of production, where producers, seeking to minimize their private costs of production impose external costs to others. Not only do the actions of some groups hurt others in the present, but they are damaging the ability of future generations to meet their needs, thus posing threats to sustainability.

Exercise 9.2

ATL Thinking and Communication

Overfishing

Overfishing occurs when more fish are caught than the population can replace through natural reproduction. Gathering as many fish as possible may seem like a profitable practice, but overfishing has serious consequences. The results not only affect the balance of life in the oceans, but also the social and economic well-being of the coastal communities who depend on fish for their way of life.

Billions of people rely on fish for protein, and fishing is the principal livelihood for millions of people around the world. For centuries, our seas and oceans have been considered a limitless bounty of food. However, increasing fishing efforts over the last 50 years as well as unsustainable fishing practices are pushing many fish stocks to the point of collapse.

More than 30 percent of the world's fisheries have been pushed beyond their biological limits and are in need of strict management plans to restore them. Several important commercial fish populations (such as Atlantic bluefin tuna) have declined to the point where their survival as a species is threatened. Target fishing of top predators, such as tuna and groupers, is changing marine communities, which lead to an abundance of smaller marine species, such as sardines and anchovies.

Source: *Overfishing*, WWF, 2019, https://www.worldwildlife.org/threats/overfishing

1. How is overfishing an example of the tragedy of the commons?
2. How is overfishing a threat to sustainability?
3. Use a negative externality of production diagram to explain how overfishing is a market failure.

Did you know?

The 17 UN Sustainable Development Goals (SDGs) obviously include many goals, targets and strategies related to environmental sustainability. We look more closely at the SDGs in Chapter 28. However, we include links to the goals here to highlight the importance of global cooperation in managing common pool resources.

"The world's oceans – their temperature, chemistry, currents and life – drive global systems that make the Earth habitable for humankind. Our rainwater, drinking water, weather, climate, coastlines, much of our food and even the oxygen in the air we breathe are all ultimately provided and regulated by the sea. Throughout history, oceans and seas have been vital conduits for trade and transportation.

Careful management of this essential global resource is a key feature of a sustainable future. However, at the current time, there is a continuous deterioration of coastal waters owing to pollution and ocean acidification is having an adversarial effect on the functioning of ecosystems and biodiversity. This is also negatively impacting small-scale fisheries.

Marine protected areas need to be effectively managed and well-resourced and regulations need to be put in place to reduce overfishing, marine pollution and ocean acidification."

Key concept

SUSTAINABILITY

Why is the atmosphere a common pool resource?

The discussion about common pool resources often centres around the resources that producers can "take out of" the commons, such as grass from the pastures, seafood from the fisheries, water from the groundwater table, timber from the forests. However, we need to also consider how the tragedy of the commons explains degradation and ruin of resources as a result of what is "put into" common pool resources. The world's atmosphere and the oceans are common pool resources. Everyone has access to them, everyone is using them, but the dire threats to sustainability as a result of the pollution and waste that are going into these resources cannot be underestimated.

In Kate Raworth's circular model of the economy (presented in Chapter 2), she demonstrates that the Earth has environmental limits. In effect these limits, or boundaries, relate to our global common pool resources. Raworth identifies eight specific boundaries, including, for example, climate change, biodiversity loss, ocean acidification and chemical pollution. As long as we live within the limits, our ability to live within the Earth's ecosystems is sustainable. However, we are not living within these limits. As she writes:

> "Humanity has been putting Earth's life-giving systems under unprecedented stress. The concentration of carbon dioxide in the atmosphere now far exceeds the [safe] boundary of 350 parts per million (ppm): it is over 400 ppm and still rising, pushing us to a hotter, drier and more hostile climate, along with a rise in sea level that threatens the future of island and coastal cities worldwide. Synthetic fertilizers containing nitrogen and phosphorus are being added to

Earth's soils at more than twice their safe levels. Their toxic run-off has already led to the collapse of aquatic life in many lakes, rivers and oceans, including a dead zone the size of Connecticut in the Gulf of Mexico. Only 62% of land that could be forested still stands as forest and even that land area continues to shrink, significantly reducing Earth's capacity to act as a carbon sink."

Raworth (2017), p. 52.

The climate-change costs that current patterns of resource use are imposing on people all around the world, and on future generations, are clearly unequitable.

How might international agreements reduce or eliminate negative externalities of production and reduce the threats to common pool resources?

Individual governments have incredibly important roles to play in ensuring that their economies reduce their own contributions to environmental threats, but given the global nature of the problems, effective international cooperation and agreements are vital. According to the International Environmental Agreements (IEA) Database Project, an international environmental agreement is "an intergovernmental document intended as legally binding with a primary stated purpose of preventing or managing human impacts on natural resources" (https://iea.uoregon.edu/node/6). There are hundreds and hundreds of international agreements on all aspects of the environment, relating to areas such as fisheries management, marine life, waste management, biological diversity, forest management, nuclear energy, pollution of all kinds and of course climate change. The point is that the "human impact" is the result of economic activities – producing and consuming goods and services. The negative impact imposed by humans can be seen as negative externalities and a threat to the globe's common pool resources.

Given the fact that climate change can be argued as the greatest global environmental threat, we focus here on the international cooperation and international agreements in the area of greenhouse gas emissions.

The United Nations Framework Convention on Climate Change (UNFCCC) provides the framework for international negotiations and agreements. The UNFCCC works with the Intergovernmental Panel on Climate Change (IPCC), which is the international body for assessing the science related to climate change. The IPCC was set up in 1988 to provide policymakers with regular assessments of the scientific basis of climate change, its impacts and future risks, and options for adaptation and mitigation. In 1990, the IPCC released its first report noting that "emissions resulting from human activities are substantially increasing the atmospheric concentrations of greenhouse gases", and this began the process of working towards a global treaty to reduce emissions.

The Kyoto Protocol was the first main agreement made under the UNFCCC. Its objective was to cut global emissions of greenhouse gases (GHGs). The treaty was negotiated in Kyoto, Japan in 1997, and came into force in February 2005. The goal was to cut GHG emissions by 5% between 2008 and 2012, relative to 1990 levels. The agreement mainly targeted the advanced industrialized nations, with developing countries being asked to comply voluntarily. Whilst the Kyoto Protocol had some success in reducing emissions from signatory countries, it was not successful for reducing global emissions. Nonetheless, the process created a foundation for the next international agreement, known as the Paris Agreement.

Key concept
SUSTAINABILITY

In December 2015, all countries of the United Nations Framework Convention on Climate Change met in Paris, and agreed to an historic commitment to *"combat climate change and to accelerate and intensify the actions and investments needed for a sustainable low-carbon future. The Paris Agreement's central aim is to strengthen the global response to the threat of climate change by keeping a global temperature rise this century well below 2 degrees Celsius above pre-industrial levels and to pursue efforts to limit the temperature increase even further to 1.5 degrees Celsius"* (https://unfccc.int/resource/bigpicture/index.html#content-the-paris-agreement).

Along with the targets to reduce emissions, the Paris Agreement also aims to "increase the ability of countries to deal with the impacts of climate change". Within the Paris agreement is the recognition of the interrelationship between human rights and climate change. Human rights include the rights to shelter, access to clean water and nutritious food. Global warming is threatening these human rights for millions of people around the world, particularly in developing countries. Included in the agreement are means to financially support developing countries and the most vulnerable countries.

Theory of knowledge

Language as a way of knowing

The *Guardian* newspaper in the UK has instructed its journalists to change the language they are using when referring to the environment, so that the language more accurately reflects the environmental crises facing the world.

The Editor-in-Chief of the newspaper commented, "We want to ensure that we are being scientifically precise, while also communicating clearly with readers on this very important issue. The phrase 'climate change', for example, sounds rather passive and gentle when what scientists are talking about is a catastrophe for humanity. Increasingly, climate scientists and organisations from the UN to the Met Office are changing their terminology and using stronger language to describe the situation we're in."

https://www.theguardian.com/environment/2019/may/17/why-the-guardian-is-changing-the-language-it-uses-about-the-environment

The following replacements are to be made in the newspaper's articles:

Use:	Instead of:
Climate crisis, climate emergency or climate breakdown	Climate change
Global heating	Global warming
Wildlife	Biodiversity
Fish populations	Fish stocks
Climate science denier	Climate sceptic

1. Explain whether or not you think that the language used by newspapers makes a difference to the way readers understand the issues.
2. Why might the "new" terminology be more effective than the former terminology used by the *Guardian* in terms of conveying the problems?

To meet the goal of limiting the increase in the global temperature, countries have to reduce the amount of emissions being released into the atmosphere, and reduce the current concentration of carbon dioxide by increasing "carbon sinks", such as forested areas. Reducing emissions and increasing sinks is known as "mitigation".

Each country sets its own Nationally Determined Contributions (NDCs) which establish its mitigation goals and plans. Unlike the Kyoto Protocol, which set binding targets, the Paris agreement gives each country the freedom to set its NDCs. Under the agreement, each country is to update its NDCs every five years, and each new target is supposed to show a higher level of commitment to mitigation, ie a lower level of emissions.

We will now look at some of the specific mitigation strategies that can be used to meet the Paris Agreement targets and reduce negative externalities of production.

"Climate change is a result of the greatest market failure the world has seen. The problem of climate change involves a fundamental failure of markets: those who damage others by emitting greenhouse gases generally do not pay. "

– Nicholas Stern, *Stern Review Report on the Economics of Climate Change*, 2006

"Climate change is now affecting every country on every continent. It is disrupting national economies and affecting lives, costing people, communities and countries dearly today and even more tomorrow. Weather patterns are changing, sea levels are rising, weather events are becoming more extreme and greenhouse gas emissions are now at their highest levels in history. Without action, the world's average surface temperature is likely to surpass 3 degrees centigrade this century. The poorest and most vulnerable people are being affected the most."

– https://www.un.org/sustainabledevelopment/climate-change/

How might tradable permits reduce or eliminate negative externalities of production and reduce the threats to common pool resources?

Tradable permits are a market-based approach to reducing negative externalities of production and reducing the ability of people to degrade a common pool resource. In a tradable permit scheme, a governing body sets a limit on the ability of users to access a resource. For example, if the common pool resource is a fishery, the governing body would set a maximum amount of fish that could be caught (allowable catch) that would allow the fish stock to be sustainable. If the common resource is a water supply, then there would be a maximum amount of water that could be extracted. In the case of the atmosphere, there is a maximum amount of greenhouse gases that can be emitted, reducing the ability of people to emit an unlimited amount of gases into the atmosphere. The governing body then divides up and allocates the total amount into individual amounts, which are essentially "permits" to use, or access the resource. Owners of the permit can use the permit themselves, or exchange them in a market. So, for example, a fishing company might be allocated a certain number of fish that it would be permitted to catch. If it did not need to reach this maximum, it could sell the remaining allowance to another fishing company.

We can look at this more closely using the example of tradable permits under the Kyoto Protocol which set up the Emissions Trading Scheme (ETS). It is also known as a "Cap and trade" scheme. Each member accepted a target for limiting or reducing emissions. This was the country's "allowed emissions" or "assigned amounts". The level of allowed emissions was divided into "Assigned Amounts Units" (AAUs), also known as carbon credits.

If countries do not use up all their units – that is, if they emit fewer gases than they are permitted – then they are allowed to sell these excess units to countries that are over their targets. It is a market-based response, because it creates a market for the emissions. An advantage of such a scheme is that it gives producers the incentive to adopt cleaner technologies, so that they do not have to buy carbon credits.

The Paris agreement also includes mechanisms whereby nations can trade in "carbon credits" to offset their own carbon emissions. This offers developing countries the opportunity to enhance their own carbon sinks (eg forests) in their own countries and sell carbon credits to developed countries. This is one way of supporting developing countries in financing their own mitigation plans.

In order to meet their own commitments to reducing GHG emissions, individual states, countries or regions have set up emissions trading systems within their own economies. There are many examples of these throughout the world.

The effectiveness of such an ETS depends on many different things, including:

- the inclusiveness of the scheme – how many participants are committed
- whether or not the original allowances are sufficient to bring about the desired change
- the way in which the allowances are allocated may be problematic
- the possibility that companies may simply absorb the extra costs of emitting, and not change their behaviour
- the ability of the administrators to accurately monitor the emissions
- the strength of the "punishments" for excess emissions
- the possibility that the system may be manipulated by stakeholders.

Economics in action

ATL Thinking, Communication and Research

Find an example of a state, country or region that has adopted an Emissions Trading System. Evaluate the success of the ETS in reducing emissions.

Did you know?

Carbon dioxide is the main GHG, and so people speak about "trading in carbon" and the "carbon market". Of course, no one is actually buying or selling carbon, but they can buy or sell the right to emit carbon.

How might carbon taxes reduce or eliminate negative externalities of production and reduce the threats to common pool resources?

A "carbon tax" is a tax imposed when fossil fuels are burned. When users of fossils fuels are taxed for their carbon emissions, it is a way of making them pay for the external costs that are not included in the market price. This follows the "polluter pays" principle, which argues that those who create pollution should be forced to pay for it – that is, it is a way of internalizing an externality.

A carbon tax is also regarded as a market-based approach. A higher tax raises the price, but the polluters still have freedom of choice. They can choose whether to reduce emissions, or go on polluting and pay the price.

A carbon tax is a Pigouvian tax aimed at eliminating the negative externalities associated with emitting carbon dioxide and forcing the producer to pay the full costs of producing the product. To completely reduce the negative externalities created when carbon is emitted, the government would have to be able to accurately calculate the external costs, and set the tax to reflect these costs. In practice, a carbon tax may not completely eliminate the welfare loss but is more likely to move the market closer to the socially efficient level of output, as shown in Figure 9.8. Most carbon taxes are set at a relatively low rate to begin with, and then increase gradually over time to allow producers and consumers time to change their patterns of production and consumption.

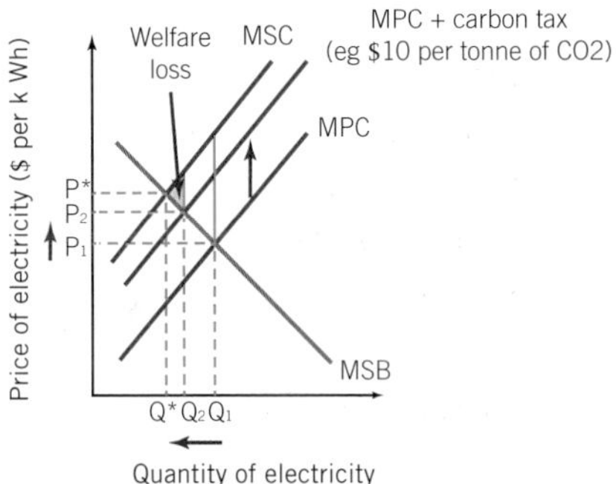

▲ **Figure 9.8** The effect of a carbon tax

When producing electricity, firms may burn fossil fuels such as coal or natural gas, and in doing so, they create external costs. The market price of P_1 does not reflect the external costs. When they must pay a tax of say, $10 per tonne of carbon that they emit, their costs of production rise from MPC to MPC + carbon tax. This raises the price of electricity to P_2. Consumption falls to Q_2, moving the market closer to the socially efficient level of output, which is Q*, and there is a smaller welfare loss.

This can bring about several benefits:

- In order to maintain their profitability, it is expected that electricity producers will invest in newer and cleaner technologies that allow them to emit less carbon.
- At higher prices, consumers will have an incentive to reduce their consumption of electricity; for example, by switching to more energy-efficient appliances.
- Consumers may seek different sources of energy, such as electricity from renewable sources.
- A carbon tax generates government revenue. This may be used to subsidize renewable energies to make them more affordable for consumers. Alternatively, many governments have promised to make carbon taxes "neutral". This means that they promise to compensate people by reducing taxes in other areas, such as indirect taxes.

'It's no longer free to pollute': Canada imposes carbon tax on four provinces

https://www.theguardian.com/world/2019/apr/01/canada-carbon-tax-climate-change-provinces

Despite the fact that any additional taxes that people are asked to pay are generally deeply unpopular, carbon taxes are favoured by many economists because they are a market-based approach, and they directly tackle a problem that all countries are committed to resolving.

Exercise 9.3

ATL Thinking and Communication

Read the article and answer the questions that follow.

Singapore Carbon Tax & Power Sector Contributions to Climate Change

In September 2016, Singapore ratified the Paris Agreement, an international treaty to reduce greenhouse gas emissions. Under the Agreement, Singapore pledged to reduce its emissions intensity by 36% from 2005 levels by 2030 and stabilize emissions with an aim of peaking around 2030.

To fulfil the country's climate change obligations under the Paris Agreement, Singapore announced the imposition of a S$5 carbon tax for every tonne of greenhouse emissions on direct emitters (which include power generating companies) from 1 Jan 2019 onwards till 2023. The aim of the carbon tax is to encourage direct emitters and downstream consumers to be more energy efficient and reduce carbon dioxide emissions.

The power sector has contributed significantly to Singapore's climate goals by achieving carbon emission reductions of 15% between 2010 and 2015. This is achieved through substantial investments in more efficient power plant units over the years. Consequently, 95% of the nation's electricity is currently being produced by natural gas-fired combined cycle gas turbines and co-generation plants. The remaining 5% is produced by solar and waste co-generation facilities. There is very limited scope for power generators to reduce carbon emission levels or switch to other fuels to avoid/reduce carbon tax based on current stock of power plants in the Singapore power system.

Singapore's land scarcity and the unsuitability of numerous renewable energy technologies (such as wind and tidal) also means power generators have limited scope to invest in zero-emission renewable energy. Therefore, end-consumers will also have to play their part by paying higher prices. The carbon tax will act as an incentive for end-consumers to improve energy efficiency and reduce overall energy consumption.

Source: *Carbon tax impact on electricity customers,* Geneco, 2019, https://www.geneco.sg/carbon-tax/

1. Using an appropriate diagram, explain how the carbon tax may reduce the external costs associated with the production of electricity.
2. Other than the carbon tax, what has Singapore done to reduce its emissions?
3. What particular problems does Singapore face in increasing the use of renewable energies?

Economics in action

ATL Thinking, Communication and Research

Evaluate the effectiveness of a carbon tax in an economy of your choice.

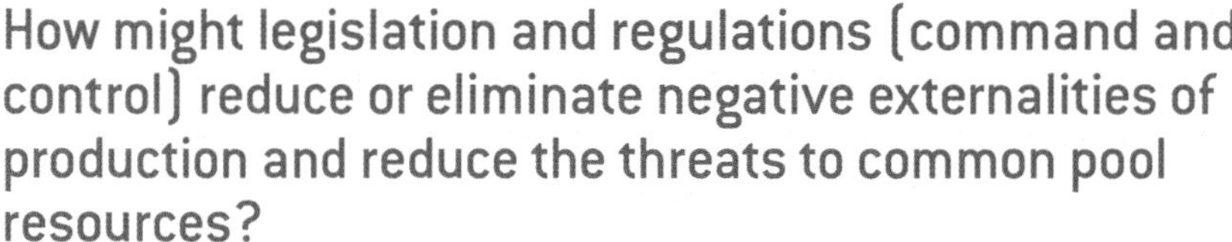

How might legislation and regulations (command and control) reduce or eliminate negative externalities of production and reduce the threats to common pool resources?

Where national governments can clearly see that economic activity creates negative externalities of production, they can enact legislation and set up regulations and regulatory agencies to prevent such impacts. Whereas tradable permits and taxes are examples of market-based responses, regulations are known as a command-and-control solution because they strictly mandate the way that producers behave. In some cases, an activity has to be severely restricted, or banned, because there is no amount of output that is acceptable. In others, the output needs to be reduced, so either a market-based approach or command and control approach could be used. For example, if a government wanted to reduce the amount of single-use plastic bags being given out by supermarkets, they could use a command-and-control approach by banning supermarkets from giving them out, or they could use a market-based approach by making the supermarkets charge a fee for the bags.

Examples of regulations include: emissions regulations, laws to protect endangered species, recycling regulations, laws concerning the disposal of waste, regulations of pollutants being discharged into rivers and laws to limit the amount of plastic waste. To meet the standards, the firms would have to spend money, thus increasing their private costs. Graphically, the solution would be shown as in Figure 9.8, replacing "MPC + carbon tax" with "MPC + increased costs". The expectation would be that such laws would incentivize producers to make different choices about the way that they produce their goods and services.

Concerns about the use of regulations include the following:

- The establishment of environmental regulations requires access to so much information that it is simply impossible for governments to realistically gather and process so much information.
- Regulations need to take into account the vast number of different circumstances facing different industries and ecosystems. This inevitably results in over-regulation in some areas, and under-regulation in others.
- Increased regulation will raise the price of their products and cause firms to be less competitive against foreign producers.
- Regulations and standards have to be strictly monitored to ensure that all stakeholders involved remain "compliant" with the rules. This is very time-consuming and very expensive.
- Excessive environmental regulations concerning new technologies discourage the development of technologies that could potentially achieve environmental benefits.
- Governments are slow-moving and resistant to change and so cannot adapt when circumstances change.

- Governments are subject to intense lobbying by stakeholders and may favour some areas of the environment over others because of the power of lobbies, or because of the desire to win votes. Alternatively, there might be a problem of "regulatory capture" where government agencies that are responsible for regulating a particular industry are heavily influenced by representatives of the industry that they are supposed to be regulating.

Exercise 9.4

ATL Thinking and Communication

Read the article and answer the question that follows

China softens "iron fist" pollution fight. Premier Li Keqiang outlines jobs-first policy at top official gathering, threatening green transition

In 2014, China declared a war against pollution when Premier Li Keqiang pledged to crackdown on polluters "with an iron fist" at the opening of the annual National People's Congress. At the time, the government was praised for its shift away from economic growth at all costs, to one that recognized the value of environmental protection.

However, things have changed in China and Li's approach was quite different at this year's conference. He outlined an "employment first" policy aimed at helping China battle a prolonged economic downturn.

While Li vowed to strengthen efforts on pollution prevention and control, he also said the government should not only regulate industries according to the law but hear their "reasonable demands" and "offer support".

"[We should] allow companies a grace period for complying with environmental requirements and avoid simply shutting down factories," Li told over 3,000 delegates.

The shift comes amid complaints that stringent environmental regulations and blanket restrictions on industrial activities have increased business costs and job losses, particularly at small private companies.

Source: Adapted from *China softens 'iron fist' pollution fight*, Dialogo Chino, March 15 2019, https://dialogochino.net/24851-china-softens-iron-fist-pollution-fight/

1. Using an MSC/MSB diagram, explain a possible consequence of Premier Li's shift in policy direction.
2. How does this article illustrate a problem that governments face when making policy choices?

Assessment advice

Question 1 in exercise 9.4 might be a little longer than a four-mark question on an exam would be, as there is quite a bit of explanation needed. However, it does raise an interesting point. When drawing microeconomics diagrams, you are advised to always indicate the relevant market either by providing a precise label on the vertical axis, or by adding a title to the diagram which indicates the market. In the extract about China, there is no specific market indicated. However, the article does refer to "industrial activities" and so the title of the diagram could be "The market for industrial output".

How might subsidies reduce or eliminate negative externalities of production and reduce the threats to common pool resources?

Greater use of renewable energy sources, such as solar or wind power rather than fossil fuels, will greatly reduce the emissions of GHGs. If the costs of this renewable power are very high, this may make their widespread use unaffordable. Furthermore, with rapidly growing populations in developing countries, there will be increasing demands for energy. If the world's commitments to emissions reductions are to be met, this will require much greater use of renewable energies. Therefore, it is argued that governments should provide subsidies to producers to reduce their costs of production and make those energies more accessible. International cooperation is needed to ensure that these technologies are affordable to those in developing countries. Indeed, Sustainable Development Goal 7 is to "ensure access to affordable, reliable, sustainable and modern energy".

Sustainable Development Goal 7

On the positive side, there is much evidence that, as a result of great improvements in technologies, the costs of renewable energy have fallen significantly. If the improvements continue, driving the price of renewable energy down further, this may help all countries reduce their GHG emissions without the need for government subsidies.

How can "collective self-governance" be used to manage common pool resources such as fisheries or forests?

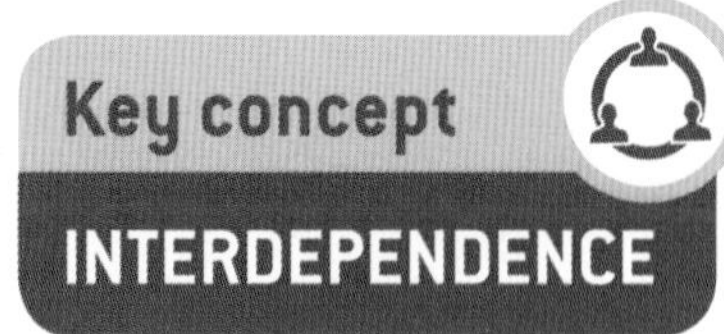

The tragedy of the commons suggests that when users of a resource act in their own self-interest, the ultimate result will be the destruction of the resource such that everyone loses. It encourages people to act selfishly, to get as much from the resource before it loses its value entirely. To prevent the tragedy of the commons, two possibilities are often suggested: either the government takes over the management of the resource and sets strict regulations for its use, or the land is privatized, with its management to be determined by the private owner.

Elinor Ostrom, who won the Nobel Prize for Economic Sciences in 2009 for her work analysing the management of common pool resources, offered a different approach and proposed that there was a way to avoid the tragedy of the commons. In her theory, based on a tremendous amount of research into current and historical examples of community management of common access resources in Maine, Nepal, Indonesia and Kenya, she demonstrated that individuals and communities could work together without top-down regulation to develop rules and institutions to manage their shared resources in a sustainable and equitable manner.

One of the key points of Ostrom's work is that there is no "one size fits all" approach to managing a particular resource, and that since the communities who use the resource have the greatest incentive to

Economics in action

ATL Thinking, Communication and Research

Referring to the work of Elinor Ostrom, evaluate collective self-governance as a means of managing a common pool resource in a community of your choice.

ensure its sustainability, they should be the ones developing the rules for its management. Furthermore, the users of the resource are more likely to implement, monitor and enforce those rules, since they were involved in the establishment of the rules and are the ones to gain when the rules are followed.

> "There is no reason to believe that bureaucrats and politicians, no matter how well-meaning, are better at solving problems than people on the spot, who have the strongest incentive to get things right"
>
> – *Elinor Ostrom, Nobel Prize for Economic Sciences, 2009.*

Key concept

INTERDEPENDENCE

Why is international cooperation so important?

As already noted, threats to sustainability are global threats because they degrade common pool resources including the atmosphere, oceans, deserts, forests and climate. The global nature of the problem underlines the interdependence among countries and emphasizes the need for cooperation. The Paris agreement and the Sustainable Development Goals represent significant progress concerning the ways that countries can and should cooperate in order to address problems related to sustainability. However, challenges clearly remain.

Despite the progress that has been made in reducing emissions through carbon pricing methods (emissions trading schemes and carbon taxes), research from the OECD reports that "governments need to raise carbon prices much faster if they are to meet their commitments on cutting emissions and slowing the pace of climate change under the Paris agreement".

Economics in action

ATL Thinking, Communication and Research

It would be valuable to assess how countries set and achieve their Nationally Determined Contributions. Choose one country as a case study and track their goals and achievements. How can international cooperation help countries to meet their own Nationally Determined Contributions?

Not all countries are as committed to the process, and at least one country has said that it will remove itself from the agreement on the grounds that the requirements will damage its economic growth. Other governments may behave similarly. Short-sighted governments may be preoccupied with achieving high rates of economic growth and short-term political popularity without considering the long-run impacts. Thus, the political will to follow through with the commitments made in the past may weaken, despite the urgent need for all countries to cooperate.

Both the Paris agreement and the Sustainable Development Goals contain detailed information about the ways in which developed countries are to support developing and least developed countries. This includes both financial and technological support. However, the mechanisms for ensuring this are not binding. This may make it difficult for developing countries and LDCs to meet their mitigation goals.

While countries have the freedom to establish their own Nationally Determined Contributions, there are concerns that there are insufficient means of monitoring and enforcing the extent to which countries meet their commitments.

Economics in action — ATL Thinking, Communication and Research

The "fast fashion" industry is now seen as a major contributor to the global waste problem and therefore a threat to sustainability.

a) Explain briefly what is meant by the "fast fashion" industry.
b) What are the negative externalities associated with the consumption of clothing?
c) Inexpensive clothes create negative externalities, but they are not considered a demerit good like cigarettes or unhealthy food. What is the difference?
d) What are the negative externalities associated with the production of clothing?
e) How are governments responding to this threat to sustainability?
f) Evaluate the success of government responses, considering the following questions:
   i) What barriers have governments faced in trying to implement policies?
   ii) To what extent have they been successful in reducing consumption?
   iii) Once the policies were implemented, what factors have limited their success?

Why is a lack of public goods a market failure?

Public goods are goods that would not be provided at all in a free market. Since they are goods that are of benefit to society, the lack of public goods in a free market is considered to be a market failure. Examples of public goods are national defence, flood barriers and streetlights on motorways.

The reason that public goods will not be provided at all in a free market is that they have two characteristics – they are *non-excludable* and *non-rivalrous* – and that makes it pointless for private individuals to provide the goods themselves. If a good does not have both of these characteristics, then it is not a public good. If a good is completely non-excludable and non- rivalrous, such as national defence and flood barriers, then it is called a *pure public good*.

A good is said to be non-excludable if it is impossible to stop other people consuming it once it has been provided. If a private individual erects a flood barrier to protect a house, the other people in the area will gain the benefit, even though they have paid nothing. This is known as the *free-rider problem*. Logically, no one will pay for a flood barrier, in the hope that someone else will do it. The good will not be provided at all by the free market. No profit-seeking private producer would have any incentive to finance the construction of a flood barrier without the ability to charge people for its use to recover the costs of production and make a profit.

A good is said to be non-rivalrous when one person consuming it does not prevent another person from consuming it as well. If a person eats an ice cream, then another person cannot consume that ice cream as well. However, if one person is protected by a flood barrier, it does not stop other people from being protected at the same time. The private benefit from a flood barrier would be very small relative to the cost, although the social benefit to all of the people who were protected by it would be huge and probably greater than the cost. Thus, there is no incentive for a private individual to erect a flood barrier.

There is much debate over what constitutes a public good. There is a category of goods known as "quasi-public goods", which have some, but not all of the characteristics of public goods. For example, a "public" area such as a beach or a park might appear to be non-rivalrous in that if one person is enjoying the area, then up to a point, others can also enjoy the area. However, one could argue that the space is only partly rivalrous; once that space becomes overcrowded, then this it is no longer possible for other people to enjoy the space.

Advancements in technology are making it increasingly possible to charge people to use things that were formerly difficult to charge for. This might make more goods "private goods" which are produced by private producers. Consider the case of roads, highways or motorways, which may be considered to be quasi-public goods. It is difficult to exclude people from driving on roads, and so private producers would not have the incentive to build roads. Toll booths to prevent people from getting onto a road can be used, but these clog up traffic, worsening other problems. Technology is now making it much easier to charge people to use roads. Electronic road pricing schemes are used all around the world to make it possible to charge people to use roads.

Key concept

INTERVENTION

How can the government reduce this market failure and increase the supply of public goods?

Governments may try to reduce this market failure by intervening in a number of ways.

- They may provide the public good themselves. This is known as "direct provision". This is usually the case with such things as national defence, flood barriers, roads, pavements, street lighting and lighthouses. The use of taxpayers' money to fund the provision spreads the cost over a large number of people who would not be prepared to pay individually.
- The government might work in partnership with the private sector, providing the financing for the establishment of the good, and then allowing the private producer to run it. This is known as "public-private partnership". It may be assumed that private producers will only engage in such a partnership if there are profits to be earned. This makes the issue of such partnerships rather controversial.

Economics in action — ATL Thinking, Communication and Research

Public-private partnerships may be very important in making it possible for an economy to enjoy more and better infrastructure, for example, but they are not without their criticisms.

Investigate the advantages and disadvantages of public-private partnerships by looking at some real-world examples.

Why is the existence of asymmetric information a market failure?

For markets to function perfectly – that is, for there to be no market failure – we assume that all parties in every transaction have what is known as *perfect information* or *perfect knowledge*. In other words, if buyers and sellers come together in a market, there will be allocative efficiency if they are all fully aware of what products are available and the range of prices.

However, in reality, this will very often not be the case and so economic decisions are frequently made based on incomplete information, resulting in market failure.

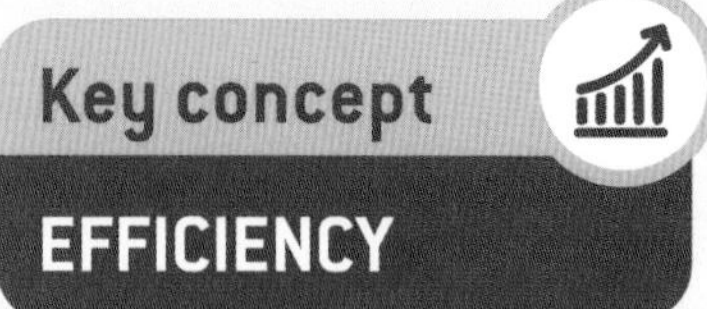

The most common example of imperfect information is known as *asymmetric information*. This is where one party in an economic transaction has access to more information or better information than the other party. We look at two types of asymmetric information: adverse selection and moral hazard.

What is "adverse selection"?

Adverse selection occurs when one party in an economic transaction has better information than the other. It may be that buyers have better information than sellers, or it may be that sellers have better information than buyers. In both cases, the result is that poor choices are made from society's point of view.

A very common illustration of adverse selection occurs in health insurance markets where the people buying the insurance have better information about their health than the insurance company. Consider the case of a heavy smoker buying health insurance. The insurance company does not know that the person is a heavy smoker, and charges them the market price for the insurance. When the person becomes ill and requires the insurance company to pay the medical costs, the insurance company then has to charge other people higher prices to cover themselves. This leads to higher prices for insurance policies, and inevitably means that some people will choose not to buy insurance. In countries where the state does not provide health care, this is a significant problem. Many cannot afford insurance because insurance companies charge higher prices to insure themselves against the higher risk people, and many people, particularly young, healthy people do not buy insurance, perhaps foolishly assuming that they will not need it. This is said to be a situation of "missing markets" as those people who should buy insurance would not be able to buy it because the market price is distorted by the higher-risk customers. It is a market failure because the price of the good is influenced by the imperfect information held by one of the parties.

Screening is seen as one solution to the problems that occur as a result of adverse selection. Screening occurs when the less informed party can find a way to get the other party to reveal the relevant information. In the case of health insurance, it is the insurance companies that are the "less informed party". They get the customers to reveal the information concerning risk factors by asking questions concerning – for example, age, weight, whether the consumer smokes, how much alcohol they drink, how active they are and whether they have any pre-existing conditions. They can then offer different insurance plans according to the risk factors. The principle is that higher-risk people should pay higher prices, so that insurance companies can sell lower priced insurance policies to people whom they know face lower risks. Governments have a role to play in the transactions between sellers and buyers, setting regulations to ensure that the insurance companies do not violate the rights of the consumers.

Adverse selection can also occur when sellers have more information than buyers. A commonly cited example of this is in the used car market. Economist George Akerlof won a Nobel Prize in Economics in 1971 for his publication, "The Market for Lemons: Quality Uncertainty and the Market Mechanism". In the market for used cars, there are inevitably some good quality cars and some poor-quality cars. (Poor-quality used cars have the nickname "lemons"). However, uninformed consumers are unlikely to be able to tell the difference between the higher quality and the lower quality cars. Therefore, used car sellers have to charge an average price. Those sellers who get an average price for their "lemon" are happy with such a transaction, as the true value of the car would be lower. However, sellers who are in possession of high-quality used cars would make a loss, as people would not be prepared to pay a higher price for a car that might be a lemon! The end result is that there would be no market for good, quality used cars, and therefore a market failure. It is argued that the adverse selection results in a situation where "bad drives out the good". (This is similar to the health insurance market where the high-risk unhealthy buyers (the "bad") drive out the healthy buyers (the "good") by causing the health insurance companies to charge higher prices).

The market for lemons

In this example, where the seller has better information than the consumer, *signalling* is seen as a possible solution. Signalling takes place when the party with more information can provide reliable information to the party with less information. In the case of the used-car sellers, they can provide accurate signals to consumers about the quality of the used car. For example, they can give warranties or guarantees to the potential buyers, with a promise to take back the car or fix any problems. This signals to the consumer that the seller knows that the car is worth the price.

What is moral hazard?

Moral hazard occurs when people have an incentive to alter their behaviour and take more risk when they know that the negative consequences of their risky decision making will be borne by others. The insurance industry can provide examples of moral hazard. For example, consider a previously safe driver who buys full insurance for their car, then changes their behaviour by starting to take risks while driving knowing that if there is any damage to the car it will be paid for by the insurance company.

Insurance companies try to get around this moral hazard by implementing "deductibles". If the reckless driver in the previous situation causes $1,000 damage to the car, they might have to pay the first $500 themselves as a "deductible". This would act as a disincentive to risky behaviour.

Moral hazard can be seen in the labour market. If a previously very good worker is promoted and guaranteed a fixed salary on a permanent contract, then the worker might choose to do the minimum amount of work required, knowing that the salary will be given to them regardless of the quality or quantity of work they do. This is why firms offer bonuses or performance-related pay to incentivize workers to work hard. Limited-term contracts are also a way of ensuring that workers maintain their productivity.

Another example is in the banking industry. Put in very simple terms, one of the reasons for the financial crisis in 2008 was said to be the irresponsibility of the profit-seeking commercial banking sector in extending far too many loans to people whom they knew would not be able to pay back their debts, packaging these loans in other financial instruments and then selling them onto other people knowing that there was a high risk that that loans would not be repaid. The inability of the people who had been encouraged to take mortgages to pay back thousands and thousands of dollars of debt should really have resulted in the collapse of those banks that had lent money carelessly. However, many banks were "bailed out" by their governments. The argument was that the banks were "too big to fail" as their collapse would have led to an even greater economic crisis. Knowing that they will be bailed out, banks can take bigger risks than they would if they knew that they would be fully responsible for the consequences. This is a moral hazard.

Moral hazard is *"any situation in which one person makes the decision about how much risk to take, while someone else bears the cost if things go wrong"*.

– Paul Krugman, Economics Nobel Prize recipient.

The solution to this type of moral hazard would be for the government to set more regulations to prevent the risky behaviour in the first place. However, as we have already mentioned, businesses object strongly when any regulations are implemented that might damage their opportunities to earn profits. Alternatively, the government can bail out the banks, but impose heavy fines on those people responsible for the excessively risky behaviour. Prior knowledge of the potential fines would ideally act as a disincentive.

What is the difference between adverse selection and moral hazard?

In the case of adverse selection, the market failure occurs **before** an economic transaction has been made. One party has more information than the other, and this gives the party an advantage going into the transaction. In the case of moral hazard, the market failure occurs **after** the economic transaction has been made. The party with greater knowledge of the risk has the advantage following the transaction.

Economics in action

ATL Thinking, Communication and Research

Find your own real-world examples to illustrate adverse selection and moral hazard.

EXAMINATION QUESTIONS

Paper 1, part (a) questions – HL & SL

Part (a) questions

1. Explain why imperfect information contributes to the overconsumption of demerit goods. [10 marks]
2. Explain why imperfect information contributes to the underconsumption of merit goods. [10 marks]

Paper 1, part (a) questions – HL only

1. Explain how consumer nudges can reduce the market failure associated with demerit goods. [10 marks]
2. Explain how screening and signalling by firms can overcome the problem of adverse selection. [10 marks]

Paper 1, full questions – HL & SL

1. **a)** Explain why negative externalities of consumption are a market failure. [10 marks]

   b) Using real-world examples, evaluate policies that could be used by governments to reduce the market failure associated with negative externalities of consumption. [15 marks]
2. **a)** Explain why the atmosphere is a common-pool resource, subject to the "tragedy of the commons". [10 marks]

   b) Using real-world examples, evaluate the role of market-based responses to managing common-pool resources. [15 marks]
3. **a)** Explain why the existence of positive externalities in a market is a case of market failure. [10 marks]

   b) Using real-world examples, evaluate to what extent governments should intervene in the market for merit goods. [15 marks]

Assessment advice

Note the use of the phrase "to what extent" in the second question. This is what we might refer to as an "evaluation" indicator as it gives you a hint as to how you would be expected to evaluate. In this example, you could explain the importance of government intervention in certain markets, but you could also identify certain merit goods where government intervention might not be as important.

10 RATIONAL PRODUCER BEHAVIOUR

REAL-WORLD ISSUE:

When are markets unable to satisfy important economic objectives and does government intervention help?

By the end of this chapter, you should be able to:

- HL Understand the concept of rational producer behaviour
- HL Be aware that neoclassical theory assumes that the aim of the firm is to maximize profits
- HL Define and explain the meaning of economic costs
- HL Distinguish between explicit costs and implicit costs
- HL Define, explain, illustrate, calculate and give examples of short run costs
- HL Define, explain, illustrate and calculate total, average and marginal revenue
- HL Explain and illustrate the relationship between average revenue, marginal revenue, total revenue and price elasticity of demand
- HL Define and explain the measurement of profit
- HL Distinguish between normal profit, abnormal profit and losses
- HL Define, explain and illustrate the concept of profit maximization
- HL Describe alternative business objectives of firms.

Exercise 10.1

ATL Thinking and Communication

A small firm has been operating for one year. During the year they have:

- paid $40,000 in wages and salaries
- paid $100,000 for raw materials
- used their own small factory, which could have been rented out for $90,000
- used $40,000 worth of electricity and services
- received $450,000 in total revenue.

In addition:

- the firm uses its own machinery, which has reduced in value by $20,000 because of wear and tear and now has a second-hand value of $70,000
- the owner of the firm has given up a job with another firm, where he would have been paid $70,000 per year
- The owner has invested $60,000 of his own money into the business (the rate of interest during the year has been 5%).

In light of the facts above:

1. identify the costs of the firm as explicit or implicit
2. calculate and explain the profits/losses made by the firm from the point of view of:
   a. an accountant
   b. an economist.

Do producers behave in a rational way? What is profit maximization?

In the neoclassical, basic theory of the firm, economists make the assumption that producers behave "rationally" by always attempting to maximize the profits that they make. This is referred to as maximizing behaviour. Simply put, profits are earned when producers' revenues are higher than their costs. However, in order to understand how producers maximize profits, it is necessary to consider these relevant concepts of costs and revenue.

1. How do economists classify costs?

Economists use the term *economic cost* when they are considering costs. The economic cost of producing a good is the opportunity cost of the firm's production. Remember that opportunity cost is the next best alternative foregone when an economic decision is made. In this case it is the opportunity cost of the factors of production (resources) that have been used in producing the good or service.

In order to work out the economic cost of production we separate the factors used by a firm into two categories:

- Factors that are purchased from others and not already owned by the firm:

  The opportunity cost of factors of production not owned by the firm is simply the price that is paid for them and the alternative things that could have been bought. For example, if a firm hires a worker for $1,000 a week then the opportunity cost to the firm is the cost of that worker's wage and the other things on which the $1,000 could have been spent. Any costs of this sort are known as **explicit costs**. Explicit costs are any costs to a firm that involve the direct payment of money.

- Factors that are already owned by the firm:

  If a firm has factors that it already owns then it will not have to pay out money when it uses them. However, there will still be an opportunity cost involved in their use which needs to be accounted for. Any costs of this sort are known as **implicit costs**. Implicit costs are the earnings that a firm could have had if it had employed its factors in another use or if it had hired out or sold them to another firm.

  Implicit costs are best understood through examples:

  a. The owner of a firm may be able to earn $100,000 per year in her next best alternative job, as a tax accountant. This opportunity cost should be included in the firm's economic costs. Indeed, some would argue that it is the most important cost that a firm needs to cover since, if it is not met, the entrepreneur would presumably close down the firm and take the job as a tax accountant. The very existence of the firm depends upon covering this cost.

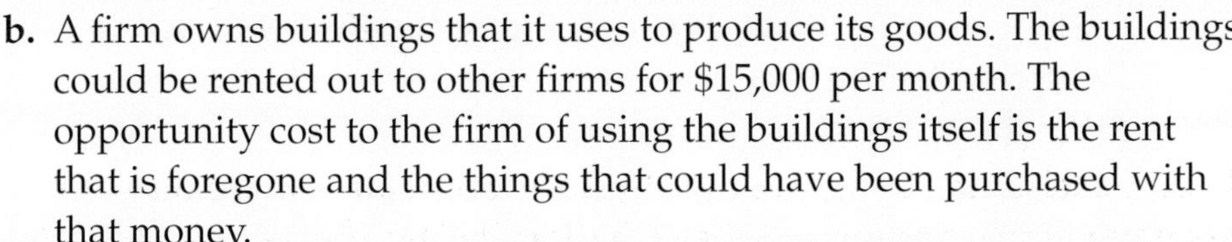

b. A firm owns buildings that it uses to produce its goods. The buildings could be rented out to other firms for $15,000 per month. The opportunity cost to the firm of using the buildings itself is the rent that is foregone and the things that could have been purchased with that money.

As we can see from above, if economists count these costs and accountants do not, then economists and accountants would report different profit levels for the same firms.

2. How do economists measure costs in the short run?

Firms have many different costs when producing whatever good or service they provide. We need to be able to understand the different types of costs that firms face and to understand where those costs originate.

We can start by looking at the example from Chapter 5, Table 5.4, and adding some more ways of measuring costs. We will assume that the cost of a machine per week is $100 (there are four machines) and that the cost of a worker is $200 per week. The outcome of this on the firm's costs is shown in Table 10.1.

Quantity of labour (V)	Total product (TP) or Output (q)	Total fixed cost (TFC)	Total variable cost (TVC)	Total cost (TC)	Average fixed cost (AFC)	Average variable cost (AVC)	Average total cost (ATC)	Marginal cost (MC)
0	0	400	0	400	–	–	–	
								20
1	10	400	200	600	40	20	60	
								13.33
2	25	400	400	800	16	16	32	
								10
3	45	400	600	1,000	8.89	13.33	22.22	
								8
4	70	400	800	1,200	5.71	11.43	17.14	
								10
5	90	400	1,000	1,400	4.44	11.11	15.55	
								13.33
6	105	400	1,200	1,600	3.81	11.43	15.24	
								20
7	115	400	1,400	1,800	3.48	12.17	15.65	
								40
8	120	400	1,600	2,000	3.33	13.33	16.67	

▲ **Table 10.1** Total, average and marginal costs per week in $

Using the figures above, we can explain the different ways of measuring costs. We tend to separate costs into two groups:

1. *Total costs*: Total costs are the complete costs of producing output. We use three measures:

   a. *Total fixed cost (TFC)*: TFC is the total cost of the fixed assets that a firm uses in a given time period. Since the number of fixed assets is, by definition, fixed, TFC is a constant amount. It is the same whether the firm produces one unit or one hundred units.

TFC is equal to the number of fixed assets times the cost of each fixed asset. In the example in Table 10.1, TFC per week is $400 (four machines costing $100 each) at every level of output.

b. *Total variable cost (TVC)*: TVC is the total cost of the variable assets that a firm uses in a given time period. TVC increases as the firm uses more of the variable factor.

TVC is equal to the number of variable factors times the cost of each variable factor. So in the current example, TVC is $200 when one worker is being employed and $1,200 when six workers are being used.

c. *Total cost (TC)*: TC is the total cost of all the fixed and variable factors used to produce a certain output. It is equal to TFC plus TVC.

So in the current example the total cost of producing 105 units of output per week is $1,600. It is the fixed cost of $400 plus the variable cost of $1,200.

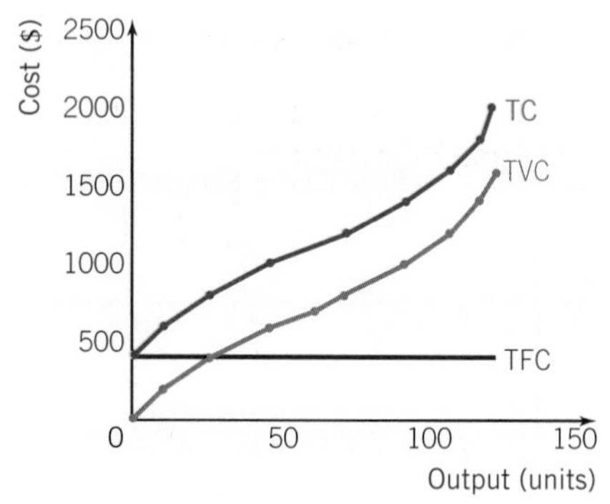

▲ **Figure 10.1** Total cost, total variable cost and total fixed cost

The different total cost curves are shown in Figure 10.1.

2. *Average costs*: These are costs per unit of output. We use three measures:

a. *Average fixed cost* (AFC): AFC is the fixed cost per unit of output. It is calculated by the equation $AFC = \frac{TFC}{q}$, where q is the level of output.

Because TFC is a constant, AFC always falls as output increases. In the current example, AFC is $40 per unit when output is 10 units and falls to $3.33 per unit when output increases to 120 units.

b. *Average variable cost (AVC)*: AVC is the variable cost per unit of output. It is calculated by the equation $AVC = \frac{TVC}{q}$, where q is the level of output.

AVC tends to fall as output increases, and then to start to rise again as the output continues to increase. This is explained by the hypothesis of eventually diminishing average returns, which we came across in Chapter 5. As more of the variable factors are applied to the fixed factors, the output per unit of the variable factor eventually falls, and so the cost per unit of output eventually begins to rise. In the current example AVC is $20 per unit when output is 10 units, falls to $11.11 per unit when output rises to 90 units and then increases to $13.33 when output continues to rise to 120 units.

c. *Average total cost (ATC)*: ATC is the total cost per unit of output. It is equal to AFC plus AVC. It is calculated by the equation $ATC = \frac{TC}{q}$, where q is the level of output.

As with AVC, ATC tends to fall as output increases, and then to start to rise again as the output continues to increase. In the current example ATC is $60 per unit when output is 10 units, falls to $15.24 per unit when output rises to 105 units and then increases to $16.67 when output continues to rise to 120 units.

3. *Marginal cost (MC)*: We have already come across marginal cost in Chapter 5. MC is the increase in total cost of producing an extra unit of output. It is calculated by the equation $MC = \frac{\Delta TC}{\Delta q}$, where ΔTC is the change in total cost and Δq is the change in the level of output.

   MC tends to fall as output increases, and then to start to rise again as the output continues to increase. This is explained by the hypothesis of eventually diminishing marginal returns. As more of the variable factors are applied to the fixed factors, the extra output from each additional unit of the variable factor added eventually falls, and so the extra cost per unit of output eventually begins to rise. In the current example MC is $20 when output rises from 0 to 10 units, falls to $8.00 when output rises from 45 to 70 units and then increases to $40.00 when output continues to rise and goes up from 115 to 120 units.

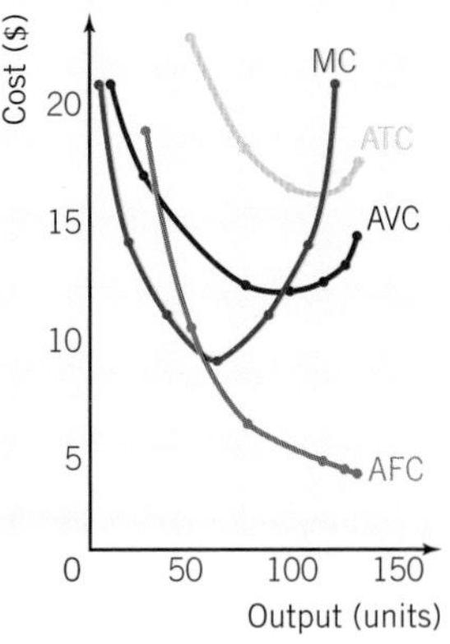

▲ **Figure 10.2** Short-run AFC, AVC, ATC and MC curves

The average and marginal cost curves from our example are shown in Figure 10.2.

It is important to recognise the relationship between the ATC, AVC and MC curves. Quite simply, the MC curve cuts the AVC and ATC curves at their lowest points. This is a mathematical relationship. AFC falls as output increases and, since it is the difference between ATC and AVC, the vertical gap between ATC and AVC gets smaller as output grows.

We have seen how to calculate the different types of average and marginal costs and draw the curves that represent the data. When economists draw costs curves to illustrate a general position, they draw them as shown in Figure 10.3.

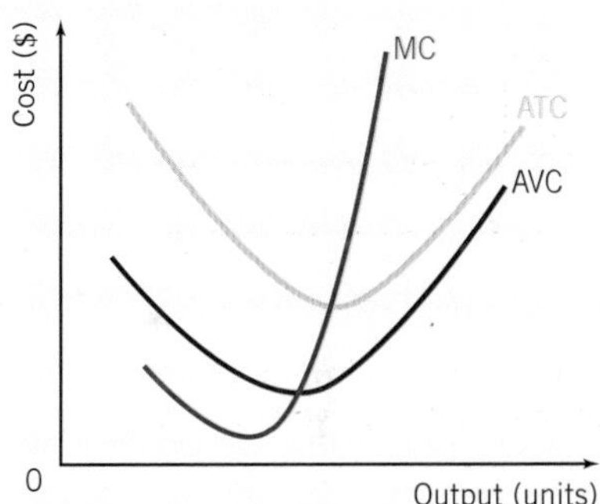

▲ **Figure 10.3** A general diagram showing short-run ATC, AVC and MC

3. How do economists measure revenue?

Revenue is the income that a firm receives from selling its products, goods and services, over a certain time period. Revenue may be measured in three ways:

1. *Total revenue (TR)*

TR is the total amount of money that a firm receives from selling a certain amount of a good or service in a given time period. It is calculated by using the formula:

$$TR = p \times q$$

where p is the price that the good or service sells for and q is the quantity of the good or service sold in the time period being considered.

If a firm sells 400 pizzas per week, at a price of $6 per pizza, then:
TR = $6 × 400 = $2,400 per week.

2. *Average revenue (AR)*

AR is the revenue that a firm receives per unit of its sales. It is calculated using the formula:

$$AR = \frac{TR}{q} = \frac{p \times q}{q} = p$$

As we can see, since TR is (p × q), q is common to the top and bottom of the formula and so AR is the same as p.

Thus, if the firm sells 400 pizzas at a price of $6 per pizza, then:

$AR = \frac{\$2,400}{400} = \$6$ (the same as the price per unit)

3. *Marginal revenue (MR)*

MR is the extra revenue that a firm gains when it sells one more unit of a product in a given time period. It is calculated by using the formula:

$MR = \frac{\Delta TR}{\Delta q}$, where Δ means "the change in".

Thus, if our pizza firm lowered the price of a pizza to $5 and found that their weekly sales rose to 500 pizzas, then:

$$MR = \frac{\$2,500 - \$2,400}{100} = \frac{\$100}{100} = \$1$$

The extra revenue gained from selling an extra unit is $1.

What happens to revenue when output increases?

We now need to consider what happens to a firm's revenue as output increases. We shall consider two different situations:

1. Revenue when price does not change with output:

If a firm does not have to lower price as output increases and it wishes to sell more of its product, then it faces a perfectly elastic demand curve. This situation only happens in theory, but it is very useful to economists when they are building their models of how markets work and they start with the theoretical market form of perfect competition (see Chapter 12).

An example of a firm that has a perfectly elastic demand curve is shown in Table 10.2.

Price ($)	Quantity demanded	Total revenue ($)	Average revenue ($)	Marginal revenue ($)
5	1	5	5	5
5	2	10	5	5
5	3	15	5	5
5	4	20	5	5
5	5	25	5	5
5	6	30	5	5
5	7	35	5	5

▲ **Table 10.2** Possible revenue figures for a firm with a perfectly elastic demand curve

We can assume that the firm is very small in terms of the size of the whole industry, and that they can increase their output without affecting

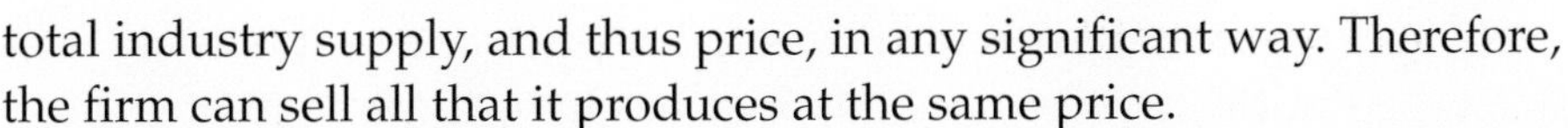

total industry supply, and thus price, in any significant way. Therefore, the firm can sell all that it produces at the same price.

If we graph the revenues, we will get the curves shown in Figure 10.4 (a) and (b).

In these graphs, we can see that, when price elasticity of demand is perfectly elastic, then price, average revenue, marginal revenue and demand are all the same. In this case, they are all $5.

Total revenue increases at a constant rate as output increases, since each extra sale adds $5 to total revenue. Marginal revenue is constant at $5.

2. Revenue when price falls as output increases (when the demand curve is downward sloping, ie when elasticity of demand falls as output increases):

When we look at what happens to TR, AR and MR as price falls when output decreases we get a very different set of curves from the ones above. If a firm wishes to sell more of its output and it can control the price at which it sells, then it will have to lower the price if it wants to increase demand. In simpler terms, it will face a downward-sloping demand curve. An example of this, and the revenue figures relating to it, is shown in Table 10.3.

(a) *AR & MR when PED = infinity*

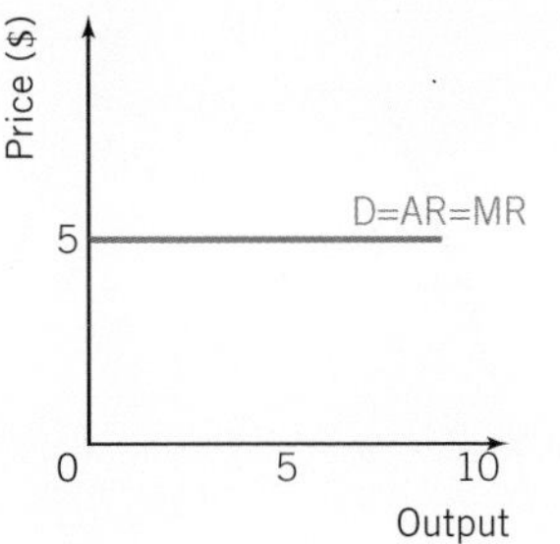

(b) *TR when PED = infinity*

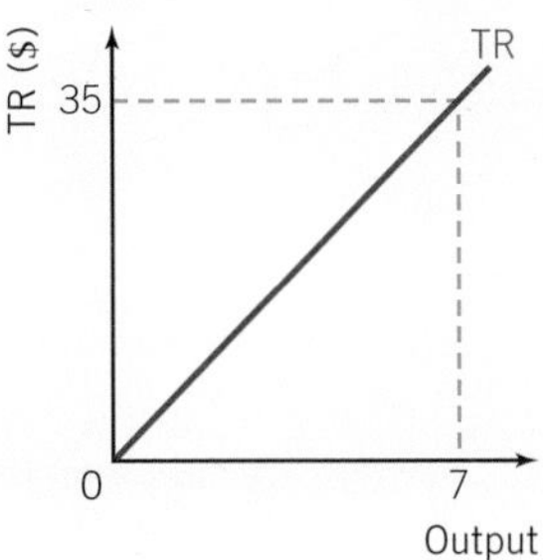

▲ **Figure 10.4** Curves for PED = infinity

Price ($)	Quantity demanded	Total revenue ($)	Average revenue ($)	Marginal revenue ($)	PED
50	0	0			
				45	
45	2	90	45		9.00
				35	
40	4	160	40		4.00
				25	
35	6	210	35		2.33
				15	
30	8	240	30		1.50
				5	
25	10	250	25		1.00
				-5	
20	12	240	20		0.67
				-15	
15	14	210	15		0.43
				-25	
10	16	160	10		0.25
				-35	
5	18	90	5		0.11
				-45	
0	20	0			

▲ **Table 10.3** Output, revenue and PED figures for a firm with a normal demand curve

Higher Level

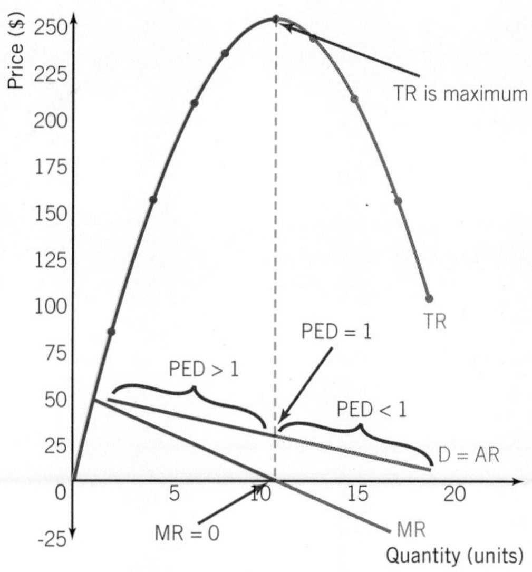

▲ **Figure 10.5** The relationship between D, AR, MR, TR and PED for a normal demand curve

As we would expect, AR is equal to price and so it falls as output increases, since the price has to be lowered in order to sell more products. This is shown clearly in Figure 10.5, where the demand curve is now labelled D = AR.

MR also falls as output increases, but at a greater rate than AR. In fact, as we can see in Figure 10.5, the MR curve is twice as steeply sloping as the AR curve and also goes below the *x*-axis. This is a relationship that holds for all downward-sloping AR curves and the MR curves that relate to them.

MR is below AR because in order to sell more products the firm has to lower the price of all products sold, losing revenue on the ones that could have been sold at a higher price in order to get the revenue from the extra sales.

For example, in Table 10.3, when price is dropped from \$40 to \$35, the quantity demanded increases from 4 units to 6. Before the price drop, the TR was \$160 (\$40 × 4). After the price drop, TR becomes \$210 (\$35 × 6).

The MR is \$25 $\left(\frac{\Delta TR}{\Delta q} = \frac{50}{2} = 25\right)$.

There are two things affecting the TR. First, two extra units of the product are sold at a price of \$35 and so TR rises by \$70. However, in order to do this, the price of the 4 units that could have been sold for \$40 has been dropped to \$35 and so there is a loss of revenue of \$20 (4 × \$5). The overall effect is an increase in revenue of \$70 – \$20 = \$50.

For a normal, downward-sloping demand curve, TR rises at first but will eventually start to fall as output increases. This is because the extra revenue gained from dropping price and selling more units is outweighed by the loss in revenue from the units that were being sold at a higher price and now have to be sold at the lower price.

For example, in Table 10.3, when price is dropped from \$15 to \$10, the quantity demanded increases from 14 units to 16. Before the price drop, the TR was \$210 (\$15 × 14). After the price drop, TR becomes \$160 (\$10 × 16).

The MR is –\$25 $\left(\frac{\Delta TR}{\Delta q} = -\frac{50}{2} = -25\right)$.

The negative MR means that TR will fall. MR is negative because, when the price is lowered, two extra units of the product are sold at a price of \$10 each, but the price of the 14 units that could have been sold for \$15 has been dropped to \$10, and so there is a loss of revenue of \$70 (14 × \$5). The overall effect is a fall in total revenue of \$20 – \$70 = –\$50.

There are some very important relationships between price elasticity of demand, MR, AR, and TR that we can identify from Figure 10.5. They are most easily explained by a logic tree, using information already discovered in the study of price elasticity and revenue.

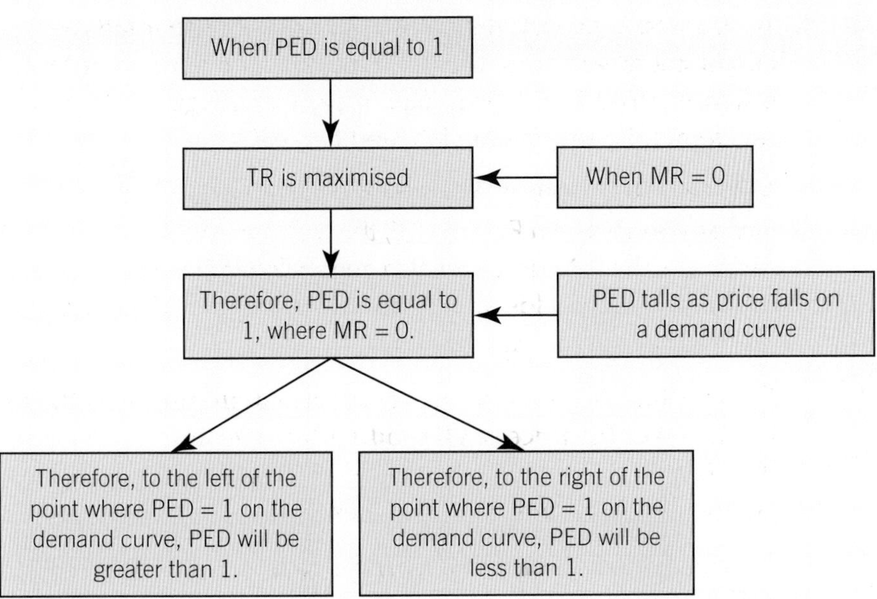

▲ **Figure 10.6** A logic tree explaining the varying values of PED on a demand curve

This knowledge of the relationship between the value of PED for a demand curve and TR is very useful for firms when they are trying to assess the impact that a change in the price of their product will have upon the total revenue that they receive.

If the firm raises price and demand is inelastic then the firm will find that total revenue will increase, because the increase in price will see a relatively smaller fall in the quantity demanded.

However, if the firm raises price and demand is elastic then the firm will find that total revenue will decrease, because the increase in price will cause a relatively larger fall in the quantity demanded.

So, if a firm knows whether their demand is elastic or inelastic, they will know what pricing policy to adopt to increase their revenue.

The basic rules are:

1. When PED is elastic any firm wishing to increase revenue should lower its price.
2. When PED is inelastic any firm wishing to increase revenue should raise its price.
3. When PED is unity then any firm wishing to increase revenue should leave the price unchanged, since revenue is already maximized.

Higher Level

Exercise 10.2

ATL Thinking and Communication

Here are some figures for the price and quantity demanded of a product:

Price ($)	Quantity demanded	Total revenue ($)	Average revenue ($)	Marginal revenue ($)	PED
20	1				
				+16	
18	2				
16	3				
14	4				
12	5		12		
10	6				
8	7				
6	8				
4	9	36			

1. Copy out the table and fill in the missing values in the other columns.
2. On a piece of graph paper, draw a vertical axis, labelled Price ($), going from −12 to +60. Then add a horizontal axis, labelled Quantity Demanded, going from 0 to 10.
3. Plot the demand curve on the graph (ie plot price against quantity demanded). Label the curve D. Plot the Average Revenue curve. What do you notice? Now add "= AR".
4. Plot the Total Revenue curve.
5. Plot the Marginal Revenue curve, remembering to plot it at the half-way marks on the horizontal axis.
6. Using the PED figures that you have calculated, try to identify:
   - the elastic region of the demand curve
   - the inelastic region of the demand curve
   - the point where PED = 1.
7. Complete the following sentences:
   - In the elastic region of the demand curve, as price falls, total revenue ____________.
   - In the inelastic region of the demand curve, as price falls, total revenue ____________.
   - Total revenue is maximized where PED is equal to ____________ and where the marginal revenue is ____________.

4. How do economists measure profits?

An economist and an accountant were talking about the accounts of a company. The accountant said that the owner of the firm, Nermin, would be very happy because the profit for the year was $80,000. The economist, however, looked at the same set of figures and said that the owner would be satisfied, but only just.

"Why is that?" said the accountant. "Profit is total revenue minus total cost and when I work that out the profit figure is very healthy."

"Yes," said the economist, "I agree with your definition of profit, but what you need to understand is that we do not take the same view on how to calculate costs. As an economist I would say that profit is total revenue minus economic cost. Economic cost includes explicit costs (costs that involve the direct payment of money) and implicit costs (earnings that the firm could have had if it employed its factors of production in other ways). In Nermin's case there is only one implicit cost that I would include that you do not include, but it is the most important cost that the firm faces."

"Which cost is that?" asked the accountant.

"I include the opportunity cost of the owner of the firm, the entrepreneur," said the economist. "If an owner does not manage to cover his or her opportunity cost in the long run then they will close the firm down and move on to their next best alternative occupation.

Thus, the opportunity cost is the most important cost for the firm to cover. It is the difference between survival and non-survival. In Nermin's case," said the economist, "I know that she expects to make $80,000 per year, since she could earn the same amount if she closed down the firm and went back to her old job as a marketing manager. That means that she is satisfied with what she has made this year, but no more."

The conversation above explains how economists measure profit.

Total profit = Total revenue – economic cost (explicit and implicit costs)

From this point forward we will assume that we are now economists and that when we say total cost we are including explicit costs and implicit costs. We can identify three profit situations, normal profit, abnormal profit and losses.

If total revenue is equal to total cost (or average revenue is equal to average cost) we say that a firm is making *normal profit* (or zero economic profit).

If total revenue is greater than total cost then we say that the firm is making *abnormal profit* (also known as economic profit).

If total revenue is less than total cost then we say that the firm is making *losses* (or negative economic profit).

	Firm A	Firm B	Firm C
Total revenue	200,000	200,000	200,000
Total fixed cost	40,000	40,000	40,000
Total variable cost	80,000	100,000	120,000
Implicit cost	60,000	60,000	60,000
Total cost	180,000	200,000	220,000

▲**Table 10.4** Revenue and cost information for one year for firms A, B and C (All figures are in US$.)

In Table 10.4 we can see these three situations.

Firm A is making an abnormal profit (economic profit) of $20,000. This means that the revenue earned by the firm is not only covering all the economic costs but is in fact $20,000 more. This will make the entrepreneur happy as she was expecting to cover her implicit costs, including opportunity costs, of $60,000 but exceeds her expectations by $20,000.

Firm B is making normal profit (zero economic profit). The revenue earned by the firm exactly covers all of the economic costs. The entrepreneur will be satisfied.

Firm C is making losses. Although an accountant would say that the firm is making a profit of $40,000 ($200,000 – $160,000), the entrepreneur will not be happy since fixed and variable costs (explicit costs) are covered, but implicit costs are not being covered. The entrepreneur will close the firm down and move on to his or her next best occupation.

For the remainder of this companion we will use the terms abnormal profit, normal profit and losses, but you must remember that these are the same as economic profit, zero economic profit and negative economic profit.

5. How do firms maximize profits?

Economists usually assume that the main aim of a firm is to maximize profits. If this is the case, then firms need to know what level of output they have to produce in order to achieve maximum profits.

If a firm finds that at its present level of output the cost of producing another unit (MC) is less than the revenue that the unit would bring in (MR), it is clear that the firm could increase its profits by producing more. Wherever the firm finds that MR > MC, it should increase production.

We can see the marginal cost and marginal revenue situation for a firm with a perfectly elastic demand curve in Figure 10.7.

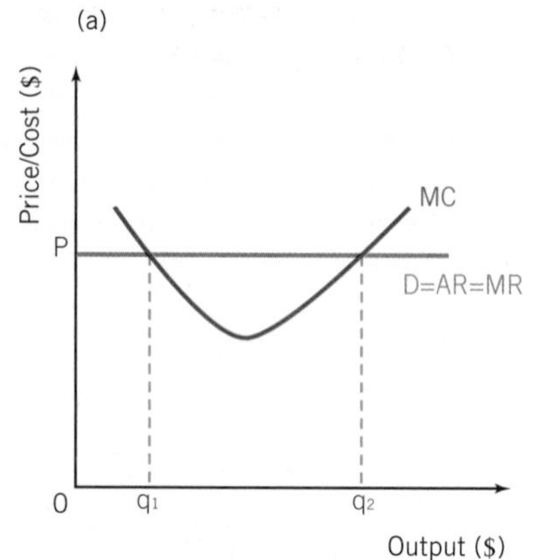

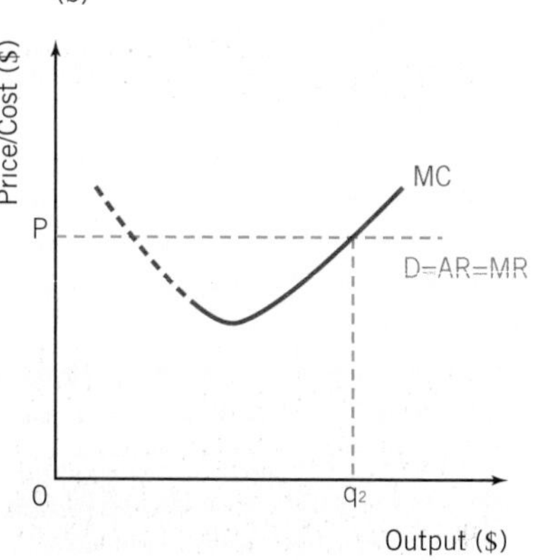

▲ **Figure 10.7** Revenue and costs for a firm with a perfectly elastic demand curve

As we can see in Figure 10.7(a), the MC curve cuts the MR curve at two points. The first point where MC = MR, q_1 is the point of profit minimization (loss maximization). The firm has made a loss on every unit produced up to this level of output, because MC is greater than MR. From q_1 to q_2, the firm makes a profit on every extra unit produced, because the MR is greater than the MC. As long as the profit made between q_1 and q_2 is greater than the loss made on the first q_1 units, then the firm will be making *abnormal profits*. Abnormal profit is when the average revenue is greater than average cost. Any unit that is produced beyond q_2 will make a loss, because MC would again be above MR. So if the firm produces more than q_2, the level of abnormal profit will begin to fall. It is at q_2 where profits are maximized.

Because profit minimization is not what a firm would want, to avoid confusion the left-hand part of the MC curve is normally omitted in diagrams. This means that only the profit maximizing output, q_2, is shown, as in Figure 10.7(b). As a general rule, we can say that:

If a firm wishes to maximize its profits, it should produce at the level of output where Marginal Cost (MC) cuts Marginal Revenue (MR) from below.

Higher Level

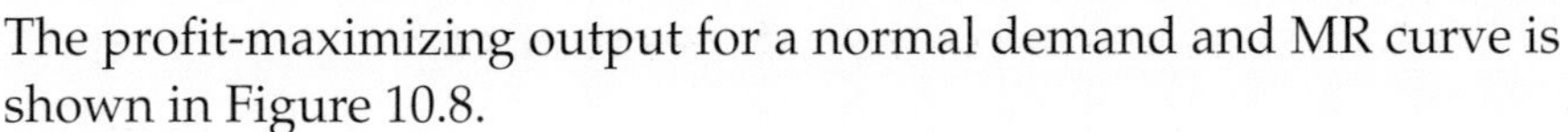

The profit-maximizing output for a normal demand and MR curve is shown in Figure 10.8.

Profit is maximized by producing where MC = MR, at a level of output of q. To find the price, we look at what consumers are willing to pay for this quantity. This is shown on the demand curve. It is found by going from q up to the demand curve and then across to the *y*-axis. This would be a price of p.

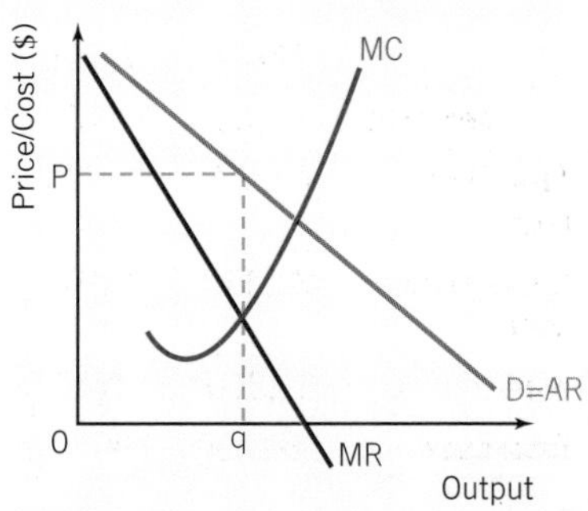

▲ **Figure 10.8** The profit-maximising level of output for a normal demand curve

In order to show a measurable amount of profit on a diagram, ie a simple shape like a rectangle, the average cost curve (AC) is added to the diagram.

You must remember to make sure that the MC curve cuts the AC curve at the lowest point on the AC.

This is shown in Figure 10.9.

The profit-maximizing output is q and the price is p. The profit per unit of producing q is the difference between AR and AC. Thus the profit per unit is a – b. Since q units are produced, the total abnormal profit is the shaded area, ab × 0Q.

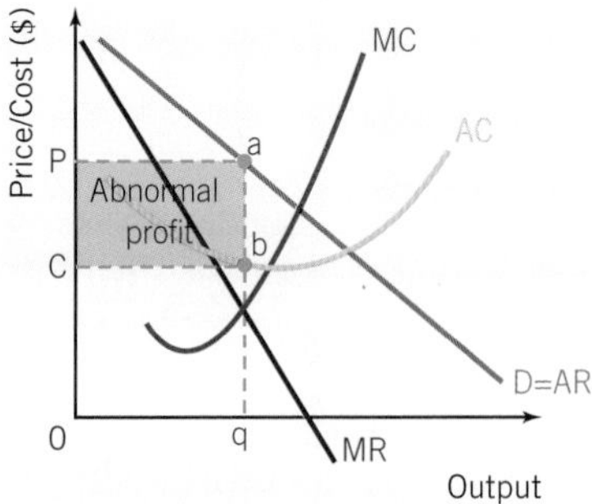

▲ **Figure 10.9** Showing an area of profit using the AC curve

Whether an abnormal profit is made will depend upon the position of the AC curve. The AC curve is a student's best friend! This is because it can be moved around to show what we want, ie *abnormal profit, normal profit or losses*. This is shown in Figure 10.10.

If the average cost is at AC, then the diagram shows an abnormal profit of pabc. If the average cost is represented by AC_1, then normal profit is being made, because p = c_1 and so there is no abnormal profit rectangle. If average cost is shown by AC_2, then a loss is being made and it is represented by the rectangle pc_2da.

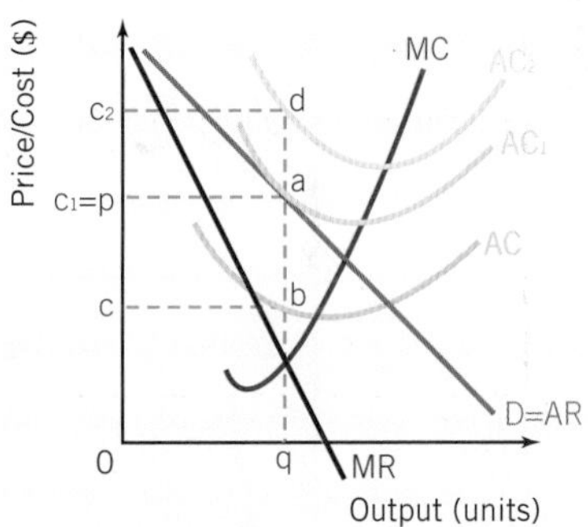

▲ **Figure 10.10** Using AC to show different profit and loss situations

Do businesses have objectives other than profit maximization? Do they always behave rationally?

In reality, the assumption that producers behave "'rationally" by only attempting to maximize profits is often not true. Firms may not always have the main aim of maximizing profits. Other aims followed by entrepreneurs may be:

1. Corporate social responsibility

Corporate social responsibility (CSR): this is where a business includes the "public interest" in its decision making. It adopts an ethical code that accepts responsibility for the impact of its activities on areas such as the workforce, consumers, the local community and the environment. Different businesses may adopt different approaches to CSR. Some may concentrate on encouraging development in the workforce and the local community through educational projects and fair trade projects. Some may concentrate on reducing their negative effect on the environment by cutting emissions and the use of sustainable resources. Some may make the provision of aid to less developed communities a priority. In some cases businesses may adopt all of the above approaches to some extent.

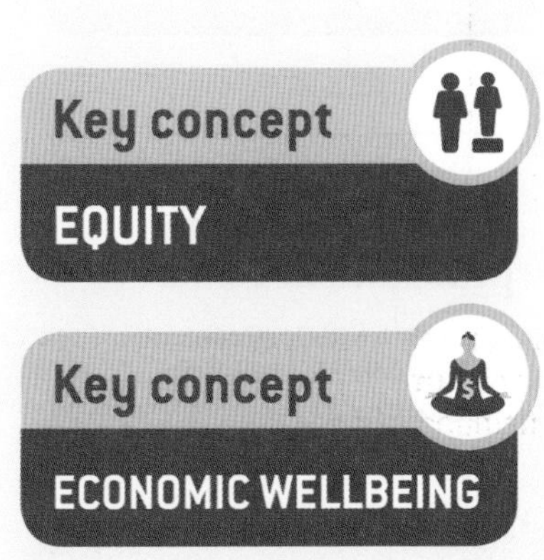

Higher Level

There are a number of advantages to adopting a CSR approach such as attracting and keeping a better workforce, building up reputation, and developing brand loyalty for being an ethical business. If companies adopt appropriate corporate social responsibility policies and are active in addressing social and environmental issues it can also reduce the need for government intervention in business activities. There has been a solid increase in "ethical consumerism" and CSR since the mid-1980s. As consumers become more aware of global and environmental issues, they are more likely to favour businesses that promote ethical considerations.

However, there have been concerns regarding CSR. Some economists have argued that companies may be adopting a CSR approach to gain a good reputation in order to take people's attention away from their main product. This has especially been suggested for companies that produce cigarettes and alcohol.

Economics in action — ATL Thinking, Communication and Research

Consider the impact of a company on others and the environment.

Using the Internet, research the corporate social responsibility policy of a large multinational company. References to the company's policies are often found on the company's homepage under the title "Corporate Social Responsibility" or "Sustainability.

Make a display poster or a PowerPoint presentation to illustrate your company's approach to CSR.

It is highly likely that the company will only present the expected positive outcomes of its actions. As you investigate, try to think critically about these policies, both to the extent to which the company fulfils its commitments and the reasons for doing so. Doing a bit more research might even uncover some negative consequences of the company's behaviour that its homepage would not reveal.

Debate the following topic with your classmates:

What are the real motivations behind corporate social responsibility?

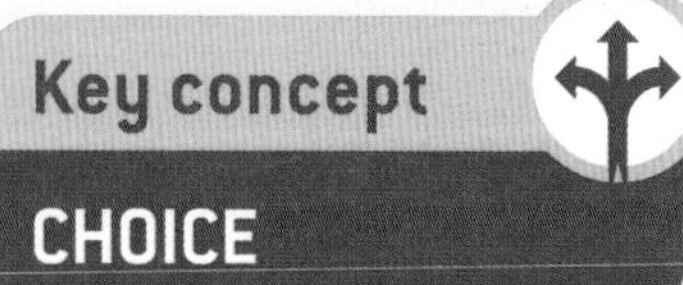

2. Satisficing

Satisficing: there are now economic theories that doubt whether entrepreneurs ever, in reality, attempt to maximize profits. They claim that what entrepreneurs actually do is to "satisfice". Satisficing is where an economic agent aims to perform satisfactorily rather than to a maximum level, in order to be able to pursue other goals. For example, if people own firms they will work hard enough to make a reasonable living (cover their opportunity costs), but will not really push themselves further, preferring to follow other goals, such as the pursuit of leisure. In many cases firms are run by people who do not actually own them. An example of this would be a firm owned by shareholders who are not involved in running the company and are therefore managed by employed non-owners.

Companies should balance profit with principles in China

https://www.ft.com/content/cd1f0fb8-9831-11e9-8cfb-30c211dcd229

In this case the managers do not have a great deal to gain if the firm makes maximum profits. It is likely that the managers will make enough profit to keep the owners of the firm happy, thereby keeping their jobs, but no more. They will "satisfice".

3. Growth maximization (increasing market share)

Growth maximization: companies may set their target to achieve growth in the short run, rather than profits, in order to gain a large market share and then dominate the market in the long run. Growth may be measured in a number of ways, such as the quantity of sales, sales revenue, employment or the percentage of market share.

4. Revenue maximization

Revenue maximization: entrepreneurs often measure success by the amount of revenue that they make. If this is the case then they may attempt to maximize their sales revenue by producing where the marginal revenue is zero. They will actually produce above the profit maximizing level of output (see Figure 10.8).

H&M, Ikea, Gap, Adidas and Nike Among Global Brands Leading on Sustainable Cotton Sourcing

https://www.csrwire.com/press_releases/42148-H-M-Ikea-Gap-Adidas-and-Nike-Among-Global-Brands-Leading-on-Sustainable-Cotton-Sourcing

Assessment advice: Calculations.

In HL Paper 3, you may be asked to calculate marginal cost, marginal revenue, average cost, average revenue and/or profit from a set of data.

EXAMINATION QUESTIONS

Paper 1, HL – Full questions

1. **a)** Explain how a firm may maximize profits. [10 marks]

   b) Using real-world examples, discuss the implications of **two** business objectives that may be followed, as an alternative to profit maximization. [15 marks]

2. **a)** Explain why the supply curve slopes upwards. [10 marks]

   b) Using real-world examples, discuss the idea that profit maximization is the best strategy for firms. [15 marks]

Paper 3, HL – Part questions

The total cost information for a firm, in dollars ($), is given in the table below:

Output (q)	Total cost (TC)	Total fixed cost (TFC)	Total variable cost (TVC)	Average fixed cost (AFC)	Average variable cost (AVC)	Average total cost (ATC)	Marginal cost (MC)
0	40			–			
1	90			40			
2	130			20			
3	160			13.33			
4	200			10			
5	250			8			
6	320			6.67			

a) Complete the cost information in the table above for all levels of output.

b) Explain why the AFC values fall as output increases.

11 MARKET POWER: PERFECT COMPETITION AND MONOPOLISTIC COMPETITION

REAL-WORLD ISSUE:
When are markets unable to satisfy important economic objectives and does government intervention help?

By the end of this chapter, you should be able to:

- HL Define market power
- HL Identify the four market forms, perfect competition, monopolistic competition, oligopoly and monopoly
- HL Explain the assumptions of perfect competition
- HL Distinguish between the demand curve for the industry and for the firm in perfect competition
- HL Explain the lack of market power in perfect competition
- HL Explain how firms maximize profits in perfect competition
- HL Explain and illustrate short run profit and loss situations in perfect competition
- HL Explain and illustrate the long run equilibrium in perfect competition
- HL Explain and illustrate the movement from short run to long run in perfect competition
- HL Explain and illustrate efficiency in the short run and the long run in perfect competition
- HL Discuss the existence or non-existence of market failure in perfect competition and the need for government intervention
- HL Define imperfect competition
- HL Explain the assumptions of monopolistic competition
- HL Explain the level of market power in monopolistic competition
- HL Explain how firms maximize profits in monopolistic competition

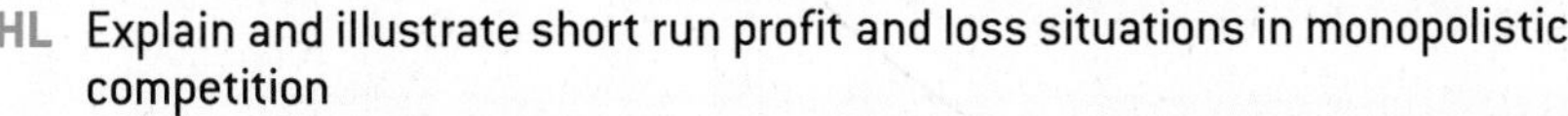

- **HL** Explain and illustrate short run profit and loss situations in monopolistic competition
- **HL** Explain and illustrate the long run equilibrium in monopolistic competition
- **HL** Explain and illustrate the movement from short run to long run in monopolistic competition
- **HL** Explain and illustrate efficiency in the short run and the long run in monopolistic competition
- **HL** Discuss the extent of market failure in monopolistic competition and whether there is a need for government intervention.

What is market power?

Market power is the ability of a firm to raise the market price of a good or service above marginal cost. The firm is able to influence market outcomes by restricting output in order to increase price.

In perfectly competitive markets, firms in the market have no market power, because they cannot do this. If they raise their prices, demand falls to zero. Because the firms cannot raise price, they are said to be *"price takers"*.

In imperfect markets, firms can raise prices without losing all of their customers. A firm with complete market power could raise prices without losing any customers. Firms that have some degree of market power are said to be *"price makers"* or *"price setters"*.

Price makers experience a normal, downward-sloping demand curve and so have the ability to alter price, or the quantity supplied, but not both. Increases in price will lead to a fall in the quantity demanded.

Reducing supply in order to increase price is considered to be bad for society, since it moves the market away from the socially-efficient level of output (MSC = MSB), thus creating a reduction in community surplus and a market failure. Because of this, many countries impose legislation to limit the market power that firms might develop and utilize.

What are the market forms?

As we already know social scientists, especially economists, are model builders. We use models to explain how things work and what might be the possible outcomes of certain economic situations.

In order to understand and predict how markets operate differently, economists have identified four *market forms*. These are perfect competition, monopolistic competition, oligopoly and monopoly. We need to look at each of the market forms and to try to understand the degrees of market power that may exist in each one. By doing this, we can try to assess the relative market intervention that governments may make in order to limit the market power.

What is perfect competition?

What are the assumptions of perfect competition?

Perfect competition is a model used as the starting point to explain how firms operate. It is a theoretical model, based upon some very precise assumptions. However, although it is purely theoretical, it is very important because once we have built our model of a perfectly competitive market we can then begin to relax the theoretical assumptions that we have made and move towards models of markets that are much more realistic.

Perfect competition is based upon a number of assumptions:

- The industry is made up of a very large number of firms.
- Each firm is so small, relative to the size of the industry, that it is not capable of altering its own output to have a noticeable effect upon the output of the industry as a whole. This means that a firm cannot affect the supply curve of the industry and so cannot affect the price of the product. Individual firms have to sell at whatever price is set by demand and supply in the industry as a whole. We say that the individual firms are "*price-takers*".
- The firms all produce exactly identical products. Their goods are "homogeneous". It is not possible to distinguish between a good produced in one firm and a good produced in another. There are no brand names and there is no marketing to attempt to make goods different from each other.
- Firms are completely free to enter or leave the industry. This means that the firms already in the industry do not have the ability to stop new firms from entering it and are also free to leave the industry, if they so wish. We say that there are no barriers to entry or barriers to exit.
- All producers and consumers have a perfect knowledge of the market. The producers are fully aware of market prices, costs in the industry and the workings of the market. The consumers are fully aware of prices in the market, the quality of products and the availability of the goods.

Although we say that it is completely theoretical, there are some industries in the world that get quite close to being perfectly competitive markets. The industries most often used as examples by economists are usually agricultural markets.

For example, let us consider the growing of wheat in the European Union (EU). There are some large wheat farms in the EU, but they are very small in relation to the whole wheat-growing industry. An individual farm could increase its output many times over without having a noticeable effect on the total supply of wheat in the EU. Thus a single farm is not able to affect the price of wheat in the EU, since it cannot shift the industry supply curve. The farm has to sell at whatever the existing industry price is. In addition, wheat is wheat, and so there is no way to tell one farm's wheat from another.

So far so good for the assumptions of perfect competition. However, although firms are relatively free to enter or leave the wheat industry, there are significant costs in doing either and these may affect the decisions of firms. Also, although information is fairly open in the industry it is unlikely that producers and consumers will have "perfect knowledge". We can say that the wheat industry in the EU may be close to being a perfectly competitive market, but is not precisely one.

How much market power exists in perfect competition?

We have said that the individual firms in perfect competition will be *price-takers*, since they cannot affect the price of the industry and so must sell at whatever the market price is. This means that we can make certain assumptions about the demand curves for both the firm and the industry.

As we can see in Figure 11.1, the industry in perfect competition will face normal demand and supply curves. We would expect producers to wish to supply more at higher prices and we would expect consumers to demand less as price rises. We would expect demand to be downward sloping and supply to be upward sloping. The industry price would therefore be P and the quantity demanded would be Q.

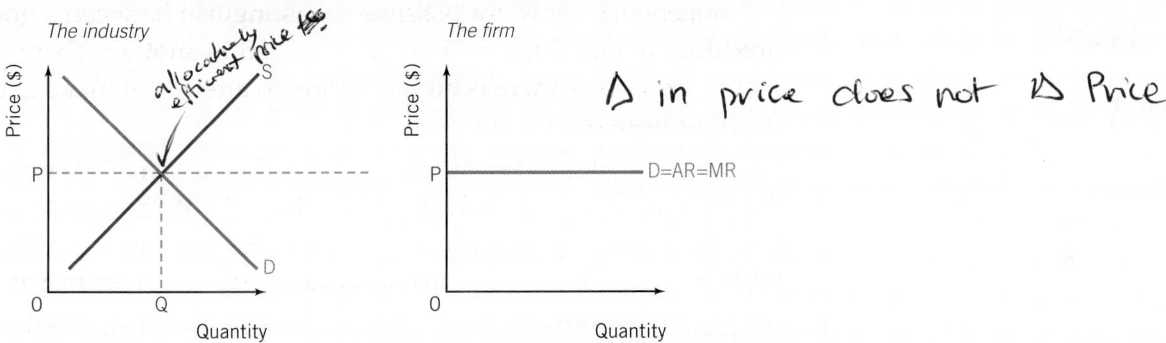

▲ **Figure 11.1** The demand curves for the industry and the firm in perfect competition

For the individual firms we know that they will have to sell at the industry price, P, because they are price-takers. If they try to sell at a higher price, then consumers will simply buy the product from another firm, since the goods are homogeneous and so there is no difference in looks or quality. If they sell at the industry price the firm can sell as much as it wants, because as it increases output it does not affect the industry supply curve and so it does not alter the industry price.

If the firm can sell all that it wishes at the price P then it must face a perfectly elastic demand at that price. In Figure 11.1 we can see that the firm derives its price of P from the equilibrium price in the industry, where the industry supply equals the industry demand. This is another explanation of the term "price-taker", because the firm has to take the price set in the industry. The firm has no market power.

Higher Level

How do firms in perfect competition maximize profits in the short run?

As we discovered in Chapter 10, firms maximize profits when they produce at the level of output where MC = MR. For perfect competition, we now have to add the marginal cost curve, shown in Figure 11.2.

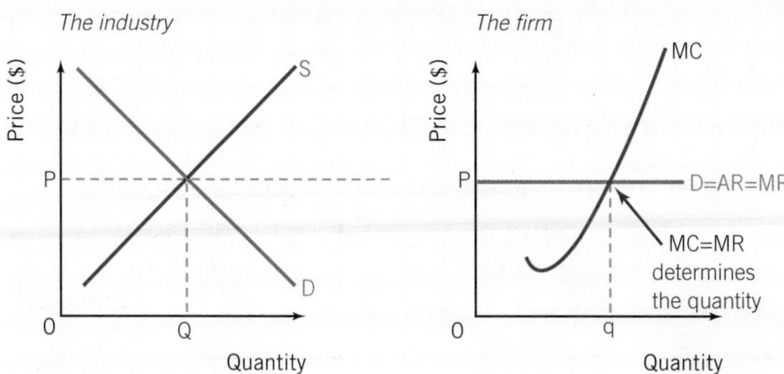

▲ **Figure 11.2** The profit-maximizing level of output in perfect competition

We can see that the firm takes the price P from the industry and, because the demand is perfectly elastic, P = D = AR = MR. Profit is maximized where MC = MR, which is at the level of output q. We must remember that although the scale of the price axis is the same for the firm and the industry, this is not the case for output. The quantity q is very small in relation to the total industry output, Q, and it would not even register on the output axis for the industry. If it could, then it would be large enough to shift the supply curve and thus alter the industry price. In that case, the firms would have some degree of market power.

In the short run in perfect competition, there are two possible profit/loss situations:

1. ***Short-run abnormal profits***: In this case, which is shown in Figure 11.3, the firms in the industry are making abnormal profits in the short run. This means that they are more than covering their total costs, including the opportunity costs.

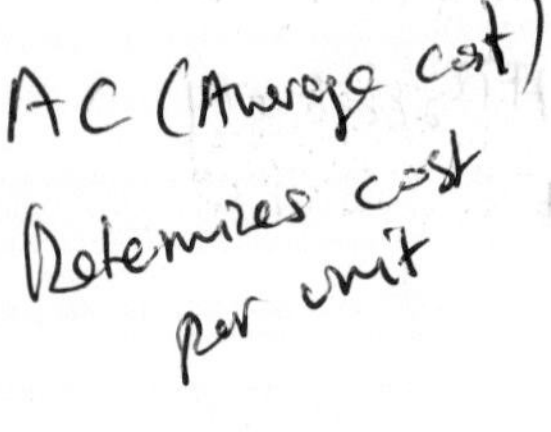

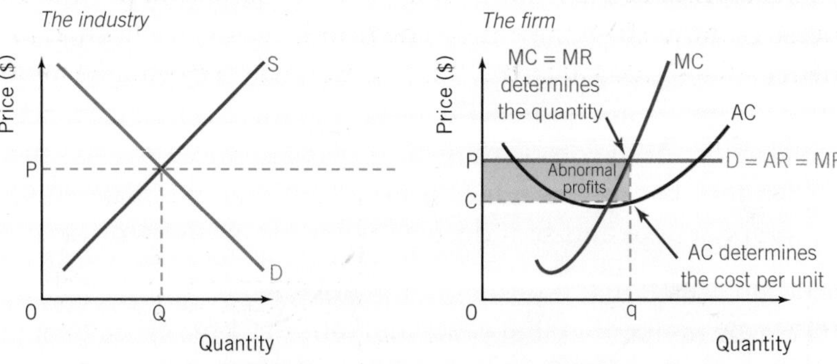

▲ **Figure 11.3** Short-run abnormal profits in perfect competion

As we can see in Figure 11.3, the firm is selling at the industry price, P, and is maximizing profits by producing at the quantity q, where MC = MR. At q, the cost per unit, average cost, is C, and the revenue per unit, average revenue, is P, so average cost is less than average revenue and the firm is making an abnormal profit of P – C on each unit. The shaded area shows the total abnormal profit.

2. ***Short-run losses***: In this case, shown in Figure 11.4, the firms in the industry are making losses in the short run. This means that they are not covering their total costs.

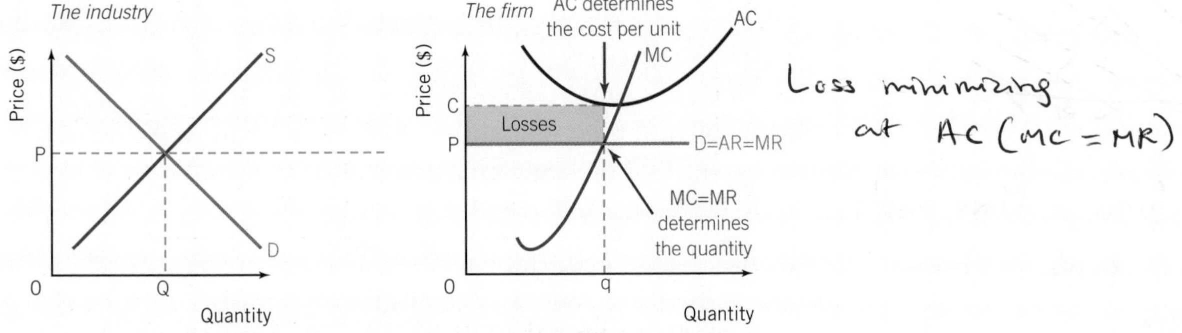

▲ **Figure 11.4** Short-run losses in perfect competition

In Figure 11.4 the firm is selling at the industry price, P, and is maximizing profits by producing at the quantity q, where MC = MR. However at output q, the cost per unit is C, which is greater than the price and so the firm is making a loss of C – P on each unit. The shaded area shows the total loss. Although making a loss, the firm is still producing at the "profit-maximizing" level of output, because any other output would create a greater loss. In effect, they are loss minimizing.

What happens to short-run profits or losses in the long run in perfect competition?

If firms are making either short-run abnormal profits or short-run losses, other firms begin to react and the situation starts to change until an equilibrium point is reached in the long run.

1. Short-run abnormal profits to long-run normal profits

Let us look first at the situation of short-run abnormal profits. The process is shown in Figure 11.5. The firm is making abnormal profits shown by the shaded area, but this situation will not continue for long.

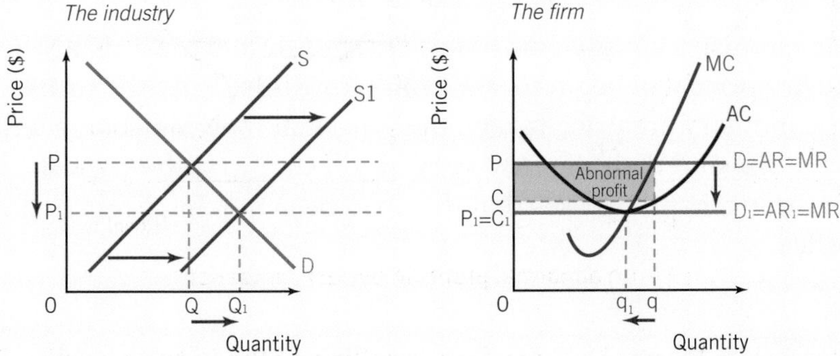

▲ **Figure 11.5** The movement from short-run abnormal profit to long-run normal profit

Higher Level

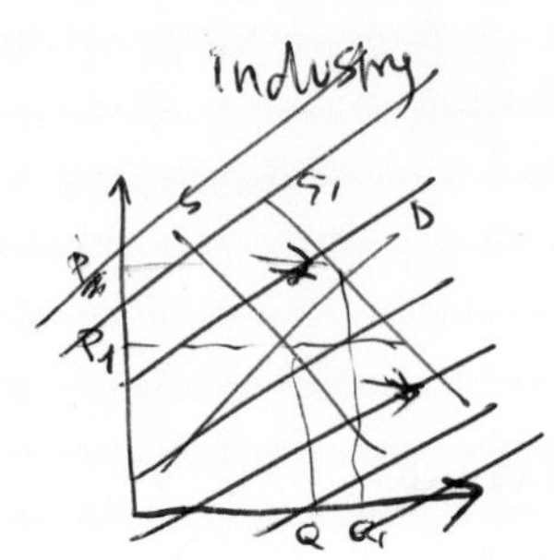

Since there is perfect knowledge and no barriers to entry, firms outside the industry that could also produce the good will start to enter the industry, attracted by the chance to make abnormal profits. At first, this will have no real effect, because the firms are relatively small. However, as more and more firms enter the industry, attracted by the abnormal profits, the industry supply curve will start to shift to the right.

As the industry supply curve starts to shift from S towards S_1, the industry price will begin to fall from P towards P_1. Because the firms in the industry are price-takers, the price that they can charge will start to fall and their demand curves will start to shift downwards. This means that the abnormal profits that they had been making will start to be "competed away".

This process will continue as long as there are abnormal profits in the industry. Eventually the industry supply curve reaches S_1, where the price is P_1. At this point, the firms are "taking" the price of P_1 and the demand curve is $D_1 = AR_1 = MR_1$. We now find that the firms are making normal profits with the price per unit equal to the cost per unit, ie $P_1 = C_1$. The entrepreneurs of the firms in the industry are satisfied, because they are exactly covering their opportunity costs. However, there is now no abnormal profit to attract more firms into the industry and so the industry is in a long-run equilibrium situation. No one will now enter and no one will now leave. The outcome is a much bigger industry producing Q_1 units, with more, smaller firms each producing q_1 units.

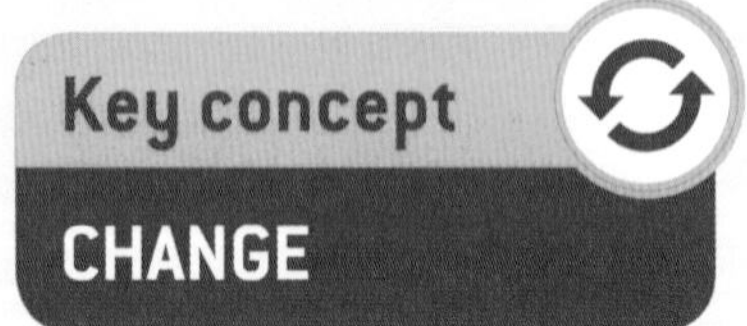

2. Short-run losses to long-run normal profits

Now take the situation of short-run losses. The process is shown in Figure 11.6. As we can see, the firm is making losses shown by the shaded area, but this situation will not remain the same.

Some firms in the industry will, after a time, start to leave the industry. At first this will have no real effect, because the firms are relatively small. However, as more and more firms leave the industry, unable to achieve normal profit, the industry supply curve will start to shift to the left.

As the industry supply curve starts to shift from S towards S_1, the industry price will begin to rise from P towards P_1. As the firms in the industry are price-takers, the price that they can charge will start to rise and their demand curves will start to shift upwards. This means that the losses that they had been making begin to get smaller.

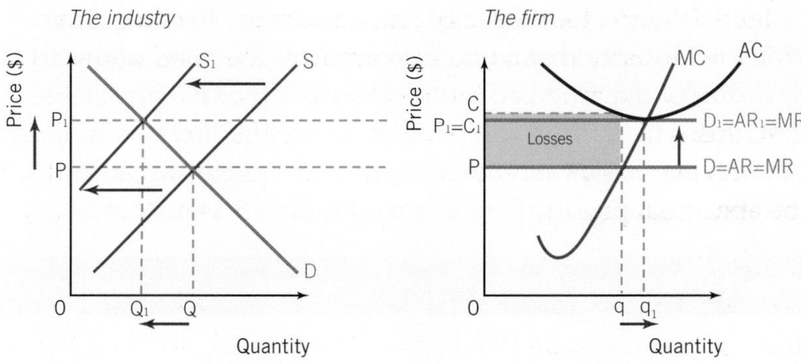

▲ **Figure 11.6** The movement from short-run losses to long-run normal profit

This process will continue as long as there are losses being made in the industry. Eventually, the industry supply curve reaches S_1, where the price is P_1. At this point, the firms are "taking" the price of P_1 and the demand curve is $D_1 = AR_1 = MR_1$. We now find that the firms are making normal profits, with the price per unit equal to the cost per unit, ie $P_1 = C_1$. Now the entrepreneurs of the firms in the industry are satisfied, because they are exactly covering all of their costs, including their opportunity costs. There is no reason to leave the industry. There are also no abnormal profits to attract new firms into the industry, so the industry is in a long-run equilibrium situation. No one will now enter and no one will now leave. The outcome will be a smaller industry producing only Q_1 units, with slightly larger firms, each producing q_1 units.

What is long-run equilibrium in perfect competition?

We can conclude that, in the long run, firms in perfect competition will make normal profits. This is because, even if they are making short-run abnormal profits or short-run losses, the industry will adjust with firms entering or leaving the industry until a normal profit situation is reached.

In Figure 11.7, the firms are making normal profits in the long run. They are selling at the price P, which they are taking from the industry. MC is equal to MR so they are maximizing profits by producing q, and at that output P is equal to AC so they are making normal profits.

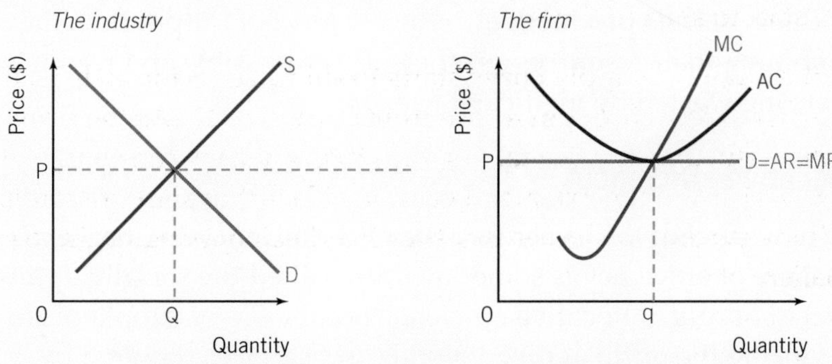

▲ **Figure 11.7** Long-run equilibrium in perfect competition

In this situation there is no incentive for firms to enter or leave the industry and so the equilibrium will persist until there is a change in either the industry demand curve or in the costs that the firms face. If this does happen, then firms will be making either short-run abnormal profits or short-run losses and the industry will once again adjust, with firms entering or leaving until long-run equilibrium is restored.

Exercise 11.1

ATL Thinking and Communication

1. Explain why a firm in perfect competition is a "price-taker".
2. Draw the following diagrams. Be sure to use a ruler and to include accurate labels for the axes. Also, be sure that your MC curves cross the minimum point of the AC curves.
   - A firm in perfect competition earning abnormal profits.
   - A firm in perfect competition making economic losses.
   - A firm in perfect competition in its long run equilibrium earning normal profits.

Key concept

EFFICIENCY

How efficient are firms in perfect competition?

When considering efficiency, we need to look at two different ways of measuring it:

1. Productive efficiency

One of the efficiency measures used by economists is that of productive efficiency. A firm is said to be productively efficient if it produces its product at the lowest possible unit cost (average cost). This is shown in Figure 11.8.

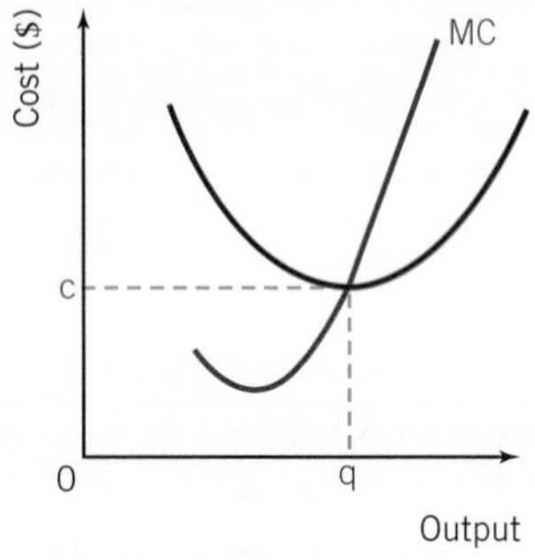

▲ **Figure 11.8** Productive efficiency

At the output q, the firm in Figure 11.8 is able to produce at the most efficient level of output, ie the lowest average cost of production. This is the cost c. So q is known as the productively efficient level of output.

We know from chapter 10 that MC always cuts AC at its lowest point, and so we can say that the productively efficient level is where:

$$MC = AC$$

Productive efficiency is important in economics, because if a firm is producing at the productively efficient level of output then they are combining their resources as efficiently as possible and resources are not being wasted by inefficient use.

2. Allocative efficiency

We have already come across allocative efficiency in Chapter 7. This measure of efficiency is sometimes also called the socially optimum level of output. Allocative efficiency occurs where suppliers are producing the optimal mix of goods and services required by consumers.

Price reflects the value that consumers place on a good and is shown on the demand curve (average revenue). Marginal cost reflects the cost to society of all the resources used in producing an extra unit of a good, including the normal profit required for the firm to stay in business. If price were to be greater than marginal cost, then the consumers would value the good more than the cost it was to make. If both sets of stakeholders are to meet at the optimal mix, then output would expand to the point where price equals marginal cost. Similarly, if the marginal cost were to be greater than the price, then society would be using more resources to produce the good than the value it gives to consumers and output would fall.

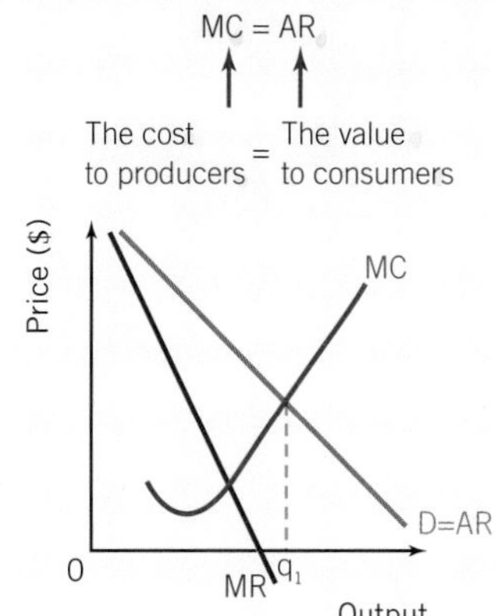

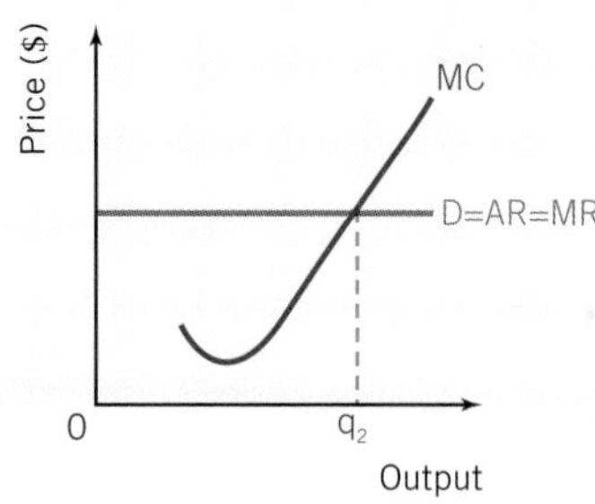

▲ **Figure 11.9** Allocative efficiency

Allocative efficiency occurs where marginal cost (the cost of producing one more unit) is equal to average revenue (the price received for a unit).

In Figure 11.9, we can see the allocatively efficient level of output for a firm with a normal demand curve and for a firm with a perfectly elastic demand curve. In both cases we are looking for the output where MC = AR, which is q_1 for the firm with a normal demand curve and q_2 when the demand is perfectly elastic.

Allocative efficiency is important in economics, because if a firm is producing at the allocatively efficient level of output there is a situation of "*Pareto optimality*" where it is impossible to make one person better off without making someone else worse off. We have already looked at this to some extent in Chapter 9.

If a firm is making abnormal profits in the short run in perfect competition, we can see from Figure 11.10 that although they are producing at the profit-maximizing level of output, q (where MC = MR), and the allocatively efficient level of output, q_2 (where MC = AR), the firm is not producing at the most efficient level of output, q_1 (where MC = AC).

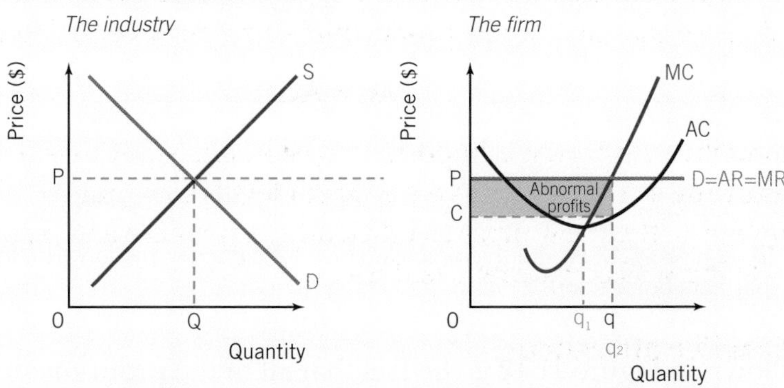

▲ **Figure 11.10** Productive and allocative efficiency with short-run profit in perfect competition

In the same way, if a firm is making losses in the short run in perfect competition, we can see from Figure 11.11 that although they are producing at the profit-maximising level of output, q (where MC = MR), and the allocatively efficient level of output, q_2 (where MC = AR), once again the firm is not producing at the most efficient level of output, q_1 (where MC = AC).

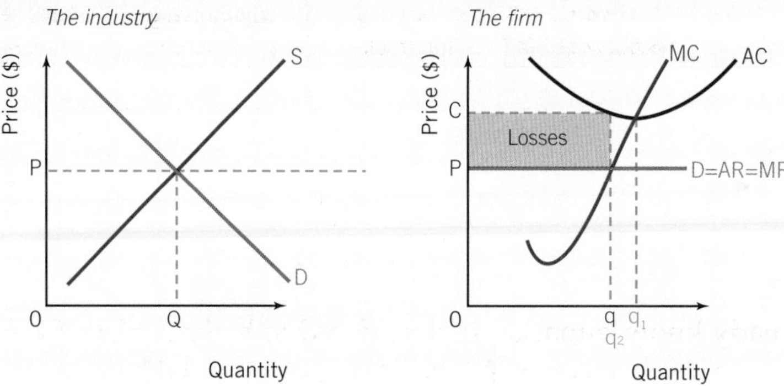

▲ **Figure 11.11** Productive and allocative efficiency with short-run losses in perfect competition

Is there a market failure that needs to be rectified in perfect competition?

As we can see in Figure 11.12, profit-maximizing firms in the long run in perfect competition all produce at the lowest point of their long-run average cost curves. Because we assume that there is perfect knowledge in the industry, all the firms will face the same cost curves, and so they are all selling at the same price and minimizing their average costs by producing where MC = AC.

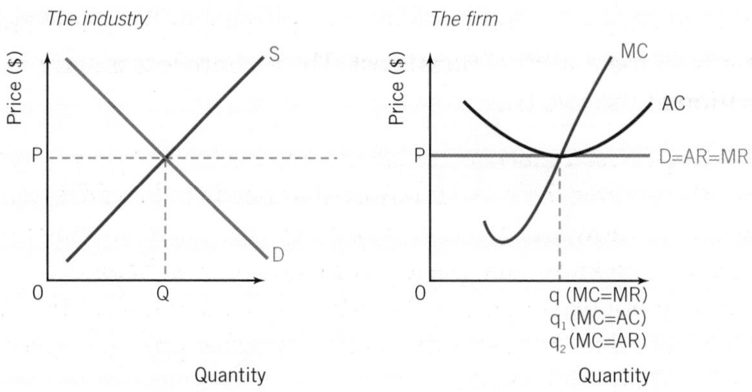

▲ **Figure 11.12** Productive and allocative efficiency in the long run in perfect competition

Also shown in Figure 11.12 is the fact that all of the profit-maximizing firms in the long run in perfect competition are also producing at the allocatively efficient level of output, because they produce where MC = AR. This means that there is no market failure involved in perfect competition, since we know that market failure exists when a firm fails to produce at the allocatively efficient level of output. This in turn means that there is no need for government intervention in perfectly competitive markets to rectify any market failure. The market power of perfectly competitive firms is non-existent, since they are price-takers.

Exercise 11.2 — ATL Thinking and Communication

Fill in the spaces in the table below with either a yes or a no.

Perfect competition	Abnormal profits possible?	Losses possible?	Allocatively efficient?	Productively efficient?
Short run				
Long run				

What is imperfect competition?

As we already know, a market is considered to be imperfect if it fails to equate marginal social cost (MSC) and marginal social benefit (MSB). This applies to all markets where the firms face a normal, downward-sloping demand curve. Monopolists and other imperfect markets may restrict output to push up prices and maximize profits, because they have market power. Because of this, they do not produce at the socially efficient level of output. This is shown in Figure 11.13.

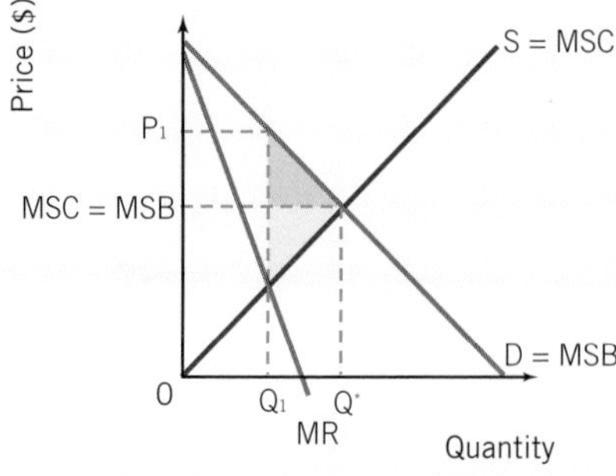

▲ **Figure 11.13** Imperfect competition

Because profits are maximized where MC = MR, Q_1 will be produced at a price of P_1 and the socially efficient level of output, Q*, is not reached. There is therefore a loss of consumer surplus, shown by the shaded dark blue triangle, and a loss of producer surplus, shown by the shaded pale blue triangle. Thus community surplus is not maximized and we have a situation of market failure. When community surplus falls from the maximum, we say that there has been a welfare loss. This is because the units Q_1 – Q* are not produced, even though the marginal social benefit is greater than the marginal social cost. The welfare loss is shown by the combination of the two triangles.

The more imperfect a market – ie the greater the market power available to firms – the greater the market failure that needs to be addressed will be. As we now know, in perfect competition, there is no market failure. However, we also know that perfect competition is a theoretical market form that may not exist in the real world. We need to look at the other market forms and try to assess the levels of market power, market failure and thus intervention needed.

What are the assumptions of monopolistic competition?

The theory of monopolistic competition was developed by Edward Chamberlin (1899–1967), an American economist. Chamberlin was dissatisfied with the two extreme theories that existed at the time, perfect competition and monopoly, so wanted to devise something more realistic that would sit between the two existing theories. In simple terms, a monopolistically competitive market is one with many competing firms where each firm has a little bit of market power. This is why we have the term "monopolistic", as firms have some ability to set their own prices. They are "mini-monopolies".

The assumptions for monopolistic competition are as follows:

- The industry is made up of a fairly large number of firms.
- The firms are small, relative to the size of the industry. This means that the actions of one firm are unlikely to have a great effect on any of its competitors. The firms assume that they are able to act independently of each other.
- The firms all produce slightly differentiated products. This means that it is possible for a consumer to tell one firm's product from another.
- Firms are completely free to enter or leave the industry. That is, there are no barriers to entry or exit.

The only difference from perfect competition is that in monopolistic competition there is *product differentiation*. Product differentiation exists when a good or service is perceived to be different from other goods or services in some way. Products may be differentiated by brand name, colour, appearance, packaging, design, quality of service, skill levels and many other methods. Examples of monopolistically competitive industries are nail (manicure) salons, car mechanics, plumbers and jewellers.

▲ **Figure 11.14** The demand curve for a firm in monopolistic competition

Although it may appear to be a small difference from the assumptions of perfect competition, this leads to a markedly different market structure. As the products are differentiated there will be some extent of brand loyalty. This means that some of the consumers will be loyal to the product and continue to buy it if the price goes up a little. For example, it may be that the customers of a certain plumber will stay with that plumber when she raises her prices above local rivals, because they believe that she is slightly more skilled than her competitors.

This brand loyalty means that producers have some element of independence when they are deciding on price. They are, to an extent, *price-makers*, and so they face a downward sloping demand curve. However, demand will be relatively elastic since there are many, only slightly different substitutes.

The demand curve facing a monopolistically competitive firm is shown in Figure 11.14.

The firm faces a downward sloping demand curve with a marginal revenue curve that is below it and produces so that it is maximizing profits where MC = MR. This means that the firm in Figure 11.14 will produce an output of q and sell that output at the price of P.

Exercise 11.3

ATL Thinking and Communication

Have you ever walked down a street in a tourist area and seen a lot of restaurants with similar menus? Explain why the restaurants might be considered to be operating in monopolistic competition.

How much market power exists in monopolistic competition?

We have said that the individual firms in monopolistic competition will be *price-makers*, since they face downward-sloping demand curves. This means that a firm is able to raise prices, so long as they are prepared to accept a fairly large fall in quantity demanded. (Demand is relatively elastic.)

However, the firm has very little market power, since it is so small relative to the size of the industry. Hence, it cannot increase the industry price by reducing output. We will see in chapter 12 that larger firms in oligopoly and monopoly are able to do this and so may develop significant market power from their size relative to the size of the industry.

How do firms in monopolistic competition maximize profits in the short run?

Just as in perfect competition, it is possible for firms in monopolistic competition to make abnormal profits in the short run. This is shown in Figure 11.15.

In this case, the firm is maximizing profits by producing at the level of output where MC = MR, and the cost per unit (AC) of C is less than the selling price of P. There is an abnormal profit that is shown by the shaded area.

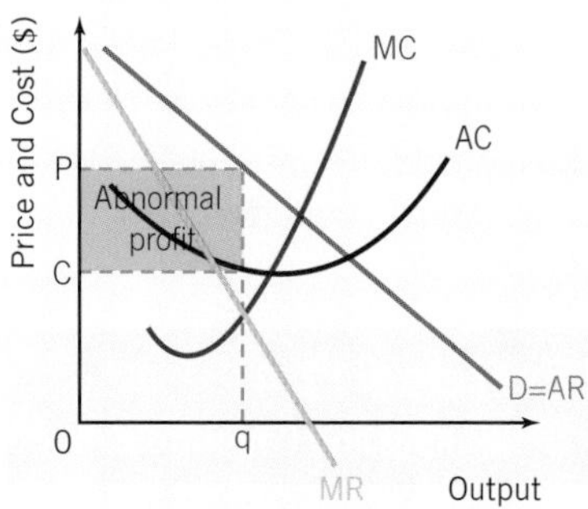

▲ **Figure 11.15** Short-run abnormal profits in monopolistic competition

It is also possible that a firm in monopolistic competition may be making losses in the short run and this is shown in Figure 11.16. Once again, the firm is producing where MC = MR, but this time the cost per unit, C, is above the price, P, and the amount of losses is shown by the shaded area.

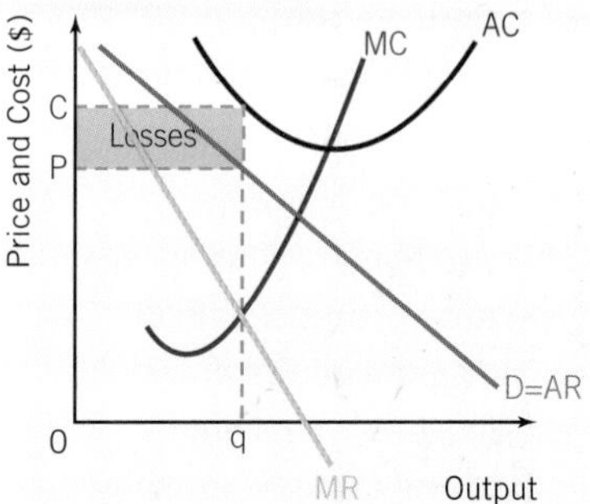

▲ **Figure 11.16** Short-run losses in monopolistic competition

What happens to short-run profits or losses in the long run in monopolistic competition?

Whether firms are making abnormal profits or losses in the short run, because of the freedom of entry and exit in the industry, there will be a long-run equilibrium, where all of the firms in the industry are making normal profits.

Key concept
CHANGE

If the firms are making short-run abnormal profits, then other firms will be attracted to the industry. Since there are no barriers to entry it is possible for these other firms to join the industry. As they enter, they will take business away from the existing firms, whose demand curves will start to shift to the left. If firms are making short-run losses, then some of the firms in the industry will start to leave. The firms that remain will find that their demand curves start to shift to the right as they pick up trade from the leaving firms.

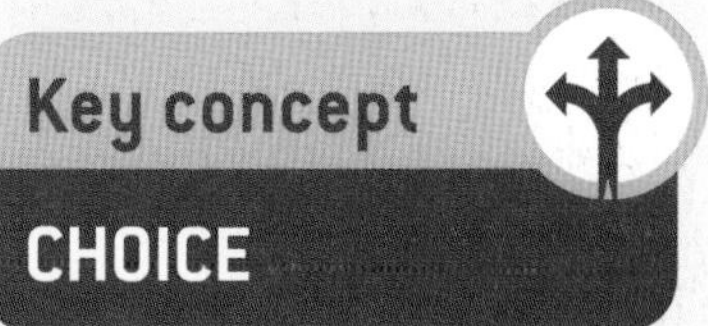

This analysis explains why it is not uncommon to see similar shops or services spring up in an area. Imagine that a new sushi restaurant opens up in a district. Soon it is so popular that there is a line outside the door every evening. Other catering entrepreneurs will be attracted to the possibility of doing so well, and so it is likely that another sushi restaurant will open up in the area. It may not happen immediately, but eventually this is likely to result in a fall in demand for the original sushi restaurant as some of its customers will switch. If demand continues to be strong, then even more restaurants will open. Each restaurant will try to distinguish itself from the others – perhaps by staying open longer, offering a "Happy Hour", special theme nights or free children's meals, to name just a few possibilities. This product differentiation is also known as non-price competition.

Higher Level

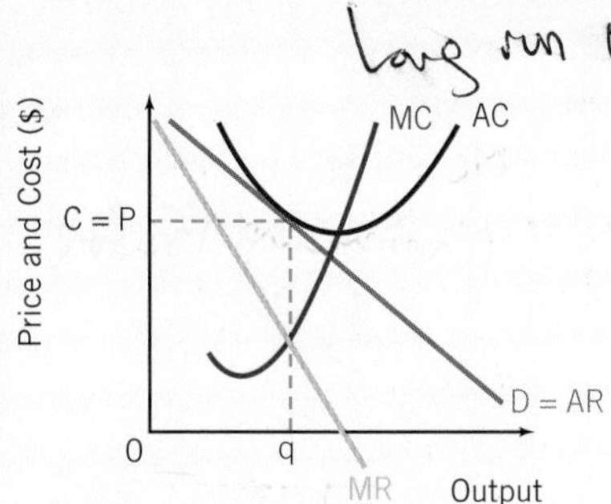

▲ **Figure 11.17** Long-run equilibrium in monopolistic competition

Whatever the short-run situation, in the long run the firms will end up in the position shown in Figure 11.17, with all making normal profits. The firms are maximizing profits by producing at the level of output where MC = MR and, at that output, the cost per unit, C, is equal to the price per unit, P. Each firm is exactly covering its costs, including its opportunity costs, and so there is no incentive for firms to leave the industry. Firms outside the industry will not enter, since they will be aware that their entrance would lead to losses for everyone.

Table 11.1 summarizes the characteristics of monopolistic competition and illustrates how Italian restaurants in a city might be considered to be close to a monopolistic competition market structure.

Characteristics of monopolistic competition market structure	Italian restaurants
Very large number of firms	✓
Each firm very small relative to the size of the market	✓
Goods ~~are~~ differentiated slightly ~~but not homogenous~~	✓ (Different menus – emphasis on pasta, emphasis on pizzas)
No barriers to entry or exit	Very low barriers (low capital costs, no special expertise, not likely to be large economies of scale, some brand loyalty)
~~Perfect information~~ Imperfect Information	Fairly open, but not perfect
Abnormal profits possible in short run, but not in long run	More and more Italian restaurants will be set up as long as the existing ones are earning abnormal profits

▲ **Table 11.1** Italian restaurants as an example of a monopolistic competition market structure

Exercise 11.4

ATL Thinking and Communication

1. Why can a firm in monopolistic competition not earn abnormal profits in the long run?
2. Draw a diagram of a firm in monopolistic competition that is in long-run equilibrium. (This is likely to be the most difficult diagram you've drawn so far, as it is challenging to draw the relationship accurately!)

Key concept

EFFICIENCY

How efficient are firms in monopolistic competition?

We know that productive efficiency is achieved at the level of output where a firm produces at the lowest possible cost per unit, the point where AC is at a minimum. This is the point where the MC curve cuts the AC curve.

Allocative efficiency is achieved at the level of output where the MC curve cuts the AR curve: the socially optimum level of output.

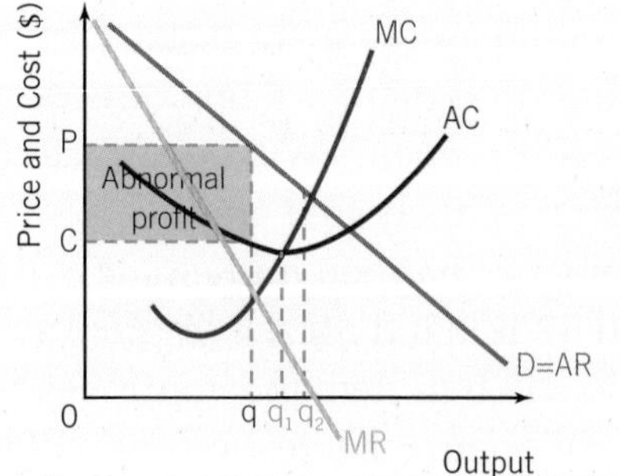

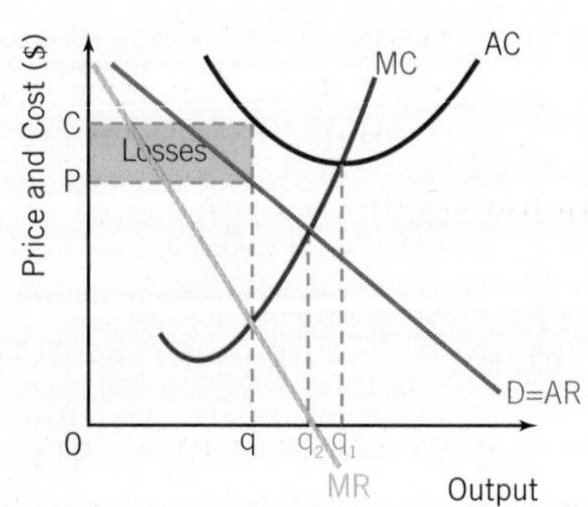

▲ **Figure 11.18** Productive and allocative efficiency in the short run in monopolistic competition

Figure 11.18 shows the two possible short-run positions in monopolistic competition and abnormal profits and losses. We see that the firm produces at the level of output where profits are maximized, q, as opposed to the productively efficient level of output, q_1, or the allocatively efficient level of output, q_2.

In the long run, the situation is the same. This is shown in Figure 11.19. The firm is again producing at the profit-maximizing level of output, q, and not at the productively efficient level of output, q_1, or the allocatively efficient level of output q_2.

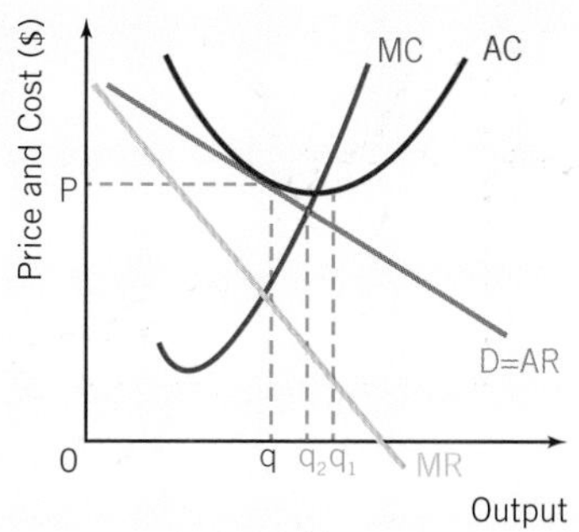

▲ **Figure 11.19** Productive and allocative efficiency in the long run in monopolistic competition

Is there a market failure that needs to be rectified in monopolistic competition?

Unlike perfect competition, where in the long run the firms are profit-maximizers, productively efficient, and allocatively efficient firms in the long run in monopolistic competition, although maximizing profits, are neither productively nor allocatively efficient.

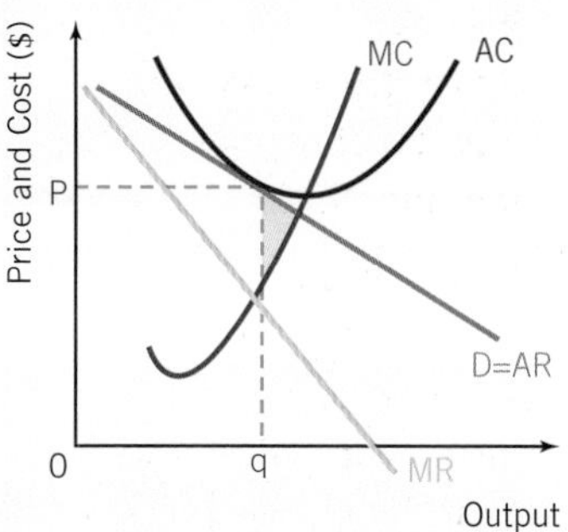

▲ **Figure 11.20** Market failure in monopolistic competition

There is a small market failure, since the firms are not allocatively efficient. This is shown by the shaded area in Figure 11.20. However, even though the firm in monopolistic competition is not allocatively efficient, because it does not produce where MC = AR, the inefficiency is not due to the firm's ability to restrict output and increase price. The inefficiency is, in fact, the result of the consumers' desires for variety. Though allocative efficiency does not occur, it is hard to argue that consumers are worse off with monopolistic competition than with perfect competition, since the difference is due entirely to consumer desire to have differentiated products.

Rather than having a perfectly competitive situation, where consumers would in theory pay lower prices but are only able to purchase a homogeneous product, monopolistic competition gives consumers the opportunity to make choices. This is why they are prepared to pay slightly higher prices for the products.

Because of the very small level of market power found in monopolistic competition, governments do not intervene in these markets to curb that power. We should remember that they might intervene to correct other market failures. For example, they may try to correct imperfect information by setting standards for trades, such as plumbers, and then giving authorization to people who reach those standards. In this way, consumers will be able to get information on which firms are approved, reducing previous imperfect information.

Economics in action

ATL Thinking, Communication and Research

Investigate the area in which you live and try to identify a market in the area that is in monopolistic competition. Try to obtain data on the number and sizes of firms, types of goods, costs of entry and exit, and existence of perfect information. Use the data to produce a detailed version of Table 11.1. Investigate any government intervention that may exist in the market that you have chosen, such as Health and Safety legislation, or qualification requirements.

EXAMINATION QUESTIONS

Paper 1, part (a) questions

1. Explain the characteristics of a perfectly competitive market structure. [10 marks]
2. Explain how it is possible for a firm in perfect competition to earn abnormal profits in the short run. [10 marks]
3. Explain how it is impossible for a firm in perfect competition to earn abnormal profits in the long run. [10 marks]
4. Explain whether or not a firm in perfect competition earning abnormal profits is productively and allocatively efficient. [10 marks]
5. Explain the characteristics of a monopolistically competitive market. [10 marks]
6. Explain how it is possible for a firm in monopolistic competition to earn abnormal profits in the short run. [10 marks]
7. Explain how it is impossible for a firm in monopolistic competition to earn abnormal profits in the long run. [10 marks]
8. Explain whether or not a firm in monopolistic competition earning normal profits is productively and allocatively efficient. [10 marks]
9. Explain the differences between the assumptions of perfect competition and monopolistic competition. [10 marks]

Paper 1, part (b) questions

1. Using real-world examples, evaluate the extent to which it is possible for a firm in perfect competition to earn abnormal profits. [15 marks]
2. Using real-world examples, discuss the existence of market power, and thus market failure, in perfect competition. [15 marks]
3. Using real-world examples, evaluate the extent to which it is possible for a firm in monopolistic competition to earn abnormal profits. [15 marks]
4. Using real-world examples, discuss the existence of market power, and thus market failure, in monopolistic competition. [15 marks]
5. Using real-world examples, evaluate the view that it would be beneficial if all markets were in perfect competition. [15 marks]

12 MARKET POWER: MONOPOLY AND OLIGOPOLY

REAL-WORLD ISSUE:

When are markets unable to satisfy important economic objectives and does government intervention help?

By the end of this chapter, you should be able to:

- **HL** Define monopoly
- **HL** Explain the assumptions of monopoly
- **HL** Define, explain and give examples of sources of monopoly power/barriers to entry
- **HL** Define, explain and illustrate a natural monopoly
- **HL** Explain the existence of market power in monopoly
- **HL** Explain and illustrate the demand curve facing a monopolist
- **HL** Explain and illustrate possible profit situations in monopoly
- **HL** Explain and illustrate levels of efficiency in monopoly
- **HL** Compare monopoly and perfect competition
- **HL** Define oligopoly
- **HL** Explain the assumptions of oligopoly
- **HL** Distinguish between collusive and non-collusive oligopoly
- **HL** Distinguish between formal collusion and tacit collusion
- **HL** Explain the role of game theory in oligopoly
- **HL** Explain and give examples of non-price competition
- **HL** Explain the existence of market failure in oligopoly
- **HL** Evaluate the risks that exist in terms of output, price and consumer choice in monopolistic and oligopolistic markets
- **HL** Evaluate different forms of government intervention in response to the abuse of significant market power in monopoly and oligopoly.

It is now time to look at the market forms where firms may have a much greater degree of market power. These are the market forms of monopoly and oligopoly. In both of these market forms, there is the possibility of significant market power existing. Indeed, in monopoly, the potential market power may be so great that the term monopoly power is often used in its place. It is the abuse of such market power that generates government intervention.

What is monopoly?

What are the assumptions of monopoly?

In the theory of monopoly, we assume that:

- There is only one firm producing the product so the firm is the industry.
- Barriers to entry exist, which stop new firms from entering the industry and maintains the monopoly.
- As a consequence of barriers to entry the monopolist may be able to make abnormal profits in the long run.

However, whether a firm really is a monopoly depends upon how narrowly we define the industry. For example, Microsoft may be the only producer of a particular kind of software, but it does not have a monopoly of all software. The vegetable shop in your area may have a monopoly of the sale of vegetables in that area, but it is not the only seller of vegetables and if the area is widened then the shop loses its monopoly.

The important question here is not whether or not a firm is a monopoly, but rather how much market power the firm has. To what extent is the firm able to set its own prices without worrying about other firms and to what extent can it keep people out of the industry? The strength of market power possessed by a firm will really depend upon how many competing substitutes are available. For example, the underground railway in a city may have the monopoly of underground travel, but it will face competition from other industries, such as buses, taxis and private transport.

Exercise 12.1 — ATL Thinking and Communication

In each case below, suggest which ones are monopolies and also define the width of the industry that you are assuming:

1. the canteen in your school
2. your doctor
3. the local refuse disposal system
4. your school
5. the national telephone service
6. the national postal service.

What gives a monopoly the ability to maintain its position and so its market (monopoly) power?

A monopoly may continue to be the only producer in an industry if it is able to stop other firms from entering the industry in some way. These ways of preventing entry to the industry are known as *barriers to entry*. There are a number of possible barriers to entry, such as:

1. **Economies of scale**

   Firms may gain significant average cost advantages as their size increases. Their unit costs of production may fall as they grow larger. These advantages are known as *economies of scale*. Economies of scale are any decreases in average costs, in the long run, that come about when a firm alters all of its factors of production in order to increase its scale of output.

   There are a number of different economies of scale that may benefit a firm as it increases the scale of its output.

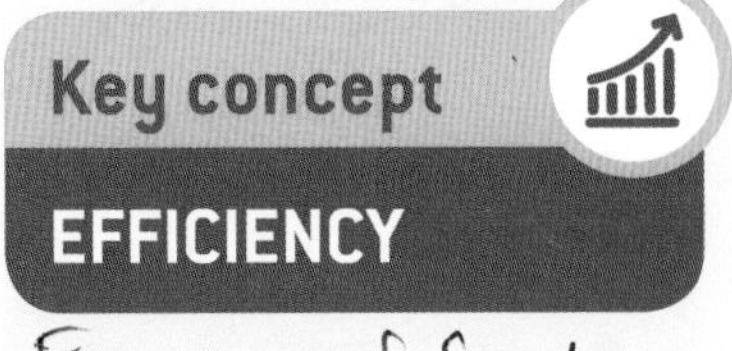

   a. *Specialization*: In small firms there are few, if any, managers and they have to take on many different roles, often roles for which they are not the best candidates. This may lead to higher unit costs. As firms grow they are able to have their management specialize in individual areas of expertise, such as production, finance, or marketing, and thus be more efficient.

   b. *Division of labour*: This is breaking a production process down into small activities that workers can perform repeatedly and efficiently. As firms get bigger and demand increases, they are often able to start to break down their production processes, use division of labour, and reduce their unit costs. A good example of this would be workers on assembly lines, where they each have a position by a conveyor belt and add parts to a product as it moves down the conveyor belt. Cars and television sets, among other things, have been produced by this sort of method.

   c. *Bulk buying*: As firms increase in scale they are often able to negotiate discounts with their suppliers that they would not have received when they were smaller. The cost of their inputs is then reduced, which will reduce their unit costs of production.

   d. *Financial economies*: Large firms can raise financial capital (money) more cheaply than small firms. Banks tend to charge

Higher Level

a lower interest rate to larger firms, since the larger firms are considered to be less of a risk than the smaller firms, and are less likely to fail to repay their loans.

e. *Transport economies*: Large firms making bulk orders may be charged less for delivery costs than smaller firms. Also, as firms grow they may be able to have their own transport fleet, which will then cost less because they will not be paying other firms, who will include a profit margin, to transport their products.

f. *Large machines*: Some machinery is too large to be owned and used by a small producer – for example, a combine harvester for a small farmer. In this case, small farmers have to hire the use of the equipment from suppliers who will then charge a price that includes a profit margin for the supplier. However, once a farm can increase to a certain size it becomes feasible to have its own combine harvester, reducing the unit costs of production.

g. *Promotional economies*: Almost all firms attempt to promote their products by using advertising or sales promotion or personal selling or publicity or a combination of the above. The costs of promotion tend not to increase by the same proportion as output. If a firm doubles its output, it is unlikely that it will double its expenditure on promotion methods, such as sales promotion and advertising. Thus, the cost of promotion per unit of output falls. This situation also applies to other fixed costs, such as insurance costs or the costs of providing security for the production unit.

Any of the above economies of scale may lead to cost savings and lower unit costs. If a monopoly is large, then they will be experiencing economies of scale. Any firm wishing to enter the industry will probably have to start up in a relatively small way and so will not have the economies of scale that are enjoyed by the monopolist. Even if the new firm were able to start up with the same size as the monopolist, it would still not have the economies that come from expertise in the industry, such as managerial economies, promotional economies and research and development.

Without equal economies of scale, a would-be entrant to the industry knows that it would not be able to compete with the existing monopolist, who would simply have to reduce price to the level of normal profits. At this level the new entrant would be making losses, because the average costs would be higher, so the lack of economies of scale acts as a deterrent to firms that might want to enter a monopoly industry.

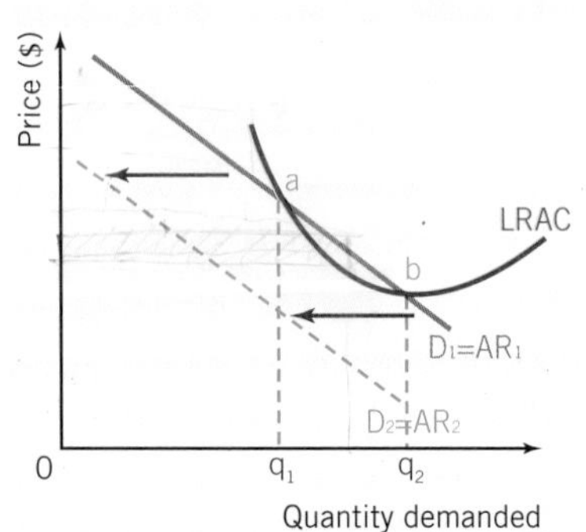

▲ Figure 12.1 A natural monopoly

2. **Natural monopoly**

Some industries are classified as natural monopolies. An industry is a natural monopoly if there are only enough economies of scale available in the market to support one firm. This is best shown by a diagram, such as Figure 12.1.

In this case, the monopolist is the industry and has the demand curve D_1. The long-run average cost curve faced by the monopolist is LRAC and its position and shape are set by the economies of scale that the firm is experiencing. The monopolist is able to make abnormal profits by producing an output between q_1 and q_2, because the average revenue is greater than the average cost for that range of output.

If another firm were to enter the industry, then the firm would take demand from the monopolist and the monopolist's demand curve would shift to the left, in this case to D_2. Since we can assume that the situation will be the same for both firms, the two firms would now be in a position where it is impossible for them to make even normal profits. Their LRACs would be above AR at every level of output.

In this industry, the LRAC, which is shaped by the economies of scale experienced by the monopolist, will only give an abnormal profit if the monopolist is able to satisfy all of the demand in the market. The industry is a natural monopoly, because the market will only support one firm. Examples of natural monopolies include the industries that supply utilities such as water, electricity and gas.

3. **Legal barriers**

In certain situations, a firm may have been given a legal right to be the only producer in an industry, ie the legal right to be a monopoly. This is the case with patents, which give a firm the right to be the only producer of a product for a certain number of years after it has been invented. Patents are usually valid for approximately 20 years. When a patent expires other producers will then be allowed to produce and sell the product. Patents exist as a means to encourage invention. If individuals or firms put time and money into inventions, only to find that they were copied as soon as they were successful, then there would be little incentive to do so. However, if a firm knows that, if its invention is successful, it will have a protected monopoly for a number of years, then it is more likely to invest in research and development.

Patents, along with copyrights and trademarks, are examples of intellectual property rights. Intellectual property refers to the creations of the mind. Just as private property rights allow people to own physical property, so patents guarantee the creators of ideas the rights to own their ideas. A very good example of patent protection is found in the pharmaceutical industry.

Another example of legal barriers is where the government of a country grants the right to produce a product to a single firm. It may do this by setting up a nationalized industry, such as a state postal service, and then banning other firms from entering that industry,

Higher Level

Exercise 12.2
ATL Thinking and Communication

Can you think of any other products that dominate the market so heavily that the product is known by its brand name rather than its product name? Can you think of any products that may have lost this market dominance to competitors?

or it may simply sell the right to be a sole supplier to a private firm, such as the right to be the only network provider for mobile phones, once again banning other firms.

4. **Brand loyalty**

It may be that a monopolist produces a product that has gained huge brand loyalty. The consumers think of the product as the brand. For example, in the early days of the vacuum cleaner they were simply known by their brand name, Hoover. If the brand loyalty is so strong then new firms may be put off from entering the industry, since they will feel that they are not able to produce a product that will be sufficiently different in order to generate such strong brand loyalty.

Exercise 12.3
ATL Thinking and Communication

Discoveries of new drugs have led to significant improvements in health and longevity. None of this would have been possible if pharmaceutical companies hadn't had the incentive to carry out the research, development and testing necessary to bring these drugs onto the market. Estimates of the costs of developing and testing new drugs in the US range from $800 million to $2 billion and it can take anywhere from 12 to 15 years to bring a new drug onto the market.

Given these figures, it is not surprising that drug developers want to have some guarantee that they will be able to be the exclusive providers so that they can recover their costs and maximize their profits. This is why patents are justified. In fact, pharmaceutical companies continually lobby governments to have increased patent protection for their products.

As soon as the patent on a drug expires, other pharmaceutical companies can produce and sell their own version of the drug. These are commonly known as generic drugs or simply generics. A generic drug is exactly the same as its patented version in terms of dosage, safety, strength, intended use, risks and benefits. They are said to be "bio-equivalent".

The producers of the generic drug can develop the drug while the brand-name drug is protected by its patent and release it as soon as the patent expires.

Generic drugs are vastly less expensive than the brand-name drugs quite simply because the pharmaceutical companies that produce the generic drug do not have the huge development and testing costs. The generics have to meet the country's health and safety standards, but it takes much less time and money than the original. With lower costs, they can charge lower prices.

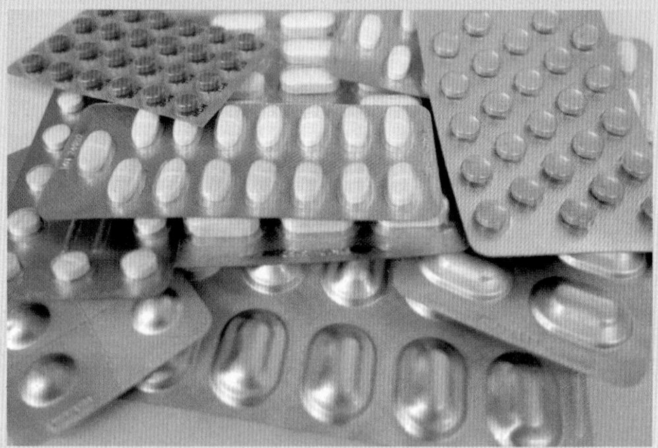

Drug companies spend a lot of money on advertising to try to make sure that the consumers of their drugs maintain brand loyalty. This is particularly important when a drug is facing its patent expiry. They hope that their consumers will stick with their drug even when cheaper generics are on the market. If the drug is a prescription drug, the pharmaceutical companies may find ways to convince doctors that they should keep prescribing the brand-name drugs.

There are deep ethical issues involved in the question of patents on life-saving drugs. The fact that people die from preventable diseases because they cannot afford to buy the patented medicines, even though generic drugs may be made available at a fraction of the price, is currently under debate.

1. Use the information above to explain the possible advantages and disadvantages of pharmaceutical patents for the different stakeholders involved.

Higher Level

5. **Anti-competitive behaviour**

A monopolist may also attempt to stop competition by adopting restrictive practices, which may be legal or illegal. For example, an established monopoly should be in a strong position to start a "price war" if another firm enters the industry. The monopoly can lower its price to a loss-making level and should be able to sustain the losses for a longer time than the new entrant, thus forcing the new firm out of the industry. Indeed, knowledge of this possibility should be enough to dissuade new firms from even attempting to enter the industry.

In 2004, the European Union Competition Commission fined Microsoft €497 million for "bundling" its Windows Media Player and messaging technologies into its Windows operating system. The commission claimed that this prevented potential competitors from reaching consumers. It also ordered Microsoft to make technical information public to allow other companies the ability to produce goods that are compatible with Microsoft to give Microsoft more competition.

In 2006, Microsoft received an additional fine of €280.5 billion for alleged failure to comply with the 2004 fine. Microsoft appealed the fine, but lost the appeal in September 2007. Microsoft was fined again in 2008 for failure to comply with the ruling, and was ordered to pay €899 million Euros, the largest fine ever given by the European Competition Commission.

That was not the end of it, however. In 2009, the EU Competition Commission again found Microsoft guilty of anti-competitive practices, this time for bundling its Internet Explorer browser into its Windows operating system. According to the commission:

"The evidence gathered during the investigation leads the Commission to believe that the tying of Internet Explorer with Windows, which makes Internet Explorer available on 90% of the world's PCs, ***distorts competition*** *on the merits between competing web browsers insofar as it provides Internet Explorer with an* ***artificial distribution advantage*** *which other web browsers are unable to match. The Commission is concerned that through the tying, Microsoft shields Internet Explorer from head-to head-competition with other browsers which is* ***detrimental to the pace of product innovation and to the quality of products which consumers ultimately obtain****. In addition, the Commission is concerned that the ubiquity of Internet Explorer creates artificial incentives for content providers and software developers to design websites or software primarily for Internet Explorer which ultimately risks undermining competition and innovation in the provision of services to consumers."*

Source: Europa press release, January 17th, 2009

Economics in action ATL Thinking, Communication and Research

At any given time, you will be able to find examples of anti-competitive behaviour being addressed in the media. Find an example of a current case, and identify what anti-competitive behaviour the firm is being accused of. Who are the "victims" in the case?

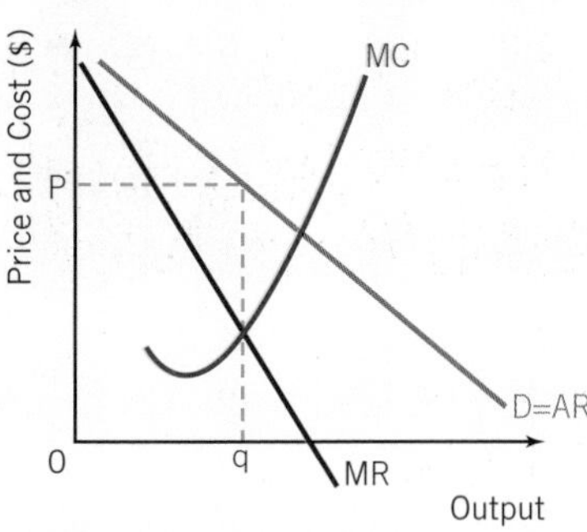

▲ Figure 12.2 The demand curve facing a monopolist

How much market power exists in monopoly?

As we know, the monopolist is the industry and so the monopolist's demand curve is the industry demand curve and is downward sloping. The monopolist can therefore control either the level of output or the price of the product, but not both. Students often assume that monopolists can charge whatever price they like and still sell their products, but this is not the case. In order to sell more they must lower their price.

The demand curve facing a monopolist is shown in Figure 12.2. The monopolist has a normal demand curve, with marginal revenue below it, and maximizes profit by producing at the level of output where marginal cost is equal to marginal revenue.

We can see that, in this case, the monopolist sells a quantity q at a price per unit of P. Because the monopoly firm is the industry, they completely control the industry output and so are easily able to restrict quantity in order to increase price. The level of market (monopoly) power is significant.

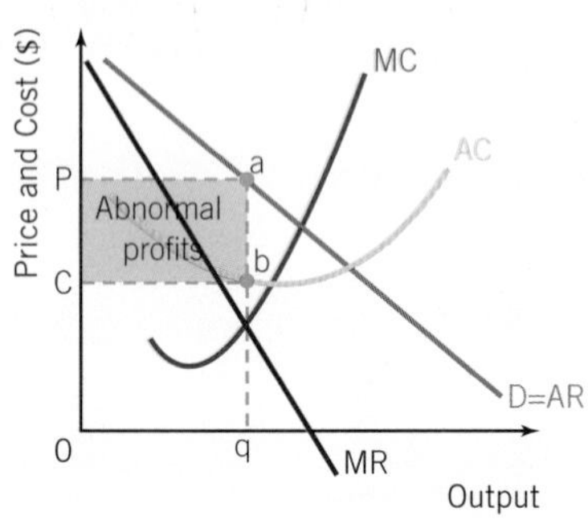

▲ Figure 12.3 Abnormal profits in the long run in monopoly

What are the profit situations facing a monopoly?

If a monopolist is able to make abnormal profits in the short run, and if the monopolist has effective barriers to entry, then other firms cannot enter the industry and compete away the profits that are being earned. In this situation, the monopolist is able to make abnormal profits in the long run, for as long as the barriers to entry hold out. This situation is shown in Figure 12.3.

The monopolist is maximizing profits and is making abnormal profits shown by the shaded area, PabC. Without the entry of new firms to the industry this situation will continue.

It is sometimes assumed that a monopolist will always earn abnormal profits, but this is not true. If the monopolist produces something for which there is little demand, then it will not earn abnormal profits. If a monopolist were making losses in the short run, then it would plan ahead in the long run to see whether changes could be made so that normal profits, at least, could be earned. If this were not possible, then the monopolist would close down the firm and, since the firm is the industry, the industry would cease to exist. This situation is shown in Figure 12.4.

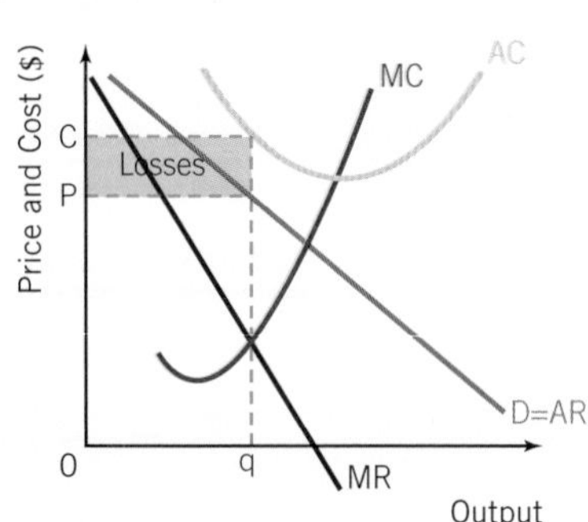

▲ Figure 12.4 A monopolist making losses in the long run

Here, the firm is not able to cover costs in the long run, since the average cost is greater than the average revenue at all levels of output. Since there is nothing that can be done to rectify the situation, this will be an industry in which no firm will be willing to produce. There will be no industry.

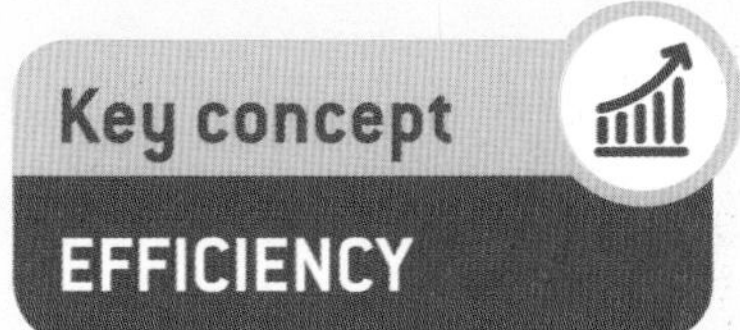

How efficient is a monopoly?

Unlike perfect competition, the monopolist produces at the level of output where there is neither productive efficiency nor allocative efficiency. This is shown in Figure 12.5.

The monopolist is producing at the profit-maximizing level of output, q. Output is being restricted in order to force up the price and to maximize profit. However, the most efficient level of output, q_1 and the allocatively efficient level of output, q_2, are not being achieved.

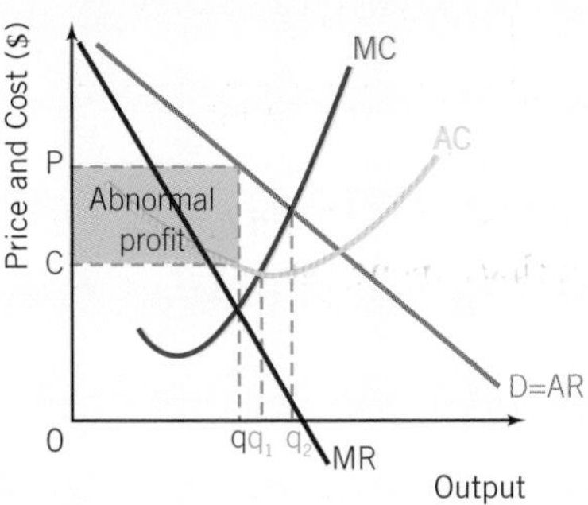

▲ Figure 12.5 Productive and allocative efficiency in monopoly

Is there a market failure that needs to be rectified in monopoly?

There is no doubt that market failure can exist in monopoly. Allocative efficiency is not achieved by a profit-maximizing monopolist and so there is clearly a market failure if firms follow the profit maximization route. However, are there advantages to monopoly that might outweigh the market failure and so make it unnecessary for governments to intervene?

a. What are the advantages of monopoly in comparison with perfect competition?

The first advantage is the existence of substantial economies of scale. Monopolies may be able to achieve large economies of scale simply because of their size. Monopolies do not have to be big, but if the industry is big, then the monopolist should gain substantial economies of scale. If this pushes the MC curve down, then it is possible that the monopolist may produce at a higher output and at a lower price than in perfect competition. This idea of relative price and output in monopoly and perfect competition is very debatable. The situation is shown in Figure 12.6.

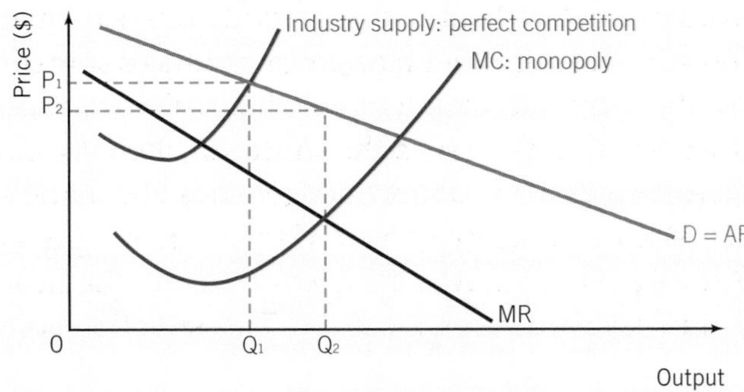

▲ Figure 12.6 Economics of scale in monopoly

In perfect competition, the equilibrium price and quantity will be where demand is equal to supply. This means that the price will be P_1 and that a total output of Q_1 will be produced. However, if the industry is a monopoly, with significant economies of scale, then the MC curve may well be substantially below the MC curve in perfect competition, which is the industry supply curve.

Higher Level

Higher Level

If this is the case, then the monopolist will produce where MC = MR, maximizing profits and producing a greater quantity than perfect competition, Q_2, at a lower price, P_2.

A second advantage may be that there will be higher levels of investment in research and development in monopolies. Firms in perfect competition are, by definition, relatively small, and so may find it difficult to invest in research and development. However, a monopolist making abnormal profits is in a better situation to use some of those profits to fund research and development. This would, in the long run, benefit consumers, who would have better products and even more **choice**.

b. What are the disadvantages of monopoly in comparison with perfect competition?

If significant economies of scale do not exist in a monopoly, then the monopoly may simply restrict output and charge a higher price than under perfect competition in order to maximize profits.

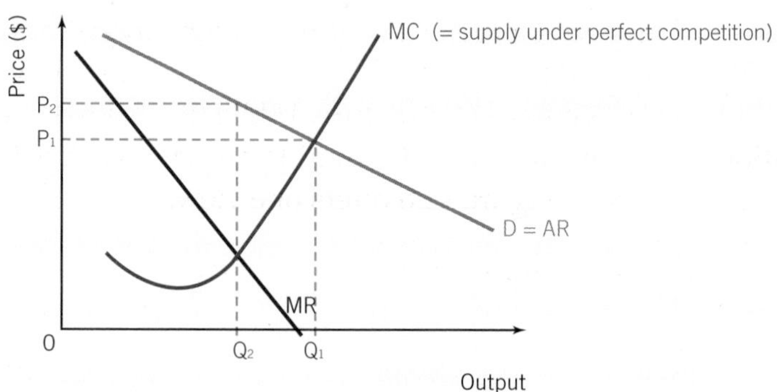

▲ **Figure 12.7** Monopoly versus perfect competition without economies of scale

In Figure 12.7, there are no differences in costs for the monopolist and the perfectly competitive market. If this is the case, then the profit maximizing monopolist will produce Q_2 at a price of P_2, where MC = MR. The perfectly competitive market will, however, produce Q_1 at a price of P_1, where industry supply meets industry demand. Thus, higher prices and lower output would exist under monopoly.

The high profits of monopolists may be considered as unfair, especially by competitive firms, or those on low incomes. The scale of the problem depends upon the size and power of the monopoly, and the extent to which the firm is abusing its market power.

To summarize, there are three possible problems associated with monopolies in comparison with perfect competition.

- They are productively and allocatively inefficient.
- They can charge a higher price for a lower level of output.
- They can exercise anti-competitive behaviour to keep their monopoly power.

These potential problems mean that monopolies can act against the public interest. There are risks in terms of lower output (and thus consumption), higher prices and lower consumer choice. As a result, all governments have laws and policies to limit the abuse of market/monopoly power, where it exists.

What is oligopoly?

What are the assumptions of oligopoly?

Oligopoly is where a few firms dominate an industry. The industry may have quite a few firms or not very many, but the key thing is that a large proportion of the industry's output is shared by just a small number of firms. What constitutes a small number varies, but a common indicator of concentration in an industry is known as the concentration ratio.

Concentration ratios are expressed in the form CR_x where X represents the number of the largest firms. For example, a CR_4 would show the percentage of market share (or output) held by the largest four firms in the industry. The higher the percentage, the more concentrated the market power of the four largest firms. While other concentration ratios such as a CR_8 are measured, it is the CR_4 that is most commonly used to make a link to a given market structure. While the line between the concentration of market share or sales in different market structures is subject to interpretation, Figure 12.8 offers one view.

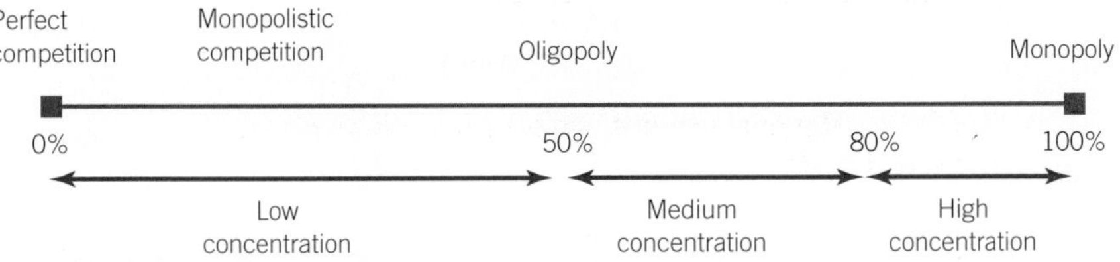

▲ **Figure 12.8** CR_4 ratios in different market structures

For example, in the US malt beverages industry, there are 160 firms, and the CR4 is 90%. Thus the four largest firms produce 90% of the industry's output and it is an industry with a high concentration of market power among the largest four companies. In the frozen fish and seafood industry, there are 600 firms and the CR4 is 19, suggesting low concentration. We may conclude that the malt beverages industry is an oligopoly and the frozen fish and seafood industry is in monopolistic competition.

Exercise 12.4

ATL Thinking, Communication and Research

How would you classify each of the following industries in the USA?

1. Breakfast cereal manufacturing: 48 firms, $CR_4 = 82.9\%$
2. Textile mills: 3,863 firms, $CR_4 = 13.8\%$
3. Breweries: 494 firms, $CR_4 = 89.7\%$
4. Wineries: 637 firms, $CR_4 = 43.2\%$

Economics in action

ATL Thinking, Communication and Research

The CR_4 tells us how the market share in the industry is concentrated among the four largest firms, but it doesn't necessarily reveal the extent of the competition in the industry. A CR_4 of 80% would suggest high concentration, but if that market share were to be divided up with the largest company having 65% of the market and the other three having 5% each, then this would be very different from each of the four having 20% equal share.

An alternative indicator of concentration in an industry is known as the Herfindahl- Herschmann index.

Research task

What is the Herfindahl-Herschmann index? How might it be a better indicator of concentration than the CR_4? What are the levels of the CR_4 values that distinguish between different categories of competition?

Oligopolistic industries may be very different in nature. Some produce almost identical products, eg petrol, where the product is almost exactly the same and only the names of the oil companies are different. Some produce highly differentiated products, eg motor cars. Some produce slightly differentiated products, eg shampoo, but spend huge budgets to persuade people that their product is better.

In most examples of oligopoly, there are distinct *barriers to entry*, usually the large-scale production or the strong branding of the dominant firms, but this is not always the case. In some oligopolies, there may be low barriers to entry. If this is the case, then the oligopoly, if profitable, should weaken as new firms enter.

Key concept
INTERDEPENDENCE

However, the key feature that is common in all oligopolies is that there is *interdependence*. Whereas in perfect competition and monopolistic competition the firms are all too small relative to the size of the market to be able to influence the market, in oligopoly there is a small number of large firms dominating the industry. As there are just a few firms, each needs to take careful notice of each other's actions. Interdependence tends to make firms want to collude and so avoid surprises and unexpected outcomes. If they can collude and act as a monopoly, then they can maximize industry profits. However, there is also a tendency for firms to want to compete vigorously with each other in order to gain a greater market share.

All in all, however, oligopoly tends to be characterized by price rigidity. Prices in oligopoly tend to change much less than in more competitive markets. Even when there are production-cost changes, oligopolistic firms often leave their prices unchanged, in fear of how their competitors may react.

What is the difference between a collusive and a non-collusive, oligopoly?

Collusive oligopoly exists when the firms in an oligopolistic market collude to charge the same prices for their products, in effect acting as a monopoly, and so divide up any monopoly profits that may be made.

There are two types of collusion:

Formal collusion takes place when firms openly agree on the price that they will all charge, although sometimes it may be agreement on market share or on marketing expenditure instead. Such a collusive oligopoly is often called a *cartel*. Since this results in higher prices and less output for consumers, this is usually deemed to be against the interest of consumers and so collusion is generally banned by governments and is against the law in the majority of countries. If a country's anti-trust authority finds that firms have engaged in anti-competitive behaviour, such as price-fixing agreements, then the firms will be penalized with fines or other punishments. Formal collusion between governments may be permitted. The prime example is OPEC (the Organisation for Petroleum Exporting Countries), which sets production quotas and prices for the world oil markets.

Tacit collusion exists when firms in an oligopoly charge the same prices without any formal collusion. This is not as difficult as it sounds. A firm may charge the same price as another by looking at the prices of a dominant firm in the industry, or at the prices of the main competitors. It is not necessary to communicate to be able to charge the same prices.

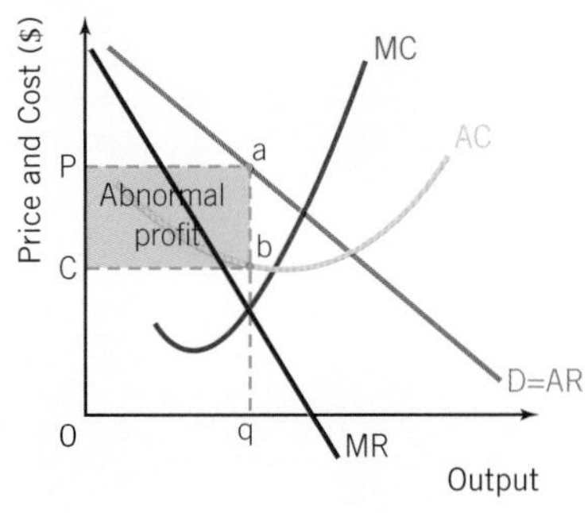

▲ **Figure 12.9** Oligopolists acting as a monopolist

In both formal and tacit collusion, the process is the same. The firms behave like a monopolist (single producer), charge the monopoly price, make monopoly profits and share them according to market share. This is shown in Figure 12.9.

Collusive oligopoly offers one explanation of price rigidity in oligopoly. If firms are colluding, either formally or tacitly, and they are making their share of long-run monopoly profits, then they may try to keep prices stable in order that the situation continues. This is the *incentive to collude* – long-run monopoly profits.

However, it should be said that, when collusion is taking place, there is always an *incentive to cheat*. This is best explained using the example of a collusive *duopoly*, an oligopoly with just two firms. In this case, the first firm to break the agreement, and to lower prices, should gain a greater market share until the other firm responds. This may lead to greater revenue and possibly profit.

But, this raises the danger of a "*price war*", since the other firm will need to lower its prices below the firm that broke the agreement first in order to gain back its market share. In the same way, since the second firm will now get back its market share and presumably take some of the market of the first firm, the first firm will need to lower its prices again and undercut the second firm. This process could continue, in a downward spiral, harming both firms.

Non-collusive oligopoly exists when the firms in an oligopoly do not collude and so have to be very aware of the reactions of other firms when making pricing decisions. We say that the behaviour of firms in an oligopoly is strategic behaviour as they must develop strategies that take into account all possible actions of rivals. In order to explain how firms behave in these situations, economists often use "game theory".

Game theory considers the optimum strategy that a firm could undertake in the light of different possible decisions by rival firms. For simplicity we will look at a situation where there are only two firms making up a market. This is known as a duopoly. We assume that the firms have equal costs, identical products and share the market evenly, so the initial demand for their goods is the same. (Rather large assumptions!)

The situation is shown in Table 12.1, where firms A and B are contemplating what would be the possible profit outcomes if they were to change the prices of their identical products.

		Firm A's price choices	
		$5.50	**$5.00**
Firm B's Price choices	**$5.50**	A & B both high prices A gets $6m B gets $6m	A low price; B high price A gets $8m B gets $2m
	$5.00	B low price; A high price B gets $8m A gets $2m	A & B both low prices A gets $4m B gets $4m

▲ **Table 12.1** The predicted profits for firms A and B with different possible price combinations

Key concept
CHOICE

Key concept
INTERDEPENDENCE

Let us start by assuming that both firms are currently charging a price of $5.50 for their products and so they are both making profits of $6 million. Now let us assume that they are not colluding, but they are both separately considering lowering their prices to $5.00.

We can start by considering firm A's choices. Firm A has two choices: it can leave its price unchanged or it can lower it.

If firm A is pessimistic, or cautious, it might consider the worst possible scenarios following its choices, where firm B responds in the way that is most damaging to firm A. If it does not lower its price and firm B does, then its profit would fall from $6 million to $2 million. If it lowers its price and firm B also lowers its price, then its profit would fall from $6 million to $4 million. This means that the best option, if one considers the worst possible outcomes, is to lower prices. The firm is maximizing its minimum profit options and is therefore known as a "maximin" strategy. The strategy is to adopt the policy that has the least worst outcome.

If Firm A is optimistic it might consider the best possible scenarios following its choices, where firm B responds in the way that is best for firm A. If it does not lower its price and firm B does not lower its price, then firm A will make $6 million. If firm A lowers its price and firm B does not lower its price, then firm A will make $8 million. Once again the best option is for firm A to lower price. The strategy of trying to make the maximum profit available is known as a "maximax" strategy. Firm A's "maximin" and "maximax" strategies are both to lower price.

If we turn the tables and look at the situation from the point of view of firm B the same logic applies and so the "maximin" and "maximax" strategies for firm B are also to lower price.

If both firms adopt the strategy of lowering prices, which seems to be logical, then they will end up making lower profits of $4 million each. Thus, a price cutting exercise is actually harmful to both firms. They would have been better leaving their prices where they were. They would have benefitted from the ability to collude, if they could have done so.

The different strategies and outcomes are shown in Figure 12.10.

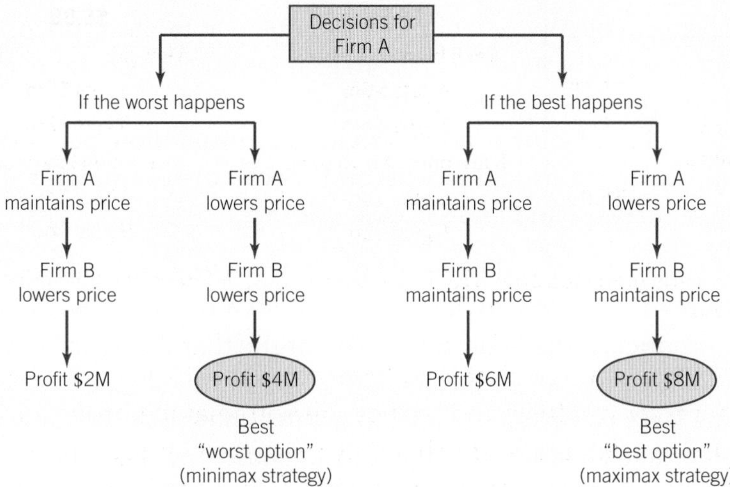

▲ **Figure 12.10** Game theory outcomes for Firms A and B

Game theory is useful for firms if they are able to predict relatively accurately the outcomes that will follow any set of decisions. However, this is not necessarily easy to do. Also, the more firms there are in an industry the more difficult it will be to estimate all the possible combinations of decisions and also outcomes. So, game theory is mostly useful when there are only a few firms in an industry, there are only a small number of possible options, and the outcomes can be accurately predicted.

Theory of knowledge

The prisoner's dilemma

The concept of the "prisoner's dilemma" was developed by Flood and Dresher and formalised by Albert Tucker in 1992. The prisoner's dilemma uses the example of two men being arrested by the police. The police require more evidence and so separate the men and offer each of them the following conditions.

1. Testify for the prosecution. If you do, you go free and your partner in crime gets 10 years in prison. Only the first one to confess gets the offer.
2. Say nothing and you get 5 years in prison.

Each prisoner has the choice of cooperating with the other and saying nothing or betraying the other, and so it raises issues of trust, cooperation and betrayal. Is it human nature to save oneself at the expense of others? Should one sacrifice one's own well being for the common good?

The principle of the prisoner's dilemma can be applied to real-world situations, such as cycling. Sometimes two riders get away from the main group of riders (known as the peloton). If the two riders cooperate, each taking a share of the lead so that the other can shelter from the wind, they will finish first and second. If they don't cooperate, the peloton will catch them up. What sometimes happens is that one rider (the cooperator) does all the hard work at the front, while the other rider (the betrayer) sits in the slipstream of the first rider (just behind the leader). The betrayer almost always wins.

Theorists have adapted the prisoner's dilemma as part of game theory. Economists apply it to the actions of firms, mainly those in oligopoly.

1. What does it mean to say that firms in an oligopoly are **interdependent**?
2. Examine some of the price and non-price strategies open to a firm in an oligopoly to improve its position in a market.
3. Do you think it is better for a firm in an oligopoly to cooperate with the others?

Higher Level

Key concept

CHOICE

How do firms compete in oligopoly?

Because firms in oligopoly tend not to compete in terms of price, the concept of *non-price competition* becomes important. There are many kinds of non-price competition, such as the use of brand names, packaging, special features, advertising, sales promotion, personal selling, publicity, sponsorship deals and special distribution features such as free delivery and after-sales service.

Oligopoly is characterized by very large advertising and marketing expenditures as firms try to develop brand loyalty and make demand for their products less elastic. Some may argue that this represents a misuse of scarce resources, but it could also be argued that competition among the large companies results in greater choice for consumers. Firms undertake all kinds of behaviour to guard and extend their market share. This serves to increase the barriers to entry to new firms. Many rivalries among firms in oligopolies are well known nationally and internationally, for example, Coke and Pepsi or Adidas and Nike.

However, many of the branded consumer goods that we purchase are produced in oligopolies and we might have no idea that there are actually just a few companies dominating the market. A walk down a supermarket aisle of washing powders might suggest a vast number of competing companies when, in reality, the majority of the brands are produced by just two companies – Unilever and Procter & Gamble. These two giant multinationals produce a vast number of brands that compete with each other in a number of industries – for example, home-care products, personal hygiene, health care and beauty products.

Economics in action

ATL Thinking, Communication and Research

1. By referring to the Internet home pages of Unilever and Procter & Gamble, make a list of 20 rival brands produced by each of these giant multinational companies.
2. Find a copy of a consumer magazine of any type (sports, computing, women's interest, men's interest). By looking at the advertisements in the magazine, identify the different ways that firms try to differentiate their products.

Is there a market failure that needs to be rectified in oligopoly?

As with any firm that faces a downward-sloping demand curve, firms in oligopoly will not be producing at the allocatively efficient level of output, if they are maximizing profits, and so there will be a market failure. The existence of market power will always create risks in terms of output, price and consumer choice.

If there is a collusive oligopoly, with formal or tacit collusion, and if there are barriers to entry, then firms will behave like a monopolist, by charging the monopoly price and splitting the monopoly abnormal profits based upon their market share. This is shown in Figure 12.11.

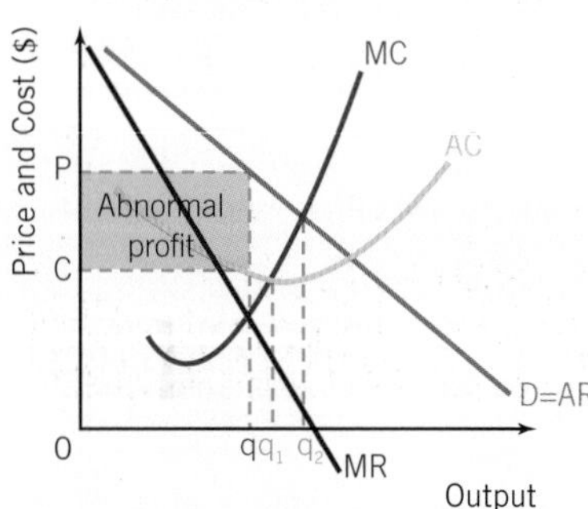

▲ Figure 12.11 Productive and allocative efficiency in a collusive oligopoly

The oligopolists will produce, in total, the profit-maximizing level of output, q. They are restricting output in order to force up the price to p. They will then share the abnormal profit created, depending upon their market share. The most efficient level of output, q_1 and the allocatively efficient level of output, q_2, will not be achieved.

In non-collusive oligopolies, the same will happen, although the level of market power may be somewhat lower.

Higher Level

So when will governments intervene to restrict significant market power in monopoly or oligopoly?

Key concept

INTERVENTION

Exercise 12.5

ATL Thinking and Communication

1. Construct a diagram to show the loss of consumer surplus in a monopoly/collusive oligopoly.
2. Explain why a government may intervene in this situation. (Make sure to identify the different stakeholders.)

We have already identified a number of situations that may lead to government intervention to restrict the abuse of market power. They are summarised in the list below:

1. **Restriction of output, higher prices and distorted resource allocation**
   As we saw earlier in the chapter, in figure 12.2, if firms with market power restrict/control output to force up market prices, then consumers will get less of the product, they will pay a higher price, and also there may be implications for resource allocation; for example, employment might be lowered. There will be a loss of consumer surplus.

   In some oligopolistic markets, firms will spend large amounts of money on marketing in order to make the demand for their product more inelastic and so to create a significant barrier to entry. This is a form of non-price competition.

2. **Lower consumer choice**

   The existence of fewer, or single, firms in an industry may lead to the production of fewer brands, leading to a lack of consumer choice.

Key concept

CHOICE

3. **Productive inefficiency**

   Going back to figure 12.2, production does not take place at the lowest possible unit cost, leading to a waste of resources.

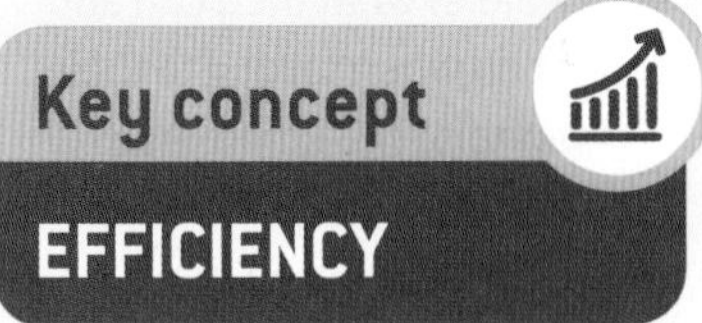

4. **Allocative inefficiency**

   There will be an underallocation of resources to the product in question, since the value put on it by consumers is greater than the cost of producing it to producers. This is also shown in Figure 12.2.

5. **Abnormal profits and inequity**

   The higher prices in an oligopoly or monopoly may exploit low income consumers and their purchasing power might be transferred to the owners of firms, entrepreneurs or shareholders, in the form of higher profits leading to more unequal distribution of income. There may be a reduction in equity.

Key concept

EQUITY

How might governments intervene in response to abuse of significant market power in monopoly or oligopoly?

The existence of significant market power in monopoly and oligopoly is considered to be socially unacceptable, if firms abuse the power. Obviously, the existence/definition of what constitutes abuse is a subjective matter and will vary from country to country. However, if abuse is in existence, then government intervention should take place.

Did you know?

Avoiding anti-competitive behaviour in New Zealand

Anyone who runs a business in New Zealand must comply with the Commerce Act, which aims to promote competition in markets for the long-term benefit of consumers.

Competitive markets help to keep prices down and ensure that the quality of goods and services remains high. Competition also ensures consumers have a range of choices, and firms have incentives to innovate, invest and operate efficiently. Anti-competitive behaviour can jeopardise all of this, as well as a company's ability to win new customers.

It is important that businesses are aware of what they can and cannot do when talking to their competitors. The Commerce Act prohibits anti-competitive agreements between firms such as agreements to fix prices, allocate markets or restrict output.

The Commission can take enforcement action against businesses and individuals who breach the Commerce Act and the court can impose significant penalties for breaches against both businesses and individuals.

Businesses should seek independent legal advice to ensure they are not at risk of breaching the Commerce Act.

Source: Commerce Commission, New Zealand, https://comcom.govt.nz/business/avoiding-anti-competitive-behaviour

Given the enormous benefits of effective competition for consumers and the allocation of resources, and the dangers associated with the abuse of monopoly power, governments usually have agencies to promote competition and prevent the abuse of monopoly power. There could be lots of different names for such an agency, including "Competition Commission" or "Commerce Department". It might be referred to as a "Monopoly watchdog". The actions of a competition authority could include the following:

- Governments usually pass laws that restrict the ability of firms to grow through *mergers* or *takeovers*. A merger is where two companies, often of similar size, agree to combine and become one larger firm. A takeover is usually the acquisition of a company by another company (normally a larger one). Takeovers are mostly "hostile", ie without the consent of the company being taken over. The laws may not permit mergers or takeovers that would give an individual firm more than a certain percentage of the market – for example, 25%. In addition, they may pass laws that do not permit mergers or takeovers that enable a specified number of the largest firms in an oligopoly to control more than a certain percentage of the market – for example, the four largest firms may be restricted to 60%.
- Governments pass laws against *price fixing*, making it illegal for firms to collude over prices, thus making collusive oligopolies illegal. This is the case in the majority of the countries in the world.
- If firms are insisting that retailers charge a certain price for their product, or if firms are refusing to supply their products to certain retailers, then governments may also legislate to stop the practice.

Such bodies are then empowered to take action, or to recommend that the government should take some action, if it can be shown that the public interest is being harmed. When anti-competitive behaviour is suspected, the competition authority will undertake intense investigations. If investigations reveal that anti-competitive behaviour has been used, governments may fine those involved, or even jail the executives responsible for the abuse of market power.

> "Dominant companies have a special responsibility not to abuse their powerful market position by restricting competition."
>
> — *European Commission*

Governments may also set up regulatory bodies for certain industries that have a duty to represent the interests of consumers, where possible by promoting competition. An example of this might be the Office of Gas and Electricity Markets (Ofgem) in the UK.

Regulatory bodies may have a number of different powers, such as:

- The ability to set price controls (*price capping*).
- The ability to impose fines for anti-competitive behaviour.

- The ability to insist on average price levels that set a "*fair rate of return*", based upon profit levels which might be expected in a competitive market.
- The ability to make firms "unbundle" their products, thus making it easier for other firms to enter the market and compete. Bundling is where firms sell a number of their products together in a "bundle". An example of this would be Microsoft, which sells Word, Excel, PowerPoint and Access as a single product.
- The ability to break up a monopoly into separate businesses, thus promoting competition. However, this rarely happens and is considered to be an extreme action.
- The ability to set standards for the quality of service in an industry.

In an extreme situation, the government may take the industry into *public (government) ownership*. In this case, the goods and services sold in the market would be produced in a *nationalized industry*, owned by the state. This is likely to be a highly-publicized issue.

Big Four accounting firms accused of 'anti-competitive' behaviour

EU fines Google $2.4b for anti-competitive behaviour

Higher Level

EXAMINATION QUESTIONS

Paper 1, part (a) questions

1. Explain the level of output at which a monopoly firm will produce. [10 marks]
2. Explain the concept of a natural monopoly. [10 marks]
3. Explain whether a monopoly is likely to be more efficient or less efficient than a firm in perfect competition. [10 marks]
4. Explain **three** barriers to entry that might allow a firm to be a monopoly. [10 marks]
5. Explain why firms in oligopolies engage in non-price competition. [10 marks]
6. Explain the difference between a collusive and a non-collusive oligopoly. [10 marks]

Paper 1, part (b) questions

1. Using real-world examples, evaluate the view that governments should always prevent firms from being monopolies. [15 marks]
2. Using real-world examples, evaluate the view that governments should maintain strong policies to control collusive behaviour by oligopolies. [15 marks]
3. Using real-world examples, discuss the possible risks involved when a market is dominated by one or a few very large firms. [15 marks]
4. Using real-world examples, evaluate possible government responses to the abuse of significant market power. [15 marks]

Economics in action

ATL Thinking, Communication and Research

Using your country, or another country of your choice, produce a brief report including the following, where appropriate:

1. The name of the competition commission/anti-trust authority, and one case that it has investigated in the last year (include a summary of who was involved, how the anti-competitive behaviour was discovered, what the charges were, and what, if any, were the outcomes).
2. The name of an industry regulatory body and a list of its powers.
3. The name of a nationalized industry and some explanation of the reason for its existence.

13 THE LEVEL OF OVERALL ECONOMIC ACTIVITY

REAL-WORLD ISSUE:

Why does economic activity vary over time and why does this matter? How do governments manage the economy and how effective are their policies?

By the end of this chapter, you should be able to:

- → List the five main macroeconomic goals
- → Distinguish between the output approach, the income approach and the expenditure approach to measuring national income
- → Calculate nominal GDP from national income data using the expenditure approach
- → Calculate GNI from data
- → Calculate real GDP and real GNI using a price deflator
- → Calculate real GDP and real GNI per capita
- → Evaluate the uses of national income statistics
- → Evaluate the appropriateness of using GDP or GNI statistics to measure economic well being
- → Explain and illustrate the business cycle and its phases
- → Illustrate short-term fluctuations and long-term growth trends in the business cycle
- → Explain alternative measures of well being
- → Distinguish between a decrease in GDP and a decrease in GDP growth.

In Chapters 3 to 12 we looked at microeconomics – the study of individual markets. In Chapters 13 to 22 we will be looking at macroeconomics – the study of a national economy. Macroeconomics is concerned with the allocation of a nation's resources and is concerned with five main variables. These variables and the macroeconomic objectives associated with each variable are shown in Table 13.1 and form the basis of the macroeconomic analysis for the next twelve chapters.

Variable	Macroeconomic objective
Economic growth	A steady rate of increase of national income
Employment	A low level of unemployment
Price stability	A low and stable rate of inflation
National debt	A sustainable level of government (national) debt
Income distribution	An equitable distribution of income

▲ **Table 13.1** Macroeconomic objectives

In studying an economy as a whole, a significant concern is the level of the economy's total output. We will see later in this chapter that this is also known as the economy's national income and we will look at the different ways in which this national income can be measured.

How is national income measured?

To understand how national income is measured, it is useful to return to the simple model of the circular flow of income that we came across in Chapter 1. This is shown below:

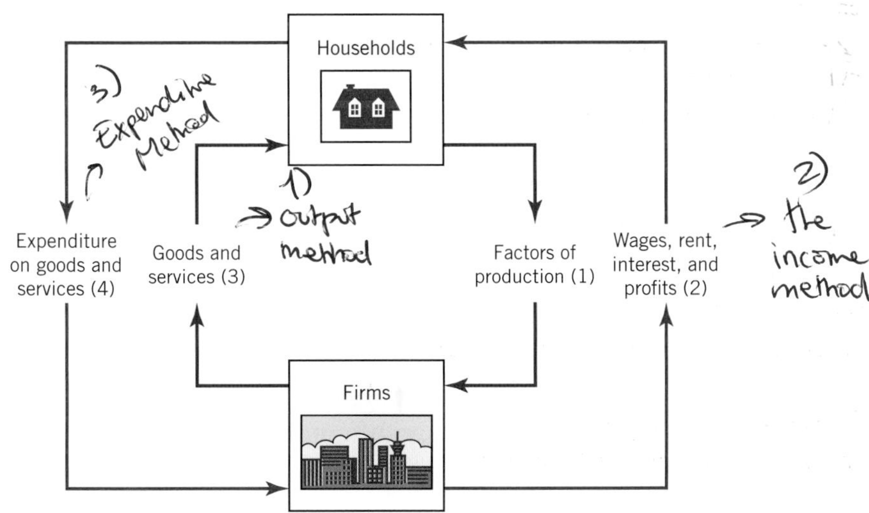

▲ **Figure 13.1** Two-sector circular flow of income model

One commonly used measure of a country's national income is gross domestic product (GDP). There are three different methods that are all used to calculate this figure.

1. *The output method*: This measures the actual value of the goods and services produced. This is calculated by summing all of the value added by all the firms in an economy. When we say value added it means that at each stage of a production process we deduct the costs of inputs, so as not to "double count" the inputs. The data is usually grouped according to the different production sectors in the economy: agriculture and mining (primary sector), manufacturing (secondary sector) and services (tertiary sector). The output method measures the value of the arrow marked as number (3) in Figure 13.1.

2. *The income method*: This measures the value of all the incomes earned in the economy. This method measures the value of the arrow marked as number (2) in Figure 13.1.

3. *The expenditure method*: This measures the value of all spending on goods and services in the economy. This is calculated by summing up the spending by all the different sectors in the economy. These include:

   - spending by households, known as consumption (C)
   - spending by firms, known as investment (I)
   - spending by governments (G)
   - spending by foreigners on exports minus spending on imports. This is known as net exports (X – M).

   The expenditure method measures the value of the arrow marked as number (4) in Figure 13.1.

Each approach measures the value of a nation's output differently by looking at different sets of data. Nonetheless, since they are measuring the same thing, their values are necessarily an equal amount. One common and highly acceptable definition of GDP is that it is the total value of all final goods and services produced in an economy in a year. This clearly reflects the output method of calculation. Another widely used definition is that GDP is the total value of all spending in the economy, algebraically expressed as GDP = C + I + G + (X – M). This reflects the expenditure method. Thus, regardless of the method chosen, in theory, accounting will result in the same final figure, whether we call it national output, national income or national expenditure.

In practice, however, the data that are collected to calculate each of the three values come from many different and varied sources, and inevitably there will be inaccuracies in the data, leading to imbalances among the final values. Some of these inaccuracies are the result of the timing of the data gathering; often figures have to be revised at later dates when full information is collected.

DEFINITION: NATIONAL OUTPUT = NATIONAL INCOME = NATIONAL EXPENDITURE

Exercise 13.1

ATL Thinking and Communication

1. Using the expenditure approach, calculate the GDP of Canada in 2018 (fourth quarter), using the data below.

	(million CAD$)
Consumer expenditure on goods and services	1,614,165
Business investment	424,259
Government expenditure	417,805
Exports	664,437
Imports	654,843

Source: Statistics Canada, www40.statcan.ca

2. What percentage of GDP is made up by each of the **four** sectors of the economy?
3. Why do economists not simply ignore the imports figure, instead of actually deducting it, when calculating GDP?

What is the difference between gross domestic product (GDP) and gross national income (GNI)?

Two definitions for gross domestic product (GDP) were given above. A third is useful to be able to make a comparison between GDP and gross national income (GNI). GDP may be defined as the total of all economic activity in a country, regardless of who owns the productive assets. For example, if an Indian multinational company (MNC) is operating in Canada and earning profits, then this income is included in the Canadian GDP and not in the Indian GDP. If the production takes place on Canadian land then it is recorded on the Canadian GDP.

Gross national income (GNI) is the total income that is earned by a country's factors of production regardless of where the assets are located.

In the example above, the profits earned by the Indian MNC would be included in Canada's GDP but not Canada's GNI, because Canada does not own the assets. Similarly, Canada's GDP would not include profits earned by a Canadian MNC operating in Brazil, but its GNI would include such profits. Thus, GNI is equal to GDP plus income earned from assets abroad minus income paid to foreign assets operating domestically. The income earned by assets held in foreign countries is known as *property income from abroad* and the difference between income earned from assets abroad minus income paid to foreign assets operating domestically is known as *net property income from abroad*.

GNI = GDP + net property income from abroad

What is the difference between nominal GDP and real GDP, nominal GNI and real GNI?

If we were to compare the GDP of a country from one year to the next we would have to take into account the fact that prices in the economy are likely to have risen. If prices of goods and services rise (inflation), then this will overstate the value of GDP. That is, GDP will rise, even if there hasn't actually been an increase in economic activity. In order to get a true picture of the change in economic activity we take the nominal GDP, which is the value at current prices, and adjust it for inflation to get the GDP at constant prices. This is done through the use of a "GDP deflator" and the value is known as real GDP. To compare GDP data over time it is necessary to use the real value so that price changes cannot distort the information.

Real GDP = Nominal GDP adjusted for inflation

The same as the above applies if we are considering nominal GNI and real GNI.

Real GNI = Nominal GNI adjusted for inflation

Assessment advice – Calculations

In SL paper 2 or HL paper 3, you may be asked to calculate real GDP or real GNI using a price deflator.

Here is an example of the kind of question that you may face and a worked solution:

The nominal GNI for country X in 2009 was US$750 billion and in 2010 it rose to US$780 billion. In the year in question country X had experienced an inflation rate of 4%.

1. Calculate the real GNI figure for 2010 for country X.
2. Explain why the real GNI figure for 2010 is not the same as the nominal figure.

Solution:

1. Real GNI for 2010 = 780 billion × price deflator* = 780 billion × 100/104 = 750 billion

   [*A GNI price deflator is calculated by the following equation:

   Nominal GNI/ Real GNI × 100.

   It actually gives a good indication of inflation in the economy over the period in question. If you wish to work out the price deflator then you need to have both the nominal and real values for GDP.

   If you are given the inflation rate and the nominal rate, as in the question above, then the price deflator is easy to calculate. The deflator is a fraction and is simply 100/(100 + the inflation rate). The fraction is multiplied by the nominal figure to give a real figure.]

2. Because there was inflation of 4% in the year, the prices of everything in the economy, on average, went up by 4%. This means that the value of the goods and services produced in the economy in the year would have been 4% greater than the previous year. Interestingly, when the inflationary effect is taken out, the real GDP figure for 2010 is the same as the figure for 2009. This means that the economy produced the same value of goods and services in both years, in real terms. The level of economic growth was 0%.

Exercise 13.2

ATL Thinking and Communication

Pick an OECD country that you can study throughout the macroeconomics part of the course. The exercises will allow you to build a good case study of this country. There are several resources that you can use to do the research – the national statistics office for the country and the OECD (www.oecd.org) are two good starting points.

For this first exercise find the following information and put it into a table. Be sure to note the source.

1. Real GDP for the last 10 years.
2. Real GDP per capita for the last 10 years.
3. Real GDP growth per year for the last 10 years.

How do we measure GDP or GNI per capita?

These are the easiest of the national income statistics to measure. In the case of GDP, it is simply the total GDP divided by the size of the population. While the total economic activity of a country is appropriately measured using the GDP figure, if one is to make any judgment about the progress of a country in comparison with other countries in terms of raising living standards then the GDP per capita figure is much more appropriate.

For example, the projected GDP of China for 2019 is US$13,457 billion, significantly higher than that of Canada, with a projected GDP of US$1,733 billion. This says that the output of China is approximately seven-and-three-quarter times larger than that of Canada. However, when we take the population into account we find that China's GDP per capita is US$9,633, while the GDP per capita of Canada is US$46,733[1]. Thus the output per person in Canada is almost five times that of China's output per person.

In the case of GNI per capita, it is simply the total GNI divided by the size of the population.

Why are national income statistics gathered?

Definitions of national income are fairly straightforward, but the job of compiling accurate accounts is extremely complicated and necessarily expensive. Every country has an organization that is responsible for calculating and reporting on the country's national accounts. The United

[1] **Source:** IMF World Economic Outlook Database, March 2019

Nations provides guidelines for such work in the System of National Accounts (SNA). The data gathered are used in myriad ways.

- National income statistics can be seen as a "report card" for a country. Economic growth is a stated objective of governments. Economic growth is an increase in a country's national income over time. Therefore, people use the statistics to judge whether or not a government has been successful in achieving its macroeconomic objective of increased growth.
- Governments use the statistics to develop policies.
- Economists use the statistics to develop models of the economy and make forecasts about the future.
- Businesses use statistics to make forecasts about future demand.
- The performance of an economy over time can be analysed (as long as real data are used).
- Because rising national income is often equated with rising living standards, people often use national income accounts as a basis for evaluating the standard of living or quality of life of a country's population. (The truth of this statement is something that we will return to numerous times in this book!)
- National income statistics are often used as a basis for comparing different countries.

What are the limitations of national income statistics in terms of accuracy, making comparisons, and appropriateness for measuring living standards (economic well being)?

Given the importance of national income statistics and their wide use, it is essential to be aware of possible limitations of the data, both in terms of the accuracy of the data, in terms of their uses for making comparisons, and in terms of their appropriateness in making conclusions about living standards.

- *Inaccuracies*: As noted above, the data that are used to calculate the various measures of national income come from a vastly wide range of sources, including tax claims by households and firms, output data and sales data. Figures tend to become more accurate after a lag time as they are revised when additional data are included. Statisticians in national statistics agencies make every effort to make their data as reliable as possible and in the more developed countries they can be assumed to be fairly reliable. The United Nations SNA works with all countries to improve the methods of gathering data. This improves the validity of comparisons.
- *Unrecorded or under-recorded economic activity – informal markets*: It is important to note that national income accounts can only record economic activity that has been officially recorded. They therefore

do not include any do-it-yourself work or other work done at home. If you paint your own home, your work will not be included in the country's GDP, but if you pay a house-painting company to do so the activity will be recorded, and GDP will rise, even though the output is identical. This is perhaps most significant for developing countries, where much of the output does not make it to any recorded market. For example, much of the food consumed in developing countries may be produced by subsistence farmers. These are people who grow their own food. Although estimates of the value of this are made, it is likely that GDP figures are undervalued. Comparisons may be difficult.

Apart from the do-it-yourself work and subsistence farming, there is another category of economic activity that goes unrecorded or under-recorded. This may be referred to as the hidden economy. This includes activity that is unrecorded because the actual work is illegal, such as drug trafficking. It also includes unrecorded activity that is legal, but the people are doing it illegally. For example, if foreign workers do not have the appropriate work permits to do work such as cleaning, building or working in restaurants, then their work will go unrecorded. It also includes work that is not recorded because people want to evade paying taxes. For example, when governments impose high taxes on cigarettes, this provides smokers with additional incentive to buy their cigarettes illegally to avoid paying the taxes. High indirect and direct taxes, along with government health and safety regulations, give employers the incentive to avoid the "official" economy and hire workers unofficially. High income taxes give people the incentive to understate their full income. For example, a lawyer will have to declare some official income, but may then pursue work that she does not declare. If she accepts cash for the extra work, then she can avoid officially claiming the income. Statisticians try to estimate the extent of the hidden economy from country to country. Table 13.2 includes some estimates for ten OECD countries.

Country	Hidden economy % of GDP (1999–2007 average figure)
Mexico	30.0
Italy	27.0
Republic of Korea	26.8
Spain	22.5
Norway	18.7
Germany	16.0
Canada	15.7
Netherlands	13.2
Japan	11.0
USA	8.6

Source: "Shadow Economies all over the World: New estimates for 162 countries from 1999–2007 (Revised version)", The World Bank Development Research Group, Policy Research Working Paper 5356, July 2010.

▲ **Table 13.2** Estimates of average size of hidden economies in 10 OECD countries

The official GDP figure of Norway might be underestimated by 18.7% due to the existence of the hidden or shadow economy, while in the US there is an 8.6% underestimation. It is argued that, for the most part, the countries with higher tax burdens have a higher amount of hidden economic activity. The fact that there are different degrees of the hidden economy in different countries, and the fact that they are estimates, means that arriving at accurate measures to compare the values of GDP among countries may be a problem.

- *External costs*: GDP figures do not take into account the costs of resource depletion. Cutting down trees leads to an increase in GDP, but there is no measure to account for the loss of these trees. GDP figures do not make deductions for the negative consequences of air and water pollution and traffic congestion, as these are external costs. Such external costs are almost certain to compromise the quality of life, even as GDP increases.
- *Other quality of life concerns*: GDP may grow because people are working longer hours or taking fewer holidays. While people may earn higher incomes as a result, they might not actually enjoy higher standards of living. GDP accounting does not include free activities such as volunteer work or people caring for the elderly and children at home. These are all activities that can lead to a better society, but might even be discouraged in the pursuit of economic growth.
- *Composition of output*: It is possible that a large part of a country's output is in goods that do not benefit consumers, such as defence goods or capital goods. If this is the case, then it would be hard to argue that a higher GDP will raise living standards.

New Zealand Ditches GDP For Happiness And Wellbeing

https://www.forbes.com/sites/jamesellsmoor/2019/07/11/new-zealand-ditches-gdp-for-happiness-and-wellbeing/#6408a9c31942

Exercise 13.3

ATL Thinking and Communication

Read the following extract concerning the oil spill in the Gulf of Mexico in 2010. How does the issue highlight the importance of valuing natural resources in national income accounts?

Referring to the BP oil spill, the U.N. urges new resource accounting

LONDON, July 13 (Reuters) - The Gulf of Mexico oil spill highlights the need for governments to include the value of natural resources, such as fisheries, when calculating the size of their economies, the United Nations environment chief said.

A U.N. Environment Programme report on Tuesday urged businesses to take more account of their impact on the natural resources which people depend on. It said the private sector would act faster if governments more explicitly valued such resources, including biodiversity, a term for the wide array of animal and plant species.

"The oil spill goes to the heart of a contradictory set of signals," said the UNEP executive director. He said that the money spent on cleaning up the spill from BP Plc's ruptured well in the Gulf of Mexico would be included in gross domestic product, the conventional measure of economic activity, but many costs to nature, including the health of fisheries and the survival of marine creatures, would not. "An oil spill could turn out to be a positive thing for the GDP indicator, while it has actually caused a far greater (negative) impact in terms of the natural wealth and natural capital of the United States."

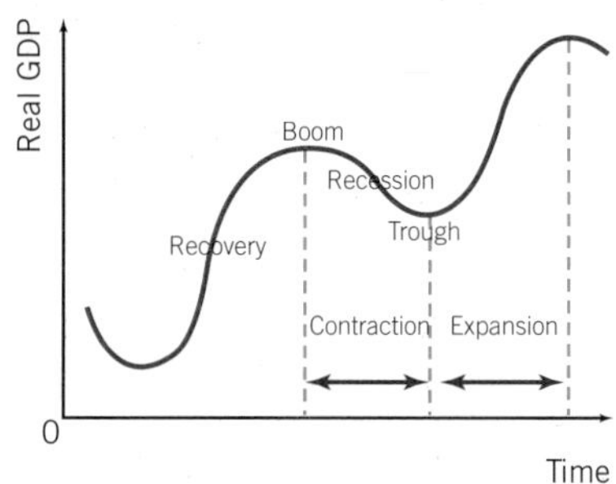

▲ Figure 13.2 The standard business cycle

What is the business cycle?

In developed country economies we can generally see a pattern where there are periods of rising growth, followed by periods of slowing growth and even falling growth. This is known as the business cycle or trade cycle. The business cycle is the periodic fluctuations in economic activity measured by changes in real GDP. The phases of the business cycle are known as boom, recession, trough and recovery. While the fluctuations are, in practice, highly irregular, the most common illustration of the business cycle shows a standard periodic cycle. This is illustrated in Figure 13.2.

In the recovery phase we see economic expansion, with GDP increasing at a rising rate. This is largely driven by an increase in what is known as aggregate (total) demand in the economy, as households and businesses are encouraged to spend more. To meet the increase in demand by households, firms increase their output and take on more workers so that unemployment falls. The newly employed workers spend their incomes on new goods and services and so household spending increases even more. Just as increasing demand for a good or service can result in an increase in its price, so can increasing aggregate demand in an economy lead to an increase in average prices. Thus, as an economy "booms" it is likely that inflationary pressure will build up and the rate of growth of GDP will fall as the economy nears its potential output. Economic policy makers are likely to react by trying to slow down the growth of the economy and this may cause a fall in total demand. This is the beginning of the recession part of the cycle.

A recession is defined as two consecutive quarters of negative GDP growth, that is, falling GDP. During a recession, falling aggregate demand will lead firms to lay off workers, so unemployment rises. If more people are unemployed, there will be even less spending. Low levels of demand result in lower rates of inflation, or even deflation.

Note

Please note that a decrease in GDP, where the economy actually gets smaller, is not the same as a decrease in GDP growth, which is where the economy continues to grow, but at a slower rate.

At some point the contraction will come to an end. This is known as the trough. Output cannot continue to fall forever as there will always be some people with jobs to maintain a given level of consumption, foreigners will demand exports, governments will continue to spend by running budget deficits, and people will be able to use savings to finance their consumption. Additionally, the low demand for money for investment will result in lower interest rates. Thus, aggregate demand will pick up, the economy will enter the recovery phase, and the cycle will repeat itself.

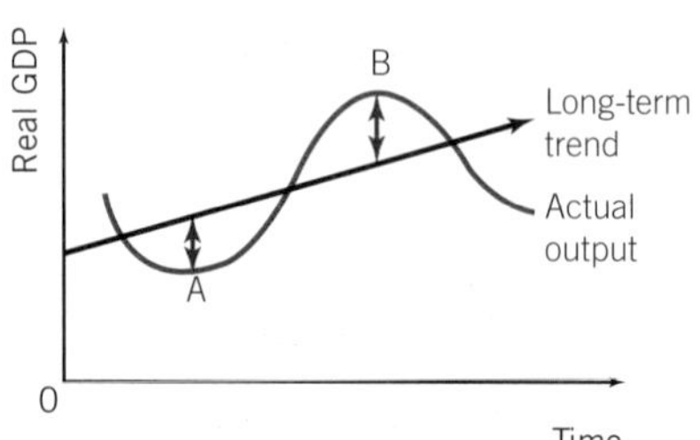

▲ Figure 13.3 Long-term and output gaps

As the diagram shows, the second recovery is at a higher level of real GDP than the first and each boom is higher than the last. This illustrates the important point that economies tend to go through periodic fluctuations in real GDP around their long-term growth trend, or long-term potential output. This is shown in Figure 13.3.

The periodic fluctuations in growth are shown as the actual output line, while the economy's long-term trend is shown as a steady increase in output. This represents the growth rate that the economy can sustain over time (but is not to be confused with sustainable development!). The difference between actual output and potential output is known as the output gap. At point A there is a negative output gap. The economy is producing below its trend and unemployment is likely to be a problem. At point B there is a positive output gap. The economy is producing above its trend, ie beyond capacity, and inflation is likely to be a problem. This illustrates an interesting feature of economics. In the short run it is quite possible that economies will face a "trade-off" between inflation and unemployment. When operating below trend unemployment will be a problem, while operating above potential will result in inflationary pressure (rising rate of inflation). This will be addressed in greater detail later.

Economists have long studied the causes of business cycles and have often hypothesised about the length and magnitude of a "typical" cycle. However, there are no straight answers to these questions. One theory (of many) is that a country's business cycle may be linked to its electoral cycle. That is, a government will stimulate an economy with expansionary policies to create a boom and lower unemployment just before an election, and then put less popular contractionary policies into place after it has been elected. A criticism of such policies is that they can widen the magnitude of the cycle, with higher levels of unemployment and inflation than there would be if the economy were left on its own.

Exercise 13.4

ATL Thinking and Communication

Make an annotated copy of the business cycle diagram, noting:

- the different phases through which an economy is likely to pass
- the positive and negative features of such phases
- the long-run potential growth line
- positive and negative output gaps.

Key concept

ECONOMIC WELLBEING

What other measures of economic well being exist?

There are many composite indicators that may be used to measure economic well being. Let us look at three of them.

1. **OECD Better Life Index**

   OECD stands for the Organisation for Economic Co-operation and Development. It was established in 1961 and its mission is to promote policies that will improve the economic and social well-being of people around the world. The OECD has 35 member countries, comprising most of the world's developed economies and a number of emerging economies. It also has "key partners", such as Brazil, China, India, Indonesia, Russia and South Africa.

   The OECD Better Life Index allows the comparison of well being across countries, based on 11 topics that the OECD has identified as essential, in the areas of material living conditions and quality of life. The 11 topics reflect what the OECD has identified as essential to well being in terms of *material living conditions* (housing, income, jobs) and *quality of life* (community, education, environment, governance, health, life satisfaction, safety and work-life balance).

Economics in action

ATL Thinking, Communication and Research

Go to the OECD Better Life Index website http://www.oecdbetterlifeindex.org/#/33325225553.

1. Explore the site.
2. Create your own Better Life Index, using the calculator on the website.
3. Write a short report on the Better Life Index results for a country of your choice.

2. Happiness Index

The Happiness Index is another composite index. It is put together by the United Nations Sustainable Development Solutions Network and the results are published in the annual World Happiness Report. The World Happiness Report 2018, ranked 156 countries by their happiness levels, and 117 countries by the happiness of their immigrants.

The data used to rank countries in each report is drawn from the Gallup World Poll, as well as other sources such as the World Values Survey, in some of the reports. The main variables considered in 2018 were GDP per capita, social support, healthy life expectancy, freedom to make choices, generosity and perceptions of corruption. The results for the top and bottom three countries are given below in Table 13.3:

Overall rank	Country	Score	GDP per capita	Social support	Healthy life expectancy	Freedom to make life choices	Generosity	Perceptions of corruption
1	Finland	7.632	1.305	1.592	0.874	0.681	0.192	0.393
2	Norway	7.594	1.456	1.582	0.861	0.686	0.286	0.340
3	Denmark	7.555	1.351	1.590	0.868	0.683	0.284	0.408
154	South Sudan	3.254	0.337	0.608	0.177	0.112	0.224	0.106
155	Central African Republic	3.083	0.024	0.000	0.010	0.305	0.218	0.038
156	Burundi	2.905	0.091	0.627	0.145	0.065	0.149	0.076

Source: The World Happiness Report 2018, http://worldhappiness.report/ed/2018/

▲ **Table 13.3** Top and bottom three countries – World Happiness Report 2018

Economics in action — ATL Thinking, Communication and Research

Go to the World Happiness Report website: http://worldhappiness.report/.

Using information from the site, update Table 13.3 and comment on any obvious changes that may have occurred.

3. **Happy Planet Index (HPI)**

The HPI measures sustainable wellbeing. It measures how well countries are doing at achieving long and happy lives, taking into account sustainability. The HPI combines four elements to show how efficiently residents of different countries are using environmental resources to lead long, happy lives.

It uses the equation shown below:

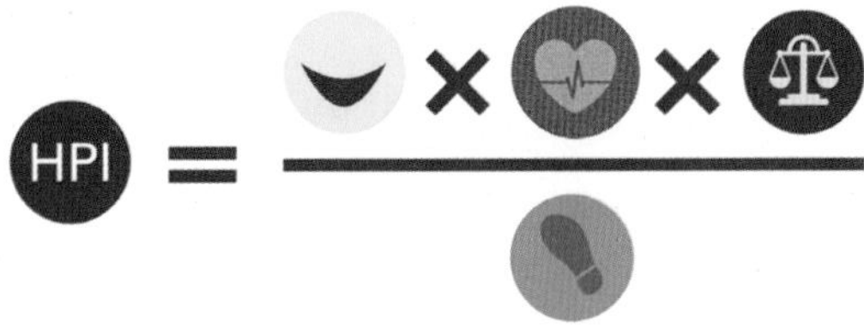

Wellbeing: How satisfied the residents of each country say they feel with life overall, on a scale from zero to ten, based on data collected as part of the Gallup World Poll.

Life expectancy: The average number of years a person is expected to live in each country based on data collected by the United Nations.

Inequality of outcomes: The inequalities between people within a country, in terms of how long they live, and how happy they feel, based on the distribution in each country's life expectancy and wellbeing data. Inequality of outcomes is expressed as a percentage.

Ecological Footprint: The average impact that each resident of a country places on the environment, based on data prepared by the Global Footprint Network. Ecological Footprint is expressed using a standardized unit: global hectares (gha) per person.

Source: The Happy Planet Index, http://happyplanetindex.org

Key concept

SUSTAINABILITY

Economics in action

ATL Thinking, Communication and Research

Go to the Happy Planet Index website, http:// happyplanetindex.org.

1. Explore the site.
2. Use the HPI map to find two countries of your choice. Write a report on the differences between the countries in relation to the HPI.

Exercise 13.5

ATL Thinking, Communication and Research

Make four graphs to illustrate the following information about your OECD country for the last five years:

1. growth rate (you have the data from exercise 13.2)
2. unemployment rate
3. inflation rate
4. current account balance.

EXAMINATION QUESTIONS

Paper 1, part (a) questions

1. Using a diagram of the circular flow of income model, explain the three ways that national income can be measured. [10 marks]
2. Distinguish between GDP, GNI, real GDP and real GNI per capita. [10 marks]
3. Explain **three** uses of national income statistics. [10 marks]

Paper 1, part (a) questions

1. Using a diagram of the circular flow of income model, explain the three ways that national income can be measured. [10 marks]
2. Distinguish between GDP, GNI, real GDP and real GNI per capita. [10 marks]
3. Explain **three** uses of national income statistics. [10 marks]
4. Distinguish between the OECD Better Life Index and the Happy Planet Index. [10 marks]
5. Explain the workings of the business cycle. [10 marks]

Paper 1, part (b) questions

1. Using real-world examples, evaluate the use of GDP figures as a means of comparing countries. [15 marks]
2. Using real-world examples, evaluate the appropriateness of using GNI statistics to measure economic well being. [15 marks]

Assessment advice: Interpreting data

A common error is for students to interpret a fall in the growth of GDP as a fall in GDP, and therefore a recession. Consider the data for Luxembourg: From 2002 to 2003 the rate of growth of GDP fell from 3.5% to 2%. You must not think that this means that the actual output of GDP was less in 2003 than it was in 2002. It means that GDP grew, but at a slower rate than it had the previous year. From 2003 to 2004 the rate of growth increased sharply to about 4.2% and then slowed slightly in the next year to 4%. In all years, the GDP of Luxembourg was rising.

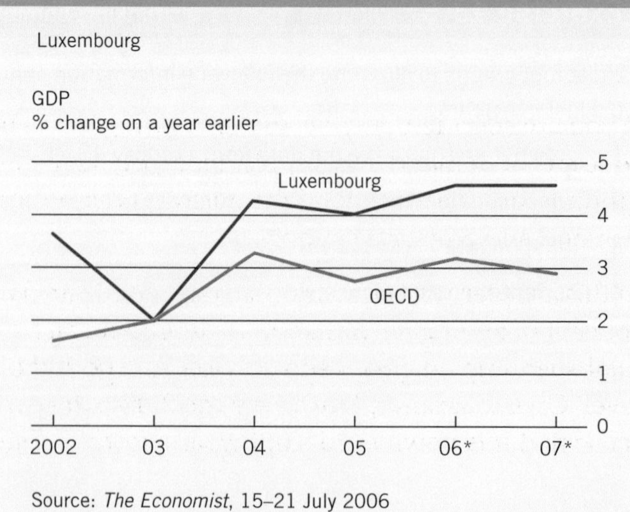

Source: *The Economist*, 15–21 July 2006

14 AGGREGATE DEMAND

REAL-WORLD ISSUE:
Why does economic activity vary over time and why does this matter? How do governments manage the economy and how effective are their policies?

By the end of this chapter, you should be able to:

- → Distinguish between demand and aggregate demand
- → Define and illustrate aggregate demand
- → Define and describe the components of aggregate demand
- → Explain the determinants of the components of aggregate demand
- → Illustrate shifts of the aggregate demand curve.

What is aggregate demand (AD)?

If you are confident in your understanding of the microeconomic concepts of demand and supply, then you have the necessary groundwork to understand the macroeconomic concepts of aggregate demand and aggregate supply.

In this chapter we begin our macroeconomic analysis by examining the concept of aggregate demand. By definition, aggregate demand is the total spending on goods and services in a period of time at a given price level. On a diagram it looks very much like the demand curve in the sense that it is downward sloping, as shown in Figure 14.1.

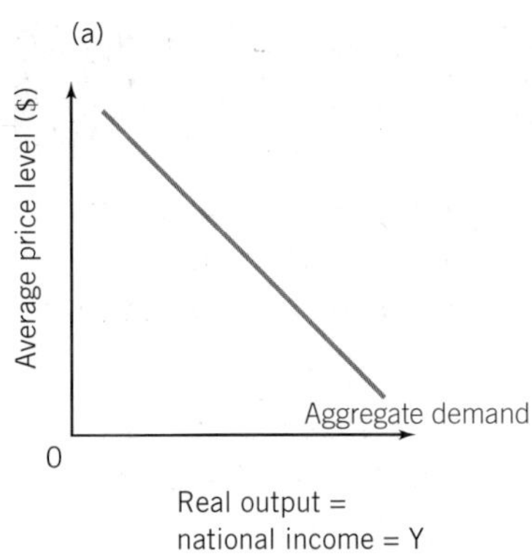

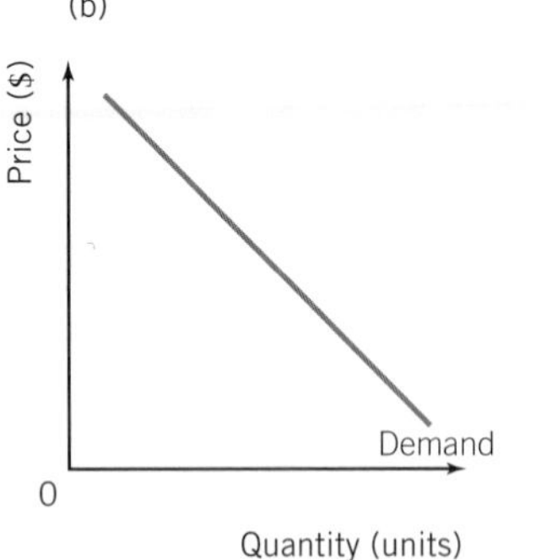

▲ **Figure 14.1** (a) Macroeconomic aggregate demand curve; (b) microeconomic demand curve

However, the demand curve shows the relationship between the price of one good – for example, soccer balls – and the demand for that one good. The fact that it is a demand curve for one market makes it a microeconomic concept. Macroeconomics considers the working of the whole economy, including all the goods and services demanded. Where the microeconomic demand curve has the "price" of the one good on the y-axis, the macroeconomic aggregate demand curve has a measure of the average price level of all goods and services. Where the microeconomic demand curve has the "quantity" of the one good on the x-axis, the macroeconomic aggregate demand curve has the total quantity of all goods and services, which is national output.

Given what you learned in Chapter 13, you will also realize that national output is equivalent to national income and national expenditure. In macroeconomic analysis the x-axis is commonly labelled "real output" (the value of national output adjusted for inflation) or national income (Y). Thus the aggregate demand curve shows the relationship between the *average price level* and *real output*. The two different diagrams are shown to help you see and learn the difference between the microeconomic concept of demand and the macroeconomic concept of aggregate demand.

The AD diagram illustrates the inverse relationship between the average price level and the total real output demanded; at a lower average price level, a higher quantity is demanded. Essentially, this is the Law of Demand on an aggregate level. The word "aggregate" means "total". Therefore, in constructing an aggregate demand curve, we look at the demand from all possible sectors within the economy. This gives us the components of aggregate demand described in the next section.

What are the components of aggregate demand?

There are four components of aggregate demand, ie there are four things that make up aggregate demand.

1. **Consumption**

   Consumption (C) is the total spending by consumers on domestic goods and services. In looking at consumer demand for goods we look at two categories of goods—durable goods and non-durable goods. Durable goods are goods such as cars, computers, mobile phones and bicycles that are used by consumers over a period of time (usually more than one year). Non-durable goods are goods such as rice, toilet paper and newspapers that are used up immediately or over a relatively short period of time.

2. **Investment**

   Investment (I) is defined as the addition of capital stock to the economy. Investment is carried out by firms. Firms have two types of investment:

   - Replacement investment occurs when firms spend on capital in order to maintain the productivity of their existing capital.
   - Induced investment occurs when firms spend on capital to increase their output to respond to higher demand in the economy.

   The economy's capital stock includes all goods that are made by people and are used to produce other goods or services, such as factories, machines, offices or computers. Investment is not to be confused with buying shares or putting money in a bank – we tend to call this "investment" in everyday English, but it is, in fact, "saving" as it is a leakage from the circular flow.

3. **Government spending**

   Governments at a variety of levels (federal, state/provincial, municipal/city) spend on a wide variety of goods and services. These include health, education, law and order, transport, social security, housing and defence. The amount of government spending (G) depends on the policies and objectives of the government.

4. **Net exports (X–M)**

   Exports are domestic goods and services that are bought by foreigners. When the firms in a country sell exports to foreigners, it results in an inflow of export revenues to the country. Imports are goods and services that are bought from foreign producers. When imports are bought it results in an outflow of import expenditure. The net trade component of AD is actually export *revenues* minus import *expenditure*, but it is simplified by noting it as exports minus imports (X–M). The figure can be either positive, whereby export revenues exceed import expenditure, or negative, whereby import expenditure exceeds export revenues. If the net figure is positive it will add to AD but if the net figure is negative it will reduce AD.

   So, aggregate demand is equal to consumption + investment + government spending + net exports, which is equivalent to GDP using the expenditure method of calculation.

Exercise 14.1

ATL Thinking and Communication

1. Make a list of five durable goods and five non-durable goods used in your household.
2. Compare the contents of your list with the lists of others in your group.

What is the shape of the AD curve?

Aggregate demand can be presented as a formula, **C + I + G + (X – M)**, and as a diagram, as shown in Figure 14.2.

When the average price level in the economy falls from PL_1 to PL_2, the level of output demanded by consumers (C) plus firms (I) plus governments (G) and the net foreign sector (X–M) increases from Y_1 to Y_2.

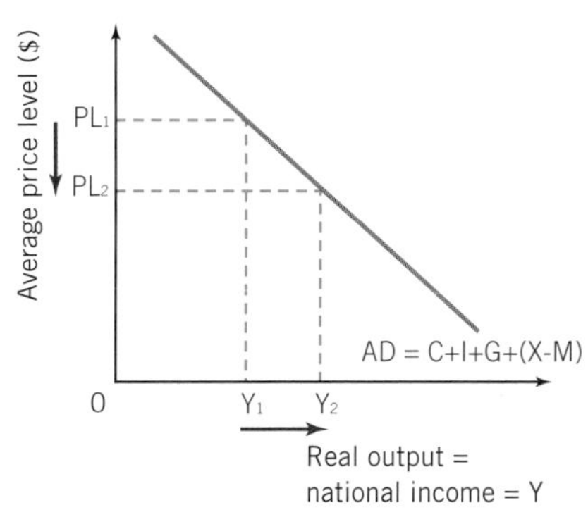

▲ Figure 14.2 The aggregate demand curve

> **Note**
>
> You will find that different books use different labels for the *x*-axis. You may find any of national income (Y), national expenditure, national output or real output. Whichever one you choose, be sure that it is distinct from simply quantity or Q, which would indicate a single market in a microeconomic analysis.

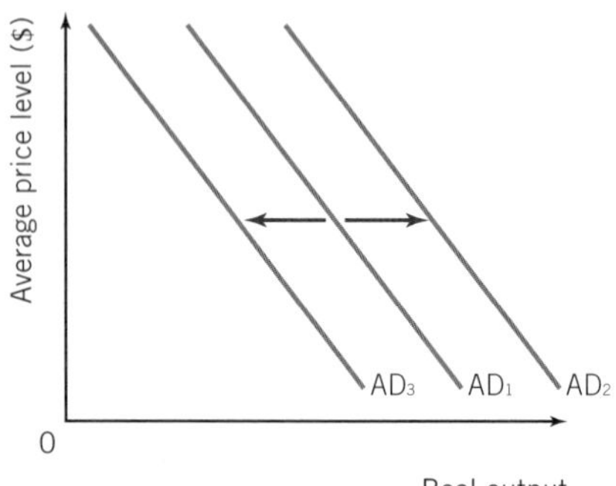

▲ Figure 14.3 Shifts in aggregate demand

So what causes changes in AD?

A change in the price level will result in a movement along the AD curve, from one level of real output to another. A change in any of the components of aggregate demand will cause a shift in the demand curve as shown in Figure 14.3.

An increase in any of the components of aggregate demand will result in an increase in aggregate demand and a shift of the AD curve to the right from AD_1 to AD_2. A decrease in any of the components of aggregate demand will result in a fall in aggregate demand and a shift of the AD curve to the left from AD_1 to AD_3.

What causes changes in consumption?

1. **Changes in income taxes**

   The most significant determinant of consumption is income. As incomes rise people have more money to spend on goods and services, so consumption increases. If there is an increase in direct income taxes (the taxes paid on income by individuals), then people will have less *disposable income*. Disposable income is the income that people have remaining for spending and saving after income taxes have been paid. With less disposable income, consumption will decrease and there will be a fall in AD. A reduction of income tax levels will lead to an increase in disposable incomes and thus an increase in consumption and AD. Government manipulation of income taxes is an element of fiscal policy, which we will look at in more detail in Chapter 17.

2. **Changes in interest rates**

   Spending on non-durable goods is carried out with the day-to-day money that people earn (their income). But some of the money that is used to buy durable goods comes from money which people borrow from the bank. When people borrow money they must pay for the borrowed money by paying interest to the bank. If there is an increase in interest rates, which is essentially the price of borrowed money, then there is likely to be less borrowing (because it is more expensive to borrow). Therefore consumption will fall, resulting in a fall in AD.

   For example, borrowed money is usually used to buy houses. To buy a house, most consumers get a loan for housing called a mortgage. If interest rates increase then this loan may become more expensive on a month-to-month basis. This means that people will have less money to spend on other goods and services, so consumption will fall. Also, a rise in the interest rate makes saving more attractive; people would prefer to put their extra income in the bank to earn money rather than spend it on goods and services. This is another reason why changes in interest rates affect consumption.

Overall, an increase in interest rates leads to a fall in consumption. On the other hand, a fall in interest rates will lead to an increase in consumption, *ceteris paribus*, as it becomes more attractive to borrow money to spend on durable goods and services. In addition, if interest rates fall then mortgage repayments may fall, leaving more money to spend on goods and services, and it becomes less appealing to save money in the bank when the return on the savings (the interest earned) is relatively low.

Exercise 14.2

ATL Thinking and Communication

Identify five goods or services that people might need a bank loan to purchase.

3. **Changes in wealth**

The amount of consumption depends on the amount of wealth that consumers have. It is very important not to confuse the concepts of "income" and "wealth". Income is the money that people earn. Wealth is made up of the assets that people own. This includes physical assets, such as houses, art, antiques or jewellery, and monetary/financial assets, such as shares in companies, government bonds or bank savings. There are two main factors that can change the level of wealth in the economy.

- *A change in house prices*: When house prices increase across the economy, consumers feel more wealthy and are likely to feel confident enough to increase their consumption by saving less or borrowing more.
- *A change in the value of stocks and shares*: Many consumers hold shares in companies. If the value of those shares increases then people feel wealthier. This might encourage them to spend more. Alternatively, they might sell those shares and then use the earnings to increase consumption.

4. **Changes in consumer confidence/expectations**

If people are optimistic about their economic future then they are likely to spend more now. For example, if they think that they are likely to get a promotion in the future due to a booming economy and strong sales then they will feel more confident about taking a loan or using up savings. Thus, high consumer confidence is likely to lead to increased consumption. However, if people expect economic conditions to worsen then they are likely to reduce their consumption today in order to save for the future. Economists regularly measure consumer confidence and put the information together in the form of a "consumer confidence index" or "consumer sentiment index". An increase in the index indicates that confidence is rising; if this is the case, then consumer spending is likely to rise as well.

Political uncertainty weighs on Thailand's consumer confidence

https://www.thailand-business-news.com/business/72338-political-uncertainty-weighs-on-thailands-consumer-confidence.html

Consumer expectations regarding the future price level will also affect consumption. If consumers expect the price level to increase in the future, ie *inflation*, then they will increase consumption now, especially on durable consumer goods. In the same way, if they expect the price level to fall, ie *deflation*, they will put off consuming now in the belief that products will be less expensive in the future. Again, this especially relates to durable consumer goods.

Exercise 14.3

ATL Thinking and Communication

Read the short text below and answer the questions that follow.

Use the data from the text to support your answers.

Consumer confidence slumps amid Brexit uncertainty

KBC Bank/ESRI consumer sentiment index falls to 86.5 in February from 98.8 in January

Shoppers could cut spending if fears of a hard Brexit and a weaker Irish economy persist, experts warn in a report today.

Consumer confidence tumbled in February following a nurses' strike and the British parliament's rejection of prime minister Theresa May's Brexit deal, according to figures released by KBC Bank and the Economic and Social Research Institute (ESRI).

"Irish consumer sentiment fell sharply in February on a notably poorer outlook for the Irish economy and jobs that translated into poorer household income prospects," the KBC Bank/ESRI index states.

KBC Bank Ireland chief economist Austin Hughes says there is no immediate threat to spending, but suggests that consumers could tighten purse strings if their concerns continue.

While the bank and economic researchers expected the uncertainty to dent consumer confidence, they say that the depth of the fall was surprising. The KBC Bank/ESRI consumer sentiment index fell to 86.5 in February from 98.8 in January, and was down sharply on the 105.2 recorded during the same month last year.

Nevertheless, Mr Hughes says he does not believe the economy's outlook or consumers' prospects deteriorated sharply last month. "Consequently, we don't envisage any sharp pullback in spending," he says. "However, the February survey period did see a number of developments that may have unnerved many consumers and prompted an outsize drop in confidence.

"If this persists we would expect consumer spending to move on to a weaker path."

Industrial unrest

Mr Hughes blames politics and industrial unrest on both sides of the Irish Sea for the fall in confidence. He believes one factor was Mrs May's failure to get her Brexit deal through parliament, increasing the risk that the UK could crash out of the European Union without an agreement. During the period, a number of reports, including documents from the Central Bank and KBC, highlighted the damage that a disorderly or "hard" Brexit could do to the Irish economy.

At home, he says that the nurses' strike and the debate over the national children's hospital cost could have reminded consumers of previous industrial relations turbulence and issues with managing public finances.

While all elements of the index fell, consumers' concerns were strongest about macroeconomic questions. The number of consumers who expected unemployment to rise jumped to almost four out of 10 from 22 per cent the previous month. However, they only modestly changed their assessments of their household finances over the previous 12 months.

"So the reality of consumers' current circumstances hasn't fundamentally changed," says Mr Hughes. "However, the risks to the future were seen to materially worsen." He argues that with reduced pessimism over Brexit and the ending of the nurses' strike, it would not be surprising to see consumer sentiment rebounding this month.

Source: adapted from *The Irish Times*, March 15, 2019 (author Barry O'Halloran)

1. Using numbers from the text, explain the difference in consumer confidence in Ireland from:
   a. January 2019 to February 2019
   b. February 2018 to February 2019.
2. Using a diagram, explain how the change in consumer confidence from 2018 to 2019 might be expected to affect Irish AD.
3. Identify and explain the reasons for the fall in consumer confidence.

5. **Levels of household indebtedness**

The extent to which households are willing and able to borrow money affects consumption. If it is easy to borrow money (easy credit) and interest rates are low then it is likely that households will take on more debt by getting loans or using their credit cards. Thus spending on goods and services will rise. However, if interest rates rise, then households will have to spend more to repay their loans and mortgages (the original amount borrowed plus the interest). In the short run they might simply continue to borrow but ultimately the debt will have to be paid and this may well leave consumers with less money to spend on goods and services. This would lead to falling AD.

Did you know?

One-in-five Canadians with debt will need to liquidate assets to pay it down in 2019

One-in-five Canadians with debt say they will need to liquidate assets (eg cash in their pension plans, get a second mortgage, sell a vehicle, etc) to help pay off (or pay down) their debt in 2019. The need to liquidate is reported as significantly higher among males (24%) versus females (14%) and those with children under 18 (23%) versus without children (16%).

The 2019 Household Debt Survey, a poll of 1,515 Canadians, was conducted to uncover financial concerns that confront Canadians on a daily basis, such as budgeting, bill payments, debt, cost of living and job security.

The survey also found that almost two-thirds of Canadians with debt (62%) anticipate taking on new forms of debt in 2019. Within this group, those under 55 years of age are significantly more likely to anticipate new forms of debt this year (67%) compared to those who are 55 and older (50%). Below are the anticipated new forms of debt:

→ New/increased credit card balance (23%)
→ New/increased line of credit (15%)
→ New/increased vehicle loan or lease (13%)
→ New/increased mortgage (12%)

With federal Finance Minister, Bill Morneau set to release the federal budget on March 19, Canada's national debt hovers above $691 billion – that's nearly $18,700 per Canadian. Much like all levels of government, Canadian households are also awash in debt. In fact, almost half of Canadians are within $200 of not being able to pay their bills.

Source: Adapted from *Financial Planning Standards Council*, March 13, 2019

Economics in action

ATL Thinking, Communication and Research

Consumption makes up most of the aggregate demand in most countries. Consider the national income data in exercise 13.1 and note the percentage of GDP that comes from consumption in Canada. You will find that this is rather typical of the developed countries.

Investigate the components of GDP (AD) for the country that you chose in exercise 13.2.

What causes changes in investment?

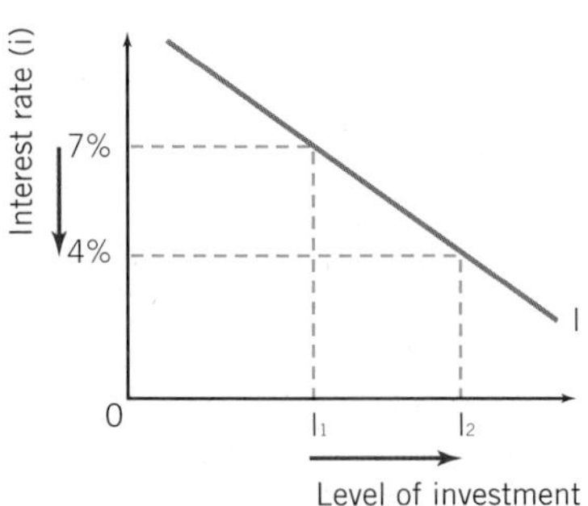

▲ Figure 14.4 The relationship between investment and the interest rate

1. **Changes in interest rates**

   In order to invest, firms need money. The money that firms use for investment comes from several sources. For example, they can use their "retained profits" or they can borrow the money. Both of these are affected by the interest rate. If the money is to be borrowed, then an increase in the cost of borrowing may lead to a fall in investment. If interest rates are high, then firms may prefer to put their retained profits in the bank to earn higher returns as savings, rather than use them to invest. Therefore, there is an inverse relationship between interest rates and the level of investment, as shown in Figure 14.4.

   A decrease in the interest rate, from 7% to 4%, will decrease the incentive to save and decrease the cost of borrowing, so is likely to lead to an increase in borrowing that is likely to result in an increase in the level of investment from I_1 to I_2. An increase in the interest rate will have the opposite effect.

2. **Changes in business taxes**

   If the government increases taxes on business profits, then it will reduce *post-tax profits*, which will mean that firms have less money to invest and so we would expect to see a fall in AD. In the same way, if the government was to lower taxes on business profits, then more investment could take place and there would be an increase in AD, ie a shift of the AD curve to the right. Government manipulation of *corporate taxes* (taxes on the profits of firms) is an element of fiscal policy, which we will look at in more detail in Chapter 17.

3. **Technological change**

   In any dynamic economy there is likely to be a quick pace of technological change. In order to keep up with advances in technology and to remain competitive firms will need to invest. This will increase AD.

4. **Changes in business confidence/expectations**

   Businesses make decisions about the amount of investment they should make based to a large extent on their expectations for the future and their confidence in the economic climate. There would be little point in investing to increase the potential output of a firm if consumer demand is likely to fall in the future. If businesses are very confident about the future of the economy and expect consumer demand to rise then they will want to be ready to meet the increases in consumer demand by investing to increase potential output and productivity. Economists regularly measure the confidence of businesses and publish data in the form of a business confidence index.

Brexit uncertainty 'hitting UK business investment'

https://www.bbc.com/news/business-48653510

Exercise 14.4

ATL Thinking and Communication

Read the following article and answer the questions that follow:

SA business confidence falls to almost two-year low

South African business confidence fell to the lowest level in almost two years in the first quarter of 2019, with more than two thirds of respondents dissatisfied with current conditions.

A gauge measuring sentiment declined to 28 in the first quarter from 31 in the final three months of 2018. The median estimate of four economists in a Bloomberg survey was 32.

Key Insights

Confidence in the retail industry is at the lowest since the end of 2013. Sentiment among retailers and builders fell the most, with the latter reflecting a dearth of new work, the survey showed. Confidence levels in four of the five sectors covered in the index fell.

President Cyril Ramaphosa's rise to power boosted business confidence in early 2018 but sentiment has slumped as trading conditions remain depressed. While his efforts to expose corruption, rebuild institutions and bolster investment will bear fruit in the longer term, "forceful, and in some instances, unpopular structural reforms must also form part of the mix," said Ettienne le Roux, the chief economist at RMB.

"South Africa will not be able to shift to a lasting, higher growth and prosperity path without more short-term pain", said Le Roux. "This time around, the country cannot rely on the global economy to counterbalance such internal adjustment costs, as global growth itself is now shifting to a lower gear." Africa's most-industrialised economy expanded 0.8% in 2018 and is struggling to gain momentum as rolling blackouts threaten to damp prospects of a recovery.

The index reflects the results of a survey of 1,700 businesspeople, with most responses received from February 13 to March 4.

Source: Adapted from *Bloomberg NEWS*, March 13 2019

1. With reference to the data, state the extent of the decrease in business confidence between the last quarter of 2018 and the first quarter of 2019.
2. Outline the reasons for the decline.
3. Use a diagram to show how the change in business expectations might influence aggregate demand.

5. **Levels of corporate indebtedness**

The extent to which businesses are willing and able to borrow money affects investment. If it is easy to borrow money (easy credit) and interest rates are low then it is likely that businesses will take on more debt and investment will rise. However, if interest rates rise, then businesses will have to spend more to repay their loans (the original amount borrowed plus the interest). In the short run they might simply continue to borrow but ultimately the debt will have to be paid and this may well leave businesses with less money to spend on investment. This would lead to falling AD.

What causes changes in government spending?

The amount and nature of government spending depends on the political and economic priorities of the government. For example, we looked at government subsidies in Chapter 8. If the government has made a commitment to financially support a given industry, then government spending will rise. If governments are obliged to spend to correct market failure, then government spending will rise. A new education or health policy might require increased public spending on schools or hospitals. Put quite simply, if government spending increases, then AD will shift to the right; if government spending falls, then the opposite will happen.

What causes changes in net exports?

Net exports are the difference between export revenues and import expenditure over a given period of time. As we know, they are expressed as (X – M) in the aggregate demand function. A positive (X – M), a *trade surplus*, will lead to a shift of AD to the right and a negative (X – M), a *trade deficit*, will shift AD to the left.

1. **Changes in the level of exports**

   Exports are goods or services that are bought by foreigners. If foreign incomes rise then their consumption of imported goods and services will rise. For example, as the Chinese national income rises, Chinese people are more willing and able to buy imported goods and services from Europe. Thus, European exports rise as the Chinese economy grows. Similarly, as China grows, investment in China expands. This is likely to involve some measure of imported capital. Thus, as China grows, German exports of capital equipment may also rise.

   Other than changes in the national income of trading partners, changes in the value of a country's currency (its exchange rate) can also affect a country's exports. If a country's exchange rate becomes stronger, then this makes the country's exports relatively more expensive to foreigners. According to the Law of Demand, this will cause the quantity of exports to fall. This will have an effect on the country's export revenues (the way in which it affects the export revenues depends on the elasticity of demand for exports; this will be addressed in a later chapter). Conversely, if the exchange rate falls in value then exports will become more competitive and may result in an increase in export revenues.

   Changes in countries' trade policies may also affect the value of a country's exports. If a country decides to adopt a policy of more liberalized (free) trade then it may reduce the tariffs that it charges on imports and effectively allows countries to export more to that country. On the other hand, if a country adopts more protectionist policies to reduce the level of imports then it will reduce the exports of other countries.

   The last broad factor to affect export revenues is the relative inflation rates among trading partners. For example, if inflation in the US were relatively higher than in Canada then US goods would be less competitive in Canada and may reduce the export revenues which the US earns from its exports to Canada. On the other hand, if the inflation rate in the US were relatively lower than the Canadian rate then American goods would be more competitive in Canadian markets, and so American export revenues might be expected to rise, *ceteris paribus*.

2. **Changes in the level of imports**

   It has already been established that when a country's national income is growing there is likely to be an increase in consumption.

As people consume more goods and services, it will necessarily be the case that some of these goods and services will be imported. Similarly, as national income rises, there is likely to be greater investment. Part of the capital goods that are purchased will be imported capital goods and/or components. Thus, as national income rises so does spending on imports. If national income falls there will be reduced spending on imports.

Using the same analysis as we used above, you should be able to see how changes in a country's exchange rate would be expected to change the level of spending on imports. An increase in the exchange rate would make imported goods less expensive and, depending on the elasticity of demand for imports, could reduce import expenditure. A decrease in the exchange rate would make imported goods more expensive and thus affect the level of import expenditure.

The type of trade policies that a country adopts will affect its level of import spending. If a country decides to adopt a more liberalized trade policy by, say, reducing tariffs (taxes) on imports, then import expenditure would be expected to rise. However, if a more protectionist set of policies were to be adopted then import expenditure would fall, *ceteris paribus*.

If the inflation rates of trade partners were to vary notably then this might also affect the level of import spending as noted above.

Thus, net exports (the difference between export revenues and import expenditure) depends on domestic national income (affecting the demand for imports), foreign national incomes (affecting the demand for exports), changes in exchange rates, changes in trade policies and relative inflation rates. We spend much more time discussing changes in trade policies and exchange rates in later chapters.

Exercise 14.5

ATL Thinking and Communication

Draw an aggregate demand diagram to illustrate an increase in AD, and one that shows a decrease in AD. Be sure to label the axes accurately. Decide whether each of the following factors would lead to an increase or a decrease in AD and write out the point beneath the appropriate diagram. In each explanation, explain which component(s) of AD is likely to be affected and why.

Example: A fall in income tax is likely to lead to an increase in AD because consumers' disposable incomes will rise, leading to an increase in consumption, *ceteris paribus*.

1. a fall in house prices
2. a rise in consumer confidence
3. an increase in foreign incomes
4. a fall in the consumer confidence index
5. a decrease in interest rates.

EXAMINATION QUESTIONS

Paper 1, part (a) questions – HL & SL

1. Explain the differences between an increase in demand and an increase in aggregate demand. [10 marks]
2. Explain the difference between the components of aggregate demand and the determinants of aggregate demand. [10 marks]
3. Explain **three** factors that could cause an increase in the level of consumption in an economy. [10 marks]
4. Explain how a change in interest rates is likely to affect the level of investment in an economy. [10 marks]

15 AGGREGATE SUPPLY

REAL-WORLD ISSUE:
Why does economic activity vary over time and why does this matter? How do governments manage the economy and how effective are their policies?

By the end of this chapter, you should be able to:

- → Define aggregate supply (AS)
- → Define and illustrate short-run aggregate supply
- → Explain the causes of shifts in short-run aggregate supply (SRAS)
- → Distinguish between short-run aggregate supply and long-run aggregate supply (LRAS)
- → Distinguish between a "Keynesian" AS and a new classical LRAS
- → Explain the sources of increases in the AS/LRAS.

What is aggregate supply?

In this chapter we continue our macroeconomic analysis by introducing the concept of aggregate supply. The concept of the "supply side" of the economy is extremely important in the study of the overall productive capacity of the economy. By definition, aggregate supply is the total amount of goods and services that all industries in the economy will produce at every given price level. It is essentially the sum of the supply curves of all the industries in the economy. In contrast to the theory of aggregate demand, however, we distinguish between the short run and the long run in looking at aggregate supply.

What does the short-run aggregate supply curve look like?

Graphically, the short-run aggregate supply (SRAS) curve looks very much like a microeconomic supply curve in that it is upward sloping. There is a positive relationship between the price level and the amount of output that a country's industries will supply.

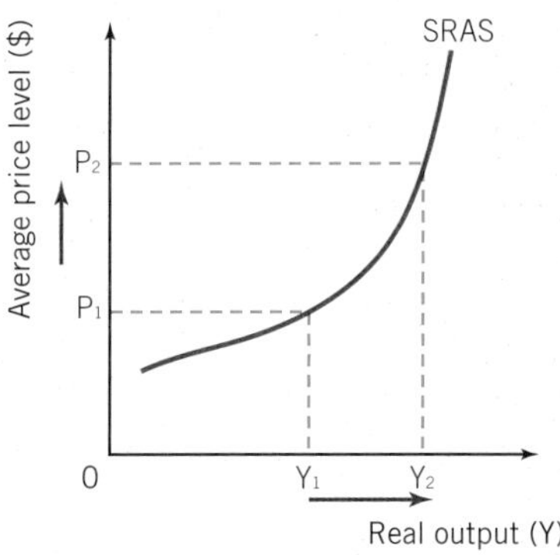

▲ Figure 15.1 The curved SRAS curve

Remember from microeconomics and the Law of Supply (Chapter 5) that supply curves are usually curved and get steeper as price rises. Thus, the SRAS curve would be the same since it is a horizontal summation of all the microeconomic supply curves. It would look like the SRAS curve in Figure 15.1.

However, for ease of analysis, economists usually draw SRAS curves as straight lines, as in Figure 15.2, and so shall we from now on.

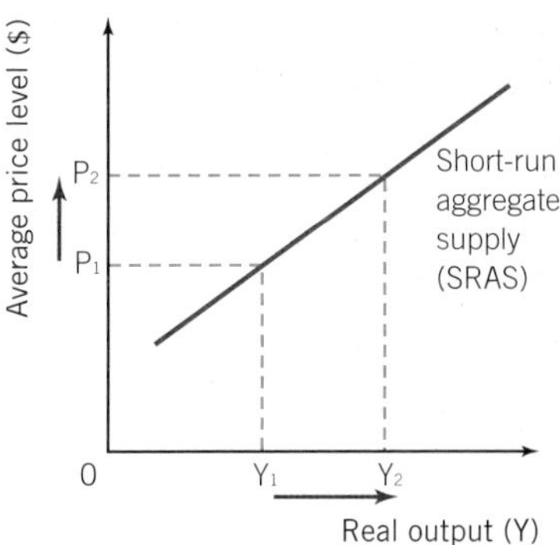

▲ Figure 15.2 The straight-line SRAS curve

At any given price level, industries will supply a certain level of output. Let us look at what happens in the short run if the country's industries want to increase the level of output. It is necessary to understand what is meant by the short run. In our macroeconomic analysis, the short run is defined as the period of time when the prices of the factors of production do not change. Most importantly, the price of labour – the wage rate – is fixed.

If a larger level of output is to be produced, firms are likely to face higher average costs of production. For example, in order to produce more, firms will have to provide incentives to workers to produce a larger amount. Most commonly this is done by paying "overtime" wages. These might be one and a half times the normal wage and so costs rise. Higher level students should recall that the law of diminishing returns means that marginal and average costs will rise as output increases in the short run. In the short run then, an increase in output will be accompanied by an increase in average costs. Industries will pass on an increase in costs in the form of a higher price level. This explains why the SRAS curve is upward sloping. In Figure 15.2, an increase in the level of output from Y_1 to Y_2 will be accompanied by an increase in the price level from P_1 to P_2.

What will shift the SRAS curve?

We have shown that the SRAS curve shows the relationship between the average price level and the level of national output under the *ceteris paribus* assumption. That is, we assume that factor costs remain constant. A change in the price level results in a change in the level of output and is shown as a movement along the SRAS curve as shown in Figure 15.3. This is similar to the microeconomic supply curve, where an increase in the price leads to an increase in the quantity supplied, and is shown as a movement along the supply curve. But, just as with the microeconomic supply curve, a change in anything other than the price will lead to a shift in the whole curve. Thus a change in any of the factors other than

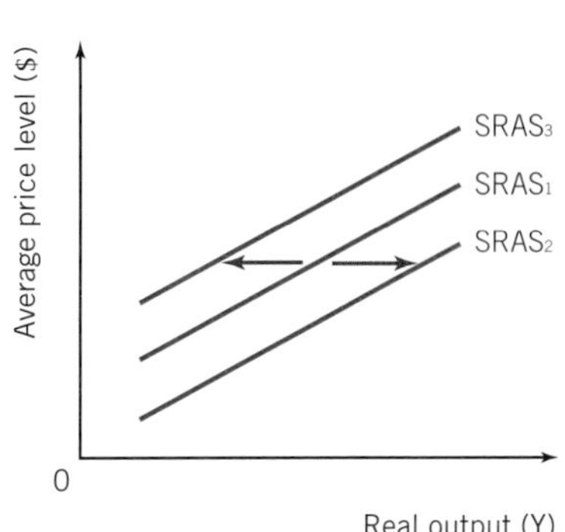

▲ Figure 15.3 Shifts in the SRAS curve

the price level will result in a shift in the SRAS curve. These may be referred to as "supply-side shocks".

Figure 15.3 shows an increase in the short-run aggregate supply ($SRAS_1 \rightarrow SRAS_2$) and a decrease in the SRAS ($SRAS_1 \rightarrow SRAS_3$).

The most straightforward explanation of supply-side shocks is that they are factors that cause changes in the costs of production. Similar to our microeconomic analysis, a decrease in costs results in an increase in aggregate supply; while an increase in costs results in a decrease in aggregate supply.

Typical examples of changes in the costs of production include the following:

- *A change in wage rates*: An increase in wages will result in an increase in the costs of production to firms and therefore a fall in aggregate supply. If, for example, the government raised the legal minimum wage it would increase labour costs. If labour unions in manufacturing industries, whose priority is usually to ensure good wages and conditions for workers, were to negotiate higher wages for manufacturing workers, then this would also result in a fall in the SRAS.
- *A change in the costs of raw materials*: For a change to have an effect on aggregate supply we are assuming an increase in the price of significant, widely used, raw materials. An increase in the price of rubber would affect industries that use rubber as a factor, but this might not be significant enough to affect aggregate supply noticeably. However, a change in the price of oil would have an impact on all industries, as oil is widely used in most production processes.
- *A change in the price of imports*: This point is linked to the previous point. If the capital or raw materials used by a country's industries are imported, then a rise in import prices will increase the costs of production. This can occur due to changes in the exchange rate of a country's currency. For example, if the value of the euro falls then this makes the import price of the raw materials and capital used by European producers relatively more expensive, raising their costs of production.
- *A change in government indirect taxes or subsidies*: An increase in indirect taxes effectively increases the costs of production to firms and therefore results in a fall in the SRAS curve. Conversely, a fall in indirect taxes will result in an increase in the SRAS curve. Since subsidies are a payment from governments to firms, then an increase in government subsidies reduces firms' costs of production, resulting in a decrease in the SRAS while a decrease in subsidies will increase firms' costs of production and shift the SRAS curve to the left.

Since indirect taxes are imposed on the majority of goods and services in an economy, any change in the rate of indirect taxation will have a clear effect on SRAS. In the case of subsidies, the granting of a subsidy for a single product will have minimal impact upon SRAS, unless the product is essential and widely used, such as fuel.

What happens when AD meets SRAS in the short run?

The economy will operate where aggregate demand is equal to aggregate supply. This is shown in Figure 15.4.

At the average price level (PL), all the output produced by the country's producers is consumed. There is no incentive for producers either to increase output or raise prices. The concept of macroeconomic equilibrium will be discussed in more detail in the next chapter.

What is long-run aggregate supply?

There is considerable debate regarding the long-run aggregate supply (LRAS) curve. There are two different "schools of thought" concerning the shape of the LRAS. The first one discussed is often referred to as the new classical (or monetarist) LRAS and this may be viewed as the more broadly used model. However, there is a model which challenges some of the assumptions of this model, known as the "Keynesian" AS. This model was developed by followers of the famous economist John Maynard Keynes, who we have already come across in Chapter 2. The different-shaped LRAS curves lie at the basis of controversies about different policies to be used by governments.

What does new classical LRAS look like?

New classical economists include a number of different branches of economists including monetarists, "supply-side economists" and economists from "the Austrian school". In very simple terms, what these economists have in common is their belief in the efficiency of market forces and their view that there should be the very minimum of government intervention in the allocation of resources in the economy.

In this view, the LRAS curve is perfectly inelastic, or vertical, at what is known as the "full employment level of output". This full-employment level of output represents the potential output that could be produced if the economy were operating at full capacity and is annotated as Y_f on a macroeconomic diagram. It is important to realize that full employment does not mean that there is zero unemployment, but this is something that we will cover in more detail later.

This view asserts that the potential output is based entirely on the quantity and quality (productivity) of the factors of production and not on the price level. Thus, the LRAS is independent of the price level. This model is illustrated in Figure 15.5. The price level might rise from P_1 to P_2 but the level of output does not change.

Exercise 15.1

ATL Thinking and Communication

1. Draw a SRAS curve and label it $SRAS_1$. (Be sure to label the axes correctly.)
2. Add a new SRAS curve demonstrating an increase in SRAS. Label this $SRAS_2$.
3. Explain two possible reasons for this increase in SRAS.

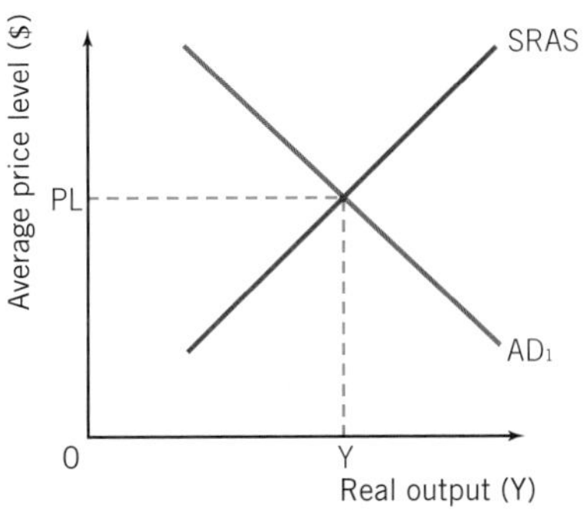

▲ Figure 15.4 Short-run macroeconomic equilibrium

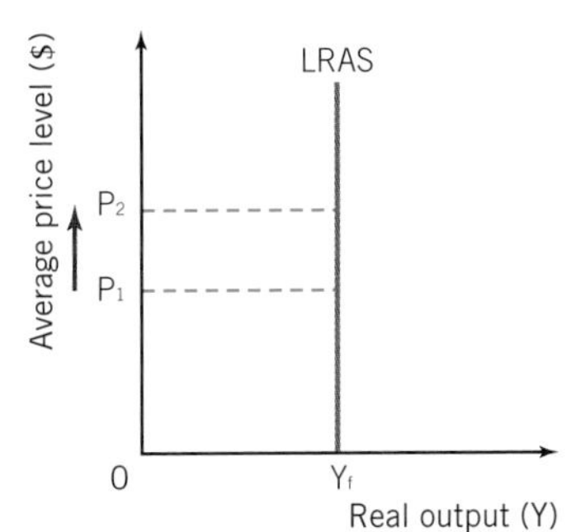

▲ Figure 15.5 New classical LRAS curve

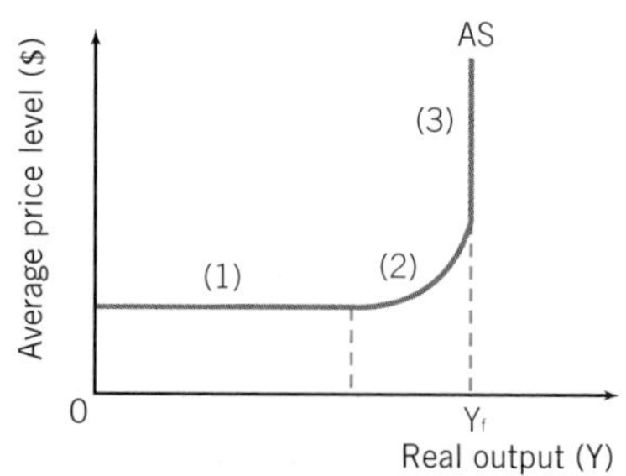

▲ Figure 15.6 Keynesian LRAS curve

What does Keynesian AS look like?

The shape of the curve that is known as the Keynesian AS shows three possible phases and does not really distinguish between the short run and the long run. These are shown in Figure 15.6 as regions (1), (2) and (3).

Phase (1) – In this phase, the aggregate supply curve will be perfectly elastic at low levels of economic activity. Producers in the economy can raise their levels of output without incurring higher average costs because of the existence of "spare capacity" in the economy. That is, there are high levels of unused factors such as unemployed labour and underutilized capital. Should there be a need for greater output, these can be used to their fullest capacity at constant average costs. This corresponds to the region (1) in Figure 15.6.

Phase (2) – As the economy approaches its potential output (Y_f) and the spare capacity is "used up", the economy's available factors of production become increasingly scarce. As producers continue to try to increase output, they will have to bid for the increasingly scarce factors. Higher prices for the factors of production mean higher costs for the producers, and the price level will rise to compensate for the higher costs. This corresponds to region (2) with an upward-sloping AS.

Exercise 15.2

ATL Thinking and Communication

Draw the Keynesian aggregate supply curve and add notes to your diagram to describe each of the phases.

Phase (3) – When the economy reaches its full capacity (Y_f), it is impossible to increase output any further because all factors of production are fully employed. This suggests that AS is perfectly inelastic and is shown as region (3). This third range corresponds exactly to the LRAS of the new classical economists. At this stage output cannot be increased without an increase in the quantity or improvement in the quality (productivity) of the factors of production.

What will shift the AS and LRAS curves?

As a country's factors of production are constantly changing we would expect to see steady increases in its AS/LRAS. This is effectively an illustration of potential economic growth. An outward shift of a country's AS/LRAS curve means that its productive potential has increased. In fact, a shift in the AS/LRAS can be likened to an outward shift of the production possibilities curve (PPC).

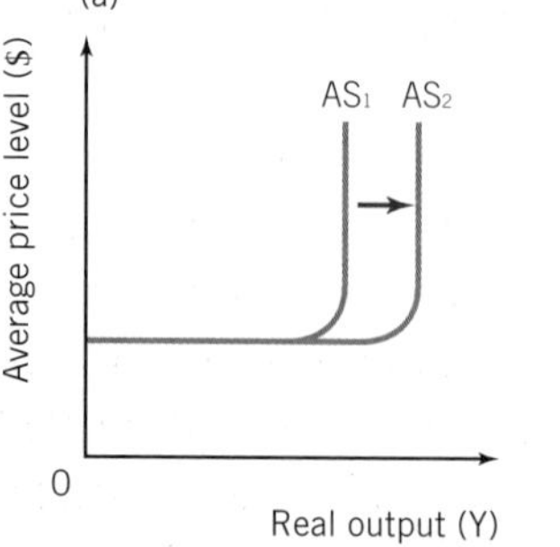

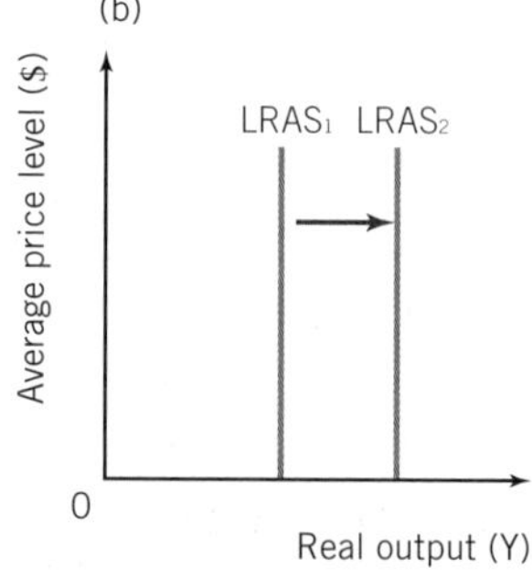

▲ Figure 15.7 A shift in the LRAS curve (a) from the Keynesian perspective and (b) from the new classical perspective

A shift in the AS/LRAS can be shown from either a Keynesian perspective, as in Figure 15.7 (a), or a new classical perspective, as in Figure 15.7 (b). The increase in the full employment level of output is equivalent to the outward shift of the PPC in Figure 15.8.

In very simple terms, the AS/LRAS curve will shift to the right if there is an improvement in the quality of the factors of production – that is, an increase in the productivity (output per unit of input) of the resources used in production – or an increase in the quantity of the factors of production. Either of these may be affected by advances in technology, so improvements in technology are of vital importance to the supply side of any economy. To see how this might come about it is worth considering each factor of production to understand how the quantity or productivity might increase. This is shown in Table 15.1.

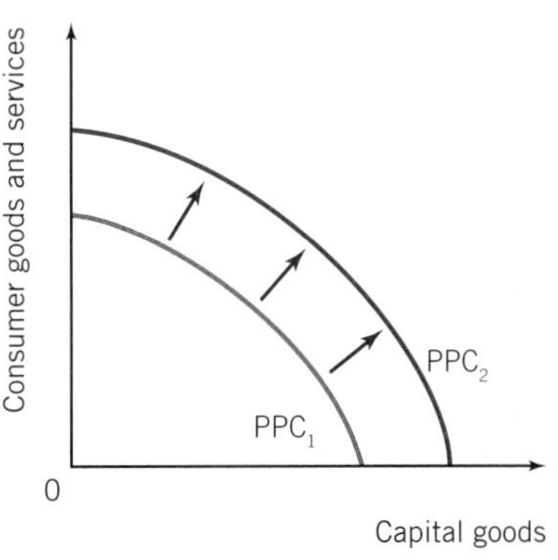

▲ Figure 15.8 An increase in productive potential equivalent to an increase in the LRAS

Factors of production	Increase in quantity	Improvement in quality (increase in productivity)
Land (all natural resources)	• Land reclamation • Increased access to supply of resources • Discovery of new resources	• Technological advancements that allow for increased access to resources or the discovery of new resources • Fertilizers • Irrigation
Labour + entrepreneurship	• Increase in birth rate • Immigration • Decrease in the natural rate of unemployment (this aspect of unemployment will be covered later)	• Education • Training • Re-training • Apprenticeship programmes
Capital	• Investment	• Technological advancements that contribute to more efficient capital • Research and development

▲ Table 15.1 Factors affecting the quality or quantity of factors of production

Many of the sources of these supply-side changes come naturally through market forces. For example, students in school are attracted to study engineering, scientific research or entrepreneurship because they have an incentive to earn higher wages. Immigrants are attracted to a country because they are similarly motivated by the incentive to achieve a higher standard of living than they would at home. Businesses are motivated by the desire to earn higher profits and will therefore engage in research and development to improve productivity of their resources.

Exercise 15.3

ATL Thinking and Communication

How might each of the following expenditures by government contribute to an increase in the LRAS curve?

1. An apprentice sheet-metal worker.
2. Construction of the Zakim Bunker Hill Bridge, Boston, Massachusetts.

Raw-material producers are similarly incentivized by the profit motive to develop improved resource extraction technologies.

Key concept
INTERVENTION

Regardless of the extent to which market forces contribute to more and better factors of production, governments also have a very important role to play. The policies that a government uses to increase the quantity or improve the quality of the factors of production are known as supply-side policies and these can be divided into two types of policies: interventionist policies and market-based policies. We will look at these policies when we consider supply-side policies in Chapter 18.

EXAMINATION QUESTIONS

Paper 1, part (a) questions

1. Explain three possible causes of a decrease in the SRAS curve. [10 marks]
2. Explain the difference between the Keynesian AS and the new classical LRAS. [10 marks]
3. Explain the concept of potential economic growth. [10 marks]

16 MACROECONOMIC EQUILIBRIUM

REAL-WORLD ISSUE:
Why does economic activity vary over time and why does this matter? How do governments manage the economy and how effective are their policies?

By the end of this chapter, you should be able to:

- → Identify the short-run equilibrium level of national income/output
- → Illustrate equilibrium output in the short run
- → Explain and illustrate the monetarist/new classical perspective on long-run macroeconomic equilibrium
- → Explain and illustrate the Keynesian perspective on long-run macroeconomic equilibrium
- → Explain and illustrate that the difference between the equilibrium level of national income and the full-employment level of national income will result in an inflationary or deflationary gap
- → Discuss the difference between Keynesian and new classical economists in their view of macroeconomic equilibrium in the long run.

Remember that national income is equivalent to the level of output that a country produces and is a key sign of the economic health of an economy. The actual level of output, and its corresponding price level, is determined by the interaction between aggregate demand and aggregate supply. Our next important concept is that of the equilibrium level of national income (or output). Simply put, the equilibrium level of national income is where aggregate demand is equal to aggregate supply. But, as shown in the previous chapter, economists distinguish between a short-run and a long-run aggregate supply curve; therefore, we have a short-run and a long-run macroeconomic equilibrium.

Although we don't get into a detailed look at unemployment and inflation until Chapters 19 and 20, there are constant references to these two major macroeconomic topics in this chapter. Joblessness and rapidly rising prices can be a significant problem in any economy.

What level of output in the economy represents short-run equilibrium?

The economy is in short-run equilibrium where aggregate demand equals short-run aggregate supply (SRAS). Graphically, it looks very much like the short-run equilibrium for a particular market, but of course the labels on the axes are different, as shown in Figure 16.1.

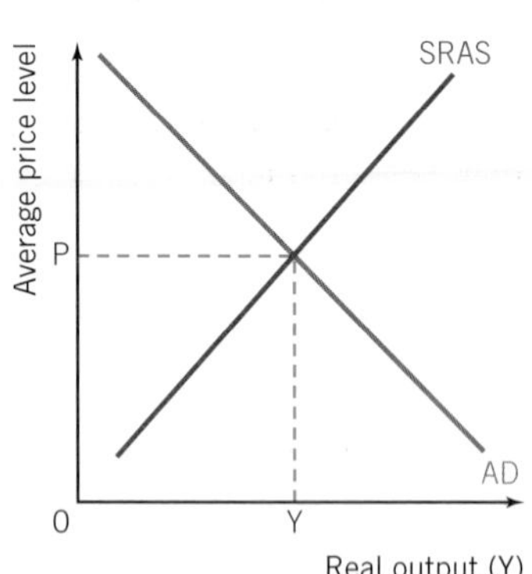

▲ Figure 16.1 Short-run equilibrium output

The economy is in short-run equilibrium where aggregate demand equals short-run aggregate supply, producing an output level of Y at the price level of P. The output produced by the economy is exactly equal to the total demand in the economy and so there is no reason for producers to change their levels of output. Because aggregate demand is equal to aggregate supply, there is no upward or downward pressure on the price level. In other words, there is no inflationary or deflationary pressure. As long as nothing changes to influence AD or AS, the economy rests at this equilibrium.

What level of output in the economy represents long-run equilibrium?

The long-run equilibrium is where aggregate demand is equal to long-run aggregate supply. Given that there is disagreement among economists as to the shape of the long-run aggregate supply curve, we distinguish between the Keynesian equilibrium output in the long run and the new classical equilibrium output.

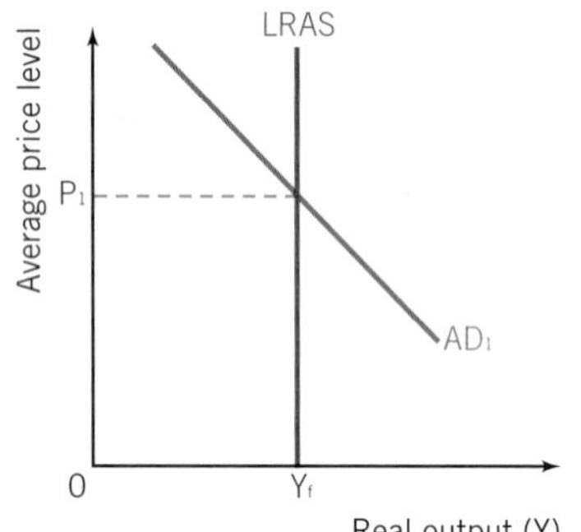

▲ Figure 16.2 The new classical perspective of long-run equilibrium

What is the new classical perspective?

According to new classical economists, the economy will always move towards its long-run equilibrium at the full-employment level of output. Thus, the long-run equilibrium is where the aggregate demand curve meets the vertical long-run aggregate supply curve as shown in Figure 16.2.

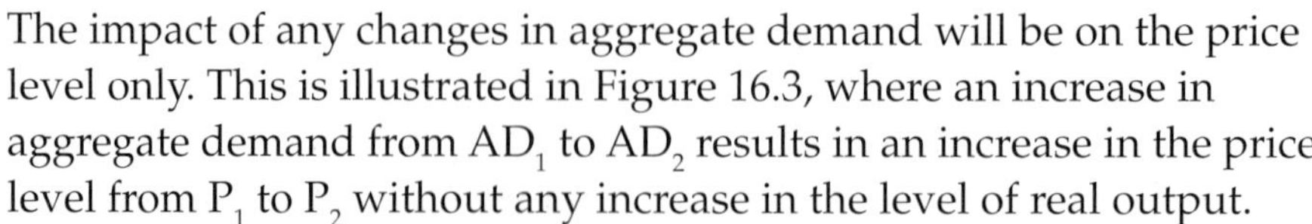
The impact of any changes in aggregate demand will be on the price level only. This is illustrated in Figure 16.3, where an increase in aggregate demand from AD_1 to AD_2 results in an increase in the price level from P_1 to P_2 without any increase in the level of real output.

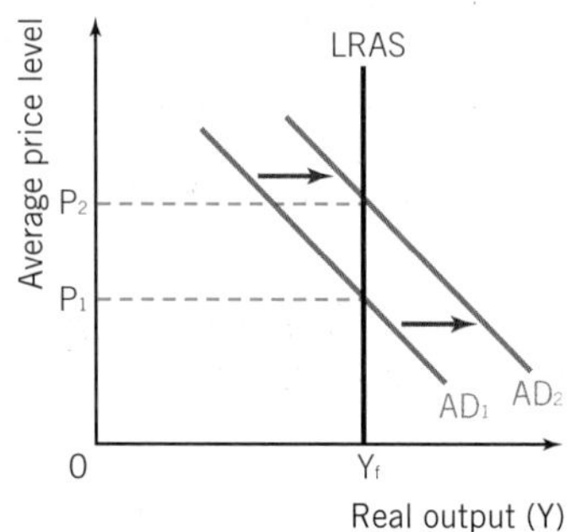

▲ Figure 16.3 The new classical perspective of the impact of an increase in AD in the long run

It is valuable to look at the adjustment from the short run to the long run in order to understand the new classical perspective. Both Keynesian and new classical economists agree on the shape of the short-run aggregate supply curve, but, as stated above, the new classical economists argue that the economy will always move automatically to its long-run equilibrium.

The word "automatically" in the last sentence means "without any government intervention" and illustrates the significance that the new classical economists place on free markets. In their view, there may be a short-run increase in output if there is an increase in aggregate demand, but the economy will always return to its long-run equilibrium.

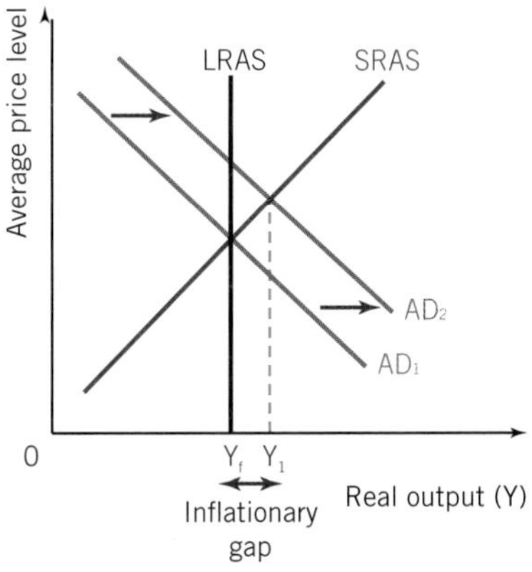

▲ Figure 16.4 An inflationary gap in the new classical model

The new classical perspective showing a combination of the short run and the long run is illustrated in Figure 16.4 and Figure 16.5. Initially, the economy is at its long-run equilibrium at Y_f. If there is an increase in aggregate demand, AD_1 to AD_2, due to changes in any of the components of aggregate demand then, in the short run, there will be an increase in output from Y_f to Y_1. In this case the economy would be experiencing what is known as an *inflationary gap*, where the economy is in equilibrium at a level of output that is greater than the full employment level of output. This is illustrated in Figure 16.4.

However, according to the new classical economists, this is only possible in the short run. It is possible for output to increase along the short-run aggregate supply curve by paying existing workers overtime wages as a short-term solution. But as the economy is originally at the full-employment level of output, there are no unemployed resources. In their effort to increase their output, the firms in the economy are competing for increasingly scarce labour and capital and, as the diagram shows, the increase in aggregate demand results in an increase in the price level from P_1 to P_2 as shown in Figure 16.5. The increase in the average price level means that, on average, all prices in the economy have risen as the firms bid up the prices of the factors of production in order to increase their output. The rise in the price level means an increase in costs to firms as the prices of the factors of production (eg the prices of labour, raw materials and capital) have risen. At this point, you must remember what happens to short-run aggregate supply when the costs of production rise. The result is a shift in the short-run aggregate supply from $SRAS_1$ to $SRAS_2$. Although firms were willing to supply a higher level of output due to the higher prices they were receiving in the short run, their higher costs of production result in no real gain, so they reduce output back to Y_f. The final result is that output returns to its full employment level, but at a higher price level of P_3.

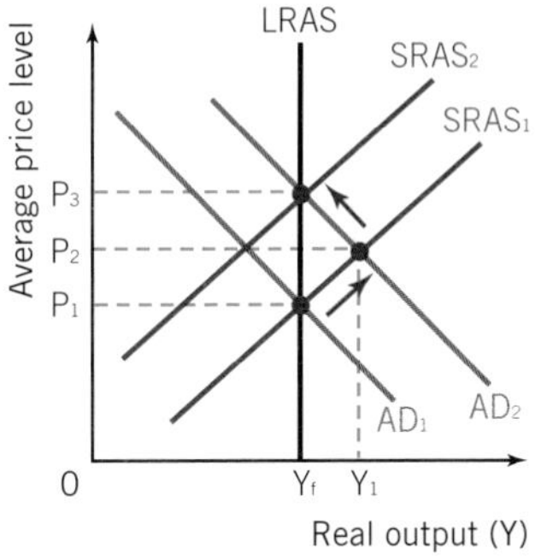

▲ Figure 16.5 The new classical perspective of the impact of an increase in AD in the short run and in the long run

We can use similar analysis to see what happens if aggregate demand falls. This is illustrated in Figure 16.7. Originally, the economy is at its long-run equilibrium where AD_1 intersects with $SRAS_1$, at output Y_f and price level P_1. A fall in aggregate demand from AD_1 to AD_2, due to changes in any of the components of aggregate demand, results in a fall in the level of national output from Y_f to Y_1 and a decrease in the price level. In this case, the economy would be experiencing what is known as a *deflationary (or recessionary) gap*, where the economy is in equilibrium at a level of output that is less than the full-employment level of output.

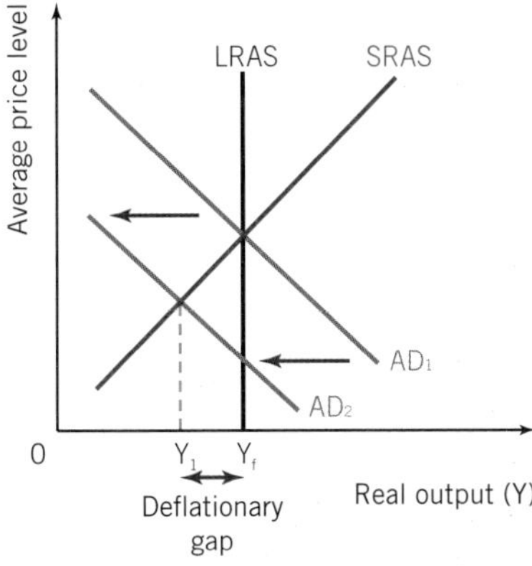

▲ Figure 16.6 An deflationary gap in the new classical model

In the short run, the economy will produce at less than full employment output; however, this deflationary gap will not persist. The fall in the

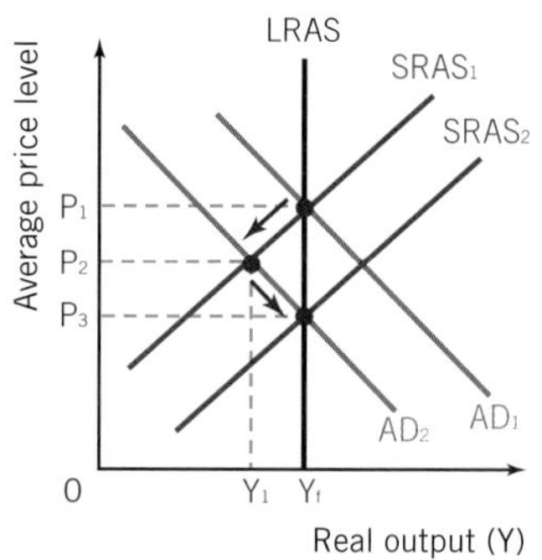

▲ Figure 16.7 The new classical perspective of the impact of a decrease in AD in the short run and in the long run

price level means that the prices of the economy's factors of production have fallen. This is shown in Figure 16.7. This means that firms' costs of production fall and this results in a shift in the short-run aggregate supply from $SRAS_1$ to $SRAS_2$. As the diagram shows, the economy returns to its long-run equilibrium at the full-employment level of output, at a lower price level.

The diagrams and explanations illustrate the new classical perspective of the long-run equilibrium in the economy. What is important is the conclusion that the long-run equilibrium level of output is equal to the full-employment level of income and that the economy will move towards this equilibrium without any government intervention as a result of free market forces. According to this model, an increase in aggregate demand will be purely inflationary in the long run and thus there is no role for the government to play in trying to deliberately steer the economy towards full employment. Although there may be deviations from full employment in the short run, new classical economists would not see a role for the government in filling these gaps. They would recommend leaving the economy to market forces, rather than using government policies to manage the level of aggregate demand.

What is the Keynesian perspective?

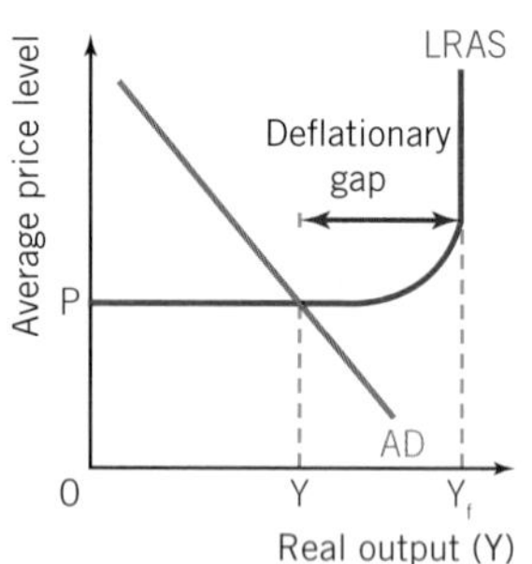

▲ Figure 16.8 The Keynesian perspective of long-run equilibrium output below the full employment level of output

In both new classical and Keynesian analysis, the equilibrium level of output is where aggregate demand is equal to long-run aggregate supply. According to the Keynesian economists, however, this equilibrium level of output may occur at different levels. Significantly, they believe that the economy may be in long-run equilibrium at a level of output below the full employment level of national income (Y_f). This will be the case if the economy is operating at a level where there is spare capacity. In this view, the equilibrium level of output depends mainly on the level of aggregate demand in the economy. Figure 16.8 illustrates this important view of the Keynesian perspective.

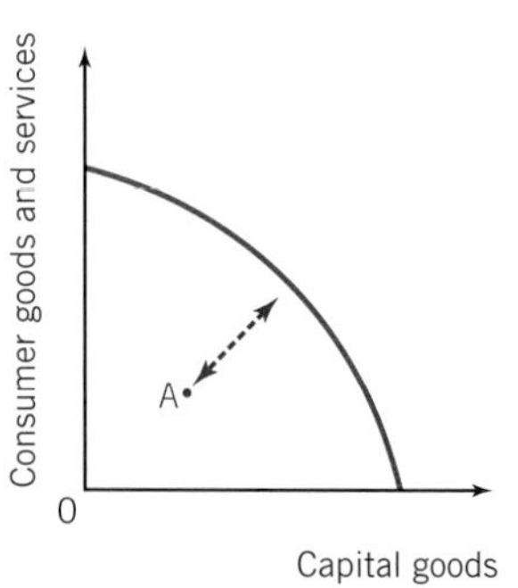

▲ Figure 16.9 Output gap illustrating the difference between an economy's actual output and its potential output

If aggregate demand is at the level shown in Figure 16.8, then equilibrium will occur at a real output level of Y, with a price level of P. As noted in the previous chapter, aggregate supply can be perfectly elastic because of the existence of spare capacity, with high levels of unused factors of production such as unemployed workers and/or underutilized capital. It is important to observe that in this case, the equilibrium level of output is below the full-employment level of output. We say that there is a deflationary gap whereby the level of aggregate demand in the economy is not sufficient to buy up the potential output that could be produced by the economy at the full-employment level of output. This may also be referred to as an *output gap* and, though not easily measurable, could be shown as the distance from a point inside a country's hypothetical production possibilities curve to a point on the curve, as shown in Figure 16.9.

In the Keynesian view, aggregate demand can increase such that there is an increase in the level of real output, without any consequent increase in the price level. This is shown in Figure 16.10.

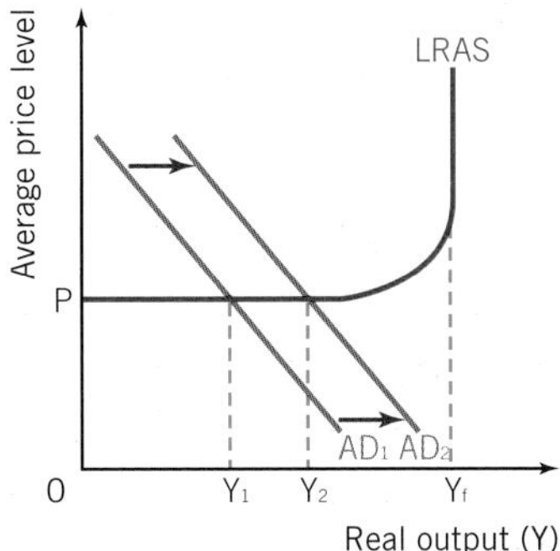

▲ **Figure 16.10** The Keynesian perspective of the impact of an increase in AD when the economy is operating below full employment

If there is an increase in aggregate demand from AD_1 to AD_2, then there will be an increase in real output from Y_1 to Y_2, but no change in the price level. This is due to the existence of spare capacity in the economy. Producers can employ the unused factors of production to increase output with no increase in costs. Thus, there is no inflationary pressure.

If aggregate demand increases further, to AD_3 as in Figure 16.11, then the economy starts to experience inflationary pressure as available factors of production become scarcer and their prices are bid up. The price level rises from P_1 to P_2 to compensate producers for their higher costs.

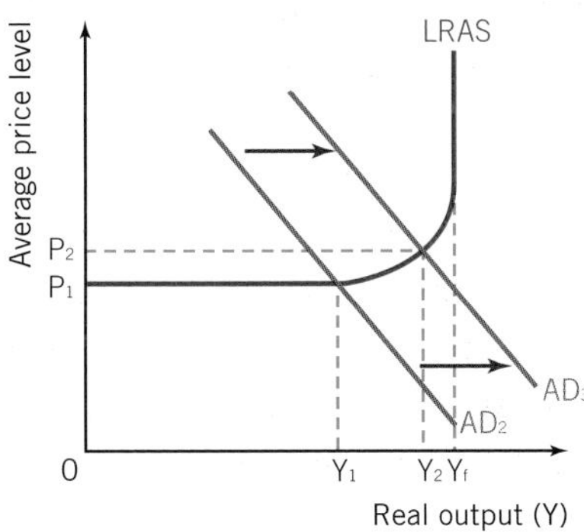

▲ **Figure 16.11** The Keynesian perspective of the impact of an increase in AD when the economy is close to full employment

If the economy is operating at full employment and there is an increase in aggregate demand, then the outcome will be "purely inflationary". That is, there is no increase in output and the only change is an increase in the price level. This is because it is impossible for the economy to produce any further increase in output in the long run, given the existing factors of production. This is illustrated in Figure 16.12.

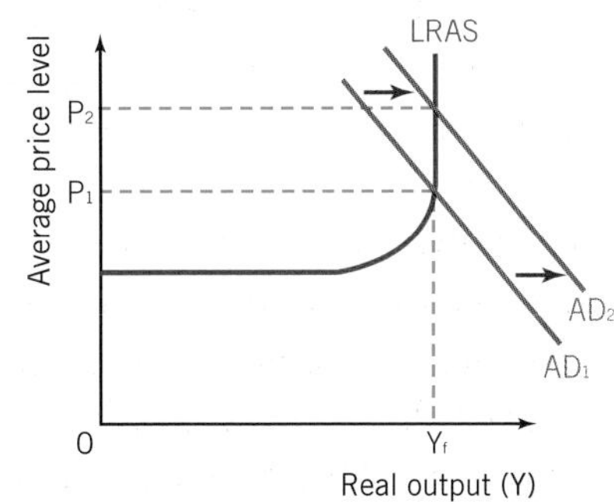

▲ **Figure 16.12** The Keynesian perspective of the impact of an increase in AD when the economy is at full employment

An increase in aggregate demand from AD_1 to AD_2 results in no change in output as the economy cannot produce output beyond the full-employment level of output. The only impact is an increase in the price level from P_1 to P_2 to allocate the scarce resources among the competing components of aggregate demand, ie consumers, producers, the government and the foreign sector.

Exercise 16.1

ATL Thinking and Communication

Using the Keynesian model:

1. Draw and fully label an AD/AS diagram with AD at a level that creates a deflationary/recessionary gap.
2. Identify the three different phases of the Keynesian AS curve on the diagram.
3. Add two AD curves to each phase of the AS curve (ie six AD curves in all).
4. Explain what will happen if there is a shift to the right in AD in each of the phases, using the AD curves that you have drawn.

Exercise 16.2

ATL Thinking and Communication

Using the new classical model:

1. Draw and label fully an AD/AS diagram with the economy in short-run equilibrium at the full-employment level of income.
2. Add and label a new AD curve to the right of the one that you have drawn.
3. Explain what will happen in the short run and the long run.

EXAMINATION QUESTIONS

Paper 1, Part (a) questions

1. Explain the difference between the equilibrium level of output and the full-employment level of output. [10 marks]
2. Explain the effects of an increase in long-run aggregate supply on national income and the price level. [10 marks]
3. Explain, from a new classical perspective, how an increase in aggregate demand will affect an economy in the short run and the long run. [10 marks]

17 Demand management (demand-side policies)

By the end of this chapter, you should be able to:

- → Define fiscal policy
- → Explain the nature of a government budget
- → Explain the goals of fiscal policy
- → Explain how expansionary and contractionary fiscal policies work
- → Discuss the effectiveness of fiscal policy
- → Discuss the potential costs of a high level of government debt
- HL Explain and calculate the Keynesian multiplier
- → Define monetary policy
- → Explain the goals of monetary policy
- → Explain how expansionary and contractionary monetary policies work
- → Discuss the effectiveness of monetary policy
- HL Explain the process of money creation by commercial banks
- HL Explain the tools of monetary policy
- HL Explain the determination of the equilibrium nominal interest rate
- → Explain and calculate the difference between the nominal interest rate and the real interest rate.

Governments have two broad categories of policies available to affect the level of aggregate demand in the economy. These are known as *fiscal policy* and *monetary policy*.

What is fiscal policy?

The word fiscal is defined as "pertaining to government revenue and expenditure".

When we refer to government or public spending, we are speaking about the total spending by all levels of government in a country, including the central (for example, federal or national) government, regional (for example, state or provincial) governments and local (municipal) governments.

Broadly speaking, there are three categories of public spending. Capital expenditures include any spending that adds to the capital stock of the economy, such as the spending on the upgrading of a national highway or the building of schools and hospitals. Current expenditure tends to be on-going spending such as the purchases of textbooks in schools or the payment of wages to public sector employees. The last category is transfer payments, which include any benefits paid to people in the economy for which no goods and services are produced in return. These include payments such as unemployment benefits, child support payments, disability payments and pensions.

Governments receive their income from different sources. These include the payment of income taxes and social security payments by households, social security payments and corporate taxes by firms, indirect taxes paid on expenditure on goods and services and tariffs paid on the purchase of imported products. Other than income from taxes, governments also earn money from the profits of government-owned (nationalized) businesses or if they sell nationalized industries. Income is also earned when governments rent out government-owned buildings or land.

Fiscal policy is defined as the set of a government's policies relating to its expenditure and taxation rates. Governments use *expansionary fiscal policy* to increase aggregate demand and *contractionary or deflationary, fiscal policy* to reduce aggregate demand.

The government budget

Each year governments issue their national budgets, where they lay out their expected spending and revenues for the coming year. This is known as the "fiscal stance". If they expect to earn more than they spend it is called a *budget surplus*. If they plan to spend more than they earn it is a *budget deficit* and if expected revenues are equal to expenditures then it is a *balanced budget*.

To finance a budget deficit (or to "run a budget deficit") the government will have to borrow money, either from the households and firms within the country or by borrowing from abroad. The government does this by selling government bonds. People buy the bonds as a form of saving; they lend money to the government and are eventually paid back, along with extra payment which is the interest paid by the government. When a government runs a deficit in one year this is added to the total debt accumulated by the government. Therefore, in any given budget, the government has to allocate some money to paying back the loans and the interest on the loans taken in the past. If a government has a budget surplus in a given year this can be used to pay back the government debt.

What are the aims of fiscal policy?

Fiscal policy may be employed by governments to help to achieve a number of economic goals:

- the maintenance of a low and stable rate of inflation
- a low unemployment rate
- a stable economic environment for long-term growth
- to reduce fluctuations in the business cycle (which we came across in Chapter 13)
- to promote an equitable distribution of income
- to achieve an external balance between export revenue and import expenditure.

What is expansionary fiscal policy?

Expansionary fiscal policy is a form of Keynesian demand management. As we already know, Keynesian economists believe that government intervention through demand management is necessary in order to control the economy, especially unemployment. They employ a range of fiscal measures to achieve their aims.

- If a government would like to encourage greater consumption, then it can lower income taxes to increase disposable income. This is likely to increase AD.
- If a government would like to encourage greater investment, then it can lower corporate taxes so that firms enjoy higher after-tax profits that can be used for investment. This is likely to increase AD.
- Governments have major investment projects themselves and may increase their spending in order to improve or increase public services. This directly impacts upon AD by shifting it to the right.

The effects of an expansionary fiscal policy can be seen in Figure 17.1. If the government follows a successful expansionary fiscal policy, then there will be a shift of aggregate demand from AD_1 to AD_2. This will have a number of economic outcomes. There will be inflationary pressure as the average price level rises from P_1 to P_2. However, there will be an increase in real output, from Y_1 to Y_2, which will mean an increase in national income, an increase in economic growth, and very probably, a decrease in unemployment.

The expansionary fiscal policy involves a 'trade-off' between lower unemployment and higher inflation. This is a topic that we shall come back to when we look at inflation and unemployment in detail.

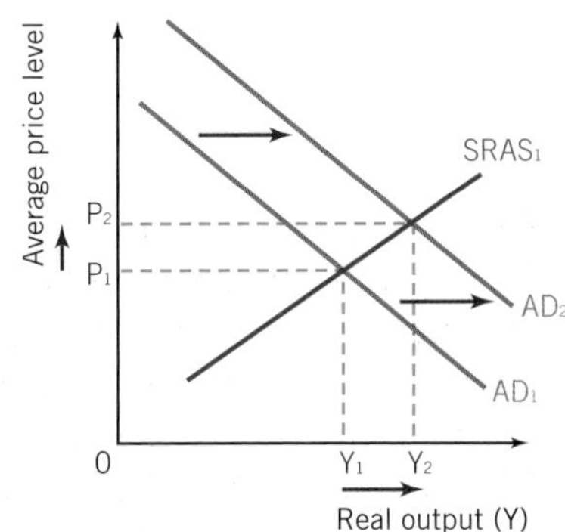

▲ Figure 17.1 An expansionary fiscal policy

Exercise 17.1

ATL Thinking and Communication

1. Explain the elements that would be involved in a contractionary fiscal policy.
2. Use a fully labelled diagram to illustrate the effects of a contractionary fiscal policy.
3. Explain the 'trade-off' that exists in the diagram.

Theory of knowledge

Paradigm shift

In Theory of Knowledge, you might come across the concept of a "paradigm shift". In 1962, Thomas Kuhn introduced this concept in the natural sciences to explain that advances in science do not come about in a gradual, evolutionary manner, but occur in a revolutionary way as scientists actually change the complete way that they look at the world. According to Kuhn, all scientists work within a given paradigm. This is essentially a framework that explains and justifies the theories of their discipline. There are different paradigms in different fields; for example, the theoretical paradigm on which all chemists base their work is that matter is composed of atoms made up of negatively-charged electrons surrounding a positively-charged nucleus. Within a given discipline, the vast majority of theorists accept the paradigm. It forms the basis of all their thinking and it accurately explains and justifies all the knowledge within that discipline.

According to the theories of Kuhn, paradigms are strikingly resistant to change. If anomalies occur that cannot be explained within the paradigm they tend to be disregarded. However, it is possible for paradigms to shift. If a significant number of anomalies arise, it may come to the point where the existing framework of theories can no longer reliably account for the discrepancies. There may be some times when the scientists cling to their old framework, believing that the discrepancies are the exception rather than the rule, but, ultimately, the old paradigm is discarded as it cannot account for mounting evidence against it. Thus, a scientific revolution occurs.

The clearest example of this in the natural sciences is the scientific revolution that occurred when the dominant worldview that the Sun, planets, and the Moon revolved around the Earth, as established by Ptolemy in the first century BCE, was eventually replaced. For about 2000 years this paradigm was widely accepted in spite of the number of anomalies that occurred. In the 1530s, Copernicus presented a radical challenge to the Ptolemaic paradigm in presenting the heliocentric system whereby the Earth revolves around the Sun. For at least a century this view was so unacceptable to astronomers and the church that one of the followers of his ideas was actually burned at the stake in 1600. It was considered to be heretical to challenge the view that Earth was at its God-given position at the centre of the universe. Ultimately, the work of many scientists, including Isaac Newton, was instrumental in establishing the heliocentric system as the new paradigm for astronomers. This is known as a paradigm shift. Kuhn's work illustrates a common feature of humankind. All disciplines have certain ways of looking at things that tend to be fairly entrenched. When new ideas come along that challenge the paradigms that guide theorists in a given field, it is very difficult to accept them. In colloquial terms, we could say that it is "hard to think outside the box."

We can apply this principle to economic theories. Before the time of John Maynard Keynes, the main economic theories were based on the work of the classical economists, whose paradigm rested on a belief in the power of the free market to achieve the most efficient allocation of resources and

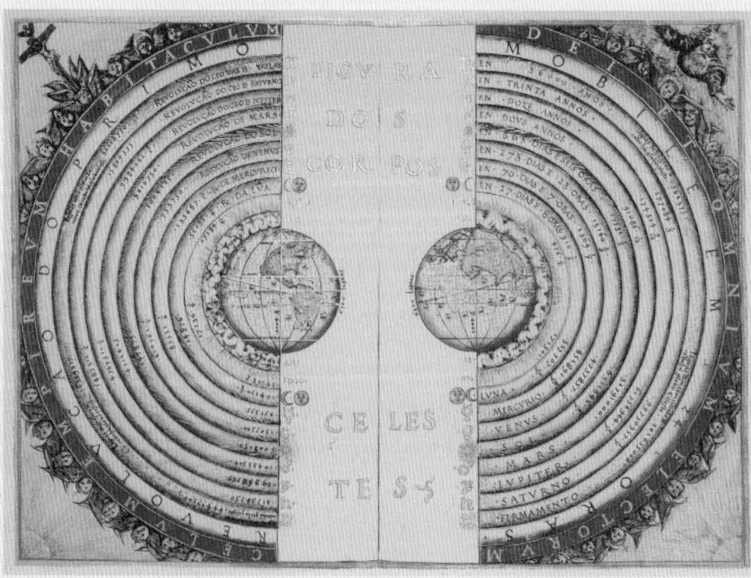

a conviction that there should be minimal government intervention in the economy. This was essentially the paradigm among most economists and their views were widely accepted among Western governments. The massive unemployment of the 1930s presented an anomaly; according to the theories of the paradigm, such unemployment should not persist. Thus, governments were not encouraged to intervene to help solve the problem. Keynes' proposition that it was actually the government's responsibility to intervene to pump aggregate demand into a sluggish economy took a very long time to be accepted, as it was such a challenge to the guiding paradigm. Ultimately it was accepted, as government after government realized that demand management could be used to fine-tune the economy. For approximately 30 years, Keynesian demand theory became the new paradigm that guided economic policy.

It should be noted, however, that a paradigm in the social sciences will be less rigid than a paradigm in the natural sciences and may not satisfy all theorists within the field. For example, while Keynesian economics dominated much public policy, there was always some opposition to the theories derived from the tenets of the paradigm. There were still classical economists opposing Keynesian economic policies and, by the 1970s, economic circumstances had changed so considerably that Keynesian policies were no longer widely acceptable.

Then, in 2008, there was a revival of Keynesian theory as his ideas made their way back into policy, although again there were opponents. Whether those opponents were "right" to challenge the demand-side intervention of economic policy makers is a question that cannot be answered with a simple yes or no. This gives rise to a number of knowledge issues.

How effective are fiscal policies?

We will see later how effective fiscal policies are in achieving specific macroeconomic objectives, such as low unemployment and a low and stable rate of inflation. However, we should now consider their effectiveness in general terms.

The great strength of fiscal policy is that it is effective, in the long run, at dealing with a deep recession. This can be seen historically in the Great Depression of the 1930s, where the countries that adopted expansionary fiscal policy through government expenditure came through the depression relatively faster than those that did not. It is interesting that in the aftermath of the world recession that began in 2008, many countries went back to Keynesian demand management policies and attempted to combat the deflation with expansionary fiscal policy based upon increased government expenditure.

Another strength is that government expenditure can be used to target specific sectors of the economy. As well as increasing AD through government expenditure and tax cuts, the government can invest the funds in areas of the economy that they believe will benefit the most from the investment and also give tax cuts to the people that they think need them the most. An example of this sort of targeting is the American Recovery and Reinvestment Act (2009) which is detailed below.

The American Recovery and Reinvestment Act (2009)

The American Recovery and Reinvestment Act (ARRA) of 2009 was a fiscal stimulus signed by President Obama on 17 February 2009. It ended the Great Recession in July 2009. Congress passed the bill based on President Obama's plan to put $787 billion into the pockets of American families and small businesses, with the aim of boosting demand and instilling confidence.

Key concept
EQUITY

Key concept
SUSTAINABILITY

Key concept
ECONOMIC WELLBEING

Key concept
EFFICIENCY

In 2012, the Congressional Budget Office (CBO) reported that Congress added to ARRA spending in subsequent budgets. It raised the total cost to $831 billion. Most of the impact occurred by 2011.

ARRA had seven components. Here are the details of each:

1. *Immediate relief for families*: through tax cuts, tax credits and unemployment benefits. ARRA stimulated demand by sending $260 billion to families. They received the funds through tax cuts, tax credits and unemployment benefits. Most of the funds were delivered in the first two years.
2. *Modernize federal infrastructure*: ARRA created jobs by funding shovel-ready public works projects. A total of $46 billion was given for transportation and mass transit projects; $31 billion to modernize federal buildings; and $6 billion in water projects.
3. *Increase alternative energy production*: This funding jump-started the alternative energy industry in America. It demonstrated that the federal government supported clean energy.
4. *Expand health care*: This component subsidized the greater health care costs that recessions create. A total of $138 billion dollars was spent on health care.
5. *Improve education*: ARRA spent $117 billion on education. Education spending is the second-best way to create jobs. According to a University of Massachusetts study, one billion dollars in federal spending creates 17,687 jobs.
6. *Invest in science research and technology*: $10 billion to modernize science facilities and fund research jobs that investigate disease cures. A total of $4 billion to increase broadband infrastructure in rural and inner-city areas. That made their businesses more competitive. $4 billion for physics and science research.
7. *Help small businesses*: Small businesses drive 70 percent of all new jobs. ARRA allocated $54 billion to help small businesses with tax deductions, credits and loan guarantees.

Source: Adapted from: *ARRA, its details with pros and cons* by Kimberly Amadeo, 9 November 2018, www.thebalance.com

There are, however, several constraints on fiscal policy, including:

1. *Time lags*: Changing fiscal policy takes time. Tax rates cannot be changed quickly. In most countries, changes to the tax structure will need to go through the democratic processes governing the country and it will take time to gain approval. This will slow down the implementation of fiscal policy.

   Also, once the fiscal changes have been made, even when successful, it is likely that it will take time before the aggregate demand begins to shift. People will have to recognize and react to the fiscal changes. It is possible that the economy may have already recovered for other reasons, by the time the fiscal policy effects take place, and so they become inflationary.

2. *Political pressure*: Government spending and taxation are often influenced by political factors, rather than economic factors. For example, deflationary fiscal policies may be needed, but they may be blocked by political parties who do not want to raise taxes for fear of losing votes.

3. *Sustainable debt*: Governments may have to run budget deficits in order to fund expansionary fiscal policies and, over time, this may accumulate into unsustainable national debt in the long run. Because of this, governments may not fund necessary public spending.
4. *The effect on net exports*: expansionary fiscal policy, especially increased government borrowing and spending, may lead to an increase in interest rates. This may lead to an increase in the exchange rate, making exports less attractive and imports more attractive. (The link between interest rates and exchange rates will be dealt with in Chapter 26.) This in turn may lead to a fall in (X-M), which will work against the desired outcome of expansion.
5. *Crowding-out effect*: If governments attempt to increase spending through increased borrowing, they then monopolize the funds available in the economy for borrowing. This means that firms may not have access to funds for investment and so investment will fall. AD will not shift as much, since the increase in government spending (G) will be partially, or completely, offset by a fall in investment (I). (Crowding out is an HL topic and will be looked at in more detail in Chapter 19).

   The increased demand for borrowing by the government will also increase the interest rate and thus will have contractionary monetary effects.
6. *Inability to achieve specific targets*: It is very difficult, if not impossible, to finely adjust fiscal policy to achieve specific targets. The government expenditure and tax changes are large and affect many different areas of the economy. It is possible to get the economy moving in the desired direction, expanding or contracting, but it is difficult to predict the precise outcome.

Why is a sustainable level of government (national) debt a macroeconomic objective?

What is government (national) debt?

We have already seen in Chapter 13 that one of the macroeconomic objectives of governments is a sustainable level of debt. This debt is known as government, or national, debt. In the USA, it is also known as federal debt. It is the accumulation of all the *budget deficits* over the years and represents the total amount of money that the government owes to its creditors, both domestic and foreign. (We looked at the concept of a government budget earlier in this chapter.)

Once the total government debt has been calculated, then it is normally expressed as a percentage of GDP. Quite simply, it shows the percentage of annual national output that the government owes, both domestically and abroad.

Country	Government debt as a % of GDP (December 2017)	Budget surplus(+) or deficit (–) as % of GDP for 2017
Japan	253.0	–4.5
Greece	178.6	+0.8
Italy	132.1	–2.1
Singapore	110.6	+0.4
France	97.0	–2.6
Canada (25)	89.6	–0.9
UK (29)	84.7	–2.0
USA (36)	105.4	–3.5
India (47)	68.7	–3.5
China (111)	47.6	–3.5
Source: Trading economics, April 2019, tradingeconomics.com		

▲ Table 17.1 Government debt and budget figures for selected countries, 2017 estimates

Economics in action

ATL Thinking, Communication and Research

Look at the latest budget and debt figures for your chosen OECD country over the last five years. Identify the trend in the level of government debt.

Table 17.1 shows the estimated government debt and budget statistics for a selection of ten countries. In all cases, with the exception of Greece and Singapore, the governments are running budget deficits and so are adding to their government debt.

What are the costs of having high levels of government debt?

In the short-term, many stakeholders in the economy will benefit from *deficit spending* by the government as it drives economic growth. However, as the government debt gets greater, year upon year, there will be long-term costs that have to be borne.

There will be an increase in *debt servicing* costs. Debt servicing is the amount of money needed to make payments on the principal and interest on a loan in a given time period. As the government debt increases, debt servicing costs increase and the government will spend more of its budget on interest costs. This may have a number of bad effects:

a) It may lead to *crowding out* of private investments. As mentioned earlier, if governments attempt to increase spending through increased borrowing, they then monopolize the funds available in the economy for borrowing. This means that firms may not have access to funds for investment and so investment will fall.

b) As interest payments increase as a percentage of government budget expenditure, this may have a damaging effect on other areas of spending. Benefits and services provided by the government may need to be cut.

c) If the government wishes to maintain the same levels of benefits and services, then this may require higher rates of taxation to fund the expenditure. However, this may in turn lead to falling output and incomes, since it is a deflationary fiscal policy.

d) It may decrease the ability of the government to respond to emergencies. Governments often have to borrow money to deal

with emergency situations, such as natural disasters, financial crises and even military actions. If the government debt is too big, the government will have fewer fiscal options available. For example, following the financial crisis of 2008, the US government had a total debt to GDP ratio of around 68%. This meant that the government was able to respond to the crisis by reducing taxes and increasing spending. Whether this would be possible, with much higher debt to GDP ratios is a matter of debate.

What is the multiplier effect?

Higher Level

If a government decides to fill a deflationary gap by increasing its own spending, the final increase in aggregate demand will actually be greater than the amount of spending. In fact, any increase in aggregate demand will result in a proportionately larger increase in national income. This is explained by the *multiplier effect*. In order to understand this concept, it is necessary to remember the concepts of injections and withdrawals introduced in Chapters 1 and 13.

Government spending and business investment are injections into the circular flow of income and any injections are multiplied through the economy as people receive a share of the income and then spend a part of what they receive.

For example, a government spends $100 million on a school building project. This $100 million goes to a vast number of people for the factors of production that they provide. The money goes as income for the labour provided by people such as architects, engineers, builders, electricians, plumbers and designers. The providers of the capital and raw materials such as concrete, steel, minerals, water and electricity also receive a share of this spending. So, $100 million ends up as income in the pockets of people who provide the factors of production for the building project.

What do the people do with this income? Some of it goes back to the government as taxes, some of it is saved, some of it is spent on foreign goods and services and the rest is spent on domestically produced goods and services. You should recognize the first three options as withdrawals from the circular flow of income. The money that is spent goes as income to a new set of recipients, who then behave in the same way – they pay some in taxes, some is saved, some is spent on imports and the rest is spent on domestic goods and services. During each "round", some income is withdrawn from the circular flow and some stays to be re-spent.

Consider this simplified numerical example. The government spends $100 million in an economy. In the economy, the average behaviour is observed as follows: 20% of all additional income goes to taxes, 10% is saved, and 10% is used to buy imports of goods and services. This means that the remaining income, which represents 60% of all additional income, is spent on domestic goods and services. This is known as the

Higher Level

Exercise 17.2
ATL Thinking and Communication

Here is an example of two questions and answers:

Question (a): Calculate the multiplier for an economy where the marginal propensity to consume is 0.75.

Answer: The multiplier = $\frac{1}{(1-0.75)} = \frac{1}{0.25} = 4.$

Question (b): By how much will national income increase in total if there is an investment of $50,000?

Answer: An investment of $50,000 will result in a final increase in national income of 4 x $50,000 = $200,000.

Showing your workings, answer the following questions:

1. An economy has a marginal propensity to consume of 0.8. Calculate:
   a) its marginal propensity to withdraw
   b) its multiplier
   c) the amount of injections that would be needed if national income is to rise by $10 million.
2. In a country, the marginal propensity to save is 0.1, the marginal rate of taxation is 0.3, and the marginal propensity to import is 0.1. How will the value of the multiplier change if the government lowers taxes, such that the marginal rate of taxation drops to 0.2?

marginal propensity to consume (MPC) and is expressed as a decimal. In this particular economy the MPC is 0.6.

When the government spends its $100 million, it goes to people such as architects, plumbers, engineers, electricians, providers of raw materials etc. They pay $20 million in taxes, $10 million leaks from the circular flow as savings and $10 million is spent on imports. The rest, $60 million, is spent. They spend it on a wide range of things such as food, clothing, entertainment, books and car repairs, and the recipients of this $60 million behave in the same way, with 40% leaving the circular flow and 60% remaining to be re-spent as other people's income.

Table 17.2 illustrates the rounds of spending and re-spending.

Initial spending by government in $millions	100.00
2nd round of spending = 60% of 100	60.00
3rd round of spending = 60% of 60	36.00
4th round of spending = 60% of 36	21.60
5th round of spending	12.96
6th round of spending	7.78
7th round of spending	4.67
8th round of spending	2.80
9th round of spending	1.68
10th round of spending	1.01
11th round of spending	0.60
12th round of spending	0.36
13th round of spending	0.22
14th round of spending	0.13
15th round of spending	0.08
16th round of spending	0.05
17th round of spending	0.03
18th round of spending	0.02
19th round of spending	0.01
20th round of spending	0.01
Total spending, including initial spending by government	$249.99m

▲ **Table 17.2** The multiplier effect

The final addition to national income, when all the money has been spent and re-spent, amounts to $250 million, ie 2.5 times the original government spending of $100 million. In this example, the multiplier is equivalent to the value 2.5. Any injection into the circular flow of this economy would contribute 2.5 times its amount to national income.

Rather than complete a rather complicated table to find the value of the multiplier, there are formulas that can be used. The value of the multiplier can be calculated by using either the marginal propensity to consume (mpc) or the value of the marginal propensity to withdraw (mpw). The mpw is the value of the marginal propensity to save (mps) plus the marginal rate of taxation (mrt) plus the marginal propensity to import (mpm).

Formulas:

$$\text{The multiplier} = \frac{1}{1 - \text{mpc}} \textbf{ OR } \frac{1}{\text{mps} + \text{mpm} + \text{mrt}} = \frac{1}{\text{mpw}}$$

From the example above, where the mpc = 0.6, the multiplier is:

$$\frac{1}{1 - 0.6} = \frac{1}{0.4} = 2.5$$

or

the mps = 0.1, mrt = 0.2, and the mpm = 0.1, the multiplier is:

$$\frac{1}{0.1 + 0.2 + 0.1} = \frac{1}{0.4} = 2.5$$

Any change in any of the withdrawals from the circular flow will result in a change in the economy's multiplier. If the taxation rate increases, for example, then the value of the multiplier will fall. If the marginal propensity to import falls, then there will be an increase in the multiplier.

If a government is planning to intervene to try to fill a deflationary gap, it must have some idea of two things. First, it must try to estimate the gap between equilibrium output and full employment output. Second, it must have some estimate of the value of the multiplier so as to be able to judge the suitable increase in aggregate demand that is necessary to inject into the economy in order to fill the gap. The difficulties in estimating both of these values illustrate one of the limitations of government fiscal policy aimed at managing aggregate demand in the economy.

What is monetary policy?

Monetary policy is defined as the set of official policies governing the supply of money and the level of interest rates in an economy. Governments use *expansionary monetary policy* to increase aggregate demand and *contractionary, or deflationary, monetary policy* to reduce aggregate demand.

In any economy, there is a vast array of different interest rates. Advertisements offering low mortgage rates or "competitive financing" are examples of the interest rates offered by private profit-making businesses, such as commercial banks. Although banks are regulated by the government, they are mainly free to set these rates themselves.

When we talk about interest rates as a tool of monetary policy we are talking about the *base rate* (*discount rate or prime rate*) that is set by a country's *central bank*. The central bank is not a private profit-making bank but is essentially the government's bank and the ultimate authority in control of the money supply in an economy. In some countries the government controls the central bank, but in most industrialized countries these days the central bank is an independent body with the primary responsibility of maintaining a low and stable rate of inflation in the economy. Changes in the central bank's base rate ultimately impact upon all borrowing and lending in the economy and are an important signal of a country's monetary policy. Even though the central bank may be largely independent we usually consider its activities as part of government monetary policy.

What are the aims of monetary policy?

Monetary policy may be employed by governments to help to achieve a number of economic goals:

- the maintenance of a low and stable rate of inflation, usually tied in with "*inflation targeting*", where the central bank sets a specific medium-term target inflation rate as a goal, for example 2%
- a low unemployment rate
- a stable economic environment for long-term growth
- to reduce fluctuations in the business cycle (which we came across in Chapter 13)
- to achieve an external balance between export revenue and import expenditure.

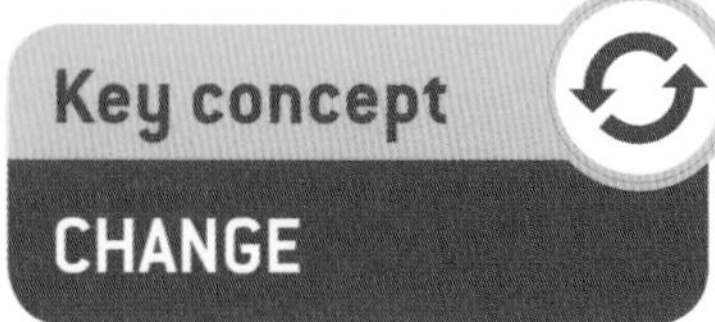

What is expansionary monetary policy?

Changes in the central bank's base rate can affect the level of AD in the economy. To increase aggregate demand the central bank might lower the base rate of interest. This ultimately reduces the cost of borrowing and can lead to increases in both consumption and investment. They could also increase the supply of money, which would lower its price, ie lower the rate of interest, since the interest rate is the price of money. This would also then increase consumption and investment. This would be known as *expansionary* or *"loose" monetary policy*.

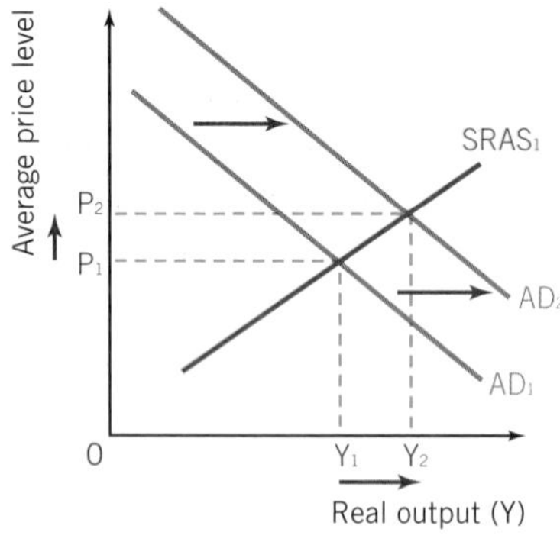

▲ **Figure 17.2** An expansionary monetary policy

The effects of an expansionary monetary policy can be seen in Figure 17.2. If the government follows a successful expansionary monetary policy, then there will be a shift of aggregate demand from AD_1 to AD_2. This will have a number of economic outcomes. There will be inflationary pressure as the average price level rises from P_1 to P_2. However, there will be an increase in real output, from Y_1 to Y_2, which will mean an increase in national income, an increase in economic growth, and very probably, a decrease in unemployment.

The expansionary monetary policy, as with expansionary fiscal policy, involves a "trade-off" between lower unemployment and higher inflation. This is a topic that we shall come back to when we look at inflation and unemployment in detail.

Exercise 17.3

ATL Thinking and Communication

1. Explain the elements that would be involved in a contractionary, "tight", monetary policy.
2. Use a fully labelled diagram to illustrate the effects of a contractionary/tight monetary policy.
3. Explain the "trade-off" that exists in the diagram.

How effective are monetary policies?

We will see later how effective monetary policies are in achieving specific macroeconomic objectives, such as low unemployment and a low and stable rate of inflation. However, we should now consider their effectiveness in general terms.

Monetary policy has a number of strengths:

1. *It is relatively quick to put into place*. In most countries, the interest rate is set by the central bank and can be altered quickly, when it is felt to be necessary.

2. *There is no political intervention*: Because the interest rate is normally adjusted by the central bank, there do not have to be political processes that are gone through before the rate can be changed. This is the opposite of fiscal policy.

   Also, because the central bank is usually independent, and not under the control of the government in power, it can implement policies, such as increased interest rates, that may be politically unpopular.

   However, this strength is somewhat theoretical. In many countries, although the central bank is said to be independent, there is no doubt that governments influence their decisions, often for political aims as opposed to economic aims.

3. *An absence of "crowding out"*: As mentioned earlier, expansionary fiscal policy involving increased government borrowing may lead to higher interest rates and a "crowding out" of private investment. This is not the case with monetary policy, where interest rates are simply lowered.

4. *The ability to make small changes*: Because interest rates may be adjusted by as little as one quarter of one percent, it is possible to be more precise than fiscal policy and to set more exact targets – for example, an inflation target of 2%. Monetary policy enables more fine-tuning of the economy. The fine tuning is also helped by the speed of implementation and the lack of political involvement that have already been mentioned.

ECB signals it will move to boost growth amid fears of low inflation

https://www.theguardian.com/business/2019/jul/25/ecb-signals-it-will-move-to-boost-growth-amid-fears-of-low-inflation

There are also, however, a number of limitations to monetary policy:

1. *Time lags*: Although they are quick to change, monetary policies still take time to have an effect on the economy. It may take a number of months before there is a noticeable effect on aggregate demand. In that time, economic factors may have changed and the policy may not be appropriate.

2. *Ineffectiveness when interest rates are low*: Expansionary monetary policy through cuts in the rate of interest cannot be used for ever. Eventually interest rates will start to approach zero and there will be no room left for further cuts.

3. *Low consumer and business confidence*: Even though interest rates are reduced, the effect on expenditure may be very much dampened by low consumer and business confidence. This is especially the case if the economy is in a deep recession.

Higher Level

Exercise 17.4

ATL Thinking and Communication

1. Showing your working, what will be the value of the money multiplier if the minimum reserve requirement is:
   a) 5%
   b) 10%
   c) 25%
2. Explain, using figures, what would happen to the money supply if a new deposit of $2 million was made in a commercial bank and the minimum reserve requirement was 40%.
3. Explain, using figures, what happens to the money supply if the minimum reserve requirement in question 2 is decreased to 25%.

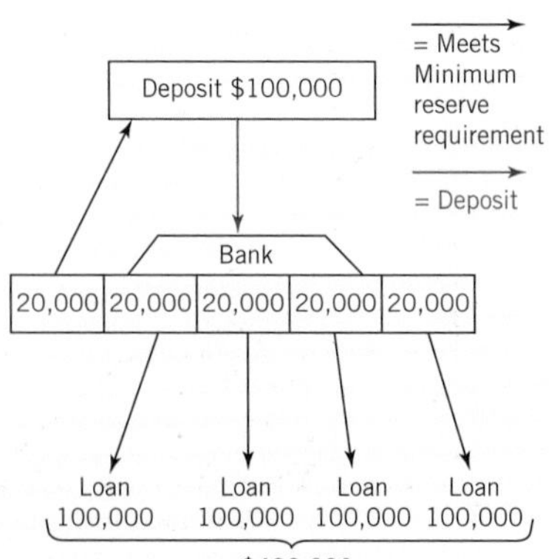

▲ Figure 17.3 The process of credit creation

How do commercial banks create money?

Commercial banks can actually create money. They do this through a process known as "credit creation". In this way, they can have a significant effect on the money supply in an economy.

Credit creation occurs when commercial banks lend money to customers, either individuals or businesses. They do this by making loans based upon the deposits that customers have made with them. However, it is not simply a case of someone depositing $100,000 dollars and a bank lending that $100,000 to someone else. If this happened, then no money would be created. The fact is that when commercial banks receive deposits, they lend out a multiple of the deposit value. They lend out more than they get! This is sometimes known as the money (or banking credit) multiplier.

The multiplier is related to a minimum reserve requirement. This is a percentage of the deposits that commercial banks are legally required to hold in reserve by the central bank, so that they can meet the cash requirements of their depositors.

The process of credit creation by commercial banks is best explained using an example. Let us suppose that a new depositor places $100,000 in a bank. The central bank in that country insists upon a minimum reserve requirement of 20%. This means that the bank has to keep $20,000 in reserve to meet the cash requirements of the depositor.

The bank now has $80,000 of the new deposit that is not being used. A business customer now asks the bank for a loan of $100,000, in order to fund investment in a new machine. The bank decides that the firm is credit worthy and so agrees the loan. The bank credits the firm's bank account with $100,000, simply a computer entry. The firm's bank account increases by $100,000 and it now also has a loan account of $100,000, a debt. At this point, $100,000 of new money has been created. In order to meet reserve requirements on the new money, the bank has to have funds of 20%, ie $20,000, in reserve. However, this can be covered with $20,000 from the $80,000 of unused new deposit and there are still $60,000 not being used.

The bank can use the remaining $60,000 of deposits to fund another three loans of $100,000. Each would be backed by $20,000 of reserves. They could equally just lend $300,000 supported by the whole $60,000. In both cases, they would be meeting the minimum reserve requirement of 20% of all loans being held in reserve. At the end of the process, the original deposit of $100,000 will have become deposits of $500,000. There is a money multiplier of 5. This is illustrated in Figure 17.3.

The size of the money multiplier can be calculated using the equation:

$$\text{Money multiplier} = \frac{1}{\text{Minimum reserve requirement}}.$$

eg if the minimum reserve requirement is 20%, then:

$$\text{Money multiplier} = \frac{1}{\frac{20}{100}} = 5.$$

What tools are available to governments to control the money supply?

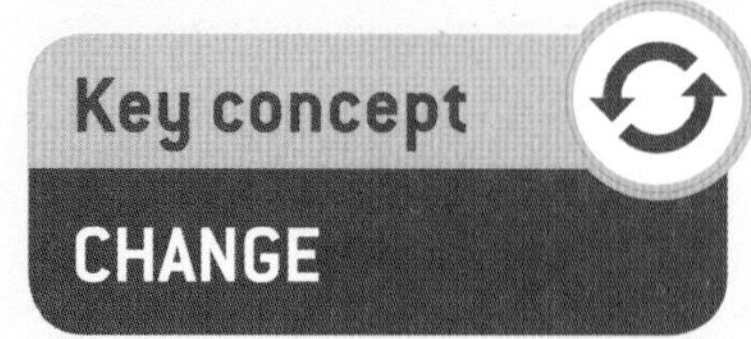

There are a number of methods that the central bank may use to affect the size of the money supply, and thus the interest rate. We shall look at four of them.

- **Minimum reserve requirements**

  We have already touched on minimum reserve requirements above. Remember that the minimum reserve requirement is the percentage of their deposits that the commercial banks are legally required by the central bank to hold in reserve, so that they can meet the cash requirements of their depositors. It should be clear from the exercise above that there is a relationship between the size of the minimum reserve requirement and the size of the money multiplier. In simple terms, the larger the minimum reserve requirement, the smaller will be the money multiplier.

  This means that if governments wish to reduce the money supply (a contractionary monetary policy) then they should increase the minimum reserve requirement. This will reduce the ability of the banks to create credit and so will reduce the money supply. This in turn will increase interest rates and thus lower AD as consumption and investment fall.

  In the same way, if they wish to increase the money supply (an expansionary monetary policy) then they should reduce the minimum reserve requirement. This will increase the ability of the banks to create credit and so will increase the money supply. This in turn will lower interest rates and thus increase AD as consumption and investment rise.

- **Open market operations**

  Open market operations involve the buying and selling of government securities in the open market by the central bank. A government security is a bond, usually issued by the central bank, that offers interest on the nominal value of the bond. They are redeemable after a given number of years. They are considered to be very low-risk, since they are guaranteed by the government.

  If the central bank wishes to reduce the money supply (a contractionary monetary policy) then they will sell more government securities to institutions, which will have the effect of reducing the money that commercial banks have to lend. This fall in supply will increase the cost of borrowing and so increase interest rates, the price of money. This is shown in Figure 17.4, where the quantity of loanable funds at the banks is reduced from S_2 to S_1, and so the interest rate rises from i_2 to i_1. The increase in interest rates will lower AD as consumption and investment fall.

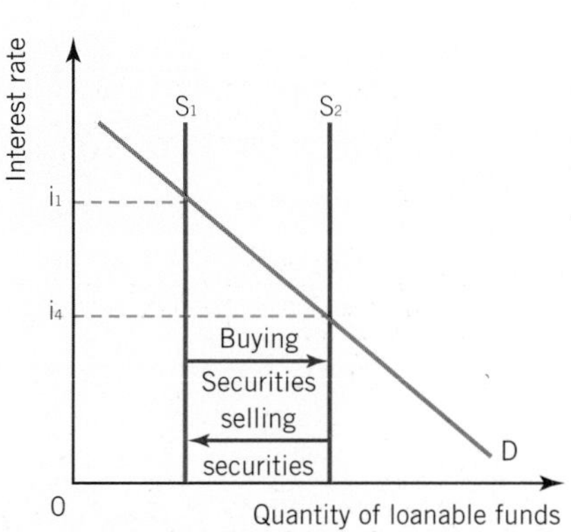

▲ Figure 17.4 Open market operations

If the central bank wishes to increase the money supply (an expansionary monetary policy) then they will buy back their own securities from institutions, which will have the effect of increasing the money that commercial banks have to lend. This increase in supply will reduce the cost of borrowing and so decrease interest rates, the price of money. This is shown in Figure 17.4, where the quantity of loanable funds at the banks is increased from S_1 to S_2, and so the interest rate falls from i_2 to i_1. The decrease in interest rates will increase AD as consumption and investment rise.

- **Changes in the central bank minimum lending rate**

  The minimum lending rate is also known as the base rate, discount rate or refinancing rate. The minimum lending rate is the rate of interest which the central bank charges on loans and advances to commercial banks. It operates as the *base rate* for the banking system, influencing the interest rates charged on bank loans, mortgages and credit transactions throughout the economy. The central bank has control over the level of the minimum lending rate and so they can raise or lower it as they wish.

  If the central bank is implementing a contractionary monetary policy, then they will raise the minimum lending rate. When this happens, commercial banks and other financial institutions, such as building societies, will increase their lending rates and also their interest rates paid to people who save. This will be likely to discourage consumers and businesses from borrowing money and will also encourage consumers to save more. This will reduce consumption and investment and so reduce AD.

  If the central bank is implementing an expansionary monetary policy, then they will lower the minimum lending rate. When this happens, commercial banks and other financial institutions, such as building societies, will lower their lending rates and also their interest rates paid to people who save. This will be likely to encourage consumers and businesses to borrow more money and will also discourage consumers from saving. This will increase consumption and investment and so increase AD.

- **Quantitative easing**

  Quantitative easing (QE) involves the introduction of new money into the money supply by a central bank. The aim is, obviously, to expand the economy and so it is a form of expansionary monetary policy.

  It has become a common form of monetary policy following the economic crisis of 2008. After the crisis, many countries trying to increase AD using lower interest rates found that even though interest rates were very low, AD was not increasing because low consumer and business confidence were preventing consumers and producers from increasing their borrowing. Another means of increasing the money supply had to be implemented and this was QE.

The process is quite simple. The central bank injects new money directly into the economy by purchasing assets, mostly securities, from commercial banks and other financial institutions with *newly created electronic cash*. This will have a number of expansionary effects, including:

- it will increase the reserves of commercial banks as they sell securities. This will increase their liquidity and encourage them to lend more to households and firms, increasing consumption and investment and so increasing AD
- it will lower interest rates, and this will reduce the debt of people and firms who have previously borrowed money; this should increase consumer and business confidence
- the lower interest rates will cause exchange rates to fall, which will make exports less expensive and imports more expensive, and should lead to an increase in (X-M), thus increasing AD.

Note

The link between interest rates and the exchange rate will be explained in Chapter 26.

Economics in action — ATL Thinking, Communication and Research

Using the Internet, write a report on an economy of your choice, considering the actual implementation of:

1. open market operations
2. minimum reserve requirements
3. changes in the minimum lending rate
4. quantitative easing.

What determines the equilibrium nominal interest rate?

Interest rates are often referred to as the price of money, but more accurately they are the opportunity cost of holding/spending money. The *nominal rate of interest* is the rate of interest available in the money market, not allowing for inflation. If the rate of interest is adjusted for inflation, then we call it the *real rate of interest*.

Note

We will look at the calculation of the real rate of interest later in this section.

If a consumer, firm, or the government holds/spends money, then they forego other things that the money could have been used for, ie saving or investment. If nominal interest rates are high, then they are giving up a large return on their savings and investment and so they will hold/demand less money. If nominal interest rates are low, then the opportunity cost of spending/holding money will be less and so they will hold/demand more money. This explains why the demand curve for money is downward sloping. This is shown in Figure 17.5.

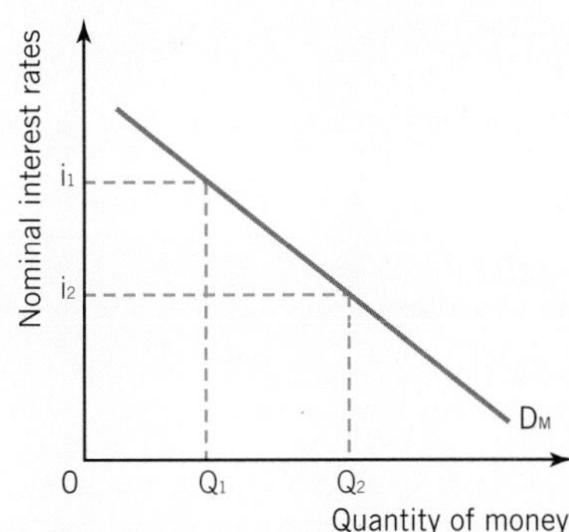

▲ **Figure 17.5** The demand curve for money

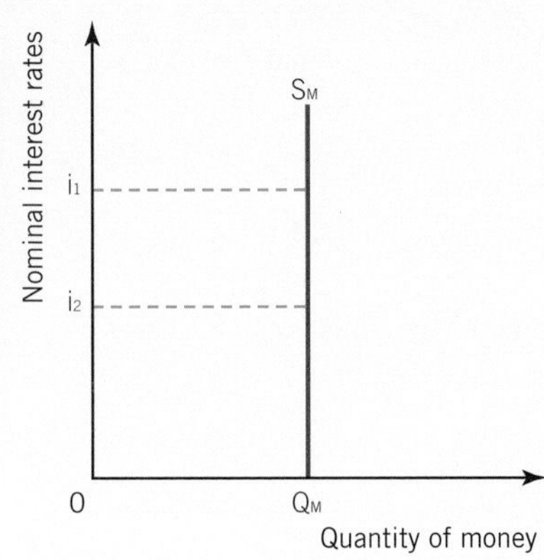

▲ **Figure 17.6** The supply curve for money

The supply of money in an economy, as we know, is controlled by the central bank, through its monetary policy, and is generally considered to be fixed at any given time. Thus it is usually shown as a perfectly inelastic supply curve. This is shown in Figure 17.6. Because it is controlled by the central bank, and not affected by the nominal interest rate, the supply will be constant at Q_M, even if the nominal interest rate shifts from i_1 to i_2.

The money market is where the demand and supply of money come together to determine the equilibrium nominal rate of interest. As with any market the equilibrium is where demand equals supply and so in this case, it is where the demand for money equals the supply of money. This is shown in Figure 17.7.

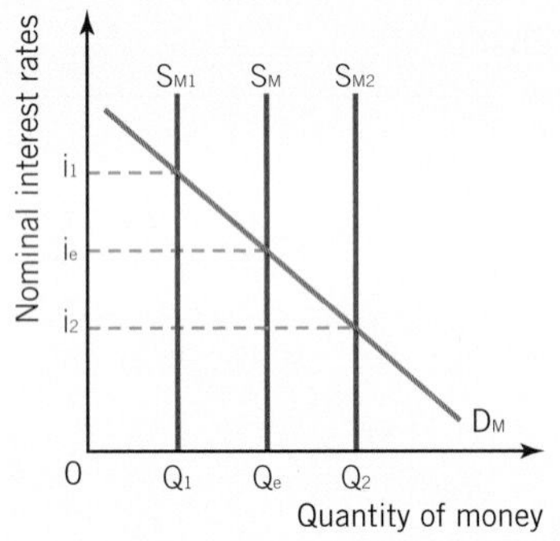

▲ **Figure 17.7** The money market

The equilibrium nominal rate of interest is at i_e, where S_M is equal to D_M. If the central bank adopted a contractionary monetary policy, using any of the tools we have covered, then the money supply would fall from Q_e to Q_1 and the new equilibrium nominal rate of interest would be i_1. If the central bank adopted an expansionary monetary policy, then the money supply would increase from Q_e to Q_2 and the new equilibrium nominal rate of interest would be i_2.

What is the difference between nominal and real interest rates?

In Paper 2, HL and SL, and in Paper 3, you may be asked to calculate real interest rates from a set of data. This is relatively simple.

As we stated earlier, the *nominal rate of interest* is the rate of interest available in the money market, not allowing for inflation. If the rate of interest is adjusted for inflation, then we call it the *real rate of interest*. So, to calculate the real rate of interest from a nominal rate of interest, we simply need to subtract the inflation rate from the nominal rate.

The real rate of interest = nominal rate of interest – inflation rate

If the rate of interest in the market is 5% and the inflation rate is 3%, then the real rate of interest is 2%. This will be important for both savers and borrowers. A person saving at a nominal rate of 5% will find that their real gain is only 2%, whereas someone borrowing at a rate of 5% will find that they are really only paying back at a rate of 2%.

This becomes especially important when real interest rates become negative. If the nominal interest rate is 2% and the inflation rate is 4%, then the real rate of interest will be –2%! This means that anyone saving money will find that the value of their savings is decreasing by 2% per year, whereas someone borrowing money is paying back 2% less than they borrowed, in real terms. This would obviously be a real deterrent to saving and a stimulus to borrowers.

Exercise 17.5

ATL Thinking and Communication

Showing your calculations, answer the following questions:

1. If the nominal interest rate in an economy is 8% and the inflation rate is 3.5%, what is the real interest rate?
2. If the nominal interest rate in an economy is 4.2% and the inflation rate is 7.5%, what is the real interest rate?
3. If the real interest rate in an economy is −2.5% and the inflation rate is 5%, what is the nominal rate of interest?

EXAMINATION QUESTIONS

Paper 1, part (a), questions

1. Explain how the government can use fiscal policy to alter the level of AD in the economy. [10 marks]

2. Explain how the government can use monetary policy to alter the level of AD in the economy. [10 marks]

3. Explain the difference between the nominal rate of interest and the real rate of interest. [10 marks]

HL 4. Explain two factors that would cause the value of a country's Keynesian multiplier to increase. [10 marks]

HL 5. Explain how commercial banks can create new money. [10 marks]

HL 6. Explain two tools available to governments to control the money supply. [10 marks]

HL 7. Explain what determines the equilibrium nominal interest rate. [10 marks]

Paper 1, part (b) questions

1. Using real-world examples, discuss the effectiveness of fiscal policy. [15 marks]

2. Using real-world examples, discuss the effectiveness of monetary policy. [15 marks]

18 SUPPLY-SIDE POLICIES

REAL-WORLD ISSUE:
Why does economic activity vary over time and why does this matter? How do governments manage the economy and how effective are their policies?

By the end of this chapter, you should be able to:

- → Define supply-side policies
- → Explain the goals of supply-side policies
- → Explain different market-based, supply-side policies
- → Discuss the effectiveness and limitations of market-based, supply-side policies
- → Explain different interventionist, supply-side policies
- → Discuss the effectiveness and limitations of interventionist, supply-side policies
- → Explain how supply-side policies and demand-side policies may be connected.

What are supply-side policies and what are their goals?

Supply-side policies are policies that are designed to increase the long-run, aggregate supply in the economy by increasing the quantity and/or quality of factors of production. They are intended to shift the AS/LRAS curve to the right. This is shown in Figure 18.1.

The main goals of supply side policies are to:

1. Achieve long-term economic growth by increasing the productive capacity of the economy
2. Improve competition and efficiency
3. Reduce labour costs and unemployment through increased labour market flexibility
4. Reduce inflation to improve international competitiveness
5. Increase firms' incentives to invest in innovation by reducing costs.

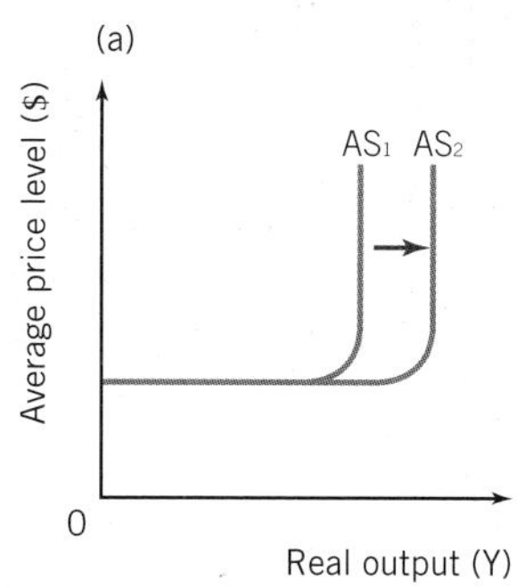

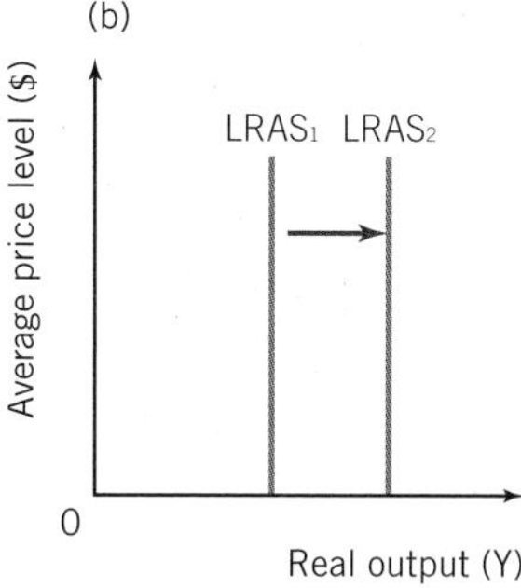

▲ **Figure 18.1** The effect of supply side policies

What are market-based, supply-side policies?

Market-based policies focus on allowing markets to operate more freely with minimal government intervention. They are advocated by those economists who believe in the efficiency of free markets in allocating resources. The word "incentives" is often used with such policies, as they are designed to increase the incentives for labour to work harder and more productively and to increase the incentives for firms to invest and to increase productivity. These may also be described as institutional changes as they affect the structures, institutions and "rules" that govern economic stakeholders.

- *Reduction in household income taxes*: When people work harder and earn more money it is possible that they will have to pay higher taxes on the higher levels of income. Higher taxes may act as a disincentive to work, as people would prefer to substitute more work for more leisure time rather than pay higher taxes on the extra income. If income taxes are reduced, so that people are not taxed more for working more, then they might have the incentive to work harder and to become more productive, thus increasing the potential output of the economy.
- *Reductions in corporate taxes*: If businesses are able to keep more of their profits then they will have more money available for investment. As investment is the addition of capital stock to the economy, greater investment means more capital, thus an increase in a factor of production. Firms also use their profits for research and development, so more profits mean more research and development which leads to advances in technology as well. If businesses know that they are going to be able to keep a larger share of their profits, rather than give it to the government in taxes, then they will have more incentive to produce efficiently. Given the importance of the profit motive in stimulating competition, the potential for the firm to earn higher profits is likely to generate positive supply-side benefits.
- Labour market reforms:
    - ➔ *Reduction in trade union power*: The responsibilities of trade unions include protecting workers' well being, rights and incomes. It may be perceived that trade unions raise the costs of

workers above the level that would be the case in a non-union environment. Thus, the argument is that reducing (or, in the extreme, eliminating) trade union power will reduce the ability of unions to negotiate higher costs of labour and therefore lower the costs of production to firms and increase the number of workers that firms may hire.

→ *Reduction or elimination of minimum wages*: By the same token, it can be argued that because a government-set, minimum wage will keep the price of labour above its free market level, a reduction or abolition of the minimum wage would decrease the cost of labour and thus increase aggregate supply.

→ *Reduction in unemployment benefits*: If unemployed people are given generous benefits from the government, it may be argued that they will have less incentive to find and take jobs that are available. Market-oriented, supply side economists recommend that unemployment benefits be reduced to encourage unemployed people to take available jobs in the economy. Of course this policy only works if jobs are in fact available.

- *Deregulation*: If governments have placed many regulations on the operations of businesses then this may increase their costs of production, thereby reducing potential output in the economy. Such regulations include environmental laws, health and safety regulations or laws concerning working hours, leave and holidays. A reduction in the number and/or the severity of regulations, ie deregulation, will help to increase aggregate supply.
- *Privatization*: This is the sale of public government-owned firms (nationalized firms) to the private sector. It is argued by free-market economists that privately-owned, profit-maximizing firms will be much more efficient than nationalized firms and will therefore increase the potential output of the economy. Nationalized firms tend to have different goals from private firms, such as maintenance of employment or the provision of a service to an isolated market, and this means that they may operate inefficiently.
- *Policies to increase competition*: Competition has the effect of encouraging greater efficiency. Therefore, any policies that increase competition, such as enforcing strict anti- monopoly laws, will increase efficiency and improve the productive potential of an economy.
- *Trade liberalization*: This is another measure designed to increase competition, but this time internationally. The elimination of subsidies, tariffs and quotas would reduce government intervention and lead to *free trade*. This would mean that exporting firms would need to be more efficient in order to compete with foreign firms. They will need to improve their efficiency and increase investment.

We need pro-market policies to boost confidence

https://punchng.com/we-need-pro-market-policies-to-boost-confidence-%E2%80%95ashade/

Note

We will look at international trade in detail when we get to the Global Economy, in later chapters.

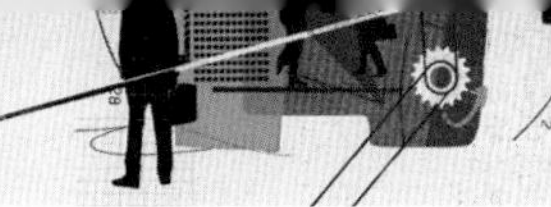

What are the limitations of market-based, supply-side policies?

We will see later how effective market-based, supply-side policies are in achieving specific macroeconomic objectives, such as low unemployment and a low and stable rate of inflation. However, we should now consider their limitations in general terms. All the market-based policies explained above emphasize the reduced role of the government in the economy and the importance of allowing all markets, especially labour markets, to operate freely, without interference. This should improve resource allocation and comes at no significant cost to the government. However, there may be limitations related to their effectiveness and/or equity.

1. The reduction in household income taxes may not lead to a great increase in the incentive to work. When people have an increase in their disposable income, it is possible that they may choose to work less.

2. Reduction in household income taxes may benefit higher wage earners more than those on lower wages and so there may be an increase in income inequality.
3. Reducing corporate taxes and thus increasing the net profits of companies will benefit the wealthy shareholders and so may once again lead to increased income inequality.
4. Labour-market reforms may lead to a possible reduction in living standards for low-income or unionized workers leading to increased income inequality.

5. Deregulation may have a number of negative effects.
   - There may be negative consequences for the environment if environmental regulations are relaxed, so that there are more negative externalities of production.
   - There is a potential reduction in worker safety, if health and safety regulations are relaxed.
   - There may be a worsening in working conditions if regulations concerning working hours are changed.

6. Privatization may not have the desired results if the process is not carried out in a transparent manner. There have been cases in some countries where nationalized industries have been sold at prices below their true value to individuals with connections to the government. The industries have enjoyed monopoly power, which means that there has been no incentive to reduce costs, reduce prices or offer more choice. Indeed, in some cases, there are increases in price and a reduction in supply.
7. In all market-based, supply-side policies, there will be time lags involved before the effects of the policies are filtered through to increased potential outcome.

What are interventionist, supply-side policies?

As the name suggests, these policies are based on the idea that the government has a fundamental role to play in actively encouraging growth.

- *Investment in human capital*: In order to constantly increase the quality/productivity of a country's labour force, education and training need to be available. You should remember that education creates positive externalities. That is, the benefits of education and training are felt not just by those people that receive the education, but are felt across the economy as a more educated and more trained workforce increases the potential output of the economy.

  Although education and training would be provided in a pure market system, it would be underprovided, and thus it is the responsibility of the government to ensure that the country's education facilities are geared to providing the necessary skills and knowledge for a dynamic economy. This involves both the skills and knowledge that young people need to enter the labour force as well as the retraining of workers to help them adjust to changing economic circumstances. Such training can take place in schools, universities, public training institutions and apprenticeship programmes. Governments can also support private schools, private universities and private training institutions with subsidies or tax benefits. They can also support firms which provide training and apprenticeship programmes. All these methods should help to raise the levels of human capital of an economy.

  In addition to education and training, the quality of human capital may also be improved by investment in the quality and quantity of health care, as well as improving people's access to health care.

Hands-on learning delivers real-work skills and more options for high school graduates

https://www.bellinghamherald.com/opinion/article233173346.html

- *Research and development (R&D)*: It is important that an economy's firms are able to stay up-to-date with modern developments, to develop new production techniques, and to seek improved methods of production. All these may increase the economy's potential output, but all involve extensive spending on research and development. Governments can actively encourage research and development by firms by offering tax incentives. For example, they could allow firms not to pay taxes on the retained profits used for R&D. This is known as a tax credit. Firms may be reluctant to spend on R&D if they think that they will not be able to reap the full benefits of their spending. Governments can thus encourage R&D by guaranteeing intellectual property rights such as patents and copyrights. Alternatively, governments themselves could finance R&D in public research facilities and universities.
- *Provision and maintenance of infrastructure*: Infrastructure may be defined as the large-scale capital, usually provided by the government, which is necessary for economic activity to take place.

It includes capital such as roads, electricity, water supply, sanitation, waste management, railways, airports, ports, telecommunications, Internet access and public transportation. We could also consider other institutions such as the education and health systems or the legal and security framework of a country as a type of infrastructure as these are necessary for economic activity. Since these are all necessary for economic activity to take place, the productive potential of an economy as illustrated by its LRAS will be enhanced by improved infrastructure.

- *Direct support for businesses/industrial policies*: Governments have agencies or ministries who are responsible for developing policies that support and encourage the development of industry (for example, a Ministry of Industry, Ministry of Industry and Trade or Commerce Department). Some of their mandates could include: improving the competitive nature of industries through the maintenance of anti-monopoly laws, helping small and medium enterprises to become established and to grow, supporting export companies in their access to markets abroad and advising government on the ways in which education can meet the needs of businesses. In addition to the tax credits that governments might make available, they also support certain industries through financial subsidies.

Economics in action

ATL Thinking, Communication and Research

Look up the name of the government agency responsible for supporting industry in your chosen OECD country. Present an overview of its responsibilities and achievements.

What are the limitations of interventionist, supply-side policies?

We will see later how effective interventionist, supply-side policies are in achieving specific macroeconomic objectives, such as low unemployment and a low and stable rate of inflation. However, we should now consider their limitations in general terms.

All the interventionist policies explained above are necessary in an economy and therefore are not considered to be controversial. They have the characteristics of merit goods in that while they could be provided by the market system, they would be underprovided. The economy would not benefit from the potential welfare gain in terms of the greatest possible increase in the long-run, aggregate supply. Therefore, government intervention is needed. However, there may be limitations related to their implementation;

1. In all interventionist, supply-side policies, there is a significant monetary cost involved. This creates two problems. Firstly, there is always an opportunity cost when governments spend money. It may be the case that, in order to implement one policy, such as increased expenditure on energy infrastructure, there is inadequate expenditure on the health care system. Secondly, the increased expenditure, if funded through borrowing, may increase the levels of government indebtedness and have future negative effects.

2. In all interventionist, supply-side policies, there will be time lags involved before the effects of the policies are filtered through to increased potential outcome.

> **Economics in action**
>
> ATL Thinking, Communication and Research
>
> In reality, all governments employ a mixture of market-based and interventionist, supply-side policies. Investigate the policies employed in your chosen OECD country

3. It is inevitable that in any democracy, the extent to which different interventionist policies are provided depends on the ideological aims of the government at the time and the power of various interest groups. If there are changes in government, then there may be significant changes in emphasis on different policies.

4. Controversies may arise concerning the provision and the funding of education. For example, governments might grapple with the question of how many resources should be allocated for the provision of science education versus arts education or people might disagree on the type of examinations which should be in the education system. The same may happen with health care funding.

How are supply-side policies and demand-side, policies connected?

Some supply-side policies will have demand-side effects and some demand-side policies will have supply-side effects.

What are the demand-side effects of supply-side policies?

Supply-side policies are, by definition, long run. However, when they are implemented, some of them will have short-run, demand-side effects.

Let us look first at market-based policies. As well as being supply-side policies, reducing household income taxes and corporate taxes will also have expansionary fiscal effects. Thus, in the short run, they can be expected to increase aggregate demand, leading to economic growth and lower unemployment, at the cost of increased inflationary pressure.

Interventionist policies will all have a demand-side implication, since they all involve government spending. The increased spending by the government represents an addition to aggregate demand in the economy and so also has expansionary fiscal effects.

It should be noted that, while the demand-side effects may be felt quite quickly, for the most part there is a fairly lengthy time-lag between the implementation of these supply-side policies and their effect on the potential output.

What are the supply-side effects of demand-side policies?

Demand-side, fiscal policies can have supply-side effects. An expansionary fiscal policy, involving lower household income taxes, may increase the incentive to work harder and to become more productive, thus increasing the potential output of the economy. In the same way, an expansionary fiscal policy to reduce corporate taxes may lead to increased investment and/or increased research and development, increasing the quality and quantity of factors of production.

Expansionary, fiscal policies involving an increase in government expenditure may have strong, supply-side effects depending upon the direction of the spending. Any government expenditure aimed at the provision of infrastructure, investment in human capital, such as education or health care and increasing research and development will not only shift aggregate demand, but will also, in the long term, increase the quantity and quality of factors of production, increasing the potential output of the economy.

EXAMINATION QUESTIONS

Paper 1, part (a) questions

1. Explain **three** different interventionist, supply-side policies. [10 marks]
2. Explain **three** different, market-based, supply-side policies. [10 marks]
3. Explain how a reduction in taxes may be considered as both a demand-side policy and a supply-side policy. [10 marks]
4. How might government spending on infrastructure be seen as both a demand-side policy and a supply-side policy? [10 marks]

Paper 1, part (b) questions

1. Using real-world examples, discuss the effectiveness of **three** interventionist policies that might be used to increase LRAS. [15 marks]
2. Using real-world examples, discuss the effectiveness of **three** market-based policies that might be used to increase LRAS. [15 marks]

Paper 2, 4-mark question

Nigeria to invest $20 bln in the infrastructure sector in the next 10 years

In the coming ten years, Nigeria will invest $20 billion into its infrastructures, the trade and investment minister indicated this week during a press conference. "Our target is that we'd like to see infrastructure spending increase to the $10 – $20 billion range over the next 5 to 10 years because we think that's the level of our need," the minister said.

Source: Adapted from *Nigeria to invest $20 billion in the infrastructure sector in the next 10 years*, 29 March 2019 www.ecofinagency.com

Using an AD/LRAS diagram, explain the effect that this investment might have on potential output.

Exercise 18.1

ATL Thinking and Communication

In Chapter 17, we came across The American Recovery and Reinvestment Act (ARRA) (2009). This was a fiscal stimulus signed by President Obama on February 17, 2009. Some of the components are restated below:

- *Modernize federal infrastructure*: $46 billion was given for transportation and mass transit projects; $31 billion to modernize federal buildings; and $6 billion in water projects.
- *Expand health care*: $138 billion dollars was spent on health care.
- *Improve education*: ARRA spent $117 billion on education.
- *Invest in science research and technology*: $18 billion was spent on research and technology.

1. Using an appropriate diagram, explain how the expenditure above would affect the demand-side of the economy.
2. Using an appropriate diagram, explain how the expenditure above would affect the supply-side of the economy.
3. Explain how each of the components of the ARRA might lead to an increase in the potential output of the economy.

19 MACROECONOMIC OBJECTIVES: LOW UNEMPLOYMENT

REAL-WORLD ISSUE:
Why does economic activity vary over time and why does this matter? How do governments manage the economy and how effective are their policies?

By the end of this chapter, you should be able to:

- → Explain what is meant by unemployment
- → Define and calculate the unemployment rate
- → Explain the difficulties involved in measuring unemployment
- → Discuss the costs of unemployment
- → Explain and illustrate the labour market
- → Distinguish between the different causes of unemployment
- → Explain the natural rate of unemployment
- → Evaluate measures that may be taken to reduce unemployment
- HL Explain the concept of "crowding out".

As we know, a low level of unemployment is one of the main macroeconomic goals of every government. Unemployment is a highly publicized topic; a low and/or falling unemployment rate is widely interpreted as a sign of improved health of an economy.

What is unemployment and how do we measure it?

According to the International Labour Organization (ILO), unemployment is defined as "people of working age who are

without work, available for work, and actively seeking employment." (International Labour Organization, www.ilo.org)

By definition, the *unemployment rate* is the number of people who are unemployed expressed as a percentage of the total labour force (not the whole population).

$$\text{Unemployment rate} = \frac{\text{Number of unemployed}}{\text{Total labour force}} \times 100$$

The labour force, otherwise known as the workforce, is essentially the "economically active population". Although it varies from country to country, there is a specified age at which people are eligible to start work and to retire. Anybody outside this age is not part of the labour force. Students attending school are not part of the labour force, as they are not looking for work. Similarly, parents who stay at home to look after children are not considered to be part of the labour force. People who are not considered to be part of the labour force would include children, students, stay-at-home parents, retired people and others who are choosing not to (or are not able to) work. Even though they do not have jobs, such groups are not considered to be unemployed. Because they are not actively seeking employment, they are not part of the labour force.

Why is it difficult to measure the level of unemployment?

It may be surprising to realize that it is actually quite difficult to measure the size of the labour force and the number of people that are unemployed.

Are there institutional differences when measuring unemployment?

Each country has its own national system for measuring the number of people that are unemployed. Information is gathered from national censuses and surveys of the population, along with administrative records such as unemployment insurance records and social security information. It is worth noting that there may be inaccuracies in such data and there may also be inconsistency in the definitions across different countries.

The following gives an example of possible differences in measurement. Unemployment data may be based on the people who are registered as unemployed, as in Austria or Switzerland. Alternatively, it may be calculated as the number of people who are claiming unemployment benefits, as in Britain and Belgium. However, even within these two approaches, there may be problems measuring the true number of people unemployed. For example, the incentive to register as unemployed is likely to depend on the availability of unemployment benefits. A person who is not entitled to any benefits is not likely to register as unemployed.

Economics in action

ATL Thinking, Communication and Research

You have already gathered the data for the unemployment rate in your chosen OECD country. Now find out exactly how the government defines and calculates the unemployment rate.

What is "hidden unemployment"?

One problem that exists in the calculation of unemployment is the existence of hidden unemployment. Hidden unemployment consists of several different groups of people. The first group includes those people who have been unemployed for a long period of time and have given up the search for work. Since they are no longer looking for work, presumably having lost hope, they are no longer considered to be unemployed. These might be referred to as "discouraged" workers.

Another group of people who make up the hidden unemployed are people who have part-time work, or temporary contracts, but would really like to be working full time or on a permanent contract. Since they are working they are obviously not considered as unemployed. They might not be earning as much as they would like, or need, and would like to find a full-time job, but have to stay in the part-time job as it provides a better income than having no job at all.

Yet another group of people hidden from official unemployment figures are people who are working in jobs for which they are greatly over-qualified. Again, such people would like to find work that utilizes their skills and pays higher income, but must stay in the lower-skilled job as it is better than no job at all.

Why does the distribution of unemployment limit the reliability of national unemployment rates?

Along with differences in methods of measurement, and the existence of hidden unemployment, it is worth pointing out another limitation of the unemployment rate. As with many other indicators, a national unemployment rate establishes an average for a whole country, and this is very likely to mask inequalities among different groups within an economy. One should be careful in using the national rate as a basis for making conclusions about different groups of people. These are some of the typical disparities that exist among different groups of people within a country:

- *Geographical disparities*: Unemployment is likely to vary quite markedly among regions in a country, as most countries do have some regions that are more prosperous than others. Inner city unemployment might be quite a bit higher than suburban or rural unemployment.
- *Age disparities*: Unemployment rates in the under-25 age group are higher than the national averages in many countries.
- *Ethnic differences*: Ethnic minorities often suffer from higher unemployment rates than the national average. This may be the result of differences in educational opportunities or possibly due to attitudes and/or prejudices of employers.
- *Gender disparities*: Unemployment rates among women have tended to be much higher than rates for men in many industrialized countries. There may be all kinds of reasons for this: differences in education, discrimination by employers or other social factors.

In India, Millennials Face A Tough Job Market With Unemployment At 4-Decade High

https://www.npr.org/2019/07/26/745731801/in-india-millennials-face-a-tough-job-market-with-unemployment-at-4-decade-high?t=1564481971761

The International Labour Organization

The International Labour Organization (ILO) is the UN specialized agency which seeks promotion of social justice and internationally recognized human and labour rights. It was founded in 1920 and is the only surviving major creation of the Treaty of Versailles which brought the League of Nations into being; it became the first specialized agency of the UN in 1946.

The ILO formulates international labour standards in the form of Conventions and Recommendations setting minimum standards of basic labour rights: freedom of association, the right to organize, collective bargaining, abolition of forced labour, equality of opportunity and treatment and other standards regulating conditions across the entire spectrum of work- related issues. It provides technical assistance primarily in the fields of:

- vocational training and vocational rehabilitation
- employment policy
- labour administration
- labour law and industrial relations
- working conditions
- management development
- cooperatives
- social security
- labour statistics and occupational safety and health.

It promotes the development of independent employers' and workers' organizations and provides training and advisory services to those organizations. Within the UN system, the ILO has a unique tripartite structure, with workers and employers participating as equal partners with governments in the work of its governing organs.

Source: www.ilo.org

Economics in action

ATL Thinking, Communication and Research

1. Read through the description of the ILO in the previous box.
2. Have a look at the homepage of the ILO (www.ilo.org) to develop an awareness of the type of work carried out by this international organization. At the time of writing, some of the flagship programmes include:
    - Occupational Safety & Health – Global Action for Prevention – The OSH-GAP promotes a culture of prevention in occupational safety & health and works to realise the fundamental right of all workers to safe and healthy work.
    - Jobs for Peace and Resilience – Jobs for Peace and Resilience is an employment generation programme for conflict-affected and disaster-prone countries, where decent work for women and men, who are vulnerable to social and political instability, could contribute to peace building, national reconciliation and social cohesion.
    - Social Protection Floors for All – Social Protection Floors for All fosters and supports the design and implementation of social protection systems, with a final goal of making social protection floors (SPFs) a reality for all people.
    - Better Work – Better Work aims to lift millions out of poverty by providing decent work, empowering women, driving business competitiveness and promoting inclusive economic growth.

Source: www.ilo.org

Make your own list and explain four contemporary issues being addressed at the ILO, at the moment.

Economics in action — ATL Thinking, Communication and Research

Investigate the distribution of unemployment in your chosen OECD country by looking at the unemployment rates for:

- different regions
- different age groups
- different ethnic groups
- men and women.

Present the information in the form of tables or graphs. Other than the national statistics office or the OECD, the ILO might be a useful resource.

What are the costs of unemployment?

The reason that governments place such importance on reducing the level of unemployment is because unemployment poses great costs on an economy. It should be pointed out that the costs of unemployment increase the longer that people are unemployed. The costs listed below are really those costs associated with *long-term unemployment*. These costs can be grouped into different categories.

- *Costs of unemployment to the unemployed people themselves*: People who are unemployed face several costs. First of all, unemployed people will receive less income than they would do if they were employed. This is assuming that they receive some unemployment benefits. Clearly if there are no unemployment benefits, then the situation is much worse. A reduction in income implies lower standards of living for those that are unemployed and, in all likelihood, their families as well. The costs worsen the longer the people are unemployed. It is quite likely that a person who remains unemployed for a long period of time could become increasingly dejected and this could contribute to high levels of stress and problems associated with stress, such as anxiety and depression. Erosion of mental health can lead to relationship break-downs and, in the extreme, higher levels of suicide.
- *Costs of unemployment to society*: The social costs of unemployment can most clearly be seen in areas where there are high levels of unemployment in the form of poverty, homelessness, higher rates of crime and vandalism, increased gang activities and so on. While it would be a simplification to blame these problems entirely on unemployment, they are not unconnected.
- *Costs of unemployment to the economy as a whole*: A production possibilities curve can be used to illustrate the key problem facing an economy with unemployment – if actual output is less than potential output due to the unemployment of the factor of production, labour, then the economy is foregoing possible output and would

be operating at a point within its production possibility curve. This loss of output and income to the unemployed has other implications for the economy as a whole. For instance, there is the opportunity cost of the government's spending on unemployment benefits. If unemployed people who have lower incomes pay less direct tax and spend less money, the government earns less in indirect taxes as well. The government may have to spend more money to solve the social problems created by unemployment.

Key concept

EFFICIENCY

Exercise 19.1

ATL Thinking and Communication

Using a production possibilities curve, explain the costs of unemployment to a country.

What are the main factors affecting the level of unemployment?

At any given point in time there will be a number of people that are unemployed. This may be referred to as the "pool" of unemployment. But this "pool" will be in a constant state of change. Unemployment is a "flow concept". At any given time people are becoming unemployed while others are gaining employment. The level of unemployment depends on the relationship between these two. If more people are becoming unemployed than gaining jobs, then the level of unemployment will rise. If more jobs are being created so that more people are gaining jobs than losing jobs, then the level of unemployment will fall. These can be referred to as the inflows and outflows into the "pool" of unemployment and are illustrated in Figure 19.1.

Economics in action

ATL Thinking, Communication and Research

Try to assess some of the problems associated with unemployment in your chosen OECD country.

These factors cause the level of unemployment to rise

Inflows (those becoming unemployed)

- People who have lost their jobs
- People who have resigned
- People who have left school, but have not yet found work
- People who are trying to return to work after having left it (eg stay-at-home parents returning to the workforce)
- People who have immigrated into the country but have not yet found work

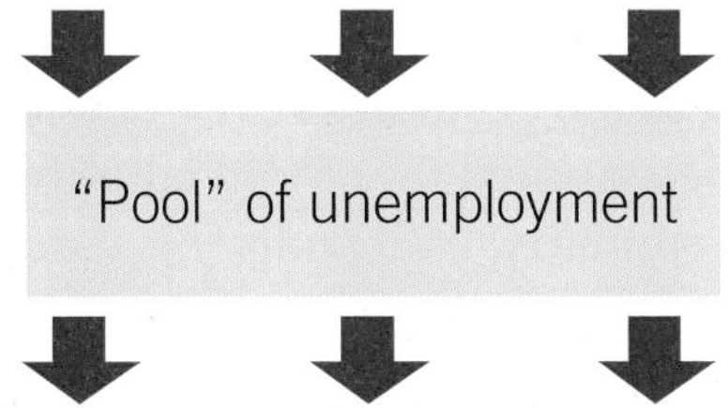

These factors cause the level of unemployment to fall

Outflows (those no longer considered to be unemployed)

- People who find jobs
- People who retire
- People who go (back) into education
- People who choose to stay at home to look after children
- People who emigrate to other countries
- People who give up the search for jobs
- People who pass away

Note that other than the first point, the rest of the people are no longer considered to be unemployed because they have left the labour force—they are no longer "people of working age who are without work, available for work and actively seeking employment".

▲ **Figure 19.1** Inflows and outflows from the 'pool' of unemployment

The movements in and out of the pool of unemployment affect the supply of labour in an economy at any given time. This, along with the demand for labour, will determine the level of employment and unemployment in an economy.

To restate, unemployment is a *flow concept* and the people that governments are concerned about are the workers who do not "flow", the *long-term unemployed*. It is the people who remain in the "pool" of unemployment and cannot get out.

What is the labour market?

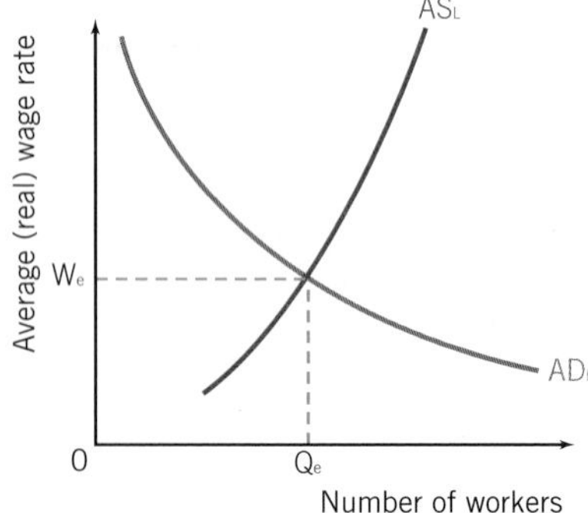

▲ Figure 19.2 Equilibrium in the labour market

Figure 19.2 shows the macroeconomic labour market. The *y*-axis on the diagram represents the price of labour, as measured by the average real wage rate. This shows the average level of wages adjusted for inflation. The *x*-axis represents the quantity of workers.

The labour market represents the demand and supply for all labour in the economy. Thus the demand for labour is more accurately called the aggregate demand for labour (AD_L) as it includes the demand not just for one type of worker but for all the labour that is involved in producing an economy's goods and services. For example, it includes the demand for teachers, assembly line workers, sales people, pizza deliverers, motorcycle mechanics and bankers, to name a few. The aggregate demand curve shows the total demand for labour at every given average wage rate. The aggregate demand curve slopes downwards, because at a lower real wage level, producers are more willing to take on more labour – ie producers' demand for workers increases. As the wage level increases, firms attempt to reduce the amount of labour that they use, perhaps by using more capital-intensive production methods.

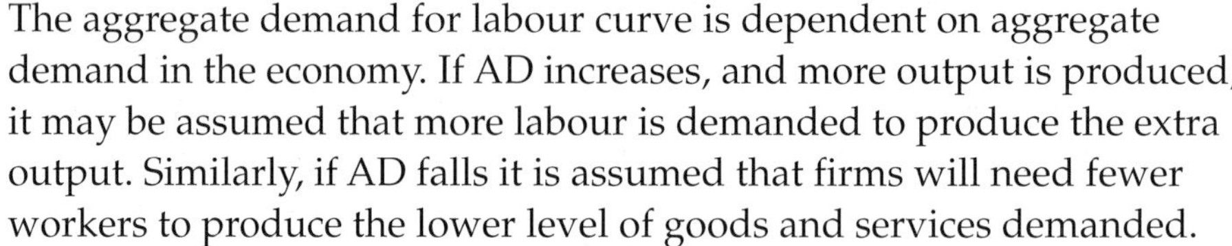

The aggregate demand for labour curve is dependent on aggregate demand in the economy. If AD increases, and more output is produced, it may be assumed that more labour is demanded to produce the extra output. Similarly, if AD falls it is assumed that firms will need fewer workers to produce the lower level of goods and services demanded.

The aggregate supply of labour curve (AS_L) illustrates the total number of an economy's workers that are willing and able to work in the economy at every given average wage rate. As the average wage rate increases, more people are willing to work and so the AS_L curve slopes upwards.

The labour market is in equilibrium where the aggregate demand for labour is equal to the aggregate supply of labour. Although it resembles any microeconomic demand and supply diagram, it is actually a macroeconomic model, as it describes aggregates in the economy. The equilibrium wage for the economy is established by this interaction of AD_L and AS_L and is shown on the diagram as W_e.

What are the causes of unemployment?

There are a number of different causes – types – of unemployment. We will consider four of them:

1. cyclical (demand-deficient) unemployment
2. structural unemployment
3. frictional unemployment
4. seasonal unemployment.

Unemployment for Singaporeans crept up in Q2 as employers grow cautious in hiring

https://www.straitstimes.com/business/unemployment-for-singaporeans-crept-up-in-q2-as-employers-grow-cautious-in-hiring

What is cyclical (demand-deficient) unemployment?

This type of unemployment is associated with the cyclical downturns in the economy. ("Cyclical" relates to the business cycle that we looked at in Chapter 13.) As an economy moves into a period of slower growth (or negative growth in the case of a recession), aggregate demand tends to fall as consumers spend less on goods and services. This is shown in Figure 19.3(a). The fall in consumer spending is likely to lead to a fall in the demand for labour. As firms cut back on production, they will need fewer factors of production and, of course, labour is one of the factors. The fall in demand for labour can be shown on a labour market diagram, as illustrated in Figure 19.3(b).

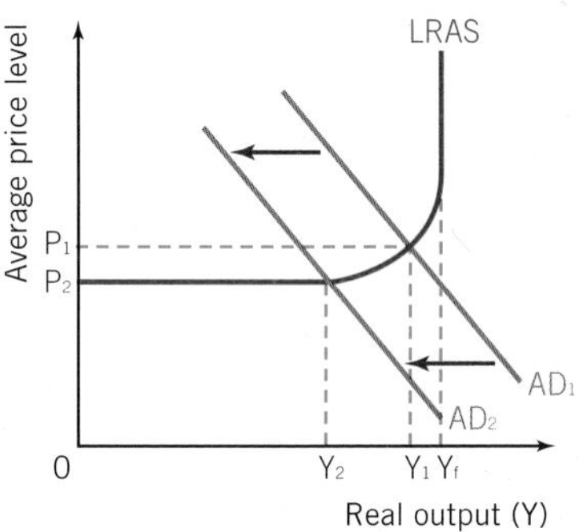

▲ Figure 19.3(a) A decrease in AD

Assume that the economy is initially operating at a high level of economic activity at Y_1 in Figure 19.3(a). There is aggregate demand for labour at AD_L in 19.3(b), so the equilibrium wage will be W_e, for Q_e workers. The labour market is in equilibrium.

If the economy slows down, aggregate demand is likely to fall as shown in Figure 19.3(a). To reduce their output, firms will reduce their demand for labour from AD_L to AD_{L1} as shown in Figure 19.3(b). If labour markets functioned perfectly, then the average real wage would fall to W_1. However, this is not the case, and we say that wages are "sticky downwards". This means that while workers' wages can easily increase, it is less likely that real wages will fall. There are several reasons for this wage "stickiness". First of all, firms realize that paying lower real wages is likely to lead to discontent and reduced motivation among workers. This may result in lower worker productivity and is undesirable. Secondly, firms may not be able to reduce wages due to labour contracts and trade union power. Since wages are likely to remain "stuck" up at W_e, the aggregate supply of labour will be greater than the aggregate demand for labour and unemployment of a – b will be created.

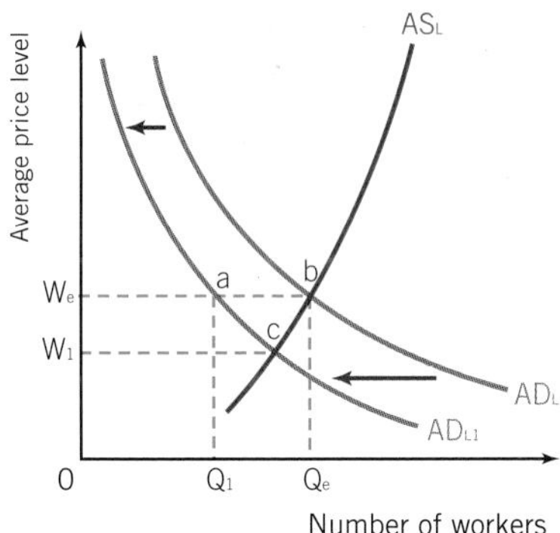

▲ Figure 19.3(b) Demand-deficient unemployment

This type of unemployment has a third name – Keynesian unemployment. As discussed in Chapter 16, Keynes observed that it was quite possible for the economy to operate well below full employment, and this was likely to result in high levels of unemployment.

How might we cure demand-deficient unemployment?

Given that the problem is due to the low level of aggregate demand, the solution to this type of unemployment should be clear – the government can intervene to bring about an increase in aggregate demand through the use of fiscal or monetary policies. That is, the government can use Keynesian demand management policies.

Exercise 19.2

ATL Thinking and Communication

Using an AD/AS diagram, explain how fiscal policy may be used to decrease demand-deficient unemployment.

Since the problem is caused by insufficient aggregate demand in the economy, the government could use fiscal policy by increasing AD itself through increased government spending, or it could lower direct and indirect taxes to indirectly increase consumption by households and investment by firms. The central bank could use monetary policy by decreasing interest rates or increasing the money supply.

What is structural unemployment?

This is by far the worst type of unemployment and occurs as a result of the changing structure of an economy. We can look at two forms of structural unemployment.

1. *A permanent fall in demand for a particular type of labour*

   One form of structural unemployment occurs when there is a *permanent* fall in demand for a particular type of labour. This is natural in a growing economy, as while there will always be new types of jobs being created (eg software engineers, financial advisors), other jobs in a country may disappear (eg coal mining), making people unemployed. One reason that it is so harmful is that it tends to result in long-term unemployment as people who lose their jobs in one area lack the necessary skills to take on the newly-created jobs. We say that they lack the *occupational mobility* to change jobs. It may be that jobs are created in one part of the country, while the unemployed are living in another part of the country. Here, we would say that they lack the *geographic mobility*.

   There are different causes of this type of structural unemployment.

   - Technological change can make workers redundant. Increasing mechanization and work done by robots has led to significant job cuts in many developed countries. This can be referred to as technological unemployment.
   - Globalization has made it increasingly possible for companies to set up their operations in countries where labour costs are lower and/or regulations are less strict. This results in a fall in demand for labour in more developed countries. Globalization has also resulted in increased trade such that producers from countries with lower costs of production have greater access to global markets. This means that demand for particular types of labour in countries with higher costs of production might fall due to lower-cost labour in foreign countries. For example, unemployment in many manufacturing industries in developed countries is blamed on imports from China.

- Changes in consumer taste may lead to a fall in demand for a particular type of labour. For example, people in some areas are increasingly concerned about the negative externalities associated with the production and consumption of coal. This has led to a search for alternatives and a fall in the demand for coal in some countries. As a result, coal miners have become structurally unemployed.

We can use a diagram to illustrate structural unemployment. We can show the fall in demand for labour in a particular market or geographical area. Consider the case of manufacturing workers in Canada, as illustrated in Figure 19.4. Given that the cost of employing labour in manufacturing in emerging/developing economies is lower than in high-income countries there has been a fall in demand (D_1 to D_2) for manufacturing labour in higher-wage countries such as Canada. The consequence of this is that there are fewer manufacturing workers employed (Q_1 to Q_2) and the wage falls from $16 per hour to $12 per hour. From this diagram we can assume that unless these workers can find other jobs there is an increase in unemployment of the amount $Q_1 - Q_2$.

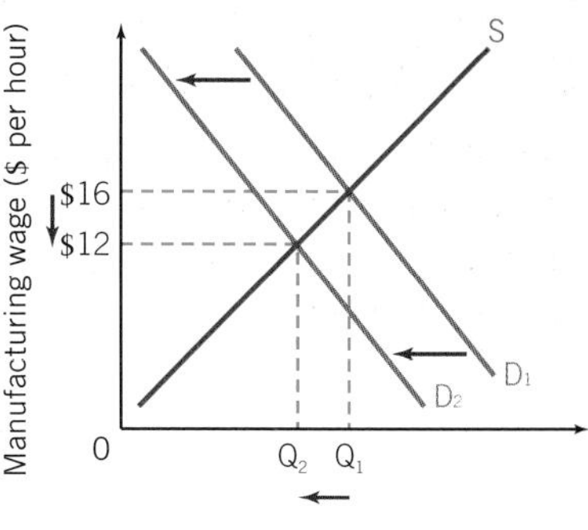

▲ **Figure 19.4** A fall in employment (structural unemployment)

Please note an important distinction between demand deficient unemployment and structural unemployment. Demand deficient unemployment is caused by an overall (and temporary) fall in the demand for all labour in the economy as a result of a slowdown in economic growth or a recession. The expectation would be that once aggregate demand picks up then the aggregate demand for labour should also increase. Structural unemployment is caused by a permanent fall in the demand for one type of labour and requires a different set of solutions.

However, it should be noted that demand deficient unemployment caused by a lengthy period of economic activity could result in structural unemployment. This could occur because, as the economy picks up, it is quite possible that new forms of labour are needed, while workers who were made redundant during a recession do not have the skills needed for the changing economic climate.

2. *A change in the institutional framework of the economy*

Another form of structural unemployment occurs when there are changes in the institutional framework of an economy that affect the labour force. Examples of this include laws governing the labour market and trade unions.

- *Laws governing the labour market* – For example, consider the case where there is a law which states that firms may not fire workers unless they give lengthy documentation and proof of inefficiency or malpractice. Most people would agree that this is a very important right that should be given to all workers. However, this law might also prevent some firms from hiring workers, as they fear the costs of dismissing them should the workers not be efficient. This would reduce the demand for labour, causing unemployment.

▲ Figure 19.5 Minimum wage and structural unemployment

Another example here would be minimum wage legislation, which we came across in Chapter 8. Let us assume that a minimum wage of $12 per hour is put in place for fast-food restaurant workers in a country. This is shown in Figure 19.5.

Before the imposition of the minimum wage, Q workers were being employed at a wage of $10 per hour. When the minimum wage of $12 is legally enforced, the quantity of labour demanded falls to Q_1 workers and so there is an increase in unemployment of $Q_1 - Q$. Interestingly, because of the higher hourly wage, there is also an increase of workers who are prepared to supply their labour from Q to Q_2.

- *Laws governing trade unions* – A key responsibility of trade unions is to protect their union members. It may be that firms are prevented from hiring certain workers, who might be willing and able to work, because the union does not allow the firms to employ non-union members. In this case the union would be contributing to the unemployment in the economy.

How might we cure structural unemployment?

Structural unemployment is best dealt with through the use of supply-side policies. We can look at possible interventionist and market-based policies.

1. *Interventionist policies*

   A key here is to try to enhance the occupational mobility of people, so that they become more able to take available jobs.

   - A long-term solution involves an education system that trains people to be more occupationally flexible. Evidence suggests that people in more developed economies will have to change jobs several times in their career. Thus it is clear that an education system must make people able to learn the skills to adapt to economic conditions that are changing rapidly.
   - Another strategy to improve occupational mobility involves spending on adult upskilling or retraining programmes to help people acquire the necessary skills to match available jobs.
   - Another possibility is for the government to give subsidies to firms that provide training for their workers.
   - If jobs exist in other parts of a country, a government might provide subsidies or tax breaks to encourage people to move to those areas. This enhances their geographic mobility.
   - Governments can also support apprenticeship programmes, such as those available in Germany and Austria, so that potential workers can acquire the skills needed in the labour force.
   - Job centres providing information about job vacancies, training opportunities and interview-training can help unemployed people access available jobs.

There are two main disadvantages to such policies. The first is that they are likely to involve a high opportunity cost as governments will have to forego spending in other areas in order to be able to afford the strategies. The second is that these policies are really only effective in the longer term.

2. *Market-based policies*
    - Some would argue that people will have little incentive to find a job if the unemployment benefits available to them in their country are generous and allow them to remain unemployed or take their time in looking. Thus, economists who prefer to allow markets to operate freely would say that governments should lower unemployment benefits to encourage unemployed workers to take the jobs that are available rather than allow them the chance to wait for a better one to come along. If unemployment benefits were reduced, then the unemployed workers might become more willing to work, thus shifting the aggregate supply of labour to the right.
    - Market-oriented economists feel that government intervention and labour market regulations reduce "labour market flexibility" and discourage businesses from hiring workers. They would argue that regulations about hiring and firing, for example, make businesses less willing to take on new workers, so they would argue in favour of deregulation of labour markets. This would involve reducing or removing the legislation that businesses must follow in their hiring, firing and employment practices.

The burden of such policies falls on two groups of people. First, people who lose their unemployment benefits will have lower living standards, and so such a policy can be said to increase inequity in an economy. Second, it can be assumed that labour market regulations are in place to protect workers from unfair treatment, such as being fired without due cause. Labour market regulations also guarantee certain conditions of work, such as working time, holidays and safety at work. If there is labour market deregulation, it would not be surprising to find worse working conditions for labour. So, although unemployment might fall and the economy's output might rise, there might be a high cost for the workers themselves. Again, this can contribute to inequity in the economy where the benefits of higher economic growth are not shared by all.

What is frictional unemployment?

This is the short-term unemployment that occurs when people are in between jobs, or they have left education and are waiting to take up their first job. Frictional unemployment is not generally perceived to be a negative outcome in any dynamic economy. If people leave one job, the assumption is that they will move on to a job where they can be more productive. As soon as such members of the labour force get a job, they will be able to contribute more to the economy.

How might we reduce frictional unemployment?

Even though frictional unemployment is not seen as a serious problem in an economy due to its short-term nature, there are ways that governments can reduce this level of unemployment if it is believed that people are remaining unemployed for too long. Some would argue that people will have little incentive to find a job if the unemployment benefits available to them in their country are generous and allow them to take their time in looking. Thus, a market-based solution would be similar to that of structural unemployment – reduce unemployment benefits.

Sometimes people who are frictionally unemployed remain without work because they are not aware of appropriate vacancies that exist. In such a case, frictional unemployment can be reduced by improving the flow of information from potential employers to people looking for jobs. This can be through such things as Internet job sites, newspapers, job centres and employment counsellors. This would reflect a more interventionist approach.

What is seasonal unemployment?

It is natural in many economies for some workers to be employed on a seasonal basis. That is, the demand for certain workers falls at certain times of the year. For example, in temperate climates where there is a cold winter there may be unemployed construction workers or farmers. The tourism industry tends to work in seasons – for example, there is not much call for a ski instructor in Austria in July.

How might we reduce seasonal unemployment?

Such unemployment can be reduced by encouraging people to take different jobs in their "off season". The methods mentioned above, reduced unemployment benefits and greater flow of information, are appropriate here as well.

What is the natural rate of unemployment?

Theoretically, the labour market may be in equilibrium, with no demand-deficient unemployment, but there might still be unemployed people. This is because some of the types of unemployment occur even when the labour market is in equilibrium.

When the labour market is in equilibrium, the number of job vacancies in the economy is the same as the number of people looking for work. However, although jobs exist, there are some workers who are either unwilling or unable to take them.

This unemployment, which is greater than the equilibrium level of unemployment, the full employment level of output, is known as the *natural rate of unemployment*. It comprises the three types of unemployment that we have encountered above – structural, frictional and seasonal unemployment.

Workers who are structurally unemployed may be unable to take jobs that are on offer because they do not have the requisite skills (occupational immobility) or because they are living in one area and the jobs are in another area (geographical immobility) or because the institutional framework relating to employment prevents them. For example, perhaps there are job vacancies in the financial services industry, but the unemployed assembly line workers are not able to take the jobs because they lack the appropriate education and skills. Or perhaps there are job vacancies in the domestic services industry, but the unemployed mechanical engineers are unwilling to take them. Or perhaps there are jobs available for computer programmers, but the unemployed computer programmers are not aware that these jobs are available. In each of these three examples, the unemployed workers are either unable (the assembly line workers and the computer programmers) or unwilling (the mechanical engineers) to take the jobs that are available.

Workers who are frictionally unemployed have voluntarily left their jobs, or are new to the labour market. This type of unemployment is easily recognizable as natural unemployment as it is natural for people to leave jobs in the hopes of finding better ones. They are searching for new and/or better jobs.

Workers who are seasonally unemployed may be unable to take jobs because their expertise is not applicable at the time of year or because they are unwilling to take jobs outside of their existing range of skills.

NATURAL RATE OF UNEMPLOYMENT = Structural unemployment + frictional unemployment + seasonal unemployment

Are demand-side policies or supply-side policies more effective in reducing unemployment?

It should be clear that the solutions to unemployment depend very much on the type of unemployment. If an economy is experiencing a downturn in economic activity, then it is likely that demand-deficient unemployment will rise, making demand-management policies suitable.

There are of course concerns associated with such policies. In order to use expansionary fiscal policy, a government may have to run a budget deficit and spend more than it takes in revenues. While not necessarily a problem, particularly in the short run, this may lead to fiscal problems in the longer run. If governments reduce taxes, there is no guarantee that people will spend their extra disposable income; if consumer confidence is low then people might prefer to save and aggregate demand might remain depressed. If governments reduce interest rates to encourage spending, there is no guarantee that it will have the desired effect of increasing consumption and/or investment. Once again, if consumer or business confidence is low then there is unlikely to be an increase in borrowing to finance consumption and investment.

Economics in action

ATL Thinking, Communication and Research

Research the labour market of the government in your chosen country. Consider the following questions:

1. How extensive are the labour market regulations (eg minimum wage, hiring and firing rules (job security), safety standards, length of work day, paid holidays)?
2. What does the government do to reduce the level of unemployment? Try to identify the policies that are interventionist and the policies that are market-oriented.

By now, you should have a complete picture of unemployment in your chosen country, including the nature of unemployment, the distribution of unemployment, the costs of unemployment and the solutions being employed to reduce unemployment.

Even when successful, there is likely to be a lag before they come into effect. It is possible that aggregate demand will increase, but by the time that it does, the economy may have already recovered, and the extra impetus can then be inflationary.

Another problem that occurs is due to the fact that even when the economy is at full employment, there will be some unemployment. We now know that this type of unemployment is natural unemployment and the solutions to these types are best found in supply-side policies. Using demand management policies to cure this type of unemployment will be unsuccessful. At full employment, the economy is producing near full capacity. Increases in aggregate demand at this point would result in inflationary pressure. We will address this further in the next chapter.

Higher Level

Fiscal policy – discretionary policy versus automatic stabilizers

We distinguish between discretionary fiscal policy and automatic stabilizers when discussing fiscal policy. Discretionary fiscal policy is a deliberate change to a government policy in order to manage aggregate demand, such as a decision to increase spending on infrastructure to expand the economy or to reduce spending on health care as a means of deflating the economy.

Automatic stabilizers, on the other hand, do not require any deliberate change to government policy in order to change the level of aggregate demand. These affect both government revenue and government expenditure. If there is high unemployment then government tax revenues will fall, as fewer people will be earning an income. It will not take any deliberate action on the part of the government to increase AD by lowering taxes. As far as the other tool of fiscal policy, government expenditure, is concerned, there will also be an increase in government spending. If there is high unemployment then there will be an increase in transfer payments to the unemployed (depending on the ability or willingness of the government to pay unemployment benefits). The government does not have to deliberately increase its own spending to increase AD, as this will happen automatically through the increased spending on unemployment benefits.

Automatic stabilizers are seen as important measures of controlling fluctuating economic activity because, since they automatically operate to increase aggregate demand when there is a slowdown in economic activity, they are not influenced by political decision making and not subject to the same time lags as discretionary policy would be.

The problem facing policy makers is that in practice it might be very difficult to distinguish between the different types of unemployment. Moreover, an economy may be suffering from several different types of unemployment. At any rate, it would be most common to see governments using a mix of demand-side and supply-side policies. Demand-side policies, particularly the manipulation of interest rates, are commonly used to narrow possible business cycle fluctuations and reduce output gaps. Supply-side policies are vital to ensure that labour is suitably skilled and flexible to adapt to changing economic conditions so that the LRAS is always shifting to the right.

What is crowding out?

When governments run budget deficits in order to stimulate an economy and reduce unemployment, there is a potential problem known as "crowding out". To run a budget deficit, the government has to borrow money. Governments do this by selling government bonds such as treasury bills or treasury bonds to financial institutions who then sell them on to people who want to save their money. What the government is essentially doing is increasing demand for the savings, or loanable funds, that are in the economy. We illustrate the consequences of this increase in demand in Figure 19.6.

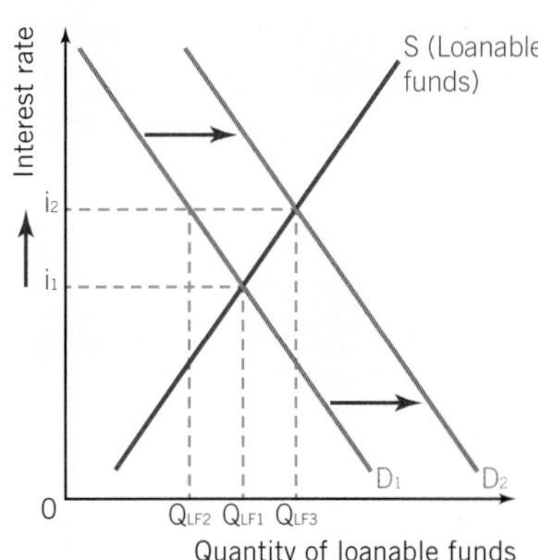

▲ **Figure 19.6** Crowding out – moderate view

There is a given amount of savings in the economy and this is represented by the supply of loanable funds curve, S_{LF}. The price of these loanable funds is the interest rate. The demand curve for private business borrowing is D_1. There is increased demand for loanable funds from D_1 to D_2 in order to finance a government spending deficit. This results in an increase in the interest rate from i_1 to i_2. Overall, total borrowing increases from Q_{LF1} to Q_{LF3}. However, the increase in government borrowing is Q_{LF2}–Q_{LF3}, the horizontal distance between D_1 and D_2. The higher interest rate will reduce the incentive for private businesses to invest and so their borrowing will fall from Q_{LF1} to Q_{LF2}. Private businesses will have been "crowded out" of the market.

So we have a situation where the government wished to increase aggregate demand by increasing government spending, but the higher interest rate causes interest-sensitive private investment to fall, which may reduce aggregate demand. The final effect on aggregate demand will depend upon whether the increase in government spending outweighs the fall in private investment or not.

Whether or not crowding out does occur and the extent to which it might occur is a subject of much debate in economics. Yet again, there is disagreement among Keynesian economists and new classical economists. To simplify the argument, Keynesian economists say that it will not occur, if the economy is producing at less than full employment. The new classical economists, who are opposed to the use of demand management policies, argue that crowding out is a significant problem of increased government spending.

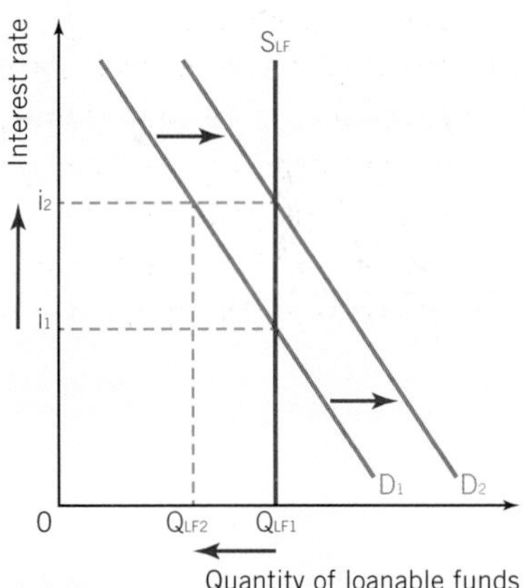

▲ **Figure 19.7** Crowding out – extreme view

Extreme new classical economists argue that the crowding out effect is even more pronounced because, at any given time, the supply of loanable funds is fixed, ie perfectly inelastic. Thus any increase in government spending leads only to an increase in interest rates and no increase at all in total borrowing. This is shown in Figure 19.7.

If the supply of loanable funds is perfectly inelastic, then the increase in government demand for borrowing leads to a large increase in interest rates from i_1 to i_2. The quantity of borrowing stays at Q_{LF1} but, with the higher interest rates, the quantity of private business borrowing falls to Q_{LF2}. There is even greater crowding out than in the moderate view.

Exercise 19.3

ATL Thinking and Communication

You have come across a number of types of unemployment in this chapter. Create a table that will show all of the different types of unemployment, their causes and their cures.

EXAMINATION QUESTIONS

Paper 1, part (a) questions

1. Explain the cause of demand deficient unemployment. [10 marks]
2. Explain **two** possible causes of structural unemployment. [10 marks]
3. Explain the costs associated with unemployment. [10 marks]
4. Explain the difficulties involved in measuring the exact level of unemployment. [10 marks]
5. Explain **two** policies that might be used to reduce the natural rate of unemployment. [10 marks]

HL 6. Explain crowding out. [10 marks]

HL 7. Explain how automatic stabilizers may reduce the effectiveness of fiscal policy. [10 marks]

Paper 1, part (b) questions

1. Using real-world examples, evaluate the effectiveness of demand-side policies in reducing unemployment.
2. Using real-world examples, evaluate the effectiveness of supply-side policies in reducing unemployment.

Paper 2 – 4-mark question

Unemployment increases as technology blossoms

Over the past five years, improvements in technology and increased investment by a large proportion of the major companies in the garment industry have led to a significant decrease in employment. This is a concern for the government.

Using a labour market diagram, explain the type of unemployment that has occurred in the garment industry.

Paper 2 – 4-mark question

Economy is moving into recession

In the last two quarters, economic growth has been –0.25% and –0.5%, respectively. This is proof that the economy is now in recession. The biggest effect of this is to be seen in the labour market, where the unemployment rate has increased from 12% to 13.5% in the last year. It is essential that the government addresses this problem.

Using an AD/AS diagram, explain the type of unemployment that has occurred in the economy.

By the end of this chapter, you should be able to:

- → Explain the concepts of inflation, disinflation and deflation
- → Explain the costs of inflation
- → Explain how inflation is measured
- → Explain the problems in measuring inflation
- → Explain and illustrate the causes of inflation
- → Evaluate measures that may be taken to reduce inflation
- → Distinguish between "good" deflation and "bad" deflation
- → Explain the costs of deflation
- HL Calculate a weighted price index.
- HL Explain and illustrate the short-run Phillips curve
- HL Explain and illustrate the long-run Phillips curve
- HL Explain the concept of the natural rate of unemployment
- HL Evaluate the extent to which there might be a trade-off between inflation and unemployment.

What is inflation?

In Chapter 13 you learned that one of a government's macroeconomic goals is price stability. Another way to express this is to say that governments desire a low and stable rate of inflation. *Inflation* is defined as a persistent increase in the average price level in the economy, usually measured through the calculation of a consumer price index (CPI). The word "persistent" is of great importance in your understanding of the concept. A single increase in prices is not called inflation. When inflation occurs there is a sustained increase in the price level. It is also very important not to confuse inflation with an increase in the price of a particular good or service.

What are the costs of high inflation?

The reason that governments wish to keep inflation at a low level is because there are a significant number of negative consequences associated with higher levels of inflation.

If inflation hits, it can be fast and devastating

https://www.telegraph.co.uk/business/2019/07/29/inflationhits-canbe-fast-anddevastating/

- *Loss of purchasing power*: If the rate of inflation is 2%, then this means that the average price of all goods and services in the economy has risen by 2%. If your income remains constant, or rises by less than 2%, then you will not be able to buy as many goods and services as you could before the increase in the average price level. We say that there is a fall in real income, which means that there is a decrease in the purchasing power of income. If income is linked to the inflation rate, so that you automatically get a 2% "cost-of-living" increase, then you will not face a fall in your real income. This is the case for many jobs, particularly where there are strong unions. However, many people have jobs that do not offer the security of inflation-linked incomes. This may be because they are on fixed incomes or because they have weak bargaining power or because they are self-employed or on temporary contracts with no security. Thus, inflation reduces the purchasing power of their incomes, and will reduce their living standards. It is important to realize that expectations about inflation are important. Even when people's incomes are linked to inflation, they can be negatively affected if the actual rate of inflation turns out to be higher than the expected rate. For example, if the expected rate of inflation is 1.5% and wages are therefore increased by 1.5%, then workers will lose purchasing power if inflation turns out to be higher than expected at 2.5%.
- *Effect on saving*: If you save $1,000 in the bank at 4% annual interest, then in one year's time you will have $1,040. If the inflation rate is 6% then the real rate of interest (the interest rate adjusted for inflation) will be negative and your savings will not be able to buy as much as they could have in the previous year. You would have been better off spending the money rather than saving it, because it will have lost some of its purchasing power. Therefore, we say that inflation discourages saving.
- *Effect on economic growth*: If people do want to save money, rather than spend on consumption, then they may choose to buy fixed assets, such as houses or art. This means that there are fewer savings available in the economy for investment purposes and this has negative implications for economic growth.

- *Effect on interest rates*: Commercial banks make their money from charging interest to people who borrow money from them. If there is a high rate of inflation then banks raise their nominal interest rates in order to keep the real rate that they earn positive.
- *Effect on international competitiveness*: If a country has a higher rate of inflation than that of its trading partners then this will make its exports less competitive and will make imports from lower-inflation trading partners more attractive. This may lead to lower export revenues and greater expenditure on imports, thus worsening the trade balance. It might lead to unemployment in export industries and in industries that compete with imports.
- *Uncertainty*: Not only might there be reduced investment due to a fall in the availability of savings and higher nominal interest rates, but firms may be discouraged from investing due to the uncertainty associated with inflation. Again, this has negative implications for economic growth.
- *Labour unrest*: This may occur if workers do not feel that their wages and salaries are keeping up with inflation. It may lead to disputes between unions and management.

So who really wins and who loses when there is significant, sustained inflation? This is shown in Table 20.1.

Winners	**Losers**
People with index-linked incomes – because their incomes will increase in line with inflation, they do not really suffer from a fall in purchasing power, although there may be a time-lag involved.	People on fixed incomes/wages – such as pensioners, people relying on state benefits or workers on long-term fixed-wage contracts. They will suffer a significant fall in purchasing power over time.
People with high wage-bargaining power – such as workers in high-demand industries, and strong trade unions. They will be able to negotiate wage increases that cover the inflation rate, or even outstrip it.	People with low-wage-bargaining power – such as workers in low-demand industries and workers who do not possess high skill levels. They may not be able to negotiate wage increases that cover the inflation rate.
Borrowers – because the real interest rate is lowered by inflation, the amount paid back by the borrower will be worth less than the amount of the loan that was taken out.	Savers/lenders – because the real interest rate is lowered by inflation, the amount received by the saver will be worth less. If the inflation rate is greater than the nominal interest rate, the saver will actually lose money.
People who are "asset rich" – in times of high inflation, there is often a "flight to assets" as people buy assets, such as houses or precious metals, as opposed to saving. This leads to increases in the price of assets, which benefits people who already own assets.	People who are "cash rich" – in times of high inflation, people who have high amounts of cash will find that the value of their cash is significantly reduced over time. This will be made worse if the cash cannot be saved at a positive real interest rate.
Importers – imports will be relatively more attractive as the prices of domestic products increase, and so demand for imports will grow.	Exporters – exports will be relatively less attractive abroad as the higher prices make them compare less favourably with foreign goods and services.

▲ **Table 20.1** The winners and losers of inflation

Economics in action — ATL Thinking, Communication and Research

Find an example of a country that is experiencing high inflation and identify the costs being experienced by the various stakeholders.

How is inflation measured?

It is necessary to have some kind of an accurate measure of the increase in the price level. The most widely used statistic to measure inflation is known as the consumer price index (CPI). In some countries this is referred to as the retail price index (RPI).

Not all prices change by the same amount over a given period of time – for example, the price of chocolate might increase by 5% in a year, while the price of petrol might increase by 10%. Neither of these is an appropriate measure of the change in the average price level. Statisticians in different countries around the world have slightly different ways of measuring the rate of inflation, but the central idea is the same. Simply put, they choose what is known as a representative "basket" of consumer goods and services and measure how the price of this basket changes over time. When the price of the basket increases then this means that the average price level has risen.

What is meant by a "representative basket of consumer goods and services"? It would be impossible to devise a measure of inflation that includes all goods and services bought by consumers. In each country the agency in charge of the compilation of economic data creates a list of the typical goods and services consumed by the average household. These items are grouped into a number of different categories. The prices of these items are measured each month to calculate the change in the price of the "basket". The change in the price of the basket is reflected in the measure called the consumer price index. It is important to point out that some of the goods and services consumed are far more important than others, because they take up a larger share of consumers' income. Thus, the categories are given a weight in the index to reflect their importance in the average consumer's income. The weights for the different categories of the UK CPI along with some examples of the items that are included are shown in Table 20.2.

Category	CPI Weight (%)
Food and non-alcoholic beverages (breads and cereals; meat; oils and fats; milk, cheese and eggs; fruit; vegetables; sugar, jam, honey, chocolate and confectionary sugar; coffee, tea and cocoa; mineral waters, soft drinks and juices)	8.0
Alcohol and tobacco (spirits; wine; beer; cigarettes and cigars)	3.2
Clothing and footwear (women's, men's and children's clothing; accessories; cleaning and repair of clothing; shoes and boots)	5.7
Housing and household goods (rents; maintenance; water supply; electricity, gas and other fuels)	29.8
Furniture and household goods (furniture and furnishings; carpets and other floor coverings; household textiles; household appliances; glassware and tableware; goods and services for household maintenance)	5.2
Health (medical products, appliances and equipment; out-patient services and hospital services)	2.2
Transport (new and second-hand cars; motorcycles and bicycles; spare parts and accessories; fuels and lubricants; vehicle maintenance and repairs; passenger transport by railway, road and air)	12.4
Communication (postal services; telephone and telefax equipment; mobile phone charges; Internet subscriptions)	2.0
Recreation and culture (audio-visual equipment and related products; data-processing equipment; recording media; repair of audio-visual equipment and related products; major durables for recreation and culture; games, toys and hobbies; equipment for sport and outdoor recreation; gardens, plants and flowers; pets, related products and services; recreational and cultural services; books, newspapers, magazines and stationery; package holidays)	12.5
Education (private school fees, evening classes and university tuition fees)	1.8
Restaurants and hotels (restaurants, take-aways and food delivery; bar charges; catering; canteens)	9.8
Miscellaneous goods and services (jewellery, clocks and watches; social protection; insurance; flower delivery; self-storage fees; funeral charges)	7.4

Source: Consumer price inflation basket of goods and services: 2019, Philip Gooding, Office for National Statistics

▲ Table 20.2 UK CPI: categories and their weights

From the data we can conclude that spending on food and non-alcoholic beverages makes up 8.0% of the spending of the "typical" or average household. Thus, changes in the prices of the food and beverage products in the basket will be given a weight of 8.0% in the calculation of the index. The components and the weighting of the basket are determined by surveys of household spending habits and will change according to changes in consumption habits (see Table 20.3 for some examples of recent changes to the UK "basket"). The price of the basket is measured regularly by collecting prices from shopping outlets throughout the country and a national average price is determined. This is the measure of the national consumer price index and changes in the index represent the "headline" inflation rate. This is the rate of inflation most commonly used and the one that we are most familiar with for judging the overall state of the country's economy.

The UK Consumer Price Index

Currently, around 180,000 separate price quotations are used every month covering 650 representative consumer goods and services for which prices are collected in around 150 areas in the UK. The categories and their weightings, along with the representative item, are revised each year to take into account changing consumption patterns by households. To give one example, there has been an increasing tendency for consumers to spend more on the category of Housing and Household goods and so the weight of this component has risen a great deal. In the last nine years, it has increased from 12.9 to 29.8! Table 20.3 gives examples of changes to the basket in 2019.

CPI Sub-Category	Change	Comment
Bread and cereals	Added — Popcorn	This item has been added due to increased spending. Its inclusion widens the range of items in this part of the basket and, in particular, improves coverage of snack items.
Coffee, tea and cocoa	Added — Flavoured tea	Added to reflect the increased expenditure and shelf-space devoted to flavoured teas more generally.
Glassware, tableware and household utensils	Added — Bakeware — baking tray or roasting tin	Added to expand the range of kitchen equipment. It reflects a large increase in expenditure over recent years and the growing popularity in baking at home.
Non-durable household goods	Added — Washing liquid/gel	Washing liquid/gel now attracts higher expenditure than powder, reflected in the different varieties available to consumers and the increased shelf-space in stores.
Equipment for the reception and reproduction of sound and pictures	Removed — Hi-fi	Removed due to low coverage and declining consumer spend. This will be replaced by a portable speaker reflecting current trends.
Pets, related products and services	Removed — Complete dry dog food	Replaced by dog treats which attract higher consumer spending and are part of the growing popularity of pet treats more generally.
Miscellaneous printed matter, stationery and drawing materials	Removed — Envelopes	Removed from an over-covered area of the basket. Envelopes are a low weighted item as a result of the increasing use of new technology for communication.

Source: Consumer price inflation basket of goods and services: 2019, Philip Gooding, Office for National Statistics

▲ Table 20.3 Changes to the CPI basket of goods in the UK in 2019

Economics in action

ATL Thinking, Communication and Research

Research the most recent changes to the CPI basket of goods in the UK. If you were researching cultural change in the UK, what could the changes to the CPI basket over the years tell you?

Theory of knowledge

In carrying out research or investigations, physical and social scientists have to deliberately choose to include or analyse certain data from a wide range of data, and their choices inevitably affect the outcomes. For example, when economists propose that one representative item be replaced with another representative item in the CPI basket they will use data concerning household spending, but there will necessarily be some judgment involved. To what extent do you think that this could affect the reliability of the statistic?

If the CPI basket is used to generate the inflation rate on which wage increases are based, how will this truly reflect the spending patterns of different groups of people?

What are the issues involved in the measurement of inflation?

- Measuring inflation using the consumer price index has one main limitation. The basket used in any country represents the purchasing habits of a "typical" household, but this will not be applicable to all people. The purchasing habits of different people will clearly vary greatly. For example, the "basket" of a family with children will be very different from that of an elderly couple or a single person with no children. There may be variations in regional rates of inflation within a country. Although regional figures are published, the national figure is the more widely-used measure and this may not be an accurate reflection for a particular area. If the national average is used as the basis for wage negotiations or pension changes then these might not accurately reflect the price changes for a particular group. This will be harmful if the group has a higher cost of living than suggested by the national average and beneficial for those whose spending costs are less than the average.
- There may be errors in the collection of data that limit the accuracy of the final results. Because it would be utterly impossible to collect the prices of all items bought by all households in all possible locations, it is necessary to take sample items in a sample of selected cities and a sample of selected outlets. The layers of sampling are likely to lead to some degree of inaccuracy. The larger the sample, the more accurate the results will be, but this is time-consuming and very costly.
- As Table 20.3 shows, statisticians try to take into account changes in consumption habits by making changes to the basket. Items are removed or added to be more representative of the typical household's demand. However, this takes a good deal of time. Moreover, if the items in the basket are changed, then this limits the ability of analysts to make comparisons from one time period to another. This is complicated by the fact that the quality of goods changes over time. For example, when a computer company upgrades a computer to include more built-in memory, then the quality of the product improves. The price of the computer may rise to reflect the improvement. If the computer is in the typical basket, then this will feed into a higher rate of inflation, yet the product is not really the same product.
- Countries measure their rate of inflation in different ways and include different components. This can make it problematic to make international comparisons.
- Prices may change for a variety of reasons that are not sustained. For example, seasonal variations in the prices of food and volatile oil prices may lead to unusual movements in the inflation rate and can be misleading. Statisticians make some effort to reduce such

distorting effects by identifying a "core" rate of inflation that uses the information of the consumer price index but excludes food and energy prices.

- The CPI (or RPI) measures changes in consumer prices and is a very important indicator of an economy's health. However, there are other price changes which are important in judging the economic health and prospects of a country. For this reason economists also measure changes in the prices of the factors of production needed by the economy's firms. One way of doing this is through a commodity price index, which tracks changes in raw material prices. There are different types of commodity price indices. One measures changes in a weighted basket of a large number of different traded commodities. Others track a particular category of commodity, such as food commodities (eg sugar or coffee) or industrial commodities, which is further divided into metals (eg tin, copper) and non-food agricultural commodities (eg wool). Upward movements in commodity prices are signals of cost-push pressures and may be leading indicators (indicators which predict that a change will occur in the future) of inflation.

Another index used is a *producer price index*, which tracks the price of goods as they leave the factories and before distributors, wholesalers or retailers (stores) add their profit margins.

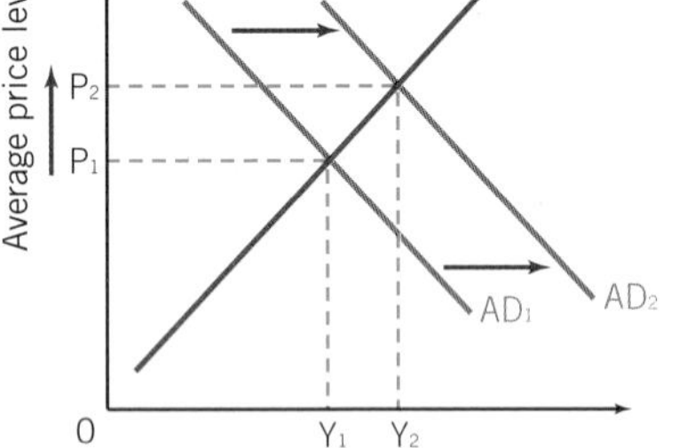

▲ Figure 20.1 Demand-pull inflation

What are the causes of inflation?

We can divide the causes of inflation into two main types: demand-pull inflation and cost-push inflation.

How does demand-pull inflation occur?

As the name suggests, demand-pull inflation occurs as a result of increasing aggregate demand in the economy. This can be seen in Figure 20.1. The increase in aggregate demand from AD_1 to AD_2 "pulls up" the average price level from P_1 to P_2.

The reasons for the increase in aggregate demand could be due to changes in any of the components of aggregate demand. For example, there could be a high level of consumer confidence, causing consumers to increase consumption; or there could be a high level of demand for a country's exports due to rising foreign incomes; or the increase might be due to an increase in government spending.

As noted in Chapter 2, there is a group of economists known as monetarists. Such economists believe that inflation is always caused by excessive growth of the money supply by the central bank.

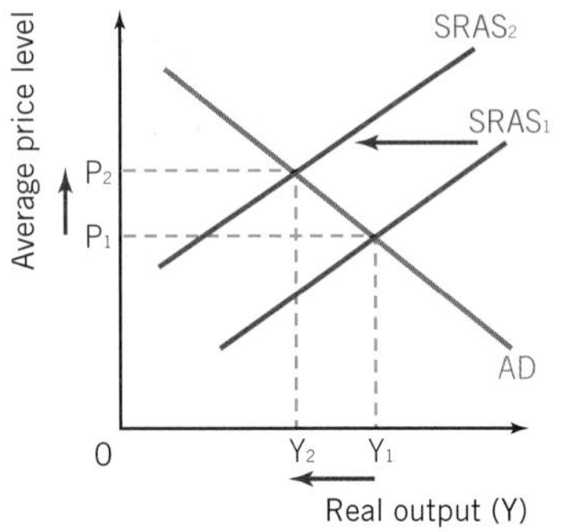

▲ Figure 20.2 Cost-push inflation

How does cost-push inflation occur?

Cost-push inflation occurs as a result of an increase in the costs of production. Cost-push inflation is illustrated in Figure 20.2. As you know, an increase in costs results in a fall in short-run aggregate supply from $SRAS_1$ to $SRAS_2$. This results in an increase in the average price level and a fall in the level of real output.

The causes of increases in costs are discussed in Chapter 16. Increases in the price level due to increases in the costs of labour may be referred to as *wage-push inflation*. Changes in the costs of domestic raw materials will increase firms' costs of production, creating cost-push pressures. Increases in the costs of imported capital, components or raw materials also increase costs of production to firms, causing *import-push inflation*. It is worth noting that a fall in the value of a country's currency can cause import-push inflation. This is because a lower exchange rate makes imported capital, components and raw materials more expensive, thereby increasing the costs of imported factors of production to the country's firms.

What happens if we have demand-pull and cost-push inflation together?

Regardless of the source of the increase in the average price level, one of the problems associated with inflation is its tendency to perpetuate itself. For example, consider what happens if there is an increase in aggregate demand due to increased wealth in the economy (perhaps due to rising house prices). Let's look at the effects in the short run as shown in Figure 20.3.

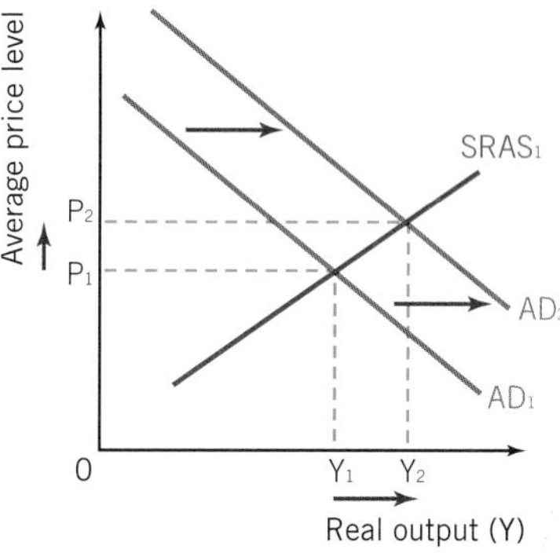

▲ Figure 20.3 Demand-pull inflation

If we assume that the economy is near full employment then the increase in aggregate demand results in an increase in demand-pull inflation as the price level rises from P_1 to P_2, as shown in movement (1) in Figure 20.4.

The diagram shows what may happen next. The higher price level means that costs of production rise. Also, because the price level increases, workers will negotiate for higher wages and this further increases the costs of production. Thus, there will be a shift in the short-run aggregate supply curve from $SRAS_1$ to $SRAS_2$ as a result of cost-push pressures. This is the movement (2) in the diagram. The cycle will not necessarily stop there. Higher wages may give households the illusion that they have more spending power and this might encourage further increases in consumption, shown as another increase in aggregate demand to AD_3 and the movement (3) in the diagram. This may be referred to as an inflationary spiral.

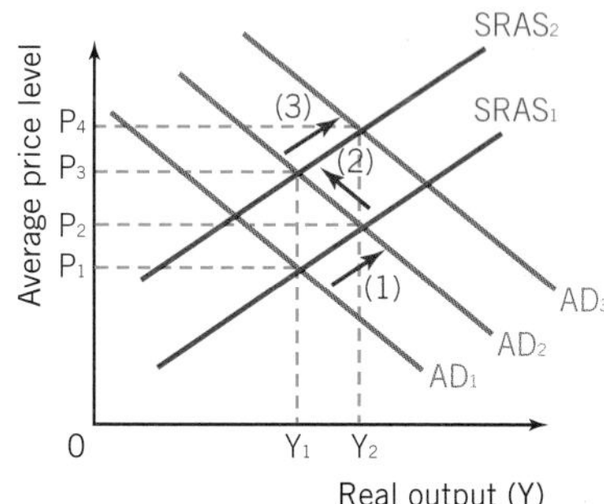

▲ Figure 20.4 An inflationary spiral

How might a government attempt to reduce inflation?

Inflation is a short-run problem and so supply-side policies to increase the long-run supply are not really suitable to cure it. Although successful supply-side policies will reduce the average price level over time, the time lag is too great for them to be an effective means of reducing inflation in the short-run.

Exercise 20.1

ATL Thinking and Communication

1. Using an AD/SRAS diagram, explain how contractionary policies could be used to reduce demand-pull inflation.
2. a) Using an AD/SRAS diagram, explain how contractionary policies could be used to reduce cost-push inflation.
   b) With reference to your diagram in 2a, explain why contractionary policies might be unpopular in an economy.

For demand-pull inflation, caused by increased aggregate demand, the solution is obvious; the government and the central bank should use contractionary fiscal and monetary policy to reduce aggregate demand. For cost-push inflation, the solution is not so obvious. Cost-push inflation is caused by rising costs of production, but policy-makers have very little control over costs of production. Therefore, as counter-intuitive as it might seem, demand-side policies are needed to fight inflation, regardless of whether this is demand-pull inflation or cost-push inflation.

There are problems associated with such contractionary policies. First of all, from a political standpoint, such policies are highly unpopular. Looking first at fiscal policy, a voting population is unlikely to be happy to accept higher taxes as it reduces disposable income and the level of consumption. A reduction in government spending will inevitably impact upon a variety of groups in the economy and this may result in less support for the government. It takes a long time for a government to bring about a change in its fiscal policy. Budgets are developed over a long period and changes need to go through lengthy legislative procedures, where there may be great opposition to any budget cuts. Therefore, there would be a long time lag involved in using contractionary fiscal policy to bring about a decrease in aggregate demand.

As far as monetary policy is concerned, higher interest rates will also harm some people in the economy, most obviously anybody who has taken a loan or mortgage. Higher interest rates mean higher loan and mortgage repayments and will therefore be unpopular. Higher interest rates may also result in less borrowing by firms, and therefore less investment, which could harm the economy in the longer run.

Furthermore, if inflation is cost-push in nature, then a higher price level is accompanied by a lower level of real GDP, and thus a higher level of unemployment. Contractionary policies will result in a fall in aggregate demand, resulting in a further fall in real GDP and possibly even higher unemployment. However, economists could argue that although this would be a very painful outcome, it would be a necessary strategy to prevent inflation from continuing to rise, since the costs of high inflation are so damaging to the economy. Since governments are less likely to make unpopular political decisions by raising taxes and/or lowering government spending, the task of fighting inflation usually falls to central banks.

Turkey's Erdogan reportedly fired his central bank chief for refusing to slash interest rates

https://markets.businessinsider.com/news/stocks/turkey-erdogan-fires-central-bank-chief-for-not-cutting-rates-2019-7-1028333541

In most industrialized countries the central bank is an independent body whose main goal is the maintenance of a low and stable rate of inflation. In theory, such central banks would be prepared to take action on monetary policy without concern for the political consequences.

Rate Cuts Needed to Defend Fed's Inflation Target

https://www.wsj.com/articles/feds-evans-rate-cuts-needed-to-defend-feds-inflation-target-11563306804

In some countries, including Poland, South Korea, Canada, England, Australia and New Zealand, the central bank sets an explicit target rate of inflation. For example, as shown in the "Did you know?" box below,

the policy of the National Bank of Poland (NBP) uses changes in interest rates (eg base rates, reserves rates or discount rates) to keep the inflation rate within the targeted range of 2.5% plus or minus 1%. Other central banks, such as the Federal Reserve in the US, have an implicit target rate of inflation. That means that there is an informal target rate that these central banks choose, rather than an officially stated one.

The movement towards independence for central banks started in many countries in the 1980s and was partially due to the tendency of governments to use monetary policy to pursue short-term political objectives. Such tendencies often resulted in unacceptably high levels of inflation as governments, keen to be popular, were reluctant to adopt policies such as higher interest rates in order to fight inflation. As a result of the greater independence for central banks and inflation targeting, many countries have successfully prevented high inflation from occurring.

Targeting inflation, whether explicitly or implicitly, is said to be beneficial as it results in a reduction in inflationary expectations. The target acts as an anchor, holding down inflationary pressure. That is, as long as people have faith in the central bank's ability to contain inflation, then they will not expect higher rates of inflation. If they do not expect higher inflation then they will not make demands for increases in wages any higher than the expected rate of inflation and this will keep the costs of labour from rising excessively. This suppresses cost-push inflationary pressure.

It is fair to say that the more independent the central bank, the more likely that price stability will be maintained. If inflation is rising or inflationary pressures are building up, then a way to bring these down would be to raise interest rates. Central banks keep very close watch on signs of inflation and are ready to raise interest rates to reduce inflationary pressure. While a government would be reluctant to do this, the central bank can make the politically unpopular decision because it does not have to worry about being re-elected!

Nowadays, monetary policy is considered to be the most effective way of managing aggregate demand in the economy and changes in interest rates are considered the best weapon in the fight against inflation. Fiscal policy is not seen to be as effective as monetary policy in battling inflation. It would be very difficult for governments to reduce their spending because of their commitments to the public. Moreover, even if governments could reduce their spending, it would take a long time for the cuts to have any effect on the price level. Thus fiscal policy is not usually used to combat inflation.

For monetarists who believe that inflation is caused by excessive growth of the money supply, then the solution is plain. The money supply should only increase by the same amount as the real increase in national output. That is, if national output is growing by 3%, then the money supply should also grow by 3%. If money supply increases by more than 3%, then the economy will face a situation where "there is too much money

Did you know?

The policy of the central bank in Poland

"Narodowy Bank Polski implements the monetary policy guidelines determined by the Monetary Policy Council. The basic goal of monetary policy is to maintain price stability.

Since 1998, NBP has been pursuing direct inflation targeting. Since the beginning of 2004, the continuous inflation target has been standing at 2.5% with a permissible fluctuation band of ± 1 percentage point. This means that every month, annual CPI should be as close as possible to 2.5%.

Narodowy Bank Polski influences the level of inflation mainly by determining the official interest rates, which define yields on monetary policy instruments. In order to influence short-term interest rates on the money market, NBP uses modern monetary policy instruments, including:

- open market operations
- credit-deposit operations
- a reserve requirement.

By using the above mentioned instruments, NBP strives to maintain such a level of interest rates in the economy, which would maximize the probability of achieving the inflation target."

chasing too few goods" and so prices will rise to ration the output. Practically speaking, although central banks can influence the level of spending in the economy through monetary policy and the changes in interest rates, it is actually very difficult for governments and/or central banks to tightly control the actual money supply in the economy.

A significant problem facing governments is the possible trade-off between their different policy objectives. They may want to fight inflation by bringing about a decrease in aggregate demand, but this might result in a higher level of unemployment. If they try to fight unemployment and increase economic output (achieve economic growth) by increasing aggregate demand, it might create inflationary pressure.

Exercise 20.2 ATL Thinking and Communication

Pakistan Raises Rate for Sixth Straight Time

Pakistan's central bank raised its key rate for a sixth straight time as inflation accelerated outside the range projected by the monetary authority and concerns about fiscal consolidation persisted.

State Bank of Pakistan, the most aggressive central bank in Asia, is seeking to restore price and economic stability. Inflation accelerated to 8.2% in February, overshooting the central bank's average forecast range of 6.5% to 7.5% for the year. The recent increase is mostly due to significant increases in the price of petrol and petroleum products, following a significant devaluation of the Pakistani rupee.

The target policy rate was raised to 10.75% from 10.25%, the State Bank of Pakistan said in a statement. The cumulative 5% rate increase since last year is also to contain the financial blow outs from Pakistan's twin current-account and budget deficits, which limited the nation's ability to repay debt and pay for much-needed imports.

Source: Adapted from *Pakistan raises rate for sixth straight time* by Faseeh Mangi 29 March 2019, www.bloomberg.com

1. Using an AD/AS diagram, explain the cause of the recent increase in the inflation rate.
2. Using an AD/AS diagram, explain how the increases in interest rates might slow the inflation rate. What would happen to the demand for cars if there was a significant increase in the level of income tax?

What is deflation?

Deflation is defined as a persistent fall in the average level of prices in the economy. There are two broad explanations for a sustained fall in the price level and economists have used these to categorize "good deflation" and "bad deflation".

How does "good" deflation work?

The first type of deflation, "good" deflation, comes about from improvements in the supply side of the economy and/or increased productivity. A simple, aggregate demand/aggregate supply diagram will illustrate that an increase in the long-run, aggregate-supply curve can result in an increase in real output and a fall in the price level. If the level of real output increases then we can assume that there is a lower level of unemployment as more workers will be needed to produce the higher level of output. This is shown in Figure 20.5. The shift from $LRAS_1$ to $LRAS_2$ can be caused, as we know, by an improvement in the quality or quantity of factors of production. When this happens, the average price level will fall from P_1 to P_2, deflation and the level of real output increases from Y_1 to Y_2, economic growth leading to increased employment. The level of the increase in employment will depend upon how *labour intensive* production is in the economy.

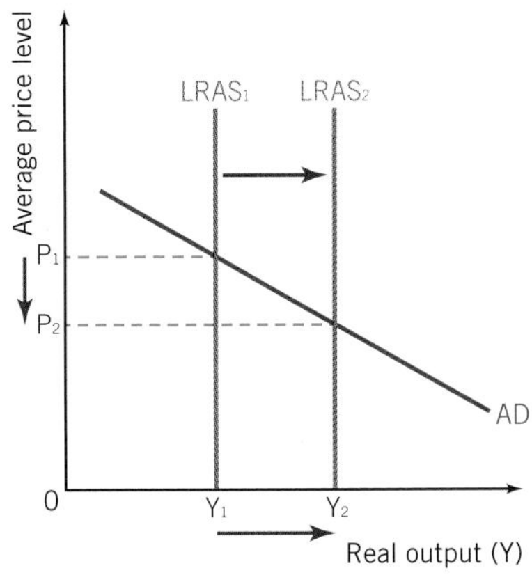

▲ Figure 20.5

How does "bad" deflation work?

The second type of deflation, "bad" deflation, finds its source in the demand side of the economy. Another simple aggregate demand/aggregate supply diagram will illustrate that a fall in aggregate demand will result in a decrease in the price level and a decrease in real output. If real output decreases then it is assumed that the level of unemployment will rise, as firms will need fewer workers if there is less demand.

Both causes of deflation result in a fall in the price level, but we might say that the first is positive because it results in an increase in real output and a fall in unemployment, while the second is negative because it results in a fall in real output and a rise in unemployment.

It is very important that you do not confuse deflation with a falling rate of inflation, which is referred to as *disinflation*. Consider Figure 20.6 which shows the inflation rate for a country for the years 1999 to 2005.

From 1999 to 2000 the inflation rate rose from 1.2% to 1.6%. From 2000 to 2001 the inflation rate fell from 1.6% to 1.3%. This means that the average level of prices rose, but at a lower rate than in the previous year. This is disinflation. In the next two years, the inflation rate continued to fall. Prices were still rising, but by a smaller and smaller amount. Moving into 2004, the country experienced deflation, where the average level of prices actually fell by 0.5%. From 2004 to 2005 the country was still in a period of deflation, where average prices fell by 0.3%.

Exercise 20.3

ATL Thinking and Communication

1. Draw, and label fully, a SRAS/AD diagram to show how "bad" deflation comes about.
2. Explain, using the diagram, how "bad" deflation is caused.
3. Draw, and label fully, a LRAS/AD diagram to show how "good" deflation comes about.
4. Explain, using the diagram, how "good" deflation is caused.

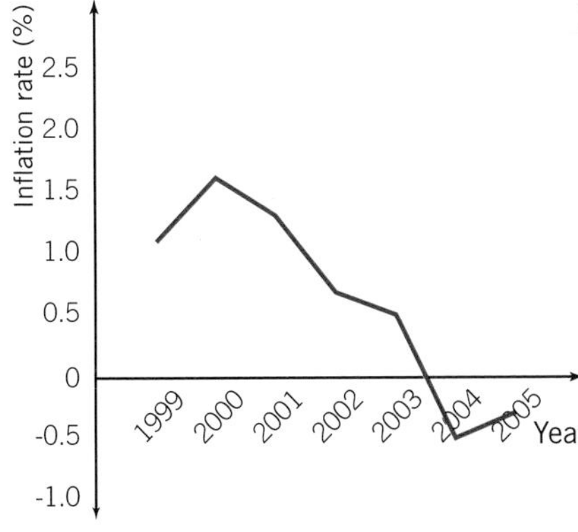

▲ Figure 20.6 Changing rates of inflation and deflation

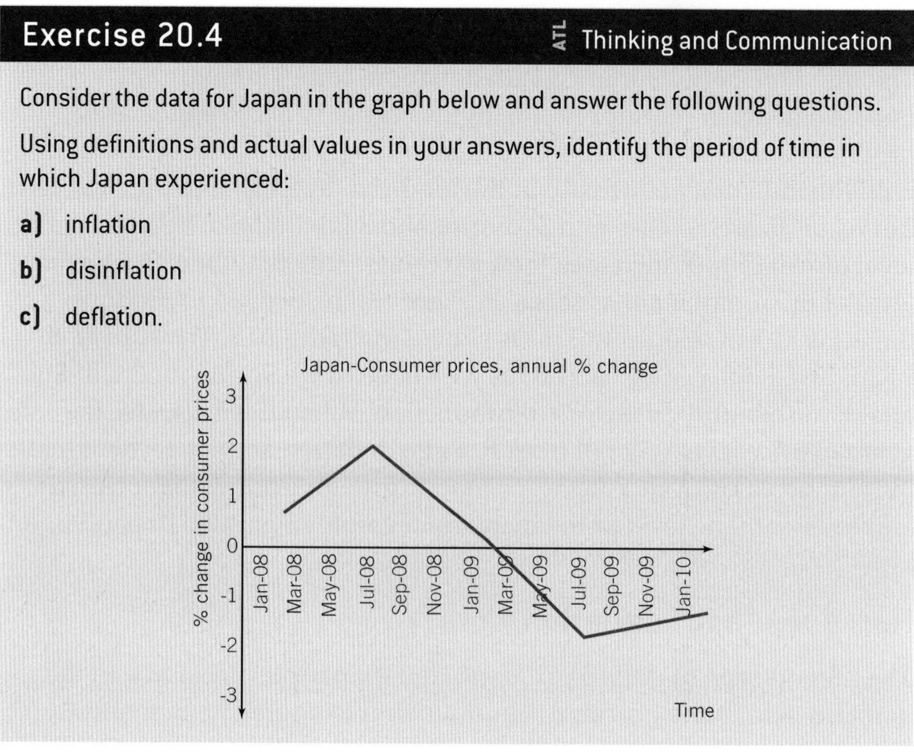

Exercise 20.4 ATL Thinking and Communication

Consider the data for Japan in the graph below and answer the following questions.

Using definitions and actual values in your answers, identify the period of time in which Japan experienced:

a) inflation

b) disinflation

c) deflation.

What are the costs of "bad" deflation?

Although, as consumers, we might be pleased to face falling prices, a significant number of problems can be associated with a sustained fall in the price level. In fact, some economists might argue that the costs of "bad" deflation are greater than the costs of inflation. The costs include:

- *Unemployment*: The biggest problem associated with deflation is unemployment. If aggregate demand is low then businesses are likely to lay off workers. This will further reduce aggregate demand. This may then lead to a *deflationary spiral*.
- *Deferred consumption*: If prices are falling, consumers will put off the purchase of any durable goods as they will want to wait until the prices drop even further. This may be referred to as deferred consumption. This can lead to a fall in aggregate demand and a *deflationary spiral*.
- *Falling consumer confidence/uncertainty*: If households become pessimistic, or uncertain, about the economic future, then consumer confidence will fall. Low consumer confidence is likely to further depress aggregate demand. Thus, a *deflationary spiral* may occur.
- *Effect on investment*: When there is deflation, businesses make less profit, or make losses. This may lead them to lay off workers. Furthermore, business confidence is likely to be low and this is likely to result in reduced investment. This has negative implications for future economic growth.

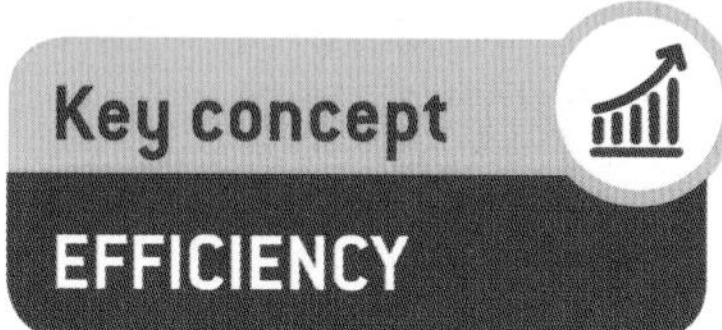

- *Costs to debtors*: Anyone who has taken a loan (this includes all homeowners who have taken a mortgage to buy their home) suffers as a result of deflation, because the value of their debt rises as a result of deflation. If profits are low, this may make it too difficult for businesses to pay back their loans and there may be many *bankruptcies*. This will further worsen business confidence.
- *Policy ineffectiveness*: Deflation makes the use of monetary policy ineffective. (See Chapter 17 for detail on monetary policy.) The very low or negative interest rates associated with deflation make expansionary monetary policy ineffective, since it is not possible to reduce interest rates substantially to increase aggregate demand.

Exercise 20.5

ATL Thinking and Communication

Read the article below and then answer the following questions:

a) Explain the difference between deflation and disinflation referred to in paragraph 1.

b) Identify and explain the advantages of deflation that are mentioned in the article.

c) Identify and explain, using an AD/AS diagram, the disadvantages of deflation that are mentioned in the article.

Deflation won't impact consumers if short term, say analysts

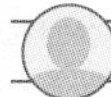
By Julia Chan and Yiswaree Palansamy, 1st March 2019

Malaysia is in a state of disinflation, and not deflation, contrary to reports stating otherwise, says economist James Alin from University Malaysia Sabah (UMS). The UMS School of Business and Economics lecturer said that the consumer price index (CPI), an indicator for inflation, has decreased but not gone into the negative as of January, 2019. "So actually we are not in deflation yet – just disinflation. The last time the country was in deflation was four years ago," he said.

He argues though that deflation has some positives, "Decreases in the consumer prices index can be a good thing in the short run, because prices of goods and services we consume daily are falling. In other words, our disposable income increases. Prices going up and down is an indication that the markets mechanism is working rather well," he said.

However, he also contended that the change in prices will not affect the average consumer by much. "Actually 45 percent of goods listed are non-durable and perishable items, one can buy more when it is cheaper but is it possible to stock? Most of those are once-in-a-while purchases. You don't buy clothing every day just because it's cheaper, unless you are rich and addicted to shopping. As an individual, they can only consume roughly the same amount of these items categorised in the CPI whether it is more expensive or cheaper," he said naming things like food, furniture, water consumption and property. So changes are minimal in impact for consumers. For high-end consumers, it may be of more impact," he said.

Alin said that the negative aspect of deflation is when the CPI hits and remains at negative rates over a long period of time, low prices of goods and services may cause small and medium-size firms to go out of business. "This is where the impact will be felt. If a person is selling things at low prices, he may not be able to sustain the business, and this will result in laying off employees or shutting down. Prolonged deflation results in impending recession – when economic growth is negative for two consecutive quarters of a year – and deflation will have worse effects compared to inflation, because interest rates can only be lowered to zero," he said.

"So it is a fine balance – too high prices and people suffer, too low and companies and employees suffer. It's a tough balance," he said.

Source: Adapted from *Deflation won't impact consumers if short term, say analysts,* by Julia Chan and Yiswaree Palansamy, 1st March 2019, www.malaymail.com

Higher Level

How do you create a weighted price index to calculate inflation?

We already know from earlier in this chapter that there are different types of price indices used to measure inflation, such as commodity price indices and consumer price indices. A weighted price index takes a "basket" of products and the products are then given a different weight (or importance), based upon the relative amounts that people spend on them.

Let us use a simple consumer price index to explain how this works. The table below shows a hypothetical, simplified basket of goods which might be bought by typical consumers in an economy and the price indices for two years:

Category	**Index for year X**	**Index for year (X + 1)**
Housing	120	130
Foodstuffs	105	105
Travel	120	125
Clothing	120	110
Entertainment	125	130
Average index	**590/5 = 118**	**600/5 = 120**

▲ **Table 20.4** Unweighted price index information for year X and year (X + 1)

In table 20.4 consumer expenditure has been split into five categories. The average price level for each year is shown by taking the price indices for each category of expenditure, totalling them, and then dividing by the number of categories. We see that over the two years the average index increases from 118 to 120. This means that we can work out the inflation rate by using the following equation:

$$\text{Inflation rate} = \frac{\text{Index for }(X + 1) - \text{Index for }X}{\text{Index for }X} \times 100$$

In our case, this gives $\frac{120 - 118}{118} \times 100 = \frac{2}{118} \times 100 = 1.69\%$

However, this is a very simplistic and inaccurate measure since it gives all of the categories an equal weighting, so a fall in the price of clothing has an equal and opposite effect to the increase in the price of housing. This is obviously not accurate, since it is highly likely that an increase in the cost of housing would have a greater impact on people's incomes than the fall in price of clothing, as people spend much more on housing per month than they do on clothing.

This is why weights are used to calculate price indices. They stress the relative importance of each category of goods. In the case of consumer price indices the weighting is based upon the relative expenditure on each category. A set of weighted figures are shown below in table 20.5.

Category	Index for year X	Weight	Index for year X times weight	Index for year (X + 1)	Weight	Index for year (X + 1) times weight
Housing	120	0.4	48	130	0.4	52
Foodstuffs	105	0.2	21	105	0.2	21
Travel	120	0.2	24	125	0.2	25
Clothing	120	0.1	12	110	0.1	11
Entertainment	125	0.1	12.5	130	0.1	13
Totals		**1.0**	**117.5**		**1.0**	**122**

▲ **Table 20.5** Weighted price index information for year X and year (X + 1)

In table 20.5 we have the same price index figures as in our earlier example, but now there are weights to represent relative expenditure. Consumers spend 40% of their income on housing and so it is given a weight of 0.4. In the same way, they only spend 10% of their income on clothing and so the weight (importance) of clothing in the weighted consumer price index is only a quarter of the weight of housing expenditure. The total of all the weights is 1.0.

The index for year X is calculated by multiplying the index for each category by its weight and then adding the individual totals, thus giving 117.5. The index for year (X + 1) is calculated in the same way, with an outcome of 122.

We can then work out the inflation rate by using the same equation as earlier:

$$\text{Inflation rate} = \frac{\text{Index for (X + 1)} - \text{Index for X}}{\text{Index for X}} \times 100$$

$$\text{This now gives us } \frac{122 - 117.5}{117.5} \times 100 = \frac{4.5}{117.5} \times 100 = 3.83\%$$

As we can see, the weighted inflation rate is significantly larger than the unweighted rate – 3.83% as opposed to 1.69%. This is because the increase in the price of housing, the most important expenditure, is given its proper importance and is not cancelled out by the fall in the price of less important expenditures.

Note

These are the types of questions you might see in HL Paper 3.

Exercise 20.6 — ATL Thinking and Communication

The price index figures for country X for two years are shown below:

Category	2022	2023
Housing	110	120
Transport	106	110
Foodstuffs	120	120
Entertainment	110	100
Clothing	105	105

Base year = 2019

1. Calculate the average index for each year.
2. Calculate the unweighted inflation rate for 2022/23.

The expenditure patterns of the population of the country are surveyed and it is discovered that the average household spends 35% of its income on housing, 25% on transport, 15% on foodstuffs, 15% on entertainment and 10% on clothing.

3. Explain, with the help of the figures above, the relative importance of the weighting.
4. Assuming that consumer expenditure patterns do not change over the period 2022/23, construct a table showing the weighted indices for 2022 and 2023.
5. Calculate the weighted inflation rate for 2022/23.
6. Explain the differences between the inflation rates that you have calculated in 2 and 5.

Higher Level

Is there a trade-off between inflation and unemployment?

Having looked at unemployment in the previous chapter, we may now consider the relationship between the two macroeconomic problems of unemployment and inflation.

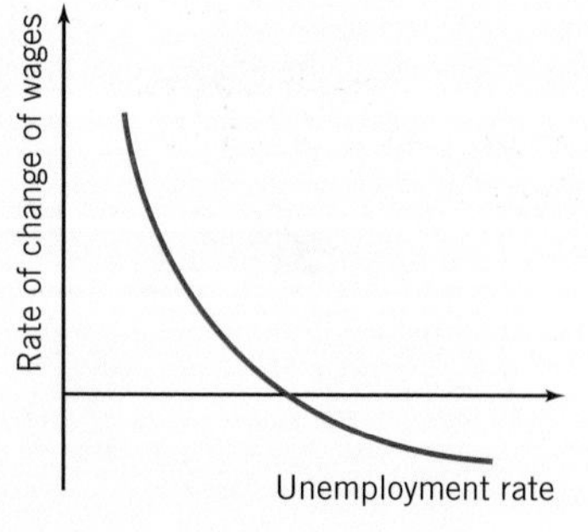

▲ Figure 20.7 The original Phillips curve

What is the original Phillips curve?

In 1958, Alban Williams Phillips, a New Zealand-born economist working at the London School of Economics, published a significant work in which he presented his argument that there was an inverse relationship between the rate of change of money wages (ie wages not adjusted for inflation) in the economy and the rate of unemployment as shown in Figure 20.7. His observation was based on his study of UK data from 1861 to 1913.

The explanation for this was that, if there was a low level of unemployment, firms would have to pay higher wages to attract labour. If unemployment was high then unemployed workers would be competing with each other to obtain available jobs, so that wages offered could be relatively low. During an economic expansion, when more output is demanded and more workers are needed, wages rise more quickly than they would if there was a contraction in activity and lower levels of demand. The rate of change of money wages could actually become negative, ie wages could fall at high levels of unemployment because workers would be willing to accept the lower wages rather than remain unemployed.

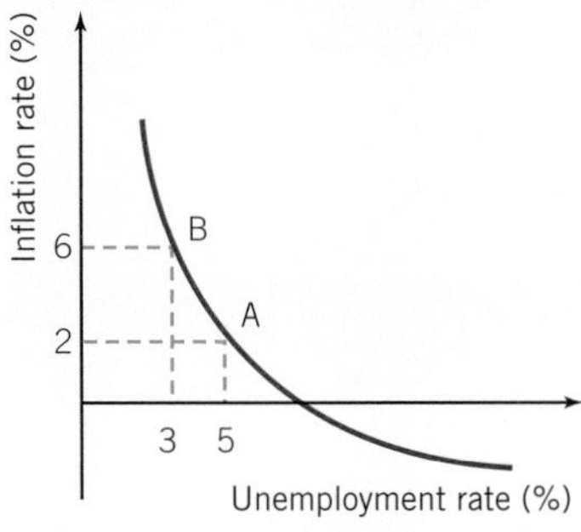

▲ **Figure 20.8** The Phillips curve as it is usually drawn

Other economists adapted the relationship established by Phillips and applied it to data from other countries to establish the pattern that we now refer to as the Phillips curve. This shows the inverse relationship between the inflation rate (rather than the change in money wages) and the unemployment rate of an economy as shown in Figure 20.8. This is due to the fact that, since wages make up a large proportion of firms' costs, changes in wages feed directly through to changes in the price level.

Another way to express this relationship is to say that there is a "trade-off" between inflation and unemployment. For example, as shown in Figure 20.8, an unemployment rate of 5% might be accompanied by an inflation rate of 2%. If unemployment were to fall to 3%, then inflation would rise to 6%. As one variable decreases, the other increases. The implication of this trade-off for government objectives is clear. If the main objective of a government is to reduce the rate of unemployment this can be done, but at the expense of a higher rate of inflation. Similarly, if inflation is perceived to be too high then it can be lowered by allowing the unemployment rate to increase. The trade-off can also be explained using aggregate demand/aggregate supply analysis, as shown in Figure 20.9.

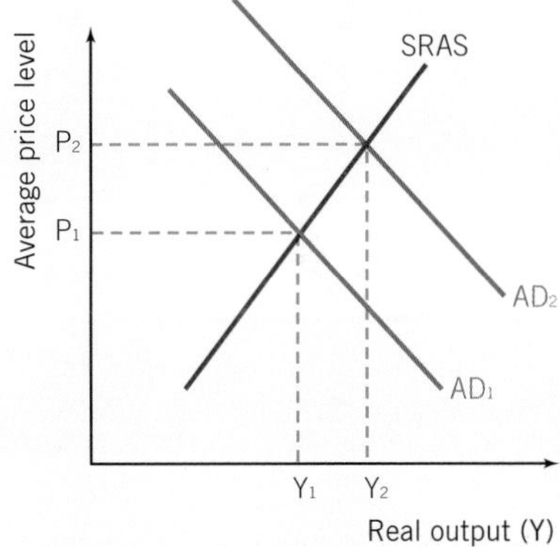

▲ **Figure 20.9** Phillips curve relationship through AD/AS analysis

The economy is initially in equilibrium at Y_1, at a price level of P_1. If the government feels there is too much unemployment at this point, then it might use Keynesian demand management techniques to bring about an increase in AD, from AD_1 to AD_2. This will result in an increase in output, which is produced by hiring more workers, so unemployment is assumed to fall. However, there is also a higher price level, that is, higher inflation. In agreement with the Phillips curve, a decrease in unemployment occurs at a cost of higher inflation. This would be like the movement from A to B in Figure 20.8.

This existence of a trade-off between inflation and unemployment was supported by data up to the 1970s. From this time on, however, evidence about inflation and unemployment began to suggest that the relationship shown by the Phillips curve was no longer valid, as both inflation and unemployment rose in many economies. The combination of high inflation and high levels of unemployment is known as stagflation. According to the Phillips curve, the two problems should not worsen simultaneously and so the model came under attack.

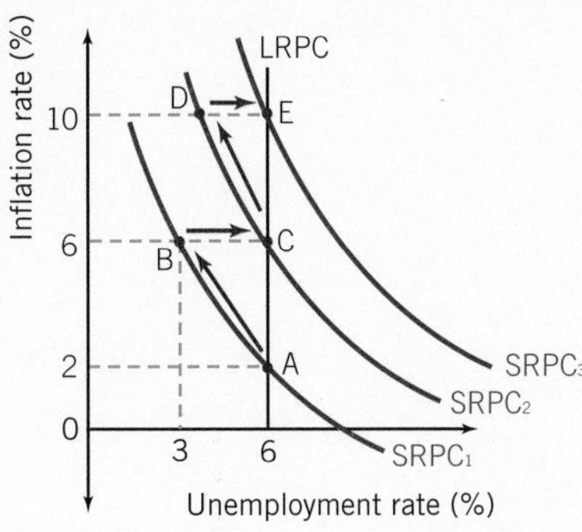

▲ **Figure 20.10** The long-run Phillips curve

What is the long-run Phillips curve?

It was the monetarist economists led by Milton Friedman who were the biggest critics of the original Phillips curve. According to their analysis there is no trade-off between inflation and unemployment. This is consistent with the explanation of the new classical long-run aggregate supply provided in Chapter 15. Recall that according to the new classical economists, the economy will automatically tend towards its long-run equilibrium at the full employment level of output.

Figure 20.10 can be used to explain this adaptation of the Phillips curve model. Assume that the economy is in long-run equilibrium at point A on $SRPC_1$. The labour market is also in equilibrium so that the only unemployment that exists is the natural unemployment of 6%. The inflation rate is 2%. People expect inflation to be 2% and negotiate any pay increases based on this expected rate. Now, consider what would happen if the government decided that they wanted to reduce unemployment and so adopted an expansionary demand-side policy – for example, increasing government expenditure. Aggregate demand would increase and this, in turn, would lead to an increase in the demand for labour and so an increase in wage levels. However, at the same time, there would be an increase in the inflation rate, in this case to 6%.

In the short run there would be a fall in unemployment as workers who had not been prepared to take jobs at existing wage levels before are now attracted by what they think are higher wages and the economy moves from A to B on the diagram. However, these are higher nominal wages and real wages have not risen. In this case, we would say that the workers have suffered from money illusion. When the workers realize that their real wages have not risen, they then leave the jobs and unemployment goes back to the natural rate, but now at an inflation rate of 6%.

The economy does not return to point A. Now that inflation is running at 6%, people will expect prices to continue to rise at 6% and negotiate an equivalent increase in wages, so the economy will be at point C on the diagram, on a new short-run Phillips curve, $SRPC_2$. Unemployment has returned to its natural rate at a higher rate of inflation. Any attempt to use demand management again to reduce the unemployment below this natural rate will only result in higher inflation (C to D to E) and a move to another short-run Phillips curve, $SRPC_3$.

The natural rate of unemployment is the unemployment rate that is consistent with a stable rate of inflation. As long as governments do not use expansionary policies, inflation will not accelerate at the natural rate of unemployment. However, if expansionary policies are used, then inflation will accelerate.

The long-run Phillips curve is vertical at the natural rate of unemployment (NRU). At any given point in time, there may be a short run trade-off between inflation and unemployment, but the economy will always return to unemployment at the natural rate. Governments cannot reduce this rate by using demand management policies. The natural rate of unemployment is the unemployment that occurs when the economy is at full employment and the labour market is in equilibrium.

Of course this is not to say that the long-run unemployment rate cannot be reduced at all! The key point here is that supply-side policies, not demand management policies, are the solution for reducing the natural rate of unemployment. Supply-side policies will reduce the natural rate of unemployment and shift the long-run Phillips curve to the left from $LRPC_1$ to $LRPC_2$ as shown in Figure 20.11. This would be the equivalent of a rightward shift in the long-run aggregate supply curve or an outwards shift in a country's production possibilities curve.

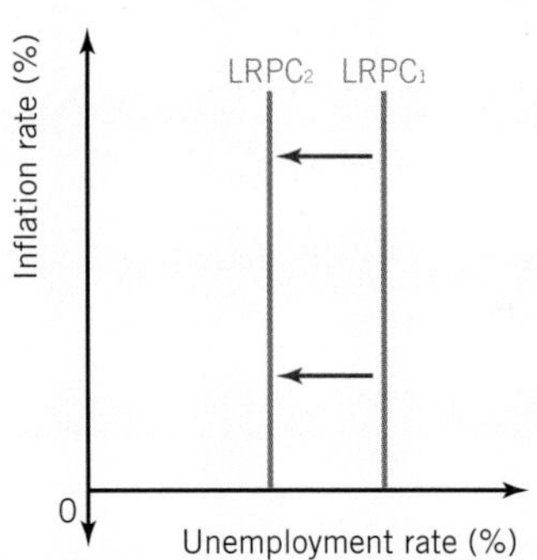

▲ **Figure 20.11** Supply-side policies can reduce the NRU

This confirms conclusions drawn about unemployment at the end of Chapter 19. Demand-side policies may be appropriate for reducing cyclical demand-deficient unemployment, but not for reducing the frictional, seasonal and structural unemployment that make up the natural unemployment.

The OECD itself admits that the natural rate of unemployment "can only be estimated with uncertainty". Nonetheless, estimates of the NRU are made. What is evident is that it varies considerably over time and between countries.

Differences between countries are due to a number of factors, including the availability of unemployment benefits, trade union power, the extent of labour market regulations and wage-setting practices by firms. Countries with more benefits and considerable regulation of labour markets tend to have a higher NRU. When organizations such as the OECD recommend that countries make labour market reforms to reduce unemployment, they are usually referring to measures that will reduce the natural rate.

EXAMINATION QUESTIONS

Paper 1, part (a) questions

1. Explain the concept of demand-pull inflation. [10 marks]
2. Explain the concept of cost-push inflation. [10 marks]
3. Explain the monetarist explanation of inflation. [10 marks]
4. Explain **three** consequences of inflation. [10 marks]
5. Explain **three** consequences of deflation. [10 marks]
6. Explain **three** problems involved in the measurement of inflation. [10 marks]

HL Explain why there may be a trade-off between inflation and unemployment in the short run. [10 marks]

Paper 1, part (b) questions

1. Using real-word examples, evaluate methods that might be used to reduce inflation. [15 marks]
2. Using real-word examples, discuss the extent to which demand-side policies are effective in reducing inflation. [15 marks]
3. **HL only** Using real-word examples, discuss the Phillips curve in terms of the trade-off between inflation and unemployment. [15 marks]
4. Using real-world examples, discuss the potential conflict between low inflation and low unemployment. [15 marks]

Paper 2: 2-mark and 4-mark questions

Consider the following data and answer the questions:

JAPAN	2014	2015	2016	2017	2018
Consumer price index (% change from previous year)	2.76	0.79	−0.12	0.47	0.98
Unemployment rate (% of labour force)	3.59	3.38	3.12	2.81	2.44

UNITED STATES	2014	2015	2016	2017	2018
Consumer price index (% change from previous year)	1.62	0.12	1.26	2.13	2.44
Unemployment rate (% of labour force)	6.17	5.29	4.87	4.35	3.90

Note: Labour market data are subject to differences in definitions across countries.

Source: OECD Data, March 2019, data.oecd.org

2-mark questions

Define the following terms, indicated in bold in the data:

a) Consumer price index [2 marks]

b) Unemployment rate [2 marks]

4-mark questions

1. With reference to the data, explain why we can say that Japan experienced deflation and disinflation between 2014 and 2016. [4 marks]
2. With reference to the data, explain the trends in inflation and unemployment in the United States, between 2015 and 2018. [4 marks]

21 MACROECONOMIC OBJECTIVES: ECONOMIC GROWTH

REAL-WORLD ISSUE:

Why does economic activity vary over time and why does this matter? How do governments manage the economy and how effective are their policies?

By the end of this chapter, you should be able to:

- → Define economic growth
- → Use a PPC curve to explain how a movement from a point inside a PPC curve to a point on a PPC curve illustrates economic growth
- → Explain the role of AD in creating economic growth
- → Use a PPC curve to explain how an outwards shift in a PPC curve illustrates economic growth
- → Use an LRAS diagram to explain how an outwards shift in the LRAS curve illustrates growth
- → Calculate the rate of economic growth from a set of data
- → Evaluate the possible consequences of economic growth.

We have now discussed two of a country's main macroeconomic objectives – low unemployment and the maintenance of a low and stable rate of inflation. We now move onto a third goal – economic growth. Very importantly, economic growth can help to achieve the first two goals.

We have already mentioned the definition of economic growth – an increase in real GDP over time. Be sure that you can remember the difference between real GDP and nominal GDP discussed in Chapter 13.

Rates of economic growth vary over time and from country to country. As we know, economies face periodic fluctuations in economic activity and growth rates, known as the business cycle. Emerging economies, such as China and India, have experienced rapid economic growth, while more developed countries have experienced more moderate rates of growth. This is illustrated in Figure 21.1.

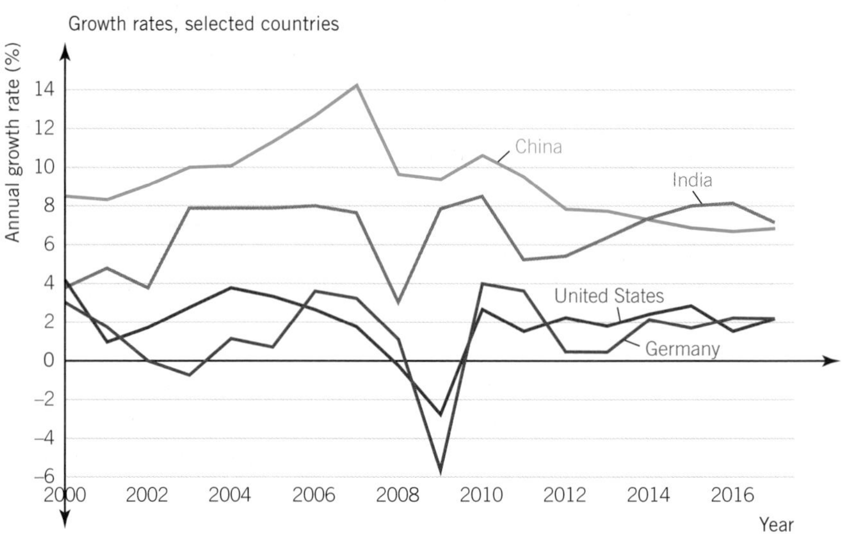

▲ **Figure 21.1** A comparison of different growth rates

Source: Word Development indicators, The World Bank

How can we use diagrams to illustrate growth?

It may be argued that demand-side factors can bring about short-term economic growth. We can illustrate this using a combination of an AD/AS model with a PPC model.

Consider an economy which is operating with a deflationary gap, as shown in Figure 21.2 (a) below. This would be equivalent to the economy operating at a point "a" within the PPC, as in Figure 21.2 (b).

In this case, the economy's resources are not being used to the fullest extent possible. That is, there is underemployment or unemployment of resources/factors of production.

If there were to be an increase in aggregate demand from AD_1 to AD_2, then the deflationary gap could be removed and there would be an increase in real output from Y_1 to Y_2 in Figure 21.3 (a). This would be an equivalent to a movement from "a" to "b" in Figure 21.3 (b). The increase in real output is an increase in real GDP, so there has been economic growth.

The increase in aggregate demand has brought about the need to employ those underemployed or unemployed resources, moving the economy towards the full employment of resources. In this case, economic growth comes about by increasing the employment of the factors of production.

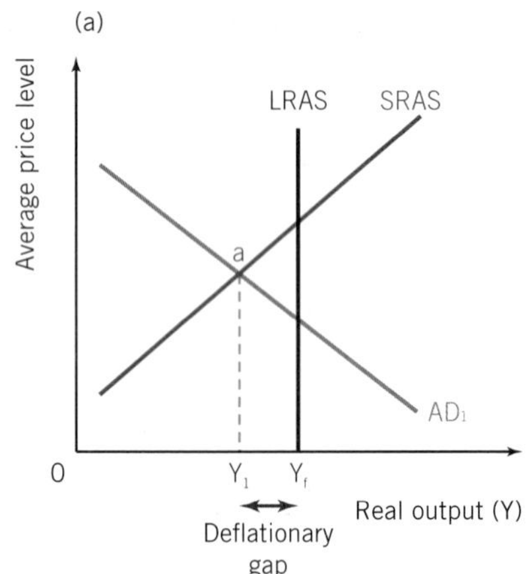

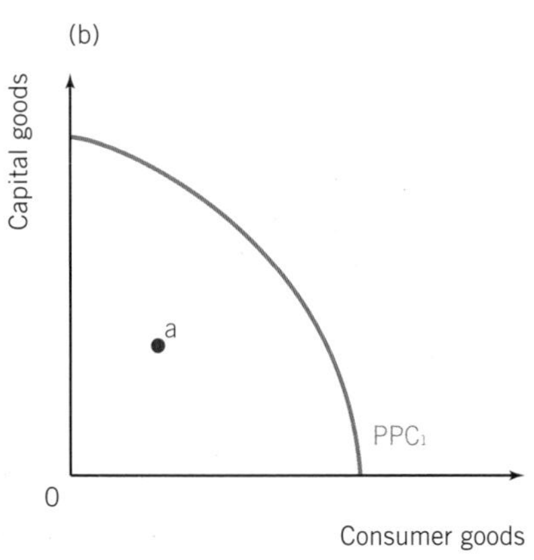

▲ **Figure 21.2** A deflationary gap/output gap

Note that in Figure 21.3 (b), point "b" is not on the PPC but just short of it. This is because an economy will never fully employ all resources to the fullest extent possible. As we discussed in Chapters 19 and 20, there will always be some unemployment in the form of natural unemployment. This is why the LRAS curve is not exactly the same as the PPC in terms of representing potential output.

The economic growth illustrated above shows an economy making better use of its existing resources and increasing GDP by moving towards the full employment level of output (at LRAS) and the potential output (on a PPC). Economic growth can also occur in the long term as a result of increasing the full employment level of output or potential output. This is shown in Figure 21.4.

In this case there is an increase in GDP in Figure 21.4 (a) as a result of the shift in the LRAS curve. The equivalent change is shown as an outward shift in the PPC in Figure 21.4 (b).

As you will recall from Chapter 15, this comes about as a result of an increase in the quantity or an increase in the quality (productivity) of an economy's factors of production and advances in technology, and may come about through market forces or government, supply-side policies – either interventionist or market-based.

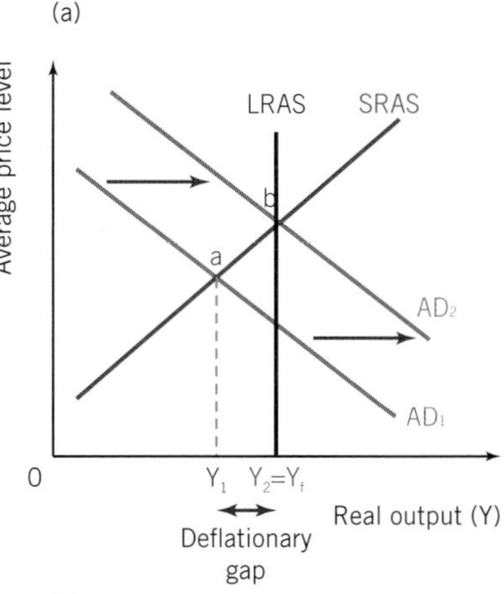

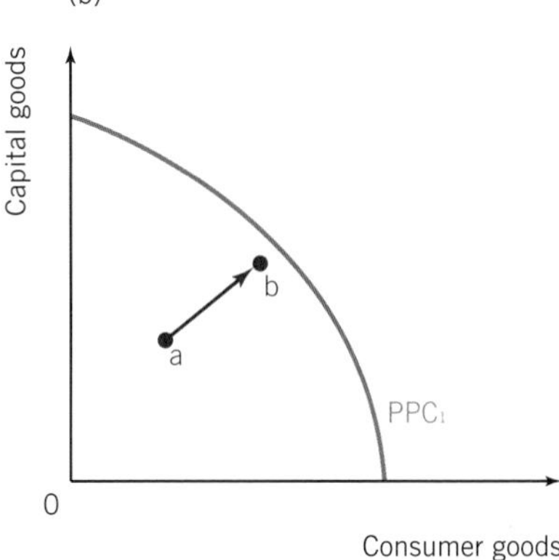

▲ Figure 21.3 Economic growth to remove a deflationary gap/output gap

How do we sum this up?

Deflationary gaps, or output gaps, may be the result of a fall in economic growth or negative economic growth in the short run and may be solved using demand management (expansionary fiscal and monetary) policies. Such policies may narrow the fluctuations in economic activity shown on a business cycle diagram.

The trend growth line shown on a business cycle diagram is influenced by the supply-side policies that generate long-term economic growth. You should be able to evaluate the consequences of both demand- and supply-side policies, in terms of their likely success in achieving their goals, their appropriateness in different situations, the consequences for different stakeholders and the possible trade-offs (opportunity costs) that occur in the pursuit of different goals.

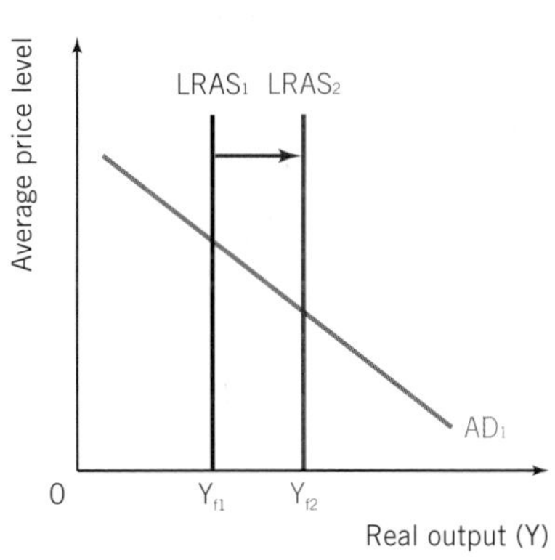

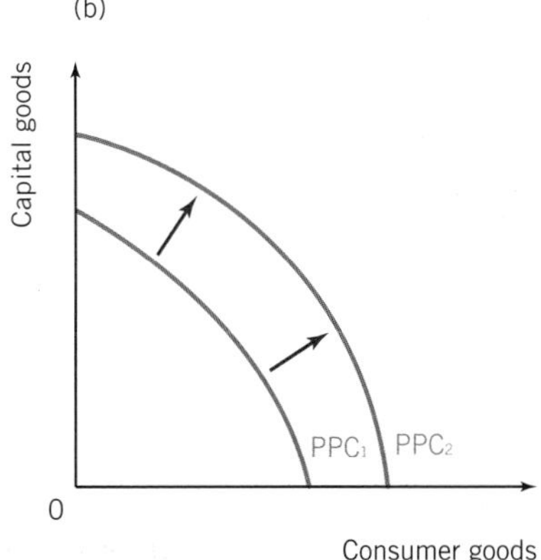

▲ Figure 21.4 Economic growth through an increase in potential output

How do we measure economic growth?

For your exams you may be asked to calculate the rate of economic growth from a set of data.

The formula for the rate of growth is:

$$\text{Growth rate} = \frac{(\text{Real GDP in year 2} - \text{Real GDP in year 1})}{\text{Real GDP in year 1}} \times 100$$

Exercise 21.1
ATL Thinking and Communication

Read the table below relating to Canada:

Year	Real GDP (millions of $)
2015	1,697,000
2016	1,721,000
2017	1,774,000

Source: The World Factbook, www.cia.gov

Calculate the economic growth rate:

a) from 2015 to 2016

b) from 2016 to 2017.

Here is a worked example using some data from Canada:

Calculation of economic growth rate

Year	Real GDP (millions of Canadian $, base year 2002)	Growth rate
2006	1,283,033	
2007	1,311,260	$\frac{(1{,}311{,}260 - 1{,}283{,}033)}{1{,}283{,}033} \times 100 = 2.2\%$
2008	1,318,054	$\frac{(1{,}318{,}054 - 1{,}311{,}260)}{1{,}311{,}260} \times 100 = 0.51\%$
2009	1,285,604	$\frac{(1{,}285{,}604 - 1{,}318{,}054)}{1{,}318{,}054} \times 100 = -2.46\%$

Source: Statistics Canada, www.statscan.gc.ca

What are the consequences of economic growth?

As we know, economic growth is a policy objective of all governments. This is due to the huge benefits that economic growth can bring to an economy. However, there are also significant negative consequences.

So, what are the positive consequences of economic growth?

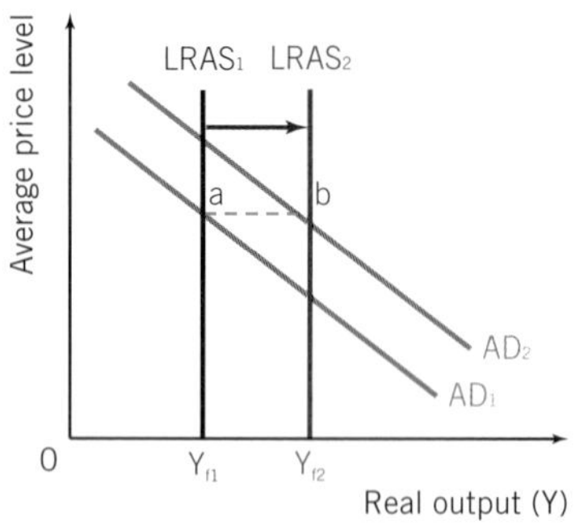

▲ Figure 21.5 Non-inflationary growth

It may be assumed that, on the whole, in the absence of periodic recessions, aggregate demand tends to increase steadily as population size and incomes grow. Without supply-side improvements to shift out the LRAS, aggregate demand would increase more than aggregate supply and there would be inflation. You should be able to draw a diagram to illustrate this. However, when economic growth occurs, pushing out the aggregate supply curve, economies can experience non-inflationary growth as shown in Figure 21.5.

The movement from AD_1 to AD_2 in Figure 21.5 indicates "normal" increases in aggregate demand due to growing populations and rising incomes. As long as the economy also makes improvements on the supply side to shift out the LRAS, then the GDP will increase, without any upward pressure on the price level, from a to b. Thus, the movement from Y_1 to Y_2 represents non-inflationary growth. It may be assumed that more labour will be needed to produce the higher level of output, so unemployment should also fall. Therefore, supply-side policies and the growth that they bring about result in lower unemployment and downward pressure on the price level.

Since economic growth is an increase in national output this is equivalent to an increase in national income. If GDP per capita also increases, which depends on population growth, then the income of the average person will increase and it would be normal to assume that this may be equated with higher living standards. Indeed, if you compare your living standards with those of your parents and grandparents when they were your age, you are likely to see a great many ways in which your material living standards have improved.

Economic growth has not only been achieved by great leaps in technology, but has contributed to great leaps in technology, leading to advancements in areas such as medicine, household appliances, computers, audio-visual equipment, transportation and entertainment, to name a few. Such advancements have the possibility of making life easier and more pleasurable, contributing to higher living standards.

Depending on the nature of a country's tax system, higher incomes are likely to lead to greater tax revenues, and this may make it possible for a government to spend more on merit goods and public goods, thereby further improving living standards. Tax systems can also redistribute income and reduce income inequalities.

We can also look at the international context. Economic growth that comes about as a result of higher productivity may also bring about an improvement in the competitiveness of a country's exports, leading to further increases in aggregate demand. However, it must also be recognized that higher national income also increases the demand for imports, so the final impact on net exports will depend on a great many factors. Nevertheless, higher economic growth certainly affects the amount of trade that an economy engages in and can have a very positive impact on living standards.

There is compelling argument that, as national incomes rises, so do levels of education and human capital and, with it, greater demands for freedoms and democracy. As Benjamin Friedman writes in his book *The Moral Consequences of Economic Growth*, "Our conventional thinking about economic growth fails to reflect the breadth of what growth, or its absence, means for a society. Growth is valuable, not only for material improvements, but also for how it affects our social attitudes and our political institutions, in other words, our society's moral character".

So, what are the negative consequences of economic growth?

It is quite possible that the drive for economic growth and higher incomes results in a poorer standard of living for individuals. Higher income may come about by sacrificing leisure time and neglect of personal relationships, which would not mean better living standards. It might also be that the more people earn the more goods and services they want and are therefore never satisfied. The resulting preoccupation with greater and greater material wants might make people less happy. Recall from Chapter 13 the international indicators which measure happiness and well-being; these are not always directly related to national income.

Economic growth involves structural change in an economy. Typically, economies move from having a larger share of output being generated from the primary sector, to a larger share from the secondary sector, to a larger share being generated from the tertiary sector. And even within the sectors

Economics in action

ATL Thinking, Communication and Research

Interview ten people older than you and try to identify ways in which your standard of living may be different from theirs were when they were your age.

The wealth gap has widened despite record economic growth

https://nypost.com/2019/07/01/why-the-wealth-gap-has-grown-despite-record-economic-growth/

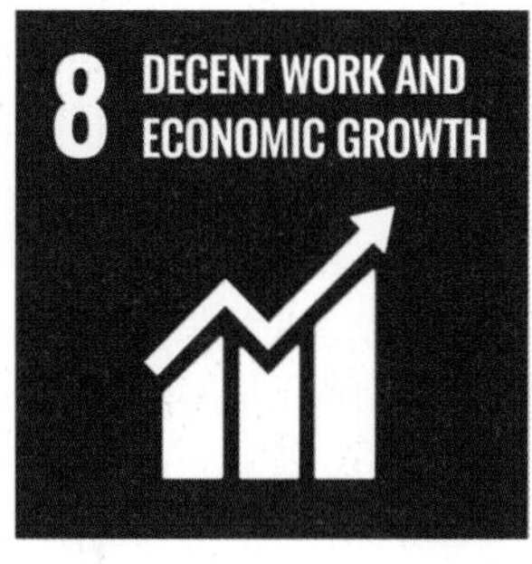

there will be changes as a result of economic growth. As these structural changes within an economy occur, the adjustments are likely to result in structural unemployment which means that not everyone benefits from the economic growth to the same extent. Technology and globalisation are contributing to a different type of structural change in economies. Both the ability of firms to relocate their production to lower-cost countries and advances in technology are reducing demand for labour in many advanced countries. The countries may be achieving economic growth, but the benefits of that growth are not being shared equitably. Thus, the goal of economic growth comes into conflict with the goal of equity.

Key concept

EQUITY

The need to ensure that the benefits of economic growth are shared more equitably is highlighted in the Goal 8 of the Sustainable Development Goals, which aims to "Promote inclusive and sustainable economic growth, employment and decent work for all" (Sustainable Development Goals, Goal 8). Growing inequalities are a topic that we look at in more detail in Chapter 22.

Key concept

SUSTAINABILITY

The catastrophic consequences of human activity on the environment is something we looked at in Chapter 9. Rapid economic growth results in higher emissions of greenhouse gases. Higher national income results in higher and higher levels of waste. Producing a higher level of output also involves the depletion of non-renewable resources. At projected rates of population growth, the "equivalent of three planets could be required to produce the natural resources needed to sustain current lifestyles" (Sustainable Development Goals, Goal 12). Thus, the goal of economic growth comes into direct conflict with the goal of sustainable economic development.

EXAMINATION QUESTIONS

Paper 1, part (a) questions

1. Explain how economic growth may bring about an increase in potential output. [10 marks]
2. Explain how investment may result in economic growth. [10 marks]

Paper 1, part (b) questions

1. Using real-world examples, discuss the possible consequences of economic growth. [15 marks]

Paper 2: 4-mark questions

Asian economic growth...

Developing countries in Asia, like Vietnam, are seeing an upturn in investment from many parts of the world, especially China. China's foreign direct investment in new projects such as renewable energy, textile factories and property in the region nearly tripled, while investment by the U.S. jumped by nearly three-quarters.

Source: Adapted from *Asian economic growth hurt by US-China trade tensions*, April 2 2019, www.marketwatch.com

1. Using an AD/AS diagram, explain how China's foreign direct investment may lead to economic growth. [4 marks]
2. Using a production possibilities curve, explain how China's foreign direct investment may lead to economic growth. [4 marks]

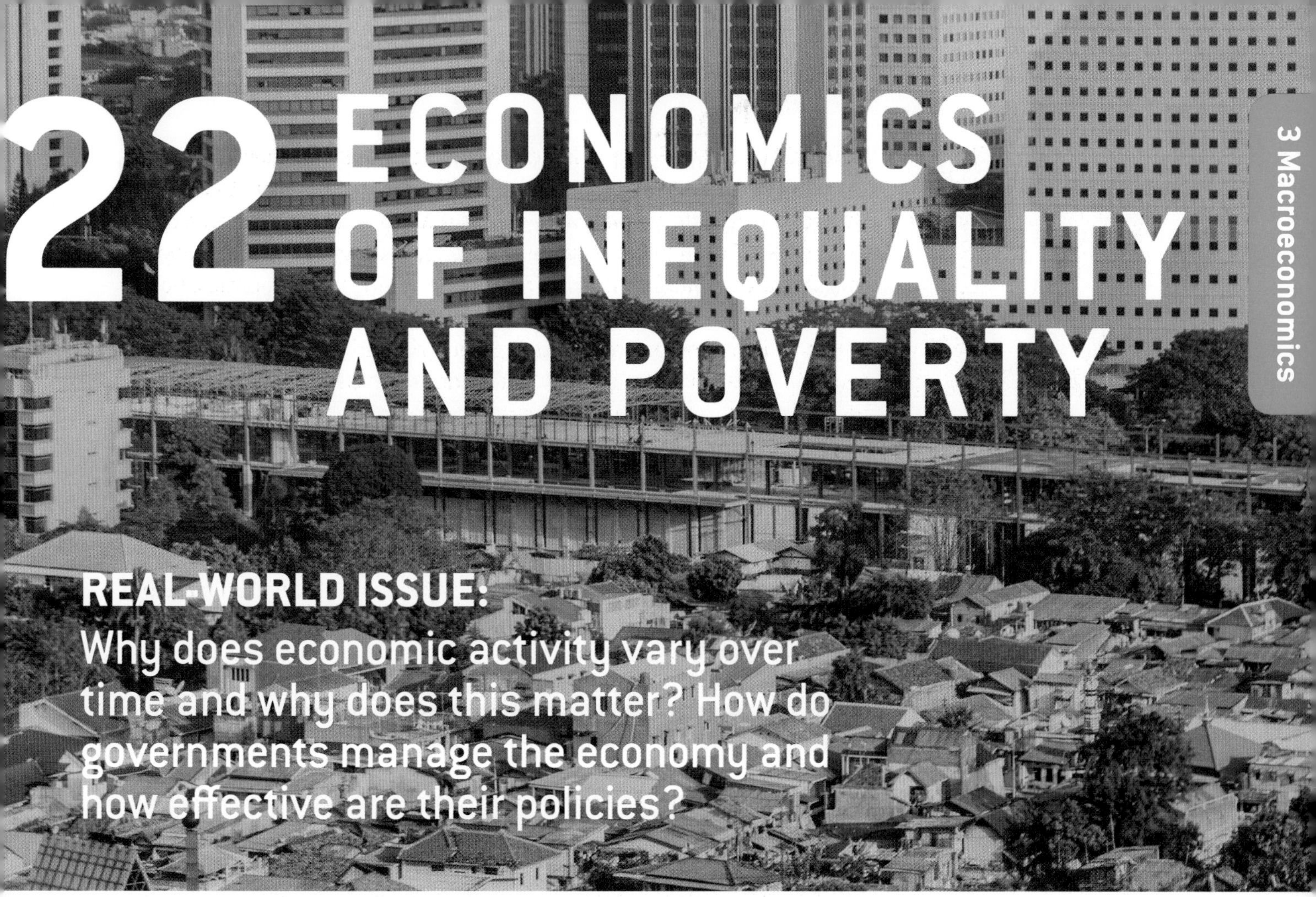

22 ECONOMICS OF INEQUALITY AND POVERTY

REAL-WORLD ISSUE:
Why does economic activity vary over time and why does this matter? How do governments manage the economy and how effective are their policies?

By the end of this chapter, you should be able to:

- → Distinguish between equity and equality
- → Explain the meaning of inequality
- → Explain how income inequality may be measured
- → Illustrate how the Lorenz curve shows inequality
- → Explain the relationship between the Lorenz curve and the Gini index
- HL Construct a Lorenz curve
- → Explain the meaning of poverty
- → Explain how poverty is measured
- → Explain the Multidimensional Poverty Index
- → Describe some of the causes of inequality and poverty
- → Discuss the impact of inequality on economic growth, living standards and social stability
- → Discuss the role of taxation in reducing poverty, income and wealth inequalities
- → Evaluate policies available to a government to reduce poverty, income and wealth inequality.

This chapter is all about equity and economic well being and so these concepts will run throughout.

As we have seen, a goal of governments is an equitable distribution of income. Inequality and poverty are national and global problems. The following article presents several of the key issues surrounding the topic of inequality and poverty. It is useful to have a look at this before developing the theory.

Richest 1 percent bagged 82 percent of wealth created last year – poorest half of humanity got nothing

Eighty two percent of the wealth generated last year went to the richest one percent of the global population, while the 3.7 billion people who make up the poorer half of the world saw no increase in their wealth, according to a new Oxfam report released today. The report is being launched as political and business elites gather for the World Economic Forum in Davos, Switzerland.

"**Reward Work, Not Wealth**" reveals how the global economy enables a wealthy elite to accumulate vast fortunes while hundreds of millions of people are struggling to survive on poverty pay.

- Billionaire wealth has risen by an annual average of 13 percent since 2010 – six times faster than the wages of ordinary workers, which have risen by a yearly average of just 2 percent. The number of billionaires rose at an unprecedented rate of one every two days between March 2016 and March 2017.
- It takes just four days for a CEO from one of the top five global fashion brands to earn what a Bangladeshi garment worker will earn in her lifetime. In the US, it takes slightly over one working day for a CEO to earn what an ordinary worker makes in a year.
- It would cost $2.2 billion a year to increase the wages of all 2.5 million Vietnamese garment workers to a living wage. This is about a third of the amount paid out to wealthy shareholders by the top 5 companies in the garment sector in 2016.

Oxfam's report outlines the key factors driving up rewards for shareholders and corporate bosses at the expense of workers' pay and conditions. These include the erosion of workers' rights; the excessive influence of big business over government policy-making; and the relentless corporate drive to minimize costs in order to maximize returns to shareholders.

Winnie Byanyima, Executive Director of Oxfam International said: "The billionaire boom is not a sign of a thriving economy but a symptom of a failing economic system. The people who make our clothes, assemble our phones and grow our food are being exploited to ensure a steady supply of cheap goods, and swell the profits of corporations and billionaire investors."

Women workers often find themselves at the bottom of the heap. Across the world, women consistently earn less than men and are usually in the lowest paid and least secure forms of work. By comparison, 9 out of 10 billionaires are men.

"Oxfam has spoken to women across the world whose lives are blighted by inequality. Women in Vietnamese garment factories who work far from home for poverty pay and don't get to see their children for months at a time. Women working in the US poultry industry who are forced to wear nappies because they are denied toilet breaks," said Byanyima.

Oxfam is calling for governments to ensure our economies work for everyone and not just the fortunate few:

- Limit returns to shareholders and top executives, and ensure all workers receive a minimum 'living' wage that would enable them to have a decent quality of life. For example, in Nigeria, the legal minimum wage would need to be tripled to ensure decent living standards.
- Eliminate the gender pay gap and protect the rights of women workers. At current rates of change, it will take 217 years to close the gap in pay and employment opportunities between women and men.
- Ensure the wealthy pay their fair share of tax through higher taxes and a crackdown on tax avoidance, and increase spending on public services such as healthcare and education. Oxfam estimates a global tax of 1.5 percent on billionaires' wealth could pay for every child to go to school.

Results of a new global survey commissioned by Oxfam demonstrates a groundswell of support for action on inequality. Of the 70,000 people surveyed in 10 countries, nearly two-thirds of all respondents think the gap between the rich and the poor needs to be urgently addressed.

"It's hard to find a political or business leader who doesn't say they are worried about inequality. It's even harder to find one who is doing something about it. Many are actively making things worse by slashing taxes and scrapping labor rights," said Byanyima.

"People are ready for change. They want to see workers paid a living wage; they want corporations and the super-rich to pay more tax; they want women workers to enjoy the same rights as men; they want a limit on the power and the wealth which sits in the hands of so few. They want action."

Source: Adapted from OXFAM International Press Release, 22 January 2018.

Some of the key points raised in the article are:

- throughout the world there is evidence of great inequalities in income and wealth
- poor people throughout the world are working hard, but lack the opportunities to improve their well-being
- inequality is caused by many factors
- inequality can harm everyone, but it is often women who are hardest hit
- it is not right that governments claim to be concerned about inequality, but then implement policies that actually increase it
- there are a number of things that governments can do, and there is widespread support for action to reduce inequality.

We will be considering all of these points as we work through this extremely important topic.

Are equality and equity the same thing?

In contrast to the concept of equality, where economic outcomes are the same for different people or different social groups, equity does not mean that everyone should be the same or get the same treatment. In recognizing that all people are different, equity is about fairness; it means that despite their differences, everyone should be given the same opportunities to succeed. Where differences exist among people due to factors such as socio-economic background, gender or race, equity is about making sure that all people be treated fairly and be given the resources and opportunities that they need to reach their full, healthy potential.

It would be hard to find someone who did not agree that equity is an important element in any economy. When it comes to the question of equality, however, economists generally agree that some degree of inequality is inevitable, and even necessary, within a market economy. When there is some gap between the rich and the poor in an economy, it gives people the incentive to work harder, and to gain a better education. It also encourages entrepreneurship, since those who innovate and do well can enjoy the financial benefits of their risk-taking. All of these are important for individuals seeking to improve their own well-being, but they are also very important for overall improvements to the productivity and output of the economy as a whole.

However, it is argued that there are a great many reasons to be concerned about growing levels of income and wealth inequalities in the world. According to findings from the World Inequality Database (WID), income inequality has increased in nearly all regions of the world in recent decades. What is important to note, however, is that this has occurred at different rates. Income inequality has grown rapidly in North America, China, India and Russia, but has grown "only" moderately in Europe. In the Middle East, sub-Saharan Africa and

Brazil, income inequality has remained fairly stable, but at high levels. Given the fact that inequality levels are very different, even for countries sharing similar levels of development, it is clear that inequality is not determined by the level of national income. It is, instead, the result of national policies and institutions that do not cater for economic growth that is "fair" or "inclusive". Because of the failings of these policies and institutions, the economic growth does not generate higher income and better opportunities for everyone.

Inequalities in income and wealth are considered to be *"inequalities in outcomes"*. The amount of income that a person earns, or the amount of wealth that they have accumulated may be the outcome of hard work, or sensible life choices and might then be seen as the reward that people deserve for their efforts and initiative. However, it is often the case that a person simply cannot earn as much, or afford to buy any assets simply because they do not have the same opportunities. This is referred to as *"inequality of opportunity"*. High levels of inequality of opportunity mean a person's education, the types of health care they can access, the jobs they can get and ultimately the amount of income they can earn, are not based on their achievements, but are based on their circumstances at birth. These circumstances include their gender, their ethnicity, the place where they were born, their parents' profession and socio-economic background.

Overall, the point is that rising levels of inequality in income, wealth, and opportunity reflect a lack of equity. It is important to gain an understanding of how such inequalities have increased and what governments and other institutions might do to reduce them.

In this chapter we look at the causes, consequences and possible solutions to issues related to inequality and poverty. It is vital to stress that inequalities and poverty are problems in all countries, regardless of the average level of income within the country. As you go through this chapter, you should be examining each of the topics in the context of your own chosen real-world examples.

How is income inequality measured?

Income inequality in an economy can be measured. The most common representation of inequality comes in the form of a Lorenz curve. This takes data about household income gathered in national surveys and presents them graphically. Consider the following data:

Country	Survey year	Lowest 20%	Second 20%	Third 20%	Fourth 20%	Highest 20%	Gini Index (2002–2007)
Bolivia	2007	2.7	6.5	11.0	18.6	61.2	58.2
Brazil	2007	3.0	6.9	11.8	19.6	58.7	55.0
Croatia	2005	8.8	13.3	17.3	22.7	37.9	29.0
Madagascar	2005	6.2	9.6	13.1	17.7	53.5	47.2

Sources: World Bank Data & UN Human Development Reports 2009

▲ Table 22.1 Income distribution for selected countries

Households are ranked in ascending order of income levels and the share of total income going to groups of households is calculated. For example, if we look at Brazil, we see that the poorest 20% of households receive only 3.0% of total household income while the richest 20% of the households receive 58.7%. This contrasts with Croatia, where the data suggest more equality in distribution, with the poorest 20% receiving 8.8% of total household income, and the richest 20% receiving 37.9%.

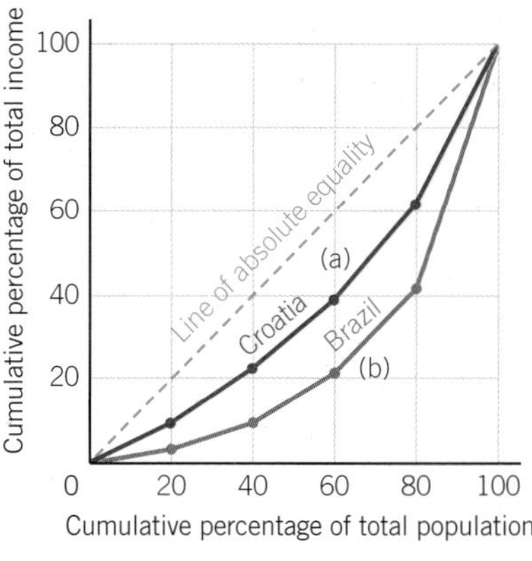

(a) = area between line of equality and Lorenz curve

(a) + (b) = total area under line of equality

▲ **Figure 22.1** Lorenz curves for Brazil and Croatia

The information can be graphed using Lorenz curves shown in Figure 22.1. The *x*-axis shows the cumulative percentage of the total population divided up in the quintiles shown in Table 22.1. The *y*-axis shows the cumulative percentage of total income earned by the quintiles. The line of absolute equality indicates a perfectly equal distribution of income where, for example, 10% of the population earns 10% of the income, and 90% of the population earns 90% of the income. Each country has its own Lorenz curve based on the income data. The farther away a country's curve is from the line of absolute equality, the more unequal is the distribution of income. In our example, the curve drawn for Brazil is further away than that of Croatia. We can quickly observe from the diagram that income is less equally distributed in Brazil than it is in Croatia.

The Lorenz Curve model is useful for two things in particular. It may be used to compare two or more countries in terms of income distribution, or it may be used to compare the change in income distribution for a single country over time.

Global inequality is on the rise – but at vastly different rates across the world

https://theconversation.com/global-inequality-is-on-the-rise-but-at-vastly-different-rates-across-the-world-88976

An indicator that neatly summarizes the information presented in the table and on the Lorenz curve is the Gini index. The Gini index is derived from the Lorenz curve and is a ratio of the area between the line of equality and a country's Lorenz curve (area (a) in Figure 22.1) to the total area under the line of absolute equality (areas (a) + (b) in Figure 22.1). The higher the Gini index, the more unequal is the distribution of income. Gini index values are given in Table 22.1. Of the four countries, Bolivia has the highest income inequality with a Gini Index score of 58.2, whereas Croatia has the lowest with a score of 29.0.

Although a reduction in income inequality may be an important objective of development, one must be very careful in using Gini index numbers as a basis for evaluating a country's development progress. While low-income countries tend to have higher levels of inequality than high-income countries, there is no hard and fast correlation between the level of development of a country measured by its Human Development Index (HDI) and its Gini index. There are countries with a high level of human development, such as the US (HDI rank 13), that have a relatively high Gini index (41.5) and countries with a low level of human development, such as Mauritania (HDI rank 159), with a much lower Gini value (32.6) (*Statistical Update 2018, Human Development Indices and Indicators*, UNDP).

Economics in action

ATL Thinking, Communication and Research

Table 22.2 provides examples of a range of Gini coefficients for different countries. The data is the latest available within the 2010–2017 time period. It is worth noting the difference between these figures and the figures in Table 22.1, which were for 2002–2007.

Madagascar, Brazil and especially Bolivia, have seen significant falls in their Gini Index values, ie income inequality has fallen. Investigate possible reasons for the fall in any one of the three countries.

Note

In the assessment advice box below, you do not have to do any calculations or show the curves accurately, you can simply draw a rough sketch to explain the change.

Table 22.2 provides examples of a range of Gini coefficients for different countries.

Country	Gini coefficient (latest figure available within 2010–2017 period)
Finland	27.1
Norway	27.5
Croatia	30.8
Canada	34.0
Ethiopia	39.1
United States	41.5
China	42.2
Madagascar	42.6
Bolivia	44.6
Brazil	51.3
Eswatini (Kingdom of)	51.5
South Africa	63.4

Source: Statistical Update 2018, Human Development Indices and Indicators, UNDP http://hdr.undp.org/sites/default/files/2018_human_development_statistical_update.pdf

▲ Table 22.2 Gini coefficients for selected countries

Economics in action

ATL Thinking, Communication and Research

The income Gini coefficient is the most commonly used statistic to measure income inequality. However, there are a great many other ways that inequality is measured. One interesting value to examine is referred to as "top income inequality" which measures the amount of income earned by the richest 1% of the population. This is also useful to assess how income inequality is changing within an economy over time.

Try to find some data to show how the income earned by the richest 1% of the population in a country of your choice has changed in the last decades. What are the implications of this change?

Assessment advice – SL & HL

In paper 2, you might be given Gini coefficient data and asked a question such as the following:

The Gini coefficient value for the United States increased from 34.6 in 1979 to 41.0 in 2013. Using a Lorenz curve diagram, explain what has happened to income distribution in the United States.

Model answer:

The Gini coefficient in the United States increased from 34.6 in 1979 to 41 in 2013. This means that the distribution of income has become more unequal. On the Lorenz curve diagram, we can see that the Lorenz curve for the U.S. moves outwards from 1979 to 2013, moving away from the line of absolute equality. This shows the increase in inequality.

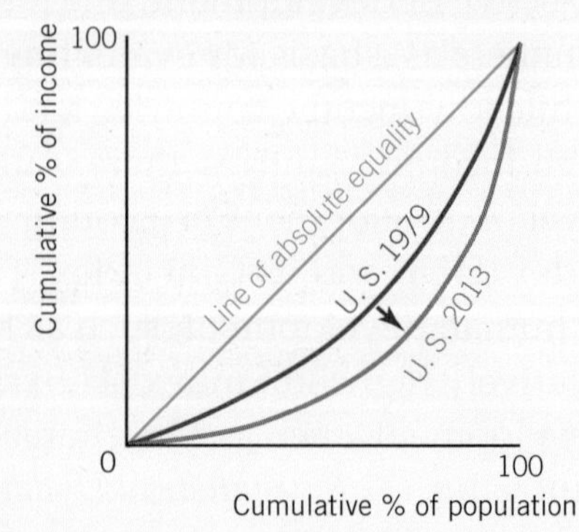

How is a Lorenz Curve constructed?

As we know, statistical data about household income is gathered in national surveys. The households are grouped into five quintiles according to their incomes, as we saw in Table 22.1. The first quintile is the poorest quintile representing the 20% of the population earning the lowest income. The fifth quintile is the richest quintile, representing the 20% of the population earning the highest income. The curve is drawn based on the cumulative income of each of the percentiles.

In HL Paper 2 or, more likely, HL Paper 3, you may be asked to construct a Lorenz curve from income quintile data.

Consider the data in Table 22.3 for Spain, where we see that the poorest 20% of the population earns 5.7% of the income, and the richest 20% earns 41.9% of the income. In the examination, you would be given the first two columns of data and then be asked to construct an accurate Lorenz curve.

In order to do this, you will need to work out the cumulative share of the income, as we have shown in column 3. With this data, you can then draw the Lorenz curve accurately, as shown in Figure 22.3. (Obviously, you would not have to put all the details for each point that we have shown, this is just there to help you understand!)

Quintile	Share of income	Cumulative share of income
1st (poorest)	5.7	5.7
2nd	11.8	17.5 (5.7 + 11.8)
3rd	17	34.5 (5.7 + 11.8 + 17)
4th	23.6	58.1 (5.7 + 11.8 + 17 + 23.6)
5th	41.9	100 (5.7 + 11.8 + 17 + 23.6 + 41.9)

Source: Our World in Data, https://ourworldindata.org/income-inequality

▲ **Table 22.3** Spanish income statistics, 2014

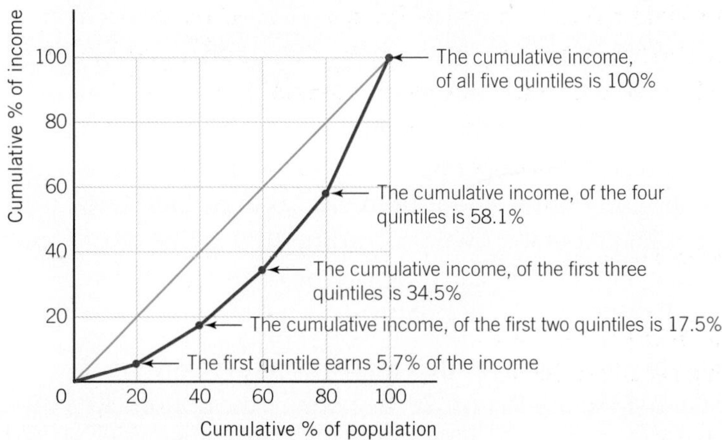

▲ **Figure 22.2** Constructing a Lorenz curve

For practice, you might like to draw Lorenz curves for Bolivia and Madagascar, using the data to be found in Table 22.1.

Exercise 22.1 ATL Thinking and Communication

Household income data, by quintile, for Sweden and South Africa are given in the following table. There is also Gini coefficient data.

	Sweden	South Africa
1st quintile (poorest)	9.0	2.5
2nd quintile	14.1	4.7
3rd quintile	17.7	8
4th quintile	22.9	15.9
5th quintile (richest)	36.3	68.9
Gini coefficient	27.2	63.4

a) On one graph, plot accurate Lorenz curves for both countries. [4 marks]

b) Comment on the difference in the distribution of income between the two countries. [2 marks]

c) Using the values for the Gini coefficients given in the last row, comment on the relationship between the Lorenz curve and the Gini coefficient. [2 marks]

What about inequality of wealth?

While there is certainly a link between income inequality and wealth inequality, they are not the same thing. Income includes all the money that people earn from wages, salaries, interest from savings and bonds, dividends earned from the ownership of stocks and shares, rent and the money that people gain from selling assets for more than the assets cost (capital gains). For tax purposes, individuals are required to submit information about all sources of income, and so statistical data about incomes and income distribution is fairly easy for governments to acquire.

Wealth may also be referred to as "net worth" and is the value of all of a person's total assets minus their total liabilities. The assets that make up wealth include houses and property, money in savings accounts, investments in stocks and bonds, and retirement savings. Liabilities include all the debts that a person owes, including things like mortgages, student loans, car loans and credit card debts. The difference between a person's assets and liabilities is their wealth.

Wealth is substantially more concentrated than income. According to the Credit Suisse Global Wealth Report 2018, globally the bottom 50% of adults owns less than 1% of total wealth, the richest 10% owns 85% of total wealth and the top 1% alone owns almost half of all household wealth.

How are inequality and poverty linked?

When there is a high level of income inequality, it means that a significant portion of the population is living in some form of poverty, and it is highly likely that this poverty will perpetuate the inequalities that exist.

What is the meaning of poverty?

Poverty in all its forms is a global problem, and is a clear sign of a lack of equity. In fact, the number one Sustainable Development Goal (SDG1) of the United Nations is to "End poverty in all its forms everywhere". Within SDG 1 are seven targets to address the different forms of poverty.

Although there are many different types of poverty (eg income poverty, food poverty, energy poverty, child poverty, old age poverty), here we address two particular types: "absolute poverty" and "relative poverty".

Absolute poverty occurs when the income of a person, or household, is not enough for them to meet even their basic needs of shelter, food, safe drinking water, health and education. The World Bank sets what is known as the "International Poverty Line"; if people earn less than this international measure, then they are said to be living in absolute, or extreme poverty. In 2015, the international poverty line was revised upwards from US$1.25 a day to US$1.90.

Obviously, when $1.90 is converted into a local currency at the official exchange rate, it will buy different amounts of goods and services in different countries. To overcome this, and allow for meaningful understanding of what the absolute poverty value really means, the figure is given in what economists refer to as "purchasing power parity" (PPP) exchange rates. These are also known as "international dollars". When the figure of US$1.90 is transferred into different currencies at the PPP exchange rate, it means that it will buy approximately the same amount of goods and services in any country.

Extreme poverty rates have fallen by more than half since 1990, according to the United Nations. While this is a remarkable achievement, millions and millions of people in developing regions live on less than $1.90 a day, and are therefore facing extreme deprivations. Furthermore, "millions more make little more than this daily amount and are at risk of slipping back into extreme poverty" (United Nations, SDG tracker, https://sdg-tracker.org/no-poverty).

Recognizing the inequity of extreme poverty, the first target of SDG1 (known as SDG1.1) is the elimination of extreme poverty by 2030. As Figure 22.3 indicates, the challenge is enormous.

1 NO POVERTY

What is extreme poverty?

According to the UN's Guiding Principles on Extreme Poverty and Human Rights, *"Persons living in poverty are confronted by the most severe obstacles – physical, economic, cultural and social – to accessing their rights and entitlements. Consequently, they experience many interrelated and mutually reinforcing deprivations – including dangerous work conditions, unsafe housing, lack of nutritious food, unequal access to justice, lack of political power and limited access to health care – that prevent them from realizing their rights and perpetuate their poverty. Persons experiencing extreme poverty live in a vicious cycle of powerlessness, stigmatization, discrimination, exclusion and material deprivation, which all mutually reinforce one another."*

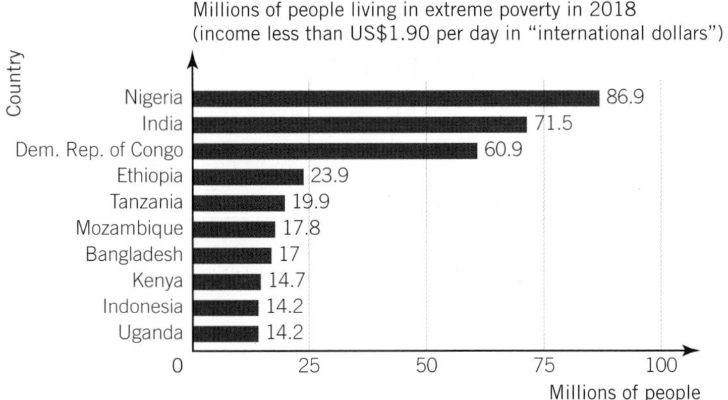

Source: Quartz Africa, https://qz.com/africa/1313380/nigerias-has-the-highest-rate-of-extreme-poverty-globally/

Figure 22.3 Extreme poverty figures for selected countries

Economics in action

ATL Thinking, Communication and Research

Investigate the progress made in reaching SDG 1.1.

What is the difference between absolute poverty and relative poverty?

The value of absolute poverty (currently at USD $1.90 PPP) may be raised from time to time (by the World Bank) but it is considered to be fixed according to the costs of achieving very basic needs. Relative poverty, on the other hand, is a comparative measure based on the living standards in a particular country. It means that a person is poor relative to the others in the country. One standard measure of relative poverty is that it includes those people who earn less than 50% of the median income. So, for example, if the median income in a country is $50,000, then a person would be living in relative poverty if their income was less than $25,000. It would be argued that a level of income below $25,000 would be inadequate for an acceptable standard of living in that country. Because poverty is defined in relative terms, this is also a measure of income inequality.

Absolute poverty is certainly a much more significant problem in developing countries. However, the global goal related to poverty is not just to eradicate extreme poverty, since people in poverty face enormous challenges and experience unacceptable low standards of living everywhere in the world. Therefore, there is also a target related to *relative* poverty in the Sustainable Goals. The second target of SDG1 (SDG1.2) aims to "reduce at least by half the proportion of men, women and children of all ages living in poverty in all its dimensions according to national definitions". In other words, it wants to cut in half the number of people living in relative poverty in every country. This SDG 1.2 also recognizes that while lifting people out of absolute poverty is the priority, living even close to this very low level of income involves very low living standards.

Economics in action

ATL Thinking, Communication and Research

Examine the nature of poverty in your chosen OECD country.

How is poverty measured?

As explained above, absolute poverty is measured by using the World Bank's international poverty line, currently standing at $US 1.90 PPP.

Economies set their own "national poverty lines" which reflect relative poverty. As we have already stated, the national poverty line is usually set at an arbitrary percentage of the median income. For example, Australia sets its national poverty line at 50% of median income. According to this value, 13.2% of the population was living in poverty in 2015–2016.

Figure 22.5 indicates the relative poverty for a selection of OECD countries. The OECD uses the 50% of median income as its threshold for relative poverty. Observe that the chart provides the total poverty rate, indicating the percentage of the total population living beneath the poverty line. It also indicates the poverty rate of two separate age groups – the child poverty rate, for people between 0 and 17 years, and the poverty rate for seniors, for people above 65 years. This data about different age groups is important, as it gives a greater picture of the nature of poverty in an economy, and it should help governments implement policies that can target the appropriate people.

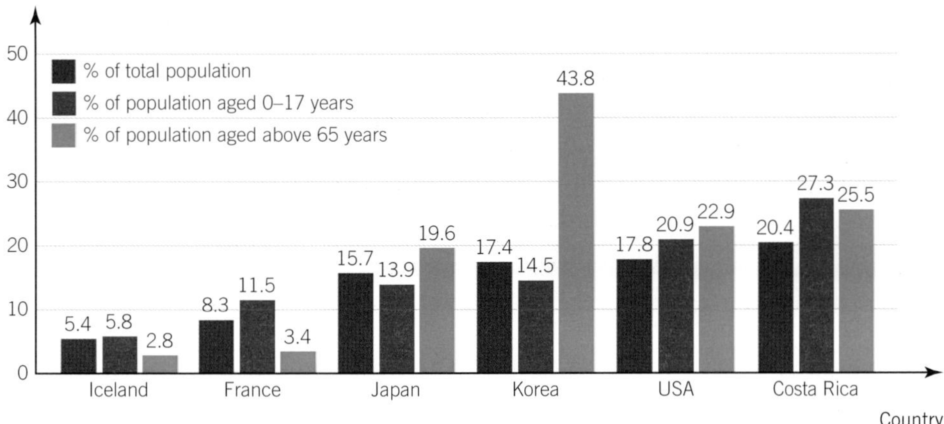

Source: OECD Data 2019 https://data.oecd.org/inequality/poverty-rate.htm#indicator-chart

▲ **Figure 22.4** Percentage of people living in relative poverty (earning less than 50% of the median income)

An alternative approach to measuring poverty in a country may be to set the poverty line at the minimum amount of income that households need to meet their basic needs for goods and services. This is similar to the World Bank's international poverty line, but takes into account the need to live beyond mere survival, and to enjoy a certain "basic" standard of living deemed to be acceptable, relative to the standards of living of people across the country. It should be noted that this is, of course, an extremely normative issue – filled with judgements and opinions, and therefore open to some controversy.

We will look at one example of a national poverty line based on a minimum income standard.

Canada uses a "market-based measure" which measures the cost of a basket of goods and services needed to live a "modest, basic standard of living". The figure is based on a family of four, with two children. Since costs of living vary across the country, the poverty line is different in different provinces to account for the different costs. Table 22.4 gives the monthly cost for the Canadian "basket" in two different provinces in 2015.

Economics in action

ATL Thinking, Communication and Research

1. Compare and contrast the levels of poverty among the OECD countries presented in Figure 22.4.
2. What particular concerns might countries face as a result of the poverty experienced by people of different ages? To do this, you need to investigate the problems associated with child poverty and poverty among senior citizens.

	Alberta (CAD$ per month)	Quebec (CAD$ per month)
Clothing and footwear	$134	$161
Transportation	$367	$192
Nutritious food	$1,036	$947
Shelter (including electricity, heat, clean water)	$980	$604
Other goods and services (personal care items, basic telephone service, reading materials, recreation, entertainment, school supplies)	$882	$835
Total	**$3,399**	**$2,739**

Source: *"Opportunity for All: Canada's First Poverty Reduction Strategy"*, Employment and Social Development Canada.

▲ Table 22.4 Monthly cost of a basket required to live a "modest, basic standard" in two selected Canadian provinces.

The conclusion from this would be that for households in the province of Alberta, the government sets the poverty line at approximately $40,780 per year. This is the minimum income that families would have to earn to enjoy a "modest, basic" standard of living. For households in Quebec, where costs are slightly lower, the poverty line is approximately $32,880. The average poverty line for a four-person household in Canada in 2015 was $37,542. This figure is adjusted for households of different sizes, such as single-parent households, or households with no children. For a single person, the line is set at around half of the household value. Based on these figures, it was estimated that in 2015, 12.1% of the population lived in poverty in Canada (Source: Adapted from *Canada's official poverty line: what is it? how could it be better?* by Professor Miles Corak, August 21, 2018 https://milescorak.com/2018/08/21/canadas-official-poverty-line-what-is-it-how-could-it-be-better/).

What is the Multidimensional Poverty Index (MPI)?

Poverty means that people lack basic necessities and exist in poor conditions. These are referred to as deprivations. People in extreme poverty are deprived of clean water, sanitation, adequate nutrition, primary education and they suffer from poor health. In this way, they are multidimensionally poor. Of course they also lack income, but to simply say that poor people do not have enough income does not reveal what their individual circumstances are. More specifically, it does not reveal what their individual deprivations are.

As stated above, SGD1 aims to "reduce poverty *in all its forms* everywhere". In recognizing that people experience poverty in many different forms, the United Nations has developed the Multidimensional Poverty Index (MPI). This is known as a "composite indicator" because it attempts to measure the many specific dimensions of poverty, rather than simply looking at income as a single indicator.

People have basic needs in three key dimensions: health, education and standards of living. Each of these three dimensions has equal weight in measuring the extent of poverty. For each of the dimensions, the

Multidimensional Poverty Index identifies specific ways to measure the dimension. These are known as the indicators. It then notes what it means to be poor or deprived in each of the indicators. For example, in the dimension of health, nutrition and child mortality are the two indicators. For the indicator of child mortality, the MPI considers the person to be poor if any child in the family has died in the five-year period prior to the time of the survey. The full tool is shown in Table 22.5.

Dimensions of poverty	Indicator	Deprived if living in the household where...	Weight
Health	Nutrition	An adult under 70 years of age or a child is undernourished.	1/6
	Child mortality	Any child has died in the family in the five-year period preceding the survey.	1/6
Education	Years of schooling	No household member aged 10 years or older has completed six years of schooling.	1/6
	School attendence	Any school-aged child is not attending school up to the age at which he/she would complete class 8	1/6
Standard of living	Cooking Fuel	The household cooks with dung, wood, charcoal or coal.	1/18
	Sanitation	The household does not have access to improved (according to SDG guidelines) or it is improved but shared with other household.	1/18
	Drinking Water	The household does not have access to improved drinking water (according to SDG guidelines) or safe drinking water is at least a 30-minute walk from home, round trip.	1/18
	Electricity	The household has no electricity.	1/18
	Housing	Housing materials for at least one of roof, walls and floor are inadequate: the floor is of natural materials and/or the roof and/or walls are of natural or rudimentary materials.	1/18
	Assets	The household does not own more than one of these assets: radio, TV, telephone, computer, animal cart, bicycle, motorbike or refrigerator, and does not own a car or truck.	1/18

Source: United Nations Development Program, 2019, http://hdr.undp.org/en/2018-MPI

▲ Table 22.5 2018 MPI: dimensions, indicators, deprivation cutoffs and weights.

A person is considered to be multidimensionally poor if they experience deprivation in at least one-third of these weighted indicators. (Don't worry – the calculations are well beyond the requirements of this course, but it is useful to see how this is done!)

The UNDP 2018 Statistical Update presents estimates for 105 developing countries with a combined population of 5.7 billion (77% of the world total). It states that about 1.3 billion people in the countries covered – 23.3% of their entire population – lived in multidimensional poverty between 2006 and 2016–17. The UNDP Human Development Report of 2018 presents the specific data for all 105 developing countries, with important summaries and comparisons.

Understanding the particular nature of poverty in a particular country is valuable as it makes it possible to implement policies targeted specifically at the deprivations in that country. For example, Tajikistan and Peru have similar levels of multidimensional poverty, but they differ notably in the composition of their poverty. This is shown in Figure 22.5.

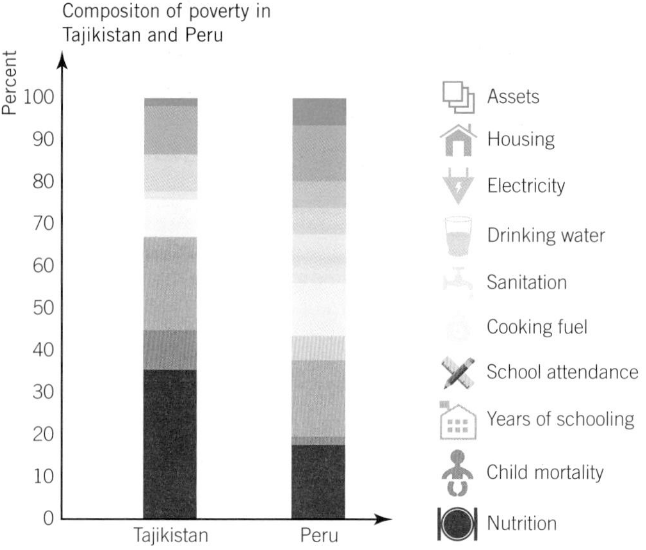

Source: https://ophi.org.uk/wp-content/uploads/info4b-1.jpg

▲Figure 22.5 Composition of poverty in Tajikistan and Peru.

In Peru, years of schooling contributes 18% to the MPI value, whereas in Tajikistan, it is only 1%. In Tajikistan, nutrition contributes approximately 35% to the MPI value, whereas in Peru it is around 18%. Clearly, the two countries would need to implement different strategies to tackle their own causes of poverty. This is evidence that a "one-size-fits-all" approach to poverty reduction is inappropriate.

> **Economics in action**
>
> ATL Thinking, Communication and Research
>
> Using any of the measures of inequality and poverty presented in this chapter, along with any others that you come across, discuss the nature of inequality and poverty in a developing country of your choice. The most recent United Nations Development Program (UNDP) Human Development Report will be a good place to start.

What are the difficulties in measuring poverty?

While it is extremely important to have a good idea of the nature and extent of poverty in an economy to be able to design and implement policies to alleviate it, there are a number of problems associated with its measurement:

- As we have noted, there are many different types of poverty including absolute poverty, relative poverty, extreme poverty, acute poverty, income poverty and multidimensional poverty. Each type of poverty has its own definition, but these may vary from country to country. Poverty can be difficult to measure because it is difficult to define.
- There are some elements of poverty which are difficult or impossible to measure – for example, people living in poverty suffer feelings of uncertainty, vulnerability, fear (eg of where the next meal is going to come from or if you can afford new shoes for your child, or how you are going to make it to the next pay day without income for food). These are all valid dimensions of poverty but they are all hard to measure; simple income measures of poverty may not capture this.

- Measures of poverty are most often based on household surveys. While surveying techniques have undoubtedly improved over the years, such surveying requires an enormous amount of resources. Results of such surveys may be of poor quality in countries where resources are stretched.
- Because governments are judged on their ability to support people in poverty, and indeed to help people lift themselves out of poverty, it is in the interest of governments to adjust their national poverty lines to reduce the extent of official poverty in the country. Simply defining the term differently will affect poverty statistics, even when the people concerned are in no better place to meet their basic needs.

What are some of the causes of inequality and poverty?

The causes of inequality and poverty are complex and interrelated. We examine some of the causes here, but this is by no means an exclusive list. While the causes discussed here are relevant to all countries, the particular problems of developing countries will be treated in Chapter 30.

- **Inequality of opportunities**

  Not only are people born into different conditions, but they also face vastly different opportunities as they grow up, get an education, find employment and grow older. The fact is that the opportunities that people face are unequal. A child born into a middle- or high-income family is likely to have educated parents who are in good health; they are likely to have good access to health care, do better in school, go to university and get a job with a decent income. They are more likely to be able to save money, and have enough collateral to be able to borrow money from the bank to buy a house. Their good health and socio-economic situation may allow them to live to an old age, with a good pension. This is not to say that life will be without challenges! But their opportunities will allow them to achieve their potential.

  On the other hand, a child born into a poor household is faced with far fewer opportunities. The mother's health and nutrition may be poor, and this may result in lower birth weight and health challenges right from the outset. They may grow up without nutritious food and go to school hungry. They may become ill because of their poor nutrition, or they might suffer problems of obesity or diabetes as people on low incomes tend to eat more high-calorie inexpensive food. Their parents may have to work long hours with no holidays and may still not be able to afford a decent standard of living. As teenagers, children living in relative poverty may quit school as early as possible because they see no future in education, and so they leave with a lower level of skills and education. This means that they find it difficult to get a job where they can earn a decent living.

They will be unable to save, needing to spend all money on meeting basic needs. As they grow older, they will struggle even more to make ends meet. Ultimately, their poor health may result in a lower life expectancy than those who were born with better opportunities. Throughout their life cycle, they may struggle to reach their potential, regardless of their effort and initiative.

The examples given above are clearly simplistic, but they do illustrate a common reality which is that both economic advantages and economic disadvantages tend to reinforce themselves through this life cycle. Sadly, children born into poverty are likely to enjoy very few opportunities to move out of poverty as they grow up. This is known as a poverty trap or poverty cycle. As noted by the OECD, *"The vicious confluence of poor educational opportunities, low skills and limited employment prospects can trap people in situations where they are also far more likely to be exposed to environmental hazards and violence. As a result of this multidimensional inequality, while some individuals, citizens and regions thrive, others fall further behind."*

Key concept
CHANGE

One problem here relates to the issue of "social mobility" which is the ability of people or households to move up or down the socio-economic "ladder". Intragenerational social mobility refers to the ability of an individual to move from one income level to a higher income level within their own lifetime. Intergenerational social mobility refers to the ability of a person to move to a higher level of income than their parents. If a child born into a low-income family where neither parent had been to university was to go to university and get a job where they earn the median income, this would be an example of upward social mobility.

However, in its report "*A Broken Social Elevator? How to Promote Social Mobility*", the OECD notes rather bleakly that both intergenerational and intragenerational social mobility is on the decline among OECD countries. Children with a disadvantaged background face too many challenges and have too few opportunities to move up the ladder, and those at the top of the ladder have the tools to pass on their advantages to their children, therefore reinforcing income and wealth inequalities. Empirical evidence suggests that in more unequal societies, characterized by both unequal incomes and unequal opportunities, people are less likely to be socially mobile and move up or down from their level on the income scale, especially if they are in the top or bottom 5% of earners.

Economics in action

ATL Thinking, Communication and Research

Find two countries that differ in terms of their social mobility. Identify possible reasons for this difference. Later, when looking at how governments can improve the opportunities available to people on lower incomes, the evidence you find here should be very useful.

The situation is even harsher in developing countries where children living in relative poverty face even fewer opportunities and greater challenges in terms of health and education. Those living in absolute poverty, especially in the Least Developed Countries have virtually no opportunities to improve their standards of living.

- **Discrimination**

  Inequality may be the result of unfair treatment, or discrimination, against certain people due to any number of factors, including their gender, race, ethnicity, age, religion, sexual orientation or socio-economic status. Discrimination manifests itself both in the opportunities that people face, and in the outcomes that they obtain. For example, as we saw above, lower-income children are discriminated against as they do not receive the same educational opportunities as higher income children, and as a result, they are unable to secure the higher-paying jobs as they move into the labour market.

  Wage discrimination is a particular type of discrimination that contributes directly to inequality. Wage discrimination occurs when workers in similar positions receive different wages on the basis of their gender, race, ethnicity, age, sexual orientation or any other characteristics that are not related to their skills or productivity.

Gender Discrimination is at the Heart of the Wage Gap

https://time.com/105292/gender-wage-gap/

Did you know?

According to the 2016 "Gender Pay Inequality Report" from the Joint Economic Committee in the United States:

- *"A woman working full time, year-round, earns $10,800 less per year than a man, based on median annual earnings. This disparity can add up to nearly half a million dollars over a career.*
- *On a percentage basis, a woman earns only 79% of what a man earns. This is known as the gender earnings ratio.*
- *Lower career earnings result in an even greater disparity in retirement income. Women 75 years and older are almost twice as likely to live in poverty as men.*
- *Women of colour face even larger gender pay gaps. Compared to white men, African-American women, on average, are paid only 60% and Latinas are paid only 55%.*
- *Women's increased participation in the paid labour force has been a major driver of economic growth in recent decades. According to the Council of Economic advisers, the US economy is $2.0 trillion bigger today than it would have been if women had not increased their participation and hours since 1970.*
- *Enacting policies that would narrow the gender pay gap and help more women work full time in the paid labour force would decrease income inequality and lift many women out of poverty."*

https://www.jec.senate.gov/public/_cache/files/0779dc2f-4a4e-4386-b847-9ae919735acc/gender-pay-inequality----us-congress-joint-economic-committee.pdf

- **Differences in human capital**

  Simple economic theory can be used to show that a person's income may be determined by supply and demand for their particular type of labour. If there is a lower supply of highly-skilled computer engineers than there is for unskilled manual work, the wages of the higher-skilled people will be higher, and so there will be inequality. This may be justified by the fact that the higher-skilled person should be rewarded for the investment in their own human capital.

  However, in the last decades, the wages of skilled workers have risen at a higher rate than those of unskilled workers leading to increasing inequality. Furthermore, a reduction in trade-union power in many countries has meant that workers in low-skilled jobs have much less job security and protection from falling real wages.

Economics in action

ATL Thinking, Communication and Research

Explain how discrimination worsens the opportunities and incomes of a particular group of people in a country of your choice. Support your reasoning with data.

Theory of knowledge

Consider the enormous amounts of money paid to famous athletes or celebrities. How can supply and demand analysis be used to justify their high incomes? Is this equitable?

- **Different levels of ownership of resources, particularly the unequal ownership of capital.**

  When people own physical capital, such as companies, they can earn profit. When they own financial capital, such as shares in companies, they can earn a share of the profits through dividends. The higher a person's income, the more physical and financial capital they will own. In contrast, lower income people tend not to own capital and the vast majority of their income comes from wages and salaries. In recent years, average profits and the value of share prices has risen at a much higher rate than average wages and salaries, translating into even higher incomes for those wealthy people with financial assets. As a result, there has been an increased concentration of wealth among the rich.

- **Globalization and technological progress have affected different types of labour differently**

  Increased global trade and the freedom of companies to locate their production facilities all around the world means that there is less demand for manufacturing workers in developed countries. Technological progress means that machinery and computerized technologies are able to do the repetitive work that skilled workers used to do, compounding the problem of falling demand for such labour. The result is that wages for manufacturing workers in developed countries have been depressed and there has been increasing structural (technological) unemployment. Yet labour markets still demand the skilled labour of people with higher education in sectors such as the financial, technology and electronic industries, so incomes of professionals in those sectors have risen, resulting in greater inequality.

  This is sometimes referred to as a the "hollowing out of the middle class", with a relatively small percentage of people earning high incomes, a notably larger percentage on low incomes, and shrinking numbers of people earning middle incomes.

Economics in action

ATL Thinking, Communication and Research

How have globalization and technological change affected the nature of jobs and employment in your chosen OECD country?

- **Market-oriented, supply-side policies**

  In the 1980s, market-oriented, new-classical supply-side policies became very popular in the UK, under Prime Minister Margaret Thatcher, and in the US, under President Ronald Reagan. There is a strong correlation between the introduction of these policies and rising inequality.

  Deregulation in financial markets greatly increased the opportunity for wealthy people to earn more income from their investments. The same deregulation is often blamed for the financial crisis in 2007 that significantly deepened inequalities. It has been argued that the deregulation allowed the financial system to take much greater risks than they would have done under effective supervision.

Labour market reforms to reduce the power of trade unions and make labour markets more flexible mean that workers have less power to use collective bargaining power with employers to protect their wages and working conditions, and this has depressed wages. Labour market reforms have also allowed firms to offer more "non-standard employment". Standard employment is when a person has a permanent and secure contract to work full-time. Non-standard employment, which includes temporary workers, part-time workers, workers on zero hours contracts and self-employed workers, offers far less security and lower incomes. On a zero-hours contract, an employer does not have to employ a worker for any given number of hours; the workers can be called upon when needed.

While there are benefits of non-standard employment, both to firms and to some workers, the International Labour Organisation (ILO) notes that the rise in non-standard employment poses many risks for workers, firms, labour markets and society. These risks include a lack of job security, lower average earnings, uncertain working hours with negative implications for work-life balance, concerns over health and safety of workers and an inability of non-standard workers to access social security benefits such as unemployment insurance or pensions.

- **Government tax and benefits policies**

  While most countries implement tax policies that are "progressive" and take a higher percentage of tax at higher levels of income, the top rate of income tax has fallen in many countries. Corporate profits are generally taxed at a lower rate than income taxes, and so owners of capital benefit. Furthermore, governments tend to tax income from savings, dividends and capital gains at a lower rate than taxes on wages and salaries. People with higher incomes and those with significant wealth benefit from such policies, and this widens inequalities in income and wealth.

  There has also been a move towards "austerity" policies in many countries, as governments have reduced spending to try to reduce their public debts. This has involved less spending by governments in all areas, including those areas which are specifically aimed at redistributing income, such as social welfare benefits like unemployment insurance, child benefits and housing allowances. These austerity policies have therefore tended to worsen the incomes and standards of living among lower-income people.

- **Unequal status and power**

  Where the ownership of resources and income in an economy are concentrated among a small percentage of the population, those wealthier people may have a disproportionate say in the development of government policies. When people running for public office finance their campaigns with donations from private individuals, they will need to gain support from wealthy citizens

Households are struggling with declining incomes due to flat wages

https://thenewdaily.com.au/money/finance-news/2019/07/30/incomes-falling-hilda-report/

and companies. When they are elected, those politicians are then more likely to develop policies that are in the interest of the wealthy people and businesses supporting them, such as reduced minimum wages, reduced business regulations and tax cuts for the wealthy, thus worsening the economic well-being of lower income people.

Low-income people are also less likely to become involved in the political process. They may lack the background, the education, the social networks or they may simply lack the time to engage in political activities. As a result, the "voice" of low-income people may not be adequately represented in government policy.

What are the consequences of inequality and poverty?

- **For economic growth**

  The debate about the link between inequality and economic growth has fueled much theoretical and empirical research. On the one hand, large gaps between high- and low-income groups provide the incentives for entrepreneurship and innovation. The attractiveness of high incomes gives lower paid workers the motivation to work harder and improve their education and skills so that they may move into the higher paid jobs. When there is more equality and the gap is smaller, there are fewer incentives. Furthermore, it is argued that high levels of investment are needed for an economy to grow, and that the pools of savings needed for investment will not be as available in a more equal society.

Key concept
EFFICIENCY

  On the other hand, it is also argued that inequality harms economic growth. Where there is high inequality and high levels of poverty, there are increasingly fewer opportunities for lower income members of society, and as we have already seen, this can become a vicious cycle. Children from poorer backgrounds are likely to leave school without appropriate skills and training. This may result in lower productivity levels, which damages economic growth. As noted by the OECD, "If a large swathe of the population is unable to invest in its skills, that's bad news for the economy." Furthermore, the social and political instability that is often associated with high levels of poverty can be a deterrent to growth. This underlines a very important point written about by a wide range of economists – that inequality is damaging for everyone, not just the poor.

- **For living standards and social stability**

  Logically, wide gaps in income mean that those living below the average level of income are living in some degree of poverty. Poverty may take all kinds of shapes, but the clear result is unacceptably low living standards and economic vulnerability.

Cornwall fuel poverty laid bare as thousands struggle to heat homes

https://www.cornwalllive.com/news/cornwall-news/cornwall-fuel-poverty-laid-bare-3037571

  People in poverty have to make difficult choices about how to use their very limited incomes – food, fuel, school supplies and

transportation. The Joseph Rowntree Foundation identifies what it means to be poor in the UK: *"Poverty means not being able to heat your home, pay your rent or buy the essentials for your children. It means waking up every day facing insecurity, uncertainty and impossible decisions about money. It means facing marginalization – and even discrimination – because of your financial circumstances. The constant stress it causes can lead to problems that deprive people of the chance to play a full part in society."*

In unequal societies, neighbourhoods and areas of cities may become identified by their income groups, with "rich" areas and "poor" areas, and this may be self-perpetuating. If government-subsidized housing is concentrated in particular areas, this will result in even greater concentration of people living with low incomes. Low-income areas are less likely to have good schools and attract good teachers, so education prospects suffer. Low-income areas may suffer from poor infrastructure and facilities, so this limits opportunities for its residents.

Social stability is precarious in situations of high inequalities. Where people are living in extremely disadvantaged circumstances, with low living standards, resentment and hostility may be high. Studies have shown that this leads to social tension and increased criminal behaviour. This is particularly the case where young people feel that they have no job prospects and legitimate ways of earning a living. There may be increased gang-related activity. People living in impoverished areas may feel unsafe, and law enforcement may not be able to deal with the dangers. Social instability may result in threats to private property.

When a significant proportion of a population lives in relative poverty and people see a system that they perceive is unfair and not working for them, they are unlikely to support the political system and democratic process. This can give rise to an unstable social and political climate and tension between low-income people and those that govern. This further emphasizes the conclusion that high levels of inequality are harmful for everyone.

Economics in action

ATL Thinking, Communication and Research

As we have already stated, inequality is not a function of national income. It is the result of national policies and institutions that shape the way in which a nation's advantages and benefits are shared. Therefore, governments have it within their power to shape institutions and develop policies that reduce inequalities in opportunities, income and wealth. The policies identified in the rest of this chapter are by no means exhaustive, and include just a few country-specific examples. It is expected that you will find your own examples of government action in different countries, so that

Exercise 22.2

ATL Thinking and Communication

Even back in 1776, Adam Smith, who became known for his support of *laissez faire* economic policies (see Chapter 2), recognized the lack of equity in a society with a large share of people in poverty. Try to translate the following into modern language!

"No society can surely be flourishing and happy, of which the far greater part of the members are poor and miserable. It is but equity that they who feed, clothe and lodge the whole body of people should have such a share of the produce of their own labour as to be themselves tolerably well-fed, clothed and lodged".

Adam Smith, *The Wealth of Nations*

Economics in action

ATL Thinking, Communication and Research

Work in pairs and choose a city in a developed country of your choice. Make a presentation to demonstrate any consequences of inequality and/or poverty that are evident in the city. Support your presentation with specific data and pictures.

you can make your own suggestions about what works and doesn't work to promote equity.

Areas for inquiry include:

- the role of a country's tax structure in achieving equity
- policies to improve people's opportunities to reach their potential
- the effectiveness of transfer payments in reducing poverty and inequality
- advantages and disadvantages of minimum wages
- Universal Basic Income as a means of reducing poverty and inequality.

What is the role of taxation in reducing poverty, income and wealth inequality?

Governments at all levels (municipal, state/provincial, national) impose a huge array of different taxes for a range of reasons. Indirect taxes may be imposed to reduce the consumption of goods whose consumption creates negative externalities, they may be used to pursue environmental goals and they may be imposed on imported goods to help domestic producers. Direct taxes may be raised or lowered to change the level of aggregate demand in the economy to achieve macroeconomic goals. Taxes are also levied so that government can finance its expenditures. In this section, we are looking at the way that different taxes and tax systems influence the distribution of income.

Households pay their direct taxes in the form of income taxes. Each year, people must fill in a tax return, noting all the different forms of income they may have received. The amount of tax that they owe depends on this income. Most governments implement a progressive income tax system as the main way of achieving greater equity. A progressive tax means that as income rises, people pay a higher percentage of this income as tax. In a progressive system, a person earning a low income might pay a small percentage of their income to the government, whereas a person earning a very high income would have to pay a larger percentage.

Many countries have property taxes as a form of a tax on wealth. The higher the value of a person's home, or property, the higher the amount of tax would be paid. A few countries have "wealth" taxes, where they charge people a tax based on the value of their financial assets. Despite the fact that relatively few countries impose such taxes, there is much political debate on the issue. In 2014, the French economist Thomas Piketty wrote a lengthy and very popular book called *Capital in the Twenty-First Century* documenting and analysing changes in wealth and income inequality over time. His great concern with rapidly increasing inequality in the last decades led him to call for a coordinated global tax on wealth. This has become a popular demand, particularly from people, politicians and economists who are greatly concerned about growing inequalities and the global concentration of wealth among a very small percentage of the world's population. A small percentage tax on the wealth of the super-rich in an economy could generate significant funds. This might allow the government to reduce income taxes on middle- and low-income earners or to finance important infrastructure initiatives.

Businesses pay taxes on their profits, known as corporate taxes. Corporate taxes vary from country to country. In some cases, the tax rate is constant, regardless of the level of profits, while in others, they may be progressive so that companies theoretically pay higher rates of taxes on higher levels of profits. In reality, despite the official corporate tax rates, companies can often take advantage of a huge number of "tax breaks" that allow them to pay a much lower "effective" tax rate than the official corporate rate. Some very large multinational companies are often in the media spotlight for the relatively small percentage of taxes they pay as a percentage of their total profits. It is argued that these very large companies are able to take advantage of different tax systems by employing global tax experts to help them minimize their tax commitments. To reduce global inequalities, it is necessary that large multinational corporations pay appropriate taxes on their profits. A statement from the International Monetary Fund acknowledges this problem in its claim that "A new approach to international corporate tax rules is urgent".

How are progressive taxes calculated?

We can see a simple example of a progressive tax system in Table 22.6.

Tax "Bracket"	"Taxable" income ($)	Tax rate
1	Up to $10,000	0
2	Over $10,000 and up to $25,000	30%
3	Over $25,000 and up to $50,000	40%
4	Over $50,000	50%

▲ **Table 22.6** Tax rates for different income levels (hypothetical)

Often (but not in all countries), there is a certain amount of income that is not taxed. In these systems, a person earning a low income (in the first tax bracket) would pay no tax at all. However, when the income rises and moves into the second tax bracket, then a certain percentage of the income will have to be paid to the government as income tax. In this case, the "marginal rate" of tax of 30% would have to be paid on all income between $10,000 and $25,000. Then if income were to rise further, moving the person into the third bracket, 40% would have to be paid on all income between $25,000 and $50,000. If a person's income increased above $50,000, this would put the additional income into the top tax bracket with a marginal rate of 50%. But note that this 50% would only be paid on incomes over $50,000.

Let's look at two examples of how this works.

Katja and Marija both live in the hypothetical economy with the tax rates as shown in Table 22.6. Katja earns $43,000 and Marija earns $80,000. How much does each of them pay in income tax? The calculations are shown below:

Katja "Taxable" Income $43,000	Marginal rate	Calculation	Tax paid
Up to $10,000	0%	10,000 × 0	0
Income between $10,000 and 25,000	30%	15,000 × 0.3	4,500
Income above $25,000 ($18,000)	40%	18,000 × 0.4	7,200
Total income $43,000			Total tax paid: $11,700

Marija "Taxable" Income $80,000	Marginal rate	Calculation	Tax paid
Up to $10,000	0%	10,000 × 0	0
Income between $10,000 and 25,000	30%	15,000 × 0.3	4,500
Income between $25,000 and $50,000	40%	25,000 × 0.4	10,000
Income above $50,000 ($30,000)	50%	30,000 × .5	15,000
Total income: $80,000			Total tax paid: $29,500

We can also calculate the average tax rate paid by each of the residents. The average tax is simply: total tax paid/total income × 100.

In this case, Katja's average tax rate is $\frac{11{,}700}{43{,}000} \times 100 = 27.21\%$.

Marija's average tax rate is $\frac{29{,}500}{80{,}000} \times 100 = 36.88\%$.

It is very important to note that the example used in Table 22.6 represents a vastly simplified tax structure. In reality, most countries have tax structures that are far more complicated. The biggest complication comes in the form of "tax deductions" and how "taxable" income is calculated. Tax deductions allow people to reduce their "taxable" income as a result of spending on certain things. For example, if a person moves from one part of the country to another to take a different job and the cost of the move is $5,000, they might be able to deduct this amount from their income, and therefore reduce their "taxable" income, reducing the amount of tax they pay. The government might do this to ease the costs of moving and encourage workers to be more willing to change jobs. A common tax deduction in many countries is when people donate money to a recognized charity; they can claim this on their tax form and reduce their taxable income. Tax deductions vary from country to country.

Assessment advice

In HL P3, you may be asked to calculate total tax, average tax and the amount of indirect tax from a set of data. Here is one example of the type of questions you might be asked. You are given half of the answers as a model.

The following table shows the tax rates for income tax in the country of Opportunia for 2018.

Tax bracket	Disposable Income	Tax rate
1	Up to $11,000	0%
2	Over $11,000 and up to $18,000	25%
3	Over $18,000 and up to $31,000	35%
4	Over $31,000 and up to $60,000	42%
5	Over $60,000 and up to $90,000	48%
6	Over $90,000 and up to $1,000,000	50%
7	Over $1,000,000	55%

In Opportunia, there is also an indirect VAT (Value added tax) on all goods and services purchased of 15%.

Samaya and Wesley both work in Opportunia. Their incomes are given in the table below. Read the information in the table and use it to answer the questions that follow. The calculations for the questions concerning Samaya are given for you in blue, so you should complete the questions for Wesley.

	Annual Income EUR (Given)	Income tax paid EUR	Disposable Income (Yd)	% of Yd spent (Given)	VAT paid	Total tax paid	Average rate of tax
Samaya	45,000	$12,180	$32,820	90	$3,852.78	$16,032.78	35.63%
Wesley	90,000			60			

a) Calculate the annual income tax to be paid by Samaya and Wesley.

For Samaya: (Bracket 1) 11,000 × 0% = 0
(Bracket 2) 7,000 × 25% = 1,750
(Bracket 3) 13,000 × 35% = 4,550
(Bracket 4) 14,000 × 42% = 5,880
= $12,180

b) Calculate the disposable income earned by Samaya and Wesley.

Samaya's disposable income (total income minus income tax) is:
45,000 – 12,180 = $32,820

c) Calculate the GST paid by Samaya and Wesley.

Samaya spends 90% of her disposable income (given).
Therefore, Samaya spends:
32,820 × .90 = $29,538

This amount that Samaya spends includes the VAT on the goods and services that she bought. Therefore, we have to work out how much of her spending was the indirect tax.

There are two different methods that you might use to work this out.

Method one

Solve the equation: X + (Indirect Tax Rate × X) = Total spending

Where X = Original expenditure

For Samaya: X + 15%X = 29,538

1.15X = 29,538

X = 25,685.22 (rounded to two decimal places, or cents)

If $25,685.22 is the original expenditure, and the total spending is $29,538, then the indirect tax is the difference of $3,852.78.

Method two

Use the equation: Total expenditure $\times \frac{\text{Indirect Tax Rate}}{(100 + \text{Indirect Tax Rate})}$

For Samaya: $29{,}538 \times \frac{15}{115} = \$3{,}852.78$

d) Calculate the total tax paid by Samaya and Wesley.

For Samaya: Total tax paid is $12,180 + $3,852.78 = $16,032.78

e) Calculate the average rate of tax (including both direct tax and indirect tax) paid by Samaya and Wesley.

Use the equation: $\frac{\text{Total tax paid}}{\text{Total income}} \times 100$

Where total tax paid = total direct tax paid + total indirect tax paid

For Samaya: $\frac{\$16{,}032.78}{\$45{,}000} \times 100 = 35.63\%$

f) Is this a progressive tax? With reference to values, explain your answer.

g) Opportunia changes its tax structure, and increases the VAT to 20%. Using a Lorenz curve diagram (with two Lorenz curves), explain how a change like this would affect its Lorenz curve.

What are "regressive" taxes?

An income tax structure is progressive if it takes a larger percentage of a larger income and a smaller percentage of a smaller income. As noted above, most direct tax structures are progressive.

On the other hand, indirect taxes are *regressive*, in that they take a larger share of income from lower income people than from higher income people. This is not a deliberate policy to harm low income people; it is simply a mathematical fact.

Consider an example of a $1.00 tax on a litre of diesel, and assume that people end up spending $50 per month in petrol taxes. For a person earning $500 per month, this $50 tax represents 10% of their income. For a person earning $2,500 per month, this same tax of $50 only takes 2% of their income. Thus, the indirect tax is regressive because it takes a larger percentage of income from lower income people than from higher income people.

Indirect taxes are an important source of revenue for governments, and they can be used to discourage the consumption of goods that create negative externalities (such as diesel). However, because they are regressive, they worsen income inequality.

Most countries have tax systems that combine elements of different types of taxes, some of which may be progressive and some of which may be regressive. A progressive income tax structure which makes the distribution of income more equal will be offset to some extent by the country's indirect taxes.

What are the arguments for and against progressive taxation as a means of achieving a more equitable distribution of income?

Since equity is about fairness, it may be argued that it would not be fair to charge all income earners the same rate of tax, since lower income households need to use more of their income to meet their needs, and taxes could substantially reduce their economic well-being. Since those with higher incomes can afford to pay more, it may be argued that it is fair that they should pay more. A progressive income tax narrows the gap between high income and low income people and it is seen as a means of achieving greater equity. A government seeking to achieve a more equal distribution of income could make its tax structure more progressive, by raising the tax rate at higher levels of income or lowering the rate of tax at lower levels of income.

Furthermore, a progressive tax structure gives the government the funds to finance its necessary expenditures and also allows for redistributive policies. This is done through the provision of transfer payments, such as child allowances, maternity and paternity benefits, unemployment insurance and pensions as a means of promoting equity.

Some countries have much more progressive tax structures than others. That is, the average tax and the marginal tax rates are relatively higher. Those countries that have more progressive taxes have a more equal distribution of income; they can also afford much more in terms of social services and social welfare programmes to support living standards of lower income households.

However, there are also arguments against progressive tax structures. As noted in Chapter 18, free market economists who support market-oriented, supply-side policies argue that higher marginal taxes create *disincentives*. According to this view:

- if people feel that their hard work is simply going to result in them having to pay a higher rate of tax, they have less incentive to work harder and improve their economic situation
- higher taxes could discourage entrepreneurial activity and even encourage entrepreneurs to leave the country in favour of more "favourable" tax climates
- taxes on interest, dividends and capital gains, which particularly affect higher income earners, could depress saving and the purchasing of stocks and shares, which would deprive financial markets of necessary funds.

Economics in action

ATL Thinking, Communication and Research

A tax is a proportional tax if the proportion of income paid in tax is constant for all income levels. It may be argued that a proportional tax structure is good for an economy as it removes the possible disincentive associated with a progressive tax. If people know that that they will not be taxed at a higher rate if they earn more money, they may have more incentive to work hard.

Can you find any examples of economies which use a proportional tax system? Why do they do this?

Key concept

EFFICIENCY

Despite these arguments, there is little evidence that such possible disincentives would have any notable effect of the economic well-being of the richest within any population. Economies which have very progressive tax structures do not demonstrate weaker economic performance. It may be argued that the benefits of greater equality far outweigh possible costs to those on very high incomes.

What further policies may be used to reduce poverty and inequalities in income and wealth?

What are transfer payments?

Governments use tax revenues to redistribute income and provide different types of assistance to groups in the economy to improve their living standards and opportunities. These are known as transfer payments since the assistance represents income that is transferred from some groups in the economy to support other groups. They may also be known as "welfare payments" or "social security payments".

There are many different types of transfer payments, including child support, maternity and paternity benefits, old age pensions, housing allowances, fuel allowances to help pay for heating and other welfare payments. Some transfers are "universal"; that is, they are given to everyone. For example, child support might be given to all parents for all children that they have. Others transfer payments are "means tested"; that is, they are given only to people whose incomes are below a certain level or they are given based on eligibility requirements. These represent targeted spending aimed at reaching those who clearly need the support and are seen as an important way to reduce poverty and inequality.

Exercise 22.4 ATL Thinking and Communication

Read the article and answer the questions that follow

Income redistribution through taxes and transfers across OECD countries

Tax and transfer systems play a crucial role in income redistribution and inequality reduction, but concerns have arisen about their effectiveness under the pressure of globalisation and the emergence of new forms of work. This has prompted vivid debates on introducing a universal basic income and reigniting tax progressivity through the taxation of top incomes and wealth.

Taxes and transfers reduce market income inequality by slightly more than 25% on average across the OECD (Figure 1); but this average masks a great deal of difference ranging from 40% in Ireland to around 5% in Chile. The level of redistribution is also highly variable in countries exhibiting similar levels of market income inequality – for example, the Gini index stands at around 38 in both Japan and Norway, but the Gini index for income after taxes and transfers stands at around 27 in Norway compared to 32 points in Japan. Such variations reflect cross-country differences in the size of the public sector, and, indeed, the level of redistribution is strongly associated with the level of public social spending on cash support to the working-age population, as well as to the level of total tax revenues.

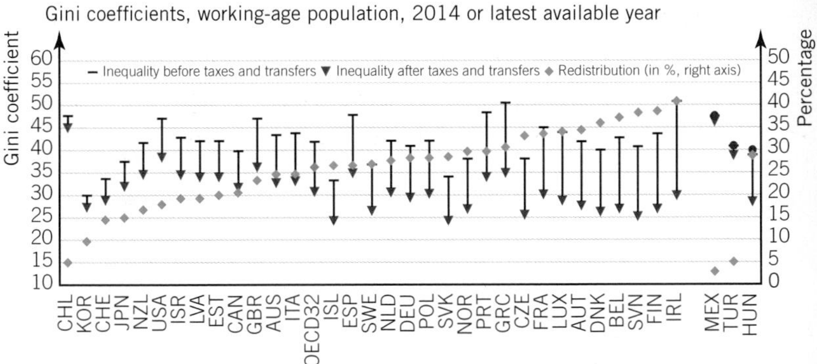

▲**Figure 1** The equalising effect of taxes and transfers varies widely across OECD countries, even for similar levels of inequality before taxes and transfers

At the same time, size is not enough to fully explain income redistribution, for instance because it says little about the extent to which social spending and transfer payments go to the poorest households. For example, in Greece, Italy, Portugal and Spain, 10% or less of total transfers accrues to bottom quintile households, by contrast with more than 40% in Australia, Finland and New Zealand.

Source: Adapted from "Income redistribution through taxes and transfers across OECD countries", Vox, CEPR Policy Report, https://voxeu.org/article/income-redistribution-through-taxes-and-transfers

▲**Figure 2** Targeting of cash transfers to low-income households differs across OECD countries

1. By comparing two contrasting countries in Figure 1, explain how the system of "tax and transfer" results in different outcomes in terms of reducing income inequality. Use numbers in your response. You might have to look up the OECD abbreviations for countries to do this. (The text shows an example of this by comparing Japan and Norway. Do not use this same example!)
2. Suggest why the share of social spending and transfer payments that reaches the poorest 20% of the population is lower in some countries.
3. With reference to the information in Figure 2, explain how Spain could reduce income inequality by adopting measures similar to New Zealand.

What are policies to promote equal opportunities through investment in human capital?

It is not enough to simply say that governments should increase their spending on education and/or health. It is not the quantity of spending that brings about improvements in human capital; it is the nature and quality of that spending. Governments need to design policies that ensure equal opportunities for people at all income levels. This requires targeted government subsidies, transfers and programmes that support lower income households who are currently locked out of many opportunities. Governments in countries, regions and cities with low levels of social mobility can learn from the evidence of successes in other areas to help to develop policies that help to break the cycle of poverty.

As the OECD points out in its report on promoting social mobility, governments need to create opportunities for improved health and education at all age levels, from pre-school to university and to adult education and training and through to retirement. Examples of policies at different levels include:

- Public health insurance (universal health care) to make sure that all households have access to the health care system.
- Programmes to provide pre-natal and post-natal care to low income families.
- Improved access to good-quality child care and preschool programmes to children from disadvantaged backgrounds. This could be done through subsidies to make early education affordable.
- Conditional cash transfers (CCTs). These are payments to families given on the condition that the parent or parents meet certain requirements related to their children's education and health. Such conditions might include immunization or a certain percentage of school attendance. Such programmes are seen to reduce current poverty by providing cash and reduce future poverty by increasing the human capital of children and youths so that they can benefit from more opportunities later.
- School food policies to make sure that children from low-income households can have nutritious meals that help them to learn more effectively.
- Health education in schools and in the media to improve diet and nutrition.
- Recruitment of quality teachers and more educational resources for schools in disadvantaged areas.
- Provision of after-school programmes to teach non-academic skills and provide safe environments.
- Targeted support for low-performing students to prevent school dropouts.
- Apprenticeships for older students to help prepare for the workplace.
- Financial support, counselling and tutoring to help students from lower-income families attend and stay in higher education.

- Training and work experience programmes to increase the employability of adults who lose their jobs.
- Community programmes to provide parenting support.
- More resources targeted towards elder care to help senior citizens struggling on low pensions.

What are policies to reduce gender and other discrimination?

In terms of basic human rights, all people in an economy should have the same access to private and public services, jobs and opportunities regardless of their gender, disabilities, race, religion, political stance or sexual orientation. It is the government's responsibility to have effective policies in place to prevent any unfair treatment, and thereby work towards decreasing the inequalities which can significantly damage people's standards of living.

Governments and most large companies have "diversity" policies to ensure that they are giving equal and fair treatment to all groups within society. There is much overlap here with the policies addressed above, as the goal is to increase the opportunities available to those who may have been denied certain opportunities as a result of their gender, race, sexual orientation etc.

Policies could include:

- Laws related to salaries and wages to ensure equal pay for work of equal value.
- Positive/affirmative action to encourage businesses and government bodies to have greater diversity in their workplaces and provide more opportunities for those groups of people who have previously been discriminated against.
- Legislation to make it illegal to discriminate against any individuals in, for example, education, an employment position, or in the rental market.
- Diversity quotas (or targets) to ensure that members of groups that have been discriminated against make up at least a certain required percentage of the people working in a particular capacity. For example, in government, there could be a requirement that a certain percentage of women be members of particular committees. This would give groups that had been disadvantaged greater representation in the government and theoretically promote their interests more effectively.
- To promote gender equality, governments might mandate that a certain percentage of company boards of directors be women.
- Requirements for accessibility so that a person cannot be excluded due to disabilities.

In-work poverty a growing crisis for 14 million struggling to make ends meet

https://www.bigissue.com/latest/in-work-poverty-a-growing-crisis-for-14-million-struggling-to-make-ends-meet/

What will increased minimum wages achieve?

By definition, a minimum wage is "the minimum amount of remuneration that an employer can legally pay a worker". According to the International Labour Organization (ILO), the "purpose of minimum wages is to protect workers against unduly low pay. They help ensure a just and equitable share of the fruits of progress to all and a minimum living wage to all who are employed and in need of such protection. Minimum wages can also be one element of a policy to overcome poverty and reduce inequality."[1]

While having a job is one important way of ensuring a decent standard of living, many countries face the problem of "working poverty" where people have jobs but are still living below their country's national poverty line. One reason for this may be to do with the fact that in some countries, the national minimum wage is not sufficient to ensure a reasonable standard of living.

It may be argued that it is simply not fair if a person is living in poverty yet working a full-time job earning the minimum wage. Given the significant negative consequences of poverty and inequality, an appropriate solution would be to raise the minimum wage to a level that guarantees an income which will allow for a reasonable standard of living.

There is significant debate on the consequences of raising minimum wages. Table 22.7 briefly presents some of the key arguments and counter arguments for not increasing minimum wages.

Arguments against:	Counter arguments:
A higher minimum wage will hurt the workers it is designed to help because firms will reduce the quantity of labour they demand and so it will lead to an increase in unemployment for those unskilled workers working at the minimum wage.	There is no obvious empirical relationship between a minimum wage and unemployment.
Employers will replace workers with machines if the price of labour increases.	Much of the work done by minimum wage workers cannot be done by machines.
Higher wages mean higher costs of production and so higher prices.	Higher wages motivate people to work harder and so their higher productivity offsets the higher wages.
Businesses that cannot afford the higher wages will go out of business, increasing unemployment.	Higher wages encourage people to stay in their jobs longer, and this reduces the costs of hiring and re-training new workers.

▲Table 22.7 Arguments against minimum wage increases and their counter arguments

[1] **Source:** The International Labour Organization: How to define a minimum wage, https://www.ilo.org/global/topics/wages/minimum-wages/definition/lang--en/index.htm

There are also a number of additional arguments for increasing the minimum wage rate:

- Higher wages encourage people to join the labour market, and so reduce unemployment.
- Higher wages result in increased consumption by low-wage workers, leading to an increase in aggregate demand and increased employment.
- The minimum wage is generally what is earned by low-skilled workers in occupations such as retail salespeople, fast-food workers, cleaners and people who care for children or the elderly. These are often the people who were deprived of the opportunities to obtain an education that would have given them the skills needed for higher-paid jobs. A higher minimum wage may allow them to escape their poverty trap and provide better opportunities for their own children.
- Many of the jobs done by minimum wage workers are done by women. Increasing the minimum wage can narrow the wage gap between men and women.
- Higher minimum wages reduce inequality.

What is Universal Basic Income?

Welfare programmes providing transfer payments, such as unemployment benefits, are essential to reduce poverty and ensure that those people who need government support are able to get it. However, many programmes require significant amounts of paperwork, conditions, resources to make sure that recipients are eligible for the benefits and sanctions for those who "cheat" the system.

Issues can arise for a vast variety of reasons. Consider one simple example, of a person receiving some form of jobless payment of $900 per month. They have the opportunity to take a job, but the pay of $950 they would receive would still leave them in poverty, and they would clearly lose the unemployment benefit. An option would be to apply for a different type of income support, but this would be time-consuming and difficult, and might leave them unable to afford the basics for some time. This would create a disincentive to take a job, which is not the intention of the benefits system! Problems with such welfare systems can leave poor people trapped in poverty.

One solution would be to give every single person a Universal Basic Income (UBI). Proponents of such a scheme have been around for centuries, and include philosophers, politicians and economists from all side of the spectrum, even free market economists such as Friedrich von Hayek and Milton Friedman.

Universal Basic Income has been nicknamed "free money for everyone", and the idea has gained popularity across the world in recent years. The observation that technology and automation is going to continue to eliminate certain forms of work and increase inequalities has lead many people to recognise that different solutions need to be found to ensure that people can live in dignity and enjoy reasonable living standards.

Did you know?

In 2019, the minimum wage in Spain increased by an impressive 22%. This was the largest increase in 40 years. The monthly salary increased from €736 to €900. Since most workers in Spain are paid 14 times a year, this results in an annual income of €12,600. The legal wage is to be paid to temporary and part-time workers, as well as domestic employees.

Spanish Prime Minister Pedro Sánchez claimed that "a rich country cannot have poor workers".

The following appeared in the royal decree that announced the increase, "The rise in the minimum wage is a decisive factor for the creation of employment and economic recovery to be translated into a progressive real reduction of poverty and of wage inequality and will serve to improve the general conditions of the economy".

In a UBI scheme, all citizens would receive a guaranteed amount, each week, or each month, with no conditions or eligibility requirements. The amount given would be enough to keep people above the poverty line and would be the same for everyone, regardless of their income or whether they are working or not working. Table 22.8 briefly presents some of the key arguments and counter arguments for not giving a UBI.

Arguments against UBI	Counter-arguments
Giving people money will make them lazy, and they will stop working, or not look for work	The amount given would be enough to meet basic needs, preventing people from living in poverty. People will still want to improve their economic well being by working to earn more. A UBI gives people opportunities to do many things, all of which can be good for themselves and the wider community/economy. Possibilities include: • Returning to school to improve skills to get a good job • Looking after children/older family members • Starting a business
It is too expensive.	There are several arguments against this: • Inequality and poverty are a problem for everyone, not just the poor. It is in the interest of the rich people that poverty and inequality be reduced and so marginal tax rates for the very rich could be increased to help finance a UBI. • In many countries, the benefits of economic growth have gone to the wealthiest few; maybe it is time for redistributive policies, such as higher taxes and wealth taxes on the very rich, to spread the benefits a little more equally. • Removing many of a country's conditional welfare payments and replacing them with an unconditional UBI would free up significant amounts of resources.
What's the point of giving it to rich people, too?	It needs to be universal and seen as a right for everyone. Any conditions or threshhold incomes make it another form of welfare, requiring resources to administer.

▲Table 22.8 Arguments against providing UBI and their counter arguments

Economics in action

ATL Thinking, Communication and Research

Different versions of Universal Basic Income schemes have been used or trialed around the world. Politicians in many countries advocate their implementation. Present your own version of the advantages and disadvantages, supporting your points with evidence.

EXAMINATION QUESTIONS

Paper 1, part (a) questions – HL & SL

1. Distinguish between equity and equality. [10 marks]
2. Explain two ways in which a country might establish its national poverty line. [10 marks]
3. Explain the difference between absolute and relative poverty. [10 marks]
4. Explain two causes of inequality. [10 marks]
5. Explain what would happen to the distribution of income if a country were to decrease the direct tax rates for top income earners, and reduce its indirect tax rate. [10 marks]

Paper 1, part (a) questions – HL only

1. Analyse the relationship between a country's Gini coefficient and its Lorenz curve. [10 marks]

Paper 1, part (b) questions – HL only

1. Using real-world examples, evaluate the consequences of a country adopting a more progressive tax structure. [15 marks]
2. Using real-world examples, evaluate the effectiveness of minimum wages in achieving a more equitable distribution of income. [15 marks]
3. Using real-world examples, discuss the extent to which transfer payments can alleviate poverty. [15 marks]
4. Using real-world examples, evaluate the view that a government's fiscal policy can be both a cause of inequality and a means of reducing inequality. [15 marks]

4-mark questions (HL P2, SL P2 or HL P3)

1. A country increases its indirect tax rate. Using a Lorenz curve diagram, explain how this may impact the country's distribution of income. (HL and SL) [4 marks]
2. Citizen A in a country earns $130,000 and pays $12,000 in taxes. Citizen B earns $55,000 and pays $10,000 in taxes. Explain whether the tax structure is progressive or regressive. (HL only) [4 marks]

Assessment advice: Internal assessment

It is required that one of your commentaries be about macroeconomics. You should be able to see that there are a large number of possible topic areas here. Your investigations into different countries should be useful here as it is possible that you used contemporary articles in gathering your information. Perhaps one of these will be suitable for a commentary. Just remember that the article you choose has to have been written no earlier than one year before you write your commentary.

Having finished macroeconomics, you are likely to be able to bring together many topics that are interwoven. This will give you an opportunity to evaluate. For example, you may find an article about a central bank's efforts to control inflationary pressures through interest rate increases. Evaluation in such a case may involve an assessment of the likely effects of this on the stakeholders and a consideration of the potential conflict among policy objectives.

When you are choosing your article, bear in mind that there must be a clear link to one of the key concepts in the course. When you write your commentary, be sure that your analysis includes meaningful references to this concept.

Please remember that all three of the articles that you use to write your commentaries must come from different sources. This not only gives you the opportunity to read articles that may come from different perspectives, but ideally, it should allow you to learn about economics in different parts of the world.

23 WHY DO COUNTRIES TRADE?

REAL-WORLD ISSUE:
Who are the winners and losers of the integration of the world's economies?

By the end of this chapter, you should be able to:

- → Define international trade
- → Identify and explain the gains from trade
- HL Define, explain, illustrate and give examples of absolute advantage
- HL Define, explain, illustrate and give examples of comparative advantage
- HL Calculate opportunity costs to identify comparative advantage
- HL Use linear PPCs to show potential gains from specialization and trade as a result of comparative advantage
- HL Discuss the limitations of comparative advantage theory.

What are the gains from international trade?

International trade is the exchange of goods and services between countries. There are a number of gains to be made from international trade and we should consider them at this point.

1. *Lower prices:* The main gain from trade is the ability to buy goods and services at a lower price than the domestic one. Consumers are able to buy less expensive products and producers are able to purchase less expensive raw materials and semi-manufactured goods. This is the main reason for trade.

Prices may be lower in some countries than others because of access to natural resources, differences in the quality of the labour forces, or differences in the quality of capital and the levels of technology. The cause of these lower prices is mainly determined by the concept of comparative advantage, which is dealt with in the next section.

2. *Greater choice:* International trade enables consumers to have a greater choice of products. They now have access not just to domestically produced products, but also to products that come from a number of different countries.
3. *Differences in resources:* Different countries possess different resources. There are some resources that a country may need, but quite simply does not have. For example, many countries do not possess copper, diamonds or oil naturally. However, they may need them in order to produce other products and so have no option but to import the commodities they lack. To do this, they will need to export goods or services, in order to earn foreign currency and so buy the required resources.

   Some countries, such as Singapore, have very few natural resources and so are dependent on trade for their survival, economic growth and well being. Singapore has to import almost every natural resource, even water! However, Singapore is able to export high levels of manufactured goods and services in order to fund their imports.

4. *Economies of scale:* When producing for an international market, as well as for a domestic one, the size of the market, and thus demand, will increase. This means that the level of production and the size of production units will also increase.

   As we know from Chapter 12, the increased levels of production should provide scope for economies of scale to be achieved and production should become more efficient. Also, larger production units will enable the amount of specialization to increase. When firms are large, individuals may specialize in specific, narrower tasks, such as accounting manager or marketing manager, and they should become more knowledgeable and so more efficient. Larger production units will also lead to greater scope for the division of labour. This is where a production process is broken down into a number of simple and basic tasks. Workers may then concentrate on a small, repetitive task and achieve a high degree of efficiency.

   In addition, if countries specialize in the production of certain commodities, such as chemicals, there will be cost benefits to be gained from acquiring experience and expertise. This is known as moving down the "learning curve" (the long-run average cost curve).

International trade, and with it larger markets and production units, should enable production in a country's export industries to become more efficient in the long run. It should also make the producers more competitive. It should lead to a reduction in long-run average costs.

5. *Increased competition:* International trade may lead to increased competition, as domestic firms compete with foreign firms. This should lead to greater efficiency and may mean that consumers gain by being offered less expensive goods and services. It is also likely that the quality and variety of goods available to consumers will increase, with increased competition.
6. *More efficient allocation of resources:* When international trade takes place freely, without government interference, then the countries that are best at producing certain goods and services will produce them; they will be able to produce these goods and services at the lowest cost and take advantage of their efficiency. If this happens in all of the different trading countries, then it is fair to assume that the world's resources are being used most efficiently when free trade is taking place.
7. *Source of foreign exchange:* International trade enables countries to obtain foreign exchange. If a country exports products, then that country will be paid in foreign currencies. For example, when Ghana sells gold and cocoa to the Netherlands, it will be paid in euro, which it can then use to buy essential products from abroad, such as industrial machinery or petroleum. This is especially important to countries such as Ghana which do not have a convertible currency – one which can be freely exchanged for other currencies on the world market. As it lacks a convertible currency, the only way that Ghana can buy goods from abroad is if it manages to sell goods abroad first, thus getting hold of foreign exchange. So, it should be clear that an important gain from international trade to all countries, but especially developing countries, is that it gives them a source of foreign exchange that can then be used to purchase goods and services from other countries.

Key concept

EFFICIENCY

Exercise 23.1

ATL Thinking and Communication

Make a list of the goods you commonly use that are imported. These can include food, clothing, electronics etc. If possible, identify the source of the goods.

Putting together the seven points above, it is clear that there are huge gains to be achieved from trade. As a concluding comment, it is fair to say that for all the reasons listed above, international trade can make a major contribution to a country's economic growth.

Economics in action

ATL Thinking, Communication and Research

A visit to the Atlas of Economic Complexity provides excellent data visualizations on a vast number of issues related to trade. The information provided on the site about the variety of goods that countries export and import and how this has changed over time is invaluable in understanding the role of trade in contributing to an economy's growth.

Here is one example for Canadian exports in 2018. When you examine such a diagram online, you can break it down further into all the different products. On the right, it shows you that you can look at each product, along with the specifics of trade with individual trade partners.

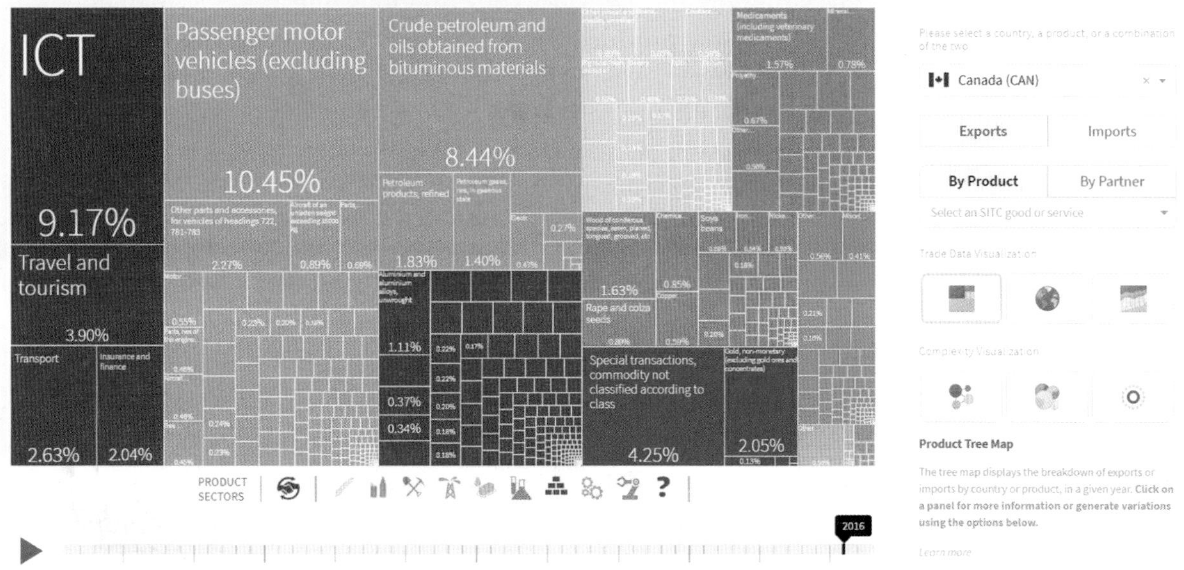

Compare the trade profile of your chosen OECD country with a country at a different level of national income.

http://atlas.cid.harvard.edu/

How does comparative advantage theory work?

We have already said that there are many advantages to international trade. But which goods should a country produce for export and which goods should it import? The answer to this question lies in the concept of comparative advantage.

What is absolute advantage?

Let us start by looking at the concept of absolute advantage. A country is said to have an absolute advantage in the production of a good if it can produce it using fewer resources than another country.

Table 23.1 shows the production outcomes where two countries, Australia and China, are using the same quantities of resources to produce lamb and cloth.

Higher Level

Country	Kilos of lamb	Metres of cloth
Australia	6	1
China	4	3
Total without trade	10	4

▲ **Table 23.1** Absolute advantage

It is clear from the table that Australia has an absolute advantage in producing lamb and that China has an absolute advantage in the production of cloth.

In this situation, the answer to our previous question, "Which goods should a country produce for export and which goods should it import?" is simple. Australia should specialize in the production of lamb and China should specialize in the production of cloth. The output of both products will be maximized when the countries specialize and, after trading, both countries will gain.

Australia would produce lamb and, if it doubled its resources, then assuming constant returns to scale, total output from the resources would be 12 kilos – an increase of 2 kilos. In the same way, China, with twice as many resources and constant returns to scale, would have a total output from its resources of 6 metres of cloth – an increase of 2 metres. Thus, total output of both goods has risen, following specialization.

The situation above, where each country has an absolute advantage in the production of one product, is known as *reciprocal absolute advantage*.

What is comparative advantage?

The whole concept of absolute advantage seems obvious, but what happens if there is not a situation of reciprocal absolute advantage as shown in the above example? In the early nineteenth century, David Ricardo was the first economist to prove mathematically that trade could still be beneficial to both countries when one of the countries had an absolute advantage in producing all goods. Ricardo considered the opportunity cost of production and used this to explain the concept of comparative advantage.

A country is said to have a comparative advantage in the production of a good if it can produce the good at a lower opportunity cost than another country. In other words, country A has to give up fewer units of other goods to produce the good in question than does country B.

This is best shown by an example. Table 23.2 shows the production outcomes where two countries, France and Poland, are using the same quantities of resources to produce wine and cheese.

Country	Litres of wine	Opportunity cost of 1 litre of wine	Kilos of cheese	Opportunity cost of 1 kilo of cheese
France	3	$\frac{4}{3}$ kilos of cheese	4	$\frac{3}{4}$ litre of wine
Poland	1	3 kilos of cheese	3	$\frac{1}{3}$ litre of wine

▲ **Table 23.2** Comparative advantage

This shows that France has an absolute advantage in the production of both goods. However, in terms of comparative advantage, France has a comparative advantage in the production of wine and Poland has a comparative advantage in the production of cheese. This is because France only has to give up $\frac{4}{3}$ kilos of cheese to produce a litre of wine, whereas Poland has to give up 3 kilos, but Poland only has to give up $\frac{1}{3}$ litre of wine to produce a kilo of cheese, whereas France has to give up $\frac{3}{4}$ litre of wine.

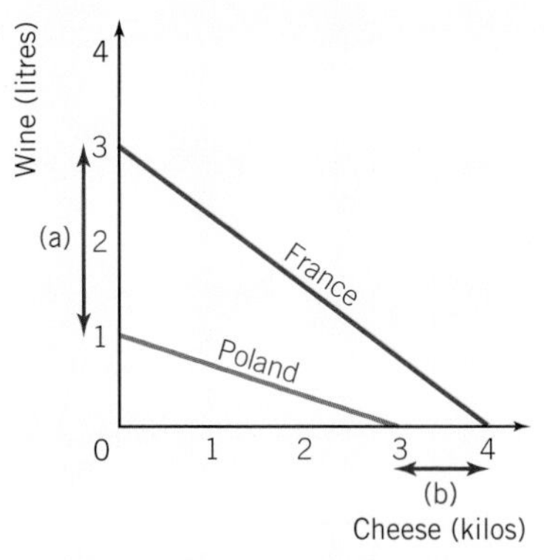

▲ Figure 23.1 Production possibilities curves to show comparative advantage

The theory of comparative advantage tells us that France should specialize in the production of wine and Poland should specialize in the production of cheese. France will then consume the wine that they wish and use any extra wine to exchange for cheese. In the same way, Poland will consume the cheese that it wants and use any extra cheese to exchange for wine. The situation can also be shown on a simple diagram as in Figure 23.1, using simplified production possibilities curves.

Figure 23.1 shows the same information as Table 23.2. However, even without the information in Table 23.2, it is possible to use Figure 23.1 to show comparative advantage.

In simple terms, when a country has an absolute advantage in producing both goods, as France has here, and the scale of the axes is the same, the comparative advantage for the better producer is in the good where the distance between the production possibilities is greatest, shown by (a) in the diagram, and the comparative advantage for the less efficient producer is in the good where the distance between the production possibilities is least, shown by (b) in the diagram. Thus, as we know, France has the comparative advantage in producing wine and Poland has the comparative advantage in producing cheese. This is not a mathematical justification, but simply a useful trick to employ when using diagrams such as this. The real reason relates to the relative slopes of the lines, since it is the slope of the lines that shows the opportunity costs, which in this model is always shown as constant opportunity cost (straight line PPC).

Exercise 23.2

ATL Thinking and Communication

Using the same quantities of resources to produce rice and cloth, China and Pakistan have the following production outcomes.

Country	Kilos of rice	Opportunity cost of 1 kilo of rice	Metres of cloth	Opportunity cost of 1 metre of cloth
China	5		4	
Pakistan	3		3	

1. Calculate the opportunity costs for the table.
2. Draw a diagram to illustrate the information in the table.
3. Should trade take place between China and Pakistan? Why?
4. In which product should each country specialize? Why?

Higher Level

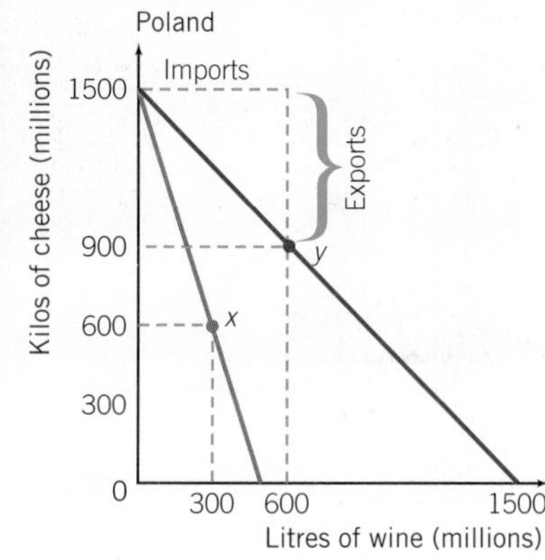

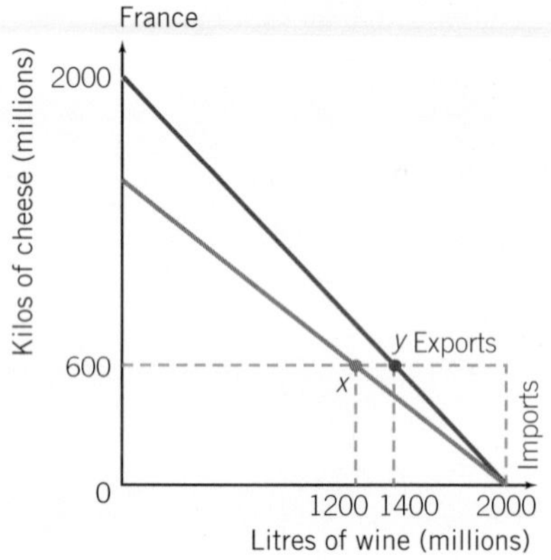

▲ **Figure 23.2** (a) & (b) The potential gains from specialization and trade

How can we use the comparative advantage model to illustrate the "gains from specialization and trade"?

This is best explained using an example. Let us take the original example from Table 23.2, with Poland and France each producing both wine and cheese. To show the potential gains from specialization for both countries, we need to consider an exchange ratio. This is the rate at which one product may be traded for another.

For simplicity, we will assume a ratio of 1:1, ie 1 kilo of cheese can be traded for 1 litre of wine. Table 23.3 shows hypothetical total outputs of wine and cheese in Poland and France, with the same opportunity cost ratios from Table 23.2.

Poland		**France**	
Cheese (kilos m)	Wine (litres m)	Cheese (kilos m)	Wine (litres m)
1,500	0	1,500	0
1,200	100	1,200	400
900	200	900	800
600	300	600	1,200
300	400	300	1,600
0	500	0	2,000

▲ **Table 23.3** Cheese and wine output, Poland and France

In Figure 23.2 (a), before specialization, let us assume that Poland is originally producing at point *x* on its PPC, consuming 600 million kilos of cheese and 300 million kilos of wine. It then specializes in cheese production, where it has a comparative advantage, and so produces 1,500 million kilos of cheese and no wine. It now agrees to export 600 million kilos of cheese to France at the exchange ratio of 1:1 and so receives 600 million litres of wine in return, ie it imports 600 million litres of wine. The country is now consuming outside of its PPC, at point *y* on the red 1:1 exchange ratio line. Poland will still have 900 million kilos of cheese that it has not exported and the 600 million litres of wine that it has imported from France. Thus, there is a gain through specialization and trade of 300 million kilos of cheese and 300 million litres of wine.

In Figure 23.2 (b), before specialization, let us assume that France is originally producing at point *x* on its PPC, consuming 600 million kilos of cheese and 1,200 million litres of wine. It then specializes in wine production, where it has a comparative advantage, and so produces 2,000 million litres of wine. It now agrees to export 600 million litres of wine to Poland at the exchange rate of 1:1 and so receives 600 million kilos of cheese in return, ie it imports 600 million kilos of cheese. The country is now consuming outside of its PPC, at point *y* on the red 1:1 exchange ratio line. France will still have 1,400 million litres of wine that it has not exported and the 600 million kilos of cheese that it has imported from Poland. Thus, there is a gain through specialization of 200 million litres of wine.

So, in this case, both countries will gain from specialization and trade by being able to consume at a point beyond their PPCs. Obviously, the relative amount of gain will depend upon the exchange rate that presides in the market, but it is clear that it is possible for both countries to benefit.

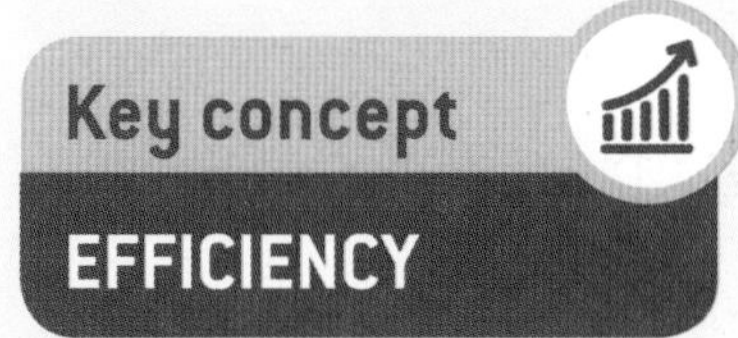

Higher Level

Exercise 23.3

ATL Thinking and Communication

Consider the hypothetical total outputs of two countries, Amazonia and Bretonia, for two products, coffee and tea. The countries are using the same quantities of resources for production.

Amazonia		Bretonia	
Coffee (kilos million)	Tea (kilos million)	Coffee (kilos million)	Tea (kilos million)
500	0	600	0
400	50	500	200
300	100	400	400
200	150	300	600
100	200	200	800
0	250	100	1,000
		0	1,200

1. Calculate the opportunity costs of producing tea and coffee:
   a) in Amazonia
   b) in Bretonia.

Let us assume that the two countries will exchange tea and coffee in the ratio of 1:1, ie 1 kilo of coffee for 1 kilo of tea.

2. Draw a PPC diagram for Amazonia including a 1:1 exchange ratio line.
   a) Show the original position on the PPC if Amazonia was producing and consuming 100 million kilos of coffee and 200 million kilos of tea.
   b) Show on the diagram, and explain in writing, what will happen if Amazonia specializes in coffee production, consumes 200 million kilos of coffee, and exports the remainder to Bretonia in exchange for tea, at an exchange ratio of 1:1.
3. Draw a PPC diagram for Bretonia including a 1:1 exchange ratio line.
   a) Show the original position on the PPC if Bretonia was producing and consuming 200 million kilos of coffee and 800 million kilos of tea.
   b) Show on the diagram, and explain in writing, what will happen if Bretonia specializes in tea production, consumes 900 million kilos of tea, and exports the remainder to Bretonia in exchange for coffee, at an exchange ratio of 1:1.

Does the theory of comparative advantage always work?

One point to bear in mind is that the theory of comparative advantage works so long as the opportunity costs faced by the two countries are different. If the two countries face the same opportunity costs (shown by parallel PPCs), then there would be no point in trade taking place. This situation is shown in Table 23.4 and Figure 23.2.

Higher Level

Higher Level

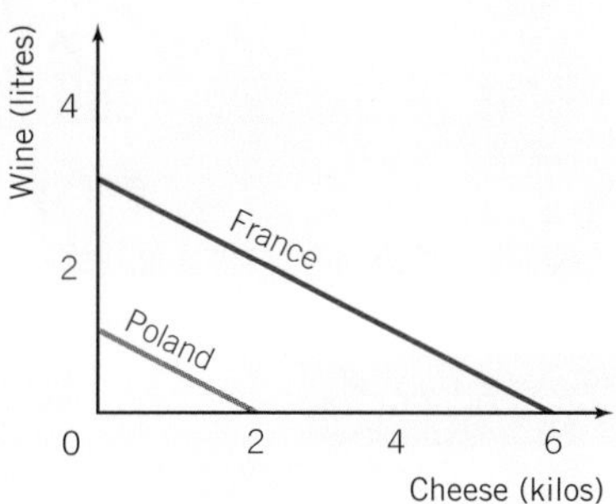

▲ **Figure 23.3**
Identical opportunity costs

Country	Litres of wine	Opportunity cost of 1 litre of wine	Kilos of cheese	Opportunity cost of 1 kilo of cheese
France	3	2 kilos of cheese	6	$\frac{1}{2}$ litre of wine
Poland	1	2 kilos of cheese	2	$\frac{1}{2}$ litre of wine

▲ **Table 23.4** Comparative advantage

As we can see in Figure 23.3, if the slopes of the two production possibilities curves are the same, then opportunity costs for each country will be identical, and there will be no gains to be made by trading.

What gives a country a comparative advantage?

To a large extent, comparative advantage is based on a country's factor endowments. A country that is "endowed" with a large amount of arable land may develop a comparative advantage in agricultural products. A country with abundant unskilled labour can develop its comparative advantage in the production of labour-intensive, low-skilled, manufactured goods. A country with abundant well-educated labour may have a comparative advantage in the output of financial services. A country with beautiful beaches and a favourable climate may develop its comparative advantage in the output of tourist services, illustrating that "climate" can actually be a factor of production! The abundance of a particular factor will make the price of this factor relatively lower than the price of other factors, thereby allowing the opportunity cost of the goods or services using that factor to be lower than it would be in other countries.

David Ricardo (1772–1823)

David Ricardo was born in London into a Dutch-Jewish family in April 1772. At a young age, and without a great deal of formal education, he joined his father working at the London Stock Exchange. When he married a Quaker woman his orthodox Jewish family disinherited him and broke off all contact.

At the age of 27, Ricardo read Adam Smith's famous work, *The Wealth of Nations*, and this encouraged him to study political economy further. It was 10 years before he was first published, in 1809, when he contributed to *The Monthly Chronicle* on the issue of inflation in England and the "bullion controversy". His views represent early monetarist thought that the inflation was caused by the willingness of the Bank of England to issue excessive amounts of bank notes.

Ricardo was very successful at the stock exchange and made a fortune as a stockbroker and loan broker. He purchased a country estate in Gloucestershire and moved there on his retirement from business in 1814. In 1815, Ricardo's publication, *Essay on the Influence of the Low Price of Corn on the Profits of Stock*, presented the theory now known as the law of diminishing returns. His study of the relationship between labour, capital and land in agriculture led him to the conclusion, now well-known, that as increasing amounts of labour and machinery are used on a fixed area of land, additions to total output will eventually diminish.

Ricardo's most famous work was *Principles of Political Economy and Taxation*, published in 1817. At the time, the protectionist British Corn Laws were in place to restrict imports of wheat into Britain. In examining comparative costs between different producers, Ricardo arrived at the conclusions that are known today as the theory of comparative advantage. His famous case study, now presented widely to economics students, looked at the production of wine and cloth in England and Portugal. Although Portugal might be better at producing both wine and cloth, Ricardo showed that both countries would benefit if each specialized and they traded freely. He was thus an early advocate of free trade.

In the same publication, Ricardo made another of his important contributions to economic thought, his explanation of the theory of rents. In studying the production of food and the need to feed increasing populations by using less productive areas of land, Ricardo was able to show that it would be landowners who would benefit from population growth the most, as they would be able to extract high levels of rent.

Throughout his career, Ricardo was influenced by his friendships with James Mill, Jeremy Bentham and Thomas Malthus, important names in nineteenth-century economic, political and philosophical thought. Ricardo died in 1823, at the age of 51. In a relatively short career of 14 years as a "professional" economist, he made several lasting contributions to the economic theory that we study today.

What are the limitations of the theory of comparative advantage?

Comparative advantage theory is based upon a number of assumptions, which tend to limit the application of the theory in real life.

- As in perfect competition, it is assumed that the producers and consumers have perfect knowledge and are aware of where the least expensive goods may be purchased.
- It is usually assumed that there are no transport costs. However, in reality, this is not true. The existence of transport costs may erode a country's comparative advantage and not make international trading worthwhile, since it may eliminate its competitiveness.
- Basic theories assume that there are only two economies producing two goods. However, this is not such a problem. The theory may be applied to more countries and more products and it is still possible to discern where the comparative advantages lie. The use of computer simulations has made the multi-country/multi-product analysis much easier to conduct.

- It is usually assumed that costs do not change and that the returns to scale are constant, ie there are no economies or diseconomies of scale. However, the existence of economies of scale would, in all probability, increase a country's comparative advantage, as relative costs of production fall even more.
- It is usually assumed that the goods being traded are identical, such as barley, cotton or bananas. However, problems arise with goods such as consumer durables. A Toshiba television will be different from a Phillips television and so it is much harder to prove that Japan has the comparative advantage in producing televisions.
- It is usually assumed that factors of production remain in the country. However, it may be the factors of production, rather than the goods, that move from country to country. For example, developed countries, rather than exporting finished goods to developing countries, may invest capital in developing countries to enable goods to be produced there. Labour may migrate from low-wage to high-wage countries.
- It is usually assumed that there is perfectly free trade among countries, but of course, in reality, there are likely to be government-imposed trade barriers in many industries.

In spite of its limitations, comparative advantage theory is at the core of international trade theory and goes a long way to explaining patterns of trade. Countries that specialize in producing goods in which they have a lower opportunity cost than other countries can capture the gains from trade listed at the beginning of this chapter.

EXAMINATION QUESTIONS

Paper 1, part (a) questions

1. Explain **three** potential benefits from international trade. [10 marks]
2. Explain potential sources of comparative advantage. [10 marks]

Paper 1, part (b) questions

1. Using real-world examples, discuss the possible limitations of the theory of comparative advantage. [15 marks]

24 FREE TRADE AND PROTECTIONISM

REAL-WORLD ISSUE:
Who are the winners and losers of the integration of the world's economies?

By the end of this chapter, you should be able to:

- → Define free trade
- → Explain, give examples of and evaluate the arguments for protectionism
- → Explain, give examples of and evaluate the arguments against protectionism
- → Explain and illustrate free trade
- → Explain and illustrate when a country can export
- → Define, explain, illustrate and give examples of types of protectionism
- → Evaluate the effect of different types of trade protection
- → Discuss the merits of free trade versus protectionism
- HL Calculate, from diagrams, the effects of imposing a tariff, setting a quota or giving a subsidy, on different stakeholders.

What is free trade?

Free trade is said to take place between countries when there are no barriers to trade put in place by governments or international organizations. Goods and services are allowed to move freely between countries.

What are the arguments in favour of protectionism?

If international trade is so good for all the countries concerned, why is it that countries do not trade freely? Why do they often protect their

Key concept

ECONOMIC WELLBEING

economies from imports? A number of reasons have been put forward for this, although the arguments are not always valid. Let us look at some of the arguments.

1. **Protecting domestic employment**

   At any given time in an economy there will be some industries that are in decline (sunset industries) because they cannot compete with foreign competition. If the industries are relatively large, this will lead to high levels of structural unemployment. Governments often attempt to protect the industries in order to avoid this unemployment.

   This argument may not be very strong, since it is likely that the industry will continue to decline and that protection will simply prolong the process. Although there will be short-run social costs, it might be argued that it would be better to let the resources employed in the industry move into other areas of the economy. However, in some cases, the negative consequences of a rapidly declining major industry may be so great that the government feels obligated to intervene and protect the market.

2. **Protecting the economy from low-cost labour**

   It is often argued that the main reason for declining domestic industries is the low cost of labour in exporting countries and that the economy should be protected from imports that are produced in countries where the cost of labour is very low. For example, there have been demands in the US to protect the domestic clothing industry against cheap imports from Asia, where wages are much lower. While trade may create many benefits for an economy as a whole, these gains may be spread widely, while the cost in terms of job losses may be concentrated in particular industries. There is much greater job insecurity among manufacturing workers throughout the more developed countries as workers lose their jobs to workers in emerging markets and developing countries. Workers and their trade unions may lobby vigorously for protection against imported goods.

   However, the argument of protection against low-cost labour goes against the whole concept of comparative advantage. It would mean that domestic consumers would pay higher prices than they should and that production in the protected economy would take place at an inefficient level. The country wishing to export would lose trade and their economy would suffer.

   It should be realized that comparative advantage changes over time, and that a country that has a comparative advantage in the production of a good at present may not have it in the future. For instance, it is quite likely that the US did have a comparative advantage in shipbuilding at one time. As relative factor costs change in different countries, it is important that resources should

Did you know?

The world shipbuilding industry provides a good example of different wage costs. In 2008 South Korea produced about 50% of the world's large commercial ships. Another low-cost producer, China, was the second largest producer, with about 35% of the world's production. Production in the USA was minimal. South Korea's dominance was based upon low costs of production, especially labour costs, which typically make up approximately 30% of the total cost of building a ship.

However, by 2017, China had overtaken South Korea in world production of large commercial ships, with approximately 45% of the market. Although exact figures are not available, economists are confident that hourly wages in China are below those in South Korea and that this accounts for the increase in demand for Chinese ships.

Source: https://www.hellenicshippingnews.com

Key concept

EFFICIENCY

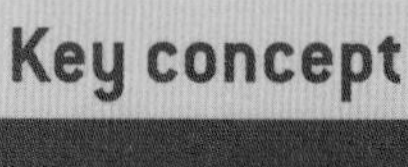

CHANGE

move as freely as possible from industries where comparative advantage is waning, into industries where it is growing. Supply-side policies that focus on labour markets emphasize the importance of making labour flexible enough to adapt to changing economic circumstances. This puts some responsibility on governments to help those workers who have lost their jobs due to increased competition from countries that have developed their comparative advantage in the production of labour-intensive goods.

3. **Protecting an infant (sunrise) industry**

   Many governments argue that an industry that is just developing may not have the economies of scale that larger industries in other countries may enjoy. The domestic industry will not be competitive against foreign imports until it can gain the cost advantages of economies of scale. Because of this, it is argued that the industry needs to be protected against imports until it achieves a size where it is able to compete on an equal footing.

   However, there are possible flaws in this argument. Most developed countries have highly efficient capital markets, which allow them access to large amounts of financial capital, even more so since the advent of globalization. Because of this, it can be argued that there is no basis for the idea that industries in developed countries will set up in a relatively small way and thus not benefit from economies of scale. With access to highly developed capital markets, it is hard to imagine that a new industry would not set up at the most efficient size. For example, the Saudi Arabian government has been diversifying into petrochemical production in recent years. It has undertaken a number of projects in partnership with large multinationals, such as Chevron, BP and Exxon Mobil. The plants constructed have been among some of the largest in the world, gaining almost immediately from economies of scale.

   It is likely that developing countries, without access to sophisticated capital markets, can use the infant industry argument to justify protectionist policies in order to assist with diversification. However, it is debatable whether they have the international political power to be able to impose protectionist policies without complaints and action from developed countries.

4. **To avoid the risks of over-specialization**

   Governments may want to limit over-specialization if it means that the country could become over-dependent on the export sales of one or two products. Any change in the world markets for these products might have serious consequences for the country's economy. For example, changes in technology could severely reduce the demand for a commodity, as the development of quartz crystal watches did for the Swiss wristwatch industry, harming the economy. The introduction of new products or changes in the patterns of demand and supply can have serious effects on the economies of developing countries, which tend to over-specialize in the production of primary products, without choice. For example, the invention of synthetic rubber had a large negative effect on the rubber industry in Malaysia; the over-supply of coffee on the world market, causing falling prices, did the same for Ethiopia.

There are no real arguments against this view. It does not promote protectionism. It simply points out the problems that countries may face if they specialize to a great extent.

5. **Strategic reasons**

   It is sometimes argued that certain industries need to be protected in case they are needed at times of war – for example, agriculture, steel and power generation. Steel is needed for many defence items such as planes and tanks and a steel industry would argue that it must be protected in order to stay competitive.

   To a certain extent, this argument may be a valid one, although it is often overstated. In many cases it is unlikely that countries will go to war or, if they do, that they will be completely cut off from all supplies. It is likely that the argument is mostly being used as an excuse for protectionism.

6. **To prevent dumping**

   Dumping is the selling by a country of large quantities of a commodity, at a price lower than its production cost, in another country. For example, the EU may have a surplus of butter and sell this at a very low cost to a small developing economy. This may ruin the domestic producers in the developing country. Where countries can prove that their industries have been severely damaged by dumping, their governments are allowed, under international trade rules, to impose anti-dumping measures to reduce the damage.

   However, it is very difficult to prove whether or not a foreign industry has actually been guilty of dumping. In addition, a government that subsidizes a domestic industry may actually support dumping. For example, developing countries argue that when the EU exports subsidized sugar, it is actually a case of dumping because the price doesn't reflect the actual costs of the EU sugar producers. So, if dumping does occur, it is more likely that there will be a need for talks between governments, rather than any form of protectionism. There is always a danger that protectionism will invite retaliatory actions by foreign governments and this reduces the benefits that can be gained by all consumers and producers in all countries.

Exercise 24.1 ATL Thinking and Communication

Beijing accuses US, EU of dumping rubber on China as trade dispute shows no signs of tiring

China has announced new tariffs on rubber imported from the United States, European Union and Singapore after an investigation found it was being sold at unfairly low prices. While the move was not directly targeted at Washington, it came just a day after a US inquiry accused China of selling heavily subsidised aluminium sheet on the American market.

China's Ministry of Commerce said in a statement on Thursday that foreign suppliers had been "dumping" chlorobutyl rubber, which is used to make tyres, on China at the expense of local companies.

In an initial ruling, importers representing companies like ExxonMobil and Arlanxeo were told to pay import duty deposits ranging from 26 percent to 66.5 percent to China customs. The statement said the anti-dumping investigation was initiated in August, but the ruling came as China and the US remain locked in a tit-for-tat trade fight, and just two days after Beijing imposed preliminary anti-dumping tariffs of 179 percent on US sorghum.

The US Commerce Department said on Tuesday that its investigations found that Chinese aluminium sheet sold in the US had been subsidized by between 31.2 and 113.3 percent. It said also that it was starting a new inquiry to determine if certain types of steel wheels imported from China were being "dumped" in the US.

While the investigations are not directly related, the recent exchange of trade moves by the world's two largest economies may undermine the limited goodwill they share and make it harder for them to avoid a full-blown trade war further down the road.

Source: Adapted from *Beijing accuses US, EU of dumping rubber on China as trade dispute shows no signs of tiring* by Sidney Leng, 19 April 2018, South China Morning Post, www.scmp.com

a) Define dumping.

b) Outline the arguments for and against the Chinese imposition of tariffs on US, EU and Singapore rubber.

c) Discuss the likely "winners" and "losers" if the US imposes tariffs on the importing of Chinese steel wheels.

7. **To protect product standards**

A country might wish to impose safety, health or environmental standards on goods being imported into its domestic market in order to ensure that the imports match the standards of domestic products. For example, the EU banned the importing of US beef in the 1980s because it was treated with hormones. The World Trade Organisation (WTO) allows countries to impose such bans, as long as the barrier is based on scientific evidence and as long as the country imposing the ban does not discriminate between countries where similar products are traded. The EU and the United States eventually reached an agreement in 2009 to grant a quota for hormone-free beef imports. The quota was for 20,000 tons per year, increasing to 45,000 tons after three years. However, under World Trade Organization rules, the first-come first-served quota also had to be made available to non-U.S. suppliers, such as Argentina, Australia, Canada and New Zealand. In 2019, the EU is proposing an exclusive, "fenced-off" quota of 35,000 tons of "not hormone-treated" beef for the US. However, it is likely that any such deal would be challenged by other producers of beef at the WTO.

Note

We will look at the WTO in detail in the next chapter.

Economics in action

ATL Thinking, Communication and Research

Research the present situation in the dealings between the EU and the US relating to beef imports. Write a report on the present state of negotiations and any conflicts that may have arisen.

The protection of standards is a valid argument, as long as the concerns themselves are valid. However, many of the reasons given for bans when standards are not reached are considered to be simply subtle means of protectionism. Certainly, there is a strong feeling amongst US cattle farmers that this is the case with beef. They say that EU doctors have no hard evidence to back up their claims that hormone-treated beef is bad for consumers and say that the ban is simply an excuse for protectionism. Where there is a dispute over product standards, a response by the exporting country might be to use retaliatory protectionist policies. In the EU–US beef dispute, the USA retaliated against the EU in May 1999 by imposing trade sanctions on imports from Europe worth $117 million. Despite the attempted intervention of the WTO, the ban/quota is still in place as we write.

Another issue relating to the use of product standards as a trade barrier is the cost involved in meeting product standards. This is a particular concern for producers in developing countries. Not only does it cost a great deal to meet the standards, but the costs of getting appropriate approval and documentation to prove that the standards have been met are extremely high. This puts producers in developing countries at a disadvantage and may make it difficult for such countries to exploit their comparative advantage successfully. The World Trade Organization recognizes this and, in cooperation with the World Health Organization, the World Bank, the World Organization for Animal Health and the Food and Agricultural Organization, has established a Standards and Trade Development Facility (STDF). This programme is designed to "help developing countries improve their expertise and their capacity to analyse and implement international standards on food safety and animal and plant health".

8. **To raise government revenue**

In many developing countries, it is difficult to collect taxes and so governments impose import taxes (tariffs) on products in order to raise revenue. The World Bank data below shows the percentage of government revenue made up by taxes on international trade for selected Least Developed Countries (LDCs).

Country	% of government revenue from taxes on international trade – 2012	% of government revenue from taxes on international trade – 2017
Burkina Faso	11.6	12.6
Lesotho	47.5	41.4
Nepal	15.2	16.0
Senegal	11.8	11.2
Solomon Islands	31.7	19.7
Togo	19.7	16.7

Source: data.worldbank.org

▲ Table 24.1 Percentage of government revenue from taxes on international trade for selected LDCs

This is not so much an argument for protectionism, but more a means of raising government revenue. In effect, the import duties are actually a tax on the consumers in the country who are buying the imports.

9. **To correct a balance of payments deficit**

   Governments sometimes impose protectionist measures in an attempt to reduce import expenditure and thus improve a current account deficit whereby the country is spending more on its imports of goods and services than it is earning for its exports of goods and services.

   However, this will only work in the short run. It does not address the actual problem, because it does not rectify the actual causes of the current account deficit. Also, if countries do this, then it is likely that other countries will retaliate with protectionist measures of their own.

Note

We will look at the topic of balance of payments, and current accounts in more detail in Chapter 27.

What are the arguments against trade protection?

The arguments against protectionism are really related to the reasons why countries trade, which were discussed in Chapter 23. In brief, the arguments against protectionism include the following:

- Protectionism may raise prices to consumers and producers of the imports that they buy.
- Protectionism would lead to less choice for consumers.
- Competition would diminish if foreign firms are kept out of a country, and so domestic firms may become inefficient without the incentive to minimize costs. Innovation may also be reduced for the same reason. On top of this, the export competitiveness of the domestic firms may be reduced.
- Protectionism distorts comparative advantage, leading to the inefficient use of the world's resources. Specialization is reduced and this would reduce the potential level of the world's output.
- Protectionism may lead to retaliation by other countries, with the potential for a "trade war" with escalating tariffs.
- For the reasons listed above, protectionism may hinder economic growth.

Key concept

EFFICIENCY

Chinese tariffs devastate Maine lobster industry

https://www.asiatimes.com/2019/05/article/chinese-tariffs-devastate-maine-lobster-industry/

Best Buy warns of higher prices for shoppers due to tariffs

https://www.citynews1130.com/2019/05/23/best-buy-warns-of-higher-prices-for-shoppers-due-to-tariffs/

Key concept

INTERDEPENDENCE

What are the main types of protectionism?

There are a number of different methods used to protect economies from imports. In order to look at them, it is best to first consider what the situation would be if a country had free trade in a given commodity – for example, wheat. We will then consider how different protectionist measures might alter the free trade situation.

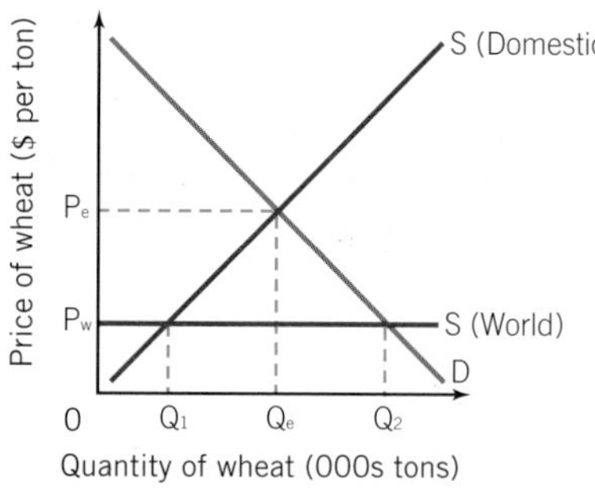

▲ **Figure 24.1** Free trade in wheat

Figure 24.1 shows the situation where free trade is taking place in a country where wheat is both produced domestically and imported.

If there were no foreign trade, then domestic farmers would produce OQ_e tons of wheat at a price of P_e per ton. If we now assume that the market is open and that foreign trade does take place, then the situation changes. Consumers find that they can import wheat at the world price and that, if they are prepared to pay the world price, they can import as much wheat as they like. This means that the supply curve faced by the importers, S (World), is perfectly elastic. S (World) must be below P_e or there would be no point in trading.

With free trade, the price of wheat in the country will be P_W. At this price, domestic farmers will only be prepared to supply OQ_1 tons of wheat. However, the demand for wheat will be OQ_2 and so the excess demand is satisfied by imported wheat. Foreign producers will supply Q_1Q_2 tons of wheat. Thus domestic consumers get to consume Q_eQ_2 more wheat at a lower price.

When can a country export?

A country is able to export a product when the country can produce and sell it at a price that is below the price that the product sells for on the world market. This is shown in Figure 24.2:

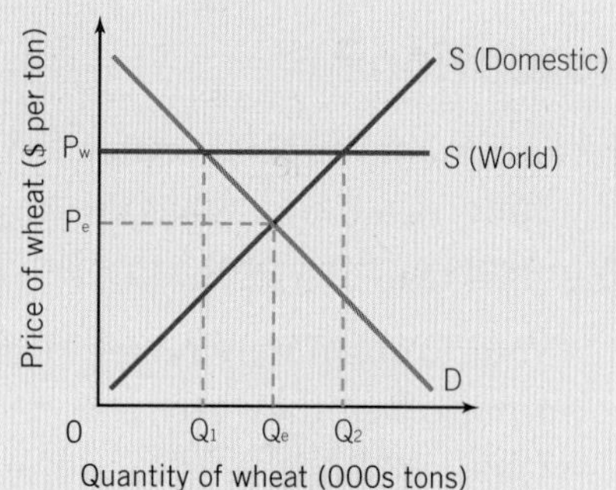

▲ **Figure 24.2** Exporting when world price is above the domestic price

If there were no foreign trade, then domestic farmers would produce OQ_e tons of wheat at a price of P_e per ton. If we now assume that foreign trade does take place, then the situation changes. Producers find that they can export wheat at the world price, P_W, which is above the price that they can sell for domestically, P_e. They increase the price of their wheat to P_W per ton and sell OQ_1 tons in the domestic market, where the quantity demanded has fallen with the higher price, and they export Q_1Q_2 tons to world markets. Thus, the producers are able to sell more wheat at a higher price by being involved in international trade.

Economics in action

ATL Thinking, Communication and Research

At any given time, there will be countless trade disputes occurring throughout the global economy. Researching one of these trade disputes will give you a chance to apply the theory, and to understand the consequences of trade protection on real-world stakeholders.

Now that we know what happens in a free-trade situation, let us look at the different types of protectionism that may be employed.

What are tariffs and how do they work?

A tariff is a tax that is charged on imported goods. As we know from Chapter 8, any tax placed upon a good shifts the supply curve upwards by the amount of the tax. In the case of a tariff, it will shift the world supply curve upwards, since it is placed on the foreign producers of the good and not the domestic producers. The effect of a tariff on imported wheat is shown in Figure 24.3.

Before the tariff, $0Q_2$ tons of wheat were being consumed at a price of P_w. Domestic production was OQ_1 and imports were Q_1Q_2. When the tariff is imposed, S (World) shifts up by the amount of the tariff to S (World) + tariff and so the market price rises to $P_w + T$. Total quantity demanded falls from OQ_2 to OQ_4, because the price has risen.

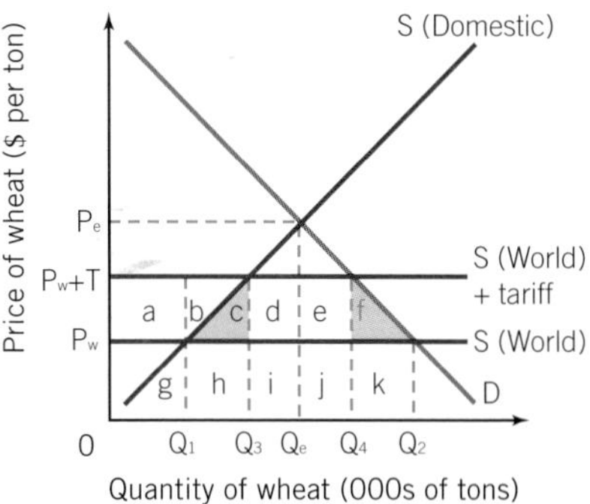

▲ **Figure 24.3** A tariff on wheat imports

Domestic producers increase production to OQ_3 and so their revenue increases from g to g + a + b + c + h. Foreign producers supply the rest, which is now Q_3Q_4. They receive P_w + T, but have to pay the tariff to the government. Thus their revenue falls from h + i + j + k to only i + j. The government now receives tariff revenue of d + e.

The importers must pay a higher price for the imported good. In the case of wheat, the higher price will be passed on to millers and eventually to the cereal companies or bakeries that buy the refined wheat. As another example, if a government introduced a tariff on automobile component parts, then this would raise the costs to car-makers and eventually lead consumers to have to pay higher prices for their cars. If the car-maker is an exporter, then the higher cost of imported components could reduce its international competitiveness.

Tariffs are the most common type of anti-dumping measure. If a country has been able to prove that dumping has taken place, then it can place a tariff on the imported goods to raise their prices and eliminate the cost advantage of the dumped imports.

There are two further outcomes.

- Q_4Q_2 tons of wheat are not now demanded. Consumers keep the amount k that they would have spent on the wheat, but there is a loss of consumer surplus equivalent to f, because the wheat is not now purchased. This is known as a dead-weight loss of welfare, because of the loss of consumer surplus.
- After the tariff, Q_1Q_3 tons of wheat are now produced by relatively inefficient domestic farmers, as opposed to more efficient foreign farmers. The foreign farmers would produce this quantity for a minimum revenue of h, whereas the domestic producers need a minimum revenue of h + c. Thus c represents the inefficiency of the domestic producers and a loss of world efficiency, since more of the world's resources are being used to produce the wheat than are necessary. This is another dead-weight loss of welfare.

Exercise 24.2

ATL Thinking and Communication

Draw your own copy of the tariff diagram, with semi-conductors in Japan as the example. Make a table with two columns, one headed "Winners" and one headed "Losers". In each column, make a list of the stakeholders who win or lose by the imposition of the tariff and give a brief explanation in each case of why the stakeholder is either a winner or loser.
Be sure to consider possible international implications. Use the letters in the diagram to specifically identify the costs and benefits.

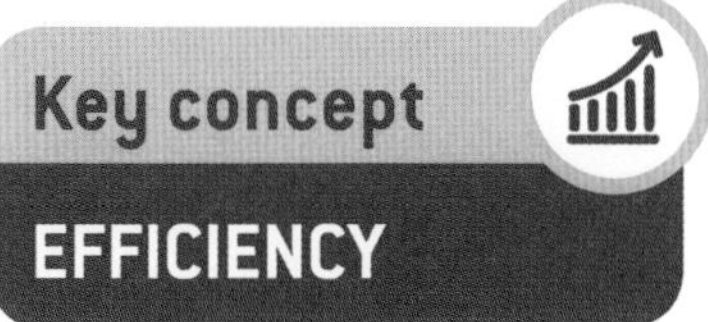

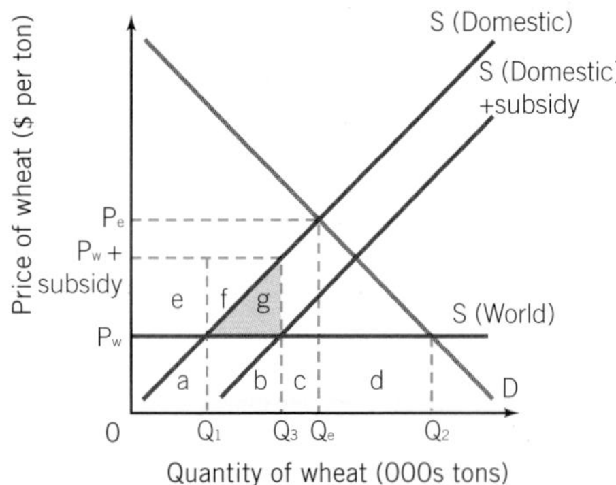

▲ Figure 24.4 A subsidy on domestic wheat production

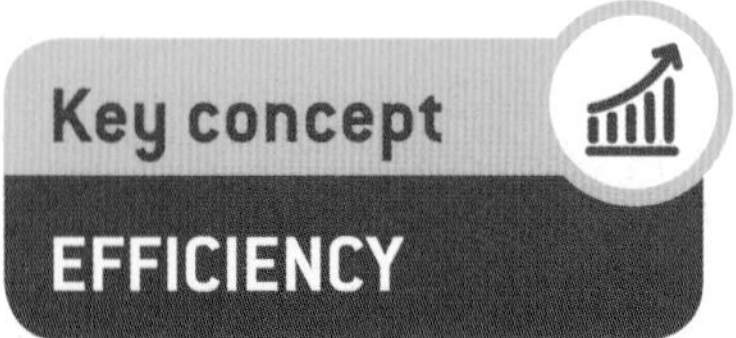

Exercise 24.3
ATL Thinking and Communication

Draw your own copy of the subsidy diagram, with cotton in the USA as the example. Make a table with two columns, one headed "Winners" and one headed "Losers". In each column, make a list of the stakeholders who win or lose by the granting of a subsidy and give a brief explanation in each case of why the stakeholder is either a winner or loser. Be sure to consider possible international implications. Use the letters in the diagram to specifically identify the costs and benefits.

What are international trade subsidies and how do they work?

As we saw in Chapter 8, a subsidy is an amount of money paid by the government to a firm, per unit of output, lowering the firm's costs. In this case, the government is giving a subsidy to domestic producers to make them more competitive and so the effect will be to shift the domestic supply curve downwards by the amount of the subsidy. If we continue with our wheat example, then the effect of a subsidy granted to domestic wheat producers is shown in Figure 24.4.

Before the subsidy, OQ_2 tons of wheat were being consumed at a price of P_w. Domestic production was OQ_1 and imports were Q_1Q_2. When the subsidy is granted, S (Domestic) shifts downwards by the amount of the subsidy to S (Domestic)+subsidy. The market price stays at P_w and so demand remains at OQ_2.

However, domestic producers increase production to OQ_3, because they are now receiving P_w+subsidy per unit that they produce. This means that their revenue increases from a to a + b + e + f + g. Foreign producers supply the rest, which is now Q_3Q_2. Thus their revenue falls from b+c+d to only c + d. The government pays the subsidy, which is shown by the area e + f + g in total.

As with a tariff, Q_1Q_3 tons of wheat are now produced by relatively inefficient domestic farmers, as opposed to more efficient foreign farmers. The foreign farmers would produce this quantity for a minimum revenue of b, whereas the domestic producers need minimum revenue of b + g. Thus g represents the inefficiency of the domestic producers and a misallocation of the world's resources, since more of the world's resources are being used to produce the wheat than are necessary. This is another dead-weight loss of welfare.

There is no loss of consumer surplus, because the price of the wheat does not change. However, consumers are indirectly affected as governments will use tax revenues to fund the subsidies. This may mean higher tax payments and also involves an opportunity cost in terms of reduced government spending on other things.

What are quotas and how do they work?

A quota is a physical limit on the numbers or value of goods that can be imported into a country. For example, the EU imposes import quotas on Chinese garlic and mushrooms. The imposition of a quota has a peculiar effect on the free trade diagram and this is shown in Figure 24.5, once more using the example of the wheat market.

Before the quota is imposed, OQ_2 of wheat is purchased at a price of P_w. Domestic supply is OQ1 and imports are Q_1Q_2. Let us now assume that the government imposes a quota of Q_1Q_3 tons of wheat.

Domestic producers supply OQ_1 at a price of P_w and the importers produce their quota of Q_1Q_3. However, once this has happened, there is an excess demand of Q_3Q_2 at the price P_w and so price begins to rise. As the price rises, importers are not allowed to supply more wheat, because they have filled their quota, and domestic producers begin to enter the market, attracted by the higher price of wheat. The domestic supply curve has, in effect, shifted to the right, above P_w. Eventually, the price settles at P_{Quota}, where demand now equals supply again and the total quantity of wheat demanded falls to Q_4.

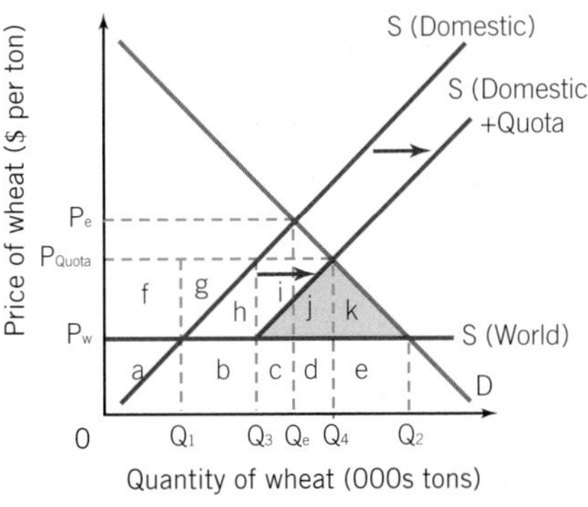

▲ **Figure 24.5** A quota on wheat imports

Domestic producers now supply $0Q_1$ and Q_3Q_4 tons of wheat at a price of P_{Quota}. Their revenue rises from a to a + c + d + f + i + j. Foreign producers now supply their quota of Q_1Q_3 tons of wheat and also receive a price of P_{Quota}. Thus their income changes from b + c + d + e to b + g + h. This is usually a fall in income but, in theory, it does not have to be.

Once again, as in tariffs, there are two areas of dead-weight loss of welfare that are caused by the imposition of the quota.

- Q_4Q_2 tons of wheat are not now demanded. Consumers keep the amount e that they would have spent on the wheat, but there is a loss of consumer surplus equivalent to k, because the wheat is not now purchased. This is a dead-weight loss of welfare, because of the loss of consumer surplus.
- After the quota, Q_3Q_4 tons of wheat are now produced by relatively inefficient domestic farmers, as opposed to more efficient foreign farmers. The foreign farmers would produce this quantity for a minimum revenue of c + d, whereas the domestic producers need a minimum revenue of c + d + j. Thus j represents the inefficiency of the domestic producers and a loss of world efficiency, since more of the world's resources are being used to produce the wheat than are necessary. This is another dead-weight loss of welfare.

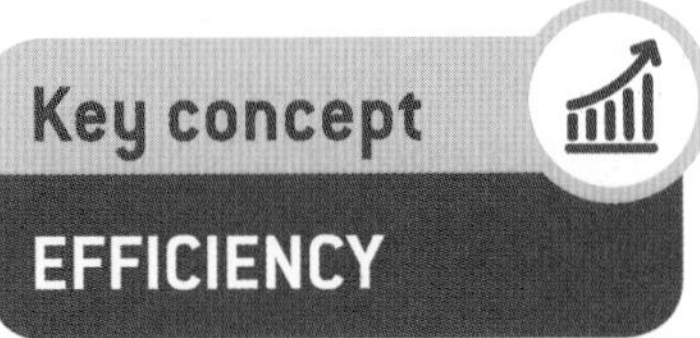

Exercise 24.4

ATL Thinking and Communication

Draw your own copy of the quota diagram, with textiles in Europe as the example. Make a table with two columns, one headed "Winners" and one headed "Losers". In each column, make a list of the stakeholders who win or lose by the imposition of the quota and give a brief explanation in each case of why the stakeholder is either a winner or loser. Be sure to consider possible international implications. Use the letters in the diagram to specifically identify the costs and benefits.

What are administrative barriers and how do they work?

We will look at three different types of administrative barriers that governments may impose.

1. **"Red tape"**

   When goods are being imported, there are usually administrative processes that have to be undertaken, which may be known as "red tape". If these processes are lengthy and complicated then they can act as a restriction to imports. For example, making importers go through complicated paperwork before they can get their goods into a country will slow down imports. In addition, if the paperwork requires a large amount of legal work, then it will slow the process down even more and raise the cost to the importer. Sometimes, countries may designate certain ports of entry that are difficult to reach and also more expensive. This may cause border delays and again raise costs.

2. **Health and safety standards and environmental standards**

   Various restrictions may be placed on the types of goods that can be sold in the domestic market, or on the methods used in the manufacture of certain goods. These regulations will apply to imports

and may restrict their entry. As mentioned earlier, while it is important that countries be able to guarantee the health and safety of the population by preventing the import of unhealthy or unsafe goods, it is extremely important that governments are legitimately keeping out imports rather than simply protecting their own country's workers.

3. **Embargoes**

   In effect, an embargo is an extreme quota. It is a complete ban on imports and is usually put in place as a form of political punishment. For example, the USA has a trade embargo on all products from Cuba. Complete embargoes are rare. More commonly, countries put in place a set of economic sanctions against an offending country. These limit the exports or imports of one or a few key products and are also used as a form of political punishment, or to achieve a desired political objective.

Economics in action

ATL Thinking, Communication and Research

Find an example of a situation where a country, or set of countries, has imposed economic sanctions on another country. Note the countries that were involved and explain why the sanctions were imposed. Also try to conclude whether the imposing country/countries achieved their objectives.

What are nationalistic campaigns and how do they work?

Governments will sometimes run marketing campaigns to encourage people to buy domestic goods instead of foreign ones in order to generate more demand for domestic goods and preserve domestic jobs. Such campaigns have happened in countries such as the UK, Australia and the US. This may be described as "moral suasion", where the government links consumption of imported goods to the creation of unemployment.

Higher Level

Assessment advice

In HL paper 3, you may be asked to calculate, from diagrams, the effects of imposing a tariff, a quota, or a subsidy on different stakeholders.

Below is an example of the kind of question that you may face and suggested responses. This graph shows the market for cooking oil in a country.

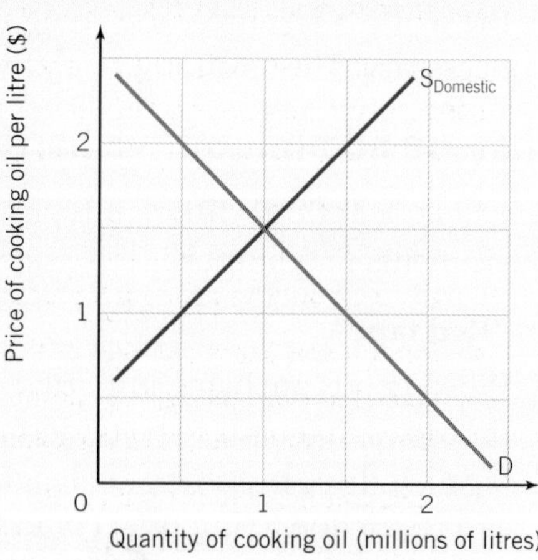

1. Indicate the domestic equilibrium price and quantity on the graph.
2. Cooking oil may be imported. The world price is $1 per litre. Add the world supply curve to the graph.
3. Explain how much cooking oil will be supplied by domestic suppliers and how much will be supplied by foreign producers when free trade takes place.
4. The government imposes a tariff of 30¢ per litre. Show the effect of this on the graph.
5. Calculate the change in consumer spending before and after the imposition of the tariff.
6. Calculate the government tax revenue after the tariff is put in place.
7. Explain the impact of the tariff on any **two** of the stakeholders in the cooking oil market.

The required diagram is shown below.

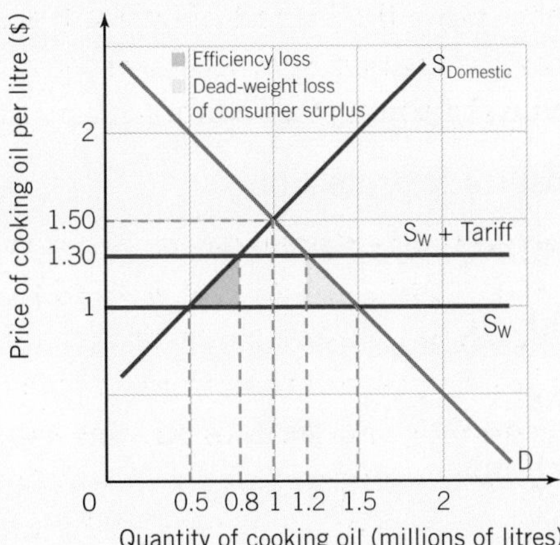

1. The equilibrium price and quantity are shown as $1.50 and 1 million litres of cooking oil.
2. The world supply curve has been added. It is a perfectly inelastic supply curve at $1.
3. Before free trade, domestic producers supplied 1 million litres of cooking oil. After free trade, the domestic supply falls to 0.5 million litres and the quantity supplied by foreign producers is 1 million litres (1.5 million – 0.5 million).
4. The effect of the tariff is shown by the upward shift of S_W from $1 to $1.30, ie SW + Tariff.
5. Consumer expenditure before the tariff was 1.5 million × $1 = $1.5 million. Consumer expenditure after the tariff was 1.2 million × $1.30 = $1.56 million. Thus, there will be an increase in consumer expenditure of $0.6 million.
6. The tax revenue will be 30¢ × 400,000 = $120,000.
7. The stakeholders in the market are domestic producers, foreign producers, consumers, the government and resource allocation. An explanation of the effect on **any two** will be sufficient. The effects are as follows.
   - *Domestic producers* are able to sell more, at a higher price, thus increasing revenue and, in all probability, profit. They will also increase employment, which should be good for the domestic economy.
   - *Foreign producers* sell less, at the same price, thus reducing their revenue and, almost certainly, their profit. This will also lower employment in the foreign economies, causing damage there.
   - *Consumers* get to consume less of the product, at a higher price, in this case paying more in total. They also suffer a loss of consumer surplus, some to domestic producers, some to the government, and a dead-weight loss, shown by the light blue triangle in the diagram.
   - *The government* will gain income from the tariff, which may then be spent. The government may also benefit from a decrease in unemployment in the economy. However, there is always the danger of retaliation from other countries for imposing the tariff.
   - *Resource allocation* in this case means that production of 0.3 million litres of cooking oil shifts from efficient foreign producers to less-efficient domestic producers. This is a welfare loss and inefficient resource allocation occurs, shown by the dark blue triangle in the diagram.

EXAMINATION QUESTIONS

Paper 1, part (a) questions

1. Explain **three** arguments in favour of trade protection. [10 marks]
2. Explain **three** arguments against trade protection. [10 marks]
3. Explain the imposition of a tariff. [10 marks]
4. Explain the granting of a subsidy. [10 marks]
5. Explain the imposition of a quota. [10 marks]
6. Explain **two** methods of protectionism. [10 marks]

Paper 1, part (b) questions

1. Using real-world examples, evaluate the arguments for protectionism. [15 marks]
2. Using real-world examples, evaluate the arguments against protectionism. [15 marks]
3. Using real-world examples, discuss the merits of free trade versus protectionism. [15 marks]
4. Using real-world examples, evaluate the effects of a tariff, or an international subsidy, or a quota on a specific market for the different stakeholders in an economy. [15 marks]

Paper 2: 2-mark and 4-mark questions

EU Stands Up For Spanish Olives Against US Tariffs At WTO

The tariffs on Spanish black olives opened a new chapter in the US-EU trade war saga last year. Now the European Union has adopted a firm stance by announcing that the European Commission will challenge the US's tariffs in the World Trade Organization (WTO). These tariffs do not only have a big impact on Spanish olive exports, but they also represent a threat to the European Common Agricultural Policy (CAP).

"The duties imposed by the United States on black olives from Spain are unjustified, unwarranted and go against the rules of the World Trade Organisation. Tomorrow, we are taking this case to the WTO dispute settlement system, requesting consultations with the US," tweeted last Monday the European Commissioner for Trade, Cecilia Malmström.

Since August 2018, the US has applied a **tariff** of 34.75% on imports of Spanish black olives in terms of anti-**subsidy** and anti-dumping duties. The argument is that Spanish producers compete at an unfair advantage because they benefit from the aid of the CAP. According to Californian olive growers, the price of Spanish olives in the US was even lower than on the Spanish domestic market, which led the US Department of Commerce (DOC) to launch an investigation last summer into unfair competition and **dumping**.

Meanwhile, the Spanish producers are already suffering the economic consequences, especially because the US is one of the main export markets of the product. It was reported that the exports of black olives to the US had fallen by 72% during the first two months of the application of the tariff. In August 2018, the first month of application of the definitive tariffs, sales to the US fell by 70%, from 3.2 million kilos in the same month of the previous year to just over 1 million kilos in 2018.

Spanish olive producers claim that if the tariff remains in place, then there is bound to be an significant increase in unemployment in the agricultural sector.

Source: Adapted from EU stands up for Spanish olives against US tariffs at WTO by Ana Garcia Valdivia, January 30, 2019, Forbes.com

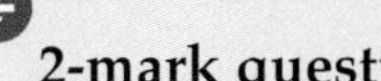

2-mark questions

Define the following terms, indicated in bold in the data:

1. tariff [2 marks]
2. subsidy [2 marks]
3. dumping. [2 marks]

4-mark questions

1. Using an international trade diagram, explain the effect of the tariff on the market for olives in the US. [4 marks]
2. Using a labour market diagram, explain the type of unemployment that might be created as a result of the tariff on olives.

HL Paper 3 Questions

Below is the market for cooking oil in a country.

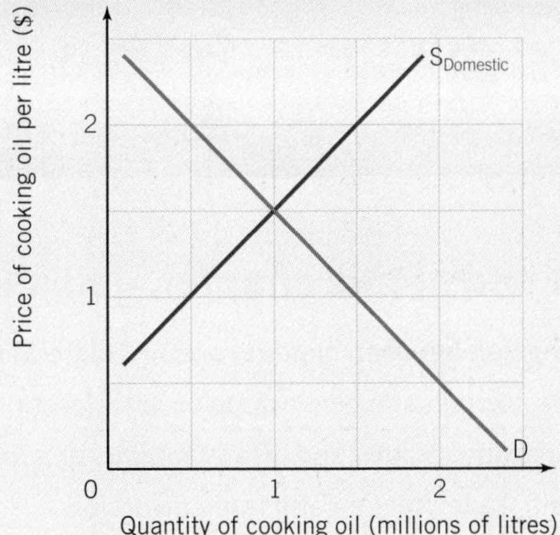

1. Indicate the domestic equilibrium price and quantity on the graph.
2. Calculate total consumer spending before imports are in the market.
3. Cooking oil may be imported. The world price is $1 per litre. Add the world supply curve to the graph.
4. Explain why domestic suppliers will reduce their production after the entry of foreign producers to the market.
5. The government gives domestic producers a subsidy of 50¢ per litre. Show the effect of this on the graph.
6. Calculate the change in consumer spending before and after the giving of the subsidy.
7. Calculate the change in the revenue of foreign producers when the subsidy is given.
8. Calculate the cost to the government after the subsidy is given.
9. Explain the impact of the subsidy on any two of the stakeholders in the cooking oil market.

25 ECONOMIC INTEGRATION

REAL-WORLD ISSUE:
Who are the winners and losers of the integration of the world's economies?

By the end of this chapter, you should be able to:

- → Distinguish between bilateral and multilateral trade agreements
- → Define, explain and give examples of different types of trading blocs
- HL Discuss advantages and disadvantages of a monetary union for its members
- HL Explain trade creation and trade diversion
- → Discuss advantages and disadvantages of membership of trading blocs
- → Describe the objectives and functions of the World Trade Organisation (WTO)
- → Discuss factors affecting the effectiveness of the WTO.

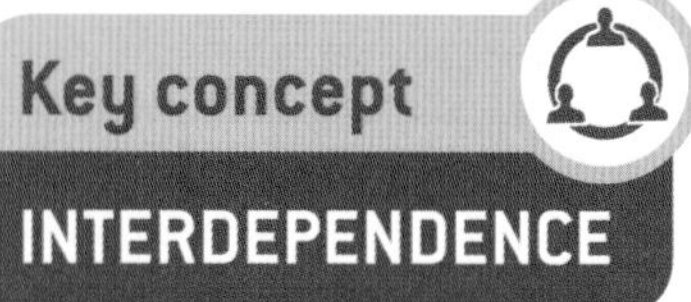

What is economic integration?

Economic integration describes a process whereby countries coordinate and link their economic policies. As the degree of economic integration increases, the trade barriers between countries decrease and their fiscal and monetary policies are more closely harmonized.

A *bilateral trade agreement* is an agreement relating to trade between two countries. The aim is usually to reduce or remove tariffs and/or quotas that have been placed on items traded between the two countries.

A *multilateral trade agreement* is an agreement relating to trade between multiple countries. It also usually aims to reduce or remove tariffs and/or quotas that have been placed on traded items, but the agreement in this case applies to all of the multiple countries involved.

What are trading blocs and what are the different degrees of economic integration?

A trading bloc is defined as a group of countries that join together in some form of agreement in order to increase trade between them and/or to gain economic benefits from cooperation on some level. This coming together is called economic integration. The Hungarian economist Béla Balassa identified six stages of economic integration:

1. **Preferential trading areas**: A preferential trading area (PTA) is a trading bloc that gives preferential access to certain products from certain countries. This is usually carried out by reducing, but not eliminating, tariffs.

   An example of a PTA is the one between the EU and the African, Caribbean and Pacific Group of States (ACP). This is an agreement between the EU and 79 countries in the ACP. Many of the countries were former colonies of EU members. It enables the EU to guarantee regular supplies of raw materials and the ACP countries to gain tariff preferences and access to special funds that are used to try to achieve price stability in agricultural and mining markets.

   Since 2008 the arrangement has been a *"reciprocal trade agreement"*. This means that the EU provides duty-free access to its markets for exports from the ACP countries and also receives duty-free access for its own exports to the ACP countries. However, it is agreed that not all of the ACP countries have to open up to EU exports. The least-developed countries in the ACP group may opt for other arrangements.

2. **Free-trade areas**: A free-trade area is an agreement made between countries, where the countries agree to trade freely among themselves, but are able to trade with countries outside of the free-trade area in whatever way they wish. This situation is shown in Figure 25.1.

In this hypothetical case, countries A, B and C have signed a free-trade agreement and are now trading freely among themselves. However, under the agreement, each country may trade with any other country in any way it sees fit. Thus, country A has political grievances with country D and so has placed a complete embargo on foreign trade. Country B protects its economy from country D by placing tariffs on a number of its imports. Country C has good relationships with country D and trades freely with it.

An example of a free-trade area is the North American Free Trade Area (NAFTA), which comprises the USA, Canada and Mexico. NAFTA was established in January 1994 and, following a final tariff reduction between Canada and Mexico in January 2003, virtually all trade in the NAFTA region is tariff-free. Over 70% of Canadian total exports now go to the USA, and Mexico's share of the US import market has grown from approximately 7% in pre-NAFTA times to approximately 13.5% today.

Economics in action

ATL Thinking, Communication and Research

The Cotonou Partnership Agreement is the legal framework ruling relations between the EU and the ACP. It was signed in 2000, lasting for a period of 20 years. In 2019, talks are going ahead to cement a new agreement, which needs to be in place by 29 February 2020, when the Cotonou Agreement expires.

By the time you read this, the trade negotiations should be resolved. Examine the current situation relating to the agreement and the outcomes for the different regions involved, ie Africa, the Caribbean and the Pacific Group of States.

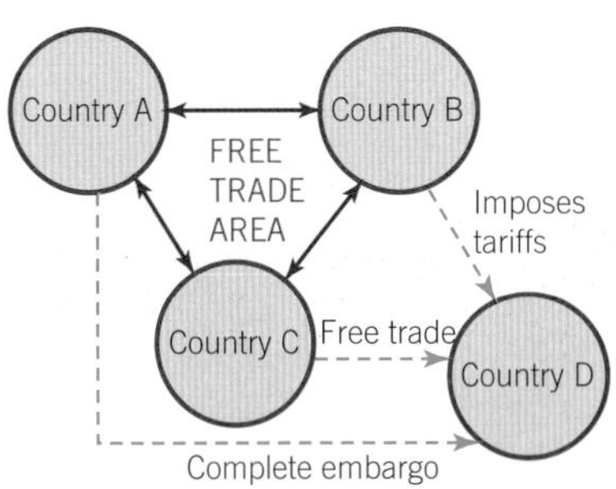

▲ Figure 25.1 A free-trade area

Economics in action

ATL Thinking, Communication and Research

In September 2018, after demands by US President Donald Trump for the preceding trade pact to be renegotiated or scrapped, the United States, Mexico and Canada reached a new agreement to govern more than $1 trillion in regional trade. However, the agreement had not been ratified by the respective parliaments by May 2019. If the agreement is not ratified, and the US pulls out of NAFTA, then the three countries would return to the trade rules that were in place before the establishment of NAFTA in 1994.

By the time you read this, the trade negotiations should be resolved. Examine the current situation relating to the agreement.

Other examples of free-trade agreements are the European Free Trade Association (Iceland, Liechtenstein, Norway and Switzerland), and the South Asia Free Trade Agreement (Afghanistan, Bangladesh, Bhutan, India, Maldives, Nepal, Pakistan and Sri Lanka).

3. **Customs unions**: A customs union is an agreement made between countries, where the countries agree to trade freely among themselves, and they also agree to adopt common external barriers against any country attempting to import into the customs union. This situation is shown in Figure 25.2.

Countries A, B and C have joined in a customs union and are trading freely with each other. If country D wishes to export goods to the customs union, the goods will be treated in the same way, no matter which country the goods enter. If the customs union has agreed to place tariffs on the products of country D, then those tariffs will be imposed, no matter what the point of entry to the customs union.

All common markets and economic and monetary unions are also customs unions, thus the EU has a customs union. Other examples would be the Switzerland–Liechtenstein customs union; the East African Community, which is a customs union comprising Burundi, Kenya, Rwanda, South Sudan, Tanzania and Uganda; and Mercosur, which is a customs union between Argentina, Bolivia, Brazil, Paraguay, Uruguay and Venezuela (although at the present time, Venezuela's membership is suspended.

4. **Common markets**: A common market is a customs union with common policies on product regulation, and free movement of goods, services, capital and labour. The best-known example of a common market is the EU. The CARICOM Single Market and Economy (CSME) is another example, which is expected to be fully implemented with harmonization of economic policy and, possibly, a single currency. The current members include Barbados, Belize, Guyana, Jamaica, Suriname, Trinidad and Tobago, Antigua and Barbuda, Dominica, Grenada, St Kitts and Nevis, St Lucia, St Vincent and the Grenadines, and Montserrat.

5. **Economic and monetary union**: An economic and monetary union is a common market with a common currency and a common central bank. The best example of an economic and monetary union is the Eurozone, which includes the member countries of the EU that have adopted the euro as their currency and have the European Central Bank (ECB) as their central bank. In 2019, the members consisted of Austria, Belgium, Cyprus, Estonia, Finland, France, Germany, Greece, Ireland, Italy, Latvia, Lithuania, Luxembourg, Malta, the Netherlands, Portugal, Slovakia, Slovenia and Spain.

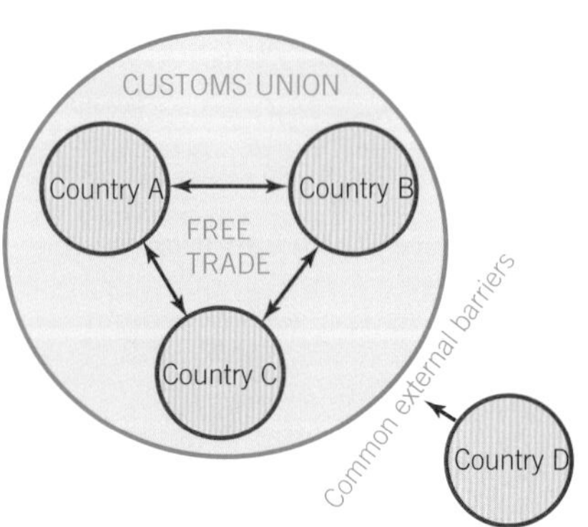

▲ Figure 25.2 A customs union

What are the advantages and disadvantages of membership of a monetary union?

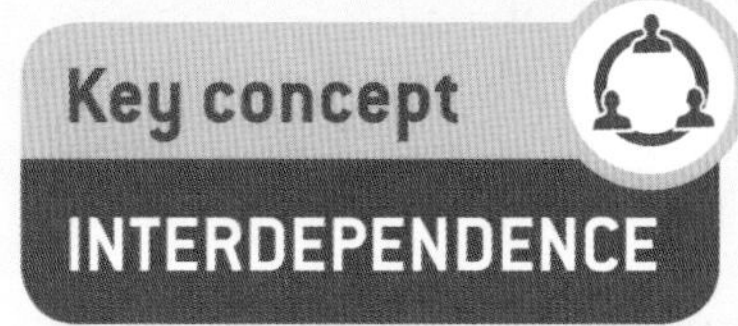

There are a number of advantages of a monetary union for the member countries.

- Exchange-rate fluctuations that used to exist between countries will disappear with a common currency and this should eliminate exchange-rate uncertainty between the countries involved, which should increase cross-border investment and trade.
- A currency which has the enhanced credibility of being used in a large currency zone should be more stable against speculation than the individual currencies were.
- Business confidence in the member countries tends to improve as there is less of a perceived risk involved in trading among the countries. This in turn should lead to both internal growth and trade growth.
- Transaction costs are eliminated within the monetary union. When countries have different currencies there is a charge when currencies are exchanged, but this will not happen with the existence of a single currency.
- A common currency makes price differences more obvious between countries and should, over time, lead to prices equalizing across borders.

There are also a number of disadvantages of a monetary union for the member countries.

- When countries enter a monetary union, interest rates are decided by the central bank. This means that individual countries are no longer free to set their own interest rates and so the tool of monetary policy (see Chapter 18) is no longer an option to influence the inflation rate, the unemployment rate and the rate of economic growth. This is especially damaging if one country in the union is experiencing an economic situation that is not being experienced by the others. For example, if one country was experiencing high inflation due to strong consumer demand, which other countries were not, it might want to increase interest rates to reduce the demand. However, with a common monetary policy, the central bank would not be able to increase the interest rate and so other measures would have to be found.
- While a common central bank is seen as a prerequisite of monetary union, many argue that without fiscal integration, in the form of a common treasury, harmonized tax rates and a common budget, a monetary union will be weak and vulnerable, since some countries will be more fiscally irresponsible than others and this may threaten the stability of the union.
- Individual countries are not able to alter their own exchange rates in order to affect the international competitiveness of their exports or the costs of their imports.

Higher Level

Key concept
CHANGE

Mercosur nations to speed up economic integration
https://www3.nhk.or.jp/nhkworld/en/news/20190718_21/

- The initial costs of converting the individual currencies into one currency are very large. The costs include such things as taking the old currencies off the market, printing and distributing the new currency, converting databases and software, rewriting all price lists and invoice systems, re-pricing all goods and services in the economy and recalibrating all machinery that takes coins and notes, such as parking meters and vending machines.

It is almost impossible to weigh up the advantages and disadvantages of membership of a monetary union. The situation will be very different in different cases. Perhaps it is best to try to determine when membership would be most beneficial and when it would make the least difference.

In a situation where there were large fluctuations between the exchange rates of the countries involved, where the union is going to create a single currency with a significant proportion of the world's foreign currency market and where business confidence will be strongly boosted between member countries, then it is likely that membership of a common currency will be beneficial to the individual countries.

Exercise 25.1
ATL Thinking and Communication

Make a table to summarize the information about trading blocs. Include the name of each of the six types of economic integration, a definition and examples. The table should illustrate how economic integration increases at each stage.

If countries are in a situation where fluctuations in exchange rates are minimal, where the common currency would not be significant on the world market, so would still be susceptible to speculation, and where business confidence is already high, then the advantages of joining a single currency would be few and the disadvantages may well be greater.

6. **Complete economic integration**: This would be the final stage of economic integration, at which point the individual countries involved would have no control of economic policy, full monetary union and complete harmonization of fiscal policy. This is what the Eurozone is moving towards.

Key concept
INTERDEPENDENCE

Key concept
CHANGE

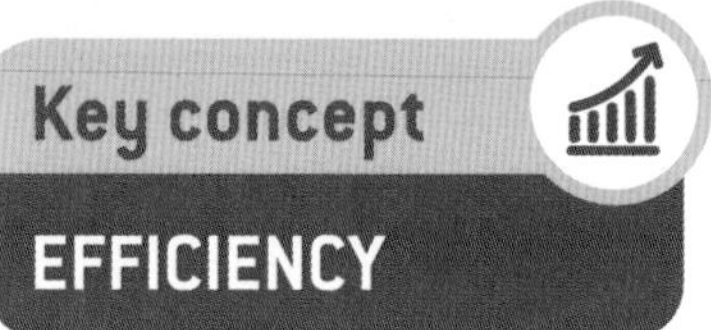

What are the advantages of membership of a trading bloc?

The extent of the advantages and disadvantages of trading blocs clearly depends on the degree of integration.

In purely economic terms, the benefits of being a member of a trading bloc are similar to those of free trade. These include:

- A greater size of market with the potential for larger export markets and economies of scale for producers as they increase their scale of production. The consequences may not be even, as some domestic producers are likely to gain from the larger market while others may find themselves unable to compete.
- Increased competition leading to greater efficiency, more choice and lower prices for consumers.

- A further stimulus for investment due to the larger market size, and foreign investment might be attracted from outside the bloc as a way of getting a foot in the door of the larger market.
- If the trading bloc includes the free movement of labour, then there may be greater employment opportunities for individuals in the member countries.
- There is an argument that, along with the economic gains, a trading bloc will foster greater political stability and cooperation.
- It is possible that trade negotiations may be easier in a world made up of a number of large trading blocs, rather than among 195 sovereign states.

Higher Level

- If the trading bloc is a customs union, then there may be *trade creation*. Trade creation occurs when the entry of a country into a customs union leads to the production of a good or service transferring from a high-cost producer to a low-cost producer. This is an advantage of greater economic integration. The concept is best explained by an example.

  Let us assume that when the UK joined the EU in 1973, it had a comparative advantage over France, a member of the EU at that time, in the production of lawnmowers. However, as a non-member of the EU, the EU had placed a tariff on UK lawnmowers. The situation is shown in Figure 25.3.

  With the tariff on UK lawnmowers in place, the French would produce OQ_2 lawnmowers themselves and would import Q_2Q_3 lawnmowers from the UK. On entering the EU, the tariff on UK lawnmowers is relaxed and the UK can now make full use of its comparative advantage. With the tariff gone, French production falls to OQ_1 and imports rise to Q_1Q_4. There are Q_3Q_4 more lawnmowers bought and thus trade has been created. In addition, the extra demand means that there is an increase in consumer surplus, shown by the shaded triangle.

  There is also a movement from high-cost to low-cost producers, since Q_1Q_2 lawnmowers, which were being made by relatively inefficient French producers, are now being made by more efficient UK producers. Although the French lawnmower producers may have lost out, there has been a world welfare gain, because fewer resources are being used to produce these lawnmowers.

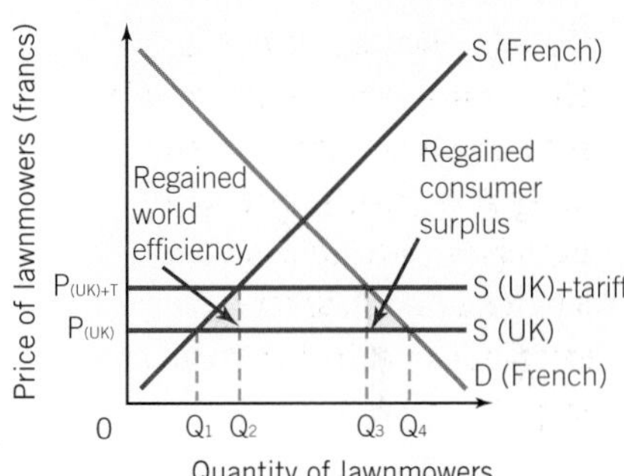

▲ **Figure 25.3** Trade creation

It should be remembered that this ought to be a two-way process. It is highly likely that, with free trade, there will also be French products that the UK will now buy more of because the French have the comparative advantage – for example, wine.

What are the disadvantages of membership of a trading bloc?

The possible disadvantages of membership of a trading bloc include:

- By their very nature, trading blocs favour increased trade among members, but enact discriminatory policies against non-members, and this can be damaging to the achievements of the multilateral trading negotiations of the World Trade Organisation (WTO) (see the next section). There is concern that the breakdown in WTO talks in 2006 and the subsequent inability to reach agreement will lead to an increase in the number of individual trade negotiations. These may undermine the international trade rules and limit the potential gains to trade achievable with more liberalized world trade. This may not be as much of a problem for large economies as it might be for small or poor economies that have little bargaining power.
- As integration becomes greater, countries will lose some degree of economic and political sovereignty. In a customs union, individual governments lose the power to make decisions on how to deal with trade with countries that are outside the union. In a common market, there are common policies on product regulation, and free movement of goods, services, capital and labour. Thus, the individual governments lose even more sovereignty. If a monetary union is joined, then individual governments lose all of the above sovereignty and the ability to manage their interest rates and exchange rates independently. In many countries, the potential loss of economic and political sovereignty acts as a strong deterrent to membership of more advanced forms of trading blocs.

Key concept
EQUITY

Higher Level

- If the trading bloc is a customs union, then there may be *trade diversion*. Trade diversion occurs when the entry of a country into a customs union leads to the production of a good or service transferring from a low-cost producer to a high-cost producer. This is a disadvantage of greater economic integration. Once again, the concept is best explained by an example.

  Let us assume that when the UK joined the EU in 1973, it had been producing textiles itself and importing textiles from Thailand, which had a comparative advantage in the product. However, once the UK joined the EU, it had to place a tariff on Thai textiles, because the EU already had one in place. The situation is shown in Figure 25.4.
- Before the entry into the EU, the UK would produce OQ_1 metres of textiles domestically and would import Q_1Q_4 metres of textiles from Thailand. On entering the EU, the UK is forced to impose the same tariff on Thai textiles as the other EU countries. With the tariff in place, Thai textiles become more expensive than textiles produced in the EU. Because of this, the UK will now produce OQ_2 metres of textiles itself and will import Q_2Q_3 metres of textiles from the EU. There will be an

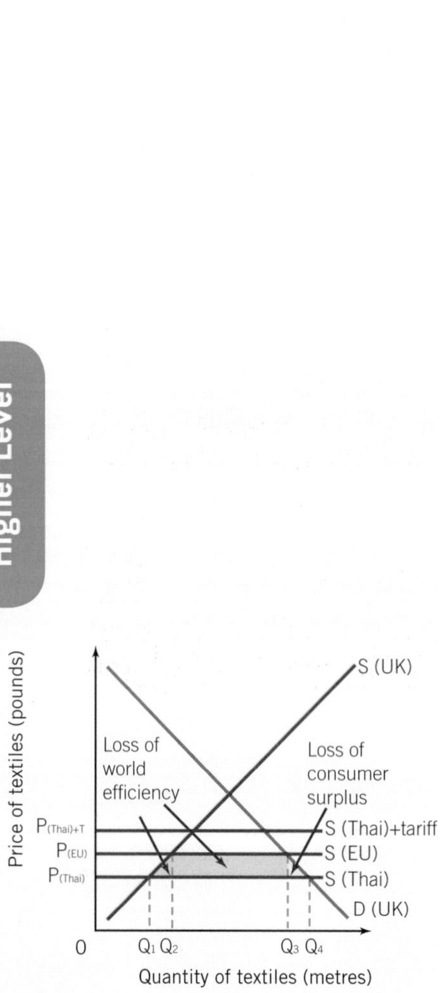

▲ Figure 25.4 Trade diversion

overall fall in the quantity demanded of textiles of Q_3Q_4 metres and so a loss of consumer surplus shown by the shaded triangle.

- There is also a movement from low-cost to high-cost producers, since Q_1Q_2 metres of textiles that were being produced by relatively efficient Thai producers, are now being produced by less efficient UK producers. Although the UK producers may have gained, there has been a world welfare loss, because more resources are being used to produce these textiles.
- To make matters worse, the production of Q_2Q_3 metres of textiles has transferred from efficient Thai producers to relatively inefficient EU producers, so the trade diversion is even greater, as is the loss of world welfare. This represents a misallocation of the world's resources, a clear disadvantage of economic integration.

Exercise 25.2
ATL Thinking and Communication

1. Choose one trading bloc to research. Make an annotated timeline to show the steps involved in its establishment and evolution. Be sure to note any significant achievements and/or setbacks.
2. Pick one country in the bloc and evaluate how it has been affected by membership of the zone.

What is the World Trade Organization (WTO)?

The WTO is an international organization that sets the rules for global trading and resolves disputes between its member countries. The WTO was established on 1 January 1995 and now, in April 2019, has 164 members and 23 observer countries, the majority of whom are seeking membership. It replaced the General Agreement on Tariffs and Trade (GATT), which had been set up after the Second World War. The WTO, along with its predecessor the GATT, is largely credited with the fact that, since 1947, average world tariffs for manufactured goods have declined from approximately 40% to 4%.

▲ Logo of the World Trade Organization

All WTO members are required to grant "most favoured nation" status to one another, which means that, usually, trade concessions granted by a WTO country to another country must be granted to all WTO members.

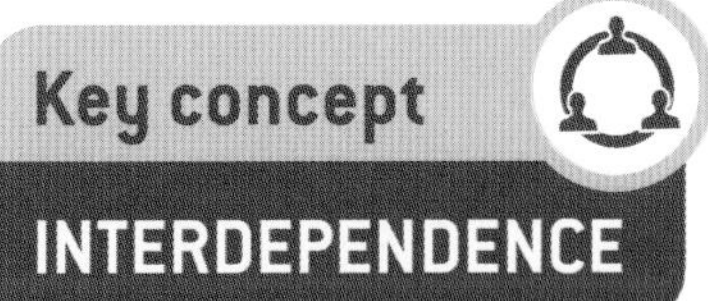

What are the aims of the WTO?

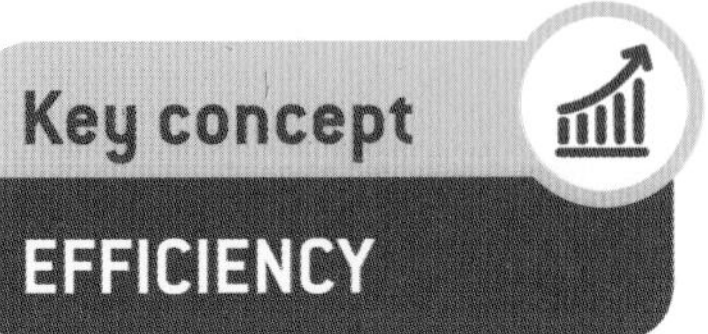

"There are a number of ways of looking at the WTO. It's an organization for liberalizing trade. It's a forum for governments to negotiate trade agreements. It's a place for them to settle trade disputes. It operates a system of trade rules." (www.wto.org)

The WTO aims to increase international trade by lowering trade barriers and providing a forum for negotiation. It has a number of stated principles:

- *Non-discrimination* – Countries should not discriminate between their own products, services, and nationals and those of foreign countries. They should also not discriminate between their trading partners.
- *More open trade* – Lowering trade barriers through negotiation is one of the most obvious ways of increasing trade. The barriers include tariffs, import bans and quotas.
- *Predictability and transparency* – All economic stakeholders, including governments, firms and investors should be confident that trade

barriers will not be raised, providing the confidence to invest, create jobs, increase consumer choice and lower prices.

- *Encouraging "fair" competition* – through discouraging "unfair" practices. These include the provision of export subsidies and the dumping of products in foreign markets in order to gain market share.
- *More beneficial for developing countries* – Giving them extra time to adjust to WTO provisions, greater flexibility and special privileges, where appropriate. Over 75% of WTO members are developing countries.
- *Protection of the environment* – WTO agreements allow member countries to legislate to protect the environment, public, animal and plant health. However, any legislation must be applied equally to domestic and foreign firms. The laws must not be disguised protectionist measures.

The functions of the WTO are to:

- administer WTO trade agreements
- be a forum for trade negotiations
- handle trade disputes among member countries
- monitor national trade policies
- provide technical assistance and training for developing countries on trade issues
- cooperate with other international organizations.

The WTO operates through a system of trade negotiations, or rounds. The first ones, held under the GATT, dealt mainly with the reduction of tariffs, but later negotiations included other areas such as anti-dumping legislation and non-tariff issues.

The current round of negotiations is called the **Doha round**, after the site of the meeting where negotiations were started in November 2001. The programme, called the Doha Development Agenda, covers many areas including agricultural tariffs, non-agricultural tariffs, trade and environment, anti-dumping, subsidies, competition policy, transparency in government procurement and intellectual property.

The negotiations have been very contentious and, at the time of writing, no agreement has yet been reached, even though there were ministerial conferences in Cancun in 2003, Hong Kong in 2005, Geneva in 2009, Bali in 2013, Nairobi in 2015 and Buenos Aires in 2017. In July 2006, Doha round negotiations broke down and were ultimately suspended as a result of an inability to come to agreement on fundamental issues. There were two key concerns. First, the EU and the USA were being urged to reduce their agricultural subsidies to improve market access for developing countries' exports. Second, the more-developed countries wanted the larger developing countries, such as Brazil and India, to lower their barriers to imports of manufactured goods. Despite a widespread view that such measures will increase growth in all countries, there has so far been no success in reaching a compromise.

What factors limit the effectiveness of the WTO in achieving its objectives?

It is widely agreed that there are a number of factors that are limiting the effectiveness of the WTO in its quest to reduce discrimination, promote more open trade, display predictability and transparency, encourage fair competition, be more beneficial for developing countries and protect the environment.

- *Unequal bargaining power of member countries* – even though all countries are said to have an equal vote, some economies, especially the USA and the EU as two of the largest markets in the world, are thought to have too much power in the WTO and its negotiations. This means that the views and aspirations of developing countries, by definition smaller, may be unheard and ignored in favour of the more powerful countries.
- *Trade rules that are unfair for developing countries* – even though many developed countries historically grew, helped by the use of tariff protection, this is not possible for developing countries under WTO rules. This may prevent them from protecting "infant industries" and diversification.
- *The growing number of trade deals negotiated outside the WTO* – this applies to such things as the Transatlantic Trade and Investment Partnership (TTIP) negotiations between the USA and the EU. Such negotiations exclude other countries and diminish the importance of the WTO by taking place outside of its jurisdiction.

Exercise 25.3

ATL Thinking and Communication

Read the following article and identify the challenges to the WTO.

Whither The WTO Doha Development Round?

by Elizabeth Morgan

In an article on December 21, 2018, the *Financial Times* declared that the World Trade Organization (WTO) Doha Round had finally died a merciful death after nearly a decade spent comatose. This reflected the view of the developed countries, which was not necessarily supported by all developing countries.

The Doha round was not launched until the fourth WTO Ministerial Conference (MC4) at Doha, Qatar, in November 2001, with much pressure exerted by the developed countries. The compromise was that the round would focus on development issues.

This Doha "Development" Round would address agricultural products, non-agricultural products (industrial, including fisheries) – known by the acronym NAMA – services, and various trade-related and development specific issues, including special and differential treatment (S&DT) and small economies.

From 2006, the Doha Round negotiations continued with limited progress. Agriculture was a particularly difficult issue, as developed countries demanded increased access into the markets of emerging developing countries and developing countries had concerns about subsidies applied in developed countries. It was also evident that development, as defined by developing countries, was not at the core of the round. Development for developed countries was all about market access.

In the intervening period, countries began to increasingly negotiate complex bilateral and plurilateral free-trade agreements mainly outside of the WTO. These included the Trans-Partnership and the Trade in Services Agreement.

By MC10 in Nairobi, Kenya, December 2015, the developed countries, the original proponents of the round, were in search of means to suspend it. The view was that they actually did not want to declare the round's death in Kenya, the first African developing country to host a ministerial conference. The Nairobi Declaration reflected the divisions in the WTO on the round's status, recognising that some members reaffirmed it, while others did not believe new approaches were necessary to achieving desired outcomes. This signalled that the developed countries had not got what they wanted and were ready to move on.

The situation at the WTO became more difficult with the election of US President Donald Trump in November 2017. The Trump administration's "America First" policy was anti-multilateralist and particularly belligerent towards the WTO. There was talk of the US withdrawing from the organisation. The administration did not favour multilateral trade negotiations, refused to approve members of the WTO Appellate Body in the dispute-settlement mechanism, moved towards more protectionist policies, unilaterally applying tariffs on steel and aluminium, and commenced a bilateral dispute with China.

Perhaps fearful of US withdrawal, feeling that the global trade environment had radically changed, and concerned about the WTO's future, some members began to look at a new direction for the organisations considering a work programme on other issues, such as e-commerce, state-owned enterprises, micro, small and medium enterprises, women's economic empowerment and investment facilitation.

The European Union, Canada and other developed countries put forward proposals and began consultations on WTO reform. For political reasons, some developing countries have joined these initiatives. Hence, the Financial Times' conclusion that the Doha Round has died.

There are still many developing countries from all regions that do not share this view of the round's demise and are uncomfortable with current proposals for WTO reform. Thus, it is reported that the atmosphere in the organisation is quite unstable as members begin to look to MC12 in Astana, Kazakhstan, in June 2020.

Source: Adapted from Wither the WTO Doha development round? by Elizabeth Morgan, The Gleaner, April 4 2019, http://jamaica-gleaner.com.

Economics in action

ATL Thinking, Communication and Research

The situation with the WTO and the Doha Development Agenda is continually changing. Research the current standing of negotiations and agreements. A good starting point for your research would be the official WTO site, www.wto.org.

EXAMINATION QUESTIONS

Paper 1, part (a) questions

1. Explain the difference between a free-trade area and a customs union. [10 marks]
2. Explain the objectives and functions of the World Trade Organization. [10 marks]
3. **HL only:** Explain trade creation and trade diversion. [10 marks]
4. Explain **two** factors that limit the effectiveness of the World Trade Organization in achieving its objectives. [10 marks]

Paper 1, part (b) questions – HL & SL

1. Using real-world examples, evaluate the advantages and disadvantages of membership of a common market. [15 marks]

Paper 1, part (b) questions – HL only

1. Using real-world examples, evaluate the advantages and disadvantages of membership of a monetary union. [15 marks]

26 EXCHANGE RATES

REAL-WORLD ISSUE:
Who are the winners and losers of the integration of the world's economies?

By the end of this chapter, you should be able to:

- → Define, explain and give examples of an exchange rate
- → Define, explain, illustrate and give examples of a fixed exchange rate system
- → Distinguish between a devaluation and a revaluation of a currency
- → Define, explain, illustrate and give examples of a floating exchange rate system
- → Distinguish between depreciation and appreciation of a currency
- → Calculate exchange rates and changes in exchange rates
- → Describe factors leading to changes in the demand for, and supply of, a currency
- → Define, explain, illustrate and give examples of a managed exchange rate system
- → Evaluate the advantages and disadvantages of high and low exchange rates
- → Explain government measures to intervene in the foreign exchange market
- HL Compare and contrast a fixed exchange rate system with a floating exchange rate system.

Exercise 26.1

ATL Thinking and Communication

Make a list of 20 different international currencies and their countries. Put together an information poster, for overseas travellers, which includes this list and illustrates some of the world's currencies.

Economics in action

ATL Thinking, Communication and Research

Australia uses a "trade weighted index" (TWI). Find out the following:

1. Why is it called the trade weighted index?
2. What are its current weightings?
3. What are the current values compared to a year ago?
4. Which currencies have contributed most to the change?

Use the website: www.rba.gov.au

What is an exchange rate?

An exchange rate is the value of one currency expressed in terms of another currency, for example, €1 = US$1.12. This means that one euro may be exchanged for 1.12 US dollars. Currencies are exchanged (traded) on the foreign exchange market, the largest market in the world in terms of cash movements. The market includes the trading of foreign currencies between governments, central banks, private commercial banks, MNCs and other financial institutions.

Did you know?

The international foreign exchange market is known as the Forex market. There are five main centres of Forex trading and these are based in London, New York, Zurich, Frankfurt and Tokyo. On any given day, the total trading in the Forex market can exceed US$1.5 trillion!

When individuals, such as travellers or importing companies, wish to buy foreign currencies, they do not buy from the Forex market. They buy from the commercial banks that charge a higher price (their commission) than is found on the Forex market. This is one of the ways that commercial banks make their profits. Charging different rates of commission is how banks can compete with each other.

Exchange rates are usually expressed as a comparison of the values of two single currencies—for example, Australian dollars for Japanese yen. However, it is possible to express one currency against a collection (basket) of other currencies, and when this is done the outcome is known as an exchange rate index. The exchange rate index is a weighted average index, like the consumer price index. In this case, it shows the exchange rate of one currency, expressed as an index, relative to the weighted exchange rates of a selection of other currencies. The currencies chosen are usually the country's major trading partners and the weighting is usually based upon the relative value of trade with each country.

What is an exchange rate system?

There are a number of different exchange rate systems operating in the world. The way that a country manages its exchange rate is known as its exchange-rate regime. There are three main types – a fixed exchange rate, a floating exchange rate, and a managed exchange rate. We will now look at each in turn.

Key concept 

INTERVENTION

How does a fixed exchange rate system operate?

A fixed exchange rate is an exchange-rate regime where the value of a currency is fixed, or pegged, to the value of another currency, to the average value of a selection of currencies, or to the value of some other commodity, such as gold. As the value of the variable that the currency is pegged to changes, then so does the value of the currency.

Deciding upon, and then maintaining, the fixed value of the currency is usually carried out by the government or the central bank. If the value of the currency, in a fixed exchange rate regime, is raised, then we say that this is a *revaluation* of the currency. If the value is lowered, then we say that this is a *devaluation* of the currency. These terms are very specific and must be used in the appropriate circumstances, ie when referring to changes in fixed exchange rates.

A fixed exchange rate is maintained by government intervention in the foreign exchange market. It is most easily explained using an example. The Barbadian $ (Bds$) has been fixed against the US dollar at a rate of 2Bds$ = 1 US$ since 1975. So, 1Bds$ = 50¢ US.

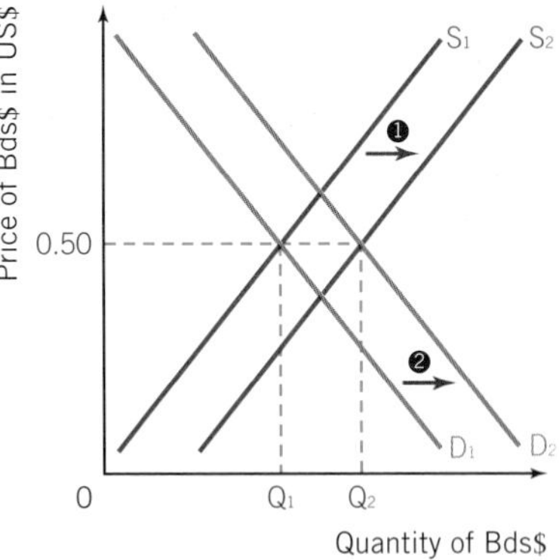

▲ Figure 26.1 An increase in the supply of Bds$

Figure 26.1 shows the situation where the supply of Barbadian dollars is increasing on the foreign exchange market. This may be caused, for example, by Barbadians purchasing greater amounts of imports. The supply curve thus shifts from S_1 to S_2 (❶) and there is an excess supply of Barbadian dollars of Q_1Q_2. Without government intervention, the exchange rate will fall. In order to maintain its fixed exchange rate, the Barbadian government needs to buy up the excess supply of its own currency on the foreign exchange market, thus shifting the demand curve from D_1 to D_2 (❷). It does this by using previously amassed reserves of foreign currencies.

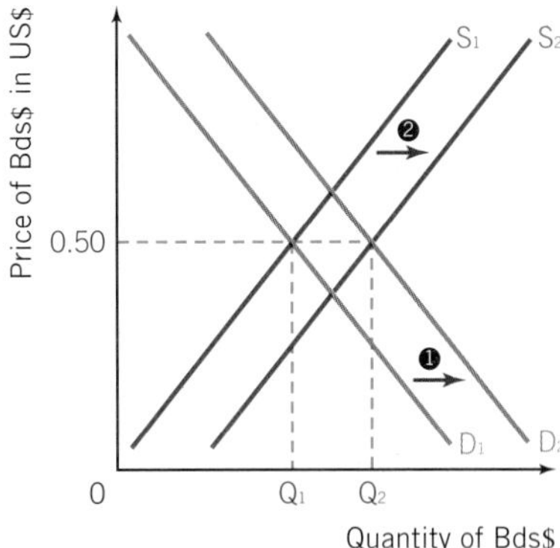

▲ Figure 26.2 An increase in the demand for the Bds$

Figure 26.2 shows the situation where the demand for Barbadian dollars is increasing on the foreign exchange market. This may be caused, for example, by more foreigners wishing to visit Barbados for their holidays. The demand curve thus shifts from D_1 to D_2 (❶) and there is an excess demand for Barbadian dollars of Q_1Q_2. Without government intervention, the exchange rate will rise. To maintain its fixed exchange rate, the Barbadian government needs to sell its own currency on the foreign exchange market in order to satisfy the excess demand, thus shifting the supply curve from S_1 to S_2 (❷). This will then increase the Barbadian reserves of foreign currencies.

One other way that a fixed exchange rate may be maintained is by making it illegal to trade currency at any other rate. However, this is hard to enforce unless the government of the country has an effective monopoly over the conversion of the currency. This was carried out with some success by the Chinese government in the 1990s to keep the yuan pegged to the US$. The danger of this sort of control is that a black market may emerge in the currency, operating at a different exchange rate.

How does a floating exchange rate system operate?

A floating exchange rate is an exchange-rate regime where the value of a currency is allowed to be determined solely by the demand for, and supply of, the currency on the foreign exchange market. There is no government intervention to influence the value of the currency.

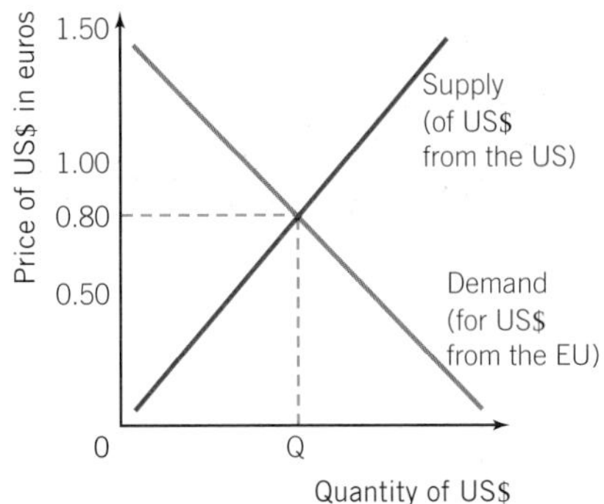

▲ Figure 26.3 A floating currency

The market for a currency is shown in Figure 26.3. In this case, it is the market for US dollars in terms of euros. As we can see, the demand curve is downward sloping and represents the demand for dollars by people in the EU, or at least people who hold euros. The supply curve is also normal and represents the supply of dollars, which comes from those who hold US dollars. The equilibrium price, the exchange rate, is US$1 = €0.80. Correct labelling, as is the case with all diagrams in economics, is crucial.

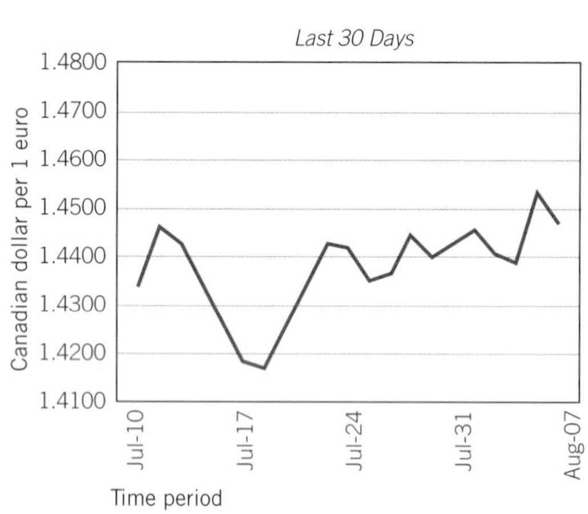

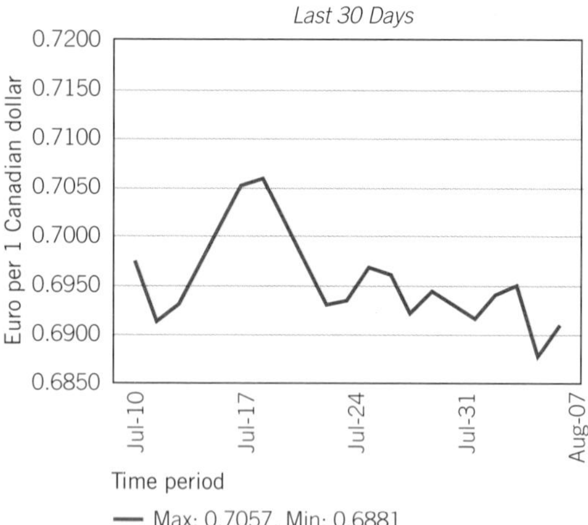

▲ Figure 26.4 Changing values of the Canadian dollar and the euro

If the value of the currency in a floating exchange-rate regime rises, then we say that this is an *appreciation* of the value of the currency. If the value falls, then we say that there has been a *depreciation* of the value of the currency. These terms must be used with floating exchange rates and must not be confused with the terms revaluation and devaluation, which relate to changes in currency values in a fixed exchange-rate regime.

Consider a change in the value of the US$ from a first exchange rate of US$1 = €0.80 to a second exchange rate of US$1 = €0.85. What does this mean?

This shows that the dollar has appreciated against the euro. In the first instance US$1 could buy €0.80 and in the second it has increased in value to be able to buy €0.85. For example, if a bottle of French wine costs €10, then under the first exchange rate this would be equal to US$12.50 [$1 = €0.8]. Under the second rate of exchange the price of the bottle of wine falls to US$11.77 [$1 = €0.85]. This shows that the purchasing power of the dollar has risen. It means that a given amount of US$ will buy more European goods.

Let's consider the euro value of dollars given the same exchange rates. If US$1 = €0.80, then €1 = US$1.25. When the exchange rate changes to US$1 = €0.85, then €1 = US$1.18. This shows that the euro has depreciated; in the first instance, it is worth US$1.25, in the second it has fallen to US$1.18. This means that a given amount of euros will buy fewer American goods.

Notice that the appreciation of the US dollar against the euro occurs at the same time as the depreciation of the euro against the US dollar. Essentially, they are two sides of the same coin. This relationship is further illustrated in Figure 26.4, which shows the value of the Canadian dollar in euros and the value of the euro in Canadian dollars for a set period of time.

Exercise 26.2

ATL Thinking and Communication

Using the data in Figure 26.4, explain how the value of the Canadian dollar has changed in terms of euros and how the euro has changed in terms of Canadian dollars for the time period shown. Look carefully at the labels on the axes.

What can you say about the relationship between the two graphs?

How do you calculate changes in exchange rates and the price of a good in different currencies?

In SL and HL paper 2, and in HL paper 3, you may be asked to make various, simple, calculations relating to exchange rates and changes in exchange rates. Here are some examples of the kind of questions that you may face and suggested responses.

1. The US dollar is currently trading against the euro at a rate of US$1 = €0.8. What is the rate for €1 in US$?
2. With the exchange rate above, what would be the cost in euros of a good that was selling for US$75?

3. If the exchange rate changes from US$1 = €0.8 to US$1 = €0.9, explain what would happen to the euro price of a US-manufactured dress shirt that was being exported to Europe from the USA at a cost of US$150?

The responses might be as follows.

1. If US$1 = €0.8, then €1 = $\frac{1}{0.8}$ = US$1.25.
2. If the good is selling for US$75, then it will cost 75 × €0.8 = €60.
3. With the original exchange rate of US$1 = €0.8, the dress shirt would cost €120 (150 × €0.8). With the new exchange rate, the value of the euro has depreciated. It now costs more euros to buy the same amount of dollars, and so the price of the dress shirt increases to €135 (150 × €0.9).

What causes a change in the value of a country's currency in terms of another currency?

We now need to consider what factors will shift the demand and supply curves for a currency. First let us look at the demand curve, using the example of the demand for US dollars by people in the EU. People in the EU will have to buy US dollars in the foreign exchange market in order to:

- buy US exports of goods and services and to travel in America
- invest in US firms (foreign direct investment [FDI] or portfolio investment)
- save their money in US banks or other financial institutions
- make money by speculating on the US dollar.

Thus the demand for the US dollar will rise if:

- there is an increase in the demand for US goods and services. This could be caused by:
  - → US inflation rates being lower than EU inflation rates, making US goods and services relatively less expensive than EU goods and services
  - → an increase in incomes in the EU, so people in the EU increase their demand for all things, including imports from the US
  - → a change in tastes in the EU in favour of US products
- US investment prospects improve, due to, for example, strong economic growth in the US, or the implementation of new business-friendly policies
- US interest rates increase, making it more attractive to save there than in EU financial institutions
- speculators in the EU think the value of the US dollar will rise in the future, so they buy it now. If they are correct, then they will be able to sell those US dollars in the future, when they are worth more, and make a financial gain.

An increase in the demand for the US dollar is shown in Figure 26.5.

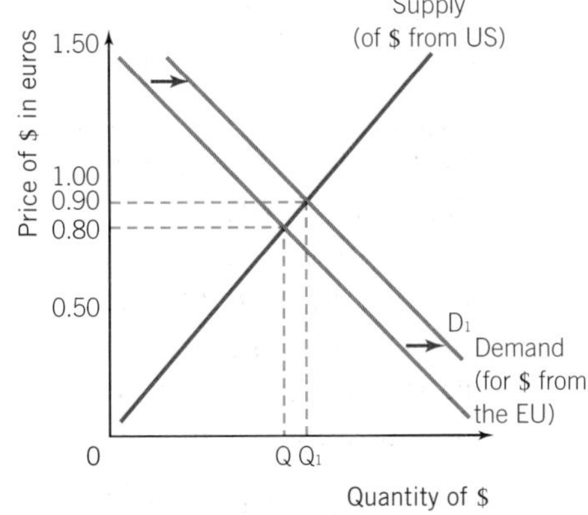

▲ Figure 26.5 An increase in the demand for the US dollar

Exercise 26.3
ATL Thinking and Communication

1. List and explain the factors that might lead to a fall in the demand for the US dollar in terms of the euro.
2. Draw a diagram to illustrate the fall in the demand for the US dollar and its effect upon the exchange rate of the US dollar in terms of the euro. Be sure to label the axes fully and accurately.

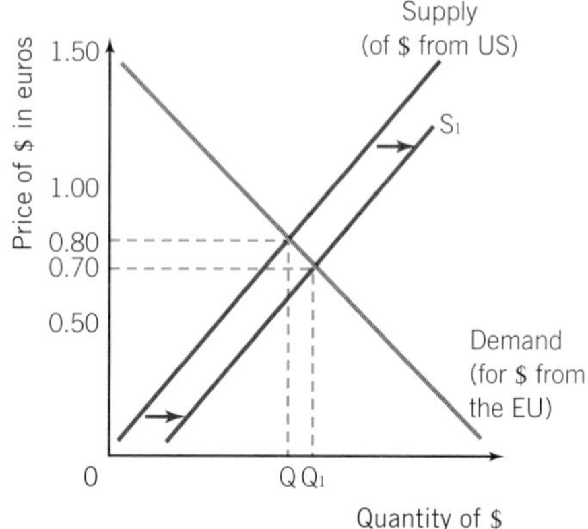

▲ Figure 26.6 An increase in the supply of the US dollar

Exercise 26.4
ATL Thinking and Communication

A newspaper article has the headline, "Indian rupee weakens against the US$ as chair of the US Federal Reserve announces an increase in its interest rate".

Using an exchange rate diagram, explain the reason for the fall in the Indian rupee.

Key concept
INTERVENTION

As we can see, an increase in the demand for the US dollar from the EU will shift the demand curve for the US dollar to the right to D_1. When this happens, the value of the dollar will appreciate and it will now be worth 0.90 euros. Each US dollar may be exchanged for a larger amount of euros.

Now let us look at the supply curve and consider the supply of US dollars, using the same example. The US dollar will be supplied on the foreign exchange market when Americans wish to:

- buy EU goods and services and to travel in Europe
- invest in EU firms (FDI or portfolio investment)
- save their money in EU banks or other financial institutions
- make money by speculating on the euro.

In all of the above cases, Americans will need euros and will have to exchange dollars to get those euros. This will increase the supply of dollars on the foreign exchange market.

Thus the supply of the US dollar will rise if:

- Americans increase their demand for EU goods and services, thus exchanging more US dollars for euros. This could be caused by:
    - → US inflation rates being higher than EU inflation rates, and thus US goods and services becoming relatively more expensive than EU goods and services
    - → an increase in incomes in the USA, so people in the USA increase their demand for all things, including imports from the EU
    - → a change in tastes in the USA in favour of EU products
- EU investment prospects improve
- EU interest rates increase, making it more attractive to save there than in US financial institutions
- speculators in the US think the value of the US dollar will fall in the future, so they sell it now and buy euros. If they are correct, they will be able to buy US dollars back again when they are less expensive and so will make a financial gain.

An increase in the supply of the US dollar is shown in Figure 26.6.

As we can see, an increase in the supply of the US dollar on the US dollar/euro market will shift the supply curve of the US dollar to the right, to S_1. When this happens, the value of the dollar will depreciate and it will now be worth €0.70. Each US dollar may be exchanged for a smaller amount of euros.

How does a managed exchange rate system operate?

In reality, there is no currency in the world that is allowed to be completely freely floating. Even where governments try to be as non-interventionist as possible, there will come times when the currency is subject to extreme fluctuations and the government, or central bank, will feel that they must intervene. In the same way, frequent changes in the exchange rate, if it is completely freely floating, may cause uncertainty for businesses, which is not good for trade, and so governments will be forced to intervene in order to stabilize the exchange rate.

Because of the above, most exchange rate regimes in the world are managed exchange rates. These are exchange rate regimes where the currency is allowed to float, but with some element of interference from the government.

The most common systems are where a central bank will set an upper and lower exchange rate value and then allow the currency to float freely, so long as it does not move out of that band. If the exchange rate starts to get close to the upper or lower level, then the central bank will intervene in the foreign exchange market for its currency. Central banks do not make the upper and lower level values public, for fear of speculation, but they do exist.

What are the possible advantages and disadvantages of high and low exchange rates?

The actual level of the exchange rate will have marked economic effects upon a country and we need to look at these now to understand fully why governments intervene to influence the value of the exchange rate. Subsequently, we look at how governments intervene.

Let us look in turn at the possible advantages and disadvantages of high and low exchange rates.

What are the possible advantages of a high exchange rate?

- *Downward pressure on inflation*: If the value of the exchange rate is high, then the price of finished imported goods will be relatively low. In addition, the price of imported raw materials and components will reduce the costs of production for firms, which could lead to lower prices for consumers. The lower price of imported goods also puts pressure on domestic producers to be competitive by keeping prices low.
- *More imports can be bought*: If the value of the exchange rate is high, then each unit of the currency will buy more foreign currencies, and so more foreign goods and services. This would include both visible imports, such as technology, and invisible imports, such as foreign travel.
- *A high value of a currency forces domestic producers to improve their efficiency*: The high exchange rate will threaten their international competitiveness so they will be forced to lower costs and become more efficient in order to maintain competitiveness. While this might result in the laying off of workers (see next point), there are other means of increasing efficiency that will result in greater economic productivity for the country.

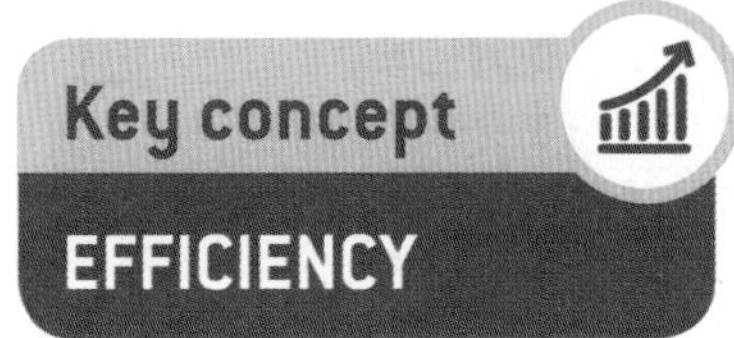

Japan's major automakers hit by strong yen; export orders down

https://www.gulftoday.ae/business/2019/08/03/japans-major-automakers-hit-by--strong-yen-export-orders-down

Thailand Tourism Suffering from Strong Baht

http://asean.travel/2019/07/02/thailand-tourism-suffering-from-strong-baht/

What are the possible disadvantages of a high exchange rate?

- *Damage to export industries*: If the value of the exchange rate is high, then export industries may find it difficult to sell their goods and services abroad, because of their relatively high prices. This could lead to unemployment in these industries.
- *Damage to domestic industries*: With greater levels of imports being purchased, because imports are now relatively less expensive, domestic producers may find that the increased competition causes a fall in the demand for their goods and services. This may lead to a further increase in the level of unemployment as firms cut back.

What are the possible advantages of a low exchange rate?

- Greater employment in export industries: If the value of the exchange rate is low, then exports from the country will be relatively less expensive and so more competitive. This in turn may lead to more employment in the export industries.
- Greater employment in domestic industries: The low exchange rate will make imports more expensive than they were. This may encourage domestic consumers to buy domestically produced goods, instead of imports, and this may also raise employment.

Exercise 26.5

ATL Thinking and Communication

1. With the help of an AD/AS diagram, explain why a high value of a currency may worsen unemployment in a country.
2. With the help of an AD/AS diagram, explain why a low value of a currency may create inflationary pressure in a country.

What are the possible disadvantages of a low exchange rate?

- Inflation: A low value of the currency will make imported final goods and services, imported raw materials and imported components more expensive. The raw materials and components are needed by firms and are costs of production that will rise, possibly leading to higher prices in the economy. The final goods and services will have higher prices. Thus there is a serious likelihood of inflation.

So what are the main points?

A high value of a currency may be good to fight inflation, but may create unemployment problems, whereas a low value of a currency may be good for solving unemployment problems, but may create inflationary pressure.

Why do governments intervene in the foreign exchange market and how do they do it?

Key concept

INTERVENTION

There are a number of reasons why governments may intervene in the foreign exchange market to influence the value of their currency. They may wish to:

- lower the exchange rate in order to increase employment
- raise the exchange rate in order to fight inflation

- maintain a fixed exchange rate
- avoid large fluctuations in a floating exchange rate
- achieve relative exchange rate stability in order to improve business confidence
- improve a current account deficit, which is where spending on imported goods and services is greater than the revenue received from exported goods and services (see Chapter 27).

Whatever the reason for the intervention, we should now consider how governments attempt to manipulate the exchange rate. There are two main methods.

1. *Using their reserves of foreign currencies to buy, or sell, foreign currencies*: If the government wishes to increase the value of the currency, then it can use its reserves of foreign currencies to buy its own currency on the foreign exchange market. This will increase the demand for its currency and so force up the exchange rate.

   In the same way, if the government wishes to lower the value of its currency, then it simply buys foreign currencies on the foreign exchange market, increasing its foreign currency reserves. To buy the foreign currencies, the government uses its own currency and this increases the supply of the currency on the foreign exchange market and so lowers its exchange rate.

2. *By changing interest rates*: If the government wishes to increase the value of the currency then they may raise the level of interest rates in the country. This will make the domestic interest rates relatively higher than those abroad and should attract financial investment from abroad. In order to put money into the country, the investors will have to buy the country's currency, thus increasing the demand for it and so its exchange rate.

   In the same way, if the government wishes to lower the value of the currency, then they may lower the level of interest rates in the country. This will make the domestic interest rates relatively lower than those abroad and should make financial investment abroad more attractive. In order to invest abroad, the investors will have to buy foreign currencies, thus exchanging their own currency and increasing the supply of it on the financial exchange market. This should lower its exchange rate.

Japan signals it will act to curb any excessive yen rises

https://japantoday.com/category/business/Japan-signals-it-will-act-to-curb-excessive-yen-rises

Economics in action

ATL Thinking, Communication and Research

Given the multitude of factors affecting the demand and supply of the world's currencies, exchange rates are in a constant state of change, with some currencies experiencing larger fluctuations than others. Find contemporary articles on the appreciation or depreciation of two different country's exchange rates. Using exchange rate diagrams, explain likely reasons for the appreciation or depreciation. Discuss the possible consequences for relevant stakeholders.

Exercise 26.6

ATL Thinking and Communication

1. Using an exchange rate diagram, explain what will happen to the value of the euro against the US dollar if the European Central Bank (ECB) buys dollars on the foreign exchange market.
2. Using an exchange rate diagram, explain what will happen to the value of the euro against the US dollar if the ECB raises the level of interest rates in the Eurozone.

What are the advantages and disadvantages of fixed and floating exchange rates?

Whatever exchange rate regime a country chooses to operate, there are bound to be advantages and disadvantages and we need to look at these in turn.

What are the advantages of a fixed exchange rate?

1. A fixed exchange rate should reduce uncertainty for all economic agents in the country. Businesses will be able to plan ahead in the knowledge that their predicted costs and prices for international trading agreements will not change.

2. If exchange rates are fixed, then inflation may have a very harmful effect on the demand for exports and imports. Because of this, the government is forced to take measures to ensure that inflation is as low as possible, in order to keep businesses competitive on foreign markets. Thus fixed exchange rates ensure sensible government policies on inflation.

3. In theory, the existence of a fixed exchange rate should reduce speculation in the foreign exchange markets. (However, in reality, this has not always been the case and there are often attempts to destabilize fixed exchange rate systems in order to make speculative gains.)

What are the disadvantages of a fixed exchange rate?

1. The government or central bank is compelled to keep the exchange rate fixed. The main way of doing this is through the manipulation of interest rates. However, this may have possible negative consequences for the domestic economy. For example, if the exchange rate is in danger of falling, then the central bank will have to raise the interest rate in order to increase demand for the currency, but this will have a deflationary effect on the economy, lowering demand and increasing unemployment. This means that a domestic macroeconomic goal (low unemployment) may have to be sacrificed.

2. In order to keep the exchange rate fixed and to instill confidence on the foreign exchange markets, a country with a fixed exchange rate has to maintain high levels of foreign reserves in order to make it clear that it is able to defend its currency by the buying and selling of foreign currencies.

3. Setting the level of the fixed exchange rate is not simple. There are many possible variables to take into account and, also, these variables will change with time. If the rate is set at a level which is too high, then export firms may find that they are not competitive in foreign markets. If this is the case, then the exchange rate will have to be devalued, but again, finding the exact right level is very difficult.

4. A country that fixes its exchange rate at an artificially low level may create international disagreement. This is because a low exchange rate will make that country's exports more competitive on world markets and may be seen as an unfair trade advantage. This may lead to economic disputes or to retaliation.

Exercise 26.7

ATL Thinking and Communication

Xi Jinping seeks to ease currency war fears as China and US near trade deal

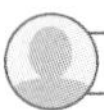

by Elizabeth Morgan

President Xi Jinping said China would avoid any currency **devaluation**, suggesting Beijing does not intend to use the currency as a trade weapon. This had the effect of pushing up the value of the yuan in the foreign exchange market.

In his keynote speech in Beijing on Friday, Xi said China would allow the market to play a "decisive" role in setting the yuan **exchange rate** while keeping the rate "basically stable", in response to allegations the country has manipulated the value of its currency to seek advantages in trade.

The promise came as Beijing and Washington are entering the final stage of their trade deal negotiations, with the yuan exchange rate reportedly part of that pact.

China's "managed floating exchange rate" system allows Beijing to dictate the value of the yuan – also known as the renminbi – against other currencies, an arrangement that has drawn frequent complaints from Washington.

During his election campaign, US President Donald Trump threatened to label China as a "currency manipulator", accusing Beijing of deliberately keeping the yuan's value low to boost Chinese exports. But he did not go ahead with that threat once he took office.

Ding Shuang, chief China economist at Standard Chartered Bank in Hong Kong, said Xi's promise that there would be no competitive devaluation did not mean the yuan would only strengthen against the US dollar.

Ding said there would be further swings in the yuan exchange rate after Beijing and Washington reached a trade deal as China reduced intervention in the exchange rate market.

"If China's balance of payments or current account deteriorates because of market forces, there's still a possibility for the yuan to weaken," Ding said.

Larry Hu, chief China economist at Macquarie Capital in Hong Kong, said China's rejection of a currency war was part of Beijing's compromise to reach a trade deal with the US. "Both sides have made some concessions to end the trade war," Hu said.

Source: Adapted from Xi Jinping seeks to ease currency war fears as China and US near trade deal, by Cissy Zhou, 26 April 2019, South China Morning Post, www.scmp.com

1. Define the following terms, indicated in bold in the text:
   a) devaluation [2 marks]
   b) exchange rate. [2 marks]
2. Using an exchange rate diagram, explain how China's "managed floating exchange rate" system might keep the value of the yuan low. (Paragraph 4) [4 marks]
3. Using an AD/AS diagram, explain how "keeping the yuan's value low" might affect the Chinese economy. (Paragraph 5) [4 marks]
4. Using an exchange rate diagram, explain how the value of the yuan might increase if there was "reduced intervention in the exchange rate market". (Paragraph 7) [4 marks]

What are the advantages of a floating exchange rate?

1. Because the exchange rate does not have to be kept at a certain level, interest rates are free to be employed as domestic monetary tools and can be used for demand management policies, such as controlling inflation.
2. In theory, the floating exchange rate should adjust itself, in order to keep the current account balanced. For example, if there is a current account deficit, then the demand for the currency is low, since export sales are relatively low, and the supply of the currency is high, since the demand for imports is relatively high. This should mean that the market will adjust and that the exchange rate should fall. Following this, export prices become relatively more attractive, import prices relatively less so, and so the current account balance should right itself. (This will actually depend upon the Marshall-Lerner condition being satisfied—see Chapter 27 HL only.)
3. Because reserves are not used to control the value of the currency, it is not necessary to keep high levels of reserves of foreign currencies and gold.

What are the disadvantages of a floating exchange rate?

1. Floating exchange rates tend to create uncertainty on international markets. Businesses trying to plan for the future find it difficult to make accurate predictions about what their likely costs and revenues will be. Investment is more difficult to assess and there is no doubt that volatile exchange rates will reduce the levels of international investment, because it is difficult to assess the exact level of return and risk.
2. In reality, floating exchange rates are affected by more factors than simply demand and supply, such as government intervention, world events and speculation. Because of this, they do not necessarily self-adjust in order to eliminate current account deficits.
3. A floating exchange-rate regime may worsen existing levels of inflation. If a country has high inflation relative to other countries, then this will make its exports less competitive and its imports relatively less expensive. The exchange rate will then fall, in order to rectify the situation. However, this could lead to even higher import prices of finished goods, components and raw materials, and thus cost-push inflation, which may further fuel the overall inflation rate.

EXAMINATION QUESTIONS

Paper 1, part (a) questions – SL & HL

1. Explain **three** factors that might lead to an increase in the demand for a currency.
2. Explain **three** factors that might lead to an increase in the supply of a currency.
3. Explain **two** methods that a central bank might employ to *devalue* its currency.

Paper 1, part (b) questions – SL & HL

1. Using real-world examples, discuss the consequences of a depreciation of a country's currency on inflation, unemployment and the standard of living.
2. Using real-world examples, discuss the consequences of an appreciation of a country's currency on the current account balance, inflation and economic growth.

Paper 1, part (b) questions – HL only

1. Using real-world examples, discuss the relative advantages and disadvantages of a floating exchange rate system in contrast with a fixed exchange rate system.

HL & SL Paper 2 – 2-mark and 3-mark questions and HL Paper 3 questions

1. The Euro is currently trading against the Singapore dollar at a rate of €1 = S$1.5. What is the rate for S$1 in €? [2 marks]
2. With the exchange rate above, what would be the cost in Singapore dollars of a good that was selling for €150. [2 marks]
3. If the exchange rate changes from €1 = S$1.5 to €1 = S$1.4, explain what would happen to the Singapore dollar price of an EU manufactured waffle maker that was being exported to Singapore from the EU at a cost of €120. [3 marks]

27 THE BALANCE OF PAYMENTS

REAL-WORLD ISSUE:
Who are the winners and losers of the integration of the world's economies?

By the end of this chapter, you should be able to:

- → Define and explain the balance of payments account
- → Define and explain the current account
- → Define and explain the elements that make up the current account
- → Define and explain the capital account
- → Define and explain the elements that make up the capital account
- → Understand that the current account balance is equal to the sum of the capital account and financial account balances
- → Calculate elements of the balance of payments from a set of data
- HL Explain how imbalances in the current account of a country may have effects on the exchange rate of a country's currency
- HL Discuss the implications of, and methods to correct, persistent current account imbalances
- HL Define, explain and give examples of expenditure-switching policies
- HL Define, explain and give examples of expenditure-reducing policies
- HL Define and explain the Marshall-Lerner condition
- HL Define, explain and illustrate the J-curve effect
- HL Discuss the implications of a persistent current account surplus.

What is the balance of payments account?

The balance of payments account is a record of the value of all the transactions between the residents of one country and the residents of all other countries in the world over a given period of time. This period is usually one year, although monthly balance of payments accounts are also produced. There are three main parts to the balance of payments account – the current account, the capital account and the financial account.

Any transaction that leads to money entering the country from abroad is known as a credit item in the balance of payments and is given a positive value. Any transaction that leads to money leaving the country to go abroad is known as a debit item in the balance of payments and is given a negative value.

Note that there are many different names used to identify the various parts of the balance of payments account in different parts of the world. The headings change from country to country and even from time to time within the same country. In order to avoid confusion, and for consistency, for the purpose of the IB curriculum and assessment, a set structure (and components) of the balance of payments is laid down and that structure will be followed in this chapter.

What are the elements of the current account?

The current account is a measure of the flow of funds from trade in goods and services, plus other income flows. It is usually sub-divided into four parts.

1. *The balance of trade in goods*

   The balance of trade in goods is also variously known as the visible trade balance, the merchandise account balance or simply the balance of trade. It is a measure of the revenue received from the exports of tangible (physical) goods minus the expenditure on the imports of tangible goods over a given period of time. It includes trade in all tangible goods, from airplanes to chickens.

   Exports occur when an international transaction relating to goods or services leads to an inflow of money into the country. Imports occur when an international transaction relating to goods or services leads to an outflow of money from the country.

   When export revenue is greater than import expenditure then we say that there is a surplus on the balance of trade in goods. When import expenditure is greater than export revenue then we say that there is a deficit on the balance of trade in goods.

2. *The balance of trade in services*

   The balance of trade in services is also known as the invisible balance, the services balance or net services. It is a measure of the revenue received from the exports of services minus the expenditure on the imports of services over a given period of time. It includes the import and export of all services such as banking, insurance and tourism. For example, an Italian tourist on holiday in Vienna would be spending money that represents an invisible export to the Austrian economy (money coming in) and so an invisible import to the Italian economy (money going out).

Exercise 27.1

ATL Thinking and Communication

Identify whether each of the following elements represents an invisible import, a visible import, an invisible export or a visible export on the UK current account.

1. UK computer manufacturers buy semi-conductors from Malaysia.

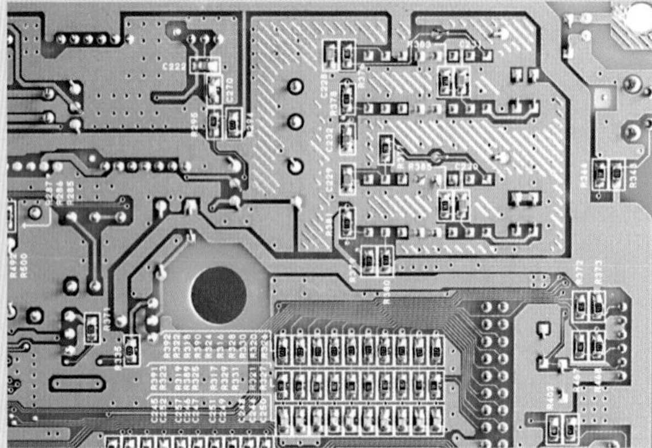

2. Lloyds of London sells insurance to Chinese shipping companies.

3. Canadian football fans buy tickets to a Manchester United game.

4. French football fans attending the World Cup 2018 stay in hotels in Russia.

5. Spanish dog lovers buy a pedigree dog from UK breeders

3. *Income*

   This is often known as net investment income (net factor income from abroad). It is a measure of the net monetary movement of profit, interest and dividends moving into and out of the country over a given period of time, as a result of financial investment abroad.

   Domestic firms may have set up branches in other countries and any profits being repatriated will count as a positive item in this account. In the same way, profits sent out of the country by foreign firms set up within the country will count as a negative item.

   Residents and institutions in the country may have invested in banks and other financial institutions in other countries and any interest received from these financial investments will count as a positive item. In the same way, any payment of interest to foreign investors that leaves the country will count as a negative item.

   Residents and institutions may have purchased shares in foreign companies and any dividends received from those companies will count as a positive item. In the same way, any dividends paid by domestic firms to foreign shareholders will count as a negative item.

4. *Current transfers*

   This is a measurement of the net transfers of money, often known as net unilateral transfers from abroad. These are payments made between countries when no goods or services change hands. At a government level these payments include things such as foreign aid and grants. At an individual level they include foreign workers sending money back to their families in their home country (remittances) or private gifts sent from a person in one country to a person in another.

Current account balance = Balance of trade in goods + Balance of trade in services + Net income flows + Net transfers

Note that any of these accounts might be in surplus or deficit at any given time—there could be a deficit on the trade in goods, a surplus on the trade in services, a surplus on net income flows, a deficit on net transfers and an overall surplus on the current account. The current account balance is an overall balance and may be in deficit or in surplus.

What are the elements of the capital account?

The capital account is a relatively small part of the balance of payments accounts and does not have a significant effect on the balance. The capital account has two components.

1. *Capital transfers*

   This is a measure of the net monetary movements gained or lost through actions such as the transfers of goods and financial assets by migrants entering or leaving the country, debt forgiveness, transfers

Did you know?

"Remittances, funds received from migrants working abroad to developing countries, have grown dramatically in recent years from US$18 billion in 1980 to over US$440 billion in 2015. They have become the second largest source of external finance for developing countries after foreign direct investment (FDI), both in absolute terms and as a proportion of GDP. Furthermore, unlike other capital flows, remittances tend to be relatively stable even during periods of economic downturns and crises."

Source: *The World Bank, www.worldbank.org*

Korea's current account balance back in surplus

https://www.asiatimes.com/2019/07/article/south-koreas-current-account-balance-swings-back-to-surplus-in-may/

relating to the sale of fixed assets (tangible assets that firms own and use in production that have a useful life of at least one year), gift taxes, inheritance taxes and death duties.

2. *Transactions in non-produced, non-financial assets*

   This consists of the net international sales and purchases of non-produced assets, such as land or the rights to natural resources, and the net international sales and purchases of intangible assets, such as patents, copyrights, brand names or franchises.

What are the elements of the financial account?

The financial account measures the net change in foreign ownership of domestic financial assets. If foreign ownership of domestic financial assets increases more quickly than domestic ownership of foreign financial assets, then there is more money coming into the country than going out, and so there is a financial account surplus. In the same way, if domestic ownership of foreign financial assets increases more quickly than foreign ownership of domestic financial assets, then there is more money going out of the country than coming in, and so there is a financial account deficit.

The financial account has three components.

1. *Direct investment*

   This is a measure of the purchase of long-term assets, where the purchaser is aiming to gain a lasting interest in a company in another economy. It includes things such as the buying of property, the outright purchasing of a business or the purchasing of stocks or shares in a business. In all cases, the asset is expected to have a positive return in the future, by making profits or by increasing in value over time. The investment does not have to be paid back and there is no guarantee that it will provide a positive return. The buyer of the asset is taking a risk.

   Much of the activity in this category is in the form of foreign direct investment (FDI, investment by multinational corporations in another country). International Monetary Fund (IMF) guidelines state that an investment in a firm is FDI if it accounts for at least 10% of the ownership of the company. However, many countries set a higher percentage of ownership for an investment to count as FDI.

2. *Portfolio investment*

   This is a measure of stock and bond purchases, which are not direct investment since they do not lead to a lasting interest in a company. This also includes the buying and selling of things such as treasury bills and government bonds. We will also include savings account deposits in this category, although in many countries that comes under the heading of "other investment".

   In all the portfolio investments mentioned above the investor is putting forward the money in order to purchase the asset, in the expectation that interest will be paid on the investment and that the money will be repaid at a given point in time. These assets are simply borrowing and lending on the international market.

3. *Reserve assets*

   These are the reserves of gold and foreign currencies which all countries hold and which are itemized in the official reserve account. It is movements into and out of this account that ensure that the balance of payments will always balance to zero. If there is a surplus on all of the other accounts combined, then the official reserve account total will increase. If there is a deficit on all of the other accounts combined, then the official reserve account total will decrease. It is net changes in the official reserve account, over the period of time being considered, that balances the accounts.

So does the balance of payments really balance?

In reality, the balance of payments accounts will not actually balance. This is because there are simply too many individual transactions taking place for the measurement to be exact. There will always be some transactions that have not yet been recorded when the figures are being put together. To resolve this, a balancing item, which we will call "net errors and omissions" is put into the accounts to ensure that they do, in fact, balance. This may also be referred to as a "statistical discrepancy". As time goes by and trading accounts are revised over the years, more data comes to light and the balancing item invariably gets smaller.

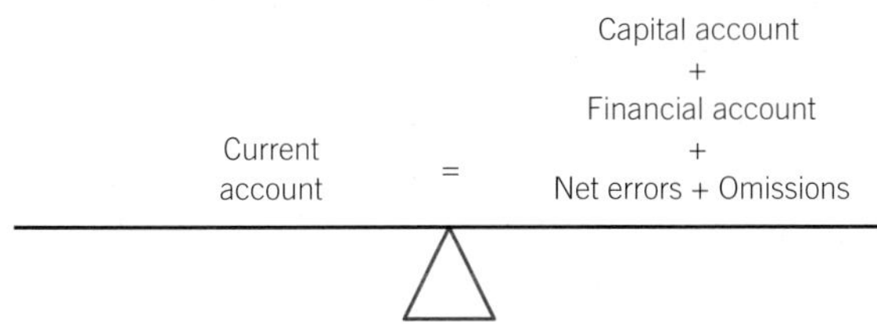

▲ **Figure 27.1** The balancing balance of payments

A selection of the balance of payments figures for the USA, from 2016 to 2018, are shown in Table 27.1. They illustrate the way that balance of payments accounts are made up.

Line	US Balance of Payments figures [millions of dollars] (Credits +; debits –)	2016	2017	2018
1	**Current account**			
2	Exports of goods	1,456,956	1,553,386	1,672,331
3	Imports of goods	–2,208,007	–2,360,877	–2,563,653
4	**Balance of trade in goods (lines 2+3)**	–751,051	–807,491	–891,322
5	Exports of services	758,890	797,687	828,424
6	Imports of services	–509,840	–542,465	–559,217
7	**Balance of trade in services (lines 5+6)**	249,050	255,222	269,207
8	Income receipts (investment income)	830,175	928,116	1,060,363
9	Income payments (investment income)	–637,153	–706,388	–816,064

Note

Summary of the structure of the balance of payments

Current account

- Balance of trade in goods
- Balance of trade in services
- Income
- Current transfers

Financial account

- Direct investment
- Portfolio investment
- Reserve assets
- Official borrowing

Capital account

- Capital transfers
- Transactions in non-produced, non-financial assets

The value of the current account = the value of the financial account + capital account + errors and omissions.

In other words:

- If the value of the current account is negative (current account deficit), this will be balanced by a positive value (surplus) on the financial account plus the capital account.
- If the value of the current account is positive (current account surplus), this will be balanced by a negative value (deficit) on the financial account plus the capital account.
- Adjustments are made via the "errors and omissions" or "statistical discrepancy".

Line	US Balance of Payments figures [millions of dollars] (Credits +; debits –)	2016	2017	2018
10	**Net income receipts (lines 8+9)**	193,022	221,728	244,299
11	Unilateral current transfers, net	–123,895	–118,596	–110,664
12	**Net income flows (lines 10+11)**	69,127	103,132	133,635
13	**Current account balance (lines 4+7+12)**	**–432,874**	**–449,137**	**–488,480**
14	**Capital account**			
15	Capital account transactions, net	–59	24,746	9,408
16	**Financial account**			
17	US-owned assets abroad, net (financial outflow)	–346,537	–1,184,436	–296,627
18	Foreign-owned assets in the USA, net (financial inflow)	741,530	1,537,684	800,915
19	Financial derivatives, net	–7,827	–23,074	20,261
20	Statistical discrepancy	47,868.9	92,521.8	–40,472.7
21	Reserves and related items	–2,101.9	1,695.2	–5,004.3
22	**Capital and financial account balance (lines 15 + 17 + 18 + 19 + 20)**	**432,874**	**449,137**	**488,480**

Source: International Monetary Fund, data.imf.org

▲ Table 27.1 US Balance of Payments statistics 2016–2018

We can see that in all three years there was a large deficit on the current account balance. Although the balance of trade in services and the net income flows were positive in every year, the balance of trade in goods was negative in every year.

In the USA, there is a slight difference in method, since as well as having a capital account and a financial account figure, there is also a separate figure for net trade in financial derivatives. In the IB model, this would be included in the financial account. However, the process still works. If all changes in asset ownership are totalled and allowance is made for the balancing item (in the US it is called statistical discrepancy), then the total capital account balance should be the opposite of the current account balance and the balance of payments should sum to zero.

This is the case in all three years in the example. In the USA net changes in the official reserve account are included in the capital and financial account and so the accounts balance.

Table 27.1 shows that the USA is experiencing persistent current account deficits (line 13), and that the size of the deficit is growing over the three years. The USA has deficits on the trade in goods balance (line 4) that are not balanced by the surpluses on the trade in services balance (line 7) or the net income flows (line 12). The current account deficit is largely financed by the foreign-owned assets in the USA (line 18). You can see that the current account balance (line 13) is equal to the capital and financial account balance (line 22).

Exercise 27.2
ATL Thinking and Communication

Using the correct terminology and actual numbers, describe the US balance of payments position in 2018, as shown in Table 27.1. Consider each of the components of the balance of payments, using real numbers to explain whether each is in surplus or deficit. Explain how the balance of payments as a whole is balanced.

The US economy entered a recession in 2008. One result of this was the significant fall in the demand for imports of goods, and to some extent services, that took place over the next few years. The deficit in 2007 was $718,094 million. This fell to $378,432 million by 2009 and $365,193 million by 2014. This illustrates the link between growth in the economy and the state of the current account introduced earlier. However, the trade gap is still large, and has been growing again since 2014, which implies that the US economy is borrowing heavily from abroad in order to finance its current international expenditure.

What is the relationship between the current account and the exchange rate?

A deficit in the current account of the balance of payments may result in downward pressure on the exchange rate of the currency. This is more of a problem in a fixed exchange rate system than in a floating exchange rate system. In a fixed exchange rate system, the implication is that the exchange rate has been set at too high a value. In the short run, the deficit may be covered by increases in the capital and financial accounts or by the government using reserve assets to balance the accounts. However, this cannot go on indefinitely, since the reserve assets will run out and so, in the end, the exchange rate will have to be devalued.

In a floating system, the deficit implies that there is an excess supply of the currency on the foreign exchange markets. This may be because the demand for exports has fallen, as has the demand for the currency, or the demand for imports has increased, leading to more demand for foreign currencies and so a greater supply of the domestic currency on the foreign exchange markets. In either case, in a freely floating exchange rate system, the exchange rate should fall, improving the competitiveness of the country's exports and increasing the domestic price of imports.

In the same way, a surplus in the current account of the balance of payments may result in upward pressure on the exchange rate of the currency. In a fixed exchange-rate system the implication is that the exchange rate has been set at too low a value. In the short run this may be offset by deficits on the capital and financial accounts or by increases in the reserve assets. In the long run, however, it is likely that other countries will be unhappy with the artificially low exchange rate and will demand higher rates or will threaten protectionist measures against the country's exports. This may result in a revaluation of the currency.

In a floating system, the surplus implies that there is an excess demand for the currency on the foreign exchange markets. This may be because the demand for exports has risen, as has the demand for the currency, or the demand for imports has fallen, leading to less demand for foreign currencies and so a lower supply of the domestic currency on the foreign exchange markets. In either case, in a freely floating exchange rate system, the exchange rate should rise, decreasing the competitiveness of the country's exports and lowering the domestic price of imports.

Key concept
CHANGE

Canadian dollar nears 8-month high after surprise swing to trade surplus

https://www.theglobeandmail.com/investing/markets/inside-the-market/market-news/article-canadian-dollar-nears-8-month-high-after-surprise-swing-to-trade/

Higher Level

Higher Level

Key concept
INTERDEPENDENCE

What are the consequences of current account imbalances?

The existence of a deficit or surplus in the current account is bound to have economic consequences that will affect the economy and we can consider some of these effects.

What are the consequences of a current account deficit?

We know that if the current account is in deficit then the capital account will have to be in surplus in order to balance out the current account deficit. This means one of three things.

1. Foreign exchange reserves may be used to increase the capital account and so to regain balance with a deficit in the current account. If reserves are taken from the official reserve account then they are a positive entry into the capital account. However, no country, no matter how rich and powerful, is able to fund long-term current account deficits from its reserves. Eventually, the reserves would run out.
2. It may be that a high level of buying of assets for ownership is financing the current account deficit. Foreign investors may be purchasing such things as property, businesses, or stocks or shares in businesses. In this case this inflow into the capital account is funding the current account deficit, but as it must be based upon foreign confidence in the domestic economy it is not considered to be harmful. However, there are sometimes fears that if foreign ownership of domestic assets were to become too great then this may be a threat to economic sovereignty. Moreover, if there is a drop in confidence then foreign investors might prefer to shift their assets to other countries. Selling the assets would result in an increase in the supply of the currency and a fall in its value.
3. It may be that the current account deficit is financed by high levels of lending from abroad. If this is the case then high rates of interest will have to be paid, which will be a short-term drain on the economy and will further increase the current account deficit in years to come. The country will be in significant debt.

   There is also always the danger that the governments or people lending the money may, at some time, withdraw their money and place it elsewhere. This would lead to massive selling of the currency and a very sharp fall in the exchange rate.
4. If a country has growing levels of economic debt, then it may get a lower credit rating from *credit rating agencies*. The three main credit rating agencies are Fitch, Moody's and Standard and Poor (S&P). These are international agencies that give advice to international investors about the location of the best and safest countries in which to invest funds. The lowest risk rating is AA1, which is also known as triple A (prime). There is a whole range of ratings down to the

highest risk ratings which are C ratings (substantial risks/extremely speculative) and D ratings (in default). If a country has its credit rating reduced, it will be more difficult to borrow and, because the risk is deemed to be greater, the interest rates charges for the loans will be higher. In September 2017, the UK's credit rating was downgraded from AA1 to AA2 based upon uncertainty caused by Brexit. In April 2019, both Fitch and S&P have warned the UK that there is a risk of a further downgrade as the Brexit process continues to make very slow progress.

5. One response to a current account deficit is for the central bank to lower interest rates in order to lower the exchange rate. If the central bank is having to use interest rate changes to control the value of the exchange rate, then it takes away the ability of the central bank to use interest rates as a means of domestic demand management (monetary policy). The lowering of the interest rate will act as an expansionary demand-side policy, causing inflationary pressure in the economy.

6. A current account deficit is a negative component of aggregate demand (AD) and, as such, may shift the AD curve to the left, reducing economic growth in the economy and having a negative effect on employment.

Economics in action

ATL Thinking, Communication and Research

1. Check the latest credit rating of the UK and discover the justification for any changes.
2. Find out the credit rating for your chosen OECD country and explain why it has the rating that it does.
3. Find out a country that has had a significant change in its credit rating and identify the reasons for the change.

What are the consequences of current account surpluses?

Perhaps the first thing we should consider is why a country may be able to run significant current account surpluses. In 2016, according to the World Bank, the ten countries with the largest current account surpluses were Germany, China, Japan, South Korea, the Netherlands, Switzerland, Singapore, Italy, Thailand and Russia. There are a number of possible factors, some structural and some more cyclical (short-term) that may account for a country being able to have persistent current account surpluses.

Key concept

CHANGE

Structural factors may be:

- A country may have built up long-run competitive advantage in producing certain products, enabling relatively low prices and thus high export demand. This is currently the case with South Korea and electronics.
- Households in a country may have high savings ratios and so expenditure on consumption in general and imports in particular may be lower than they might be in countries with a lower personal savings ratio. For example, in Germany, which has continuous current account surpluses, the personal savings ratio from disposable income is around 11%.
- There may be a significant increase in the prices of a country's main exports on the world markets, such as oil, leading to higher export revenues when the demand for the product is inelastic.

- A country may have been able to achieve significant increases in productivity and research and development funding – for example, Singapore.

Cyclical (short-term) factors may be:

- A depreciation of a country's currency increasing competitiveness in world markets.
- An increase in foreign consumer demand in a country's main export markets, such as the increased global demand for electronic products.
- Cyclical improvements in the global economy leading to increased demand and higher prices for a country's exports.
- An increase in net income flows and current transfers in a country, for example increases in profits earned abroad and remittances received from citizens working abroad.

If the current account is in surplus, there may be both positive and negative consequences.

1. A current account surplus allows a country to have a deficit on its capital account by building up its official reserve account or by purchasing assets abroad.

   In many countries that run current account surpluses, reserves have been transferred into *Sovereign Wealth Funds (SWFs)* that manage national savings for international investment. Table 27.2 shows the top five world countries ranked in terms of asset values in their SWFs. Some countries have multiple SWFs. For example, China has four funds, the China Investment Corporation (CIC), the State Administration of Foreign Exchange (SAFE), the National Social Security Fund (NCSSF) and the China-Africa Development Fund (CADF).

Rank	Country	Assets (US$ billion)
1	China	1,554.8
2	UAE	1,298.7
3	Norway	1,063.0
4	Saudi Arabia	697.0
5	Singapore	556.0

Source: Sovereign wealth fund institute, 2018, www.swfinstitute.org

▲ Table 27.2 Top 5 countries ranked in terms of SWF asset values

2. In the short-term, a current account surplus implies a shift of AD to the right, as (X–M) increases, with an increase in real national output, increased employment and an increase in inflationary pressure.

3. In the long-term, a persistent current account surplus may cause an appreciation of the currency on the foreign exchange market, as it implies an increase in demand for the currency. This will make imports cheaper, so reducing inflationary pressures, but will also make exports more expensive, which harms exporters. This may threaten employment in export industries and industries that compete with imports.

Exercise 27.3

ATL Thinking and Communication

1. Using an AD/AS diagram, explain point 2.

4. Persistent current account surpluses may lead to a decrease in domestic consumption and domestic investment. In effect, if the extra revenue that is being received from exports is not being spent on imports, but is instead being used to purchase assets abroad and to bolster reserves, then it is like the government saving. Like any saving, this will reduce potential consumption and will also reduce potential domestic investment, since the funds are not available for domestic use.

5. Any current account surplus must be someone else's deficit. Thus, if a country is persistently achieving surpluses, other countries must be experiencing deficits. This may lead to retaliation in other countries, in the form of increased protectionism, as they attempt to 'protect' their economies from the adverse consequences of trade deficits.

How big is a "big" current account deficit or surplus?

There are two ways to interpret the size of a country's current account deficit or surplus. One is to consider the value of the total—for example, the current account surplus in Germany was US$287 billion in 2017, while the current account deficit in the US was US$488.5 billion. However, it is easier to understand the magnitude of the deficit if it is placed in the context of the country's GDP. This would be similar to understanding how much a person is in debt. A billionaire who owes US$1,000 to a credit card company is in a very different situation to an unemployed student who owes US$1,000.

The burden of a deficit depends on the ability to pay. This is not so much a concern when a country has a current account surplus, although there are possible problems arising from the appreciation of the currency, but it is a problem when current account deficits reach a certain percentage of GDP. In the case of the US the current account deficit was approximately 2.4% of its GDP in 2017 and for Germany, the surplus was approximately 7.8%.

How might a government correct a persistent current account deficit?

For the most part, governments try to ensure a favourable current account balance by making sure that the supply side of the economy is efficient and productive, making the country's exports competitive on international markets and ensuring that domestic producers can compete with imports. Thus, it may be said that supply-side policies are valuable in **preventing** a large current account deficit. However, if a country is running a large and persistent current account deficit, the government may have to turn to two other types of policies: expenditure-switching and expenditure-reducing.

What are expenditure-switching policies?

Expenditure-switching policies are any policies implemented by the government that attempt to switch the expenditure of domestic consumers away from imports towards domestically produced goods and services. If successful, then expenditure on imports will fall and so the current account deficit should improve.

Examples of this type of policy are:

- *Government policies to depreciate or devalue the value of the currency*: If the government adopts policies that will reduce the level of the exchange rate then exports should become less expensive and imports should become more expensive. Depending upon how responsive domestic consumers and foreign consumers are to these price changes, this should see an improvement in the current account as export revenue rises and import expenditure falls.
- *Protectionist measures*: The government may attempt to restrict the imports of products either by reducing their availability using embargoes, quotas, voluntary export restraints, and administrative, health and safety and environmental barriers, or by increasing their prices using tariffs. If this happens then domestic consumers will switch their expenditure from imports to domestic products.

  However, governments are often reluctant or unable to use such measures because they tend to lead to retaliation and are often against WTO agreements. Also, protecting domestic industries reduces competition, which may encourage them to be inefficient. Therefore, it is not a long-run solution.

What are expenditure-reducing policies?

Expenditure-reducing policies are any policies implemented by the government that attempt to reduce overall expenditure in the economy, so shifting AD to the left. If this occurs then expenditure on all goods and services should fall and, since this would include expenditure on imports, the current account deficit should improve. The size of the fall in imports will depend upon the level of the marginal propensity to import.

However, there is a conflict here between external and internal objectives. Deflating the economy may reduce the current account deficit but the policy is likely to lead to a fall in domestic employment and a fall in the rate of economic growth. This makes it a difficult decision for a government to make.

Examples of this type of policy are:

- *Deflationary fiscal policies*: Increasing direct tax rates and/or reducing government expenditure. Clearly, these would be politically unpopular and a government might be reluctant to use such a policy.

- *Deflationary monetary policies*: Increasing the rate of interest and/or reducing the money supply. Interestingly, the higher interest rates should also increase capital flows from abroad, as foreigners put money into financial institutions attracted by the higher rates. This would lead to an inflow on the financial account, which helps to offset the current account deficit. This type of policy would also be politically unpopular as higher interest rates will increase people's mortgage, loan and credit card payments. Moreover, the higher costs of borrowing as a result of higher rates of interest may act as a disincentive to domestic investment and limit potential growth.

The economic costs of reducing a large current account deficit suggest why it is important to prevent it from occurring. To avoid these costs many governments are actively pursuing export promotion policies, which may include government-run trade missions, hoping to develop new markets, and government-sponsored advertising campaigns.

What is the Marshall-Lerner condition?

Theoretically if a country's currency depreciates or is devalued then this will lead to an increase in exports (they become less expensive in foreign markets) and a decrease in imports (they become more expensive domestically). This should result in an improvement in a country's current account, but this is not necessarily the case. We know that the effect of price change on spending or revenues depends on price elasticity of demand. The price of exports might fall because of depreciation of the currency and, according to the law of demand, the quantity demanded will increase, but whether or not this leads to an increase in export revenues depends on foreigners' price elasticity of demand for exports. Similarly, the price of imported goods will rise if a currency falls in value and, according to the law of demand, the quantity demanded will fall, but whether or not this leads to a fall in expenditure on imports depends on the price elasticity of demand for imports.

The Marshall-Lerner condition is a rule that tells us how successful a depreciation or devaluation of a currency's exchange rate will be as a means to improve a current account deficit in the balance of payments. The condition states that reducing the value of the exchange rate will only be successful if the total value of the price elasticity of demand for exports and the price elasticity of demand for imports is greater than one. It may be written as an equation, stating that a fall in exchange rate will reduce a current account deficit if

$$PED_{exports} + PED_{imports} > 1$$

This is a fairly straightforward application of the concept of elasticity of demand. If the demand for exports was price inelastic and price fell as a result of a fall in the exchange rate, then the proportionate increase in the quantity of exports demanded would be less than the proportionate

Higher Level

Exercise 27.4

ATL Thinking and Communication

1. Using a supply and demand diagram, draw revenue boxes (as shown in Chapter 4) to illustrate the following:
   a) the effect of a depreciation or devaluation of a currency on export revenues when the demand for exports is inelastic
   b) the effect of a depreciation or devaluation of a currency on export revenues when the demand for exports is elastic
   c) the effect of a depreciation or devaluation of a currency on import expenditure when the demand for imports is inelastic
   d) the effect of a depreciation or devaluation of a currency on import expenditure when the demand for imports is elastic.
2. Under which of the conditions above will a current account deficit improve, ie become smaller?

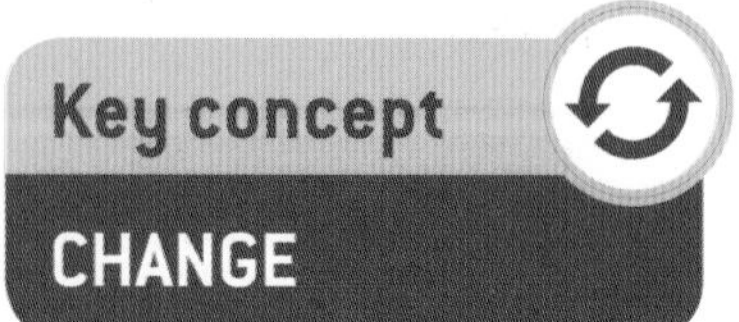

decrease in the price of exports and export revenue would fall. In the same way, if the demand for imports was price-inelastic and price rose following a fall in the exchange rate, then the proportionate fall in the demand for imports would be less than the proportionate increase in the price of imports and import expenditure would actually increase. The current account deficit would become worse.

We know that one of the determinants of elasticity of demand is the time period under consideration. Remember that demand becomes more elastic over a longer period of time. This applies to the elasticity of demand for exports and imports.

A study of trade elasticities in 2000 produced estimates of short-run and long-run price elasticities of demand for exports and imports for a number of countries. These are shown in Table 27.2. Although the data is somewhat dated, it is still useful from a conceptual point of view.

Country	Short-run $PED_{exports}$	Short-run $PED_{imports}$	Total short-run PED	Long-run $PED_{exports}$	Long-run $PED_{imports}$	Total long-run PED
Canada	0.5	0.1	0.6	0.9	0.9	1.8
France	0.1	0.1	0.2	0.2	0.4	0.6
Germany	0.1	0.2	0.3	0.3	0.6	0.9
Italy	0.3	0.0	0.3	0.9	0.4	1.3
Japan	0.5	0.1	0.6	1.0	0.3	1.3
UK	0.2	0.0	0.2	1.6	0.6	2.2
US	0.5	0.6	1.1	1.5	0.3	1.8

Source: *Trade elasticities for the G-7 countries*, Hooper, Johnson & Marquez, Princeton Studies in International Economics, No.87, August 2000

▲ Table 27.2 Short-run and long-run PED values in the G-7 countries

The figures show the following.

1. In almost all cases the short-run elasticity values are lower than the long-run values. This is exactly what we would expect to find from the theory stated in Chapter 4, which tells us that price elasticity values increase over time.
2. Only the US would meet the Marshall-Lerner condition in the short run, but all countries, other than France and Germany, meet the condition in the long run.

What is the J-curve?

If a government is facing a current account deficit, it may reduce the exchange rate of its currency in order to make exports relatively less expensive and imports relatively more expensive. If this happens and the Marshall-Lerner condition is satisfied, ie

$$PED_{exports} + PED_{imports} > 1$$

then we would expect an improvement in the current account deficit.

Exercise 27.5

ATL Thinking and Communication

Use the data in Table 27.2 to answer this question.

If Japan was experiencing a current account deficit and brought about a fall in the value of the yen, what would you expect to happen to the deficit:

1. in the short-run? Why?
2. in the long-run? Why?

However in the short run this is not the case and the current account deficit actually gets worse before it gets better. This is known as the J-curve effect. The J-curve shows what happens to a current account deficit over time when the exchange rate is devalued or depreciated. It is shown in Figure 27.2.

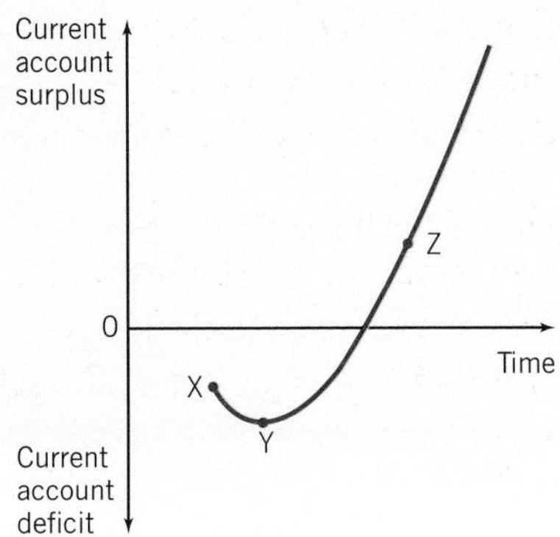

▲ **Figure 27.2** The J-curve

Let us assume that a country's current account deficit is at X and the government lowers the exchange rate. The price of exports will fall, but communication is not perfect and it will take time for other countries to realize that the prices in this country have fallen. Also, other countries will have entered into contracts for goods and services that cannot be broken quickly, so they cannot change their suppliers immediately. This means that, in the short run, the PED for exports will be inelastic and export revenue will fall as prices have fallen by proportionately more than demand will have risen. This will increase the current account deficit and start moving from X to Y on the J-curve.

In the same way the price of imports will rise but purchasers of imports will take time to find new suppliers. Also, they may be tied into contracts and will have to wait for them to expire before they can move to other suppliers. This means that, in the short run, the PED for imports will also be inelastic and import expenditure will increase, as prices have risen by proportionately more than demand will have fallen. This will further increase the current account deficit and add to the movement from X to Y on the J-curve.

As we saw in Table 27.2, the value of PED for exports and imports increases with time. By the time that the current account deficit reaches the point Y, the values of PED for exports and imports have increased to the point where, when added together, they are greater than one, so the Marshall-Lerner condition is satisfied. From this point onwards the less expensive exports and more expensive imports should lead to increased export revenue and decreased import expenditure and therefore an improvement in the current account balance, as shown by the movement from Y towards Z on the J-curve.

Economics in action

ATL Thinking, Communication and Research

Research the balance of payments position of the country that you studied earlier. Consider the following questions.

- Does it have a current account surplus or deficit?
- How is the balance distributed between the visible balance and invisible balance?
- Can you explain why there is a surplus or deficit? (If there is a deficit you may be able to link this to the business cycle. If there is a surplus it may be due to the type of goods that it exports.)
- Is this surplus or deficit of a worrying level? Why or why not?
- If there is a deficit, how is it being financed?

EXAMINATION QUESTIONS

Paper 1, part (a) questions – HL only

1. Explain expenditure-switching as a means to correct a current account deficit. [10 marks]
2. Explain why a current account deficit may result in a depreciation of a country's currency. [10 marks]
3. Explain expenditure-reducing as a means to correct a current account deficit. [10 marks]
4. Explain the link between the Marshall-Lerner condition and the J-curve. [10 marks]

Paper 1, part (b) questions – HL only

1. Using real-world examples, discuss the implications of a persistent current account deficit for the exchange rate, interest rates and the foreign ownership of domestic assets. [15 marks]
2. Using real-world examples, evaluate the effectiveness of expenditure switching and expenditure reducing measures in correcting a persistent current account deficit. [15 marks]
3. Using real-world examples, evaluate the implications of a persistent current account surplus. [15 marks]

HL & SL Paper 2 – 2-mark and 4-mark questions

BSP unfazed by PH's current account deficit

"Running a **current account deficit** is not necessarily a cause for concern given the underlying trends," said the governor of the Philippine Central Bank (BSP). The country's negative current account position should not be a cause for concern, as the economy continues to receive structural foreign exchange inflows

The governor also said, "I am not at all worried about the current account deficit, especially because it is less than 3 percent of our GDP. If you look at the composition of our imports they are indeed for raw materials, equipment, etc.".

The current account hit an all-time $7.9-billion deficit last year as robust economic activity resulted in a wider trade gap. However, the governor stressed that the Philippines' payments balance position is manageable and provides resilience against external headwinds.

He said that the country's external position "continues to be adequately supported by structural sources of foreign exchange inflows, such as overseas Filipinos' **remittances**, IT-business process outsourcing (BPO) revenues, as well as increasing tourism receipts."

Latest available data show that remittance flows hit $5.302 billion in the year to February, a 2.3% increase from $5.182 billion in the comparable 2018 period. BPO industry receipts, meanwhile, totaled $10.4 billion in 2018, 21 percent higher than the year-before amount.

"And to add to that, the Philippines has attracted a lot of interest from foreign investors," the governor said, adding that **foreign direct investment** (FDI) for the last two years was about $10 billion. "That's easily three times higher than the average for the last eight years," he claimed.

The governor's view was consistent with Standard & Poor's Global Ratings' latest assessment on the current account. In a recent statement, the credit rater said it believes that "the deficit is largely investment driven, and that this is a healthy development in light of its historical underinvestment" despite some observers' fear that the country's rising current account deficit could signal overheating risks.

Source: Adapted from BSP unfazed by PH's current account deficit, by Mayvelin U. Caraballo, The Manila Times, May 6, 2019, www.manilatimes.net

2-mark questions – HL & SL

Define the following terms, indicated in bold in the data:

a) current account deficit [2 marks]

b) remittances [2 marks]

c) foreign direct investment [2 marks]

4-mark questions – HL only

1. Using an exchange rate diagram, explain the likely effect of the current account deficit on the exchange rate for the Filipino peso. [4 marks]
2. Using an AD/AS diagram, explain the likely effect of the $7.9 billion current account deficit on the Philippine economy. (Paragraph 3) [4 marks]

Paper 2, 15-mark question – HL only

1. Using information from the text/data and your knowledge of economics, discuss the possible implications of the persistent current account deficits for the economy of the Philippines. [15 marks]

Assessment advice

In HL & SL Paper 2 and in HL Paper 3, you may be asked to calculate elements of the balance of payments from a set of data.

Here is an example of the kind of question that you may face, although the data set may be a lot smaller in some questions.

An extract from the balance of payments figures for country X is shown below.

1. Fill in the six missing values in the table, indicating whether they are credits (+) or debits (–) to the accounts. [6 marks]
2. Explain the relevance of reserve asset funding to the balance of payments. [4 marks]
3. Explain the concept of current transfers. [4 marks]
4. **HL only:** Country X has a free floating exchange rate. Explain what you would expect to happen to the exchange rate as a result of the international trade that has taken place in 2020. [4 marks]

Line	Balance of payments figures for Country X (millions of dollars) (Credits +; debits –)	2020
1	**Current account**	
2	Exports of goods	?
3	Imports of goods	–661,200
4	**Balance of trade in goods**	–273,400
5	Exports of services	162,800
6	Imports of services	–122,400
7	**Balance of trade in services**	?
8	Income receipts (investment income)	276,500
9	Income payments (investment income)	–243,400
10	**Net income receipts** (net investment income)	33,100
11	**Current transfers, net**	–38,500
12	**Net income flows**	?
13	**Current account balance**	?
14	**Capital account**	
15	Capital transactions, net	130
16	**Financial account**	
17	Direct investment, net	105,885
18	Portfolio investment, net	84,700
19	Reserve asset funding	?
20	Errors and omissions	26,500
21	**Capital and financial account balance**	?

28 ECONOMIC DEVELOPMENT AND SUSTAINABLE DEVELOPMENT

REAL-WORLD ISSUE:
Why is economic development uneven?

By the end of this chapter, you should be able to:

- → Distinguish between economic growth and economic development
- → Explain the relationship between economic growth and economic development
- → Define sustainable development
- → Outline the current status of the Sustainable Development Goals
- HL Explain the relationship between sustainability and poverty
- → Explain and give examples of common characteristics of developing countries
- → Explain and give examples of the diversity that exists between developing countries.

Key concept 
EQUITY

"Development can be seen, it is argued here, as a process of expanding the real freedoms that people enjoy. Focusing on human freedoms contrasts with narrower views of development, such as identifying development with the growth of gross national product, or with the rise in personal incomes, or with industrialization, or with technological advance, or with social modernization.

Development requires the removal of major sources of unfreedom: poverty as well as tyranny, poor economic opportunities as well as systematic social deprivation, neglect of public facilities as well as intolerance or overactivity of oppressive states. Despite unprecedented increases in overall opulence, the contemporary world denies elementary freedoms to vast numbers – perhaps even the majority of people.

Sometimes the lack of substantive freedom relates directly to economic poverty, which robs people of the freedom to satisfy hunger, or to achieve sufficient nutrition, or to obtain remedies for basic illnesses, or the opportunity to be adequately clothed or sheltered, or to enjoy clean water or sanitary facilities. In other cases, the unfreedom links closely to the lack of public facilities and social care, such as the absence of epidemiological programmes, or of organized arrangements for health care or education facilities, or of effective institutions for the maintenance of local peace and order. In still other cases, the violation of freedom results from a denial of political and civil liberties by authoritarian regimes and from imposed restrictions of the freedom to participate in the social, political, and economic life of the community."

–Amartya Sen, *Development as Freedom*, Oxford University Press (1999).

What is meant by economic development?

The national income statistics discussed in Chapter 13 provide important information about a country's economic activity. They form the basis for assessing a country's economic growth. However, economic growth is very much a one-dimensional concept. It is, quite simply, an increase in the real output of an economy over time. Traditional economic theory has tended to make the assumption that increased output of an economy, along with the pattern of industrialization that accompanies economic growth, is equivalent to economic development. This is a simplistic and incorrect assumption.

The last decades have seen the evolution of a new branch of economics—development economics. At the core of this study is the fact that economic growth is **not** equivalent to economic development. Economic development is a far more complex and multidimensional concept. For economic development to occur, growth must be *inclusive*, that is, it must benefit all people in the economy, not just a small percentage of high-income people. Furthermore, economic growth is of no use if it comes with a cost that must be borne by future generations and so real economic progress must be development that is sustainable.

A very basic definition of development might be an improvement in living standards or economic well being, or welfare. However, this is somewhat simplistic so we now expand on this notion. Yet we must always keep in mind the very subjective nature of the concept and be aware that there is a wide range of possible explanations.

For example, development economist Amartya Sen (see the biography box) makes a powerful link between development and freedom.

Amartya Sen (1933–present)

Amartya Sen was born in West Bengal, India. At the age of 9, he had his first encounter with suffering, on meeting victims of the Bengal famine in which three million people died. Later, his work on famine research led to the publication of Poverty and Famines: An Essay on Entitlement and Deprivation, addressing the inequalities in access to food.

While at secondary school, Sen was uncertain as to what academic discipline he should study. In his own words, "I seriously flirted, in turn, with Sanskrit, mathematics and physics, before settling for the eccentric charms of economics."

At the age of 18, Sen left India to study economics at Trinity College, Cambridge, where he earned both his Bachelor of Arts and then his doctorate. He has held several teaching positions, including at the University of Calcutta, Jadavpur University, Delhi, the University of Oxford, London School of Economics, Harvard and Cambridge.

While working at Harvard, he teamed up with an old friend Mahbub ul Haq, a reputed Pakistani economist. Together, they contributed to the establishment of the Human Development Index and the Human Development Report, published annually by the United Nations Development Programme (UNDP). Such developments have allowed economic development to be evaluated on a range of measures, rather than on the classical macroeconomic indicators such as GNP or GDP.

Having published an impressive number of books and publications, Sen has also received a number of awards, including the Nobel Prize for Economics in 1998 for his contribution to welfare economics. He has had a powerful influence on the study of development economics as well as on international institutions and national governments.

Amartya Sen's brief quotation at the start of the chapter demonstrates the multidimensional nature of development. Development is about increasing people's freedoms. It is about reducing poverty so that people can be adequately fed and sheltered. It is about the public provision of education, health care and the maintenance of law and order. It is about the guarantee of civil liberties and the opportunity for civic participation.

Did you know?

The United Nations Development Programme (UNDP) "works in about 170 countries and territories, helping to achieve the eradication of poverty and the reduction of inequalities and exclusion. We help countries to develop policies, leadership skills, partnering abilities, institutional capabilities and build resilience in order to sustain development results.

In September 2015, world leaders adopted the 2030 Agenda for Sustainable Development to end poverty, protect the planet and ensure that all people enjoy peace and prosperity. UNDP is working to strengthen new frameworks for development, disaster risk reduction and climate change. We support countries' efforts to achieve the Sustainable Development Goals, or Global Goals, which will guide global development priorities through 2030.

UNDP's Strategic Plan (2018–2021) has been designed to be responsive to the wide diversity of the countries we serve. The diversity is reflected in three broad development contexts:

- eradicate poverty in all its forms and dimensions
- accelerate structural transformations
- build resilience to shocks and crises.

To respond to these issues, and better focus its resources and expertise to deliver on the 2030 Agenda, UNDP has identified a set of approaches that we call our Signature Solutions:

- keeping people out of POVERTY
- GOVERNANCE for peaceful, just and inclusive societies
- crisis prevention and increased RESILIENCE
- ENVIRONMENT: nature-based solutions for development
- clean, affordable ENERGY
- women's empowerment and GENDER equality.

In all our activities, we encourage the protection of human rights and the empowerment of women, minorities and the poorest and most vulnerable."

Source: www.undp.org.

Theory of knowledge

Three core values

Another economist, Michael Todaro, developed the work of Denis Goulet to present his view of the essential features of development.

At the outset is his observation of "development as the sustained elevation of an entire social system toward a 'better' or 'more humane' life". The use of the words "better" and "more humane" are reminders of the subjective nature of the discussion. However, he identifies three "core values" or fundamental human needs. If life is to be made "better" then there must be progress in meeting these three core values.

1. *Sustenance:* The ability to meet basic life-sustaining needs for food, shelter, health and protection.
2. *Self-esteem:* The ability of people and communities to develop a sense of self worth, identity, dignity and respect.
3. *Freedom from servitude and the ability to choose:* This involves expanding the range of choices for people and societies and granting them freedom from oppression from external factors.

Does the subjective nature of the topic make it impossible to accept that these are "universal truths"?

Key concept

EQUITY

Key concept

ECONOMIC WELLBEING

Economics in action

ATL Thinking, Communication and Research

To supplement the brief description of Amartya Sen, prepare an annotated timeline of his life, making notes on the key stages in his life along with his major achievements and contributions. See his autobiography written for the Nobel Prize organisation as a starting point (http://nobelprize.org).

Does economic growth lead to economic development?

In order to consider this question, we should first look at where economic growth comes from and then we can consider its implications for economic development.

What are the sources of economic growth?

These may be identified under four simple headings:

1. Natural factors

   Anything that will increase the quantity and/or quality of a factor of production should lead to an increase in potential growth. Increasing the quantity of land available is not really very easy, although countries like Holland and Singapore have done so by means of land reclamation. However, this will only have a very small effect upon total land area and thus production capability, unless the land area is very small to start with, as is the case with Singapore. Using landfill methods Singapore has increased its land area from 581.5 square kilometres in 1965, when it gained independence, to 721.5 square kilometres at the present time, an increase in land area of around 24%. However, if its neighbour, Malaysia, was to gain the same increase through landfill, 140 square kilometres to add to its existing 329,847 square kilometres, this would represent an increase of 0.04% of land area!

   Thus, most countries will attempt to improve the quality of their natural factors, rather than the quantity. The quality of land may be improved by fertilization, better planning of land usage, improved agricultural methods and building upwards, as opposed to outwards, as is the case in places like Hong Kong.

2. Human capital factors

   The quantity of human capital may be increased either by encouraging population growth or by increasing immigration levels. However, the majority of developing countries would not be keen to increase population size and, even if they were (like Singapore), the process is very long term.

   Thus, most emphasis is put on improving the quality of the human capital. The main methods of doing this would be improved health care, improved education for children, vocational training and re-training for the unemployed. In addition, the provision of fresh water and sanitation can very much improve the health and thus the quality of human capital.

3. Physical capital and technological factors

   Economic growth may be achieved by improving the quantity and/or quality of physical capital. Physical capital includes such things as factory buildings, machinery, shops, offices and motor vehicles. [Social capital is items such as schools, roads, hospitals and houses.] Obviously, the quantity of physical capital is affected by the level of saving, domestic investment, government involvement and foreign investment. The quality of physical capital is improved by higher education, research and development and access to foreign technology and expertise.

   We identify two concepts here:

   - *Capital widening:* This exists when extra capital is used with an increased amount of labour, but the ratio of capital per worker does not change. In this case, total production will rise, but productivity (output per worker) is likely to remain unchanged.
   - *Capital deepening:* This exists when there is an increase in the amount of capital for each worker. This often means that there have been improvements in technology. Capital deepening will usually lead to improvements in labour productivity as well as increases in total production.

   Physical capital enabling extraction, or improved extraction, of primary products, such as oil drilling or improved mining techniques, may be very important in terms of economic growth since they will, in effect, increase the quantity of a factor of production.

4. Institutional factors

   A prerequisite for meaningful economic growth is the existence of certain institutional factors. These are factors such as an adequate banking system, a structured legal system, a good education system, reasonable infrastructure, political stability and good international relationships. Some of these factors are also sources of economic development, as we will see later in the section.

The possible benefits of economic growth cannot be overstated, and indeed, there is significant evidence that economic growth has enabled countries to raise millions of people out of poverty. Economic growth enables citizens to enjoy higher incomes and higher material standards of living. Higher incomes result in greater tax revenues for governments, which can be used to invest in development objectives such as spending on health services, education and infrastructure. However, it should not be assumed that growth always leads to economic development, and is certainly not the case that economic growth will lead to sustainable development.

What is sustainable development?

"Endless economic growth, based on the consumption of finite resources, cannot continue indefinitely..."

–*IB syllabus, Conceptual understanding.*

The World Commission on Environment and Development was formed by the United Nations in 1983, and in 1987 the report, *Our Common Future*, was published. The Commission was of the opinion that economic growth cannot be sustained into the future if environmental degradation is taking place and non-renewable resources are being used up at too fast a rate. The term "sustainable development" was introduced and defined as "development that meets the needs of the present without compromising the ability of future generations to meet their own needs". In economics we learn about the advantages of economic growth, and may even tend to assume that all countries seek to achieve high rates of economic growth. However, it becomes increasingly vital to appreciate the possible negative consequences of economic growth in terms of the effects on the environment and the ability of future generations to meet their needs. When we examine how resources should be allocated we must consider how such resource allocation affect future generations.

As economies grow, so does the demand for more and more goods and services and more and more energy to produce these goods and services. Factories, power plants and households all consume vast amounts of resources and energy to meet their demands resulting in earth-threatening global problems. In Chapter 9, we saw that these environmental challenges, including the 'climate crisis' can be examined using the economic theories of negative externalities of consumption and production, along with threats to common access resources.

The economist, Herman Daly, talks about "uneconomic growth" and has defined it as occurring "when increases in production come at an expense in resources and well being that is worth more than the items made". We can conclude that economic growth based on current consumption patterns is clearly not sustainable and is, in reality, uneconomic growth.

The effects on humans will be felt most severely in the developing countries. Most tragically, those that will be most harmed by the climate crisis are those that contributed the least to the greenhouse gas emissions that have created the crisis.

- Access to safe water will become even more precarious. Even now more than one billion people do not have access to safe water.
- Tropical diseases may spread further north.
- Droughts will become more frequent and intense in Asia and Africa, and flooding will likely become a bigger problem in temperate and humid regions.
- Food production in the tropics and sub-tropics is likely to suffer. Food production could become easier in middle and high latitudes but there is no guarantee that this will lessen the risk to food security.
- Millions of people will be affected by rising sea levels. This includes coastal areas along with low-lying islands in the Caribbean Sea and Pacific Ocean.

As we mentioned earlier, economic progress needs to be measured in terms of economic development that can be achieved in a sustainable manner.

Dr Gro Harlem Brundtland (1939–present)

Gro Brundtland was born in Oslo, Norway in 1939. At the age of 7, she followed in the shoes of her political activist father by becoming enrolled as a member of the Norwegian Labour Movement and she has been a member ever since. When she was 10 years old, her family moved to New York where her father had been granted a Rockefeller Scholarship. It was there that she learned English. Her commitment to social issues and the fact that she was always encouraged to be independent and outspoken meant that she had a mature sense of global awareness at a young age.

Brundtland received a medical degree in Oslo in 1963, when she was 24. After receiving a Master's degree at Harvard, she returned to Oslo to work in public health. This, along with her active role in promoting women's rights, led her into politics and she became environment minister in 1975. An oil spill caused by an explosion on an oil-drilling platform in the North Sea was her first big test as environment minister and she became a strong advocate of measures to prevent future environmental disasters.

She was elected as the first woman Prime Minister of Norway in 1981. In 1983, she was asked by the Secretary General of the United Nations to chair the World Commission on Environment and Development, whose mandate was to evaluate the planet's critical environmental and developmental problems and to provide possible solutions. To staff this commission, Brundtland selected 21 representatives from around the world, ensuring that half of the representatives came from developing nations.

The Brundtland Commission released its report, Our Common Future, in April 1987. It was in this widely-distributed publication that the concept of "sustainable development" was identified and promoted. The recommendations of the commission led to the Earth Summit in Rio de Janeiro in 1992, attended by almost 200 world leaders.

In 1986, Brundtland was elected as Prime Minister of Norway once again, and served until 1989. She was re-elected in 1990 for the next six-year term. In 1998, she was appointed as Director General of the World Health Organization, a post that she occupied until 2003.

Dr Brundtland was trained as a scientist and physician. She has worked as a politician and a diplomat. As an advocate for the environment, sustainability, women's rights, poverty alleviation and public health, she is a role model for students in all disciplines.

What are the sustainable development goals?

SUSTAINABLE DEVELOPMENT GOALS

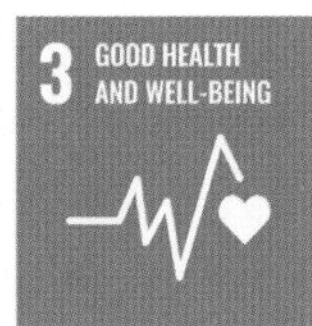

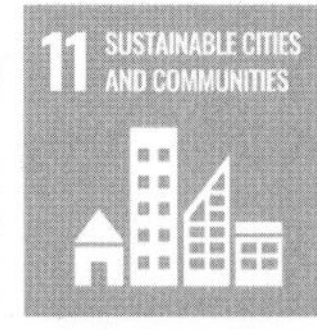

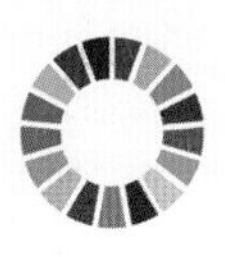

Throughout this Course Companion, there have been references to this very important example of global cooperation. We now look at this more closely.

The Sustainable Development Goals (SDGs) were born at the United Nations Conference on Sustainable Development in Rio de Janeiro in 2012. The objective was to produce a set of universal goals that met the urgent environmental, political and economic challenges facing the world.

The SDGs replace the Millennium Development Goals (MDGs), which started a global effort in 2000 to tackle the indignity of poverty. The MDGs established measurable, universally agreed objectives for tackling extreme poverty and hunger, preventing deadly diseases, and expanding primary education to all children, among other development priorities. The objectives were set to be met by the year 2015.

From 2000 to 2015, the MDGs drove progress in several important areas: reducing income poverty, providing much needed access to water and sanitation, driving down child mortality and drastically improving maternal health. They also kick-started a global movement for free primary education, inspiring countries to invest in their future generations. Most significantly, the MDGs made huge strides in combating HIV/AIDS and other treatable diseases such as malaria and tuberculosis.

Key MDG achievements were:

- More than 1 billion people have been lifted out of extreme poverty (since 1990)
- Child mortality dropped by more than half (since 1990)

- The number of out of school children has dropped by more than half (since 1990)
- HIV/AIDS infections fell by almost 40 percent (since 2000)[1].

The SDGs came into effect in January 2016 and will continue until 2030.

The SDGs are a bold commitment to tackle some of the more pressing challenges facing the world today. They are also an urgent call to shift the world onto a more sustainable path. All 17 Goals interconnect, meaning success in one affects success for others. Dealing with the threat of climate change impacts how we manage our fragile natural resources, achieving gender equality or better health helps eradicate poverty, and fostering peace and inclusive societies will reduce inequalities and help economies prosper. Figure 29.1 outlines the 17 SDGs.

Goal	Detail
1 NO POVERTY	End poverty in all its forms everywhere
2 ZERO HUNGER	End hunger, achieve food security and improved nutrition and promote sustainable agriculture
3 GOOD HEALTH AND WELL-BEING	Ensure healthy lives and promote well being for all at all ages
4 QUALITY EDUCATION	Ensure inclusive and equitable quality education and promote lifelong learning opportunities for all
5 GENDER EQUALITY	Achieve gender equality and empower all women and girls
6 CLEAN WATER AND SANITATION	Ensure availability and sustainable management of water and sanitation for all
7 AFFORDABLE AND CLEAN ENERGY	Ensure access to affordable, reliable, sustainable and modern energy for all
8 DECENT WORK AND ECONOMIC GROWTH	Promote sustained, inclusive and sustainable economic growth, full and productive employment and decent work for all
9 INDUSTRY, INNOVATION AND INFRASTRUCTURE	Build resilient infrastructure, promote inclusive and sustainable industrialization and foster innovation

Goal	Detail
10 REDUCED INEQUALITIES	Reduce inequality within and among countries
11 SUSTAINABLE CITIES AND COMMUNITIES	Make cities and human settlements inclusive, safe, resilient and sustainable
12 RESPONSIBLE CONSUMPTION AND PRODUCTION	Ensure sustainable consumption and production patterns
13 CLIMATE ACTION	Take urgent action to combat climate change and its impacts
14 LIFE BELOW WATER	Conserve and sustainably use the oceans, seas and marine resources for sustainable development
15 LIFE ON LAND	Protect, restore and promote sustainable use of terrestrial ecosystems, sustainably manage forests, combat desertification, and halt and reverse land degradation and halt biodiversity loss
16 PEACE, JUSTICE AND STRONG INSTITUTIONS	Promote peaceful and inclusive societies for sustainable development, provide access to justice for all and build effective, accountable and inclusive institutions at all levels
17 PARTNERSHIPS FOR THE GOALS	Strengthen the means of implementation and revitalize the global partnership for sustainable development

Source: undp.org

▲ **Table 28.1** The Sustainable Development Goals

[1] Source: www.undp.org

Although the goals may seem rather broad and general, each of the goals is supported by more specific targets. For example, the targets for goal number 1, no poverty, are:

- By 2030, reduce at least by half the proportion of men, women and children of all ages living in poverty in all its dimensions according to national definitions
- Implement nationally appropriate social protection systems and measures for all, including floors, and by 2030 achieve substantial coverage of the poor and the vulnerable
- By 2030, ensure that all men and women, in particular the poor and the vulnerable, have equal rights to economic resources, as well as access to basic services, ownership and control over land and other forms of property, inheritance, natural resources, appropriate new technology and financial services, including microfinance
- By 2030, build the resilience of the poor and those in vulnerable situations and reduce their exposure and vulnerability to climate-related extreme events and other economic, social and environmental shocks and disasters
- Ensure significant mobilization of resources from a variety of sources, including through enhanced development cooperation, in order to provide adequate and predictable means for developing countries, in particular least developed countries, to implement programmes and policies to end poverty in all its dimensions
- Create sound policy frameworks at the national, regional and international levels, based on pro-poor and gender-sensitive development strategies, to support accelerated investment in poverty eradication actions.[2]

What is the relationship between sustainability and poverty?

There is a vicious cycle that exists between poverty and environmental damage. To meet their basic needs, poor people tend to rely more on the environment than rich people. The environment may be the direct source of their food, fuel, sanitation and facilities for waste disposal. Yet their use of the environment results in further environmental problems.

Consider the problem of deforestation using the concept of common access resources. Low-income people in rural areas of developing countries often depend on wood as their only source of fuel for cooking and use common sources of wood. When the existing trees are cut down, there are consequences. The households who need the wood must travel greater distances to acquire wood for fuel. This is most often the responsibility of women and leaves them with less time to earn income for their households. This is quite likely to keep low-income households

Economics in action

ATL Thinking, Communication, Research and Social

You need to have some idea of the current status of the Sustainable Development Goals. In order to do this, you need to have up-to-date information. You can gain this information by going to https://sustainabledevelopment.un.org/sdgs.

Here, you will find the Sustainable Development Goals Knowledge Platform. By clicking on any one of the SDG icons, you will be taken to a brief progress report on that SDG.

As a group activity:

1. allocate each of the SDGs amongst the group
2. read through the progress report for your SDG
3. create your own summary report
4. share the summary reports amongst the group.

Higher Level

[2] Source: undp.org

trapped in a vicious cycle and one result will be the persistent overuse of the resources.

Poor people are unable to own their land. They may have to use common-pool land which is not well-suited to the growing of food. The lack of 'land tenure', insufficient knowledge of good agricultural practices and inability to afford irrigation and fertilizers are likely to lead to low levels of agricultural productivity and crop yields. This is another vicious cycle. Their poverty pushed them to more and more marginal lands, with the consequences of greater areas of soil erosion and land degradation. The threat is not only to the low-income households, but to the long-term sustainability of the land as a natural resource.

Key concept
ECONOMIC WELLBEING

Key concept
EQUITY

Poor people are far more vulnerable to floods and other environmental catastrophes that are the result of climate change, yet they were the people that contributed the least to the global problem. Although they are the most affected, poor countries are also the ones that are least likely to be able to afford the costs of mitigation needed to avert the climate crisis. Within the Paris Agreement, there are mechanisms to support developing countries in this regard, but the consequences of the crisis will continue to have a disproportionate effect on poor people.

Economics in action

ATL Research, Thinking and Communication

By choosing one recent natural disaster that is a consequence of climate change, investigate the claim that poor people are more vulnerable to environmental catastrophes.

Do developing countries have common characteristics?

The development economist, Michael P. Todaro, produced a list of the common characteristics of developing nations[3]. He said that the common characteristics could be classified into seven broad categories:

1. *Low standards of living characterized by low incomes, inequality, poor health and inadequate education*: In developing countries low standards of living tend to be experienced by the majority of the population. The main indicators of these low living standards are high poverty levels (ie very low incomes), high levels of inequality, very poor housing, low standards of health, high infant mortality rates, high levels of malnutrition and lack of education.
2. *Low levels of productivity (output per person):* This is common in developing countries. The main causes are the low education standards within the countries, the low levels of health amongst workers, lack of investment in physical capital and lack of access to technology.
3. *High rates of population growth and dependency burdens:* Developing countries tend to have crude birth rates that are more than double, on average, than the rates in developed countries. The crude birth rate is the annual number of live births per 1,000 of the population.

[3] Michael P Todaro, Economic Development, 7th Edition, Addison Wesley Longman, 2000

The world average in 2018 was 18.2, but in some developing countries it can be over 40. For example, it was 44.2 in Niger and Angola in 2017. Most developed countries tend to have figures below 15 and some are well below, such as Spain, with 9.2 and Japan, with 7.7[4].

High crude birth rates in developing countries tend to be transformed into high-dependency ratios. The high crude birth rates mean that there are a lot of young people, under the age of 15, in developing countries. Thus, those of working age, usually assumed to be 15 to 64, have to support a much larger proportion of children than the workforce in developed countries. However, interestingly, developed countries have high numbers of the population over the age of 64, who also need to be supported by the workforce.

The dependency ratio may be expressed in a number of forms. One is the child dependency ratio, which is the percentage of those who are non-productive, under the age of 15, expressed as a percentage of those of working age, usually 15 to 64. The equation would be:

$$\text{Child dependency ratio} = \frac{(\text{\% of population under 15})}{(\text{\% of population 15 to 64})}$$

Another is an old age dependency ratio, which is the percentage of those who are non-productive, over the age of 65, expressed as a percentage of those of working age, usually 15 to 64. The equation would be:

$$\text{Old age dependency ratio} = \frac{(\text{\% of population over 65})}{(\text{\% of population 15 to 64})}$$

As we can see in Table 28.2, the three developed countries have child dependency ratios of about 28% and they have old age dependency ratios ranging from 24% to 32% (and these are predicted to continue to grow). The developing countries have much higher child dependency ratios, ranging from 49% to 91%, and significantly lower old age dependency ratios, ranging from 5% to 11%.

Country (HDI rank)	Child dependency ratio (%)	Old age dependency ratio (%)
Australia (3)	29	24
France (24)	29	32
UK (14)	28	29
Bolivia (118)	51	11
Botswana (101)	49	6
Burkina Faso (183)	86	5
Cambodia (146)	49	7
Congo, Dem. Rep. (176)	91	6

Source: World Bank Group US, data.worldbank.org 2019

▲ Table 28.2 Examples of dependency ratios in developed and developing countries (all figures are for 2017)

[4] Source: World Factbook 2009, CIA, US

The differences tend to highlight the high crude birth rates and the low life expectancy levels in developing countries as opposed to developed countries. They also highlight the different problems faced in terms of dependency ratios. It is interesting to note that a significant number of developed countries are considering increasing the retirement age in order to keep people working longer and to thus reduce the old age dependency ratio.

4. *High and rising levels of unemployment and underemployment:* Developing countries tend to have relatively high rates of unemployment, typically between 10% and 20% of the labour force, but in a number of countries much greater. Although it is a difficult thing to measure accurately in a developed economy, let alone a developing economy, some estimated figures are shown in Table 28.3.

Country (HDI ranking)	Unemployment rate (%)
Bangladesh (136)	4.4
Botswana (101)	20
Burkina Faso (183)	77
India (130)	8.5
Mozambique (180)	24.5
South Africa (113)	27.5

Source: The World Factbook, CIA, 2019

▲ Table 28.3 Unemployment rates for selected developing countries

Although the unemployment figures in developing countries are worrying enough, there are three more groups that need to be considered. Firstly, there are those who have been unemployed for so long that they have given up searching for a job and no longer appear as unemployed. Secondly, there are the hidden unemployed, those who work for a few hours in the day on a family farm or in a family business or trade of some sort, and so do not appear as unemployed. In Table 28.3, the unemployment figure for Bangladesh look very good at 4.4%. However, it is estimated that there is huge underemployment in the country and that around 40% of the workforce is underemployed, working only a few hours per week at very low wages.Then, lastly, there are the underemployed. Those who would like full-time work, but are only able to get part-time employment, often on an informal basis.

It is when all of these groups are put together that the full extent of unemployment in developing countries can begin to be understood. Although it is impossible to be accurate, it would be fair to say that in many developing countries the true rate of unemployment is over 50%. When we consider high birth rates, as discussed earlier, then the situation is only likely to worsen.

5. *Substantial dependence on agricultural production and primary product exports:* Many developing countries, but certainly not all, are heavily dependent on the exports of one or two commodities for their export revenue. This is illustrated in Table 28.4.

Country	Primary commodities (%)	Manufactures (%)
Benin*	84	16
Burkina Faso*	91	9
Ethiopia*	93	7
Côte d'Ivoire*	92	8
Angola**	98	2
Yemen**	83	17
Bangladesh†	4	96
Nepal†	32	68

Source: World Bank Group US, data.worldbank.org 2019

* Non-oil-exporting LDC

† Manufactures-exporting LDC

** Oil-exporting LDC

▲ Table 28.4 Share of primary commodities and manufactures in total merchandise exports for selected LDCs

We see that for the first six countries listed, the dependence on the export of primary commodities, as compared with the export of manufactured products, is very strong. For example, 93% of all Ethiopia's merchandise export earnings come from the sale of primary commodities. In the same manner, Côte d'Ivoire earns 93% of its merchandise export earnings by exporting primary commodities.

However, notice the difference between the first four countries and the next two, as noted in the key. The first four are known as non-oil-exporting LDCs, while Angola and Yemen are characterized as oil-exporting LDCs. Almost all of the export revenue for Angola and Yemen comes from the sale of oil.

The last two countries, Bangladesh and Nepal, are different again. They concentrate on the export of low-skill manufactured products, especially textiles.

We can see from Table 28.5 that there is one more group of LDCs that need to be identified, which are the services-exporting LDCs, such as Cape Verde and the Maldives. These countries make most of their export revenue from tourism.

Country	Merchandise trade (%)	Services (%)
Cape Verde‡	5	95
Maldives‡	30	70

Source: Trade profiles, WTO, 2019

‡ Services-exporting LDC

▲ Table 28.5 Share of merchandise trade and services in total exports for selected LDCs

We will focus on the developing countries that are dependent on the export of non-oil commodities. While there is no doubt that the long-run trend in commodity prices was downward in the last 50 years of the 20th century, there has been a short-run upward movement, since about 2003, although the global economic crisis of 2008 (ask your teacher!) did dent the short-run trend.

Year	All primary commodities, weighted average	Non-oil commodities	Agricultural raw materials	Metals
2009	117.0	98.1	96.1	121.4
2010	146.3	123.1	129.6	185.8
2011	182.7	147.7	161.0	209.4
2012	174.5	136.2	127.9	172.1
2013	169.2	128.8	122.3	165.4
2014	159.6	121.8	113.1	143.5
2015	108.7	101.1	100.0	105.6
2016	100.0	100.0	100.0	100.0
2017	113.6	106.4	105.2	122.1
2018	128.4	108.1	107.2	129.8

Source: International Monetary Fund, 2019

▲ Table 28.6 Real primary commodity prices, 2009–2018

Recent movements in commodity prices are shown in Table 28.6. The data illustrates a major problem for commodity-exporting developing countries. As we discovered in Chapter 7, commodity prices tend to be volatile, due to relatively inelastic demand and supply. If we look at the data, prices in all columns peaked in 2012, before falling significantly by 2016, and then rising again by 2018.

As a result of the volatile prices, countries dependent on non-oil commodity exports are vulnerable to circumstances that are simply beyond their control. The fact that export prices can fluctuate significantly over a short period of time can make it very difficult for countries to plan effectively for the future.

6. *Prevalence of imperfect markets and limited information:* The trend in developing countries, in the last twenty years, has been towards a more market-oriented approach to growth. This has sometimes been promoted, or "encouraged", by international bodies such as the International Monetary Fund and the World Bank. However, this is possibly problematic, since whilst market-based approaches may work well in economies where markets are efficiently functioning, many developing countries face imperfect markets and imperfect knowledge.

   Developing countries lack many of the necessary factors that enable markets to work efficiently. They lack a functioning banking system, which enables and encourages savings and then investment. They lack a developed legal system, which ensures that business takes place in a fair and structured manner. They lack adequate infrastructure, especially in terms of transport routes of all types which would enable raw materials, semi-finished products, and final goods to move around the country and out of the country efficiently and at relatively low costs. They lack accurate information systems for both producers and consumers, which often leads to imperfect information, the misallocation of resources and misinformed purchasing decisions.

7. *Dominance, dependence and vulnerability in international relations:* In almost all cases, developing countries are dominated by developed countries, because of the economic and political power of the developed countries. In addition, they are dependent upon them for many things such as trade, access to technology, aid and investment. It is not really possible for economically small, developing countries to isolate themselves from world markets. For these reasons developing countries are vulnerable on the international stage and are dominated by, and often harmed by, the decisions of developed countries, over which they have no control. Some would argue that what is needed is for the developing countries to act as a bloc, rather like a trade union, in order to gain from "collective bargaining".

All of the above factors are characteristics of developing economies and can also represent hindrances to economic growth and thus, possibly, economic development.

How much diversity is there among developing countries?

As useful as a list of common characteristics is, we have to be aware that no two developing countries are the same. Developing countries display notable diversity in a number of areas:

1. *They have different resource endowments:* There is a tendency to assume that developing countries must be poorly endowed with resources, both physical and human. However, this is not necessarily the case. Whilst it is common for the human resources to be undernourished and poorly educated, and thus low-skilled (we may refer to this as low levels of human capital), endowment in terms of physical resources can vary immensely between developing countries. Angola possesses oil and diamonds and yet is still very much a developing country. Chad had been considered a country that lacked physical resources, but the discovery of oil and subsequent production, since 2003 may make a large difference to the country. Bangladesh, on the other hand, is very poorly endowed with physical resources and synthetic products have now replaced the one major resource that they did have, jute. It should be remembered, however, that a lack of physical resources does not necessarily mean that a country cannot be successful. Japan is not well endowed with physical resources and Singapore has almost literally none, yet both countries have created "economic miracles" in the last 50 years.

Economics in action

ATL Thinking, Communication, Research and Social

Find out which European countries held colonies and make a list of the places that each country colonized. Better yet, if possible, get a world map and colour in the places that were colonized according to their colonial powers.

Did you know?

- The country Nauru is the world's smallest island nation.
- It covers 21 km^2.
- It is the smallest independent republic in the world.
- It is the only republican state in the world without an official capital.

Economics in action

ATL Thinking, Communication, Research and Social

Now find out more about Nauru!

2. *They have different historical backgrounds:* A large proportion of developing countries were once colonies of developed countries. However, the extent to which this has affected these countries varies greatly. Much depends upon the length of time that the countries were colonized and whether the eventual independence was given freely or whether it had to be fought for. It could be argued that some countries gained some positive outcomes from colonization, such as Singapore and Hong Kong, and some countries did not, such as Vietnam and Angola.

   Colonized or not, there is no doubt that whatever developing countries we consider, there will be marked historical differences that will set the countries apart from each other socially, politically and economically.

3. *There are different geographic and demographic factors:* Developing countries differ hugely in terms of geographical size and also in terms of population size. Some developing countries are truly huge, such as China, Brazil, India and the Democratic Republic of the Congo, whereas others are very small in terms of land mass, such as Swaziland, Jamaica and, especially Nauru.

   In terms of population, it is a common mistake to assume that all developing countries have large populations. This is, in fact, not the case. Developing country populations range from China (approx. 1,420 million in 2019), India (approx. 1,369 million in 2019), and Indonesia (approx. 270 million in 2019), three of the four most populated countries in the world at one end of the spectrum, down to Fiji, Guyana and Djibouti, who all have populations of less than one million people.

4. *There are differences in ethnic and religious breakdown:* Developing countries have a wide range of ethnic and religious diversity. High levels of ethnic and religious diversity within a country increase the chances of political unrest and internal conflict. We have seen examples of this in Rwanda, Sri Lanka, Angola and Myanmar in the last 20 years. However, this is not the case in all developing countries.

5. *There are different structures of industry:* It is widely assumed that all developing countries depend upon the production and exportation of primary products. Whilst this may be true of many, we should not forget the evidence that was presented in Tables 28.4 and 28.5. Developing countries such as Burkina Faso and Ethiopia may be typical of many, in terms of primary product export dependence, but other countries, such as Bangladesh and Nepal, are exporters of manufactured products and others, such as Cape Verde and the Maldives, are mainly exporters of services, in the form of tourism.

6. *There are differences in per capita income levels:* Although it is often thought that all developing countries have very low levels of income per capita, we should be aware that there are marked differences in per capita income from developing country to developing country. Table 28.7 shows a range of developing countries and their GDP per capita (PPP US$).

Country	HDI rank	GDP per capita (PPP US$)
Mauritius	65	20,189
Thailand	83	15,516
Jamaica	97	7,846
Botswana	101	15,534
India	130	6,353
Pakistan	150	5,311
Ethiopia	173	1,719

Source: Human Development Report 2018, UNDP

▲ Table 28.7 GDP per capita (PPP US$) for selected countries in 2017

7. *There are differences in political structure:* Developing countries have varying political structures. These include:
   - democracies
   - monarchies
   - military rule
   - single-party states
   - theocracies
   - transitional political systems, where a country is in transition, often caused by conflict and civil war, and so cannot be classified.

Within each of these structures there are of course many sub-structures. For example, democracies may be presidential systems, semi-presidential systems, parliamentary republics or constitutional monarchies. The main point is that, with developing countries being so diverse in their systems of government, it is very difficult to establish one-size-fits-all solutions to developmental problems.

In conclusion, we can say that, while there are some common characteristics that are held by developing countries to a certain degree, there are also several significant differences. One must be very cautious in making generalizations that imply that all developing countries are the same.

Economics in action

ATL Thinking, Communication and Research

Find at least one developing country that represents each of the above political structures.

EXAMINATION QUESTIONS

Paper 1, part (a) questions – HL & SL

1. Distinguish between economic growth and economic development. [10 marks]
2. Using a PPF diagram, explain how it is possible for a country to achieve economic growth. [10 marks]
3. Outline **three** of the Sustainable Development Goals. [10 marks]

Paper 1, part (a) questions – HL only

1. Explain the relationship between sustainability and poverty. [10 marks]

Paper 1, part (b) questions – HL only

1. Using real-world examples, discuss the view that economic growth will always lead to economic development. [15 marks]

29 MEASURING ECONOMIC PROGRESS

REAL-WORLD ISSUE:
Why is economic development uneven?

By the end of this chapter, you should be able to:

- → Explain the multidimensional nature of economic development
- → Compare and contrast GDP per capita figures and GNI per capita figures for different countries
- → Compare and contrast GDP per capita figures and GNI per capita figures, at purchasing power parity (PPP) prices, for different countries
- → Compare and contrast health and education indicators for different countries
- → Explain and give examples of economic/social inequality indicators, energy indicators and environmental indicators
- → Explain and give examples of composite indicators, including the human development index, the gender inequality index, the inequality adjusted human development index and the Happy Planet index
- → Discuss the strengths and limitations of approaches to measuring economic development
- → Discuss possible relationships between economic growth and economic development.

We have already discovered, in Chapter 28, the multidimensional nature of economic development. This multidimensional nature makes the measurement of economic development extremely difficult. We shall now consider some of the ways that development is assessed.

What is a single indicator?

Single indicators are solitary measures that may be used to assess development. The indicators tend to be either financial measures, health measures, education measures or institutional measures.

What financial measures are used?

1. Single financial measures, such as GDP per capita and GNI per capita figures, are often used to assess growth and/or development. These were introduced in Chapter 13.

   GDP per capita may be defined as the total of all economic activity in a country, regardless of who owns the productive assets, divided by the number in the population. This means that the income of foreign companies producing within a country would be included in the national income of that country, but the activity of its own companies producing outside of the country would not.

   GNI per capita is the total income that is earned by a country's factors of production, regardless of where the assets are located, divided by the number in the population. This means that the income of foreign companies producing within a country would not be included in the national income of the country, but the activity of its own companies producing outside of the country would.

   In this century, there has been an increase in the annual flow of foreign direct investment (FDI) to developing countries. It has increased by approximately 250% between 2000 and 2017. In developing economies, in 2017, FDI inflows amounted to US$671 billion, almost double the value of FDI outflows (US$381 billion). Developing economies in Asia and Oceania accounted for more than two thirds of all developing economy inflows. Developed economies, by contrast, generate more FDI than they receive. In 2017, they recorded inflows of US$712 billion and outflows of US$1 trillion.[1]

   If a developing country has a large amount of FDI then its GDP figures will be significantly higher than its GNI figures, since they will include profits that may well have been repatriated. Because the repatriated profits do not remain within the economy, they cannot be used to make contributions to the country's progress, This is the main reason why GNI figures tend to be used to measure the status of developing countries.

   For developed countries whose firms are heavily involved in FDI, the GDP figure will be significantly lower than the GNI figure. Table 29.1 shows the GDP per capita and GNI per capita figures for a selection of developed and developing countries.

[1] Source: Unctad, Handbook of statistics- economic trends, 2019

Country	GDP per capita (current US$) 2017	GNI per capita (Atlas method) (current US$) 2017	GNI – GDP (% of GDP)
USA	59,927.9	59,160	−1.3
UK	39,953.6	40,600	1.6
France	38,484.2	38,160	−0.8
Botswana	7,595.6	6,730	−11.4
Cameroon	1,451.9	1,370	−5.6
India	1,979.4	1,790	−9.6
Indonesia	3,846.4	3,540	−8.0
Vietnam	2,342.2	2,160	−7.8

Source: World Bank databank

▲ Table 29.1 GDP per capita and GNI per capita figures for selected countries

As we can see for the developed countries, the UK has a GNI figure that is greater than the GDP figure, suggesting that they have significant earnings from assets owned abroad (net property income from abroad – see Chapter 13). It is interesting to note that the USA and France have negative figures in the final column, which means that they have a negative flow in terms of net property income from abroad.

As we would expect for developing countries, Botswana, Cameroon, India, Indonesia and Vietnam all have larger GDP figures than GNI figures, suggesting that there is a significant movement of earnings from assets leaving the countries to go abroad. In the case of Botswana, it is greater than 10% of GDP.

Although the repatriation of profits is usually far greater in value, developing countries do often have one other important inflow of earnings, which is money sent home to the country by workers who are abroad. This is known as worker remittances. For developed countries this figure is normally less than one percent of GDP. However, for some developing countries it is a significant figure. Examples of the developing countries with the highest remittances levels are shown in Table 29.2.

Country	Remittance inflows as a % of GDP
Tonga	34.24
Kyrgyzstan	32.86
Tajikistan	31.56
Haiti	29.25
Nepal	28.31
Liberia	26.89

Source: UNDP Human Development Report 2017

▲ Table 29.2 Remittance inflows as a % of GDP

2. Another set of single financial measures that are often used are GNI per capita figures and GNI per capita figures at purchasing power parity (PPP).

   When making financial comparisons between countries a problem arises because goods and services simply don't cost the same amount in different countries. That means that the purchasing power of a person's income will be different in different countries. For example, a loaf of bread will cost less in India than it will in Austria. In fact, the price of most things will be less in India than in Vienna. When we convert the Indian GNI per capita into US dollars we get US$1,790 (2017 figure). However, that $1,790 actually has a much higher purchasing power in India than it would in Vienna because things cost less.

To avoid this problem economists calculate what is called the purchasing power parity (PPP) exchange rate. This exchange rate attempts to equate the purchasing power of currencies in different countries. It is calculated by comparing the prices of identical goods and services in different countries. The PPP that is most widely used is the one calculated by the World Bank. The Economist magazine also calculates a PPP rate based on the price of Big Macs in different countries. They call it the Big Mac index and refer to the study as Burgernomics!

Economics in action

ATL Thinking, Communication and Research

The Economist magazine calculates what is known as the Big Mac index to estimate purchasing power parity exchange rates. Go to the website of the magazine to get the latest data, along with further information on its uses.

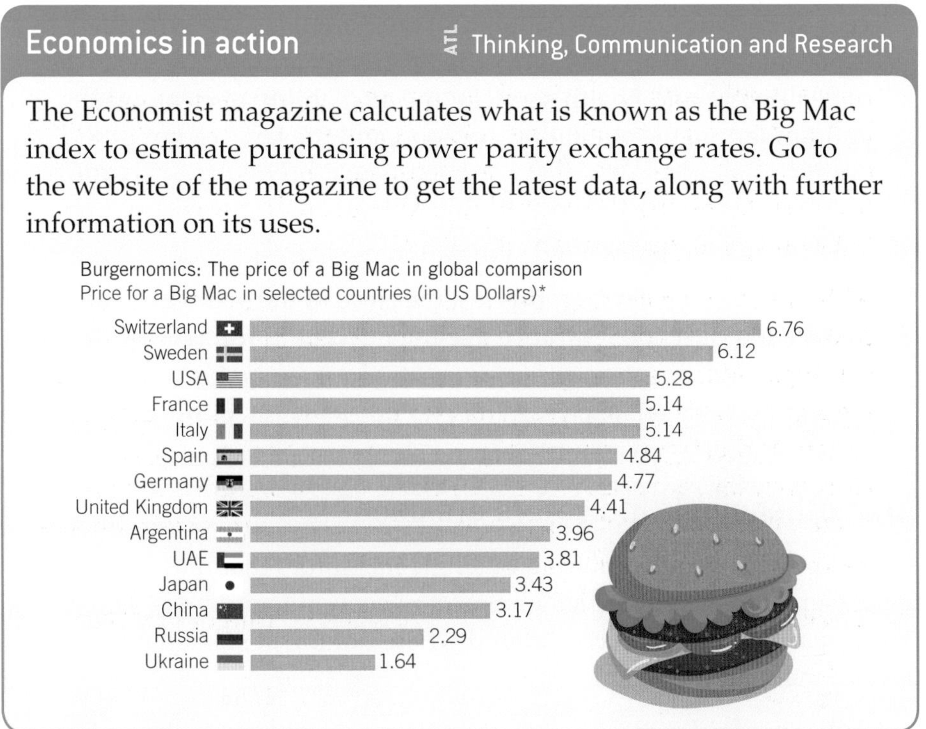

While there are limitations to the reliability of the data, when we convert GNI figures into US dollars at the PPP rates we get a more valid figure for making judgments about the ability of people to meet their basic needs. The Indian GNI per capita converted at the PPP rate into US dollars is $6,950 (2017 figure). While this is still a relatively small figure, and represents a low income, it is more realistic than the $1,790 converted at official exchange rates. Typically, the difference between the GNI converted into the US dollar at official rates is considerably lower than the GNI converted at PPP rates for lower income countries.

Key concept

ECONOMIC WELLBEING

Economics in action

ATL Thinking, Communication and Research

Using the UNICEF website at www.unicef.org/statistics, find the following data for one very high human development country (HDI > 0.8); one high human development country (0.8 > HDI > 0.699); one medium human development country (0.7 > HDI > 0.554); and one low human development country (0.555 > HDI):

1. Life expectancy at birth (years)
2. Infant mortality rate (deaths per 1000 live births)
3. Mean of years of schooling (for those aged 25 and over)
4. Expected years of schooling (for children of school entering age).

Comment upon any differences that you perceive in the four measures as as one moves from "very high human development" countries to the "low human development" countries.

What health measures are used?

Here are two examples of single health measures:

1. *Life expectancy at birth:* This is a measure, usually expressed on a country by country basis, of the average number of years that a person may expect to live from the time that they are born. It is sometimes separated into male and female life expectancy. It is one of the measures used in the Human Development Index, as you will see later in this chapter. There are many factors that may lead to a relatively high life expectancy figure for any country, such as a good level of health care and health services in the country; the provision of clean water supplies and adequate sanitation; the provision of nationwide education; reasonable supplies of food; healthy diets and lifestyles; low levels of poverty; and a lack of conflict, such as war or civil war. The lack of these factors may lead to relatively low life expectancy figures.
2. *Infant mortality rate:* This is a measure of the number of deaths of babies under the age of one year per thousand live births in a given year. It does not include babies that are born dead. As with life expectancy at birth, the figure will be greatly affected by the level of health care and health services, the availability of clean water and sanitation, the availability of food and the level of poverty.

What education measures are used?

Here are two examples of single education measures:

1. *Expected years of schooling:* this is a measure of the years of schooling that a child of school entrance age may expect to receive.
2. *Mean years of schooling:* this is a measure of the average years of schooling that have been received by those people in the economy who are aged 25 years and over.

What other single indicators are used?

As we know, there are a myriad of single indicators that may be used to measure or assess a particular aspect of economic progress. Three more areas that are often considered when looking at sustainable development are:

1. *Economic/social inequality indicators:* These would be measures in areas such as income and wealth distribution, pay inequality, asset ownership and access to credit.
2. *Energy indicators:* There is no clear agreement when it comes to defining *energy poverty.* The most common definition seems to be the inability to maintain the home at an adequate temperature or to provide essential energy services to ensure decent living conditions. Thus, useful measures to assess energy poverty could be data such as access to electricity, the impact of energy bills on household budgets and the ability to maintain a home at an adequate temperature.

3. *Environmental indicators:* Once again, the number of environmental indicators is huge and it really depends upon which environmental issue one is considering, such as air pollution, climate change, biodiversity, waste, water resources and so on. Table 29.3 suggests indicators that might be applied to assess different environmental issues.

Environmental issue	Indicator
Climate change	Ocean temperatures
Ozone depletion	Level of greenhouse gas emissions
Biodiversity	Bird migration patterns
Waste	Municipal waste (kgs per capita)
Water resources	Water withdrawal and waste water treatment
Forest resources	Intensity of use of forest resources
Fish resources	Measurement of fishing catches
Soil degradation	Level of desertification
Coastal zones	Oil spill data, coastal flooding

▲ Table 29.3 Environmental issues and selected measurement options

As we know, single indicators are too specific to fully highlight economic progress and so they are mostly used as part of a composite index in order to attempt to cover a complicated area.

What is a composite indicator?

Given the multidimensional nature of economic development, it is hardly surprising that it is difficult to measure. Rather than using single indicators, like those above, institutions have started using composite indicators, which combine a number of single indicators with weighting, to give a single, combined figure.

What is the Human Development Index (HDI)?

The United Nations Development Program (UNDP) provides the Human Development Index as one measure of development. The HDI is a composite index that brings together three variables. There are three basic goals of development that can be "measured". These are a long and healthy life, improved education and a decent standard of living. A long and healthy life is measured by life expectancy at birth on the assumption that people who live longer have benefited from good health. Education is measured by mean years of schooling for adults aged 25 years and more, and expected years of schooling for children of school entering age. The standard of living, or the ability to meet basic needs, is measured by the GNI per capita, converted at PPP US$ (see earlier section). The three indicators are combined to give an index value between 0 and 1, with higher values representing a higher level of development. The UNDP classifies countries into four categories according to their HDI. These categories are shown in Table 29.4.

Category	HDI value range
Very high human development	0.800 and above
High human development	0.700 to 0.799
Medium human development	0.555 to 0.699
Low human development	Less than 0.555

▲ Table 29.4 HDI country classifications

How useful is HDI information?

Prior to the establishment of the HDI in 1990, GDP per capita had been the yardstick for measuring development, under the assumption that higher national income translated directly into a higher level of development.

These days, the UNDP uses GNI per capita as a more accurate measure of income. If we compare a country's ranking in terms of its HDI with its ranking in terms of its GNI per capita, we may make some useful conclusions about the country's success in translating the benefits of national income into achieving economic development.

Consider the data in Table 29.5. Norway has the highest HDI value, but it is ranked 6th in terms of GNI per capita. United States is ranked 11th in terms of its GNI per capita, but 13th in terms of its HDI. Had we simply used GNI per capita figures to make conclusions about development concerns, the data would have been misleading. There are even more extreme discrepancies. Consider South Africa, ranked 90th for its GNI per capita, but 113th for its HDI. It has a GNI per capita that is significantly higher than that of Tunisia, but its HDI ranking is 18 places below Tunisia. It may be possible to make hypotheses about South Africa's national policies aimed at promoting development objectives based on this information.

The UNDP observes that one of the uses of the HDI is to "re-emphasize that people and their capabilities should be the ultimate criteria for assessing the development of a country, not economic growth" (http://hdr.undp.org).

Category	Country	HDI value	HDI rank	GNI per capita (PPP US$)	GNI per capita (PPP US$) rank	GNI per capita (PPP US$) rank minus HDI rank*
Very high human development (59 countries)	Norway	0.953	1	68,012	6	5
	Sweden	0.933	7	47,766	16	9
	USA	0.924	13	54,941	11	−2
	Italy	0.880	28	35,299	31	3
High human development (51 countries)	Turkey	0.791	64	24,804	50	−14
	Serbia	0.787	67	13,019	85	18
	Mexico	0.774	74	16,944	68	−6
	Tunisia	0.735	95	10,275	102	7
Medium human development (39 countries)	South Africa	0.699	113	11,923	90	−23
	India	0.640	130	6,353	125	−5
	Bangladesh	0.608	136	3,677	145	9
	Cambodia	0.582	146	3,413	149	3

Category	Country	HDI value	HDI rank	GNI per capita (PPP US$)	GNI per capita (PPP US$) rank	GNI per capita (PPP US$) rank minus HDI rank*
Low human development (38 countries)	Tanzania	0.538	154	2,655	160	6
	Uganda	0.516	162	1,658	175	13
	Guinea	0.459	175	2,067	164	−11
	Niger	0.354	189	906	187	−2

* A positive figure indicates that the HDI rank is higher than the GNI per capita (PPP US$) rank, a negative the opposite.

Source: UNDP, 2019, hdr.undp.org

▲ Table 29.5 GNI per capita and HDI for selected countries

Exercise 29.1

ATL Thinking and Communication

Use the data provided in Table 29.5 to draw conclusions about how the following pairs of countries differ in terms of their GNI per capita ranking and their HDI ranking. What might this say about the countries' national policies on health and education?

1. Uganda and Guinea
2. South Africa and Bangladesh

Is the HDI sufficient as the only guide to a country's development?

Certainly not, but it is more effective than the simple GDP figure. The fact remains that there are many different aspects to development other than the three included in the HDI. It should also be noted that the country's HDI is still an average figure that can mask inequalities within the country. Inequalities that are likely to occur are between rural and urban citizens, between men and women and between different ethnic groups. There are several other composite indicators and a vast number of single indicators, ie indicators that measure one thing, that attempt to measure the different dimensions of development.

What other indices are there out there?

There are, as we have already said, many more indices, both single and composite. Let us look at three of them:

1. **The Gender Inequality Index (GII)**

   As we already know from Chapter 22, gender inequality represents a major barrier to human development. The disadvantages facing women and girls are a major source of inequality. All too often, women and girls are discriminated against in such areas as health, education, political representation and the labour market. This has a negative impact upon the development of their capabilities and their freedom of choice.

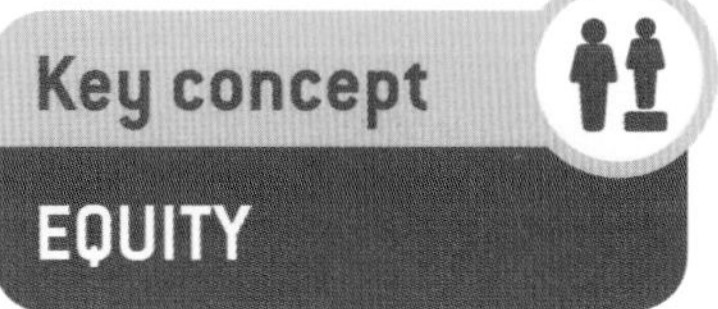

   "The GII is an inequality index. It measures gender inequalities in three important aspects of human development – reproductive health, measured by maternal mortality ratio and adolescent birth rates; empowerment, measured by proportion of parliamentary seats occupied by females and proportion of adult females and males aged 25 years and older with at least some secondary education; and economic status, expressed as labour market participation and measured by labour force participation rate of female and male populations aged 15 years and older. The GII is built on the same framework as the IHDI *(see next section)* – to better expose differences in the distribution of achievements between women and men. It measures the human development costs of gender inequality. Thus the higher the GII value, the more disparities between females and males and the more loss of human development."[2]

The GII considers the position of women in 160 countries, yielding insights in gender gaps in major areas of human development. Figure 29.1 shows the elements that make up the GII.

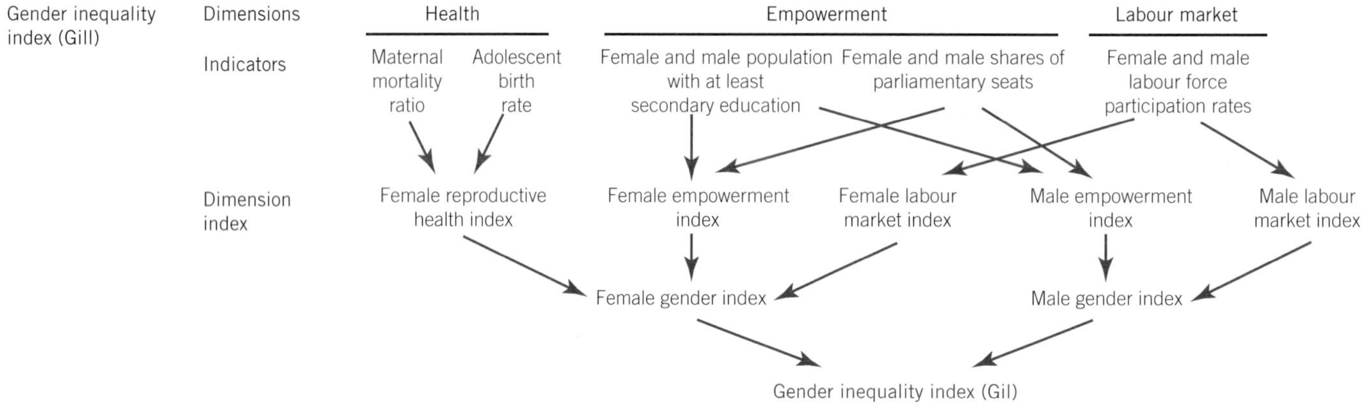

Source: UNDP, 2019, hdr.undp.org

▲ **Figure 29.1** The elements of the GII

Exercise 29.2
ATL Thinking and Communication

a) Examine the data in Table 29.6. Do you think there is a correlation between income and gender equity? Explain your answer.

b) Investigate current data to see whether your answer to part (a) is confirmed.

Table 29.6 shows GII figures for eight countries. Remember that the higher the GII value, the greater the level of gender inequality.

Country	HDI Rank	GII value
Yemen	178	0.835
Papua New Guinea	153	0.741
Chad	186	0.708
Mali	182	0.678
Netherlands	10	0.044
Sweden	7	0.044
Denmark	11	0.040
Switzerland	2	0.039

Source: UNDP, 2019, hdr.undp.org

▲ **Table 29.6** GII values (2017) for selected countries

Key concept
EQUITY

2. Inequality adjusted Human Development Index (IHDI)

The IHDI is basically the HDI, but taking into account the human development costs of inequality. Each of the components of the HDI, life expectancy, years of schooling and income/consumption, is adjusted downwards by its level of inequality. If a country had perfect equality, then the IHDI value would equal the HDI value. Without perfect equality, the IHDI value will be below the HDI value. Figure 29.2 shows the elements that make up the IHDI.

[2] http://hdr.undp.org/en/content/gender-inequality-index-gii

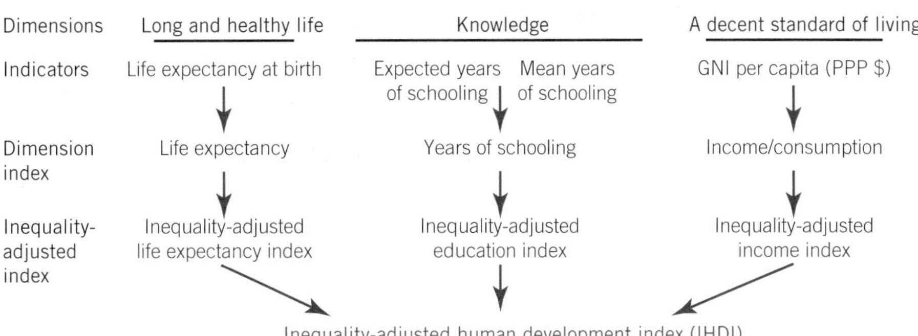

Source: UNDP, 2019, http://hdr.undp.org

▲ Figure 29.2 The elements of the IHDI

The difference between the IHDI value and the HDI value represents the loss to human development owing to inequality. The IHDI is calculated for 151 countries. Table 29.7 shows IHDI figures for selected countries. Countries with lower inequality should find that their IHDI rank is higher than their HDI rank In the same way, countries with higher inequality should find that their IHDI rank is lower than their HDI rank.

Country	HDI value	HDI rank	IHDI value	IHDI rank	HDI rank – IHDI rank
Norway	0.953	1	0.876	2	−1
Iceland	0.935	6	0.878	1	5
Hong Kong	0.933	7	0.809	21	−14
Japan	0.909	19	0.876	3	16
Brazil	0.759	79	0.578	96	−17
Kyrgyzstan	0.672	122	0.606	100	22

Source: UNDP, 2019, hdr.undp.org

▲ Table 29.7 IHDI values (2017) for selected countries

Let's compare two countries to see what the data might tell us. Hong Kong is ranked 7th in terms of its HDI rank, while Japan is ranked 19th. However, when inequality is taken into account, the IHDI value for both countries is lower than the HDI values. Furthermore, the rankings are reversed; Japan moves up many places to rank 3rd, while Hong Kong's ranking drops to 21st. This suggests that when inequalities are taken into account, both countries experience a lower level of development than their HDI values would suggest, and that inequality poses less of a problem in Japan than it does in Hong Kong.

Exercise 29.3 ATL Thinking and Communication

a) Using the data in Table 29.7, compare Norway and Iceland.

b) Using the data in Table 29.7, compare Brazil and Kyrgyzstan..

3. Happy Planet Index (HPI)

We have already come across the HPI in Chapter 13. The HPI measures sustainable well being. It measures how well countries are doing at achieving long and happy lives, taking into account sustainability. Go back and look at the earlier explanation for more details.

Key concept
ECONOMIC WELLBEING

Key concept
EQUITY

4. **The Multidimensional Poverty Index. (MPI)**

   We have already come across the MPI in Chapter 22. This measures the deprivations experienced by the poor people in a country in three key areas: health, education and standards of living. In each area, specific data is gathered to assess how poor the people are in each area. The following table indicates the indicators that are measured in each area.

Health	• Nutrition • Child mortality	
Education	• Years of schooling • School attendance	
Standards of living	• Cooking fuel • Sanitation • Drinking water	• Electricity • Housing • Assets

▲ Table 29.8 Components of the Multidimensional Poverty Index

Refer back to Chapter 22 for a reminder of how this is done, and what the values mean.

5. **The Inclusive Development Index (IDI)**

   The IDI is a project of the World Economic Forum's System Initiative on the Future of Economic Progress. It is an annual assessment of 103 countries' economic performance that measures how countries perform on eleven dimensions of economic progress in addition to GDP. It has 3 pillars: growth and development, inclusion, and intergenerational equity and sustainability. Figure 29.3 shows the elements that make up the IDI.

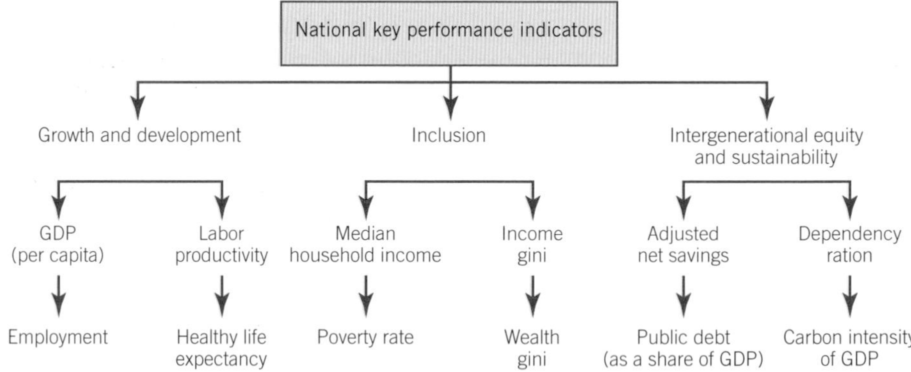

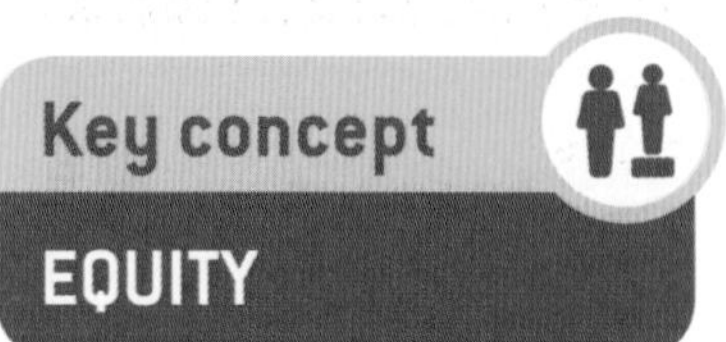

Source: The Inclusive Development Index 2018 Summary and Data Highlights, World Economic Forum, 2019

▲ Figure 29.3 The elements of the IDI

The index takes into account numerous variables in assessing development. What is particularly valuable is its recognition of the importance of including measures of inclusion and sustainability in assessing a country's progress.

It separates countries into 'Advanced economies' and 'Emerging economies' for the sake of comparison. There are figures for 29 advanced economies and 74 emerging economies. The index also employs a colour coded dashboard, representing quintiles, to show the relative position of a country in terms of other countries in its group, for each of the performance indicators. Table 29.7 shows selected data for 2018.

Country	Growth & Development				Inclusion				Intergenerational equity & sustainability			
	GDP Per Capita $	Labour productivity $	Healthy life expectancy Years	Employment %	Net income Gini	Poverty rate %	Wealth Gini	Median income $	Adjusted net savings %	Carbon intensity Kg per $ of GDP	Public debt %	Dependency ration %
Advanced Economies												
Norway	89,818	126,236	72.0	61.7	24.9	8.1	80.5	63.8	20.6	16.3	33.2	52.5
USA	52,196	111,712	69.1	58.9	37.8	16.8	85.9	48.9	7.5	46.4	107.4	51.7
Emerging Economies												
Lithuania	15,873	60,196	66.1	53.9	34.2	2.7	51.6	18.2	18.8	63.7	40.0	60.5
Indonesia	3,974	23,390	62.1	63.6	45.7	33.8	83.7	4.6	25.6	126.6	27.9	48.9

Rank

Bottom 20% Top 20%

Source: The Inclusive Development Index 2018 Summary and Data Highlights, World Economic Forum, 2019

▲ Table 29.9 IDI values 2018 for selected countries

In Table 29.9, we can see that Norway, which is ranked first in advanced economies, is in the top 20% for eight out of the twelve elements of the IDI. It is, however, in the bottom 20% when we consider the wealth Gini coefficient, ie how much of the country's wealth is owned by a certain percentage of the population. The USA is ranked 23rd and is in the bottom 20% in five elements, including income and wealth inequality.

Lithuania is ranked first in the emerging economies and, by comparison with other countries in the same group, is in the top 20% for five of the twelve elements. Indonesia is ranked 36th out of the 74 emerging countries. It is in the bottom 20% of countries for income and wealth inequality.

The ability to make comparison between similar countries should make it easier for policymakers to highlight specific weak areas that need focus and to act upon the data.

What have we learned?

In this chapter we have looked at some of the reasons why GNI statistics are not a good indicator of living standards. We have furthered that discussion with an emphasis on measuring development in developing countries. It is now important to consider one alternative measure of welfare that has been established in the more developed countries. This is known as the genuine progress indicator (GPI). This indicator attempts to measure whether a country's growth, which is simply an

Exercise 29.4

ATL Thinking, Communication and Research

Look up the Inclusive Development Index for two further countries, one advanced economy and one emerging economy. Comment on the significance of each country's values.

Exercise 29.5

ATL Thinking and Communication

Using information in this chapter, discuss the strengths and limitations of the following means of measuring economic progress:

1. the HDI
2. the GII
3. the IHDI
4. The MPI
5. the HPI.

increase in the output of goods and services, has actually led to an improvement in the welfare of the people. To the GNI figures, it adds a measure of non-monetary benefits such as the benefits of household work, parenting and volunteer work. Given that economic growth generates many costs, an indicator of genuine progress needs to deduct such costs, rather than add them to GNI. These include estimates of:

- environmental costs such as air, water and noise pollution; loss of farmland, wetlands and forests; resource depletion; ozone depletion; pollution abatement
- social costs such as family breakdown, crime, personal security (eg home security systems), loss of leisure time
- commuting costs
- costs of automobile accidents.

While such variables are, of course, difficult to measure, the realization that rising GNI does not equate with rising welfare means that welfare economists and environmental economists are constantly looking for ways to measure the consequences of growth so that developed and developing countries can aim for growth that is equitable and sustainable.

Economics in action — ATL Thinking, Communication and Research

Pick one developing country and assess its level of economic development by using the indicators mentioned in this chapter.

Exercise 29.6 — ATL Thinking and Communication

1. Define economic growth.
2. Define economic development.
3. Define sustainable development.
4. Explain how economic development can be measured.
5. With reference to the following data, and by comparing GDP per capita with the HDI explain the importance of the HDI. Be sure to use numbers from the data to support your answer. You could begin with the words, *"Even though…"*

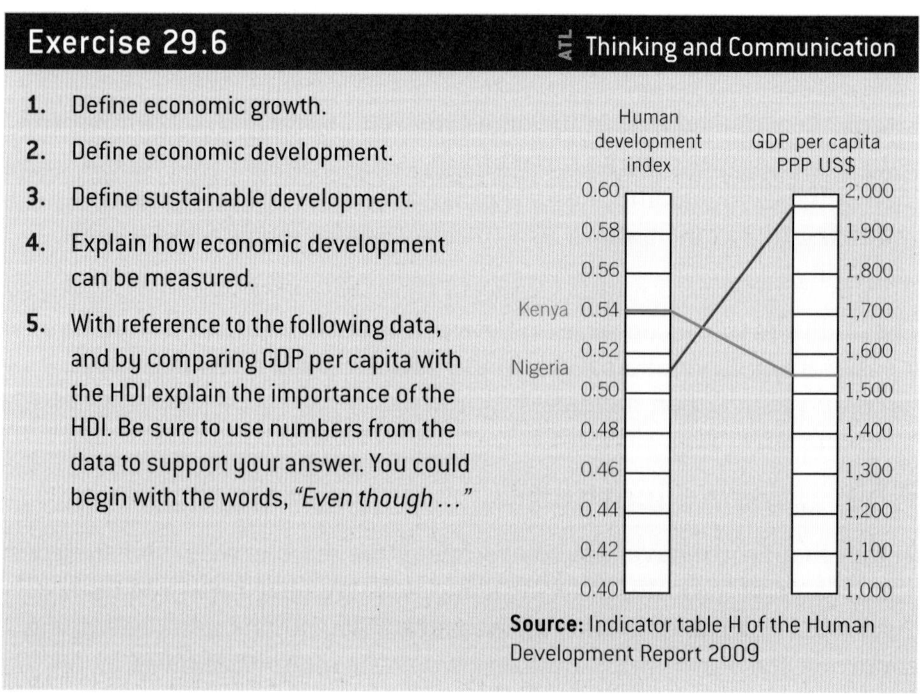

Source: Indicator table H of the Human Development Report 2009

EXAMINATION QUESTIONS

Paper 1, part (a) questions – HL & SL

1. Explain the difference between GDP per capita and GNI per capita as a means of measuring economic growth. [10 marks]
2. Explain two single indicators that might be used to measure health. [10 marks]
3. Explain how economic development might be measured. [10 marks]
4. Explain the three non-monetary indicators used in the human development index (HDI). [10 marks]
5. Explain the elements making up two different composite indicators of economic development. [10 marks]

Paper 1, part (b) questions – HL only

1. Using real-world examples, discuss the strengths and limitations of two different approaches to measuring economic development. [15 marks]
2. Using real-world examples, discuss the possible relationship between economic growth and economic development. [15 marks]

HL & SL Paper 2 – 2-mark and 4-mark questions

Country	HDI rank	HDI value	GDP per capita (PPP US$)	Unemployment rate (% of labour force)	Child dependency ratio (%)
Switzerland	2	0.944	57,625	3.2	22.0
China	86	0.752	15,270	3.9	24.3
Kenya	142	0.590	2,961	40.0	73.7
Cambodia	146	0.582	3,413	0.3	49.2
Mali	182	0.427	1,953	7.9	96.8

Source: Adapted from UNDP Human Development Report 2018 and CIA World Factbook 2019

2-mark questions – HL & SL

Define the following terms, indicated in bold in the data:

a) HDI [2 marks]

b) (PPP US$) [2 marks]

4-mark questions – HL & SL

1. Explain why a high child-dependency ratio might contribute to low levels of economic development. [4 marks]
2. Explain **two** reasons why unemployment rates are not reliable indicators of economic development. [4 marks]
3. Explain how Cambodia can have a higher GDP per capita figure and yet a lower HDI rank than Kenya. [4 marks]

30 BARRIERS TO DEVELOPMENT

REAL-WORLD ISSUE:
Why is economic development uneven?

By the end of this chapter, you should be able to:

- → Define, explain, give examples of and illustrate poverty cycles
- → Explain and give examples of economic barriers to economic growth and development
- → Explain and give examples of political and social barriers to economic growth and development
- → Discuss the significance of different barriers to economic development.

Key concept 
EQUITY

Key concept 
ECONOMIC WELLBEING

This chapter is all about equity and economic well-being and so these concepts will run throughout.

What are poverty traps (poverty cycles)?

There are many barriers to economic development. However, the situation is made worse when one realizes that the barriers are often connected in a cyclical fashion so that countries may be caught in a poverty trap. A poverty trap is any linked combination of barriers to growth and development that forms a circle, thus self-perpetuating unless the circle can be broken.

These traps may be illustrated by the use of a poverty cycle. Poverty cycles are also sometimes known as development traps. Examples of two poverty cycles are shown in Figure 30.1. As we can see, on the left is a well-known poverty cycle that illustrates how low incomes perpetuate low incomes, thus harming economic growth. On the right we can see a different cycle, where low incomes perpetuate low incomes, but this time harming economic development.

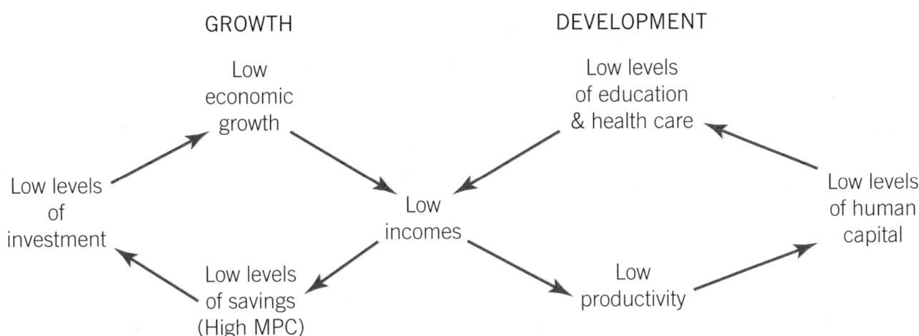

▲ Figure 30.1 Examples of poverty cycles

> **Exercise 30.1**
> ATL Thinking and Communication
>
> Devise circular problem charts (poverty cycles) beginning and ending with the following and suggest ways that the circles may be broken.
>
> 1. Poor health
> 2. Lack of technology
> 3. Low consumption levels
> 4. HIV/AIDS
> 5. Falling commodity prices
> 6. A barrier of your own choice

What are the economic barriers to development?

There are many and varied barriers to sustainable development and economic progress and we will now consider a number of them:

How does rising economic inequality hinder economic progress?

We have already looked at this in Chapter 22. Although all countries in the world have income inequality, it is fair to say that the gap between the rich and poor in developing countries is generally greater than that in developed countries.

High income-inequality can be a barrier to growth and development for a number of reasons. Firstly, there tend to be low levels of saving, because the poor save a very small proportion of their income. As we know, low saving means low investment and so low growth. Secondly, the rich tend to dominate both politics and the economy and this tends to mean that policies are followed that are more in their favour and so we do not have *pro-poor growth*. Pro-poor growth occurs when economic growth leads to a fall in some agreed measure of poverty. Thus, this type of growth benefits the poor. Thirdly, high income-inequality in developing countries tends to be marked by the rich moving large amounts of funds out of the economy in the form of capital flight. Also, a large proportion of the goods purchased by the rich are foreign produced and so their consumption does not really help the domestic economy. Thus, although we usually link income inequality simply to a consequence of low levels of development, we can also see that it can act as a barrier to growth and development.

How does a lack of access to infrastructure and appropriate technology hinder economic progress?

1. *Lack of access to infrastructure*

   A full definition of infrastructure might be "the essential facilities and services such as roads, airports, sewage treatment, water systems, railways, telephone and other utilities that are necessary for economic activity". It should be obvious that improvements in infrastructure will lead to greater economic development. For example, better roads and better public transport allow children to get to school, adults to get to the market and goods to get to potential buyers.

A developed radio and television network can make it possible for people to link up with, and participate in, wider communities. The availability of gas and electricity is important to households for activities such as cooking and food preservation. Sewage treatment improves the lot of the population, if it is universal, as does an adequate water system. Any improvement in infrastructure will, in some way, improve the well being of the people. Table 30.1 identifies different categories of infrastructure and also gives examples of each.

Category	Examples
Transport	• Roads • Railways • Seaports • Airports • Public transport • Sidewalks
Public utilities	• Electricity • Gas • Water supply • Sewers
Public services	• Police service • Fire service • Education service • Health service • Waste management
Communication services	• Postal system • Telecommunication • Radio and television

▲ **Table 30.1** Categories and examples of infrastructure

Exercise 30.2

ATL Thinking and Communication

Choose one example of each type of infrastructure listed in Table 30.1 and explain how it supports and contributes to economic activity.

2. *Lack of access to appropriate technology*

Appropriate technology is technology that is appropriate for use with existing factor endowments. This applies to both production and consumption. In terms of production, in years gone by developing countries were urged to modernize and industrialize their output. However, development economists argued that this was not "appropriate". In most developing countries there is a surplus of labour and so the appropriate technology to use would be technology that makes use of the abundant labour supply. An example of this would be giving workers capital equipment to use that is cheap to make and requires labour for its use. A well known example is the Universal nut sheller, which is a simple machine, turned by hand, that is used to shell nuts. It is cheap to make, has a long life and has a one-to-one capital to labour ratio. When used industrially, they provide greater employment than automated systems and so add to development.

In terms of consumption, a good example of appropriate technology is the solar cooker. The cooker is made from aluminium foil and plastic film, which are very cheap to purchase, and it requires sunshine to operate, which is abundant in many developing countries. The cooker aids development in many ways. It does not require wood and so there is no loss of trees, it eliminates the daily search for firewood, which frees up time for other activities, and so it helps to improve the position of women, who are most commonly responsible for cooking in developing countries.

How do low levels of human capital – lack of access to education and health care – hinder economic progress?

1. *Lack of access to education*

   Improvements in education improve the well being of the population, both the educated themselves and the society as a whole. That is, education provides external benefits. Although, as we have already seen, it leads to a more efficient workforce, it actually does much more. Increased levels of education mean that people are better able to read and to communicate. This, in turn, makes discussion and debate more likely and, as a consequence, may lead to social change. Changing attitudes may achieve a number of developmental aims. The benefits are widespread, but include the following.

   - *Improve the role of women in society:* There is no doubt that women are empowered by education and that there are high correlations between women's education and child survival rates and fertility rates (the annual number of live births per 1,000 women of childbearing age). The role of women in society is hugely important in terms of development. As Amartya Sen says, "Nothing, arguably, is as important today in the political economy of development as an adequate recognition of political, economic and social participation and leadership of women."[1]
   - *Improve levels of health:* Improved education levels, in particular literacy rates, improve levels of health in society. People, especially women, are able to communicate more fully and thus become aware of some of the hazards that face them and of some of the opportunities that exist. Individuals are able to read about, and be informed about, dangers such as HIV/AIDS, poor sanitary habits and poor dietary habits. In addition, they are able to find out about the possibilities of such things as inoculations and water filtering.

Theory of knowledge

"There are three kinds of lies – lies, damned lies, and statistics". (This is a quotation that is attributed to Benjamin Disraeli and was popularized by Mark Twain.)

Why is this statement particularly meaningful in the field of economics?

[1] *Development as freedom*, Amartya Sen, OUP, 1999

Progress has been made in the provision of education, particularly primary education, throughout the world. Enrolment in primary education in developing countries has reached 91%. However, 57 million primary age children remain out of school. More than half of the children that are out of school live in sub-Saharan Africa. An estimated 50 per cent of out-of-school children of primary school age live in conflict-affected areas. In addition, 617 million youth worldwide lack basic mathematics and literacy skills.[2]

Sustainable Development Goal 4 targets

4.1 By 2030, ensure that all girls and boys complete free, equitable and quality primary and secondary education leading to relevant and Goal-4 effective learning outcomes

4.2 By 2030, ensure that all girls and boys have access to quality early childhood development, care and pre-primary education so that they are ready for primary education

4.3 By 2030, ensure equal access for all women and men to affordable and quality technical, vocational and tertiary education, including university

4.4 By 2030, substantially increase the number of youth and adults who have relevant skills, including technical and vocational skills, for employment, decent jobs and entrepreneurship

4.5 By 2030, eliminate gender disparities in education and ensure equal access to all levels of education and vocational training for the vulnerable, including persons with disabilities, indigenous peoples and children in vulnerable situations

4.6 By 2030, ensure that all youth and a substantial proportion of adults, both men and women, achieve literacy and numeracy

4.7 By 2030, ensure that all learners acquire the knowledge and skills needed to promote sustainable development, including, among others, through education for sustainable development and sustainable lifestyles, human rights, gender equality, promotion of a culture of peace and non-violence, global citizenship and appreciation of cultural diversity and of culture's contribution to sustainable development

4.A Build and upgrade education facilities that are child, disability and gender sensitive and provide safe, nonviolent, inclusive and effective learning environments for all

4.B By 2020, substantially expand globally the number of scholarships available to developing countries, in particular least developed countries, small island developing States and African countries, for enrolment in higher education, including vocational training and information and communications technology, technical, engineering and scientific programmes, in developed countries and other developing countries

4.C By 2030, substantially increase the supply of qualified teachers, including through international cooperation for teacher training in developing countries, especially least developed countries and small island developing states

Source: UNDP, 2019, www.un.org/sustainabledevelopment/education/

[2] UNDP, 2019, www.un.org/sustainabledevelopment/education/

Sustainable development Goal number 4 relates to "Quality Education". The targets for goal 4 are shown in Table 30.2. If the goals could be achieved, then there is no doubt that one of the largest barriers to economic progress would be eradicated. However, achieving the targets is going to be a massive challenge.

At the most basic level, the provision of education requires vast funding and this simply may not be available in sufficient quantities. Within a country there may be large disparities in the provision of education, with urban areas receiving more of the education funds than rural areas. There are also family economic conditions that prevent children from attending school; they may be needed to work within the home or farm or they may be involved in external work as "child labourers". For the most part, it is children from poor households and from families where the mothers also received no formal education who do not attend school. Enrolment in secondary schools tends to be far lower than in primary schools, with the necessity of earning an income as the greatest obstacle to attending school. There is also the problem of glaring gender inequity in terms of girls' access to education.

2. *Lack of access to health care*

As we have already seen, greater levels of health care, especially when combined with greater educational opportunities, will improve the levels of economic development. Although there are many factors that influence life expectancy, it would be fair to assume that there would be a strong correlation between health care and life expectancy and the HDI figures would seem to concur. Look at table 30.2.

Country (HDI rank)	Current health expenditure (% of GDP)	Life Expectancy at birth (years)	Government expenditure on education (% of GDP)	GDP (PPP US$) Billions	Population (millions)
Norway (1)	10.0	82.3	7.7	342.3	5.3
Australia (3)	9.4	83.1	5.2	1,098.3	24.5
Canada (12)	10.4	82.5	5.3	1,615.8	36.6
Turkey (64)	4.1	76.0	4.4	2,029.1	80.7
Mexico (74)	5.9	77.3	5.3	2,239.2	129.2
Tunisia (95)	6.7	75.9	6.6	125.1	11.5
Philippines (113)	4.4	69.2	3.5 (est)	797.3	104.9
Morocco (123)	5.5	76.1	5.3	271.6	35.7
Pakistan (150)	2.7	66.6	2.8	991.9	197.0
Tanzania (154)	6.1	66.3	3.5	149.3	57.3
Uganda (162)	7.3	60.2	2.3	72.8	42.9
Ethiopia (173)	4.0	65.9	4.5	181.6	105.0

Source: Adapted from Tables 1-15 of UNDP 2018 Human Development Statistical Update

▲ **Table 30.2** Health, education, GDP and population data for selected countries

Table 30.2 shows data for three "very high human development" countries, three "high human development" countries, three "medium human development" countries, and three "low human development" countries. With the usual warning that there are many factors that affect a single outcome, let us consider some of the relationships. It would appear that countries that spend a higher proportion of GDP on healthcare tend to have a higher life expectancy. This is obvious when we look at the specific comparison between Canada and Morocco.

Canada spends 10.4% of $1,615.8 billion on its 36.6 million inhabitants. Morocco, with a similar population, spends 5.5% of $271.6 billion on its 35.7 million inhabitants. Even though there are other factors in play, it is hardly surprising that life expectancy is considerably higher in Canada and that the Canadian HDI ranking is much higher than that of Morocco.

The close correlation throughout the table between the life expectancy figures and the education expenditure figures is also worth noting, but may be difficult to fully justify with so many other variables to consider.

There has been much progress made by many developing countries in terms of the training of doctors and nurses, the building of hospitals and clinics, and the provision of public health services such as improved access to safe water and sanitation and the widespread availability of immunisations. Throughout the world infant mortality rates have fallen, life expectancy has increased, more children are immunized than ever before and maternal mortality rates are falling. Nevertheless, there are still significant shortcomings, particularly among the low-income countries. Table 30.3 provides some evidence of the disparities that exist. While it is a very small sample it gives us an idea of the figures involved.

Country (HDI rank)	Current health expenditure per capita, PPP (current international $) 2016	Births attended by skilled health personnel (%) 2012–2017	Physicians (per 10,000 people) 2007–2017	Population using improved drinking water sources (%) 2015	Population using improved sanitation facilities (%) 2015
Australia (3)	4,529	99.7	43.9	100.0	100.0
Finland (15)	4,112	99.9	32.0	100.0	99.4
Thailand (83)	635	99.1	4.7	98.2	95.0
Guyana (125)	333	85.7	2.1	95.1	86.2
Namibia (129)	969	88.2	3.7	78.8	33.8
Nigeria (157)	87	43.0	4.0	67.3	32.6
Niger (189)	34	39.7	0.2	45.8	12.9

Source: Adapted from Tables 1-15 and Dashboard 1 of UNDP 2018 Human Development Statistical Update and The World Bank, data.worldbank.org, 2019

▲ Table 30.3 Selected health indicators

Economics in action

ATL Thinking, Communication and Research

Choose a Low Human Development country, as classified by the United Nations, and research its performance in terms of provision of education and provision of health care.

How does dependence on primary sector production hinder economic progress?

While the share of manufactured goods produced by developing countries as a percentage of total world trade is growing, a number of developing countries are dependent on primary commodities for a significant share of their export revenues, as explained in Chapter 28.

Rising commodity prices may, therefore, be beneficial to those countries. It will increase their rate of economic growth and if the revenues are used to finance education, health and infrastructure, then this can set off a positive cycle in terms of development and future growth. However, if the prices fall then the economies experience deteriorating economic circumstances. Current account deficits are likely to increase and it will be very difficult for countries to finance current expenditure and necessary imports. Unless they can change the pattern of their export trade, those countries that are dependent on a narrow range of primary exports will find it difficult to gain much growth through international trade.

Zambia – economy still dependent on copper and producing few jobs

https://africasustainableconservation.com/2015/09/21/zambia-economy-still-dependent-on-copper-and-producing-few-jobs/

Regardless of the types of goods exported, be they commodities, manufactured goods or even services like tourism, if a country is dependent on a narrow range of exports, then they face great vulnerability and uncertainty. For example, economic growth in a tropical country that is reliant on tourism revenues will be limited if the global tourist trade is damaged as a result of terrorism or as a result of a global slowdown in economic growth. It is also vulnerable to other forces outside of its control such as tsunamis. Countries that were dependent on the export of a small range of low-skill manufactured goods such as textiles were damaged when China joined the WTO and sharply increased the supply of textiles on world markets, driving down their prices.

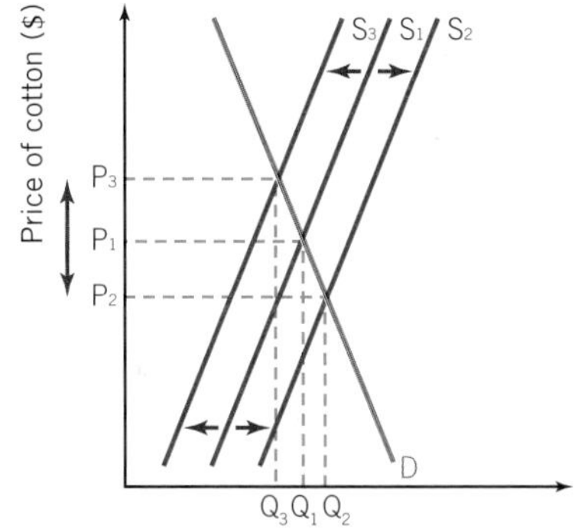

▲ Figure 30.2 The world market for cotton

Both the price elasticity of demand for commodities and the price elasticity of supply for commodities, on the world market, tend to be relatively inelastic. This is shown for the world cotton market in Figure 30.2.

With such inelastic demand and supply, any change in the demand or supply conditions for resources, in this case cotton, will lead to large price fluctuations. In Figure 30.2, a fall or increase in supply, possibly caused by either bad or good weather conditions, would have noticeable increases or decreases in price, from P_1 to P_3, when supply falls, and from P_1 to P_2 when supply increases.

This will have a marked impact on the export revenue of the countries that are selling the commodities. This price volatility, and subsequent export revenue volatility, makes it very difficult for producers and governments in developing countries to plan ahead. This in turn has an impact on investment in companies, and thus growth, and on government planning for education, health care and infrastructure and thus development.

Figure 30.3 shows the breakdown of exports of Nigeria for 2016 as a percentage of total export revenue, which was US$40 billion.

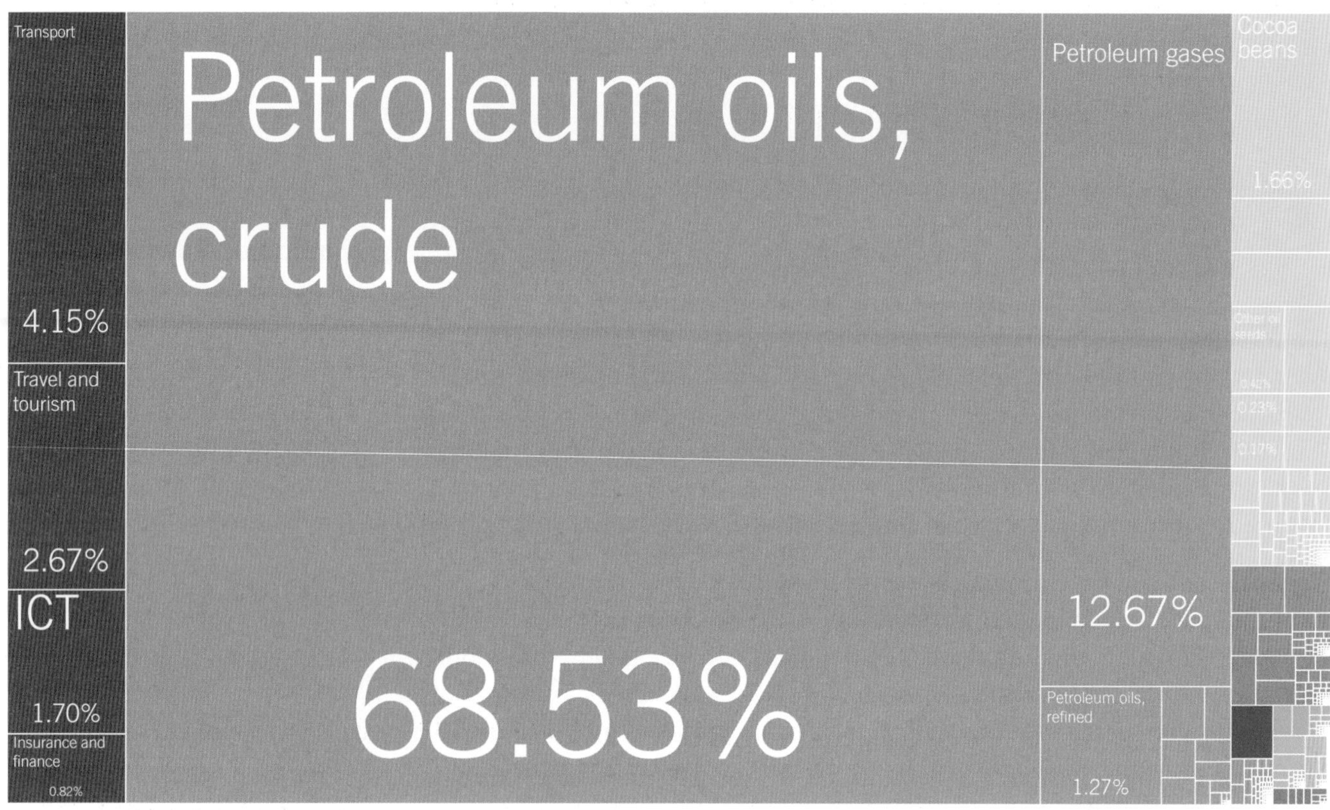

Source: Atlas of Economic Complexity, 2019 http://atlas.cid.harvard.edu

▲ Figure 30.3 Breakdown of Nigerian exports 2016

> **Economics in action**
>
> ATL Thinking, Communication and Research
>
> Using the Low Human Development country that you chose earlier in the chapter, research its main exports by going to the Atlas of Economic Complexity. Highlight any problems that the main exports may face on the world market.

How does a lack of access to international markets hinder economic progress?

As we know, protectionism is any economic policy that is aimed at supporting domestic producers at the expense of foreign producers. We have already come across forms of protectionism, such as tariffs, subsidies, quotas and non-tariff barriers, in Chapter 24. Protectionist measures by developed countries against the exports of developing countries may be very harmful. If the measures prevent developing countries from utilizing their comparative advantages and exporting to developed countries, then developing countries will be limited in their ability to earn foreign exchange.

Protectionism in any market is damaging for developing countries, but it is especially the case in primary product markets. If we take the example of cotton; since 1995, America's 25,000 cotton farmers have shared an average of $2.1 billion in government subsidies each year. This encourages farmers to produce more, forcing down the world price, and export their surplus to developing countries that do not have the benefits of subsidies. This is then immensely damaging for the developing country producers. The US does the same with maize, rice and dairy products. Meanwhile, in the same way, protected EU farmers overproduce and export sugar, cereals and dairy produce, lowering world prices and severely damaging markets and local suppliers in developing countries. As these products are sold at lower prices than would be the case without subsidies, it is argued that they are "dumped" in foreign markets. Small-scale farmers in developing countries are effectively deprived of the ability to earn a living, provide for their families and afford schooling for their children, which is clearly a significant barrier to development.

Many countries are limited in their access to global markets due to the fact that they are landlocked and/or have insufficient infrastructure to be able to physically get their products to markets. Furthermore, selling in international markets requires countries to meet certain product standards. The process of doing this is very costly.

Another factor that prevents developing countries from gaining access to international markets is that many of them have non-convertible currencies. These are currencies that can only be used domestically and that are not accepted for exchange on the foreign exchange markets. Most developing countries operate a fixed exchange rate system, where the domestic currency is pegged to a more acceptable currency, often the US dollar, at a certain rate.

Non-convertibility means that trade is less likely to occur. Traders would be taking more of a risk dealing in a non-convertible currency and are likely to go elsewhere to conduct their business. The same is true of foreign investment.

Non-convertible currencies are often over-valued at their official, pegged exchange rate. This will usually mean that a black market for the convertible currency will arise and this may be very damaging for the economy. In some cases, the domestic currency will become almost unacceptable within the country and this damages local trade as well as international trade.

Economics in action

ATL Thinking, Communication and Research

Using the Low Human Development country that you chose earlier in the chapter, research possible international trade barriers that may be hindering its growth and development.

How does the existence of an informal economy (informal sector) hinder economic progress?

The informal sector of the economy, also known as the informal economy, or grey economy, is the part of an economy that is neither taxed nor administered by any form of government. The economic activities of the informal economy are not included in a country's gross national income. The International Labour Organization reported that in 2018, 2 billion people, more than 61% of the world's employed population, were making their living in the informal economy.

In Africa, 85.8 percent of employment is informal. The proportion is 68.2 per cent in Asia and the Pacific, 68.6 per cent in the Arab States, 40.0 per cent in the Americas and 25.1 per cent in Europe and Central Asia.

The level of education is a key factor affecting the level of informality. Globally, when the level of education increases, the level of informality decreases. People who have completed secondary and tertiary education are less likely to be in informal employment compared to workers who have either no education or have only completed primary education.

Economics in action

ATL Thinking, Communication and Research

Using the Low Human Development country that you chose earlier in the chapter, research the size of the informal sector in the country. Outline possible problems that the informal sector may present.

People living in rural areas are almost twice as likely to be in informal employment as those in urban areas. Agriculture is the sector with the highest level of informal employment – estimated at more than 90 per cent. Not unsurprisingly, 93 percent of the world's informal employment is in emerging and developing countries.[3]

For workers involved in the informal sector, there is a lack of social protection, rights at work, and decent working conditions. For businesses in the informal sector, there are low levels of productivity and difficulties in accessing investment.

The non-payment of taxes in the informal sector will, obviously, impact upon government revenues and the ability of governments to fund programmes that may lead to economic development, such as education and health care.

How does capital flight hinder economic progress?

Capital flight is the movement of large sums of money out of a country as a reaction to events such as political instability or economic instability. In developing countries, there is often risk involved in holding domestic assets. These risks could include such things as the danger of hyperinflation, the threat of government compulsory purchase of assets, an expected devaluation of the currency or worry regarding the security of the banking industry.

Obviously, any domestic capital that leaves a country could have been used internally and so restricts growth. Also, capital flight may cause a depreciation of the currency as the supply of the domestic currency increases on the international money markets in response to the increased demand for foreign currencies for overseas investment/saving.

How does indebtedness hinder economic progress?

One of the major drawbacks to growth and development in developing countries is the level of debt repayments that these countries have to make on money that was borrowed previously.

Developing countries incur debt whenever borrowing from abroad takes place. This borrowing is mostly carried out by the government, although there is a small amount of private borrowing. As with any loan, although there are short-run positives, in the long run, the amount of the loan (the principal) has to be repaid, along with interest at whatever rate was agreed. The repayment of interest on a loan is known as debt servicing. If interest on an international loan is being paid, then that represents funds leaving the country. The need to service debt means that governments are

[3] Source: *Women and men in the informal economy: a statistical picture*, International Labour Organization, April 2018

unable to spend money on other areas of the economy. This is a case of opportunity cost that has a detrimental effect on two fronts. First, it slows down economic growth. For example, governments do not have funds to invest in improving infrastructure. Second, it slows down development, because governments cannot afford to provide essential services.

Indebtedness has only really been a problem for developing countries in the last fifty years. Before the 1970s, the amount of borrowing by developing countries was low, and tended to be in the form of bilateral official aid at concessionary (very low) interest rates. However, in 1973, the OPEC countries steeply increased oil prices, which led to a massive increase in oil revenues for the oil-exporting countries. These revenues, known as "petro-dollars", were deposited in Western commercial banks and interest rates started to fall sharply because of the large supply of available funds. The banks needed to lend the OPEC money to third parties in order to make profits. There was so much money now available that the usual borrowers did not take the full amount and so the banks offered loans to developing countries.

The developing countries started to borrow money from the Western banks, but these loans were made at market interest rates, not "soft" rates. They were also repayable in "hard" currencies not the currencies of the developing countries. Although the banks lent huge amounts of money they did not monitor what the money was being used for. Unfortunately, relatively little of the money borrowed was used for development purposes. Some went into large infrastructure projects that failed, approximately 20% of the money was spent on arms, and large amounts went into the private bank accounts of dictators, generals and corrupt politicians.

The borrowing by developing countries grew at an alarming rate in the 1970s, but the countries managed to keep up their repayments. However, with a worldwide recession in the early 1980s, there was a sharp fall in the demand for, and prices of, commodities and countries found that they were unable to make their loan repayments. Mexico was the first country in 1982 to default on its loans. The Mexican government said that they could not "service their debt", that is pay back the loan and its interest. Over the next few years, several countries followed Mexico in their inability to repay their debts. By the 1990s, there was what came to be known as the "Third World Debt Crisis".

In 1996, the World Bank and the International Monetary Fund (IMF) launched a new program. This was known as the Heavily Indebted Poor Countries (HIPC) Initiative. The program was reviewed and modified in 1999 and, in 2005, it was supplemented by the Multilateral Debt Relief Initiative, in order to accelerate progress towards meeting the Millennium Development Goals.

As with earlier programmes, assistance under the HIPC Initiative is conditional upon the governments of the countries in question achieving certain criteria, committing to poverty reduction through policy changes and demonstrating a "good track-record" over time. The conditions that must be met, ie the criteria, and changes have been the subject of much debate.

Up to 2019, debt reduction packages have been approved for 36 countries, 30 of them in Africa, providing $76 billion in debt-relief over time. Three additional countries are eligible for HIPC Initiative assistance.

Even now, many developing countries still have major problems with indebtedness. Figures released by the Jubilee Debt Campaign, based on IMF and World Bank databases, show that developing country debt payments increased by 60% between 2014 and 2017.

Zambia sacrificing social sector spending to avoid debt default

https://www.themastonline.com/2019/09/02/zambia-sacrificing-social-sector-spending-to-avoid-debt-default-saasa/

Average government external debt repayments in the 126 developing countries where data was available increased from 6.7% of government revenue in 2014 to 10.7% in 2017. The rapid increase came after a lending boom due to global interest rates being very low following the 2008 global financial crisis. External loans to developing countries rose from $200 billion per year in 2008 to $390 billion in 2014. From 2015 to 2017, they fell back to around $325 per year, a figure well above the levels before the 2008 crisis.

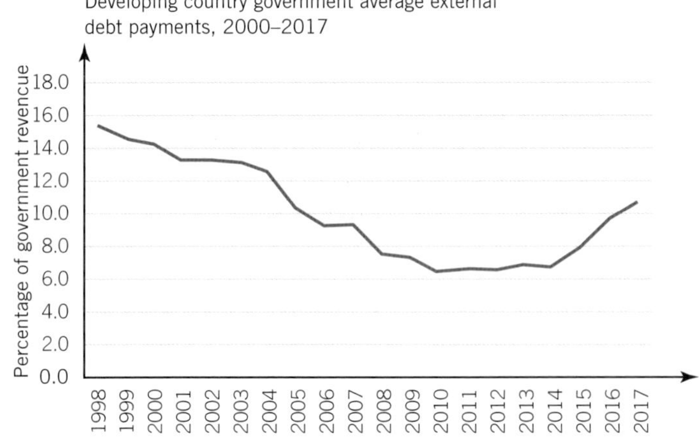

▶ Figure 30.4 External debt payments for developing countries

Source: Jubilee Debt, 2019

Figure 30.4 shows average external debt payments (as a percentage of government revenue) by developing countries between 2000 and 2017. Developing country external debt payments fell between 2000 and 2010, because of the rising prices of commodities on the world markets and the HIPC Initiative, which cancelled almost $130 billion of debts for the 36 approved developing countries.

Commodity prices reached a high in the middle of 2014, but then collapsed over the next 18 months. They reached a low in early 2016 and have recovered to some extent, but they are still 40% lower that they were in 2014. The fall in world commodity prices in 2014 reduced the incomes of many developing country governments and, in addition, this has caused exchange rates to fall against the US dollar, which increases the size of the debt repayments, because external debts are most commonly settled in US dollars. There are grave concerns that rising interest rates in developed countries will further worsen the ability of developing countries to service their debts.

The IMF states that in 2017, of 67 impoverished states that they assess, 30 are now in debt distress or are at a high risk of being so. This has doubled from 15 countries in 2013. Table 30.4 shows the top ten countries with the highest levels of debt relief as a percentage of government revenue.

Country	External government debt payments as a proportion of revenue % (2017)	Particular issues	Recipient of HIPC debt relief
Angola	55.4	Oil exporter	No
Lebanon	44.1	Ongoing debt crisis, Syrian refugees	No
Ghana	42.4	Oil and gold exporter	Yes
Chad	39.7	Oil exporter	Yes
Bhutan	34.0	Small state, large debts linked to hydropower	No
Gabon	26.9	Oil exporter	No
Tunisia	26.7	Inherited dictator debts	No
Jamaica	26.0	Small state, high debt for many years but no meaningful cancellation	No
Grenada	25.0	Small state, high debt since hurricanes in 2004 and 2005	No
Sri Lanka	24.5	High debt for many years but no meaningful cancellation	No

Source: Adapted from *Debt Sustainability Analysis Low-Income Countries*, IMF, 2019

▲ Table 30.4 Countries with highest debt payments as percentage of government revenue

Economics in action

ATL Thinking, Communication and Research

Research one of the Heavily Indebted Poor Countries to understand the causes and consequences of a high level of indebtedness. Investigate possible solutions to the problem for this country.

How do geographical factors hinder economic progress?

We shall look at two geographical factors here:

1. *Landlocked countries* – Landlocked countries trade less and have slower growth rates than countries that have coasts. The countries pay more and have to wait a longer time for imports to be delivered and they also have problems in exporting. Transport costs add to the cost of their exports and then there may be other costs, such as bribery and border delays. 16 of the world's 31 landlocked developing countries are among the poorest in the world.[4]
2. *Tropical climates and endemic diseases* – Countries that are in the tropics tend to be less developed and their geographical location is a factor in this. The development of production technology in the tropical zone has been far slower than in the temperate zone for two key areas, agriculture and health.

Bolivia landlocked: How lack of ports hinders economic growth

https://theconversation.com/bolivia-landlocked-how-lack-of-ports-hinders-economic-growth-104672

[4] Source: *"The Cost of Being Landlocked: Logistics Costs and Supply Chain Reliability,"*, World Bank, 2017.

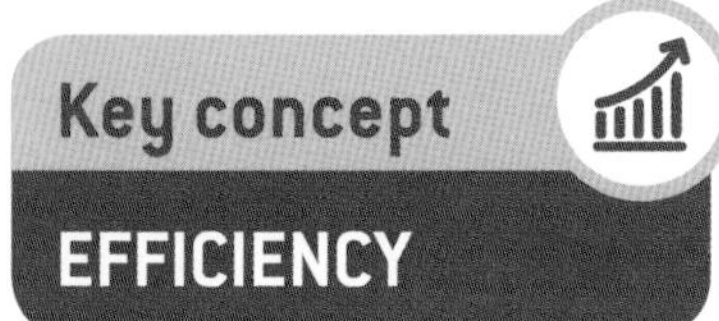

Agricultural productivity in major crops, such as maize, rice and wheat, is significantly lower in tropical countries than in temperate countries. The economist, Jeffrey Sachs, estimated that in 1995, productivity in grain production was approximately 50 percent higher in temperate zone countries than in tropical zone countries[5]. The explanation includes such things as soil formation and erosion, pests and parasites, water availability and the effects of tropical climates on plant respiration. The lower productivity may lead to poor nutrition and thus poor health, affecting the quality of the human resources.

The prevalence of disease is considerably higher in the tropical zone than in the temperate zones. Vector-borne diseases, such as malaria and helminthic infections caused by worms are common in tropical climates and have proven to be hard to control. Again, this affects the quality of human resources.

It is worth noting that countries that are both landlocked and tropical – including Bolivia, Chad, Niger, Mali, Burkina Faso, Uganda, Rwanda, Burundi, Central African Republic, Zimbabwe, Zambia, Lesotho and Laos – are amongst some of the poorest in the world.

What are the political and social barriers to development?

There are a number of political and social barriers to development that we should consider.

How does a weak institutional framework hinder economic progress?

- **Legal system and property rights**

  An honest and fully functioning legal system is almost essential if development is to be achieved. In many developing countries the legal system does not function well. Where this is the case there is no way to create and enforce contracts and there is no way to uphold property rights. Social scientists consider property rights to be essentially a "basket" of legal rights. This basket includes:

  → the right to own assets, such as land or buildings
  → the right to establish the use of our assets, such as adding to the building – for example an owner might want to add sanitation to a house
  → the right to benefit from our assets, such as renting out our land
  → the right to sell our assets
  → the right to exclude others from using or taking over our assets.

[5] Source: *Tropical Underdevelopment (NBER Working Paper No. 8119)*, Jeffrey Sachs, February 2001

Property rights allow people to own and benefit from private property, so long as the legal system and security system can support and protect these rights. If a person cannot guarantee his or her ownership of a property, then there is no incentive to improve that property, since it is possible that the property will then be lost and the investment will have been wasted. If there are no enforceable property rights, as may be the case in many developing countries, then investment and growth will be very much reduced and economic growth may be limited. Development will be thwarted for all of the reasons above.

Peruvian economist, Hernando de Soto uses the term 'dead capital' to refer to assets that cannot easily be bought, sold, valued or used as an investment because no one actually owns them or has the **right** to exchange them. De Soto points out that despite obvious poverty, people in developing countries actually have enormous assets, but they don't formally own them. That is, they lack formal property rights.

Low tax collection in developing economies has a more devastating impact than we thought

https://qz.com/africa/1573957/developing-countries-will-benefit-from-better-tax-collection/

People in more developed countries generally enjoy a legal system which guarantees the establishment and maintenance of property rights. This means that they have the right to own property and know that the legal system will honour and protect their property. Private property rights are important for three reasons. Firstly, when people own property, they can use their initiative and entrepreneurial skills to earn an income from the property. Secondly, when people own property, they have the incentive to improve the value of these assets because they know that if they sell these assets, they will earn the profit from the increased value (the 'capital gains'). Thirdly, when they own property such as a home, they can use their property as collateral to secure a loan from the bank and they can use this loan to start a business.

Nigeria: Strengthening Anti-Corruption War

https://allafrica.com/stories/201908150440.html

De Soto argues that the lack of property rights traps people in developing countries in poverty. Despite substantial capital, the lack of property rights means that the capital is 'dead' and can't be used to improve their well-being.

- **Ineffective taxation structure**

  Tax revenue provides governments with the means to finance necessary public services, such as education and health care, and generally to improve the infrastructure of the country. However, this is very difficult to do if governments do not earn a great deal of tax revenue.

  It is very difficult for governments to collect tax revenue in developing countries. We can consider reasons for this. Firstly, as a result of tax exemptions and inefficient or corrupt administration, it is estimated that less than 3% of the populations in developing countries pay income tax, as opposed to 60% – 80% in developed countries. Secondly, corporate tax revenues tend to be low, since there is relatively little corporate activity in developing countries (although it is growing) and they also often offer large tax incentives in order to encourage domestic corporate activity and to attract FDI.

Resource-rich DR Congo, a country wracked by political instability and violence

https://www.france24.com/en/20181220-dr-congo-drc-kabila-violence-election-ebola-africa-cholera-resource

Thirdly, the main source of tax revenue in developing countries comes from export, import and excise (customs) duties. These taxes are relatively easy to collect, since they are paid when the goods pass through the country's border posts. However, it is only possible to gain significant tax revenue if the country is heavily involved in foreign trade. It is worth noting that the international trading system through the WTO, with its emphasis on liberalization of trade, may have negative implications for countries that do earn significant revenue from tariffs. Finally, as has been stated above, developing countries have problems with the administration of their tax systems in terms of inefficiency, lack of information and pure corruption. These elements, when combined, often mean that people are able to evade paying the taxes that they should.

Another factor that needs to be considered is the size of the informal market. When we looked at informal markets earlier in the chapter, we discovered that the size of informal markets as a percentage of GDP is far greater in developing countries than in developed countries. It would also appear that informal markets are growing in almost all countries in the world.

Large informal markets lead to much lower tax revenues for governments in developing countries. If the incomes of people are not recorded because they are earned in informal markets, then there will be no tax paid on such income. Lower tax revenues make it difficult for governments to promote growth and achieve development objectives.

- **Banking system**

  Developed and independent financial institutions are essential, if economic growth and development is to be achieved, and these are often underprovided in developing countries. Most developing countries have what is known as dual financial markets. Financial markets may be defined as the institutions where lending and borrowing is carried out. The "official" financial markets are small and tend to be dominated by foreign commercial banks, which often have an outward looking emphasis to their operations and restrict their lending to foreign businesses and the already established large manufacturing local businesses. The "unofficial" markets are not legally controlled and are thus illegal. Their main operation is to lend money, usually at very high interest rates, to those who are desperate and poor enough to have to borrow it.

  Saving is necessary to make funds available for investment and investment is necessary for economic growth. Saving is difficult enough in countries where there are high levels of poverty, but it is even harder if there is nowhere to save money that is safe and will give a good return. When there are weak and untrustworthy financial institutions, people with investment income tend to buy assets, such as livestock, or they tend to invest their money outside the country (capital flight).

Financial services are necessary if low-income people are to be able to manage their assets and to allow them to increase in value, thus enabling them to then invest in things that will lead to their economic development, such as health care, shelter and education. The difficulties associated with saving and borrowing money are a significant barrier to economic growth and development. It makes it exceedingly difficult for poor people to raise themselves out of poverty.

In developing countries poor people find it almost impossible to gain access to traditional banking and financial systems, since they lack assets to use as collateral, are often unemployed, and lack savings. Therefore, even if there is great entrepreneurial spirit, it is very difficult for people to start up businesses. If they can find a way to borrow money it is often at exorbitant interest rates.

How does gender inequality hinder economic progress?

We have already come across some of the problems associated with gender inequality in Chapter 22. In many developing countries the role of women is very much subservient to that of men. There is no doubt that giving women more empowerment, especially in terms of education, as stated earlier, could be a huge factor in the achievement of economic development. As such, it is clear that the lack of empowerment is a huge factor hindering development.

Improving the welfare of women through greater education and improved social standing obviously leads to economic development for the women themselves. However, there are also extremely important externalities that occur when women become more empowered.

- The well-being of their families is improved, especially in terms of the health of their children. With improved education, women are better informed about health care, hygiene and diet, all of which improve the welfare of the family.
- The education of children in the family group improves. The women pass on their own education and also see education as being more important, thus striving to achieve it for their children.
- Because of the two points above, the quality of the workforce in the country will, over time, improve, with significant effects upon growth and development.
- With greater empowerment women earn more money. Research shows that increases in the levels of income of women in developing countries lead to greater increases in health levels of families than similar increases in the income levels of men.
- With better education and social standing women have more control over contraception, marry later, and so tend to have smaller families, thus lowering the rate of population growth.

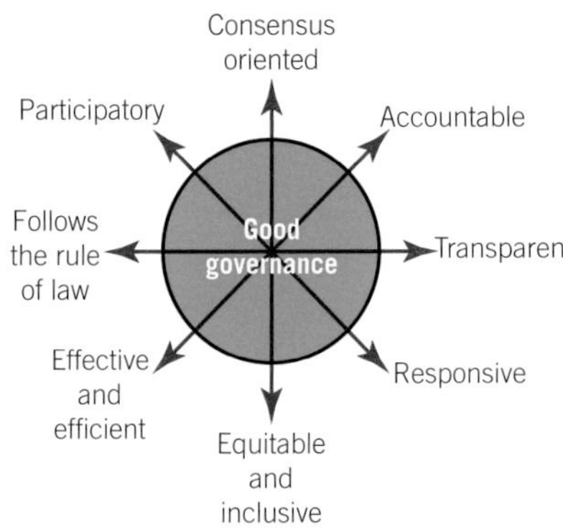

▲ **Figure 30.5** The elements of good governance

Exercise 30.3
ATL Thinking and Communication

Identify the elements of good governance that would be missing in the list above.

How do a lack of good governance and corruption hinder economic progress?

It may be argued that good governance has eight elements. It is deemed to be participatory, equitable and inclusive, responsive, consensus oriented, effective and efficient, accountable, transparent and lawful.

A lack of good governance can have many damaging effects, including corruption, political instability, and unequal political power and status, all of which can threaten economic growth and development.

1. **Corruption**

   Corruption is defined here as the dishonest exploitation of power for personal gain. It poses a huge challenge to economic growth, economic development, and sustainable development. Corruption occurs in every country in the world, to some extent. It tends to be most prevalent where:

   - governments are not accountable to the people, especially military governments
   - governments spend large amounts on large-scale capital investment projects
   - official accounting practices are not well formulated or controlled
   - government officials are not well paid
   - political elections are not well controlled, or are non-existent, ie there is no democracy
   - the legal structure is weak
   - freedom of speech is lacking.

Unfortunately, many of these conditions are to be found in a high proportion of developing countries. This may explain the high levels of corruption that exist in many countries.

There are many forms of corruption. These include bribery, extortion, fraud, patronage, influence peddling and nepotism. The effects of corruption are likely to hinder growth and development with a number of causative factors.

- Electoral corruption means that the wishes of the people are not heeded. This will put a government in place that has not been voted for by the majority. It is likely that such a government will not adopt policies to benefit the electorate. Governance will not be equitable or inclusive.
- Corruption of any sort reduces the effectiveness of the legal system. If people can "buy" their way out of trouble there may be an incentive to act illegally.
- Corruption leads to an unfair allocation of resources. If contracts go to the highest bidder, as opposed to the most efficient producer, then there is a market failure and resources are being misallocated. It often sustains inefficient producers, by shielding them from competition. It hinders sustainable development.

- Bribes increase the costs of businesses, in cash terms and in terms of management negotiation time. This will invariably lead to higher prices.
- Corruption reduces trust in an economy. As a result, countries may find it harder to attract foreign investment, which will often be diverted to less corrupt countries.
- Corruption increases the risk of contracts not being honoured and this, in turn, acts as a serious deterrent to investment, both internal and external.
- Corruption means that officials will often divert public investment into capital projects where bribes are more likely. This tends not to be important areas, such as education and health care, so it reduces the quality of government services for the people.
- Corruption often means that officials turn a blind eye to regulations, such as those regarding construction or the environment. This can obviously have a damaging effect on individuals and the country as a whole. Again, it hinders sustainable development.
- The monetary gains from corruption are often moved out of the country. This is a form of capital flight and it reduces the capital available for internal investment.
- The constant paying of small bribes reduces the economic well being of the ordinary citizen.

Transparency International publishes a yearly Corruption Perceptions Index (CPI). The index, which ranks 180 countries and territories by their perceived levels of public sector corruption, according to experts and businesspeople, uses a scale of zero to 100, where zero is highly corrupt and 100 is very clean. The top and bottom countries are shown in Figure 30.6.

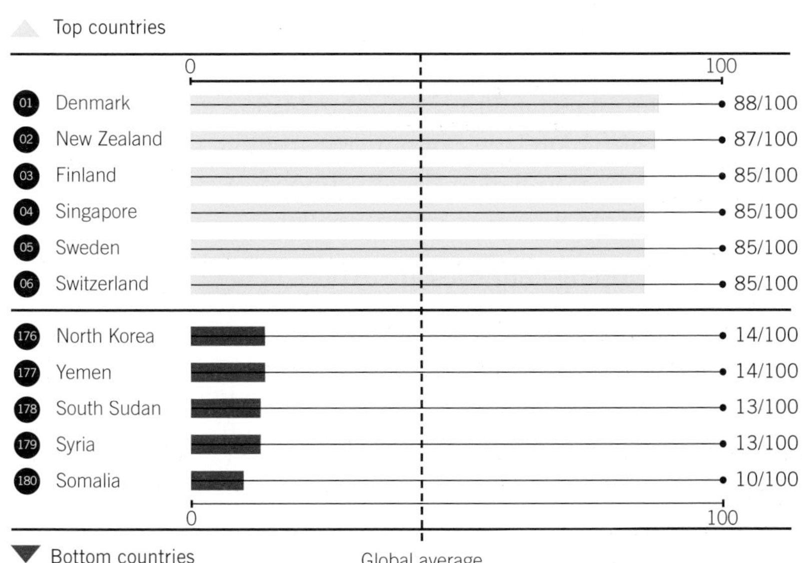

Source: Transparency International, 2019, www.transparency.org

▲ **Figure 30.6** Top and bottom countries in the Corruption Perceptions Index 2019

Economics in action

ATL Thinking, Communication and Research

a) Go to the Transparency International website.
b) Select five different countries with different levels of economic development.
c) Research the trends in the CPI index between 2015 and the present day.
d) Comment upon your findings.

In 2019, two-thirds of countries scored below 50 on the CPI, with an average score of just 43. While there are exceptions, the data shows that despite some progress, most countries are failing to make serious inroads against corruption.

There is no doubt that corruption disproportionately affects vulnerable populations and hits the poor the hardest, especially women, who represent a higher share of the world's poor. In their traditional role as caregivers in many parts of the world, women constantly experience corruption in their daily lives—from interactions with school officials to health care providers. Corruption presents a barrier for women to gain full access to their civic, social and economic rights. Corruption affecting women has an impact at both the global and local level.

2. Political instability

Countries that have political stability are more likely to attract Foreign Direct Investment (FDI) and aid, and it is more likely that domestic savings and profits will stay in the country and be able to contribute to the economy. Increased access to FDI may be more likely to contribute to increased growth rather than development, but increased access to aid may increase development.

When there is political stability, citizens are more likely to have an input into the running of the country. Government planning is likely to be more structured and long-term and the law is likely to be more enforceable. All of these elements of good governance should lead to higher living standards for the population.

Political instability causes uncertainty and, at its most extreme, complete economic breakdown. Sudan, in Africa, is a case in point. Civil wars from 1955 to 1972, and then from 1983 to 2005, had a devastating economic and social impact. South Sudan was given independence in 2011, but tribal civil unrest reappeared in 2013 and, in the following five years, there were more than 50,000 deaths and one quarter of the population was displaced. Such extreme political instability is bound to lead to very poor economic performance and also high levels of poverty and low standards of living for the majority of the population. The likelihood of attracting foreign investment, or even aid, becomes much smaller.

A number of developing countries are experiencing civil wars as a result of ethnic and/or religious conflict or border conflicts. For example, since 2003, there have been ethnic and/or religious based conflicts, internal or external, in Afghanistan, Armenia, Azerbaijan, Bahrain, Cameroon, Central African Republic, Chad, Côte d'Ivoire, Democratic Republic of Congo, India, Iran,Iraq, Israel, Kyrgyzstan, Lebanon, Libya, Mali, Mozambique, Nigeria, Pakistan, Palestine, Paraguay, Russia, Somalia, South Sudan, Syria, Tunisia, Turkey, Ukraine and Yemen. The loss of life, damage to infrastructure, loss of investment and sometimes aid, and political instability have undoubtedly hindered, if not stopped, economic growth and development in these countries.

3. Unequal political power and status

As was stated in Chapter 22, where the ownership of resources and income in an economy are concentrated among a small percentage of the population, as is very much the case in developing countries, those wealthier people may have a disproportionate say in the development of government policies. Many developing countries have a lack of democracy and the governments fail to display most, if not all, of the elements of good governance. Politicians, when in power, are more likely to develop policies that are in their own interests and not in the interests of the lower income citizens.

In addition, low income people are also less likely to become involved in the political process. They may lack the background, the education, the social networks, or they may simply lack the time to engage in political activities. As a result, the 'voice' of low income people may not be adequately represented in government policy. This can be a significant barrier to economic development.

EXAMINATION QUESTIONS

Paper 1, part (a) questions – HL & SL

1. Explain, using **two** examples, poverty traps/ poverty cycles. [10 marks]
2. Explain **three** economic barriers to development. [10 marks]
3. Explain **three** political and social barriers to development. [10 marks]

Paper 1, part (b) questions – HL & SL

1. Using real-world examples, discuss the significance of any **two** of the following as barriers to development: the informal economy, indebtedness, a weak institutional framework, lack of good governance and corruption. [15 marks]

Economics in action

ATL Thinking, Communication and Research

Group activity

1. Half the members of the class should each select a Medium Human Development country and the other half should each select a Low Human Development country. This will ensure a range of examples.
2. Each person should research their country of choice, identifying economic, political and social barriers to development.
3. Each person should then rank the significance of the different barriers for their country.
4. Each person should then prepare a short presentation to share with the rest of the class.
5. The class should then discuss the group findings and identify common barriers to development in the countries considered.

31 STRATEGIES TO PROMOTE ECONOMIC GROWTH AND ECONOMIC DEVELOPMENT

REAL-WORLD ISSUE:
Why is economic development uneven?

By the end of this chapter, you should be able to:

Explain and evaluate the role of each of the following in achieving economic growth and development:

- → Trade strategies, including import substitution, export promotion and economic integration
- → Diversification
- → Market based supply-side policies
- → Foreign direct investment
- → Social enterprise
- → Redistribution policies
- → Merit goods
- → Institutional change
- → Foreign aid, including official development assistance, non-governmental organisations and multilateral development assistance
- → Debt relief.

In Chapter 30, we considered the barriers to economic growth and economic development. Now, we need to consider different strategies that might reduce or eliminate those barriers and enable developing countries to achieve economic progress. You must always be aware that economic growth is a one-dimensional concept relating only to an increase in real GDP. In contrast, economic development is a multidimensional concept relating to a myriad of improvements in well being. The importance of economic growth is not being questioned here. As noted in the Sustainable Development Goals, "Economic growth **can** lead to new and better employment opportunities and provide greater economic security for all"[1]. The word 'can' is key here. Economic growth will not contribute to economic development if the benefits of the growth are not shared equitably. Thus, the priority must be to achieve *inclusive growth* and adopt *'pro-poor' strategies* that directly confront the problem of poverty.

Economics in action — ATL Thinking, Communication and Research

In this section, we present a range of strategies, with just a few real-world examples, Therefore, for each strategy, it is expected that you will research your own real-world examples, so that you can come to your own conclusions about the strengths and limitations of the strategies in different contexts.

What strategies will enable the achievement of economic growth and/or economic development?

How can trade strategies be used to achieve economic growth and/or development?

International trade can undoubtedly contribute to economic growth and, when well-regulated, can definitely result in economic development. We look here at three different approaches that countries may adopt:

1. **Import substitution**

   Import substitution is more fully known as import substitution industrialization (ISI). It may also be referred to as an inward-oriented strategy. It is a strategy that says that a developing country should, wherever possible, produce goods domestically, rather than import them. This should mean that the industries producing the goods domestically will be able to grow, as will the economy, and then the industries will be able to be competitive on world markets in the future, as they gain from economies of scale. It is the opposite of export-led growth and is not supported by those economists who believe in the advantages of free trade based on comparative advantage.

   In order for the strategy to work there are some necessary conditions:

   - The government needs to adopt a policy of organizing the selection of goods to produce domestically. Historically, this has been labour-intensive, low-skill manufactured goods, such as clothing or shoes.

[1] **Source:** United Nations Statistics Division, Goal 8, https://unstats.un.org/sdgs/report/2016/goal-08/

- Subsidies are made available to encourage domestic industries.
- The government needs to implement a protectionist system with tariff barriers to keep out foreign imports.

There are a number of perceived advantages and disadvantages with ISI:

Investment projects for import substitution to be implemented in Kazakhstan

https://en.trend.az/business/economy/3109530.html

Advantages

- ➔ ISI protects jobs in the domestic market, since foreign firms are prevented from competing, which means that domestic firms can dominate the market.
- ➔ ISI protects the local culture and social habits by practically isolating the economy from foreign influence.
- ➔ ISI protects the economy from the power, and possibly bad influence, of multinational corporations.

Disadvantages

- ➔ ISI may only protect jobs in the short run. In the long run, economic growth may be lower in the economy and the lack of growth may lead to a lack of job creation.
- ➔ ISI means that the country does not enjoy the benefits to be gained from comparative advantage and specialization, so producing products relatively inefficiently, when they could be imported from efficient foreign producers.
- ➔ ISI may lead to inefficiency in domestic industries, because competition is not there to encourage research and development.
- ➔ ISI may lead to high rates of inflation due to domestic aggregate supply constraints.
- ➔ ISI may cause other countries to take retaliatory protectionist measures.

The main countries to adopt ISI strategies were in Latin America, including Argentina, Brazil, Mexico, Chile and Uruguay. As former colonies gained their independence many also adopted inward-oriented strategies. These included India, Nigeria and Kenya. These policies showed some success in the 1960s and 1970s, but the policies started to fail in the early 1980s and were abandoned. At the present time, ISI does not seem to be a chosen option for economic growth.

2. Export promotion

Export promotion, often called export-led growth, is an outward-oriented growth strategy, based on openness and increased international trade. It is where growth is achieved by concentrating on increasing exports and export revenue as a leading factor in the aggregate demand of the country. Increasing exports should lead to increasing GDP and this in turn should lead to higher incomes and, eventually, growth in domestic and exporting markets. The country concentrates on producing and exporting products in which it has a comparative advantage of production. In addition, the country may attempt to 'manage' its exchange rate, keeping the rate as low as possible against other currencies and thus making its exports more attractive.

In order to achieve export-led growth, it is assumed that a country will need to adopt certain policies. These include:

- Liberalized trade: Open up domestic markets to foreign competition in order to gain access to foreign markets.
- Liberalized capital flows: Reduce restrictions on foreign direct investment.
- A floating exchange rate.
- Investment in the provision of infrastructure to enable trade to take place.
- Deregulation and minimal government intervention.

The list illustrates the theoretical "package" of policies associated with export-led growth. In reality, countries that adopt an outward-oriented strategy do not necessarily adopt all of these policies.

Developing countries may attempt to export either primary products and/or manufactured products (some have tried to export services, usually in the form of tourism). We should consider the differences involved in using the export of primary or manufactured products as the engine for growth.

- Many developing countries depend upon the export of primary products in order to gain export revenue. However, the overall trend in primary product prices, with the exception of oil and some metals, has been downward for many years. This is due to increasing supply and relatively insignificant increases in demand for many commodities. This, combined with increased protectionism by developed countries, means that export-led growth based on the export of primary products is unlikely to be achieved.
- The focus of export-led growth is usually on increasing manufacturing exports. The historic success of countries such as Japan, South Korea, Hong Kong, Singapore and Taiwan, known as the "Asian tigers", is usually used to illustrate the effectiveness of such a strategy. These countries exported products in which they had a comparative advantage, usually based upon low-cost labour, and were extremely successful in doing so. Over time, the type of product being exported by the majority of these countries has also tended to change from products that were produced using labour-intensive production methods, requiring low skill levels from the workers, to more sophisticated products, using capital-intensive production methods and more highly skilled workers. Improvements in education systems were essential for this.

Although it would appear that export-led growth is an obvious way to gain success, this is not necessarily the case. There are a number of problems associated with export-led growth:

- The success of the "Asian tigers", since around 1965, and the emergence of China as an exporting powerhouse, has led to increased protectionism in developed countries against manufactured products from developing countries. Trade unions and workers in developed countries argued that they could not compete against the imports from low-wage developing countries and that this was unfair. They lobbied their governments to put tariffs and quotas on the lower-priced goods. Price increases as a result of tariffs effectively removed the comparative advantage of the exporting countries. *Tariff escalation* also reduced the ability of the developing countries to export processed goods and assembled products, forcing many to export primary products and low-skilled manufactured goods instead.
- Certain assumptions were made about the necessary conditions for export-led growth. If we look at the successful countries, these conditions were not necessarily met. Many economists would argue that the role of the state in successful export-led growth is vital and that minimizing government intervention is not the way forward. In the "Asian tiger" countries, governments played an important role by providing infrastructure, subsidizing output through low credit terms via central banks, and promoting savings and improvements in technology. In addition, governments adopted policies where they protected domestic industries that were not yet able to compete with foreign firms and promoted the industries that were ready for competition in export markets. This illustrates the "infant industry" argument for protection. This topic is one of great debate amongst development economists and many argue that intervention is vital. Others argue that state intervention in these economies actually slowed down growth rates.

- If countries attempt to kick-start their export-led growth by attracting MNCs, there is always the fear that the MNCs may become too powerful within the country and that this may lead to problems.
- It is argued by some economists that free-market, export-led growth may increase income inequality in the country. If this is the case, then economic growth may be achieved at the expense of economic development.

Nigeria eager to implement free continental trade agreement

https://www.africanews.com/2019/07/29/nigeria-eager-to-implement-free-continental-trade-agreement/

3. **Economic integration**

Over the past decades, developing countries have been involved in many preferential access schemes and regional free-trade agreements. Such agreements offer important opportunities for countries to achieve economic growth and development. However, there are also challenges. To a large extent, the opportunities and challenges depend on the extent of the integration. That is, whether the integration is simply preferential access for particular goods, a free-trade area, a customs union or a common market.

Possible advantages/opportunities associate with economic integration:

- Larger export markets, may allow producers to gain economies of scale.
- Larger markets may encourage diversification and reduce dependence on a narrow range of commodities.
- Integration is likely to encourage regional cooperation in areas such as infrastructure, including transport and telecommunications.
- For landlocked countries, regional integration may offer vital links to ports and other infrastructure networks in neighbouring countries.
- There should be further stimulus for inward foreign direct investment, as foreign companies will benefit from the larger market size.
- If there is free movement of labour, this provides opportunities for workers to work in other member countries, and send remittances home.
- If there is free movement of capital, integration provides opportunities for companies to invest in other member countries.
- There may be greater political stability and cooperation, which can result in higher levels of investment.
- Greater efficiency as domestic producers will have to compete with lower priced imports from other member countries.
- As part of a trading bloc, individual countries may increase their bargaining power in multilateral trade negotiations.
- Consumers may have access to less expensive imported goods and services. (However, this might be limited if trade diversion takes place and the new common external tariff makes some imported products more expensive **HL only**).
- Trade creation will benefit producers who can import inputs without tariffs (**HL only**).

Possible disadvantages/challenges associated with economic integration

- The role of the WTO might be undermined, since it allows member countries to look inwards.
- Trade can become more complicated with agreements with other trading blocs.
- Unemployment may arise, as less efficient companies (with higher labour costs), may not be able to compete with lower priced imports from other member countries.
- We may encounter trade diversion (**HL only**).

What is "aid-for-trade"?

In recognising the vast opportunities that trade offers in terms of growth **and** poverty reduction, the 2030 Agenda for Sustainable Development is calling for increasing "aid-for-trade" support for developing countries. The Aid for Trade initiative was launched in 2006 through the World Trade Organisation, and aims to provide:

- technical assistance to help countries negotiate trade strategies and implement outcomes of trade negotiations
- transport infrastructure to connect domestic and international markets and storage facilities
- support for agriculture, energy generation and supply
- investment in industries so that countries can diversify and build on comparative advantage
- adjustment assistance to help with the costs associated with tariff reductions and loss of preferential treatment.

Although there is no specific trade goal within the SDGs, there are around 20 targets in different SDGs that relate directly to international trade. Importantly, Target 8.A calls to "increase aid-for-trade support for developing countries, in particular least developed countries".

With such attention and international cooperation in expanding trade capacities and access to developing countries, it is hoped that trade will be a positive force for economic growth and poverty reduction.

Higher Level

Economics in action — ATL Thinking, Communication and Research

There are many examples of regional economic integration (trade blocs) among developing countries. Find an example and identify the challenges and opportunities that membership in the bloc brings to its members. How might "aid-for-trade" help to overcome the challenges?

How might diversification of economic activity help to achieve economic growth and/or development?

As we have already discovered, one major problem for a number of developing countries has been over-dependence upon exporting a limited range of primary commodities. In many cases countries have been dependent upon export earnings from one, or possibly two, commodities.

The Advancing Economic Diversification in Ethiopia Project launches

https://www.africanews.com/2019/08/23/launch-of-the-advancing-economic-diversification-in-ethiopia-project/

Many countries are now pursuing export diversification as a means to gain economic growth. The aim is to move from the production and export of primary commodities and to replace these with the production and export of manufactured and semi-manufactured products. In doing this they hope to protect themselves from the volatile changes in primary product prices, to stabilize or increase export revenue and to stabilize or increase employment. There will also be an increased use of technology and an increased demand for more highly skilled workers.

There are a number of barriers to the strategy of diversification. One is the practice of tariff escalation, whereby the rate of import tariffs on goods rises the more the goods are processed. So, the importing country protects its processing and manufacturing industries by putting lower tariffs on imports of raw materials and components and higher tariffs on processed and finished products. There is little incentive for developing countries to diversify away from producing raw materials to processing them, as the higher prices caused by the tariffs will make their processed goods uncompetitive.

A second barrier is the need for a more highly qualified workforce in order to produce relatively more sophisticated products. As we already know, many developing countries have relatively low educational standards and find it difficult to fund an improving educational system. If this is the case, then the country is in a poverty trap. Low education leads to the production of low profit commodities and components, which leads to low incomes for governments and individuals, which perpetuates the low ability to fund education.

How can market-based supply-side policies impact economic growth and/or development?

There are three market-based supply-side policies that are most often put forward as a means of achieving economic growth. These are:

1. **Trade liberalization**

   Trade liberalization is the removal, or at least reduction, of trade barriers that block the free trade of goods and services between countries. It involves the elimination of such things as tariff barriers, quotas, export subsidies and administrative legislation.

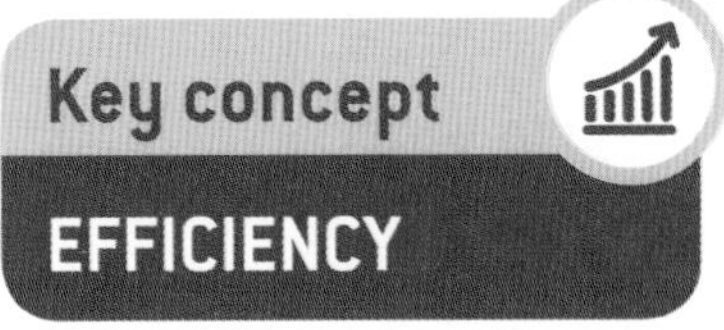

   The belief is that trade liberalization will increase world trade and will enable developing countries to concentrate on the production of goods and services in which they have a comparative advantage. The advantages of free trade are covered in Chapter 23.

   However, many developing countries and in particular, the least developed countries, lack the infrastructure and institutions that are necessary to gain the full benefits from trade liberalization. In addition, protectionist policies employed by developed countries to block developing countries from exporting higher-value manufactured goods can reduce the effectiveness of trade liberalization for developing countries. Subsidies given by developed country governments to their producers can also damage the ability of producers from developing countries to compete in international markets.

   The challenges that developing countries face in terms of benefiting from trade liberalisation underscore the need for international cooperation through aid-for-trade strategies.

2. **Privatization**

   This is the sale of public government-owned firms (nationalized firms) to the private sector. It is argued by free market economists that privately-owned, profit-maximizing firms will be more efficient than nationalized firms and will therefore increase the potential output of the economy. Nationalized firms tend to have different goals from private firms, such as maintenance of employment or the provision of a service to an isolated market, and this means that they may operate inefficiently.

   However, privatization will only generate economic gains if the process is carried out and managed well. The process of privatization requires careful design and sequencing, the creation of a regulatory infrastructure, assessment of possible poverty and social impacts, and transparent public communication. This is often challenging in developing countries.

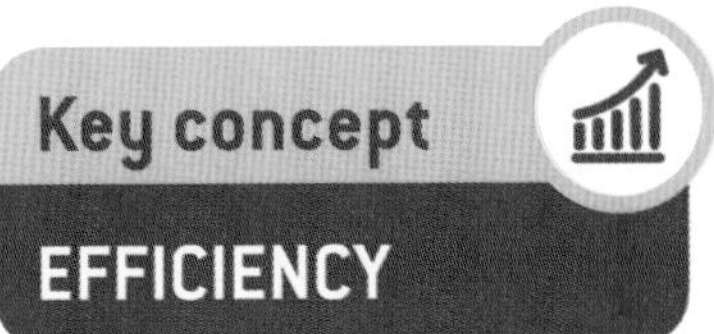

   Furthermore, it may be necessary for some goods and services to be provided by nationalized firms in order that they be accessible and affordable to everyone, particularly low income people. Should such industries be privatized, the result might be that certain operations are closed down because they are not profit-marking, or the price of the product might become unaffordable.

Civil society fights Jakarta water privatization during Annual Meetings in Bali

https://www.brettonwoodsproject.org/2018/09/civil-society-fights-jakarta-water-privatisation-annual-meetings-bali/

Consider the case of the provision of water and sanitation. Access to safe and affordable drinking water and sanitation is seen as a human right, and is an essential feature of any fight against poverty. Given the huge expense of providing such infrastructure, governments in developing countries have often turned to the private sector. Indeed, in some examples, governments were required to privatize such sectors in order to receive support from international agencies. Given that private companies have the financial resources to undertake the large investments necessary for such infrastructure projects, it is not difficult to see why privatization is an appealing option for cash-strapped governments. However, left purely to market forces, a lack of competition and regulation in the water industry means that the development goal of increased access to water at affordable prices is unlikely to be met. Therefore, if such an industry is to be privatized, it is necessary that the government is involved in establishing and enforcing regulations to ensure that the goal of providing safe and affordable water is reached.

3. **Deregulation**

   As we know from Chapter 15, if governments have placed many regulations on the operations of businesses then this may increase their costs of production, thereby reducing potential output in the economy. Such regulations include environmental laws, health and safety regulations or laws concerning working hours, leave and holidays. A reduction in the number and/or the severity of regulations, ie deregulation, will help to increase aggregate supply and thus generate economic growth.

Key concept

EFFICIENCY

In many developing countries, there is much 'red tape' involved when starting up a business and, if this is the case, then it will deter both domestic and foreign investors. Reducing the difficulty of the process may well increase investment.

The World Bank *Ease of Doing Business Index* measures how simple it is to conduct business in a country. The ease of doing business score measures the gap between an economy's performance and a measure of best practice across 41 indicators for 10 Doing Business topics. The topics considered are Starting a business; Dealing with construction permits; Getting electricity; Registering property; Getting credit; Protecting minority investors; Paying taxes; Trading across borders; Enforcing contracts; and Resolving insolvency. Table 31.1 shows a selection of figures for 2018 and 2019.

Country (DB rank)	Doing business score 2018	Doing business score 2019
New Zealand (1)	86.6	86.6
Singapore (2)	85.0	85.2
Denmark (3)	84.0	84.6
South Sudan (185)	33.3	35.3
Libya (186)	33.2	33.4
Yemen (187)	33.0	32.4
Venezuela (188)	30.9	30.6
Eritrea (189)	22.9	23.0
Somalia (190)	20.0	20.0

Source: *Doing Business*, The World Bank, 2019 http://www.doingbusiness.org

▲ Table 31.1 Doing Business Index scores for top and bottom countries, 2018 & 2019

However, it should be remembered that deregulation does have its drawbacks and detractors. If the deregulation of labour laws to attract investment damages the safety and rights of workers, then any benefits in terms of economic growth will not be inclusive. In the same way, if deregulation of the banking system leads to debt-driven growth as opposed to growth through industrial development and infrastructural change, then again, there will be growth at the cost of development. Lastly, if deregulation relates to the relaxing of environmental laws, then any growth will be at the cost of sustainable development.

How can foreign direct investment impact economic growth and/or economic development?

Foreign direct investment (FDI) is long-term investment by private multinational enterprises/corporations (MNEs or MNCs) in countries overseas. FDI usually occurs in one of two ways. MNCs either build new plants or expand their existing facilities in foreign countries (is known as greenfield investment) or MNCs merge with or acquire (buy) existing firms in foreign countries.

MNCs are attracted to developing countries for a number of reasons:

- The countries may be rich in natural resources, such as oil and minerals. MNCs have the technology and expertise to extract such resources. For example, among the top recipients of FDI in Africa are those countries with valuable natural resources, such as Nigeria and South Africa.
- Some developing countries, such as Brazil, China and India, represent huge and growing markets. If MNCs are located directly in the markets then they have much better access to the large

number of potential consumers. With growing incomes, demand for all sorts of consumer goods is rising and MNCs wish to be there to satisfy the demand.

- The costs of labour are much lower than in more developed countries. Lower costs of production allow firms to sell their final products at lower prices and make higher profits.
- In many developing countries government regulations are much less severe than those in developed countries. This makes it easier for companies to set up but, more significantly, it can greatly reduce costs of production. Additionally, many developing country governments offer tax concessions to attract foreign direct investment. Over the last fifteen years many countries, both developed and developing, have adopted policies that have been more and more favourable to foreign direct investment. This often takes the form of reducing corporate tax rates.

We should now consider the possible advantages and disadvantages that may arise for developing countries from receiving FDI from MNCs:

Possible advantages associated with FDI are:

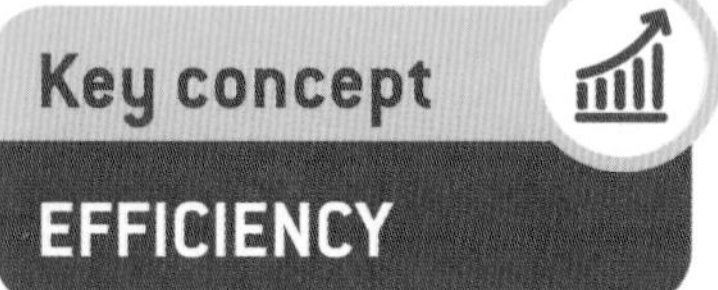

- As we know from macroeconomics, a necessary condition for growth is increased savings and developing countries tend to suffer from a *savings gap*. FDI helps to fill that savings gap and thus may lead to economic growth.
- MNCs will provide employment in the country and, in many cases, may also provide education and training. This may improve the skill levels of the work force and also the managerial capabilities.
- MNCs allow developing countries greater access to research and development, technology and marketing expertise and these can enhance their industrialization.
- Increased employment and earnings may have a multiplier effect on the host economy, stimulating growth.
- The host government may gain tax revenue from the profits of the MNC, which can then be used to gain more growth by investing in infrastructure, or to improve public services, such as health and education, to promote economic development.
- If MNCs buy existing companies in developing countries, then they are injecting foreign capital and increasing the aggregate demand.
- In some cases, MNCs may improve the infrastructure of the economy, both physical and financial, or they may act as a spur for governments to do so, in order to attract them.
- The existence of MNCs in a country may provide more choice and lower prices for consumers. They may be able to provide essential goods that are not available domestically.
- MNC activities along with liberalized trade can lead to a more efficient allocation of world resources.

It is clear that there are vast gains to be made from FDI. This can be clearly shown using China as an example. Although it is difficult to isolate FDI in terms of its effect on China's economic growth, it is reasonable to assume that it has played a significant role. Since 1978, China has actively tried to attract foreign investment as a way to stimulate economic growth. A significant proportion of China's exports are produced by foreign firms. Through joint ventures with foreign firms, Chinese firms have grown rapidly and successfully and China itself is now the source of a large outflow of foreign direct investment. As China grows, so does its demand for raw materials and much of Chinese FDI abroad is its investment in natural resources.

Possible disadvantages associated with FDI are:

- Although MNCs do provide employment, it is argued that they often bring in their own management teams, simply using inexpensive low skilled workers for basic production, and providing no education or training. This also limits the ability of host countries to acquire new technologies.
- In some cases it is argued that MNCs have too much power, because of their size, and so gain large tax advantages or even subsidies, reducing potential government income in developing countries. Along the same lines, it is argued that MNCs have too much power internationally. Their incomes and size allow them to exert too much influence on policy decisions taken in institutions such as the WTO.
- MNCs practise transfer pricing, where they sell goods and services from one division of the company to another division of the company in a separate country, in order to take advantage of different tax rates on corporate profits. In this way, developing countries with low tax rates to encourage MNCs to invest, reap little tax reward and developed countries also lose out on potential tax revenue. Given that approximately one-third of all international trade is made up of sales from one branch of a firm to another firm, this represents a potentially large loss of revenue to governments. Governments have rules to prevent firms from abusing their ability to use transfer pricing to minimize their tax payments, but these are difficult to monitor and enforce, particularly for developing country governments.
- It is argued that MNCs situate themselves in countries where legislation on pollution is not effective and thus they are able to reduce their private costs while creating external costs. Whilst this is good for the MNC it is obviously damaging for the environment of the host country. In the same way MNCs may set up in countries where labour laws are weak allowing the exploitation of local workers in terms of both low wage levels and poor working conditions.
- It is argued that MNCs may enter a country in order to extract particular resources, such as metals or stones, then strip those

resources and leave. There may be significant unrest as host country nationals see that the profits from their resources are being sent out of the country to foreigners.

- Economists have argued that MNCs may use capital-intensive production methods to make use of abundant natural resources. This will not greatly improve levels of employment in the country. It is argued that the MNCs should use appropriate technology, where production methods are aligned to the resources available. Since developing countries usually have a large supply of cheap labour, the argument is that labour-intensive production methods would be more appropriate.
- In most cases, where MNCs buy domestic firms, the owners of the firms being bought are paid in shares (stocks) from the MNC. This means that it is likely that the actual money will never be used in the developing country's economy.
- MNCs may repatriate their profits, which means that they transfer their profits out of the country back to the MNC's country of origin.

Uganda is surrendering trillions in tax agreements to multinational firms

https://www.monitor.co.ug/Business/Prosper/Uganda-trillions-tax-agreements-multinational-firms-/688616-5232786-77d0njz/index.html

Whilst most would agree that FDI is a positive factor for current economic growth, the main concerns relate to the possible negative effects of MNCs on sustainable economic development. The extent to which FDI is able to contribute to this development very much depends on the type of investment and the ability of the host country governments to appropriately regulate the behaviour of the MNCs and use the benefits of the investment to achieve development objectives.

To address some of the the concerns, the OECD *Guidelines for Multinational Enterprises*, provides a very detailed and extensive list of guidelines to all multinationals operating in, or coming from, any of the 48 countries that adhere to the Guidelines. The Guidelines provide "non-binding principles and standards for responsible business conduct in a global context, consistent with application laws and internationally recognised standards. They are the only multilaterally agreed and comprehensive code of responsible business conduct that governments have committed to promoting,"[2] Each member country has an agency serving as a National Contact Point (NCP) to promote and implement the Guidelines. These agencies also serve as a mediator for resolving issues.

Included in the many guidelines are the expectations that MNEs should:

- contribute to the economic, environmental and social progress with a view to achieving sustainable development
- respect internationally recognized human rights

[2] OECD Guidelines for Multinational Enterprises, 2011, http://www.oecd.org/daf/inv/mne/48004323.pdf\

- encourage local capacity building
- encourage human capital formation through providing employment and training opportunities
- provide full financial and operating information.

There have always been concerns related to MNC activity, such as the possible exploitation of workers, the use of child labour, the inability of workers to form trade unions, and business practices that cause immediate or future environmental damage. With the increasingly fast flow of information through the media and the internet and strong public interest groups acting globally, it is becoming difficult for MNCs to conceal activities that may contribute to these problems. They do not want to be perceived as being a cause of problems and are keen to promote their image in positive ways. As a result, firms are more and more likely to develop and publicize a set of policies to show that they are acting responsibly and ethically and "doing their bit" to promote sustainable development. As discussed earlier in this companion, this is known as Corporate Social Responsibility (CSR). Companies publish and promote their CSR policies through their annual reports, websites and advertising. The policies outline the firm's commitment to support human rights, employee rights, environmental protection, sustainable development and community involvement. The extent to which such policies are consistently followed and the extent of their actual effect on workers, the workers' communities and the environment is uncertain, but it is usually regarded as a step in the right direction!

Did you know?

FDI remains the largest external source of finance for developing economies. FDI makes up 39 per cent of total incoming finance in developing economies as a group, but less than a quarter in the LDCs, with a declining trend since 2012.

- → FDI flows to developing economies remained stable in 2017 at $671 billion, seeing no recovery following the 10 per cent drop in 2016.
- → FDI flows to Africa continued to slide, reaching $42 billion, down 21 per cent from 2016. The decline was concentrated in the larger commodity exporters.
- → Flows to developing Asia remained stable, at $476 billion. The region regained its position as the largest FDI recipient in the world.
- → FDI to Latin America and the Caribbean rose 8 per cent to reach $151 billion, lifted by that region's economic recovery. This was the first rise in six years, but inflows remain well below the 2011 peak during the commodities boom.
- → FDI in structurally weak and vulnerable economies remained fragile. Flows to the least developed countries fell by 17 per cent, to $26 billion. Those to landlocked developing countries increased moderately, by 3 per cent, to $23 billion. Small island developing states saw their inflows increase by 4 per cent, to $4.1 billion.

Source: UNCTAD World Investment Report 2018

Economics in action

ATL Thinking, Communication and Research

Research and write a brief report explaining the CSR policies of any multinational company with respect to its work in a developing country. This is easily done by going to the homepage of the company. How does the company seem to be adhering to the OECD Guidelines that MNEs should "contribute to the economic, environmental and social progress with a view to achieving sustainable development"?

Warning – you will obviously be getting a one-sided view of their efforts!

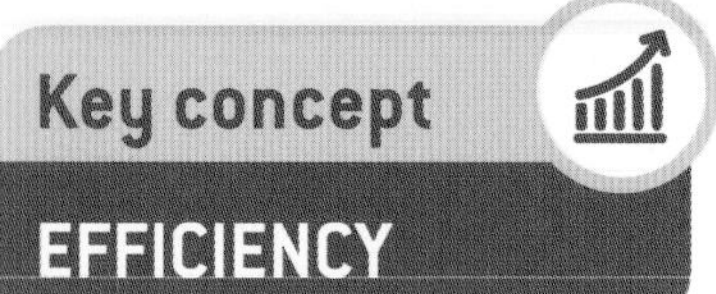

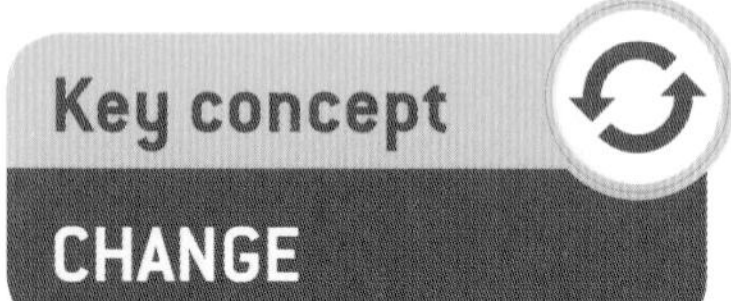

How might social enterprise promote economic development?

Social enterprises are organizations that have specific social objectives as their primary goal. They may be for-profit, or non-profit organizations, but profit is a secondary goal. Most social enterprises aim for the creation of social wealth, a viable business model and environmentally responsible operation.

The principal objective and purpose of a social enterprise is to overcome, or alleviate, a global or local issue, such as poverty, a lack of education, a lack of health care, technology access or an environmental problem. However, as with any other business, the financial figures and cash flow must be capable of providing a sustainable, long-term existence. In addition, social enterprises are both gender sensitive and environmentally conscious.

A good example of a social enterprise is Sunny Money, an enterprise that aims to provide solar powered products to rural and off-grid communities in Africa. They produce a number of products, such as solar torches, solar lights and solar battery chargers, which they sell at very low prices. The selling is done through agents and so the businesses also create employment in the areas where they sell.

Some would argue that giving away the products would be better, ie providing them through a charity. However, the managing director of Sunny Money argues that "We have taken a market-based approach because we believe that only by helping to create a viable market, which serves the needs of customers, will any intervention be sustainable. Giving away products runs the risk of destroying a market which responds to the needs of the people. How can an entrepreneur in Kenya, for example, make a living out of selling solar lights if a nearby NGO is busy giving them away for free?"[3]

[3] **Source:** Adapted from *African social enterprises pave the way for solar power while stimulating the local economy,* May 2019, www.theguardian.com

The managing director is referring to the wider impact social enterprises are hoping to have. They don't only plan to provide affordable lighting, they also want to provide economic opportunities and help local entrepreneurs carve out their own successful solar power businesses.

Economics in action — ATL Thinking, Communication and Research

Go to the website of Solar Sister: solarsister.org.

1. Identify the products that the enterprise offers.
2. Identify the social aims of the enterprise.
3. Explain the distribution system that the enterprise uses.
4. Explain the environmental elements of the operation.
5. Explain the different positive effects on development and sustainable development that are likely to be created by the activities of this enterprise.

Another valuable exercise would be to find your own example of a social enterprise working in a developing country, and explain its aims and achievements.

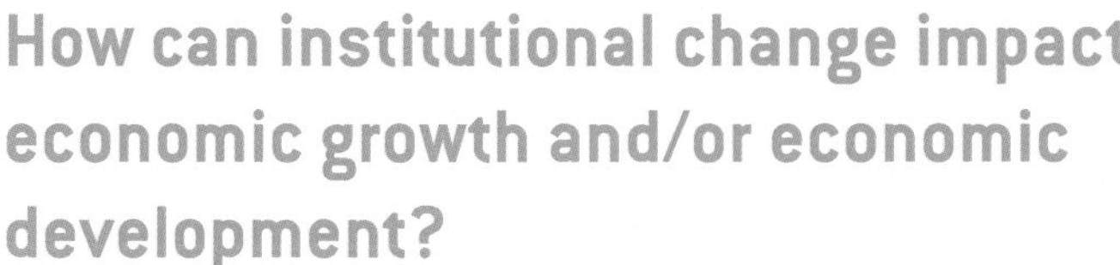

How can institutional change impact economic growth and/or economic development?

Key concept
CHANGE

We have already discovered that countries face certain institutional barriers to growth and development. It therefore follows that if the institutional framework can be reformed, then development is more likely. While there are a great many that could be investigated, we will consider three strategies that might promote favourable institutional changes:

1. **Improved access to the banking system**

   Developing countries face enormous challenges as a result of their weak financial systems. Anything that improves the access of individuals to the banking system will help with both growth and development. Two billion people worldwide still lack access to regulated financial services. Financial access and the underlying financial infrastructure taken for granted in rich countries, such as savings accounts, debit cards or credit as well as the payment systems on which they operate, still aren't available to many people in developing countries. This limits the ability of households and businesses to save, it affects the ability of people to buy and sell goods and services and very importantly, it limits the ability of entrepreneurs and firms to gain credit to start and expand businesses.

Africa's biggest bank is going after the continent's informal markets

https://qz.com/africa/1696196/standard-bank-signs-deal-with-nomanini-to-reach-informal-traders/

We will look at two areas of possible improvement:

- *Microfinance* – There is a type of financial service that is geared specifically to the poor. This is known as micro-finance and is the provision of financial services, such as small loans, savings accounts, insurance and even cheque books.

  The provision of small loans to individuals who have no access to traditional sources is known as micro-credit. A key element of original micro-credit schemes is that they did not originate in the developed world, but rather had their beginnings in developing countries. The first schemes began in the mid-1970s with projects such as Opportunity International (1972), ACCION International (1973), Muhammad Yunus/Grameen Bank (1974/76), FINCA International (inc 1985) and The SEEP Network (1985).

  Usually, the micro-credit loans are given to enable poor people to start up very small-scale businesses, known as micro-enterprises. These may include such things as roadside kiosks, bicycle repair services, market stalls, rice wine making, knitting and woodworking. The loans give protection against unexpected occurrences and seasonal problems, and may help families to gain a regular income, start to build wealth and thus escape from poverty.

  Women have tended to be the main recipients of micro-credit, for many reasons. It is thought that women are a better credit risk – they are more likely to pay back loans. Women are usually responsible for caring for children and so any reductions in a woman's poverty will translate into improvements for the children. In many documented cases, this has allowed for more poor children to go to school. When women take loans and can begin to earn an income, their social and economic status is raised and economic development is enhanced.

- *Mobile phone banking* – Access to banking services has been increased in recent times in developing countries with the advent of mobile phone banking and mobile money. In mobile banking a person who wants to send money does so by sending the amount via text to the receiver's phone number. The person who receives the money goes to an authorized local shop and withdraws the cash.

  Many mobile phone companies are taking over banking services in less developed countries. Africa is known as the "unbanked continent". Mobile banking is changing this. In Kenya and Tanzania, British operator *Vodafone* has over 33 million customers who send money to other people in the country and abroad via their M-Pesa system. Formal financial inclusion in Tanzania has increased from 44 percent in 2009 to over 65 percent at the present time.

  In Pakistan, Norwegian mobile phone company *Telenor* has been offering mobile banking since 2008. They have over 40 million subscribers. People can withdraw money at over 11,000 shops throughout the country. Pakistan itself has only 8,000 banks.

There are countless examples where mobile banking has contributed to development. For example, hospitals in Tanzania send money to women so that they can pay for the bus fare to the hospital. In Afghanistan the government pays its policemen by mobile phone. Coffee plantation owners in East Africa send workers their money via text. People who work in other countries, can much more easily, cost-effectively and securely send remittances home by using mobile bank services.

2. **Increasing women's empowerment**

Empowerment is the process by which women gain power and control over their own lives and acquire the ability to make strategic choices. As we discovered in Chapter 30, there are important externalities that occur when women become more empowered.

"Providing women and girls with equal access to education, health care, decent work and representation in political and economic decision-making processes will fuel sustainable economies and benefit societies and humanity at large. Implementing new legal frameworks regarding female equality in the workplace and the eradication of harmful practices targeted at women is crucial to ending the gender-based discrimination prevalent in many countries around the world"[4].

A strategy for women's empowerment should include:

- increasing support for the education of females
- increasing access to healthcare for women
- creating a safe environment in the home, the workplace and society
- establishing the right for women to own property and other assets
- increasing female involvement in decision making, both within the home and outside of it.

Economics in action ATL Thinking, Communication and Research

Go to the United Nations Development Program (UNDP) website: www.undp.org.

1. Find Goal 5, gender equality by clicking on the Goal 5 icon.
2. Make a note of the facts and figures offered.
3. View the Goal 5 targets.
4. Evaluate the success of your own country, or a country of your choice, in achieving the Goal 5 targets

[4] **Source:** SDG Goal 5, Gender equality, United Nations, www.un.org/sustainabledevelopment/gender-equality/

Exercise 31.1

ATL Thinking and Communication

Read the following article and summarize the benefits of women's empowerment in terms of climate change.

Education and family planning as tools to fight climate change

In 2017, an international coalition of well-known researchers, scientists and policy makers collaborated to offer a comprehensive set of 80 solutions to climate change in their book, *Drawdown, The Most Comprehensive Plan Ever Proposed to Reduce Global Warming*.

All of the solutions are economically viable, and all of them are already being used in various communities around the world. The challenge is to raise the profile of these solutions in order to slow down the earth's warming and reach 'drawdown', the point where the level of greenhouse gases in the atmosphere hit a peak and begin to fall, thus reversing global heating.

Many of the recommendations are well-known to us, and commonly recommended ways to reduce carbon emissions. The list below present the top ten. (You might have to look up 'silvopasture'!)

1	Refrigerant management
2	Wind turbines (onshore)
3	Reduced food waste
4	Plant-rich diet
5	Tropical forests
6	Educating girls
7	Family planning
8	Solar farms
9	Silvopasture
10	Rooftop solar

Two less well-known solutions are on the list at numbers 6 and 7 – the education of girls and family planning.

Let's look at Recommendation Number 6. The link between the education of girls and a smaller carbon footprint isn't as intuitively obvious as many of the others. However, there is ample evidence to support it. It's clear that if more girls go to school and get a quality education, the social benefits are profound: reduced incidence of disease, increased knowledge of nutrition, better employment opportunities, fewer forced marriages,

better job opportunities, higher life expectancies, and fewer children. Better educational access and attainment not only equips women with the skills to deal with the effects of climate change, but it empowers them to work with their communities to mitigate against it. Yet the education of girls lags far behind the education of boys in so many countries as both poverty and culture or tradition continue to mean that boys' education is prioritised.

Raising girls' education levels leads to Recommendation Number. 7 – access to family planning. The planet is overpopulated, and the demands of its citizens greatly exceed the natural resources provided by our environment.

Contraception and prenatal care is unavailable to women across the world, including developed and developing countries. It's either not available, not affordable, or social and/or religious motives mean that it's banned or heavily restricted. Without increasing awareness of, and granting access to family planning, the world's population will rise rapidly, consume ever more resources and require more and more energy to fuel its demands for goods and services. Carbon dioxide will continue to accumulate in the atmosphere.

In *Drawdown*, the authors calculated that the empowerment of women through educating girls and providing them access to family planning, would slow down the growth of the world's population and could lead to a reduction of 120 billion tons of emissions by 2050. This would be equivalent to 10 years' worth of China's annual emissions as of 2014.

Source: Adapted from The Wired, "To stop climate change, educate girls and give them birth control", https://www.wired.com/story/to-stop-climate-change-educate-girls-and-give-them-birth-control/

Key concept

EQUITY

3. Reducing corruption

We have already seen in Chapter 30 that corruption is a significant barrier to development. There is not a country in the world, developed or developing, that is immune to corruption. The abuse of public office for personal gain destroys people's trust in government and institutions, makes public policies less effective and fair, and takes taxpayers' money away from merit goods and public goods, such as schools, roads and hospitals.

Corruption limits the government's ability to help grow the economy in a way that benefits all citizens. As a result of corruption, governments receive lower tax revenue, because people pay bribes to avoid paying taxes. In addition, if people believe that the government itself is corrupt, then they will try to avoid paying taxes, since they know that the money will be misspent. In a recent IMF report, it was estimated that least corrupt governments can collect 4 percent more of GDP than similar countries with higher levels of corruption. For some countries, anti-corruption reforms have generated even higher GDP increases. For example, in Georgia, corruption was reduced significantly and tax revenues more than doubled, rising by 13 percentage points of GDP between 2003 and 2008. Reforms in Rwanda to fight corruption, since the mid-1990s, were successful, and tax revenues increased by 6 percentage points of GDP.[5]

Fighting corruption requires political will to create strong fiscal institutions that promote integrity, transparency and accountability throughout the public sector. The IMF suggest a number of measures that would help to reduce corruption:

- *Invest in high levels of transparency and independent external scrutiny.* This allows audit agencies and the public at large to provide effective oversight. For example, Colombia, Costa Rica and Paraguay are using an online platform that allows citizens to monitor the physical and financial progress of investment projects.
- *Reform institutions.* The chances for success are greater when countries design reforms to tackle corruption from all angles. For example, reforms to tax administration will have a greater payoff if tax laws are simpler and they reduce officials' scope for discretion.
- *Build a professional civil service.* Transparent, merit-based hiring and merit-based pay reduce the opportunities for corruption. The heads of agencies, ministries and public enterprises must promote ethical behavior by setting a clear tone at the top.
- *Keep pace with new challenges as technology and opportunities for wrongdoing evolve.* Focus on areas of higher risk – such as

[5] **Source:** Fiscal Monitor, International Monetary Fund, April 2019

procurement, revenue administration and management of natural resources – as well as effective internal controls. In Chile and Korea, for example, electronic procurement systems have been powerful tools to curtail corruption by promoting transparency and improving competition.

- *More cooperation to fight corruption.* Countries can join efforts to make it harder for corruption to cross borders. Countries can also aggressively pursue anti–money laundering activities and reduce transnational opportunities to hide corrupt money in opaque financial centers.[6]

We have already seen that corruption disproportionately affects vulnerable populations, the poor in general and women in particular. Corruption presents a particular barrier for women to gain full access to their civic, social and economic rights.

▲ The logo of Transparency International

Transparency International have suggested several ways that countries could reduce the problem of gender and corruption:

- *Collect, analyse and disseminate gender desegregated data.* Timely access to sufficient, accurate and up-to-date information is essential in order to design, implement and monitor effective public policies and to better integrate gender into anti-corruption policies.
- *Recognize and address specific gendered forms of corruption.* Sexual extortion (sextortion), a form of corruption where sex is the currency of the bribe, is only one form of corruption that disproportionately affects women. Other forms of abusive behaviour are not always recognized as corruption and are less likely to be reported due to a culture of shaming and victim blaming. Countries should ensure their judicial systems have the necessary tools and awareness to address sextortion cases.
- *Include women in anti-corruption decision making.* To ensure fairer access to political rights, women have to be part of the formulation, implementation, monitoring and evaluation of anti-corruption policies.
- *Empower women.* Women are less likely to report abuse, as they are often unaware of their rights and entitlements, which makes them easier targets for corruption. Governments, international organizations, businesses and civil society organizations can and should play a key role to help ensure women have full knowledge of their rights through campaigns and information on gendered forms of corruption.
- *Gender sensitive reporting mechanisms.* Safe, accountable, accessible and, most importantly, gender sensitive mechanisms should be created to report corruption. These mechanisms

[6] **Source:** Adapted from *Tackling corruption in government*, by Vitor Gaspar, Paolo Mauro and Paulo Medas, April 4 2019, IMF, blogs.imf.org

should take into account cultural context and gender issues that might hinder reporting.[7]

4. **Promoting secure property rights and land tenure rights**

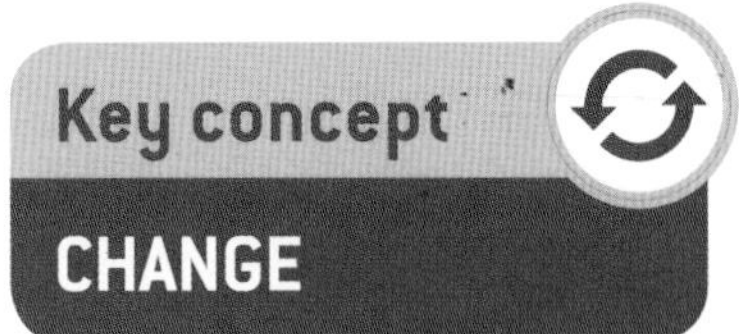

The prize-winning Peruvian economist Hernando de Soto divides the world into two groups: the ones who have defined property rights and those who do not. About two billion people have full rights to the property they live in and the land they farm, according to de Soto. For the 5.3 billion who do not have such rights, the implications are bleak: people are unable to use their resources to create wealth, and their assets become "dead capital" which cannot be used to generate income or growth. He argues that the poor are trapped by the "tragedy of the commons" that we looked at in Chapter 9. Because they don't own their property or land, their unregistered assets can effectively be stolen by more powerful entities.

It is often the case that poor people have the ability to use land for subsistence agriculture, or for grazing or for gathering firewood, but they lack the statutory, or legal right to determine its use, sell it, use it for collateral or leave it to their children. De Soto argues that legally protected property rights are the key source of the developed world's wealth and prosperity, and the lack thereof is the reason why many nations remain trapped in poverty. He estimates that providing the world's poor with titles for their land, homes and unregistered businesses would unlock $9.3 trillion in assets, an enormous sum to reduce poverty. Reforming legal structures to ensure property titles would allow the poor to use their small homes or land in order to borrow money and start businesses.[8]

The World Bank and other development organisations such as Oxfam, the International Development Law Organisation (IDLO) and the Food and Agricultural Organisation (FAO) work to raise awareness and improve the rights of people to own property and secure land tenure rights. The World Bank notes that there are seven key reasons why legal reforms to improve property and land rights are necessary for economic growth and development:[9]

1. **Secure land rights are an important pillar for agriculture**

   When farmers have secure land titles and know that their land rights will be guaranteed, they have the incentive to invest in their land and borrow money for agricultural inputs or to make improvements to the land.

---

[7] **Source:** Adapted from *Gender and corruption: where do we go from here?*, by M Amelia Berazategui, March 20 2019, Transparency International, voices.transparency.org

[8] **Source:** *The Mystery of Capital*, by Hernando de Soto, 2003, Black Swan

[9] **Source:** 7 reasons for land and property rights to be at the top of the global agenda. The World Bank Group, March 2019. https://blogs.worldbank.org/voices/7-reasons-land-and-property-rights-be-top-global-agenda

2. **Secure land rights are essential for urban development.**

   The formation of large informal settlements or slums in many cities is the result of a failure to clarify land rights. In order to create affordable and livable urban areas, effective urban planning is needed, but this is impossible without guaranteed land rights.

3. **Secure property rights help protect the environment.**

   When property rights are secure, people have far more incentive to look after their land, and ensure its sustainability.

4. **Secure property rights and access to land are crucial for private sector development and job creation.**

   The private sector needs land to build factories, commercial buildings and residential properties. Land or property rights give collateral to companies to help them finance their operations, expand their business or open new businesses, thus creating more jobs.

5. **Secure property rights are important for empowering women.**

   Access to land rights can help empower women.

   As we saw above, access to assets is essential for women's empowerment. However, millions of women are denied land and property rights for several reasons: many legal systems require women to have a male guardian in order to own property; men may not register their land or property in the name of their wife, and so women lose the property in the event of divorce or death of their husband; despite the fact that women may have the legal right to inherit land or properties,in practice they may be denied these rights by male relatives. Legal reforms are necessary to reduce the vulnerabilities women face as a result of insecure property rights and land tenure.

6. **Secure property rights help secure indigenous peoples' rights.**

   Despite the fact indigenous people have lived on their land for centuries, many countries do not always legally recognize these rights, and take over, or use the land without the consent of the indigenous people. Recognizing indigenous peoples' land rights is not only a human rights issue, but it also makes economic and environmental sense. Once their land rights are recognized, indigenous peoples will be able to use the resources on their land more sustainably, thus improving their economic and social status as a constructive force in society.

7. **Secure property rights are vital for keeping peace.**

   War and conflicts have forced millions of people to flee, leaving their properties behind. Without their property rights legally protected at home, displaced people will not be able to go back to their homes and livelihoods. Peace cannot be fully achieved if land and property rights are not well addressed, potentially triggering further conflict.

> *"Land is vital to our livelihoods. Whether we use it for building a home, operating a business, growing food, or for mere enjoyment, land sustains us all.*
>
> **Source:** Oxfam, Securing Quality and Dignity of Life

Economics in action

ATL Thinking, Communication and Research

Go to the United Nations Development Program (UNDP) website: www.undp.org.

1. Find Goal 16, 'Peace, justice and strong institutions' by clicking on the Goal 16 icon.
2. Make a note of the facts and figures offered.
3. View the Goal 16 targets.
4. Evaluate the success of your own country, or a country of your choice, in achieving the Goal 16 targets

Key concept

INTERVENTION

What interventionist strategies can promote economic growth and/or development?

Many development strategies aim to grow the economy in the belief that economic growth will lead to economic development. However, interventionist strategies are used to try to ensure that economic growth is inclusive.

Inclusive strategies aim to ensure that the the assets and capabilities of poor people are improved. They directly target the poor and allow the poor people themselves to be directly involved in the process. Such strategies may be implemented by governments or by NGOs.

To be effective, strategies need to be focused towards areas directly associated with the poor. Therefore, they should be aimed at:

- the sectors of the economy in which the poor work (for example, agriculture and the informal economy)
- the areas in which the poor live (for example town ghettos or underdeveloped rural regions)
- the factors of production which the poor possess (ie unskilled labour)
- the products which the poor consume (for example, food).

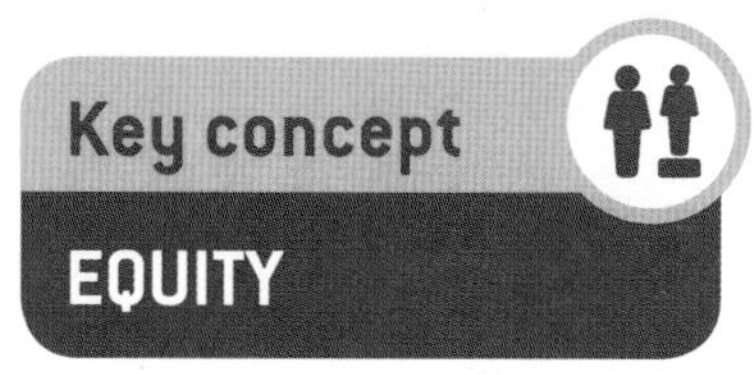

How can redistributive fiscal policies promote economic growth and/or development?

In developed countries, fiscal policy can be an effective tool for redistributing income. Governments earn money from taxes, and redistribute through transfer payments. However, developing countries have far less scope to redistribute income this way, because their ability to raise revenues from taxes (their *'fiscal capacity'*) is quite limited. As a result, their ability to provide transfer payments and finance merit goods such as health services, education and infrastructure is also limited.

There are several reasons why governments in developing countries struggle to raise tax revenues. Table 31.2 lists some of the challenges governments face in raising taxes along with possible strategies to overcome these.

Challenge	Strategy
The large size of the informal economy, whose economic activity is not taxed.	Strategies to mobilize informal workers and enterprises into the formal sector.
There is heavy reliance on indirect taxes, because they are considerably easier to set and collect, but indirect taxes tend to generate lower revenues. Furthermore, indirect taxes are regressive, so worsen income inequality.	Impose higher taxes on goods such as alcohol, cigarettes, gambling and luxury goods, which are consumed more by high-income people.
Extensive tax exemptions and loopholes in the tax structure, which mean that high income people may not pay their fair share.	Improve the tax structure to remove loopholes and ensure that the tax exemptions are meaningful
High tax rates on high levels of income may give incentives to people to evade paying taxes.	Lower rates of tax at high incomes to encourage people to pay. The lower rate could be offset if more people pay their share.
There are high levels of non-compliance, where people avoid paying taxes. Possible reasons for this include: • corruption in government so that people do not trust the government to use revenues • a lack of transparency in government so that people are not aware of how their tax revenues are used • a weak sense of national identity.	Measures to overcome non-compliance include: • commitments to reduce corruption so that people believe that the tax revenues will be spent appropriately • provide access to details concerning government budgets, so that governments are accountable to the public about what happens with the taxes they pay • public awareness campaigns to increase compliance by teaching people about the role of taxes and building a sense of national identity and responsibility • empower people to engage in open discussions about the uses of taxes.

▲ **Table 31.2** Challenges and strategies for increasing tax revenues

Sustainable development goal 17.1:

"Strengthen domestic resource mobilization, including through international support to developing countries, to improve domestic capacity for tax and other revenue collection"[10]

[10] **Source:** SDG 17, https://sustainabledevelopment.un.org/sdg17

Economics in action ATL Thinking, Communication and Research

In its publication, *Building Tax Culture, Compliance and Citizenship*, the OECD shows how governments can use tax education to "transform their tax cultures."

In the publication, they present information on innovative programmes that governments have implemented including:

- a television soap opera called "Binding Duty" in Nigeria
- computer games about taxes in Uruguay
- a "Time for Taxes" calendar in Lebanon
- National Income Tax Day in Bangladesh
- classes on taxes and accounting for businesses in Bhutan
- tax camps for secondary school children in Malaysia to instil a sense of responsibility for paying taxes.

Investigate one (or more!) of these to gain an appreciation of the objectives of the government and to see what they are doing in their programme.

How can transfer payments impact economic development?

Governments in developing countries face the challenge of allocating their very limited revenues to investment in merit goods and public goods, such as education, health and infrastructure, which have a significant effect on future poverty, or spending on transfer payments, which tends to have a greater impact on current poverty. In terms of achieving economic growth and development, the gains to investment in education, health and infrastructure are substantial. The complexities and costs of administering transfer payments are also a challenge.

However, a programme that has demonstrated positive outcomes in many developing countries is conditional cash transfers (CCT). Conditional cash transfer programmes are transfer payments targeting low income people. They aim to reduce poverty by making welfare programs conditional upon the actions of the person receiving the money. The government (or a non-government organization) only transfers the money to poor people in return for fulfilling specific behavioural conditions. These conditions may include, for example, children's school attendance, up-to-date vaccinations, or regular visits to a health care facility by pregnant women. CCTs have direct effects on poverty by, firstly, increasing the immediate income of the poor, but also by having a positive impact upon the socio-economic well being of the recipient (and their families). Thus, CCTs can alleviate poverty and improve the quality of human capital.

CCTs do not themselves create jobs, but they permit children more access to education and health care, which will make them more productive in the future and in turn should lead to higher income, taking them out of poverty. The size of the CCT is not enough in itself to raise a recipient out of poverty. It simply adds to the income that the recipient is currently receiving and provides some compensation for parents who send their children to school as opposed to working or begging.

The use of CCTs started in the 1990's in Latin America, where one of the first schemes was the *Progresa* program in 1997 (later called *Oportunidades* and now called *Prospera*). This scheme provided cash transfers to households with the conditions of regular school attendance and health clinic visits. It was designed to encourage improved education, improved health care and improved nutrition for poor families.

Exercise 31.2

ATL Thinking and Communication

Read the following article and answer the questions that follow it.

Conditional Cash Keeps Girls in School

Keeping girls in school has become a priority for those fighting poverty around the globe, and for good reasons. Research shows that the longer a girl stays in school, the more likely she is to delay marriage and avoid early pregnancy. This means lower maternal and child mortality rates, fewer abortions and improved child health. In addition, a 2011 World Bank study shows that investing in girls' continued education can boost labour force participation, lifetime earnings and **GDP**. However, even though it is clear that investing in girls' education spurs economic growth and lessens poverty and social instability, millions of girls around the world still face cultural and economic barriers that keep them out of school.

One way to counter this phenomenon is to offer poor households conditional cash transfers (CCTs). CCTs give money to poor people in return for fulfilling specific conditions, such as accessing basic health services, vaccinating children or sending daughters to school. These programs offer a two-fold approach that breaks the **poverty cycle** by both providing the poor with additional income and also strengthening human capital with healthcare and education services.

The success of one education-specific CCT program, the Female Secondary School Assistance Program (FFSAP), illustrates that providing girls with a small stipend to stay in school has far-reaching benefits. FFSAP, a joint program founded by the World Bank, Asian Development Bank and Government of Bangladesh, provided female students in grades six through ten with a monthly stipend on three conditions: that the girls maintained a 75 percent attendance rate, scored at least 45 percent on their exams and remained unmarried.

According to a study assessing the FFSAP, CCT money enabled girls to extend their education up to two years, which in turn had significant economic and social impacts. Continued education for girls in Bangladesh led to a 3.6 to 10.6 percent increase in women's labour force participation. Girls enrolled in the program also delayed marriage by 1.4 to 2.3 years, which is particularly meaningful given that Bangladesh has one of the highest child marriage rates in the world; 66 percent of Bangladeshi girls are married before the age of eighteen. Some data even suggests that the age of marriage for men also went up in part thanks to the program.

The initiative in Bangladesh is just one of many impactful CCT programs that have been implemented around the world. International development leaders should consider expanding these types of programs; it is clear that giving every girl the opportunity to complete her education benefits not only women, but entire communities and economies.

Source: Adapted from *Conditional cash keeps girls in school*, by Gayle Tzemach Lemmon, October 24th 2013, Council on Foreign Relations, www.cfr.org

a) (i) Define the term *GDP* indicated in bold (paragraph 1). [2 marks]

(ii) Define the term *poverty trap* indicated in bold (paragraph 2). [2 marks]

b) Explain how the CCT may break the poverty trap (paragraph 2). [4 marks]

c) Explain **two** factors that might make it difficult for a developing country to promote such conditional cash transfers. [4 marks]

What is the role of minimum wages in promoting economic development?

As established in Chapter 22, the purpose of minimum wages is to "protect workers against unduly low pay and ensure an equitable share in the fruits of progress to all and a minimum living wage to all who are employed and in need of such protection"[11] Therefore the establishment of a minimum wage can be seen as a valuable tool to reduce poverty and inequality. When minimum wages exist, but do not provide a 'living wage' (a wage that ensures a worker can meet their basic needs), a development strategy would be to increase the minimum wage.

Minimum wages exist in more than 90% of the 187 member countries of the International Labour Organization, including the majority of developing countries. And while minimum wages are credited with having a positive impact in terms of reducing poverty, and should form part of any poverty-reduction strategy, it is argued that they have only a moderate impact and can not be considered as a major tool to combat poverty. There are a few reasons for this:

- According to an ILO report issued in April 2018, around 61% of the world's employed population works in the informal sector. In Africa 85.8% of employment is informal. In Asia and the Pacific, the proportion is 68.2%. In the Arab States, 40% of employed are in the informal sector[12]. Workers in the informal sector are not under contract, do not receive social protection, are not guaranteed decent working conditions and are not protected by the rule of the law. They may work in dangerous and vulnerable positions. Because workers in the informal sector do not receive any legal benefits or protection, they do not receive minimum wages, and so any policy to reduce poverty through minimum wages will not be effective at reducing the poverty among informal workers. This is one of the many reasons the International Labour Organization emphasises the urgency of tackling informality and promoting the formalization of employment.

[11] **Source:** The International Labour Organization: How to define a minimum wage, https://www.ilo.org/global/topics/wages/minimum-wages/definition/lang--en/index.htm

[12] **Source:** The International Labour Organization: Women and Men in the Informal Sector: A Statistical Picture, April 2018. https://www.ilo.org/wcmsp5/groups/public/---dgreports/---dcomm/documents/publication/wcms_626831.pdf

"The incidence of informality is a major challenge for the realization of decent work for all and sustainable and inclusive development."

Source: International Labour Organization. https://www.ilo.org/global/about-the-ilo/newsroom/news/WCMS_627189/lang--en/index.htm

- Even in the formal sector, where workers are entitled to receive a minimum wage, there are always issues with "compliance and enforcement". That is, it may be relatively easy for firms to pay less than the minimum wage and escape any form of punishment. In their support of labour throughout the world, The International Labour Organization promotes methods to improve compliance with minimum wages, and advocates measures such as: information and awareness raising campaigns; better design of minimum wage policies; empowering workers to claim their rights through collective action; effective punishments that act as a disincentive to non-compliance; targeted labour inspections and monitoring practices within global supply chains to ensure that multinational companies ensure that legal regulations for labour are being observed when they operate with local suppliers.[13]

- There is a risk that although minimum wages may improve the incomes of some, they may also disadvantage others. It is possible that a minimum wage (or a higher minimum wage) will cause some employers to lay off workers. If those workers live in low-income households, poverty will increase, particularly if the worker was the only earner in the household. Another possible negative outcome is that if workers are laid off from jobs in the formal sector, they may seek jobs in the informal sector, putting downward pressure on wages there.

Minimum wages must not be discounted as a means of reducing poverty. However, their effectiveness is limited by the sheer size of the informal sector, and the extent of non-compliance that may prevent workers from being paid the legal minimum wage. Sustainable Development Goal 8 recognizes these challenges and has set targets to "encourage the formalization and growth of enterprises" and "protect labour rights" for all workers.

Economics in action ATL Thinking, Communication and Research

Investigate the effectiveness of minimum wages in a developing country.

[13] **Source:** International Labour Organization, How to Enforce Minimum Wages, https://www.ilo.org/global/topics/wages/minimum-wages/enforcement/lang--en/index.htm

How might the provision of merit goods promote economic growth and/or development?

As you know, merit goods are underprovided in a market. Merit goods such as health services and education provide tremendous private and external benefits; but developing countries face the enormous challenge of providing such merit goods. A brief look at the health and education statistics for developing countries reveals a huge range of outcomes, with some countries experiencing tremendous progress in some areas, while others make little progress at all. Yet, regardless of the level of economic development of a country, the gains from effective investments in these areas are enormous, and the key for economic growth and development.

Access to quality health care and education has the potential to raise the human capital of a country's population. Significant challenges exist in terms of identifying the needs, choosing appropriate services, financing the programmes and ensuring that all people have access to the services. Countries face different priorities and these need to be taken into account. These are the challenges that have been clearly identified in many of the Sustainable Development Goals.

To support the economic development of a population, extensive investments must be made in all types of infrastructure, including clean energy, transport, telecommunications, and clean water and sanitation. Again, the challenges of providing appropriate essential infrastructure have been identified throughout many of the SDGs.

The increased supply of merit goods may be provided through many means, such as domestic government investment, foreign direct investment, microfinance, social enterprise or from international cooperation through foreign aid. It is hoped that the commitment made by all countries to the SDGs will ensure that each country can make progress in meeting the challenges of providing these essential merit goods.

Key concept 

EQUITY

The Multidimensional Poverty Index

It would be inappropriate for countries to adopt a one-size-fits-all approach to poverty reduction, as the nature of poverty differs from country to country. Look back at the information in Figure 22.7. This demonstrated that Peru and Tajikistan experience similar levels of multidimensional poverty. However, the data shows that children in Peru experience greater deprivation in terms of accessing education than Tajikistan, as schooling contributes 18% to the MPI index in Peru and only 1% in Tajikistan. In Tajikistan, nutrition contributes 35% to the MPI index, while in Peru, the figure is 18%. This information could help governments and international partners devise country-specific strategies to reduce poverty.

How might foreign aid help to achieve economic growth and/or development?

Foreign aid is any assistance that is given to a country that would not have been provided through normal market forces. Aid may be provided to developing countries for a number of reasons including:

- to help people who have experienced some form of natural disaster or war
- to help developing countries to achieve economic development
- to fill the savings gap that exists in developing economies
- to improve the quality of the human resources in a developing country
- to strengthen institutions
- to improve levels of technology
- to fund specific development projects

Key concept 

INTERDEPENDENCE

- to enable a country to increase their capacity to benefit from international trade opportunities (Aid-for-trade)
- to help meet the Sustainable Development Goals.

What is humanitarian aid?

Humanitarian aid is aid given to save lives and alleviate suffering in response to emergencies such as natural disasters (eg earthquakes, monsoons, prolonged drought) or human-made crises (eg international wars, civil wars, refugee crises). It may also be used in response to a medical crisis, such as the Ebola outbreak. While essentially short-term in nature, humanitarian aid may be prolonged if a host government is unable to take over control of the crisis and the human suffering continues.

What is development aid?

Development aid is given by governments, multilateral organisations and non-government organisations in order to alleviate systemic poverty and promote the economic, social, environmental or political development in recipient countries. In contrast to humanitarian aid, which is a short-term response to an emergency, development aid is long term assistance in response to systematic problems.

What is "official development assistance"?

"*Official development assistance*" (ODA) is defined by the OECD Development Assistance Committee (DAC) as 'government aid that promotes and specifically targets the economic development and welfare of developing countries[14]'. ODA is given either by a government, through its official aid agency or through any one of the multilateral international institutions to which the country contributes. These include the United Nations and its many affiliated organisations (eg UN Development Programme, UN Children's Fund, UN Industrial Development Organisation, the World Health Organization, the International Labour Organization), the World Bank, and the International Monetary Fund. When a government gives aid directly to another country, it is known as *bilateral aid*. When a government gives aid money to one of the recognised international agencies, it is known as *multilateral aid.*

SDG 17 emphasises the need for the global partnership in achieving sustainable development and target 17.1 specifically identifies the role of ODA in meeting this goal. It calls for "developed countries to implement fully their official development assistance commitments, including the commitment by many developed countries to achieve the target of 0.7% of GNI"[15], as measured by the OECD Development Assistance Committee (DAC).

The DAC has very specific eligibility requirements to measure whether a particular programme meets the criteria to be considered as ODA.

---

[14] **Source:** OECD, Official Development Assistance, http://www.oecd.org/dac/financing-sustainable-development/development-finance-standards/official-development-assistance.htm

[15] **Source:** Sustainable Development Goals, SDG 17.

To meet eligibility requirements, the foreign aid must be must be provided by official agencies and it must be *'concessional'*; this means that it must be either a grant or a soft loan. A soft loan is a loan which is either interest-free, or at below market interest rates and is usually to be repaid over a longer period than commercial loans. Furthermore, the aid must have the promotion of the economic development and welfare of developing countries as the main objective.

ODA does not include military aid or aid that is donated to pursue the donor's security interests.[16] So, for example, a UK "train and equip" project to strengthen the Lebanese Armed Forces (LAF) Land Border Regiment was deemed 'non-ODA eligible' as it aimed to build defenze capacities of the partner country's armed forces. Similarly, a Portuguese project to support health-care services and medical assistance to treat military personnel of partner countries was also deemed non-eligible as it provides medical care that was not available in the partner country and was aimed at strengthening the military. On the other hand, an Austrian project to strengthen the "Transnational Crime Units" to help police fight against drug trafficking, organized crime and drug abuse in five West African countries was deemed "ODA eligible" as it followed stated rules to help partner country police prevent and address criminal activities.[17] Thus, it could be seen to support domestic institutions of partner countries in a way that benefited the population as a whole.

Economics in action

ATL Thinking, Communication and Research

How are countries doing in terms of meeting the goal of contributing 0.7% of their GNI to ODA?

Which countries are meeting the UN goal? Find the most recent data to see if any improvements have been made.

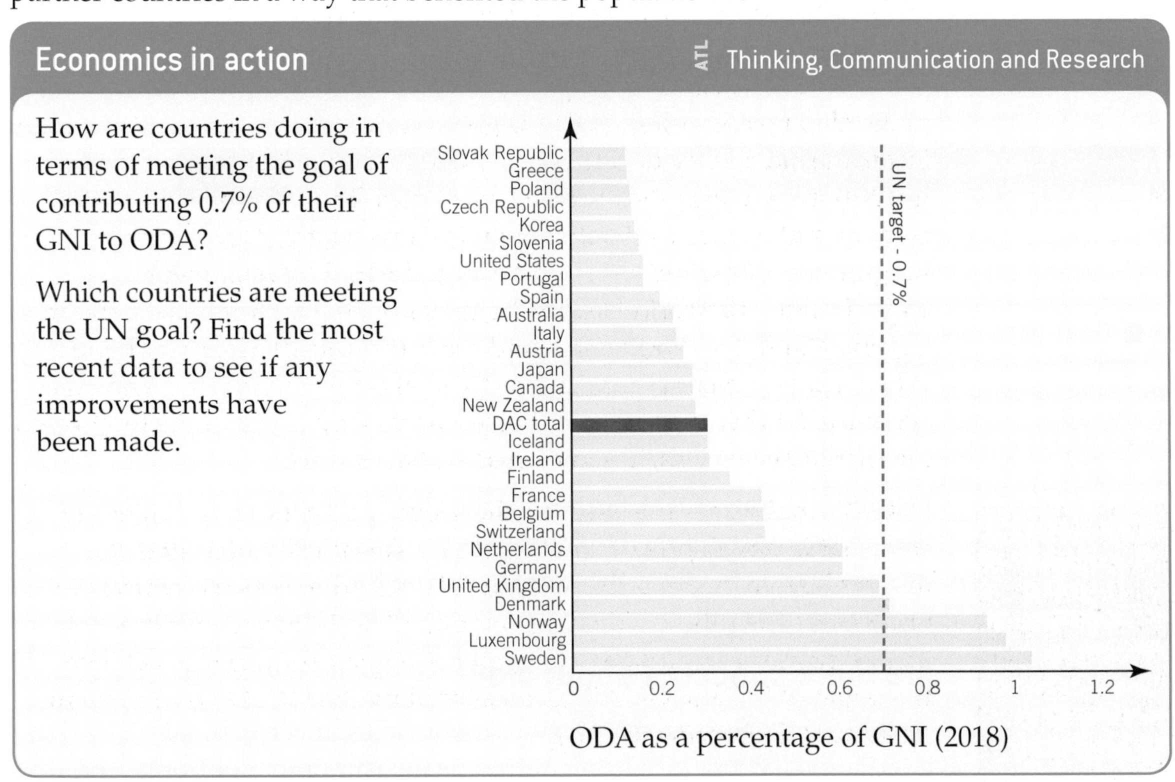

ODA as a percentage of GNI (2018)

[16] **Source**: OECD, Official Development Assistance, http://www.oecd.org/dac/financing-sustainable-development/development-finance-standards/official-development-assistance.htm

[17] Examples taken from OECD Financing for Sustainable Development, SDG DAC Eligibility Database, http://www.oecd.org/dac/financing-sustainable-development/development-finance-standards/oda-eligibility-database/

1.1.1. Top 10 ODA receipts by recipient
USD million, net disbursements in 2017

1	Syrian Arab Republic	10,361	6%
2	Ethiopia	4,117	3%
3	Afghanistan	3,804	2%
4	Bangladesh	3,740	2%
5	Nigeria	3,359	2%
6	Yemen	3,234	2%
7	Turkey	3,142	2%
8	India	3,094	2%
9	Jordan	2 921	2%
10	Iraq	2,907	2%
	Other recipients	122,123	75%
	Total	162,802	100%

1.1.3. Trends in ODA

	2016	2017	% change
ODA net disbursements (2016 constant USD million)	158,218	160,780	1.6%
ODA gross disbursements (2016 constant USD million)	181,529	187,511	3.3%
ODA commitments (2016 constant USD million)	186,501	192,946	3.5%
Population (thousands)	6,100,285	6,180,222	1.3%
Net ODA per capita (USD)	25.9	26.3	–

1.1.2. Top 10 ODA donors
USD million, net disbursements in 2017

1	United States	30,006	18%
2	Germany	19,818	12%
3	EU Institutions	16,054	10%
4	United Kingdom	11,335	7%
5	IDA	9,513	6%
6	Japan	8,080	5%
7	Turkey	7,950	5%
8	France	6,649	4%
9	Global Fund	4,226	3%
10	United Arab Emirates	3,835	2%
	Other donors	45,334	28%
	Total	162,802	100%

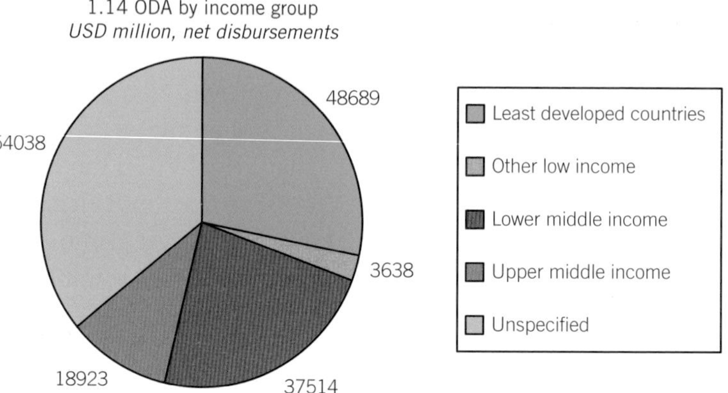

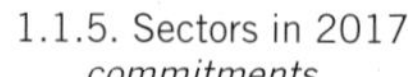

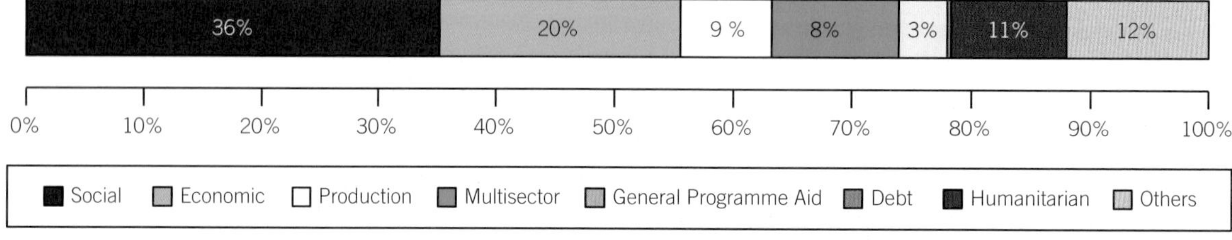

Source: *World Development Aid at a Glance, 2017*, OECD, www.oecd.org

▲ **Figure 31.1** ODA statistics for 2017

Figure 31.1 shows ODA figures for the top developed country donors that are members of the DAC for the year 2017, the main recipients of this aid, trends in ODA, the areas receiving the aid and the uses to which the money was put.

Are there concerns about aid?

To achieve the Sustainable Development Goals, it is clear that international cooperation is required on a vast number of fronts, and it is clear that developed countries have a responsibility to partner with developing countries in order to achieve these goals. Financial support through Official Development Assistance and Non-governmental organizations is one way of doing this.

Nevertheless, there are concerns about the nature, disbursement and uses of aid, which must be addressed as countries cooperate to achieve the global development goals. These concerns include the following:

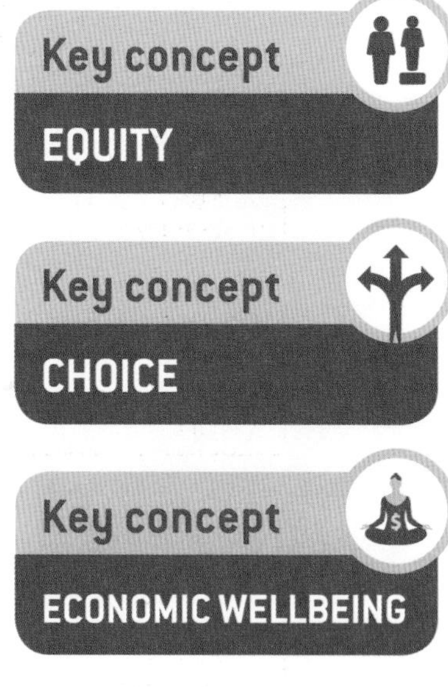

- If the government in power does not have the welfare of the majority of the population at heart, it may mean that when aid is received, it goes to a small sector of the population or a particular sector of the economy that does not need the support.
- Aid is sometimes given for political reasons rather than being given to countries where the need is greatest. It is argued that the developed countries tend to give aid to those countries that are of political or economic interest to them. One result of this is that the poorest people in the world actually receive less aid than people in middle-income countries.
- Aid is often linked to the political views of the donor governments. If these views change due, for example, to a change in government, then this can have serious consequences for the countries receiving aid.
- One form of bilateral aid is '*tied aid*'. This is when a country gives money for a particular aid project on the condition that the recipient country uses the money to buy goods and services from the donor country. The result may be that the donor country ends up paying more for the goods and services than they would have done in an open market. It also may reduce possible trade between developing countries who may have been able to provide the products less expensively. It calls into question the real motivation for the aid. Some economists have argued that tied aid is often politically motivated and is little more than a subsidy to industries in the donor country. The provision of tied aid has fallen in recent years and it has actually been phased out in some countries.For example, the UK made the giving of tied aid illegal in 2002.
- While the short-term provision of food aid may be essential, long-term provision of large quantities of food may force down domestic prices and make matters worse for domestic farmers.
- Some economists view aid as creating a culture of dependency that can actually limit long term economic development. A country may become so dependent on aid that the the government has little incentive to implement strategies of its own. This will be particularly damaging if the domestic economic situation in donor countries worsen and they reduce the amount of aid that they give.
- Some argue that aid is often focused on the modern industrial sector and may cause a greater gap in incomes and living standards between those in that sector and those in the traditional agricultural sector.
- Aid is often only available if the country agrees to adopt certain economic policies. Donors may argue that aid will only be effective if it is given to countries that adopt what it considers to be "sound" economic policies and these often reflect policies that emphasize the free market principles of liberalization, deregulation and

White House moving forward with plan to cancel foreign aid, teeing up fight with Congress

https://edition.cnn.com/2019/08/16/politics/omb-rescission-package-foreign-aid-funding/index.htm

privatization to promote economic growth. It is argued that these policies might be more in the interest of the developed countries and its multinational companies and not necessarily in the best interest of developing countries.

- Despite the fact that loans may be concessional, they still need to be repaid. Repayments on financial aid may lead to massive problems of indebtedness for developing countries.

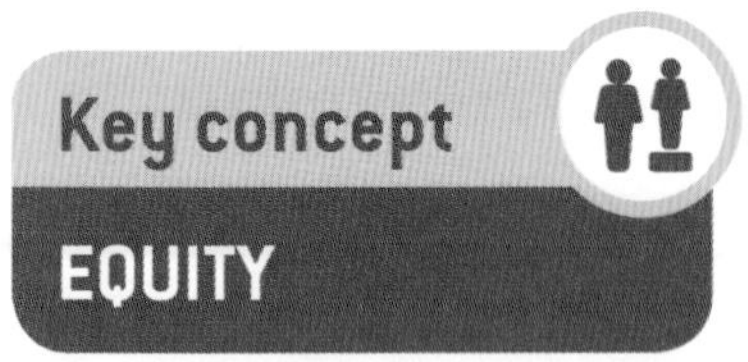

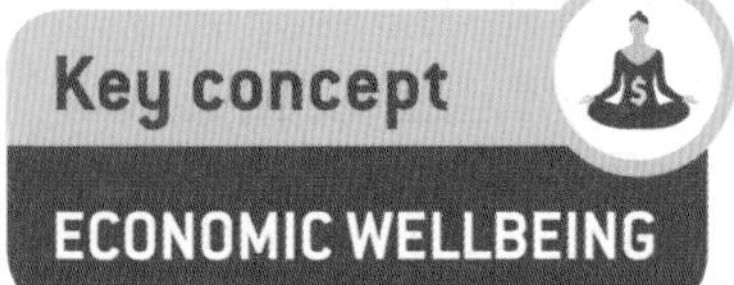

What are Non-governmental organizations (NGOs)?

Non-governmental organizations (NGOs) have a major role in terms of promoting economic growth and economic development. It is very difficult to generalize about NGOs as they are incredibly diverse—in size, purpose, outlook, nationality, income and success. However, we can say that, for the most part, the priority of NGOs is to promote economic development, humanitarian ideals and sustainable development. Although some NGOs receive funding from governments, they operate independently, without the influence of government. Their work might be to provide emergency relief in cases of disasters or to provide long-term development assistance. Examples of international NGOs are Oxfam, CARE, Mercy Corps, Cafod, Greenpeace, Amnesty International, Global 2000 and Doctors Without Borders (Médecins Sans Frontières).

NGOs carry out two main types of activities. They have operational activities, where they plan and implement specifically targeted projects in developing countries and they carry out advocacy activities where they try to influence public policy in areas such as poverty reduction, workers' rights, human rights and the environment. Some NGOs do one or the other of these activities, and some do both, by actively raising funds and raising awareness of the issues. This can result in public pressure on governments that might affect the amount and type of official aid that is given. They can also influence the buying patterns of consumers in ways that contribute to better working conditions and the promotion of sustainable development.

As NGOs often work directly in the field, it may be argued that they can develop a much deeper understanding of the issues and challenges facing the poor than official aid donors may do. In this way, they can attack poverty directly. They may work in areas that official aid cannot reach and work with groups that might be isolated from official aid. Much of what is done by NGOs focuses on working directly with poor people to enhance their human capital. This may be done in a variety of ways such as literacy programmes, health education, AIDS prevention projects, agricultural education and support, micro-credit schemes, immunization and vocational training.

As noted earlier, many NGOs focus their attention on women in particular, and we have already recognized the value of raising women's incomes and status in achieving overall economic development.

NGOs can be credited with making significant contributions in terms of raising awareness and implementing highly successful programmes in developing countries. And just like any other organisation, NGOs working in developing countries should demonstrate good governance, accountability and transparency in their activities. Nonetheless, there are concerns and criticisms of their work. These include:

- Obviously, NGOs rely on funding in order to carry out their programmes and advocacy work. Such funding comes from a variety of sources including private individuals, corporations, charitable foundations and governments. It may be that what the NGO can or can't do depends on where their funding came from and it may limit the effectiveness of what they do. In theory, NGOs operate independently of a government, but if a significant amount of their funding comes from the government, then their activities will inevitably be impacted by political views. For example, in 2018, the US government enacted a ban preventing any aid organisations receiving US government money for providing abortions or even providing any information about family planning that included information on abortions. This change in funding was expected to have grave consequences on women's health throughout the developing world, with an anticipated rise in maternal deaths due to unsafe illegal abortions.
- It may be the case that there are many NGOs operating in a developing country, resulting in uncoordinated and wasteful activities. For example, an NGO might use health workers in one area, or sector, reducing the availability in other areas. It may even be the case that NGOs draw workers away from local government projects, and thereby undermine the local government's ability to determine how to address an issue.
- NGOs may have a political or religious bias, that determine its activities, and they may promote their own bias on people in other communities.
- NGOs, unlike governments, are unaccountable; they are not elected by the people that they are representing.
- NGOs are sometimes accused of spending more money on advertising and promoting their activities, rather than allocating the money to the actual projects they are operating.

Economics in action

ATL Thinking, Communication and Research

Choose one NGO that works in the field of economic development in a developing country. Put together a report on this NGO, identifying its goals, its strategies, its successes and its challenges. Try to make references to the SDGs. Share this information with your classmates.

As a CAS initiative, you might want to try to do some work with this NGO or raise funds to support it.

How can multilateral assistance contribute to economic growth and/or economic development?

The most well-known providers of multilateral assistance are the World Bank and the International Monetary Fund (IMF).

The World Bank

The World Bank is made up of two closely-linked organisations – the International Bank for Reconstruction and Development (IBRD) and the International Development Agency. The World Bank provides financial support and technical assistance to developing countries, with the purpose of reducing poverty and supporting development. According to its mission statement, "The World Bank has two goals, to end poverty and promote shared prosperity in a sustainable way."[18]

First established following the end of World War II, the IBRD, was founded to lend money to countries in West Europe that needed help re-building their war-torn countries. Nowadays, the IBRD makes loans to middle-income and credit worthy developing countries. The funds for these loans are generated by the issue of World Bank bonds in global capital markets. Repayment of the bonds is guaranteed by the member states and by the government of the borrowing country. Because of this the bonds are seen as very safe and the IBRD is able to get the funds at relatively low interest rates. Thus the IBRD can lend to developing countries at rates that are below the rates that the countries would have to pay if they borrowed the money from other sources.

Economics in action

ATL Thinking, Communication and Research

Pick (at least) one of the World Bank development topics. Research its goals and some of its projects in this area. How do projects undertaken by the Bank help to reach any of the SDGs?

The International Development Agency (IDA) was founded in 1960, and is the part of the World Bank that works with the world's poorest countries. According to its mission statement, "The IDA provides grants and zero-to low-interest loans to the poorest countries to help boost their economic growth, reduce inequalities and improve people's living conditions.[19] The poorer the country, the more favourable the loan conditions.

In its early years, the World Bank tended to provide loans to finance large scale infrastructure projects such as electricity generation and transportation. Nowadays the focus is on smaller scale projects that aim to directly target and benefit the poorest people. A look at their website gives an idea of the huge numbers of programmes in which they are involved and information about all these projects. The projects are grouped into 27 different development topics, shown in Table 31.3. [20]

Agriculture and food	Digital development	Environment	Forests	Health	Poverty	Transport
Climate change	Disaster risk management	Extractive industries	Fragility, conflict and violence	Inequality and shared prosperity	Social development	Urban development
Competitiveness	Education	Financial inclusion	Gender	Jobs and development	Social protection	Water
Debt	Energy	Financial sector	Governance	Nutrition	Trade	

▲ **Table 31.3** World Bank Development Topics

The International Monetary Fund

The IMF was proposed at the Bretton Woods Agreements in 1944 at the same time as the International Bank for Reconstruction and Development.

According to its mission statement, "The IMF is an organization of 189

[18] **Source: The World Bank, IBRD, IDA,** https://www.worldbank.org/

[19] **Source, What is IDA?** http://ida.worldbank.org/about/what-is-ida

[20] **Source,** The World Bank Development Topics, http://www.worldbank.org/en/topic

countries, working to foster global monetary cooperation, secure financial stability, facilitate international trade, promote high employment and sustainable economic growth and reduce poverty around the world."[21]

The IMF's primary purpose is to ensure the stability of the international monetary system – the system of exchange rates and international payments that enables countries (and their citizens) to transact with each other. The Fund's mandate was updated in 2012 to include all macroeconomic and financial sector issues that bear on global stability."

The responsibilities of the IMF are set out in its Articles of Agreement as being:

- promoting international monetary cooperation
- facilitating the expansion and balanced growth of international trade
- promoting exchange stability
- assisting in the establishment of a multilateral system of payments
- making its resources available (under adequate safeguards) to members experiencing balance of payments difficulties.

The IMF uses three practices to meet its objectives. These are surveillance, financial assistance and capacity development (technical assistance and training). The IMF conducts an annual in-depth survey of each of its member countries and their economic performance. They then discuss, with the government of the country in question, the policies that are best suited to achieving stable exchange rates and economic growth. This is known as surveillance. These reports are normally published to encourage transparency.

The IMF offers technical assistance and training to its member countries, usually free of charge, in areas such as fiscal and monetary policy, exchange rate policy, banking and finance, and statistics.

When member countries are having problems in financing their balance of payments, the IMF can offer financial assistance in the form of loans. The IMF is funded by a system of "quotas", where each member country deposits money with the IMF. The size of the quota reflects each country's size in economic terms. The loans are made from these quotas. As a condition for receiving the loan, the IMF demands the implementation of a policy programme, agreed by the government of the country and the IMF. Support only continues if the policies are effectively carried out. At the present time, the IMF has approximately $1 trillion available for lending to its member countries.

Working independently, and in partnership with the World Bank, the IMF provides concessional lending through the Poverty Reduction and Growth Trust, at zero interest, and debt relief under the Heavily Indebted Poor Countries (HIPC) Initiative. In 2015, the IMF also created the Catastrophe Containment and Relief Trust. Under the new trust the IMF can join international debt relief efforts for poor countries hit by the most catastrophic of natural disasters and assist those battling public

[21] **Source:** The International Monetary Fund, https://www.imf.org/en/About

Did you know?

The World Bank Group

When we speak about the World Bank, we are referring to the combined work of the International Bank for Reconstruction and Development (IBRD) and the International Development Agency (IDA). In addition to these two organisations, there are three additional organisations that make up the World Bank Group.

These three additional organisations are:

The International Finance Corporation (IFC)

Founded in 1956, the IFC arm of the World Bank group, aims to promote private sector investment in developing countries. The IFC lends funds to private customers to finance development projects in developing countries.The IFC is also involved in giving technical assistance, both to companies and to governments.

The Multilateral Investment Guarantee Agency (MIGA)

Founded in 1988, MIGA promotes foreign direct investment in developing countries to support economic growth and reduce poverty. They do this by selling political risk insurance to MNCs. This insurance covers potential risks such as war, terrorism, the confiscation of assets by the government and the freezing of funds within a country.

The International Centre for Settlement of Investment Disputes (ICSID)

Founded in 1966, ICSID facilitates the settlement of investment disputes between member countries and individual international investors. Over 150 countries are now members of the ICSID.

health disasters – such as infectious diseases epidemics – with grants for debt service relief. Three Ebola-afflicted countries (Guinea, Liberia, Sierra Leone) received such assistance, totalling about $100 million in February and March 2015[22].

Both the World Bank and the International Monetary Fund are essential organizations for providing financial support and technical assistance to developing countries. Their overarching goals are consistent with international development goals in general, and the Sustainable Development Goals in particular. Nonetheless, there are concerns about both institutions that include (but are not limited to) the following:

- Both were established in the United States and their neighbouring headquarters are in Washington D.C. Despite their stated goals and the relevance of their projects to economic development and reducing poverty, they have been accused of promoting free market, business-friendly policies which mainly help companies in developed countries and high-income people in developing countries.
- By tradition, the head of the World Bank is appointed by the American president. Clearly, this raises concerns that the chosen person will direct policy in ways that are primarily in the interest of the U.S.
- A particularly negative impression of the IMF is associated with the conditions that it may set on countries who take IMF loans. Following the "Third World Debt Crisis" in the early 1980s, the IMF lent money to countries on the grounds that they would adopt certain policies to reduce fiscal deficits and encourage economic growth in order to be able to repay the loans. These policies were known as IMF Structural Adjustment Policies (SAP). The SAPs, reflected the free market school of thought which dominated the IMF and the World Bank. The policies were known as the Washington Consensus. and commonly included the following free market reforms:
  - ➔ trade liberalization
  - ➔ encouraging the export of primary commodities
  - ➔ devaluing the currency
  - ➔ liberalized capital flows
  - ➔ encouraging FDI
  - ➔ privatization of nationalized industries
  - ➔ elimination of subsidies and price controls
  - ➔ austerity measures to reduce government spending, including spending in areas such as education and health.

IMF Says It Cares About Inequality. But Will It Change Its Ways?

http://thecorner.eu/world-economy/imf-says-it-cares-about-inequality-but-will-it-change-its-ways/81224/

With the focus on economic growth following free market principles, countries may have been able to repay loans, but the consequences of SAPs were widely seen as damaging to the poor, and a failure in terms of contributing to economic development.

With its stated goal of reducing poverty, the approach of the IMF has changed from the days of the SAPs, but concerns remain.

[22] **Source:** IMF, www.imf.org

Exercise 31.3

ATL Thinking and Communication

Read the article and answer the questions that follow:

Ecuador agrees to a $4.2 billion financing deal with the IMF

Ecuador has reached a $4.2 billion financing deal with the International Monetary Fund (IMF), President Lenin Moreno said on Wednesday, as the Andean country grapples with a large **budget deficit** and heavy external debt.

The country will also receive $6 billion in loans from multilateral institutions including the World Bank, the Inter-American Development Bank, and the CAF Andean development bank, Moreno said in a message broadcast on national television and radio.

The OPEC nation's debt grew under former leftist President Rafael Correa. President Moreno earned Correa's support during the 2017 election campaign, but has implemented more market-friendly economic policies since taking office.

President Moreno said the maturities on the loans extended "up to 30 years" and that the interest rates "on average" did not exceed 5 percent. "This money will create work opportunities for those who have not yet found something stable," he said.

Moreno has begun to implement an austerity plan that includes layoffs of workers at state-owned companies and cuts to gasoline subsidies. There are also plans to find a private operator for state-run telecoms company CNT and other state-owned firms. Moreover, allowing for less rigidity in wages and prices could help support external adjustment. This can be achieved through policies that remove rigidities in the labour and product markets and in the financial sector.

Other reforms to make the country an attractive business destination and to boost growth and more formal employment include reviewing the system of taxation and removing obstacles to business formation and operation. Other key reforms include taking steps to encourage private investment, opening international trade and creating better conditions for participation of women in the labour market.

According to the IMF, Ecuador has made substantial gains in reducing poverty and inequality over the past two decades, since the country adopted dollarization (using the US dollar as its currency). Ecuador's gini index fell from 58 in 1999 to 45 in 2016. The percentage of the population living in **relative poverty** has fallen from 64.4 percent in 2000 to 21.5 percent in 2017 and the share of the population living in **absolute poverty** fell from 28.2 percent in 2000 to 3.6 percent in 2016.

While these are notable achievements, poverty rates among the rural and indigenous populations remain high. While social assistance spending is high by regional standards and there is good coverage of those in the bottom 20 percent of the income distribution, the authorities see scope to do more. Therefore, the government included measures in the plan to continue protecting the poor and most vulnerable. These include:

- increasing spending on social assistance programs, such as Bono de Desarrollo Humano, Bono Joaquin Gallegos Lara as well as extending the coverage of pensions
- developing a social registry to improve targeting of social programs
- increasing the efficiency and quality of primary education and health spending to enhance human capital and external competitiveness of the economy.

Skepticism of the IMF runs strong in Ecuador and throughout Latin America, where many blame Fund-imposed austerity policies for economic hardship.

a) Define the following terms used in the article:

i) budget deficit [2 marks]

ii) relative poverty [2 marks]

iii) absolute poverty. [2 marks]

b) Using a Lorenz curve diagram, explain what happened to income distribution in Ecuador from 1999 to 2016. [4 marks]

c) Identify market-oriented approaches that Ecuador has undertaken or is planning to undertake. [4 marks]

d) Identify interventionist approaches that Ecuador has undertaken or is planning to undertake. [4 marks]

e) Evaluate possible consequences of the different types of policies in terms of their effects on economic growth and economic development. [15 marks]

Economics in action

ATL Thinking, Communication and Research

1. Select two countries with HDI index values below 0.500.
2. Go to the website www.oecd.org.
3. Search for "Aid at a Glance, by recipient".
4. Select "Aid at a glance charts – OECD" from the list
5. Select ODA flows for recipients
6. Under "Interactive summary charts by aid (ODA) recipients" choose "Open interactive charts"
7. Select each of the countries you have chosen in the top left-hand corner, recipient country scroll down box.
8. Now write a report, maximum 500 words, where you compare and contrast the amount of aid received, the types of aid received, the sources of the aid and what the aid is used for, for each of the countries.

To help you, the "Aid at a glance" chart for Benin is given below:

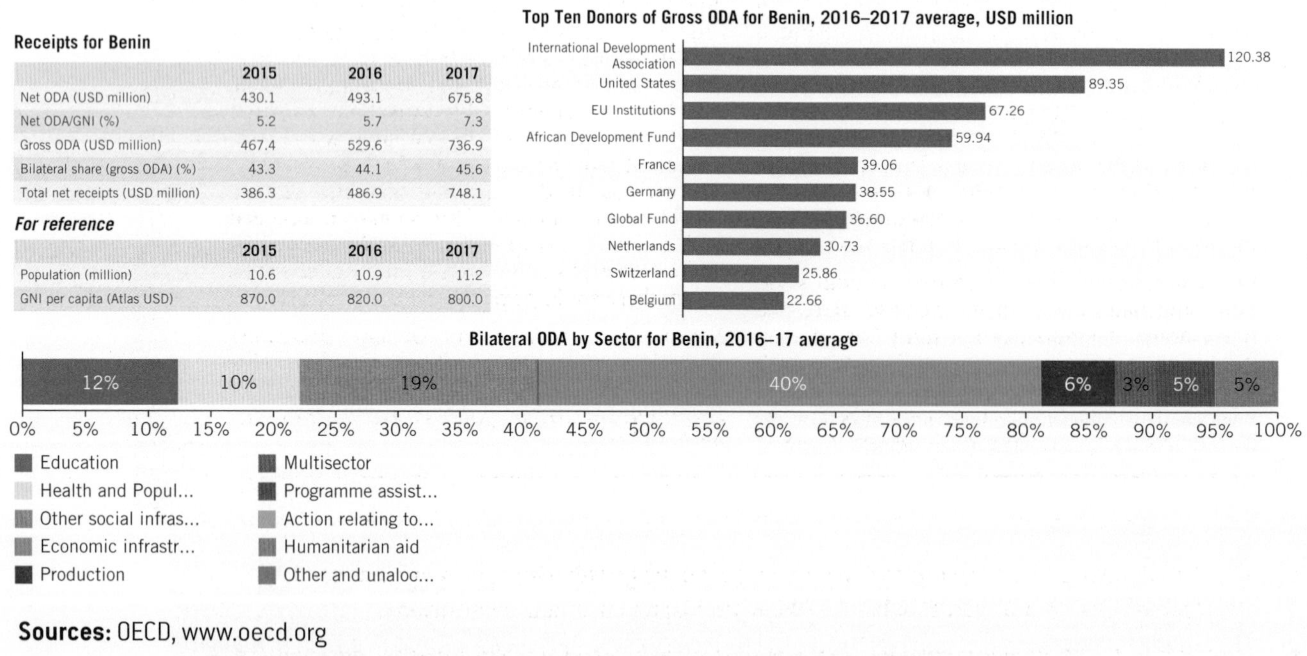

Receipts for Benin

	2015	2016	2017
Net ODA (USD million)	430.1	493.1	675.8
Net ODA/GNI (%)	5.2	5.7	7.3
Gross ODA (USD million)	467.4	529.6	736.9
Bilateral share (gross ODA) (%)	43.3	44.1	45.6
Total net receipts (USD million)	386.3	486.9	748.1

For reference

	2015	2016	2017
Population (million)	10.6	10.9	11.2
GNI per capita (Atlas USD)	870.0	820.0	800.0

Sources: OECD, www.oecd.org

Total ODA receipts are in the top left table, as is the percentage of bilateral aid. The aid sources are in the top right box. The uses/targets of the aid are given in the bottom boxes.

Economics in action

ATL Thinking, Communication and Research

Research the extent to which investment, loans and aid from China are contributing to economic growth and development in African countries.

Exercise 31.4

ATL Thinking and Communication

Read the article and answer the questions that follow.

Jobless Growth in Bangladesh

According to official statistics, between 2013 and 2016–17, on average, **gross domestic product** (GDP) in Bangladesh grew annually by 6.6 percent, and there has been a net increase of 2.8 million new jobs on top of the 60.7 million jobs that existed in the economy in 2013. This suggests that the number of jobs grew by only 0.9 percent per annum or less than one-eighth of the rate at which the economy grew during those five years. It seems that the growth experienced by Bangladesh is "jobless growth" when an economy experiences growth without a corresponding expansion of jobs.

One of the most alarming features is that manufacturing jobs declined by 0.77 million—from 9.53 million in 2013 to 8.76 million in 2016–17—an annual average decline by 1.6 percent, despite a strong manufacturing output growth of 10.4 percent. While male manufacturing jobs increased by only 0.17 million (from 5.73 million to 5.9 million), female manufacturing jobs actually saw a big drop by 0.92 million (from 3.78 million to 2.86 million). This suggests that the success of generating female employment in the manufacturing sector over the past few decades is at risk now.

One can interpret these outcomes as both good news and bad news. On the positive side, one might argue that labour productivity has gone up due to technological improvement. However, such arguments do not provide any comfort to those who see these numbers as bad news. It is obvious that the economy's rapid growth, which is one of the fastest in the world in recent years, has failed to generate jobs on a large scale, and thus has not been able to translate into the desired reduction in poverty. Consequently, the economy's growth is far from becoming "inclusive growth" as aspired to by the government in its national development plans. This has contributed to widening income inequality too in recent years as is evident from the growing Gini index.

Achieving a high rate of economic growth alone, in terms of a mere increase in the GDP growth rate, should not be treated as a solution for all problems.. The quality of growth is important, and in particular, growth must be able to produce jobs and livelihoods for as many people as possible. In order to avoid "jobless growth", the pattern, structure and strategies of growth have to be revisited. The economic growth momentum needs to be tuned for "meaningful" diversification and structural transformation of the economy where promotion of labour-intensive and high-productivity sectors, both in the farm and non-farm sectors, would be fundamental. This should be coupled with interventions to enhance productivity, jobs and incomes in traditional and informal activities where there are large pools of surplus labour.

Source: Adapted from "An Anatomy of Jobless Growth in Bangladesh', The Daily Star, May 28, 2019 https://www.thedailystar.net/opinion/economics/anatomy-jobless-growth-bangladesh-1572829

a) Use the information from the text to explain why economic growth may not result in economic development. As always, you should try to think of a diagram that you could include.

b) Explain how the strategies suggested by the author might be used to make economic growth more inclusive in Bangladesh.

How can debt relief contribute to economic growth and development?

The IMF published the following regarding the importance of debt relief in pursuing economic development:

- *Debt relief frees up resources for social spending:* Debt relief is one part of a much larger effort, which also includes aid flows, to address the development needs of low-income countries and make sure that debt sustainability is maintained over time. For debt reduction to have a tangible impact on poverty, the additional money needs to be spent on programs that benefit the poor.
- *Boosting social spending:* Before the Highly Indebted Poor Countries (HIPC) Initiative, eligible countries were, on average, spending slightly more on debt service than on health and education combined. Now, they have increased markedly their expenditures on health, education and other social services. On average, such spending is about five times the amount of debt-service payments.
- *Reducing debt service:* For the 36 countries receiving debt relief, debt service paid has declined by about 1.5 percentage points of GDP between 2001 and 2015.
- *Improving public debt management:* Debt relief has markedly improved the debt position of post–completion point countries, bringing their debt indicators down below those of other HIPCs or non-HIPCs. However, many remain vulnerable to shocks, particularly those affecting exports, as seen during the global economic crisis. To reduce their debt vulnerabilities decisively, countries need to pursue cautious borrowing policies and strengthen their public debt management.[23]

Despite improvements, the problem of high levels of indebtedness seems to be rising again. The Jubilee Debt Campaign reported that its study of 126 developing countries revealed that on average, countries were spending more than 10% of their revenues to pay the interest on the money that had been borrowed. This was the highest level of indebtedness since before the 2005 agreement of G7 countries to cancel the debts of the world's poorest countries. There are calls for there to be more accountability in terms of the way that private lenders provide loans to developing countries to avoid the accumulation of debt.

Is a new debt crisis mounting in Africa?

https://www.worldfinance.com/special-reports/is-a-new-debt-crisis-mounting-in-africa

[23] Debt Relief Under the Heavily Indebted Poor Countries (HIPC) Initiative, March 19 2019, IMF

Government Intervention versus market-oriented approaches to achieving economic growth and/or development

Throughout this Course Companion, you have learned about different strategies to achieve economic goals. As you will have seen, they may be grouped into two main categories: interventionist strategies and market-oriented strategies. All of these strategies are employed to achieve economic growth and development, but in many cases, economic growth can come at the cost of economic development and at the cost of sustainability. Therefore, it must be concluded that for any country in the world, regardless of its national income, a complementary package of policies should be adopted when approaching any economic issue, in order to achieve inclusive, sustainable economic development.

Exercise 31.5

ATL Thinking and Communication

The list below is a very simplified summary of the broad types of policies that fall into the categories of interventionist and market-oriented strategies. You should be sure that you can explain what each of them is, provide examples of where they are used and explain the strengths and weaknesses of each of them in achieving inclusive, sustainable economic growth and development.

Market-oriented approaches	Interventionist approaches
• Policies to support competition • Taxes and tradable permits • Deregulation • Privatization • Labour market policies • Tax cuts • Trade liberalization	• Direct provision of merit goods • Direct provision of public goods • Regulations and legislation (command and control) • Consumer nudges • Subsidies • Tax and transfer policies • Price controls such as minimum wages and rent controls • Policies to reduce inequalities • Interventionist supply-side policies • Demand-side policies (to impact short term macroeconomic outcomes) • Trade protection

EXAMINATION QUESTIONS

Paper 1, part (a) questions – HL & SL

1. Explain **two** strategies that might be used to promote economic growth. [10 marks]
2. Explain how increased foreign direct investment might promote economic growth. [10 marks]
3. Explain the difference between import substitution and export promotion. [10 marks]
4. Explain **two** market based supply-side policies that might promote economic growth. [10 marks]
5. Explain **two** areas of institutional change that may promote economic development. [10 marks]
6. Explain the role of the World Bank in promoting economic development. [10 marks]
7. Explain how non-government organizations operate as a means of promoting economic development. [10 marks]

Paper 1, part (b) questions – HL & SL

1. Using real-world examples, discuss the effectiveness of foreign direct investment in achieving economic growth and economic development. [15 marks]
2. Using real-world examples, evaluate the effectiveness of supply-side policies in promoting economic growth and economic development. [15 marks]
3. Using real-world examples, evaluate the effectiveness of foreign aid in promoting economic growth and economic development. [15 marks]
4. Using real-world examples, evaluate the strengths and limitations of strategies for promoting economic growth and economic development. [15 marks]
5. Using real-world examples, evaluate the success of a country of your choice in achieving any **two** Sustainable Development Goals. [15 marks]

32 ASSESSMENT ADVICE

By the end of this chapter, you should be able to:

- → Understand strategies for revision
- → Understand the demands of Paper 1, the essay paper
- → Understand how to approach Paper 1
- → Understand the demands of Paper 2, the data response paper
- → Understand how to approach Paper 2
- → Understand the demands of HL Paper 3, the policy paper
- → Understand how to approach HL Paper 3
- → Understand evaluation and synthesis
- → Understand different means of evaluation
- → Understand the demands of the Internal Assessment component
- → Understand approaches to writing the Extended Essay in economics
- → Understand opportunities for service activities in economics

How do you prepare for your economics examinations?

Hopefully, you will be able to start preparing for your exams well in advance. There are hundreds of approaches to exam revision, so we will not go into them here. However, there are several pieces of advice that we would like to share.

First, one thing that you have to do on all papers is show a clear understanding of all of the key terms. Thus, one element of your revision should involve making sure that you know accurate definitions of economic words. You will find a glossary of terms and definitions on our website. However, as a learning tool, you should actively write out your own glossary and test yourself to ensure that you can remember the definitions.

Second, it is also recommended that you compile a collection of diagrams. Again, it is not enough to simply look at the diagrams in your notes or in your textbooks. You need to practise drawing them yourself, from memory, to ensure that you can include accurate labels and show the correct relationships between variables on the graphs. The key to remembering the graphs is to make sure that you are familiar with the story that they are telling.

Third, marks are awarded for the inclusion of real-world examples wherever appropriate. Thus, as you are preparing your own revision notes, you are encouraged to note down current and relevant real-world examples. For instance, if you are studying negative externalities of consumption, note the example of the external costs of consuming sugary foods. If you are studying international trade barriers, then include an example of the specific protectionist measures taken by the US against Chinese tyres. If you are studying unemployment, then note some of the key facts about the OECD country that you have studied in the Economics in Action exercises.

> **Reminder**
> Revision notes should include definitions, diagrams and real-world examples.

Fourth, a very important skill that the examination assesses is the skill of evaluation. We provide a separate explanation of this later in this chapter. You must pay close attention to it if you are to do well.

What advice works for all the written examination papers?

This follows on from the information above. Marks are specifically given for defining the key terms, so make sure that you do this in all papers and questions. At the very least, the economics words that are stated in the question must be defined.

Always draw diagrams where they are appropriate and draw as many diagrams as you need to make the points clear. Make sure you put **accurate** labels on the axes and all the curves and remember to show the correct relationships between the variables. Draw arrows to indicate the direction of changes in variables. Be sure to provide explanations and make references to your diagrams in your writing. While titles are not required, they are very useful in showing that you know what market you are illustrating.

The presentation of diagrams is very important. Use a ruler and draw your diagrams in pencil so that you can make corrections if necessary. Don't try to squeeze a diagram into a small space on the page. A small diagram may be difficult to interpret properly and it may be difficult to incorporate all the necessary information if it is too small.

What is Paper 1 and how do you approach it?

Paper 1 is an essay paper. For Higher Level students, this paper is worth 20% of the final IB economics grade. For Standard Level students, it is worth 30% of the final grade. There are three questions on this paper and you are required to answer **one** of the questions in one hour and fifteen minutes.

The questions are drawn from the four units of the syllabus, so they could be on any topic area. For SL students, the questions will **not** be drawn from HL extension material and topics studied at HL only. It is highly likely that each question will be from a different unit, ie introduction, microeconomics, macroeconomics or the global economy.

Each essay question in Paper 1 consists of two parts, (a) and (b). Part (a) is worth 10 marks and part (b) is worth 15 marks.

You will be given five minutes of reading time before you can start writing, so this gives you time to consider all the questions carefully, so that you can make the right choice of essay title.

In this paper you want to be able to show that you have some in-depth understanding of specific topics, but you will not do this if you have not read the question carefully. A very common error is that students don't **read the questions carefully** enough and write a lot of economic theory that isn't directly relevant to the question. Remember that it is the quality of the answer that is important, not the quantity!

Once the five minute reading time is over and you are able to start writing, it is a good idea to make a plan before you start to write the actual essay. You might think that there is not enough time, but a plan will help you to stay on track once you have started writing. You do not want to get sidetracked and lose your focus on the question. A quick plan can help you to manage your time properly and ensure that you cover the main points.

For part (a), your plan could simply be a list of which terms to define, what theory needs to be explained, and what diagrams, if any, need to be drawn. For part (b), the plan would be the same elements, but added to it would be the real-world examples that you could use and the evaluation that you would attempt.

How do you answer part (a)?

In part (a), you will be asked to explain a particular economic concept or theory or to distinguish between related economic concepts. You need to be able to illustrate the skills of knowledge and understanding, application, and analysis. There are a number of "command" terms that could be used in these questions. Command terms are the words at the beginning of a question that indicate what skill you are to use. The most common command term used in part (a) questions is 'Explain', but there are other possibilities.Here are some examples of the command terms, along with sample part (a) questions:

- **Explain** *three* reasons for an increase in aggregate demand – "explain" means to give a detailed account, including reasons or causes.
- **Analyse** the relationship between the Gini coefficient and the Lorenz curve – "analyse" means to break down in order to bring out the essential elements or structure.
- **Distinguish** between trade creation and trade diversion [HL only] – "distinguish" to make clear the differences between two or more concepts or items.
- **Suggest** two approaches that a central bank could take to reduce inflation – "suggest" means to propose a solution, hypothesis or other possible answer.

Level 5 (9–10 marks)

- The response indicates full understanding of the specific demands of the question.
- Relevant theory is fully explained.
- Relevant economic terms are used appropriately throughout the response.
- Where appropriate, relevant diagram(s) are included and fully explained.

Reminder

As you write part (a), always check back to the essay title to make sure that you are still sticking to the question and that you have not been diverted.

Please observe that even though it is not explicitly stated in the question, each of the questions above would benefit enormously from a diagram, and so you should include one (or more). On the front of the examination paper, under instructions to candidates, it is stated, "Use fully labelled diagrams where appropriate".

In order to know how to best answer an exam question, it is very important that you are aware of how you are going to be assessed on your answer. Therefore, we have provided a list of descriptors taken from the top level of the mark scheme. This is shown here and it tells you what is required for an excellent answer.

It should be clear, looking at the descriptors above, that if you define your terms accurately and use them appropriately; use and explain the correct theory; and provide a relevant diagram and explain it fully; then you must achieve the top level of response for part (a).

How do you answer part (b)?

In part (b) you will be asked to move beyond an explanation towards the evaluation or synthesis of a particular economic policy or theory. You do not need to repeat the definitions that you wrote in part (a), but it is likely that there will be some new terms to define. If you have drawn diagrams in part (a) that are useful then you can refer back to them, but it is likely that you will be extending the information in part (b) and so it may be more useful to re-draw the diagrams and add the necessary information. For example, you might be asked to distinguish between demand-deficient and structural unemployment in part (a) and then asked to evaluate the policies that a government might use to reduce unemployment in part (b). It is likely that you will have drawn diagrams to support your answer in part (a), but you would need new diagrams to illustrate the solutions in part (b). In part (b), the skills involved are the skills of evaluation and synthesis. The most common command terms used in part (b) questions are 'Evaluate' and 'Discuss', but there are other possibilities. Here are some examples of the command terms, along with sample part (b) questions:

- Using real-world examples, **evaluate** the policies that a government could use to reduce negative externalities of production. – "Evaluate" means to make an appraisal by weighing up the strengths and limitations (more on this later).
- Using real-world examples, **discuss** the view that "the provision of aid is essential to enable less developed countries to achieve economic development". – "Discuss" means to present a considered and balanced review that includes a range of arguments, factors or hypotheses. Opinions or conclusions should be presented clearly and supported by appropriate evidence.
- Using real-world examples, **to what extent** might it be argued that demand management is best carried out by a central bank? – "To what extent" means that you have to consider the merits or

otherwise of an argument or concept. Opinions and conclusions should be presented clearly and supported with appropriate evidence and sound argument.

- Using real-world examples, **compare and contrast** the use of fiscal and monetary policies in reducing inflation. – "Compare and contrast" means to give an account of similarities and differences between two (or more) items or situations, referring to both (all) of them throughout.

As you will have noticed, a key element of all part (b) questions is "using real-world examples". The use of a real-world example in your response to part (b) is essential if you are to be successful. This is why we have encouraged you to investigate the real world throughout this Companion. The list of descriptors for the top level of the mark scheme for part (b) is shown here.

Note the additional two descriptors, over and above part (a). It should be clear that you need to do a bit more in part (b) to be successful. You need to define your terms accurately and use them appropriately; use and explain the correct theory; provide a relevant diagram and explain it fully; evaluate the situation; and write the answer in the context of a real-world example.

Level 5 (13–15 marks)

- The response indicates full understanding of the specific demands of the question.
- Relevant theory is fully explained.
- Relevant economic terms are used appropriately throughout the response.
- Where appropriate, relevant diagram(s) are included and fully explained.
- The response contains evidence of effective and balanced synthesis or evaluation.
- A relevant real-world example(s) is identified and fully developed to support the argument.

What is Paper 2 and how do you approach it?

Paper 2 is a data response paper. For Higher Level students this paper is worth 30% of the final IB economics grade. For Standard Level students it is worth 40% of the final grade. There are two questions on this paper and you are required to answer **one** of them. You are given one hour and 45 minutes to complete the question. Each question is worth forty marks. Each question will cover all areas of the syllabus in its question parts.

Reminder

The use of a real-world example to support your writing is essential in part (b). You need to ensure that you have examples that you can use to support all areas of the syllabus.

Both questions will follow the same format. There will be a number of sets of data in the form of pieces of written text and tables or graphs displaying numerical data. On this paper you are allowed to use a calculator as the part (b) questions usually involve some numerical analysis.

The five minutes of reading time are incredibly important here. You'll get a chance to skim all the questions to see which questions ask things you know about. Do not decide to do a question simply because you can define the two words given in part (a). It is more important that you can answer enough questions to earn as many marks as possible. When you can begin to write, it is recommended that you annotate the text – underline, highlight, make notes in the margin – anything to make you familiar with the data.

Effective time management is also extremely important. You have to do seven question parts in one and three quarter hours, but the last question part (g) carries 37.5% of the marks. It is essential that you leave yourself ample time to address that question part fully. If you have learned your definitions and diagrams effectively then you should be able to move relatively quickly through parts (a) to (f), thus leaving yourself sufficient time to thoughtfully carry out the evaluation required in part (g).

Each data response question has seven sub-questions, as described below:

- Part (a) – You are asked to define two words that are in the text. Each definition is worth two marks. A very common problem here is that students often write far too much on the definitions, thus wasting valuable time. An accurate definition is all that is required, there is no need for diagrams, explanations or examples.
- Part (b) – This will require the completion of two, simple, calculation questions. The questions will be worth a total of five marks. The areas where calculations are required have been explained in this Companion as we have gone through the topics.
- Parts (c) to (f) – These sub-questions require you to apply a specific piece of economic theory and are worth four marks each. The questions will cover all areas of the syllabus, microeconomics, macroeconomics and the global economy. In many cases you will be asked to draw a diagram. The question will tell you which diagram to use, for example, "Using an AD/AS diagram, ...). When you draw your diagrams be sure to label the axes with the variables noted in the text. For example, if the text is about the price of chickens in Indonesia, then the *y*-axis label might be price of chickens in rupiah. On these sub-questions, you must assess carefully what the question is asking. You will be under time pressure and should not write more than necessary as it will cut into your time for the other questions. Always try to make use of the text to support your use of the theory. Use a decent amount of space for the diagrams and the explanations. Examiners do not like to see writing and diagrams squeezed into small spaces.
- Part (g) – This sub-question asks you to use the information from the text and your knowledge of economics to evaluate something related to the text. This part of the question carries the most weight as it is worth fifteen out of the forty marks. The most common command terms used in the sub-question are 'Evaluate', 'Discuss' and 'To what extent'.

A key problem here is that students forget to use information from the text, even though the instructions specifically ask for this. Therefore, you are encouraged to use quotations or numerical data from the data in your answers. The section on evaluation later in this chapter should help you to know how you can be evaluative.

The list of descriptors for the top level of the mark scheme for part (g) is shown here.

Level 5 (13–15 marks)

- The response indicates full understanding of the specific demands of the question.
- Relevant theory is fully explained.
- Relevant economic terms are used appropriately throughout the response.
- Where appropriate, relevant diagram(s) are included and fully explained.
- The response contains evidence of effective and balanced synthesis or evaluation.
- The use of information from the text/data is appropriate, relevant and is used to support the analysis/evaluation.

Not surprisingly, the descriptors are almost identical to the ones used in the essay paper for part (b). The only difference is that here, there is a need to use information from the data provided to support the argument, as opposed to real-world examples. So, you need to define your terms accurately and use them appropriately; use and explain the correct theory; provide a relevant diagram, if appropriate, and explain it fully; evaluate the situation; and write the answer in the context of information from the text/data.

Reminder

The use of information from the text/data to support your writing is essential in part (g).

What is Higher Level Paper 3 and how do you approach it?

Paper 3 is a policy paper. This paper, written only by Higher Level students, tests topics across the whole syllabus, but especially the Higher Level extension topics. This paper, lasting one hour and 45 minutes has two questions and you will need to answer both of them. Each question is worth 30 marks. The paper is worth 30% of the final IB economics grade.

This paper is physically different from the other two papers, as you will be given an examination booklet in which to write your answers, draw your diagrams, and provide any calculations. Of course, if you need any extra space, you can include and attach extra sheets.

On this paper you are allowed to use a calculator as the questions involve some numerical analysis, where you calculate things like total revenue/expenditure, changes in the volume of exports/imports, the multiplier, terms of trade or elasticity to name a few.

All the numerical calculations require either whole numbers, or values to two decimal places. If you make an error in an early calculation then you can still earn marks for the later answers, as long as you use the correct reasoning, since the examiners will follow a rule known as the "Own Figure Rule".

Each Paper 3 question has nine sub-questions, as described below:

- Parts (a) to (h) – These sub-questions are normally asking for a response to stimulus material that is provided in the paper. The material may be such things as graphs, tables of values, and short texts including data. The questions may be asking for definitions, calculations or explanations. They will not require any evaluation or synthesis.
- Part (i) – This sub-question asks you to "Recommend a policy....". The command term 'recommend' requires a candidate to "present an advisable course of action with appropriate supporting evidence/reason in relation to a given situation, problem or issue". An example of a part (i) question might be – "Using the data provided, your knowledge of economics and your answers to parts (a) to (h), **recommend** a policy which could be introduced by the government of Country Y to address the problem of obesity."

  The list of descriptors for the top level of the mark scheme for part (i) is shown here.

Level 5 (9–10 marks)

- The response identifies and fully explains an appropriate policy.
- The response uses relevant theory effectively to support the recommendation.
- Relevant economic terms are used appropriately throughout the response.
- The use of information from the text/data is appropriate, relevant and supports the analysis/evaluation effectively.
- The response contains evidence of effective and balanced synthesis or evaluation.

Higher Level

Reminder

You must identify and explain an appropriate policy in part (g).

Not surprisingly, the descriptors are very similar to the ones used in the essay paper for part (b) and the data response paper for part (g). The difference is that here, there is a need to use information from the data provided and from your previous answers to support the argument. So, you need to identify and explain a policy; define your terms accurately and use them appropriately; use relevant theory to support your proposal; and evaluate the situation in the context of information from the text/data, your previous answers, and your wider economic knowledge.

What is evaluation/synthesis?

There are several places on your exam where you are asked to evaluate/synthesize something. One place is part (g) on the data response question, another is in part (b) of the essay question, and the third is in parts (i) of the policy questions. You are also expected to illustrate the skill of evaluation/synthesis in your internal assessment commentaries. As we already know, the command terms to indicate that you should evaluate/synthesize include the words, "evaluate", "discuss", "examine", "justify", "compare and contrast", "recommend" and "to what extent".

What does evaluation mean?

Two dictionary definitions of evaluate are as follows:

- *v: to examine and judge carefully; appraise*
- *v: place a value on; judge the worth of something*

How can you evaluate?

In the final analysis you must show evidence that you have examined something carefully and that you have come to a reasoned decision or conclusion. It is not quite enough to simply finish a sentence that begins, "On the other hand . . ." but it is a good start.

- **Prioritize the arguments**
  After giving a list of points, you need to make a conclusion in which you could state which one is the most (or least) significant or important point and then explain why.

  Example 1: "The **most important argument** against protectionism in international trade is that it represents a global misallocation of resources. This is because, when countries erect protectionist barriers, they are supporting inefficient domestic producers at the expense of more efficient producers in foreign countries that are exploiting their comparative advantage."

  Example 2: "The **least effective way** to reduce the negative effects of smoking effectively is to increase taxes. This is because the demand for cigarettes is inelastic and the increase in price due to taxes is likely to result in a proportionately smaller fall in quantity demanded. However, the government may earn high tax revenues which can be used to pay for the external costs and finance no-smoking campaigns.

Note that it in each case it is not enough to say which is the most important; you also need to explain why.

- **Long run versus short run**
  It is quite possible that the short-run consequences of an economic policy or event might be different from the long-run consequences. If you distinguish between the two time frames you will be providing an appraisal of the difference and so you will be evaluating.

  Example 1: "**In the short run**, abnormal profits can be earned in perfect competition. However, **in the long run** this is not possible. The existence of abnormal profits, perfect information and lack of barriers to entry means that industry supply will increase, driving down the price taken by individual firms so that only normal profits may be earned."

  Example 2: "**In the short run**, it may be possible to justify the infant industry argument as it is possible that, protected by tariffs, some firms will develop the economies of scale necessary to be internationally competitive. However, the danger is that **in the long run**, the industry will not become internationally competitive due to the lack of effective competition.

- **Consider the issue from the points of view of different stakeholders**
  What is a stakeholder? One dictionary definition is as follows: *a person or group that has an investment, share or interest in something.*

  In terms of economic theory, examples of stakeholders could be domestic producers, consumers, foreign producers, high-income people, low-income people or the government. When you consider an issue from the perspective of different stakeholders and then come to a conclusion about the nature of these different effects, then you are evaluating.

  Example 1: "A high exchange rate may be **good for consumers** because it makes imported goods less expensive and forces domestic producers to be more efficient so that they compete with the less expensive imports. On the other hand, it is clearly a **disadvantage for those domestic producers** who suffer from the competition from imports which become less expensive with the higher value of the currency."

  Example 2: "Supply-side policies may be very good in terms of creating a more flexible labour force and achieving economic growth. However, it may **lower the standards of living of workers** who may suffer from deregulation of the labour laws."

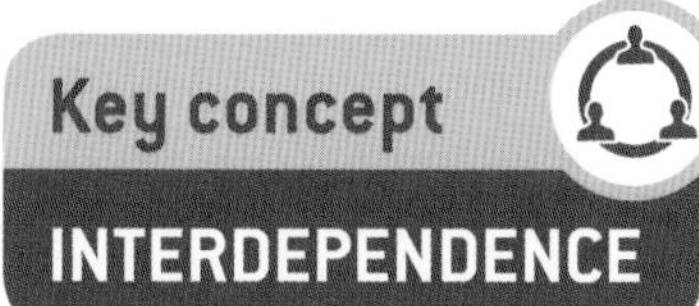

Key concept
SCARCITY

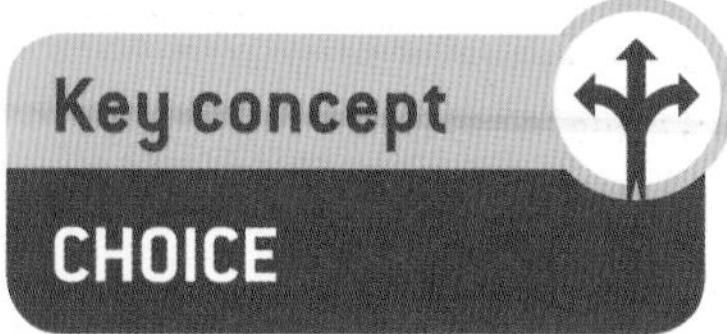

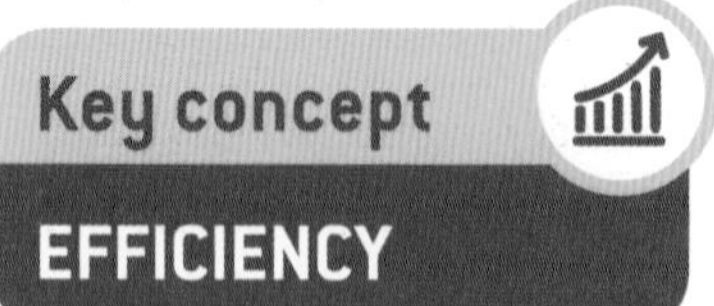

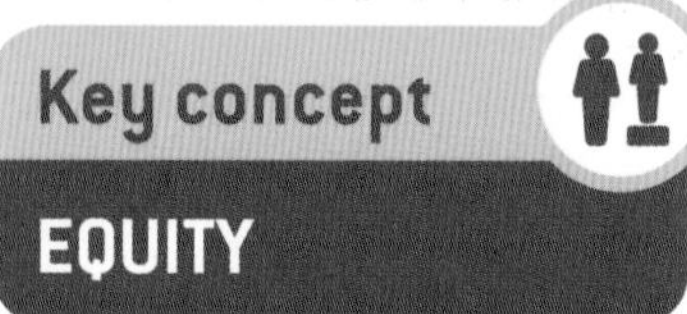

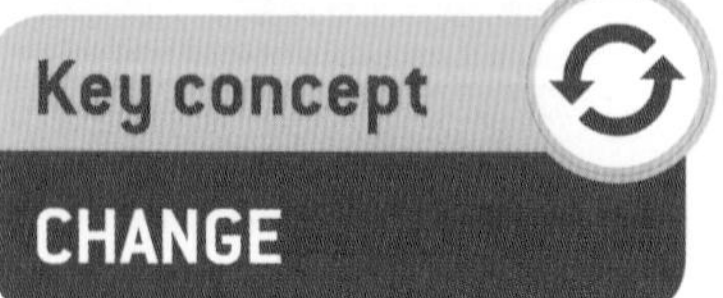

Internal Assessment

Every IB Economics student completes a portfolio containing **three "commentaries"**, each a **maximum of 800 words**. You select your own articles from published news media and write a commentary in which you apply economic theory to the real-world example discussed in the article. Ideally, the three commentaries are written as the course progresses, as you learn more and more economic theory.

Each commentary **must be based upon a different unit of the syllabus**, but not the Introduction unit, so the three commentaries **must cover Microeconomics, Macroeconomics and the Global Economy**. In addition, each commentary **must refer to a different key concept** from the syllabus. Remember that the key concepts are: scarcity; choice; efficiency; equity; economic well being; sustainability; change; interdependence; and intervention.

The portfolio as a whole is worth 20% of the final grade for HL students and 30% of the final grade for SL students. Assessment of the portfolio is identical for both groups and is based on five criteria. These mirror the skills that are emphasized in the examinations, but without the time pressure of an exam! The criteria are listed and briefly explained in Table 32.1.

Criterion	Title	What is expected	Marks available
A	Diagrams	An ability to construct and explain relevant diagrams.	3
B	Terminology	An ability to use appropriate economic terminology accurately.	2
C	Application and analysis	An ability to apply economic theory with effective economic analysis.	3
D	Key concept	An ability to identify and link a key concept to a real-world situation.	3
E	Evaluation	An ability to make judgements supported by effective and balanced reasoning.	3
Total			**14 marks**

▲ **Table 32.1** Internal Assessment Criteria

In addition to the 14 marks that are available for each commentary, there are an additional three marks to be awarded based on the way that you manage to **meet the rubric requirements** (each article is based on a different unit of the syllabus, each article is taken from a different and appropriate source, each commentary includes reference to a different key concept).

Therefore, the total marks available for the portfolio is 45 marks (14 × 3 commentaries + 3 for rubric requirements). It is not possible to provide the full assessment details in this companion so it is absolutely vital that you are given access to the full IB document about internal assessment. This includes sample commentaries that will help you have an understanding of the end result.

The first step in approaching the task of writing a commentary is to find a suitable current article. Nowadays, the bulk of articles come from internet sources and there are a number of search engines that are useful in finding appropriate articles. Ideally, you will find articles that highlight the theory that you have just finished studying. This way, the material will be fresh, and hopefully you will have been discussing relevant examples in class. Table 32.2 provides some examples of words that can be used on search engines to generate articles on topics once they have been studied.

Topic covered	Possible search words or phrases
Market failure (Unit 2)	External costs, air pollution, water pollution, road-pricing, cigarette taxes, alcohol taxes, sustainable development
Market power (Unit 2)	Monopoly power, price-fixing, collusion, competition commission, competition watch dog
Macroeconomics (Unit 3)	Consumer confidence, interest rate changes, aggregate demand, unemployment, inflation
International trade (Unit 4)	Trade disputes, tariffs, subsidies, quotas
Exchange rates and balance of payments (Unit 4)	Value of the euro (or any other currency), current account deficit, trade deficit
Economic development (Unit4)	Aid, MNCs, micro credit, agricultural subsidies, debt, foreign direct investment

▲ **Table 32.2** Suggestions for finding articles

You should **not** take the first article that you find. You should read through several and take your time to select the one that allows you to write down relevant definitions, apply the theory through the use of graphs and written explanation, and illustrate evaluative skills. Short articles, concerned with real economic matters, are recommended. The article that you choose may be written in any language, but you are required to provide a translation of the article if it is not in the working language of your school. This allows you to choose one in your own language, but will give you some extra work. Please note that as part of the requirements, you must choose the three articles from three different sources.

One danger in the writing of commentaries is that students often simply summarize or paraphrase their article. This is not the correct approach. You might provide a brief introduction in which you summarize what the issue is about, but the bulk of the commentary must include definitions, diagrams, analysis and evaluation.

As with any of the assessments carried out in economics, it is very important to include diagrams. Just as in any data response exercises that you do, make sure that you label the axes accurately and use the relevant data from the text. For example, if the article is about sugar subsidies to European farmers, don't just write price on the *y*-axis, write price of sugar in euros. If there are any figures in the text, then try to use them on the diagrams.

The presentation of your portfolio will be enhanced if you adopt a common format throughout the portfolio. That is, use a common font, size and style for each of the commentaries. According to the IB guidelines, a standardized cover sheet that includes the following information must accompany each commentary:

- the title of the article
- the source of the article (including the date of access to the site if taken from the internet)

- the date the article was published
- the date the commentary was written
- the word count of the commentary
- the unit of the syllabus to which the article relates
- the key concept being referred to.

Reminder

It is essential that you identify a different key concept in each commentary and explain the link between that concept and the article you have chosen.

Once the final portfolio is complete, you will need to upload it to the IB (through IBIS). Your teacher will then mark the portfolio and submit the marks to the IB. These marks will be subject to moderation by an external examiner.

What is the Extended Essay?

As you undoubtedly know, an Extended Essay is a 4,000 word research paper that you need to complete as part of your IB diploma. An Extended Essay in economics provides you with the opportunity to undertake in-depth research in economics in an area of personal interest. It gives you the opportunity to develop research skills, to apply economic theory to real-world situations, and to analyse and evaluate the outcomes of your research. The outcome of the research should be a coherent and structured analytical essay, which effectively addresses the particular research question.

Undoubtedly the most important information available to you when you write your Extended Essay, regardless of the subject area, is the IB assessment criteria. Quite simply, no matter how good a writer you are, if you are not aware of the specific guidelines and assessment criteria published by the IB, then you are not likely to write a successful essay. In fact, we often compare the assessment criteria to a recipe. If you are trying to cook something new, then you should definitely follow a recipe to achieve best results.

How should you choose your topic?

First of all, you should obviously choose something that interests you. However, more importantly, you must choose a topic that allows you to apply the economic theory that you have learnt in the course. While there is a lot more to economic theory than simply the material that is in the IB course, you do not want to have to do a lot of extra learning on the side! While you are likely to expand on the knowledge that you acquire in the course by doing an Extended Essay, it should not be something completely new. Perhaps the best reason for choosing and expanding on a topic covered in class is that this will ensure that you are choosing an appropriate economics topic.

In choosing your topic, you will need to think of the research that you are able to do. There is no requirement that you carry out primary research, but it may be seen as a good way to generate new research in an areas. This may be done through questionnaires, surveys or interviews. There are highly successful essays that are based on useful secondary data, particularly statistical data. The key is that the topic chosen should provide opportunities for some critical analysis of the information collected. Even where you cannot carry out surveys or questionnaires, you might try to arrange an interview (in person or by email) with a local economist, university professor or journalist. These people are often very useful sources of information.

After choosing your topic, the most important task is to develop your research question (RQ). This should definitely be able to be phrased as a question, but, ideally, it would not be a yes/no question. Nor should it be a double question, such as "Do the petrol stations in Haastown operate in an oligopoly and, if so, do they collude?"

Topics should not be historical. They should relate to economic information, policies, outcomes or events that are no more than approximately five years old. Topics that are too retrospective, such as "What was the impact of the global financial crisis on unemployment in the United States from 2007–2010?" almost invariably become descriptive. Essays should also not be based on future economic events. For example, "What will be the effect of the 2026 Football World Cup on the economy of Country X?" would not be suitable as it would be entirely speculative and unsupported.

It is incredibly important that you narrow the focus of your essay to ask something that is very specific in its scope. In doing this, you should be able to demonstrate some detailed economic understanding and critical analysis. Do not choose a question that investigates the impact of an economic event or policy on a whole economy, eg "What are the effects of the World Cup on the South African economy?" is far too large in scope. A similarly broad and problematic essay would be, "What is the effect of the global financial crisis on Croatia?"

The following examples of titles for economics extended essays are intended as guidance only. The pairings illustrate that focused topics (indicated by the first title) should be encouraged rather than broad topics (indicated by the second title).

> *To what extent has the increase in the minimum wage in Bangladesh affected the Dhaka garment workers?* **is better than** *What has been the effect of the minimum wage on Bangladesh?*
>
> *To what extent has the increase in the exchange rate of the euro affected the tourist industry in La Marina, Spain?* **is better than** *How has the increase in the exchange rate of the euro affected the Spanish economy?*
>
> *What has been the economic effect of water privatization on the farming industry in my region of Zambia?* **is better than** *How has the privatization of water affected Zambia?*

Every school has its own timetable for the completion of the Extended Essay, but it is hoped that you will have plenty of time to change your focus if it turns out that you have asked a question that you are unable to answer because there is simply not enough information.

When writing your essay, it is vital that you integrate relevant economic theory with the evidence obtained through the research. One common error is to present pages and pages of economic theory separate from the findings of the research. This is not appropriate. Any theory that you present must be delivered in the context of your research question. Additionally, you should not try to expand your essay by including irrelevant material or information that you cannot directly link to the question. It should be evident throughout the entire essay that the research question is being answered. A valid and persuasive argument needs to be developed in a clear and structured way with some awareness that there may be alternative viewpoints. You should also attempt to show critical awareness of the validity of your information and the possible limitations of their argument. Very importantly, the essay should clearly note any assumptions that have been made in setting out the argument and reaching the conclusions.

You will be "measured" by your ability to use the language and concepts of economics. All important terms that are included should be defined and the concepts should be explained. This will obviously be enhanced through the use of diagrams that, as always, must be accurately labelled. The diagrams should reflect the evidence acquired through your research. Thus, if you are doing an essay on local prices, the diagram should illustrate the domestic currency and should include some actual numbers.

One of the criteria measures the presentation of your essay. This refers to several things and these are described clearly in the assessment criteria. It includes a measure of the physical layout of the essay with the required elements such as a table of contents and page numbering. It considers your ability to compile an appropriate bibliography and cite the sources of all the information that you have used. There are several different methods for doing this. The key is that you adopt one of the accepted standardized methods and stick to it. Please be sure that, as soon as you start your research, you keep a very detailed list of all the material that you use so that you can put it all together in the bibliography. It is very difficult to track down resources several months after you have used them. This is particularly the case for any internet sites that you use. Be sure to note the full address, the date accessed, and the title of any articles that you use. Also included in the criteria for presentation is a measure of its appearance, so do your best to make sure that you produce a final essay that you can be proud of! This includes appropriate headings and neatly and accurately presented graphs and tables.

The essay must include a clear conclusion and you are advised to set this out under a separate heading. In your conclusion you should summarize the main points and provide the final answer to your research question, noting possible limitations to the validity of your research. Make sure that you do not introduce new information.

An overview of the assessment criteria used for grading the extended essay is shown below in Table 32.3.

Criterion A: focus and method	Criterion B: knowledge and understanding	Criterion C: critical thinking	Criterion D: presentation	Criterion E: engagement
• Topic • Research question • Methodology	• Context • Subject specific terminology and concepts	• Research • Analysis • Discussion and evaluation	• Structure • Layout	• Process • Research focus
Marks	Marks	Marks	Marks	Marks
6	6	12	4	6

Total marks available: 34

▲ **Table 32.3** Assessment criteria

During the process of writing your Extended Essay, you are required to have three reflection sessions with your supervisor. Undoubtedly, you will have more meetings with your supervisor to discuss your progress, but three will be identified as "reflection sessions". These are likely to be near the beginning of the process, around the time of your draft, and at the close of the process. After each reflection session, you will record your reflections on a "Reflections on Planning and Progress Form (RPPF)". The total number of words for the reflections must not exceed 500. These reflections are uploaded to IBIS along with the essay and are assessed in Criterion E. They are obviously important, since they account for 6 of the 34 marks available. They should not be treated as something that does not matter so much. The best advice we can give you for your RPPF reflections are to be genuine. Do not simply describe what you did; try to inject your own meaningful response to challenges and the learning experience.

What service opportunities might be available in Economics?

As economists, you might decide to take the opportunity to raise awareness of the economic implications of world issues in your school community. There are several days throughout the year that have been designated by the United Nations to recognize important issues and challenges facing the world's people and environment. You could use these days as focal points to look at the economic implications for the stakeholders involved.

You might set up a permanent club to carry out the task throughout the year or work independently when issues that interest you arise. If you do pursue such activities, it may be useful for you to record them as part of your CAS programme as you will be working to raise awareness of the issues.

Activities to highlight the issues and share your findings might include:

- displays/exhibitions in the hallway
- computer-assisted presentations to an assembly of your peers or other schoolmates
- newsletters
- events to publicize the issues.

The official international days are listed below.(Please note that the actual day might vary from year to year, so you should check). Attached are brief suggestions of possible links to economic theories. In each case, country case studies could be carried out to illustrate the issue or problem.

- 21 September *International day of peace*; the costs of war in terms of the damage to the factors of production and potential output.
- 5 October *World Teachers Day*; while there are significant links between quality teaching and human capital development, we have put this in just to remind you to show appreciation for your teachers!
- 17 November *International literacy day*; the importance of literacy in terms of raising human capital; correlation between literacy rates and growth and development.
- 1 December *World AIDS day*; the economic costs of HIV/AIDS.
- 10 December *Human Rights day*; the significance of the respect for human rights in the process of development.
- 11 February *International Day of Women and Girls in Science*; the role women in developing technologies to promote sustainable development
- 1 March *Zero Discrimination Day*; the consequences of discrimination in education and the workplace, the inequalities in opportunities that people have due to discrimination
- 8 March *International women's day*; inequalities between women and men, the importance of the education of girls and women; discrimination faced by women in the workplace, varying levels of unemployment among men and women; the role of women in micro-credit schemes.
- 22 March *World day for water and world biodiversity day*; external costs of economic growth; the importance of clean water for health and economic development.
- 24 March *World tuberculosis day*; the effects and the costs of the continuous presence of the illness in developing countries.
- Last week in April *World Immunization Week: the private and external benefits of immunizations, the importance of immunizations in improving children's health*
- 31 *May World no tobacco day*; the external costs of smoking; the direct costs of smoking; a comparison of measures taken around the world to reduce the costs of smoking.

If there are no official days designated, you can still declare a day, or week, to promote a particular issue. For example, some schools establish a "Fairtrade Week" to promote Fairtrade products and spread awareness of the Fairtrade movement. You might run your own "Make Trade Fair", "Drop the Debt", or "End Poverty Now" campaigns. These are all campaigns that have been carried out by international non-government organizations and they have resources available to students who would like to raise awareness of global issues (see www.oxfam.org).